my first cookbook

Fun recipes to cook together

. . . with as much mixing,
rolling, scrunching, and
squishing as possible!

Library of Congress Cataloging-in-Publication Data

Names: America's Test Kitchen (Firm), editor, publisher.

Title: My first cookbook : fun recipes to cook together...with as much mixing, rolling, scrunching, and squishing as possible

Description: Boston, MA : America's Test Kitchen, [2020] | At head of title: America's Test Kitchen Kids.

Identifiers: LCCN 2019054244 | ISBN 9781948703222 (hardcover) | ISBN 9781948703239 (epub)

Subjects: LCSH: Cooking--Juvenile literature.

Classification: LCC TX652.5 .M93 200 | DDC 641.5--dc23

LC record available at https://lccn.loc.gov/2019054244

America's Test Kitchen

21 Drydock Avenue, Boston, MA 02210

Manufactured in the United States of America

10 9 8 7 6 5 4 3 2 1

Distributed by Penguin Random House Publisher Services

Tel: 800.733.3000

Pictured on front cover: Strawberry-Mango Smoothie Bowls (page 20)

Pictured on back cover: Cheese Pupusas (page 63), Snack Toasts (page 44), Parmesan Chicken Tenders (page 66), Rice Noodle Bowls with Peanut Sauce (page 83), Applesauce Mini Muffins (page 41)

Editor in Chief: Molly Birnbaum

Executive Food Editor: Suzannah McFerran

Senior Editor: Katie Leaird

Associate Editor: Afton Cyrus

Test Cook: Andrea Morales

Deputy Editor, Education: Kristin Sargianis

Editorial Assistant: Katy O'Hara

Creative Director: John Torres

Associate Design Director: Tabitha Rodrigue

Art Directors: Scott Murry, Olivia Sheldon

Graphic Designers: Emma Kurman-Faber, Karina Masri

Illustrators: Gabriela Homonoff, Scott Murry

Photography Director: Julie Bozzo Cote

Senior Staff Photographer: Daniel J. van Ackere

Staff Photographer: Kevin White

Food Styling: Ashley Moore, Elle Simone Scott

Photography Producer: Meredith Mulcahy

Photo Shoot Kitchen Team:

    Manager: Tim McQuinn

    Lead Test Cook: Eric Haessler

    Assistant Test Cooks: Hannah Fenton, Jacqueline Gochenouer

Senior Manager, Publishing Operations: Taylor Argenzio

Imaging Manager: Lauren Robbins

Production and Imaging Specialists: Tricia Neumyer, Dennis Noble, Jessica Voas, Amanda Yong

Copy Editors: Christine Campbell, April Poole, Rachel Schowalter

Chief Creative Officer: Jack Bishop

General Manager, Kids: Claire Oliverson

Digital Marketing Manager, Kids: Kelsey Hopper

Executive Editorial Directors: Julia Collin Davison, Bridget Lancaster

contents

The Power of Cooking Together!

Cooking is not only fun, it's a powerful learning tool. It's an amazing way to learn about the world. But even more important, cooking is one of the best ways to spend time *together*.

In the kitchen, your family can leave screens (and worries) behind and enjoy making something delicious to share. What the young chef or the grown-up takes on will differ depending on age, ability, and interest. Don't be afraid to try new things or to make mistakes. The good news is that the results will be tasty no matter how you get there.

All the recipes in this book are kid tested and kid approved. This means that thousands(!) of kids (and their grown-ups) across the country tested these recipes at home, giving us feedback to help make sure that everything we publish is as delicious and doable as possible. Happy cooking!

Hey, Kids!

So you're about to cook! That is so cool. You're going to make some delicious food. There are just three things to remember:

1 **Wash your hands**

2 **Listen to your cooking partner**

3 **Have fun!**

How to Use This Book

Understanding the Symbols

To help you find the right recipe for you, this book relies on a system of symbols to designate skill level as well as type of cooking required.

⊛ beginner recipe

⊛⊛ intermediate recipe

⊛⊛⊛ advanced recipe

🔪 requires use of sharp knife

🔲 requires use of microwave

🍳 requires use of stovetop

🔲 requires use of oven

🥣 no knives or heat required

adult help! "Adult help!" is needed when the recipe step includes heat or sharp or heavy equipment. Depending on the young chef's age and ability, adults may lead other steps as well.

How to Use the Recipes

Cooking from a recipe is actually a three-step process, and the recipes in this book are written to reflect that, with three distinct sections. First, **gathering your equipment** guarantees that no one will have to run through the kitchen frantically looking for the right-size saucepan halfway through cooking the recipe. Second, **preparing your ingredients** in advance makes the act of cooking easier, reducing mistakes because no one will need to hunt for a missing ingredient or take an unexpectedly long time chopping something while food is already heating in the pan. And then, of course, **start cooking!**

Gather Equipment

The first step of every recipe is to gather the cooking tools you will need to prepare your ingredients and follow the instructions, and place them on the counter.

Prepare Ingredients

Next, read through the list of ingredients and prepare them as directed. Measure or chop ingredients. Wash fruits and vegetables. Use prep bowls to keep ingredients organized.

Start Cooking!

It's finally time to mix ingredients together and heat things on the stovetop or in the oven.

Introducing . . . Kitchen Language!

Reading a recipe can sometimes feel like reading a foreign language. Here are some common words in many cookbooks (including this one!) and what they really mean.

Peel

To peel means to remove the outer layer from a food. You can peel an apple with a vegetable peeler and an orange with just your fingers!

Chop

To chop means to cut food with a knife into small pieces, usually on a cutting board. For example, you chop vegetables into small pieces for a salad.

Shred

Shredding means to cut food into small, uniform pieces using the large holes on a box grater or the shredding disk of a food processor. You often shred cheese (think pizza!) but also some vegetables and fruits.

Zest

To zest is to remove the flavorful colored outer peel from citrus fruits, such as lemons, limes, or oranges (the colored skin is called the zest). Try not to include the white layer (called the pith) under the zest—it's bitter!

Whisk

To whisk means to combine ingredients with a whisk until evenly incorporated. To make scrambled eggs, you need to whisk whole eggs together before you cook them.

Stir

To stir means to combine ingredients, usually in a bowl with a rubber spatula or wooden spoon.

Melt

To melt means to heat solid food (such as butter or chocolate) on the stovetop or in the microwave until it becomes a liquid.

Boil

When water boils, it is very hot and has large bubbles rapidly breaking the surface. You boil water to cook pasta.

Toast

To toast means to heat food (often nuts or bread) in a skillet, toaster, or oven until golden brown, crispy, and fragrant.

Wet Ingredients

When baking, we often use this term to describe liquid (or wet!) ingredients, such as eggs, oil, melted butter, juice, and vanilla.

Dry Ingredients

When baking, we often use this term to describe fine, dry ingredients, such as flour, baking soda, sugar, and salt.

And . . .
Let's Talk About Equipment!

Tools are important in the kitchen, and the right gear is essential. We put together a list of the tools that you will use over and over and divided them into different categories—knives, cookware, kitchen basics, prep tools, and cooking tools.

Knives

Chef's knife

Paring knife

Cutting board

Large saucepan

Traditional skillet (12-inch)

Cookware

Nonstick skillets (12-inch and 10-inch)

Dutch oven

Kitchen Basics

Prep bowls

Oven mitts

Garlic press

Citrus juicer

Can opener

Vegetable peeler

Ruler

Prep Tools

Rasp grater

Measuring spoons

Liquid measuring cup

Box grater

Dry measuring cups

Spatula

Whisk

Cooking Tools

Tongs

Pastry brush

Colander

Instunt-read thermometer

Wooden spoon

Potato masher

Fine-mesh strainer

Rubber spatula

10 Helpful Prep Steps

Most ingredients must be prepared in some way before they can be used in a recipe. Here are a handful of helpful prep steps perfect for young chefs to learn to do on their own, plus a few helpful steps for either prepping or using equipment, especially for baking! (Other prep steps, such as chopping onions, are best done with help.)

How to Crack and Separate Eggs

Unless you are hard-cooking eggs, you need to start by cracking them open. In some recipes, you will need to separate the yolk (the yellow part) and white (the clear part) and use them differently. Cold eggs are much easier to separate.

1

2

3

To crack: Gently hit side of egg against flat surface of counter or cutting board.

Pull shell apart into 2 pieces over bowl. Let yolk and white drop into bowl. Discard shell.

To separate yolk and white: Use your fingers to very gently transfer yolk to second bowl.

How to Melt Butter

Butter can be melted in a small saucepan on the stove (use medium-low heat), but we think the microwave is easier.

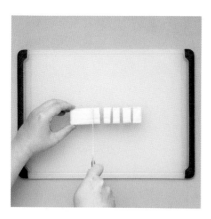

1

Cut butter into 1-tablespoon pieces. Place butter in microwave-safe bowl and place small plate on top.

2

Heat in microwave at 50 percent power (see page 12) until melted, 30 to 60 seconds (longer if melting a lot of butter).

How to Grate or Shred Cheese

Cheese is often cut into very small pieces to add to pasta, egg dishes, quesadillas, and more. When grating or shredding, use a big piece of cheese so your hands stay safely away from the sharp holes.

To grate: Hard cheeses such as Parmesan can be rubbed against a rasp grater or the small holes of a box grater to make a fluffy pile of cheese.

To shred: Semisoft cheeses such as cheddar or mozzarella can be rubbed against the large holes of a box grater to make long pieces of cheese.

How to Zest and Juice Citrus Fruit

The flavorful colored skin from lemons, limes, and oranges (called the zest) is often removed and used in recipes. If you need zest, it's best to zest before juicing. After juicing, use a small spoon to remove any seeds from the bowl of juice.

1

2

3

To zest: Rub fruit against rasp grater to remove colored zest. Turn fruit as you rub to avoid bitter white layer underneath zest.

To juice: Cut fruit in half through equator (not through ends).

Place 1 half of fruit in citrus juicer. Hold juicer over bowl and squeeze to extract juice.

How to Prep an Avocado

Avocados are so yummy, but they can be tricky to work with.
Here's an easy way to open a ripe avocado and remove the pit.

1 Use butter knife to cut avocado in half lengthwise (the long way) around pit.

2 Using your hands, twist both halves in opposite directions to separate.

3 Use soupspoon to scoop out pit; discard pit.

4 Use soupspoon to scoop out avocado from skin; discard skin. Avocado can now be sliced, chopped, or mashed.

Microwave 101

Most microwaves have a power setting that lets you cook things at reduced power levels. It's important to melt butter and chocolate at 50 percent of full power. The controls can vary from microwave to microwave, but often you have to set the power level before setting the time.

How to Weigh and Measure

Measuring ingredients is very important—too much or too little of an ingredient and the final result may not taste as delicious as it could! That's why it's essential to learn how to measure accurately when cooking or baking. There are two ways to measure ingredients: by weight, using a scale, or by volume, using measuring cups and spoons.

Kitchen Math

You can get carried away learning all the math behind measuring. Memorize the following measurements and you will be set.

3 teaspoons = 1 tablespoon

16 tablespoons = 1 cup

16 ounces = 1 pound

Using a Scale

1

Turn on scale and place bowl on scale. Press "tare" button to zero out weight (that means that the weight of the bowl won't be included).

2

Slowly add ingredient to bowl until you reach desired weight. Here we are weighing 5 ounces of all-purpose flour (equal to 1 cup).

How to Measure Dry and Liquid Ingredients

Dry ingredients should be measured in dry measuring cups—small metal or plastic cups with handles. Each set has cups of varying sizes. Dip the measuring cup into the ingredient and sweep away the excess with the back of a butter knife.

Liquid ingredients should be measured in a liquid measuring cup. Set the measuring cup level on the counter and bend down to read the bottom of the concave arc at the liquid's surface. This is known as the meniscus line.

How to Make an Aluminum Foil Sling

Lining a baking pan with two pieces of aluminum foil makes it supereasy to get baked brownies, cakes, and even granola bars out of the pan. The pieces of foil should be the same width as the pan and long enough to hang over the sides.

For an 8-inch square pan, both sheets of foil should measure 8 inches wide and roughly 13 inches long.

For a 13-by-9-inch pan, one sheet should measure 13 inches wide and the other 9 inches wide. Both sheets should be about 18 inches long.

1

Fold 2 long sheets of aluminum foil to match width of baking pan. Sheets should be same width for square baking pans but different widths for rectangular baking pans.

2

Lay sheets of foil in pan so that sheets are perpendicular to each other. Let extra foil hang over edges of pan. Push foil into corners and up sides of pan, smoothing foil so it rests against pan.

How to Line a Cake Pan with Parchment Paper

To help remove cakes from their pans, we often line the pan with parchment paper before baking. Otherwise, the cake could stick and break into pieces while removing it!

1

Place cake pan on sheet of parchment paper and trace around bottom of pan.

2

Cut out parchment with scissors.

3

Place parchment into greased pan.

How to Remove Cakes from Pans

Some cakes cool completely in their pans, while others need to be removed when they are still warm so they can cool on wire cooling racks.

Run butter knife around edge of cake to release cake from pan.

Place cooling rack on top of cake. Hold bottom of cake pan with one hand (use oven mitt if pan is still hot) and place second hand on top of cooling rack.

Turn over pan so cake falls gently onto rack.

Carefully peel parchment paper away from cake and discard.

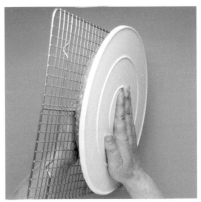

Place platter on top of cake. Hold bottom of cooling rack with one hand and place second hand on top of platter.

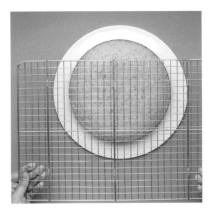

Flip cake right side up onto platter. Remove cooling rack.

after-
school
snacks

These fun snacks are perfect for a quick afternoon in the kitchen. Make some to share!

Yogurt and Berry Swirl

Serves 1

Total Time: 10 minutes

If you like your yogurt sweeter, use the full 2 teaspoons of maple syrup.

Gather Equipment

Dry measuring cups

Measuring spoons

2 small bowls

Spoon

Fork

Prepare Ingredients

½ cup plain **Greek yogurt**

1–2 teaspoons **maple syrup**

¼ cup (1¼ ounces) **blackberries** or **raspberries**

Toppings (optional) (see Make It Your Way, right)

Do the Swirl

To make swirly spirals in your yogurt, stir the mashed berries in a circle three times. 1, 2, 3, SWIRL! If you stir too much, you will mix them together completely and the pretty swirl will disappear.

Start Cooking!

Mix

Add yogurt and maple syrup to bowl.
Stir with spoon.

Mash

Place blackberries in second bowl.
Mash blackberries with fork.

Swirl

Spoon blackberries over yogurt mixture. Stir in
circles to make swirls. Add your favorite toppings
(if using).

make it YOUR way

Add your favorite toppings to your yogurt swirl for
an extra-delicious snack! We like **granola**, extra
**whole berries, sliced almonds, mini chocolate
chips,** or **toasted coconut.** You can also sweeten
the yogurt with honey instead of the maple syrup.

Strawberry–Mango Smoothie Bowls

Serves 2

Total Time: 15 minutes

It's important to use a food processor and not a blender here so you can make a smoothie that's thick enough to eat with a spoon.

Gather Equipment

Dry measuring cups

Measuring spoons

Food processor

Rubber spatula

2 serving bowls

Prepare Ingredients

1 cup (5 ounces) **frozen strawberries**

1 cup (5 ounces) **frozen mango chunks**

⅓ cup **plain yogurt**

½ ripe **banana**, peeled and broken into pieces

2 teaspoons **honey**

Pinch **salt**

Toppings (see Make It Your Way, right)

try it **THIS** way

Green Smoothie Bowls

Want to make a bright green, leprechaun-ready smoothie? Look no further. Use 1½ cups (7½ ounces) **frozen pineapple chunks** instead of the strawberries and 1 cup (1 ounce) **baby spinach** or **kale** instead of the mango. Add ½ **avocado** with banana in step 2.

Start Cooking!

1

Chop

Add strawberries and mango to food processor and lock lid into place. Hold down pulse button for 1 second, then release. Repeat until fruit is finely chopped, about twenty 1-second pulses.

2

Blend

Remove lid and scrape down bowl with rubber spatula. Add yogurt, banana, honey, and salt and lock lid back into place. Process until smooth, about 1 minute, stopping halfway to scrape down bowl.

3

Top

(adult help!) Remove lid and carefully remove processor blade (ask an adult for help). Divide smoothie between two serving bowls using rubber spatula. Add your favorite toppings.

make it YOUR way

Topping Edition

Smoothie bowls are all about the toppings. We like to arrange combinations of fresh, crunchy, and sweet toppings in fun patterns on top of the smoothie base.

Fresh toppings: whole blueberries, raspberries, blackberries; sliced strawberries, bananas, peaches, or kiwi; chunks of fresh mango or pineapple

Crunchy toppings: granola, pepitas, sunflower seeds, sliced almonds, chia or flax seeds

Sweet toppings: shredded coconut or coconut chips; a drizzle of honey or maple syrup

Frozen Banana Bites

Makes about 14 bites

Total Time: 10 minutes, plus freezing time

Gather Equipment

Dry measuring cups

Rimmed baking sheet or large serving platter

Parchment paper

Cutting board

Butter knife

Small microwave-safe bowl

Spoon

Prepare Ingredients

2 ripe **bananas**, peeled

¾ cup **semisweet** or **milk chocolate chips**

Toppings (optional) (see Make It Your Way, right)

make it YOUR way

In step 3, you can sprinkle **peanuts**, **sprinkles**, **sweetened shredded coconut**, **sesame seeds**, or even crunchy cereal such as **Rice Krispies** over the chocolate-dipped part of each banana slice.

"Fun, messy, delicious."

—ABIGAIL, 5

Start Cooking!

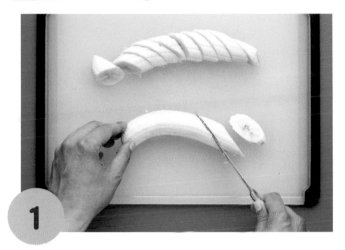

1

Cut

Line baking sheet with parchment paper. Cut bananas on diagonal into ½-inch-thick pieces.

2

Melt

Place chocolate chips in bowl. Heat in microwave at 50 percent power (see page 12), stirring occasionally with spoon, until chocolate is melted, 2 to 3 minutes. Stir chocolate until smooth.

3

Dip

Dip half of 1 banana slice in melted chocolate. Let excess drip off. Place banana on baking sheet. Repeat with remaining banana slices. Sprinkle chocolate-dipped parts of bananas with toppings.

4

Freeze

Freeze until banana slices are frozen solid, about 45 minutes.

Cranberry-Almond No-Bake Energy Bites

Makes 12 bites

Total Time: 15 minutes, plus 30 minutes chilling time

You can add 1 tablespoon of chia seeds or ground flax seed to oat mixture in step 1, if desired. Energy bites can be refrigerated in an airtight container for up to three days.

Gather Equipment

Dry measuring cups

Measuring spoons

Large bowl

Rubber spatula

Plate

Plastic wrap

Prepare Ingredients

¾   cup (2¼ ounces) **old-fashioned rolled oats**

⅓   cup **peanut, almond,** or **sunflower butter**

⅓   cup **sliced almonds**

⅓   cup **dried cranberries**

2   tablespoons **honey**

⅛   teaspoon **salt**

Fun Fact!
Where Does Energy Come From?

FOOD! But different types of food can give you different types of energy. Sweet foods such as cookies and candy give you a lot of energy, and fast—but that energy lasts for only a little bit of time, since sugar moves quickly through your body. But foods such as these energy bites that combine complex carbohydrates (oats!), protein (nut butters!), and fiber (oats and nut butters!), as well as some sugar give you longer-lasting energy. Power up!

Start Cooking!

1

Mix

Stir all ingredients in bowl with rubber spatula until well combined.

2

Shape

Use your wet hands to roll mixture into 12 balls (about 1 tablespoon each). Place balls on plate and cover with plastic wrap.

3

Chill

Refrigerate balls until firm, at least 30 minutes.

try it THIS way

Chocolate-Raisin No-Bake Energy Bites

Use ⅓ cup **chocolate chips** instead of the almonds and ⅓ cup **raisins** instead of the dried cranberries.

Blueberry-Coconut No-Bake Energy Bites

Use ⅓ cup **sweetened coconut flakes** instead of the almonds and ⅓ cup **dried blueberries** instead of the dried cranberries.

Smashed Cucumber Salad

Serves 2

Total Time: 35 minutes

If you don't have Persian cucumbers (the small ones), you can use one larger English cucumber, ends trimmed, cut crosswise into three equal lengths (but it will be harder to smash).

Gather Equipment

Measuring spoons

Large zipper-lock bag

Small skillet or rolling pin

Colander

2 medium bowls

Wooden spoon

Prepare Ingredients

5 (3 ounces) **Persian cucumbers**

¼ teaspoon **salt**

2 teaspoons **rice vinegar**

1½ teaspoons **low-sodium soy sauce**

½ teaspoon **toasted sesame oil**

½ teaspoon **sugar**

½ teaspoon **sesame seeds, toasted**

Hot Tip

Smashing Equals More Flavor

Why smash the cucumbers instead of neatly slicing them? When you smash them up, you expose more surface area and create little nooks and crannies that the flavorful dressing can sneak into.

"Getting to help Mommy put the ingredients in the bowl was my favorite part."

–CAMMIE, 5

Start Cooking!

Smash

Place cucumbers in bag and seal. Smash with skillet until each cucumber is flattened and split into 3 or 4 spears.

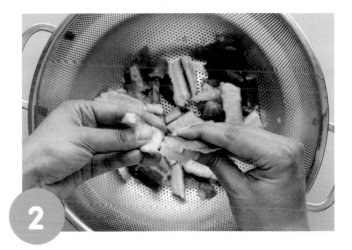

Tear and salt

Place colander in bowl. Tear cucumber spears into small pieces and place in colander. Add salt to cucumbers and toss to combine. Let cucumbers sit for at least 15 minutes or up to 30 minutes.

Make dressing

While cucumbers sit, stir vinegar, soy sauce, oil, and sugar in second bowl with wooden spoon until sugar has dissolved.

Mix

Transfer drained cucumbers to bowl with dressing and stir to combine. Discard drained liquid. Sprinkle cucumbers with sesame seeds.

Creamy Yogurt Dip

Serves 4 to 6 (Makes 1 cup)

Total Time: 10 minutes

We prefer Greek yogurt in this recipe for a creamy, thick dip. You can use plain yogurt, but the dip will be much looser.

Gather Equipment

Dry measuring cups

Chef's knife

Cutting board

Measuring spoons

Scissors

Medium bowl

Rubber spatula

Prepare Ingredients

4 **fresh chives** (optional)

1 cup **plain Greek yogurt**

1 tablespoon **lemon juice**, squeezed from ½ lemon

1 tablespoon **milk**

½ teaspoon **salt**

¼ teaspoon **pepper**

¼ teaspoon **garlic powder**

Fun Fact!
Is Greek Yogurt from Greece?

Greek-style yogurt has been drained of excess liquid so it's superthick and creamy. While people in Greece do eat strained yogurt (called *straggisto*), the Greek-style yogurt you will find in the United States usually isn't from Greece.

Start Cooking!

1 Snip

Snip chives (if using) into little pieces over bowl using scissors.

2 Mix

Add yogurt, lemon juice, milk, salt, pepper, and garlic powder to bowl with chives. Stir until well combined. Serve with your favorite things to dip in your dip, below.

make it YOUR way

Things to dip in your dip: **carrot sticks, celery sticks, sliced bell peppers, sliced cucumbers, crackers, pita chips,** and anything else you can think of.

Avocado Toast

Serves 2

Total Time: 15 minutes

Gather Equipment

Measuring spoons

Chef's knife

Cutting board

Butter knife

Medium bowl

Fork

Toaster

Prepare Ingredients

1 tablespoon **extra-virgin olive oil**

1 teaspoon **lime juice**, squeezed from ½ lime

Pinch **salt**

Pinch **pepper**

1 ripe **avocado**, halved and pitted (see page 12)

2 (½-inch-thick) slices **crusty bread**

Toppings (optional) (see Make It Your Way, right)

Fun Fact!

Avocados: Fruit or Vegetable?

Because of their dark, wrinkly skin and teardrop shape, avocados are sometimes called "alligator pears." Although they don't taste sweet or fruity like pears do, did you know that avocados are actually a fruit? Avocados are the berry of the avocado tree, which grows in warm places such as California, Mexico, and the Dominican Republic. The pit inside is the seed—and any produce that contains a seed or seeds is a fruit!

"I like squashing the avocado."
—DAVID, 5

Start Cooking!

1

Make dressing

Add oil, lime juice, salt, and pepper to bowl. Mix with fork until well combined.

2

Mash

Hold avocado halves over bowl with dressing. Squeeze avocado out of skins into bowl (discard skins). Break avocado into large pieces with fork, then mash into dressing until mostly smooth.

3

Toast

Toast bread until golden on both sides, 1 to 2 minutes. Spread avocado mixture evenly on toasts. Add toppings (if using).

make it YOUR way

You can dress up your avocado toast by adding toppings! We like adding quartered **cherry tomatoes**, crumbled **bacon**, **pomegranate seeds**, chopped **herbs**, or a sprinkle of **everything bagel seasoning**. To turn this snack into a meal, you can even top your toast with a **fried egg**!

English Muffin Pizzas

Makes 2 pizzas

Total Time: 15 minutes

If you are not using the pepperoni, you can top the pizzas with torn fresh basil leaves after the pizzas have cooled in step 4. You can use a conventional oven instead of a toaster oven for this recipe—adjust the oven rack to the upper-middle position and heat the oven to 450 degrees. Note that the total time for the recipe will be longer, because you will need to let the oven preheat.

Gather Equipment

Fork

Measuring spoons

Toaster oven with pan

Aluminum foil

Spoon

Oven mitts

Cooling rack

Prepare Ingredients

1   **English muffin**, split in half using fork

4   teaspoons **jarred pizza sauce**

3   tablespoons **shredded mozzarella cheese** (¾ ounce)

2-4   slices **pepperoni** (optional)

Fun Fact!

Who Invented English Muffins?

As legend has it, the first English muffin was baked more than 135 years ago. Its inventor was named Samuel Bath Thomas. He called it a "toaster crumpet" and went on to found the Thomas company, which makes most English muffins in our kitchens today!

Start Cooking!

1

Toast

Line toaster oven pan with aluminum foil; set aside.
Toast English muffin in toaster oven until light
golden. Remove from toaster. Heat toaster oven
to 450 degrees.

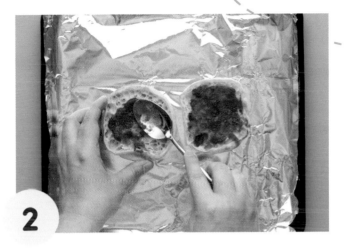

2

Sauce

Place English muffin, split side up, on toaster oven
pan. Divide pizza sauce evenly between each
English muffin half and spread into even layer with
back of spoon.

3

Top

Sprinkle mozzarella evenly over pizza sauce.
Top each pizza with 2 slices pepperoni (if using).

4

Bake

adult help! Bake pizzas in toaster oven until cheese is
melted, 5 to 7 minutes. Let pizzas cool on
cooling rack for 5 minutes.

Bean and Cheese Quesadillas

Serves 2
Total Time: 25 minutes

Gather Equipment

Can opener

Colander

Dry measuring cups

Measuring spoons

Medium bowl

Fork

Rimmed baking sheet

Pastry brush

Oven mitts

Cooling rack

Cutting board

Chef's knife

Prepare Ingredients

⅓ cup **canned black beans**, rinsed

2 teaspoons plus 1 teaspoon **extra-virgin olive oil**, measured separately

2 (8-inch) **flour tortillas**

⅔ cup **shredded Monterey Jack cheese** (2⅔ ounces)

Fun Fact!
Magical Fruit

Did you know that there are more than 40,000 types of beans? Only a few types are grown on a large enough scale to purchase in stores. Some beans are sold dry, while others, such as the black beans used in these quesadillas, are sold already cooked and in cans.

"When you put the quesadilla together, I liked to smash it down! I also liked washing the beans because I rinsed them off with the faucet handle."

Start Cooking!

–SARAH, 5

Heat and mash

Adjust oven rack to middle position and heat oven to 450 degrees. Add beans and 2 teaspoons oil to bowl. Mash beans with fork to chunky paste.

Brush

Place tortillas on baking sheet. Brush tortillas with remaining 1 teaspoon oil. Flip tortillas so oiled side is on baking sheet.

Assemble

Spread bean mixture over half of each tortilla. Sprinkle cheese over bean mixture. Fold tortillas in half, forming half-moon shape, and press to flatten.

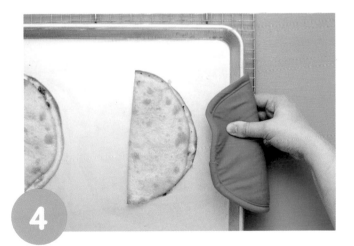

Bake

adult help! Bake quesadillas until spotty brown, 5 to 7 minutes. Let quesadillas cool on cooling rack about 5 minutes. Transfer to cutting board and cut into wedges.

Cheesy Zucchini Crisps

Serves 2 to 4 (Makes 12 crisps)

Total Time: 40 minutes

Serve these zucchini crisps with our Creamy Yogurt Dip (page 28).

Gather Equipment

Dry measuring cups

Fork

2 bowls (1 large, 1 small)

Measuring spoons

Rimmed baking sheet

Parchment paper

Dish towel

Cutting board

Box grater

Rubber spatula

Oven mitts

Cooling rack

Prepare Ingredients

Vegetable oil spray

1 **small zucchini** (6 ounces)

⅓ cup **panko bread crumbs**

¼ cup **shredded cheddar cheese** (1 ounce)

1 **large egg**, lightly beaten

½ teaspoon **garlic powder**

⅛ teaspoon **salt**

turn the page!

1

Heat and grease

Adjust oven rack to upper-middle position and heat oven to 425 degrees. Line baking sheet with parchment paper and spray with vegetable oil spray.

2

Shred

adult help! Place dish towel on cutting board, and place box grater on top. Shred zucchini on large holes of box grater.

3

Squeeze

Gather ends of towel together, twist tightly, and squeeze over sink to drain as much liquid as possible. Transfer zucchini to bowl.

4

Mix

Add panko, cheddar, egg, garlic powder, and salt to bowl with zucchini. Stir mixture with rubber spatula until combined.

Portion and flatten

Use 1-tablespoon measuring spoon to scoop and drop zucchini mixture onto baking sheet in 12 mounds (about 1 heaping tablespoon each). Gently press each mound to flatten into thin circle.

Bake

adult help! Bake crisps until edges are browned, 14 to 16 minutes. Use oven mitts to remove baking sheet from oven and place baking sheet on cooling rack. Let crisps cool for 10 minutes.

How Much Water?

Water, water, everywhere! Squeezing some water out of the shredded zucchini in this recipe prevents the crisps from turning soggy. Can you guess which of these ingredients has the MOST water?

A. Zucchini   **B. Apples**   **C. Oranges**

· ·

Answer Key: A. Zucchini! Zucchini is made up of 94% water (so, it's mostly water). Apples and oranges have a lot of water, too (86% and 89%).

Applesauce Mini Muffins

Makes 24 mini muffins

Total Time: 45 minutes

Muffins can be stored at room temperature in a zipper-lock bag for up to three days or frozen for up to one month. If muffins are frozen, thaw at room temperature, and then refresh muffins by placing them on a rimmed baking sheet and warming them in a 300-degree oven for about 10 minutes.

Gather Equipment

Dry measuring cups

Measuring spoons

Small microwave-safe bowl and plate

Liquid measuring cup

24-cup mini muffin tin

2 bowls (1 large, 1 medium)

Whisk

Rubber spatula

2 spoons

Toothpick

Oven mitts

Cooling rack

Prepare Ingredients

Vegetable oil spray

1½ cups (7½ ounces) **all-purpose flour**

1 teaspoon **baking soda**

½ teaspoon **salt**

½ teaspoon **ground cinnamon**

1 cup **unsweetened applesauce**

8 tablespoons **unsalted butter**, melted and cooled (see page 10 for how to melt butter)

½ cup (3½ ounces) **sugar**, plus extra for sprinkling

¼ cup **apple cider** or **apple juice**

1 large **egg**

Fun Fact! The Oldest Apple

There are many kinds of apples—from McIntosh to Pink Lady, Fuji to Golden Delicious. Which ones are your favorites? "Heirloom" apples are apples that have been grown for more than 50 years. The oldest kind of apple, the Decio, is from Italy. It dates back more than 1,500 years—a long time ago! A Roman general named Ezio supposedly took it with him as he chased Attila the Hun.

turn the page!

Start Cooking!

1 Heat and grease

Adjust oven rack to middle position and heat oven to 375 degrees. Spray muffin tin well with vegetable oil spray.

2 Whisk dry

In large bowl, whisk together flour, baking soda, salt, and cinnamon.

3 Whisk wet

In medium bowl, whisk applesauce, melted butter, sugar, cider, and egg until well combined.

4 Mix

Add applesauce mixture to flour mixture and use rubber spatula to gently stir until just combined and no dry flour is visible. Do not overmix.

Portion

Scoop batter into each muffin tin cup with 2 spoons (fill muffin cups to top). Sprinkle top of muffins with a little extra sugar.

Bake

adult help! Bake until muffins are deep golden brown and toothpick inserted in center of 1 muffin comes out clean, 12 to 14 minutes.

Cool

Place muffin tin on cooling rack and let muffins cool for 15 minutes. Gently wiggle muffins to loosen from muffin tin and transfer directly to cooling rack. Let muffins cool for at least 5 minutes.

"These are delicious, and if you gave them to a moose, they would love them too."

—EVA, 7, FAN OF THE BOOK
IF YOU GIVE A MOOSE A MUFFIN

make it YOUR way
Snack Toasts

Toast is simple, delicious, and perfect for getting CREATIVE. Here are some tips for tasty snack toasts, from simple to . . . animalistic!

Cream cheese

Nut butter (peanut butter, almond butter)

Sliced apples

Whole berries

2 Then add your favorite TOPPINGS

1 Start with a BASE

Spread 1 to 2 tablespoons of sticky or creamy ingredients on a slice of your favorite toasted bread.

Sliced strawberries

Nutella

Ricotta cheese

Seed butter (sunflower butter)

Sliced bananas

Raisins or other dried fruit

try it THIS way

Make Animals if you want

Here are a few animal shapes to try. You can also use your imagination to come up with your own design!

Sliced pears

Chocolate chips

Shredded coconut

Sprinkle of ground cinnamon

Drizzle of honey

Bear Circle of Nutella, 3 banana slices, and 3 blueberries

Fish Oval of ricotta cheese, 1 banana slice, 1 blueberry, 10 strawberry slices, 3 half-moon-shaped apple slices

Cat Circle of nut butter, 6 apple sticks (apple slices cut into thin sticks), 3 strawberry slices, and 2 blueberries

breakfast, lunch, and dinner

Happily, every day needs a breakfast, lunch, and dinner. (And don't be afraid of breakfast *for* dinner!)

Banana-Oat Pancakes

Serves 4 to 6 (Makes 15 pancakes)

Total Time: 50 minutes

Gather Equipment

Dry measuring cups

Measuring spoons

Liquid measuring cup

2 bowls (1 large, 1 medium)

Whisk

Large fork or potato masher

12-inch nonstick skillet

Spatula

Serving plates

Prepare Ingredients

1¼ cups (6¼ ounces) **all-purpose flour**

2½ teaspoons **baking powder**

¼ teaspoon **salt**

2 ripe **bananas**

1½ cups (12 ounces) **milk**

1 cup (3 ounces) **old-fashioned rolled oats**

2 large **eggs**

3 tablespoons **vegetable oil**

3 tablespoons **sugar**

Vegetable oil spray

Fun Fact! [That's Bananas!]

Did you know that bananas grow in bunches on trees in warm parts of the world? Most of the banana bunches that you'll see in the supermarket have six or seven bananas. The largest bunch of bananas ever recorded was grown on the island of El Hierro in the Canary Islands of Spain and had 473 bananas! That's a lot of banana pancakes!

turn the page!

Start Cooking!

1

Whisk dry

In large bowl, whisk together flour, baking powder, and salt.

2

Mash

Peel bananas and place in medium bowl. Mash bananas well with large fork or potato masher.

3

Soak

Add milk and oats to bananas and whisk until combined. Let sit until oats are softened, about 5 minutes.

4

Whisk wet

Add eggs, oil, and sugar to bowl with banana mixture and whisk until well combined.

"It was fun to make and eat. I did it **all by myself!**"

—LOGAN, 5

5

Mix

Add banana mixture to flour mixture. Whisk until just combined.

6

Cook

adult help! Spray skillet with vegetable oil spray and heat over medium heat until hot, about 1 minute. Use ¼-cup dry measuring cup to scoop 3 portions of batter into skillet.

7

Flip

adult help! Cook pancakes until first side is golden, 2 to 3 minutes. Flip and cook until second side is golden, 2 to 3 minutes. Transfer to plates. Repeat steps 6 and 7 with remaining batter in 4 batches.

Hot Pancake Tips!

To cook more pancakes at a time, you can use an electric griddle set at 350 degrees instead of the skillet.

To keep the pancakes warm and serve them all at once, transfer them to a cooling rack set in a rimmed baking sheet in a 200-degree oven as you make them.

Top the pancakes with your favorite toppings, such as **sliced bananas**, **maple syrup**, or **chopped nuts**.

Sheet Pan French Toast

Serves 4

Total Time: 40 minutes

Gather Equipment

Measuring spoons

Liquid measuring cup

Butter knife

Small microwave-safe bowl and plate

Rimmed baking sheet

Large bowl

Whisk

Oven mitts

Prepare Ingredients

Vegetable oil spray

3 large **eggs**

1 tablespoon **vanilla extract**

2 teaspoons packed **brown sugar**

½ teaspoon **ground cinnamon**

¼ teaspoon **salt**

1 cup **milk**

2 tablespoons **unsalted butter**, melted and cooled (see page 10 for how to melt butter)

8 slices **hearty white sandwich bread**

Fun Fact! The Name Game

Some say French toast gets its name from *pain perdu*, which is French for "lost bread" (since it's a great recipe to help use up stale bread that otherwise might be "lost" or thrown away). But this custardy breakfast dish has been called all sorts of other names: everything from eggy bread to German toast to poor knights of Windsor! No matter what you call it, it's one tasty breakfast.

turn the page!

Heat and grease

Adjust 1 oven rack to lowest position and second rack 5 to 6 inches from broiler element. Heat oven to 425 degrees. Spray baking sheet well with vegetable oil spray.

Whisk

In large bowl, whisk eggs, vanilla, brown sugar, cinnamon, and salt until well combined and sugar is dissolved, about 30 seconds. Add milk and melted butter and whisk until combined.

Pour

Pour egg mixture into greased baking sheet.

Soak

Place bread slices in 2 rows on baking sheet. Working quickly, flip each slice in same order you placed them on baking sheet. Let bread sit until slices absorb custard, about 1 minute.

Bake

(adult help!) Bake on lower rack until bottoms of slices are golden brown, 10 to 15 minutes.

Broil

(adult help!) Use oven mitts to transfer baking sheet to upper rack and heat broiler. Broil until tops of slices are golden brown, 1 to 4 minutes (watch carefully to prevent burning!).

try it THIS way

We developed this recipe to work with a very specific kind of bread: supermarket presliced white bread that measures 4 by 6 inches and is ¾ inch thick. (The size of the slices is the key to soaking up the right amount of custard on the baking sheet.) If you want to use whole-grain sandwich bread, you will need a little more custard. The whole-grain breads are drier, so they absorb more of the custard.

Whole-Grain French Toast

To use **whole-wheat, oatmeal,** or **multigrain sandwich bread** instead of the white bread, use 4 **eggs** and increase the **milk** to 1⅓ cups. Make sure the slices measure about 4 by 6 inches and are ¾ inch thick to ensure that they soak up all the custard on the sheet before baking.

Cheesy Scrambled Eggs

Serves 4

Total Time: 15 minutes

Gather Equipment

Measuring spoons

Butter knife

Dry measuring cups

Large bowl

Fork

12-inch nonstick skillet

Rubber spatula

Prepare Ingredients

8 **large eggs**

⅛ teaspoon **salt**

Pinch **pepper**

2 tablespoons **unsalted butter**

¼ cup shredded **extra-sharp cheddar cheese** (1 ounce)

Fun Fact! Rainbow Eggs

Eggs do not have only white shells. Yes, some are brown, too. But did you know that they can also be green, pink, or even blue? Different types of chickens lay eggs with different-colored shells. Inside, though, they're all the same, with a yellow yolk surrounded by a clear liquid called the "white."

Start Cooking!

1 Beat

Add eggs, salt, and pepper to bowl and beat with fork until very well combined, about 30 seconds.

2 Cook

adult help! In skillet, melt butter over medium-high heat, swirling to coat skillet. Add egg mixture and use rubber spatula to constantly scrape bottom and sides of skillet until eggs begin to clump, 1 to 2 minutes.

3 Add cheese

Reduce heat to low. Sprinkle cheddar over eggs. Gently and constantly stir eggs until clumped and slightly wet, about 1 minute. Turn off heat.

make it YOUR way

You can try out different cheeses such as shredded **Monterey Jack**, crumbled **feta**, or grated **Parmesan** to see which you like best with your eggs. Along with the cheese, you can add 1 tablespoon of chopped fresh herbs (such as **chives**, **parsley**, or **dill**), 2 cups of chopped **baby spinach**, ¼ cup of chopped **deli ham** or halved **cherry tomatoes**, or one or two slices of crumbled cooked **bacon**.

Kale Salad with Maple-Balsamic Dressing

Serves 4
Total Time: 20 minutes

Gather Equipment

Measuring spoons

Chef's knife

Cutting board

Dry measuring cups

Large bowl

Small jar with lid

Tongs

Prepare Ingredients

8 ounces **curly kale**

3 tablespoons **extra-virgin olive oil**

1 tablespoon **balsamic vinegar**

1 teaspoon **maple syrup**

½ teaspoon **Dijon mustard** or **mayonnaise**

¼ teaspoon **salt**

1 **apple**, cored and chopped

¼ cup **sliced almonds**

make it YOUR way

You can dress up this salad with anything you like! Try using a **pear** instead of the apple or **chopped pecans**, **walnuts**, or **pistachios** instead of the almonds. You can also add a sprinkle of crumbled **cheese**, dried fruit (such as **dried cherries**, **cranberries**, or chopped **apricots**), **sunflower seeds**, or **pepitas**.

Start Cooking!

1 Tear

Tear kale leaves from stems and discard stems. Tear kale into small bite-size pieces.

2 Massage

Place kale pieces in bowl. Squeeze and massage kale until leaves soften and turn dark green, 1 to 2 minutes.

3 Shake

In small jar, combine oil, vinegar, maple syrup, mustard, and salt. Cover jar tightly with lid and shake until mixture is well combined, about 30 seconds.

4 Dress

Add apple, almonds, and dressing to bowl with kale. Use tongs to toss salad until kale is well coated with dressing.

Oven Grilled Cheese

Serves 4

Total Time: 30 minutes

Gather Equipment

- Butter knife
- Small microwave-safe bowl and plate
- Dry measuring cups
- Rimmed baking sheet
- Aluminum foil
- Pastry brush
- Oven mitts
- Cooling rack

Prepare Ingredients

- 8 slices **hearty white** or **whole-grain sandwich bread**
- 3 tablespoons **unsalted butter**, melted (see page 10 for how to melt butter)
- 1⅓ cups shredded **Monterey Jack cheese** (6 ounces)

make it YOUR way

Add your favorite fillings to your grilled cheese to make it extra-special. Some classic add-ins are **tomato slices** or **deli ham**, but you can also try thinly sliced **apples** or even **pickles** or cooked **bacon** for an unexpected treat.

Start Cooking!

Heat and line

Adjust oven rack to lower-middle position and heat oven to 400 degrees. Line baking sheet with aluminum foil.

Brush

Place 4 bread slices on baking sheet. Brush half of melted butter evenly over top of each slice. Flip bread slices, buttered side down.

Assemble

Divide Monterey Jack evenly among bread slices. Place remaining 4 bread slices on top and press down gently. Brush tops with remaining melted butter.

Bake

 Bake until cheese is melted and bread is golden brown, 10 to 15 minutes. Place on cooling rack.

Cheese Pupusas

Serves 4 to 6 (Makes 8 pupusas)

Total Time: 1 hour

Gather Equipment

Dry measuring cups

Measuring spoons

Liquid measuring cup

Medium bowl

Rubber spatula

Plastic wrap

Scissors

Large zipper-lock plastic bag

Large plate

Dish towel

Ruler

Clear pie plate or 8-inch square glass baking dish

12-inch nonstick skillet

Spatula

Serving platter

Prepare Ingredients

2 cups (8 ounces) **masa harina**

¾ teaspoon **salt**

1½ cups (12 ounces) warm **water**

1 teaspoon **vegetable oil**

. **Vegetable oil spray**

2 cups shredded **Monterey Jack cheese** (8 ounces)

Cabbage Slaw (optional) (see page 65)

What's a Pupusa?

Pupusas are thick corn tortilla cakes stuffed with savory ingredients such as cheese, beans, or pork. They are especially popular in El Salvador, where they are fried in oil and sold on the street as snacks. They are made with masa harina—a finely ground and treated corn product—which you can find in the international aisle or near the flour in your grocery store. A clear pie plate or baking dish makes it easy to see the size of your pupusa as you press the dough flat.

turn the page!

1

Stir

In bowl, stir together masa harina and salt. Add warm water and oil. Stir well until no dry masa remains and soft dough forms, about 1 minute. Cover with plastic wrap and let rest for 15 minutes.

2

Cut

While dough rests, use scissors to cut side seams of large zipper-lock plastic bag, leaving bottom seam intact. Open bag and spray inside of bag lightly with vegetable oil spray. Set aside.

3

Portion

When dough is ready, roll dough into 8 equal balls (about ⅓ cup each). Place on large plate and cover with damp dish towel.

4

Fill

Pat 1 dough ball into 4-inch circle. Squeeze ¼ cup Monterey Jack into ball. Place cheese ball in center of dough circle, pull sides over, and pinch at top. Roll into smooth ball. Repeat with remaining dough.

Press

Open bag, place 1 filled pupusa ball inside, and fold over top of bag. Place pie plate on top of bag and press ball into 4-inch circle. Return pressed pupusa to large plate and cover with damp dish towel. Repeat with remaining 7 filled pupusa balls.

Cook

adult help! Spray skillet lightly with vegetable oil spray. Heat over medium-high heat until hot, about 1 minute. Add 4 pupusas to skillet and cook until spotty brown, 6 to 8 minutes, flipping halfway through cooking. Repeat with remaining 4 pupusas.

Testing, Testing, 1 2 3

To test whether the dough is ready in step 3, make a golf-ball-size ball of dough and gently press it flat. If many large cracks form around the edges of the ball when squeezed, the dough is too dry and needs more water. Stir in more warm water, 1 teaspoon at a time, until the dough is soft and no longer makes big cracks when pressed.

too dry   **just right**

Cabbage Slaw

Pupusas are traditionally served with *curtido*, a fresh and crunchy cabbage slaw. **To make it:** In medium bowl, combine 3 cups shredded **green coleslaw mix**, ¼ cup fresh **cilantro leaves**, 1 tablespoon **lime juice**, and ¼ teaspoon **salt**. Use rubber spatula to stir mixture together. Let sit for at least 10 minutes before serving.

Parmesan Chicken Tenders

Serves 4

Total Time: 35 minutes

Gather Equipment

Dry measuring cups

Measuring spoons

Shallow dish

Wooden spoon

Large bowl

Whisk

Large plate

12-inch nonstick skillet

Tongs

Instant-read thermometer

Serving platter

Prepare Ingredients

1 cup shredded **Parmesan cheese** (3 ounces)

1 cup **panko bread crumbs**

½ teaspoon plus ¼ teaspoon **salt,** measured separately

3 **large eggs**

3 tablespoons **all-purpose flour**

1 pound **chicken tenderloins**

2 tablespoons plus 2 tablespoons **extra-virgin olive oil,** measured separately

Fun Fact!
Chickens Don't Have Fingers

Have you ever noticed that chicken tenders are sometimes called chicken fingers? What the heck?! Some people say they got their name because when they are all fried up, you can eat them with your fingers (rather than using a knife and fork). No matter where their name came from, rest assured, they are certainly not fingers!

Start Cooking!

Mix

In shallow dish, stir together Parmesan, panko, and ½ teaspoon salt.

Coat

In bowl, whisk together eggs, flour, and remaining ¼ teaspoon salt. Add chicken to egg mixture and turn to coat well.

Dredge

Remove 1 piece of chicken, letting extra egg drip off, and add to dish with Parmesan mixture. Gently press Parmesan mixture onto chicken. Transfer to plate. Repeat with remaining chicken.

Cook

adult help! Heat 2 tablespoons oil in skillet over medium heat for 1 minute. Add half of chicken and cook until registering 165 degrees, 6 to 7 minutes, flipping halfway. Repeat with remaining chicken.

Meatballs

Serves 4 (Makes 12 meatballs)

Total Time: 45 minutes

Gather Equipment

Dry measuring cups

Liquid measuring cup

Can opener

Measuring spoons

Large bowl

Rubber spatula

Dutch oven with lid

Large plate

Prepare Ingredients

½ cup **panko bread crumbs**

½ cup **milk**

1 (28-ounce) can **crushed tomatoes,** opened

1 tablespoon **extra-virgin olive oil**

¼ teaspoon **sugar**

¼ teaspoon plus ½ teaspoon **salt,** measured separately

1 pound 85 percent **lean ground beef**

½ cup grated **Parmesan cheese** (1 ounce)

½ teaspoon **garlic powder**

½ teaspoon **dried oregano**

Fun Fact!

World's Largest Meatball

The world's largest meatball clocked in at 1,707 pounds and 8 ounces! It was made in South Carolina in 2017. It took almost a week—and a special custom-made oven—to cook.

turn the page!

Start Cooking!

Soak

Add panko and milk to bowl and stir with rubber spatula to combine. Let mixture sit for 5 minutes.

Make sauce

In Dutch oven, combine tomatoes, oil, sugar, and ¼ teaspoon salt and stir with clean rubber spatula to combine.

Mix

Add beef, Parmesan, garlic powder, oregano, and remaining ½ teaspoon salt to bowl with panko mixture and mix together with your hands.

Shape

Divide beef mixture into 12 portions (about 3 tablespoons each) and place on plate. Use your slightly wet hands to roll each portion into ball.

> **"I liked getting to mix the meatballs and roll them out!"**
> —AMELIA, 5

5 Place

Add meatballs to sauce in pot.

6 Cook

adult help! Bring to simmer over medium heat. Cover and cook until meatballs are cooked through, 15 to 18 minutes, stirring halfway through cooking.

Fun Fact!

Spaghetti and Meatballs Are NOT Italian!

You read that right. While Italians do eat spaghetti, and they do eat *polpette* (the Italian word for "meatballs"), they very rarely eat them together. (It's we Americans that are the spaghetti-and-meatball combo lovers!) And when they do eat meatballs, they are usually small (like golf balls) and are only sometimes made with ground beef. Think about what you want to do with YOUR meatballs. Spaghetti? A meatball sub? Something else entirely? (If you serve it with pasta, this recipe makes enough sauce to coat 12 ounces of pasta.)

Baked Macaroni and Cheese

Serves 4 to 6

Total Time: 1 hour

Make sure to use thinly sliced American cheese from the deli section of your grocery store in this recipe, not individually wrapped cheese "singles"—they are made from different ingredients.

Gather Equipment

Dry measuring cups

Measuring spoons

Liquid measuring cup

8-inch square glass baking dish

Rubber spatula

Aluminum foil

Oven mitts

Cooling rack

Prepare Ingredients

2 cups **elbow macaroni** (8 ounces)

1 cup shredded **mild cheddar cheese** (4 ounces)

8-10 thin slices **deli American cheese**, torn into small pieces (4 ounces)

1 tablespoon **cornstarch**

½ teaspoon **dry mustard**

½ teaspoon **salt**

2 cups **water**

1 cup **milk**

½ cup **frozen peas** (optional)

Fun Fact!

Where Does Mac and Cheese Come From?

Macaroni and cheese was born in Italy. Since Italy is the land of pasta, that's not very surprising . . . But did you know that an American president was the first to bring mac and cheese here? Yup. In the 1800s Thomas Jefferson tried macaroni and cheese on a trip to Europe and brought a hand-written recipe back to the White House.

Start Cooking!

Heat and mix

Adjust oven rack to middle position and heat oven to 400 degrees. In 8-inch square glass baking dish, toss together macaroni, cheddar, American cheese, cornstarch, mustard, and salt.

Add liquid

Pour water and milk over macaroni mixture.

Bake

adult help! Cover dish with aluminum foil. Bake until macaroni is tender, about 35 minutes. Use oven mitts to remove baking dish from oven and place on cooling rack.

Stir

adult help! Uncover and carefully stir mixture together until it looks creamy (dish will be hot!), about 1 minute. Stir in peas (if using). Let cool for 10 minutes. Stir again before serving.

Cake Pan Pizzas

Serves 4 to 6 (Makes two 9-inch pizzas)

Total Time: 1 hour

Gather Equipment

Measuring spoons

Liquid measuring cup

Dry measuring cups

2 dark-colored 9-inch round cake pans (light-colored pans will also work, but the crust will be a little softer and less crisp)

Plastic wrap

Spoon

Oven mitts

Cooling rack

Spatula

Cutting board

Chef's knife

Prepare Ingredients

2 tablespoons **extra-virgin olive oil**

1 pound **pizza dough**

½ cup **pizza sauce** or **marinara sauce**

1 cup shredded **mozzarella cheese** (4 ounces)

2 tablespoons grated **Parmesan cheese** (¼ ounce)

Fun Fact!
Yes, There Is a Pizza Olympics!

This recipe makes it easy to make a perfectly round pizza since it bakes in a round pan, but some professional pizza makers throw and spin their dough in the air to turn it into a perfectly round shape. Pizza makers can even compete every year in the World Pizza Games, which is like the Olympics of pizza and features a dough-tossing competition!

turn the page!

Start Cooking!

1 Heat and grease

Adjust oven rack to middle position and heat oven to 450 degrees. Divide oil evenly between two 9-inch round cake pans. Spread oil evenly over bottoms and sides of pans using your fingers.

2 Divide

Divide dough in half. Pat and flatten each piece of dough into circle. Place 1 dough circle in each cake pan and turn to coat with oil.

3 Rise

Cover cake pans loosely with plastic wrap. Let dough rise on counter until slightly puffy, about 30 minutes.

4 Stretch

When dough is ready, gently push and stretch dough to cover bottoms of pans (all the way to edges).

"My favorite part was making the pepperonis
into a smiley face on the pepperoni pizza."
—JAMES, 7

5

6

Top

Spoon pizza sauce evenly over both dough circles and spread into even layer, leaving ½-inch border. Sprinkle each pizza evenly with mozzarella and Parmesan.

Bake

adult help! Bake until cheese is beginning to brown, 10 to 15 minutes. Use oven mitts to remove cake pans from oven and place on cooling rack. Let pizzas cool in pans for 5 minutes. Use spatula to transfer pizzas to cutting board. Cut into wedges.

try it THIS way
Pesto Cake Pan Pizzas

Use ½ cup **pesto** instead of the pizza sauce.

make it YOUR way

Add some toppings to make your pizza just the way you want it! Before baking, try adding a cooked protein (such as **pepperoni slices**, **bacon**, or **chicken**), chopped or sliced vegetables (such as **cherry tomatoes**, **bell peppers**, or **mushrooms**), or extra cheese (such as **crumbled feta** or **goat cheese**). After baking, you can sprinkle your pizza with torn **fresh basil**, a handful of **baby spinach**, or extra grated **Parmesan cheese**.

Sheet Pan Barbecue Chicken and Broccoli

Serves 4

Total Time: 35 minutes

Gather Equipment

Measuring spoons

Liquid measuring cup

Rimmed baking sheet

Aluminum foil

Paper towels

Pastry brush

Large bowl

Instant-read thermometer

Oven mitts

Cooling rack

Prepare Ingredients

Vegetable oil spray

4 (6- to 8-ounce) **boneless, skinless chicken breasts**

¼ teaspoon plus ⅛ teaspoon **salt**, measured separately

¼ cup **barbecue sauce**

1 pound **broccoli florets** (6 cups)

2 tablespoons **extra-virgin olive oil**

Fun Fact!
Veggie Cousins

Did you know that plants have families, just like people do? Broccoli, cauliflower, cabbage, and kale are all part of the same plant family called *Brassicaceae*. They have similar flavors, so if you like broccoli, try one of its cousins!

"It was fun to make. Even touching the slimy chicken!"

—HADEN, 6

Start Cooking!

1

Heat and grease

Adjust oven rack to upper-middle position and heat oven to 450 degrees. Line baking sheet with aluminum foil. Spray lightly with vegetable oil spray.

2

Season chicken

Use paper towels to pat chicken dry. Place chicken in center of baking sheet. Sprinkle chicken evenly with ¼ teaspoon salt. Brush chicken evenly with barbecue sauce.

3

Prep broccoli

Place broccoli in bowl. Break any large florets into small pieces. Add oil and remaining ⅛ teaspoon salt and toss with your hands until broccoli is coated with oil. Arrange broccoli around chicken on baking sheet.

4

Bake

adult help! Bake until chicken registers 165 degrees, 12 to 14 minutes. Place baking sheet on cooling rack.

Fancy Fish in Foil

Serves 4

Total Time: 35 minutes

Gather Equipment

Measuring spoons

Rasp grater

Chef's knife

Cutting board

Aluminum foil

Small bowl

Spoon

Rimmed baking sheet

Instant-read thermometer

Oven mitts

Cooling rack

4 serving plates

Prepare Ingredients

1 teaspoon **fresh thyme leaves**

½ teaspoon **grated lemon zest**, plus lemon wedges for serving (see page 11 for how to grate zest)

½ teaspoon **salt**

⅛ teaspoon **pepper**

4 (6-ounce) **skinless cod fillets**, 1 to 1½ inches thick

4 tablespoons **unsalted butter**, cut into 4 pieces

Hot Tip!
Add Some Crunch

If you want a simple bread-crumb topping for your fish, give this a try: In small microwave-safe bowl, stir together ¼ cup **panko bread crumbs**, 1 teaspoon **extra-virgin olive oil**, and pinch **salt**. Cook in microwave for 1 minute. Stir mixture and continue to cook in microwave until panko is golden brown, 30 seconds to 1 minute longer. Sprinkle over your baked Fancy Fish in Foil just before serving.

Start Cooking!

1

2

Heat and cut

Adjust oven rack to middle position and heat oven to 450 degrees. Cut 4 large pieces of aluminum foil.

Assemble

Add thyme, lemon zest, salt, and pepper to bowl and stir with spoon to combine. Place 1 fillet on 1 side of each piece of foil. Sprinkle thyme mixture evenly over fillets and top with butter.

3

4

Seal

Fold empty side of foil over cod. Fold up edges of foil and pinch together to create sealed packet. Transfer packets to baking sheet.

Bake

adult help! Bake until cod registers 140 degrees, 12 to 15 minutes. Use oven mitts to remove baking sheet from oven. Transfer packets to plates and carefully open. Serve with lemon wedges.

Rice Noodle Bowls with Peanut Sauce

Serves 4

Total Time: 40 minutes

Gather Equipment

- Dry measuring cups
- Measuring spoons
- Chef's knife
- Cutting board
- Liquid measuring cup
- Vegetable peeler
- Box grater
- Large saucepan
- Wooden spoon
- Large bowl
- Whisk
- Colander
- Tongs
- 4 serving bowls

Prepare Ingredients

- 12 ounces (¼-inch-wide) **rice noodles**
- 1½ cups **frozen edamame**
- ½ cup **creamy peanut butter**
- 3 tablespoons **low-sodium soy sauce**
- 3 tablespoons **lime juice**, squeezed from 2 limes
- 1 tablespoon **honey**
- ¼ cup **hot water**, plus extra for cooking noodles
- 2 **carrots**, peeled and shredded (about 1 cup)
- ⅓ cup **dry-roasted peanuts**, chopped
- 8 **fresh Thai basil** or **sweet Italian basil leaves**, torn into pieces

turn the page!

Start Cooking!

Boil

adult help! Fill large saucepan halfway with water. Bring to boil over high heat. Carefully add noodles and edamame and stir with wooden spoon to combine. Return to boil and cook for 3 minutes.

Soak

Turn off heat. Stir to separate noodles and let sit until tender, about 10 minutes.

Make sauce

While noodles and edamame sit, in large bowl, whisk peanut butter, soy sauce, lime juice, and honey until smooth, about 1 minute. Whisk in ¼ cup hot water until fully combined.

Drain

adult help! When noodles and edamame are ready, drain noodles and edamame in colander in sink. Rinse with hot water and drain well.

Toss

Add noodles and edamame to bowl with peanut sauce. Use tongs to toss noodles and edamame until evenly coated with sauce.

Assemble

Divide noodles and edamame among serving bowls. Top each bowl with carrots, peanuts, and basil.

Fun Fact! Rice Noodles

Rice noodles are noodles . . . made out of rice! They come in all sorts of shapes and sizes and are made to float in soup or soak up sauce. Some of the most common are rice vermicelli (superthin and delicate), rice sticks (straight and flat, used in this noodle bowl), and chow fun (wide, flat, and chewy). Rice noodles are especially popular in Vietnamese, Thai, and Chinese cooking.

Couscous with Carrots and Raisins

Serves 4 to 6

Total Time: 30 minutes

Gather Equipment

Liquid measuring cup

Dry measuring cups

Measuring spoons

Chef's knife

Cutting board

Can opener

Colander

Vegetable peeler

Box grater

Medium saucepan with lid

Wooden spoon

Large bowl

Fork

Prepare Ingredients

1⅓ cups **water**

1 cup **couscous**

¾ teaspoon **salt**

3 tablespoons **extra-virgin olive oil**

3 tablespoons **lemon juice**, squeezed from 1 lemon

1 (15-ounce) can **chickpeas**, rinsed

2 **carrots**, peeled and shredded (about 1 cup)

½ cup **raisins**

Fun Fact!

What Is Couscous?

Did you know that couscous is actually pasta? Pasta noodles are made by mixing flour with water to make dough that is then formed into shapes. Couscous is traditionally made by rubbing flour and water by hand to form small balls about the size of bread crumbs.

Start Cooking!

Cook couscous

adult help! In medium saucepan, bring water to boil over high heat. Turn off heat. Carefully add couscous and salt to saucepan and stir with wooden spoon to combine. Cover and let sit for 10 minutes.

Make dressing

While couscous sits, in bowl, beat together oil and lemon juice with fork. Add chickpeas, carrots, and raisins and stir until coated with dressing.

try it THIS way

Couscous with White Beans and Feta

Use 1 (15-ounce) can **white beans** instead of the chickpeas. Omit carrots and raisins. Add ½ cup **crumbled feta** and ½ cup torn **fresh mint** or **basil** to bowl at end of step 3 and stir to combine.

Assemble

adult help! When couscous is ready, carefully transfer couscous to bowl (saucepan will be hot!). Use fork to break up clumps of couscous, then use wooden spoon to gently stir until combined.

Roasted Green Beans

Serves 4

Total Time: 35 minutes

Gather Equipment

- Measuring spoons
- Chef's knife
- Cutting board
- Rimmed baking sheet
- Aluminum foil
- Oven mitts

Prepare Ingredients

- 1 pound **green beans**
- 1 tablespoon **extra-virgin olive oil**
- ¼ teaspoon **sugar**
- ½ teaspoon **salt**
- ⅛ teaspoon **pepper**
- **Lemon wedges** for serving

Fun Fact!

So. Many. Beans.

Did you know that green beans are part of a group of plants called legumes? There are thousands of different types of legumes growing around the world. Can you guess which of these plants are legumes, like green beans?

A. Sugar snap peas

B. Chickpeas

C. Lentils

D. Kidney beans

Answer key: All of them!

Start Cooking!

1 Heat

Adjust oven rack to lowest position and heat oven to 450 degrees.

2 Trim

adult help! Line up several green beans on cutting board and cut off tough ends. Repeat trimming remaining green beans in small batches.

3 Toss

On baking sheet, toss together green beans, oil, sugar, salt, and pepper. Spread green beans into even layer on baking sheet. Cover baking sheet tightly with aluminum foil.

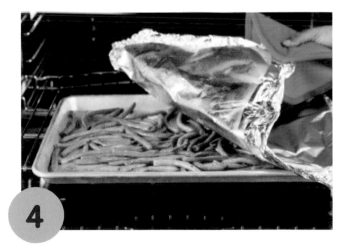

4 Roast

adult help! Roast for 10 minutes. Use oven mitts to remove foil, and roast (uncovered) until green beans are spotty brown, 3 to 4 minutes. Serve with lemon wedges.

make it YOUR way
Baked Sweet Potato Bar

Sweet potatoes are delicious and nutritious. They are simple to bake and are perfect for a potato bar complete with your favorite toppings!

Avocado

Shredded cooked chicken

2 Then add your favorite TOPPINGS

1 Start with BAKED SWEET POTATOES

Set up your topping bar while the potatoes bake! Put your favorite toppings in fun bowls with spoons so everyone can top their sweet potato just the way they like it.

Simple Baked Sweet Potatoes

Adjust oven rack to middle position and heat oven to 425 degrees. Set cooling rack in aluminum foil–lined rimmed baking sheet. Spray with **vegetable oil spray**. Use fork to prick 4 small **sweet potatoes** (about 8 ounces each) lightly in 3 places per potato. Place potatoes on greased cooling rack. Bake until potatoes are lightly browned and feel very soft when gently squeezed with tongs, about 1 hour. Use oven mitts to remove baking sheet from oven. Place baking sheet on second cooling rack and let cool for 10 minutes. Use clean dish towel to hold 1 potato steady and carefully use knife to cut slit in potato lengthwise. Use dish towel to hold ends of potato and squeeze gently to push flesh up and out of slit. Repeat with remaining 3 potatoes.

Parsley

Crumbled cooked sausage

Crumbled cooked bacon

Halved cherry tomatoes

Basil

Ranch dressing

Sour cream or yogurt

Salsa

Cilantro

Shredded cheddar or Monterey Jack

Chopped chives

Rinsed canned beans

Crumbled blue cheese

Grated Parmesan

Crumbled feta cheese

try it THIS way

Here are a few of our favorite combinations to help get your creative juices flowing—or come up with your own special topping combo!

Buffalo Chicken Potato

Top with quick **Buffalo chicken** (in bowl, stir together 1 cup shredded cooked chicken, 1 to 2 tablespoons Frank's hot sauce, and 1 tablespoon butter and heat in microwave until butter is melted and chicken is hot, 2 to 3 minutes), **crumbled blue cheese** or dollop of **sour cream**, and chopped fresh **chives**.

Thai-Style Potato

Top with **crushed dry-roasted peanuts** (crush in zipper-lock bag with rolling pin) and **fresh cilantro leaves** and drizzle with easy **Coconut-Peanut Sauce** (¼ cup canned coconut milk, 2 tablespoons creamy peanut butter, and 1 tablespoon lime juice, stirred in bowl until smooth).

Taco Potato

Top with **black beans** (1 can rinsed and heated in microwave with 1 teaspoon vegetable oil and 1 teaspoon chili powder in bowl), chopped **avocado**, and crumbled **cotija cheese**.

sweet treats

Sweets are made to share with family or friends. And everything tastes better if it's made at home!

M&M Cookies

Makes 12 cookies

Total Time: 40 minutes, plus cooling time

Gather Equipment

Dry measuring cups

Measuring spoons

Butter knife

Small microwave-safe bowl and plate

Rimmed baking sheet

Parchment paper

2 bowls (1 large, 1 medium)

Whisk

Rubber spatula

Oven mitts

Cooling rack

Prepare Ingredients

1 cup (5 ounces) **all-purpose flour**

¼ teaspoon **baking soda**

¼ teaspoon **salt**

¾ cup (5¼ ounces) **sugar**

4 tablespoons **unsalted butter**, melted (see page 10 for how to melt butter)

1 **large egg**

1 teaspoon **vanilla extract**

⅓ cup **M&M's**

turn the page!

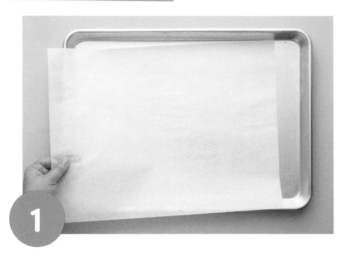

1

Heat and line

Adjust oven rack to middle position and heat oven to 325 degrees. Line baking sheet with parchment paper.

2

Whisk dry

In medium bowl, whisk together flour, baking soda, and salt.

3

Whisk wet

In large bowl, whisk sugar and melted butter until smooth. Add egg and vanilla and whisk until well combined.

4

Mix

Add flour mixture and use rubber spatula to stir until no dry flour is visible and soft dough forms.

> **"The cookies were yummiest while they were still warm."**
> —BRAYDEN, 6

5

Portion

Use your hands to roll dough into 12 balls (about 1 heaping tablespoon each). Place dough balls on parchment-lined baking sheet, leaving space between them.

6

Press and top

Gently flatten each dough ball. Press candies into each cookie (about 5 candies per cookie).

7

Bake

adult help! Bake until edges of cookies are just set and centers are still soft, 11 to 13 minutes. Let cookies cool completely on baking sheet, about 30 minutes.

Marvelous M&M's!

The *M*'s printed on M&M's stand for the last names of their inventors: Forrest Mars and Bruce Murrie. These two businessmen teamed up to make M&M's in 1941 and started by selling their candy exclusively to the U.S. armed services (the candy-coated shells made M&M's heat resistant and good for travel).

Molasses Cookies

Makes 12 cookies

Total Time: 40 minutes, plus cooling time

Gather Equipment

Dry measuring cups

Measuring spoons

Butter knife

Small microwave-safe bowl and plate

Liquid measuring cup

Rimmed baking sheet

Parchment paper

2 bowls (1 large, 1 medium)

Whisk

Rubber spatula

Shallow dish

Oven mitts

Cooling rack

Prepare Ingredients

1 cup plus 2 tablespoons (5⅔ ounces) **all-purpose flour**

½ teaspoon **baking soda**

¾ teaspoon **ground cinnamon**

½ teaspoon **ground ginger**

¼ teaspoon **ground cloves**

⅛ teaspoon **salt**

6 tablespoons **unsalted butter**, melted (see page 10 for how to melt butter)

⅓ cup packed (2⅓ ounces) **dark brown sugar**

¼ cup (3 ounces) **molasses**

1 **large egg yolk** (see page 10 for how to separate eggs)

½ teaspoon **vanilla extract**

¼ cup (1¾ ounces) **sugar**

turn the page!

1

Heat and line

Adjust oven rack to middle position and heat oven to 375 degrees. Line baking sheet with parchment paper.

2

Whisk dry

In medium bowl, whisk together flour, baking soda, cinnamon, ginger, cloves, and salt.

3

Whisk wet

In large bowl, whisk melted butter and brown sugar until smooth. Add molasses, egg yolk, and vanilla and whisk until well combined.

4

Mix

Add flour mixture and use rubber spatula to stir until no dry flour is visible and soft dough forms.

5

Roll and coat

Place sugar in shallow dish. Use your hands to roll dough into 12 balls (about 1 heaping tablespoon each). Place dough balls in dish and roll to coat with sugar.

6

Press

Place sugar-coated dough balls on parchment-lined baking sheet, leaving space between them. Gently flatten each ball.

7

Bake

adult help! Bake until edges of cookies are just set and centers are still soft and puffy, 7 to 9 minutes. Let cookies cool completely on baking sheet, about 30 minutes.

Fun Fact!

Where Does Molasses Come From?

Sugarcane! Molasses comes from the same place most regular white granulated sugar does: the tall, thick grass called sugarcane. Molasses is made by boiling sugarcane juice into a sweet, sticky syrup. It can be boiled just once to make "mild" or "light" molasses, twice to make "full" or "dark" molasses, or three times to make "blackstrap" molasses. You can use light or dark molasses in this recipe, but don't use blackstrap molasses here—its flavor is too bitter and intense.

Trail Mix Cookies

Makes 12 cookies

Total Time: 40 minutes, plus cooling time

Gather Equipment

- Dry measuring cups
- Measuring spoons
- Chef's knife
- Small microwave-safe bowl and plate
- Cutting board
- Rimmed baking sheet
- Parchment paper
- 2 bowls (1 large, 1 medium)
- Whisk
- Rubber spatula
- Oven mitts
- Cooling rack

Prepare Ingredients

- ½ cup (2½ ounces) **all-purpose flour**
- ½ teaspoon **salt**
- ¼ teaspoon **baking soda**
- ½ cup packed (3½ ounces) **light brown sugar**
- 6 tablespoons **unsalted butter**, melted (see page 10 for how to melt butter)
- ⅛ teaspoon **ground cinnamon**
- 1 **large egg**
- ½ teaspoon **vanilla extract**
- 1½ cups (4½ ounces) **old-fashioned rolled oats**
- ¼ cup **dried cranberries**
- ¼ cup **pecans**, chopped
- ¼ cup (1½ ounces) **chocolate chips**

Fun Fact! Trail . . . What?

Trail mix got its odd name because it's a mixture of high-energy portable foods easily taken on the (yes!) trail by hikers. Sometimes it's called "gorp" for "good old raisins and peanuts" or "granola, oats, raisins, and peanuts." In New Zealand, it's called "scroggin." What do YOU call it?

turn the page!

1
Heat and line
Adjust oven rack to middle position and heat oven to 375 degrees. Line baking sheet with parchment paper.

2
Whisk dry
In medium bowl, whisk together flour, salt, and baking soda.

3
Whisk wet
In large bowl, whisk brown sugar, melted butter, and cinnamon until smooth. Add egg and vanilla and whisk until well combined.

4
Mix
Add flour mixture and use rubber spatula to stir until no dry flour is visible. Add oats, cranberries, pecans, and chocolate chips and stir until evenly distributed.

"Don't be hesitant about the healthy ingredients because **they are delicious!"**

—MIRIAM, 7

Portion and press

Use 1-tablespoon measuring spoon to drop 12 mounds of dough (about 2 tablespoons each) onto parchment-lined baking sheet. Leave space between dough mounds. Gently flatten each dough mound.

Bake

adult help! Bake until edges of cookies are set and lightly browned but centers are still soft, 8 to 10 minutes. Let cookies cool completely on baking sheet, about 30 minutes.

Oat's About Time

Oats are the seed of a tall, grass-like plant. Rolled oats (also called old-fashioned or regular oats) are whole oats that have been steamed and then rolled. If these same oats are rolled very thinly, they are called quick oats because they cook, well, more quickly. Instant oats are cooked and then dehydrated, so they don't need any more cooking, just hot water. Not all brands of rolled oats are the same—some are denser than others (they weigh more). For these cookies, we had the best luck using Quaker old-fashioned rolled oats. Don't use quick, instant, or extra-thick rolled oats in this recipe.

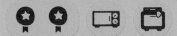

Chocolate Brownie Cookies

Makes 12 cookies

Total Time: 50 minutes, plus cooling time

We recommend using Dutch-processed cocoa powder in this recipe. If you use natural cocoa powder, the cookies will be a bit drier in texture and lighter in color.

Gather Equipment

- Dry measuring cups
- Measuring spoons
- Butter knife
- Rimmed baking sheet
- Parchment paper
- 2 bowls (1 large microwave-safe, 1 medium)
- Whisk
- Rubber spatula
- Oven mitts
- Cooling rack

Prepare Ingredients

- Vegetable oil spray
- ½ cup (2½ ounces) **all-purpose flour**
- 2 tablespoons **Dutch-processed cocoa powder**
- ½ teaspoon **baking powder**
- ¼ teaspoon **salt**
- 2 tablespoons **unsalted butter**
- ½ cup (3 ounces) plus ½ cup (3 ounces) **semisweet chocolate chips**, measured separately
- ½ cup packed (3½ ounces) **light brown sugar**
- 1 **large egg**

Chocolate Lovers Only

Do you really love chocolate? Like REALLY love it? If you do, you will really REALLY love these cookies. There's not one, not two, but three forms of chocolate in each bite: cocoa powder, melted chocolate, and chocolate chips.

turn the page!

Start Cooking!

1 **Heat and line**

Adjust oven rack to middle position and heat oven to 325 degrees. Line baking sheet with parchment paper and spray parchment with vegetable oil spray.

2 **Whisk dry**

In medium bowl, whisk together flour, cocoa, baking powder, and salt.

3 **Melt**

In large bowl, combine butter and ½ cup chocolate chips. Heat in microwave at 50 percent power until melted (see page 12), about 2 minutes. Use rubber spatula to stir mixture until smooth.

4 **Whisk wet**

Add brown sugar and egg to melted chocolate mixture and whisk to combine.

5

Mix

Add flour mixture and use rubber spatula to stir until combined and no dry flour is visible. Stir in remaining ½ cup chocolate chips.

6

Portion

Use 1-tablespoon measuring spoon to drop 12 mounds of dough (about 1 heaping tablespoon each) onto parchment-lined baking sheet. Leave space between dough mounds. Let sit for 10 minutes.

7

Roll and press

Use your hands to roll each dough mound into ball, then place back on parchment-lined baking sheet. Gently flatten each ball (if dough is sticky, use wet hands).

8

Bake

(**adult help!**) Bake until edges of cookies are just set and centers are still soft and starting to crack, 11 to 13 minutes. Let cookies cool completely on baking sheet, about 30 minutes.

Blondies

Makes 16 blondies

Total Time: 50 minutes, plus 2 hours cooling time

Gather Equipment

Dry measuring cups

Measuring spoons

Chef's knife

Small microwave-safe bowl and plate

Cutting board

Aluminum foil

8-inch square metal baking pan

2 bowls (1 large, 1 medium)

Whisk

Rubber spatula

Oven mitts

Cooling rack

Prepare Ingredients

Vegetable oil spray

1 cup (5 ounces) **all-purpose flour**

¼ teaspoon **baking powder**

¼ teaspoon **salt**

1 cup packed (7 ounces) **light brown sugar**

8 tablespoons **unsalted butter**, melted (see page 10 for how to melt butter)

1 **large egg**

1 teaspoon **vanilla extract**

⅔ cup **pecans**, chopped

½ cup (3 ounces) **chocolate chips**

turn the page!

1

Heat and line

Adjust oven rack to middle position and heat oven to 350 degrees. Make aluminum foil sling for 8-inch square metal baking pan (see photos, page 14). Spray foil with vegetable oil spray.

2

Whisk dry

In medium bowl, whisk together flour, baking powder, and salt.

3

Whisk wet

In large bowl, whisk brown sugar and melted butter until combined. Add egg and vanilla and whisk until combined.

4

Mix

Add flour mixture and use rubber spatula to stir until no dry flour remains. Add pecans and chocolate chips and stir to combine. Scrape batter into foil-lined baking pan and smooth top.

5

Bake

 Bake until top is shiny and cracked and feels firm to the touch, 25 to 27 minutes.

6

Cool

Let blondies cool completely in pan on cooling rack, about 2 hours. Use foil to carefully lift blondies out of pan and transfer to cutting board. Cut into squares.

Fun Fact!

The Difference Between Blondies and Brownies

Is the only difference between blondies and brownies . . . the color?! Yes and no. Blondies and brownies are both delicious bar treats that look similar—except brownies are dark brown and blondies are a light golden brown. Brownies are dark brown due to all the chocolate in them. Blondies rely on brown sugar instead of chocolate for sweetness. That's why blondies taste more like chocolate chip cookies (but are softer and moister) than brownies.

S'mores Rice Cereal Treats

Makes 16 bars

Total Time: 25 minutes, plus 1 hour cooling time

Do not use mini marshmallows here (they don't melt as well).

Gather Equipment

Butter knife

Measuring spoons

Dry measuring cups

8-inch square metal baking pan

Rubber spatula

Large microwave-safe bowl

Oven mitts

Cutting board

Chef's knife

Prepare Ingredients

Vegetable oil spray

1 (10-ounce) package **large marshmallows**

4 tablespoons **unsalted butter**

1 teaspoon **vanilla extract**

⅛ teaspoon **salt**

5 cups (5 ounces) **crisped rice cereal**

½ cup (3 ounces) **chocolate chips**

3 whole **graham crackers**, broken into small pieces

try it THIS way

Peanut Butter–Pretzel Rice Cereal Treats

In step 2, add 2 tablespoons **creamy peanut butter** to bowl with marshmallows before microwaving. In step 3, break 1 cup **pretzel sticks** into small pieces and add to bowl. Leave out chocolate chips and graham crackers.

Nutella Rice Cereal Treats

In step 2, add ¼ cup **Nutella** to bowl with marshmallows and butter. Leave out chocolate chips and graham crackers.

Start Cooking!

Grease

Spray inside bottom and sides of 8-inch square metal baking pan well with vegetable oil spray. Spray rubber spatula with vegetable oil spray.

Melt

adult help! In large bowl, combine marshmallows, butter, vanilla, and salt. Heat in microwave until marshmallows are puffed, about 2 minutes. Use greased rubber spatula to stir until smooth.

Mix

Add cereal, chocolate chips, and cracker pieces to bowl. Stir until well combined. Scrape cereal mixture into greased baking pan.

Press

Lightly wet your hands and press cereal mixture into flat, even layer. Let sit for 1 hour to set. Run butter knife around edge of cereal treats and transfer treats to cutting board. Cut into squares.

Pumpkin Snack Cake

Serves 12

Total Time: 1 hour, plus 2 hours cooling time

Gather Equipment

Dry measuring cups

Measuring spoons

Liquid measuring cup

8-inch square metal baking pan

8-inch square piece of parchment paper (see page 14)

2 bowls (1 large, 1 medium)

Whisk

Rubber spatula

Toothpick

Oven mitts

Cooling rack

Cutting board

Chef's knife

Prepare Ingredients

Vegetable oil spray

1 cup (5 ounces) **all-purpose flour**

1 teaspoon **ground cinnamon**

1 teaspoon **baking powder**

½ teaspoon **baking soda**

½ teaspoon **salt**

⅛ teaspoon **ground allspice**

⅛ teaspoon **ground ginger**

1 cup (7 ounces) **sugar**

2 **large eggs**

½ cup **vegetable oil**

1 cup **unsweetened pumpkin puree**

turn the page!

Start Cooking!

1

Heat and line

Adjust oven rack to middle position and heat oven to 350 degrees. Spray inside bottom and sides of 8-inch square metal baking pan with vegetable oil spray. Line bottom of pan with parchment paper.

2

Whisk dry

In medium bowl, whisk together flour, cinnamon, baking powder, baking soda, salt, allspice, and ginger.

3

Whisk wet

In large bowl, whisk sugar, eggs, oil, and pumpkin until combined.

4

Mix

Add flour mixture and use rubber spatula to stir until just combined and no dry flour is visible.

Bake

 Use rubber spatula to scrape batter into parchment-lined baking pan and smooth top. Bake until toothpick inserted in center of cake comes out clean, 30 to 35 minutes.

Cool

Let cake cool completely in pan on cooling rack, about 2 hours. Remove cake from baking pan (see page 15), discard parchment, and flip right side up on cutting board. Cut cake into squares.

Fun Fact! Canned Pumpkin(s)

At America's Test Kitchen, we have tested all different kinds of canned pumpkin. And every type of canned pumpkin is made with just one ingredient: pumpkin! But even so, each brand of canned pumpkin had a different color and texture. What gives? It turns out there aren't strict guidelines about what can legally be labeled "pumpkin." While you probably can't label a zucchini as a pumpkin, even though they are both squashes, botanists define pumpkins as "any squash with a firm shell, round body, and golden flesh." There are many different varieties of pumpkins—not just the ones we carve for Halloween—which is why one can of pumpkin might look different from the next one.

Strawberry Cream "Shortcake"

Serves 12

Total Time: 1 hour and 15 minutes, plus 2 hours cooling time

Gather Equipment

Dry measuring cups

Measuring spoons

Liquid measuring cup

Chef's knife

Small microwave-safe bowl and plate

Cutting board

9-inch round metal cake pan

9-inch round piece of parchment paper (see page 14)

3 bowls (1 large, 2 medium)

Whisk

Rubber spatula

Toothpick

Oven mitts

Cooling rack

Serving platter

Prepare Ingredients

Vegetable oil spray

1½ cups (7½ ounces) **all-purpose flour**

1½ teaspoons **baking powder**

¼ teaspoon **salt**

¾ cup (5¼ ounces) plus 1 tablespoon **sugar**, measured separately

⅔ cup (5⅓ ounces) **milk**

2 **large eggs**

6 tablespoons **unsalted butter**, melted (see page 10 for how to melt butter)

1½ teaspoons **vanilla extract**

2 cups (10 ounces) **strawberries**, hulled and quartered

2 cups **whipped cream** (see Whipped Cream, page 123 or store-bought)

Fun Fact!

What's a Shortcake?

Is a shortcake just a smaller version of a tall cake? Actually, no. Shortcakes are originally from England and are called "short" because that also means "crispy." Shortcakes have lots of butter and are more like American biscuits than cake. While the classic strawberry shortcake uses biscuits, we made a strawberry shortcake using a traditional cake. Maybe we should call it Strawberry Tallcake?!

turn the page!

Start Cooking!

1

Heat and line

Adjust oven rack to middle position and heat oven to 350 degrees. Spray inside bottom and sides of 9-inch round cake pan with vegetable oil spray. Line bottom of cake pan with parchment paper.

2

Whisk dry

In medium bowl, whisk together flour, baking powder, salt, and ¾ cup sugar.

3

Whisk wet

In large bowl, whisk together milk, eggs, melted butter, and vanilla.

4

Mix and pour

Add flour mixture and use rubber spatula to stir until just combined. Use rubber spatula to scrape batter into parchment-lined cake pan and smooth top.

5

Bake

adult help! Bake until toothpick inserted in center of cake comes out clean, 26 to 30 minutes.

Let cake cool completely in pan on cooling rack, about 2 hours.

6

Sweeten

Meanwhile, in second medium bowl, use clean rubber spatula to combine chopped strawberries and remaining 1 tablespoon sugar. Let sit while cake cools.

7

Top

Remove cake from cake pan (see page 15) and discard parchment. Spread whipped cream over top of cake. Arrange strawberries over whipped cream. Cut into wedges.

Whipped Cream

Makes 2 cups

If you don't have a mixer, you can use a whisk and whip cream by hand—but be prepared for a workout! It's okay to substitute whipping cream for the heavy cream, but do not substitute light cream or half-and-half.

To Make It: In large bowl, combine 1 cup cold **heavy cream**, 1 tablespoon **sugar**, and 1 teaspoon **vanilla**. Use electric mixer to whip cream on medium-low speed for 1 minute. Increase speed to high and whip until cream is smooth and thick and soft peaks form, about 1 minute.

Chocolate Glazed Cupcakes

Makes 12 cupcakes

Total Time: 1 hour, plus 1 hour and 20 minutes cooling time

We highly recommend using Dutch-processed cocoa powder in this recipe. If you use natural cocoa powder, the cupcakes will be drier in texture and lighter in color. You can use bittersweet or semisweet chocolate chips here, but we do not recommend milk chocolate chips.

Gather Equipment

Dry measuring cups

Measuring spoons

Large liquid measuring cup

Butter knife

12-cup muffin tin

12 paper cupcake liners

3 bowls (1 large, 1 medium, 1 small microwave-safe)

Whisk

Toothpick

Oven mitts

Cooling rack

Rubber spatula

Serving platter

Prepare Ingredients

1 cup (5 ounces) **all-purpose flour**

1 cup (7 ounces) **sugar**

½ cup (2 ounces) **Dutch-processed cocoa powder**

1 teaspoon **baking soda**

½ teaspoon **baking powder**

¼ teaspoon **salt**

1 cup (8 ounces) **milk**

½ cup **vegetable oil**

1 **large egg**

1 teaspoon **vanilla extract**

½ cup (3 ounces) **semisweet chocolate chips**

3 tablespoons **unsalted butter**, cut into 3 pieces

Fun Fact! From Cacao to Cocoa

The recipe doesn't actually call for any chocolate in the cupcake batter, just cocoa powder. Cocoa comes from the seeds of cacao plants. The seeds are fermented, dried, roasted, ground up, and separated from cocoa butter to make cocoa powder. While cocoa powder has tons of concentrated chocolate flavor, it has none of the sweetness of chocolate. On its own, cocoa powder is really bitter!

turn the page!

1

Heat and line

Adjust oven rack to middle position and heat oven to 350 degrees. Line 12-cup muffin tin with 12 paper liners.

2

Whisk dry

In medium bowl, whisk together flour, sugar, cocoa, baking soda, baking powder, and salt.

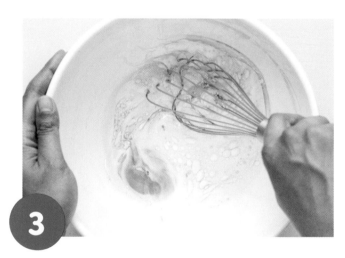

3

Whisk wet

In large bowl, whisk milk, oil, egg, and vanilla until well combined.

4

Mix

Add flour mixture and whisk until just combined and no dry flour is visible.

Portion batter

Pour batter into large liquid measuring cup. Divide batter evenly among muffin tin cups (each cup should be filled almost to top).

Bake and cool

adult help! Bake cupcakes until toothpick inserted in center of 1 cupcake comes out clean, 20 to 22 minutes. Let cupcakes cool completely in muffin tin on cooling rack, about 1 hour.

Melt

In small bowl, combine chocolate chips and butter. Heat in microwave at 50 percent power (see page 12) for 2 minutes. Stir with rubber spatula until smooth.

Glaze

Remove cooled cupcakes from muffin tin. Turn each cupcake upside down and dip top in chocolate glaze. Turn cupcake right side up and let glaze set and harden, about 20 minutes.

Ice Cream Cake

Serves 16

Total Time: 45 minutes, plus 2 hours freezing time

You can substitute your favorite flavors of ice cream for the chocolate and mint chocolate chip ice cream, if desired.

Gather Equipment

Butter knife

Small microwave-safe bowl and plate

Dry measuring cups

Large zipper-lock plastic bag

Rolling pin

Large bowl

Rubber spatula

9-inch springform pan

Ice cream scoop

Plastic wrap

Chef's knife

Prepare Ingredients

36 **Oreo cookies** (1 package), broken into large pieces

4 tablespoons **unsalted butter**, melted (see page 10 for how to melt butter)

2 pints **chocolate ice cream**

2 pints **mint chocolate chip ice cream**

¼ cup **sprinkles**

turn the page!

Start Cooking!

Smash

Place cookie pieces in large zipper-lock plastic bag. Seal bag, making sure to press out all air. Use rolling pin to gently pound bag to break cookies into crumbs.

Mix

Transfer cookie crumbs to bowl. Add melted butter and use rubber spatula to stir until combined.

Press

Transfer half of cookie mixture to 9-inch springform pan. Press mixture into even layer in bottom of pan. Place in freezer and chill for 15 minutes. Let ice cream soften on counter while crust chills.

Make first layer

Remove springform pan from freezer. Use ice cream scoop to scoop softened chocolate ice cream into pan. Cover ice cream with plastic wrap. Use your hands to gently push ice cream into even layer.

Sprinkle

Sprinkle remaining cookie mixture on top of chocolate ice cream layer. Use your hands to gently press cookie mixture into ice cream in even layer.

Make second layer

Repeat step 4 with softened mint chocolate chip ice cream. Sprinkle top of cake with sprinkles.

Freeze

Cover pan with plastic wrap. Place in freezer and chill until firm, at least 2 hours or up to 1 week. To serve, run butter knife around edge of cake to release cake from pan. Remove side of pan. Cut cake into wedges.

Fun Fact!
Keep It Chill

We wouldn't be able to make a very good ice cream cake without using the freezer. Have you ever wondered how food was stored before everyone had a refrigerator? Before the electric refrigerator and freezer were invented in the 1920s, people had iceboxes in their homes to keep food cold. Iceboxes were metal-lined cabinets with a compartment that held a large chunk of ice that cooled food in other compartments. Ice was often delivered daily to homes so everyone could keep their iceboxes cool!

Peach-Raspberry Crisp

Serves 8

Total Time: 1 hour, plus cooling time

Gather Equipment

Measuring spoons

Dry measuring cups

Chef's knife

Small microwave-safe bowl and plate

Cutting board

2 bowls (1 large, 1 medium)

Rubber spatula

Colander

8-inch square baking dish

Oven mitts

Cooling rack

Prepare Ingredients

1¾ pounds **frozen sliced peaches**, thawed

⅛ teaspoon **salt**

¼ cup packed (1¾ ounces) plus ¼ cup packed (1¾ ounces) **light brown sugar**, measured separately

⅔ cup (3⅓ ounces) **all-purpose flour**

½ cup (1½ ounces) **old-fashioned rolled oats** (see page 105)

5 tablespoons **unsalted butter**, melted (see page 10 for how to melt butter)

2 cups (10 ounces) **raspberries**

1 tablespoon **cornstarch**

1 tablespoon **lemon juice**, squeezed from ½ lemon

1 teaspoon **vanilla extract**

turn the page!

1 Heat

Adjust oven rack to upper-middle position and heat oven to 400 degrees.

2 Toss

In large bowl, use rubber spatula to gently toss peaches with salt and ¼ cup brown sugar. Let sit for 10 minutes.

3 Mix

Meanwhile, in medium bowl, use clean rubber spatula to stir together flour, oats, and remaining ¼ cup brown sugar. Drizzle melted butter over top and toss until mixture comes together.

4 Drain

Drain peaches in colander in sink. Return peaches to large bowl.

"The raspberries and peaches give it a **very fresh** feeling."

—HANNAH, 6

5 Toss

Add raspberries, cornstarch, lemon juice, and vanilla to bowl with peaches. Use clean rubber spatula to gently toss until combined.

6 Sprinkle

Transfer fruit mixture to baking dish and press gently with spatula into even layer. Sprinkle oat topping evenly over fruit mixture.

7 Bake

adult help! Bake until topping is well browned and fruit is bubbling around edges, 30 to 35 minutes. Let crisp cool on cooling rack for at least 30 minutes before serving.

Fun Fact!
What a Peach!

When we think about peaches, we often think about Georgia, but did you know that peaches originally come from China? People have been growing peach trees in China for more than 8,000 years! Spanish explorers brought peaches to the Americas in the 16th century, but American farmers did not start growing peaches until the 1800s.

Key Lime Cups

Serves 4

Total Time: 35 minutes, plus 1 hour and 45 minutes cooling and chilling time

Gather Equipment

Chef's knife

Dry measuring cups

Can opener

Rasp grater

Measuring spoons

Cutting board

Large zipper-lock plastic bag

Rolling pin

2 microwave-safe bowls (1 large, 1 small)

Rubber spatula

Whisk

4 (4-ounce) ramekins

Rimmed baking sheet

Oven mitts

Cooling rack

Plastic wrap

Prepare Ingredients

1½ **graham crackers**, broken into pieces

1 tablespoon **unsalted butter**

¼ cup (2 ounces) **cream cheese**

1 (14-ounce) can **sweetened condensed milk**

1 teaspoon grated **lime zest** plus ⅓ cup **juice**, zested and squeezed from 3 limes (see page 11 for how to zest and juice limes)

2 tablespoons **water**

1 **large egg yolk** (see page 10 for how to separate eggs)

Pinch **salt**

Whipped Cream, optional (page 123)

Fun Fact!

What Is a Key Lime, Anyway?

Key limes are NOT the same as the limes you see in the supermarket! Key limes are smaller and have more seeds, a thinner skin, and a tarter taste. They get their name from the Florida Keys, where they were first grown. Don't worry, you don't have to hunt down key limes, even though these are called "Key Lime Cups"—we developed this recipe with regular Persian limes!

turn the page!

1 Heat

Adjust oven rack to middle position and heat oven to 300 degrees.

2 Smash

Add graham cracker pieces to large zipper-lock plastic bag. Seal bag, making sure to press out all air. Use rolling pin to gently pound bag to break crackers into crumbs.

3 Mix

(adult help!) Add graham cracker crumbs and butter to small bowl. Heat in microwave until toasted, about 1 minute. Stir with rubber spatula to combine.

4 Soften

In large bowl, microwave cream cheese for 10 to 15 seconds. Whisk softened cream cheese until very smooth.

"I liked squishing the graham crackers! It was `hard to wait` to try it while it was in the fridge."

—ISABELLE, 6

5

Whisk

Add condensed milk, lime zest and juice, water, egg yolk, and salt to bowl with cream cheese. Whisk until well combined and smooth.

6

Fill

Divide filling evenly among ramekins. Place ramekins on baking sheet.

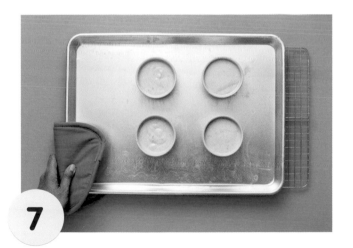

7

Bake and cool

adult help! Bake until filling is set and no longer jiggles when baking sheet is gently shaken, about 6 minutes. Let key lime cups cool on cooling rack for 45 minutes.

8

Chill

Cover ramekins with plastic wrap and refrigerate until filling is chilled and firm, at least 1 hour or up to 2 days. To serve, dollop with Whipped Cream, if using, and sprinkle with graham cracker topping.

Mango Lassi Popsicles

Makes 6 popsicles

Total Time: 15 minutes, plus 6 hours freezing time

Gather Equipment

Dry measuring cups

Measuring spoons

Chef's knife

Cutting board

Food processor

Rubber spatula

Large liquid measuring cup

6 ice pop molds (about 3 ounces each)

6 ice pop sticks

Prepare Ingredients

1½ cups (10 ounces) **fresh or frozen chopped mango**

1½ cups **plain yogurt**

¼ cup **honey**

1 tablespoon **lime juice**, squeezed from ½ lime

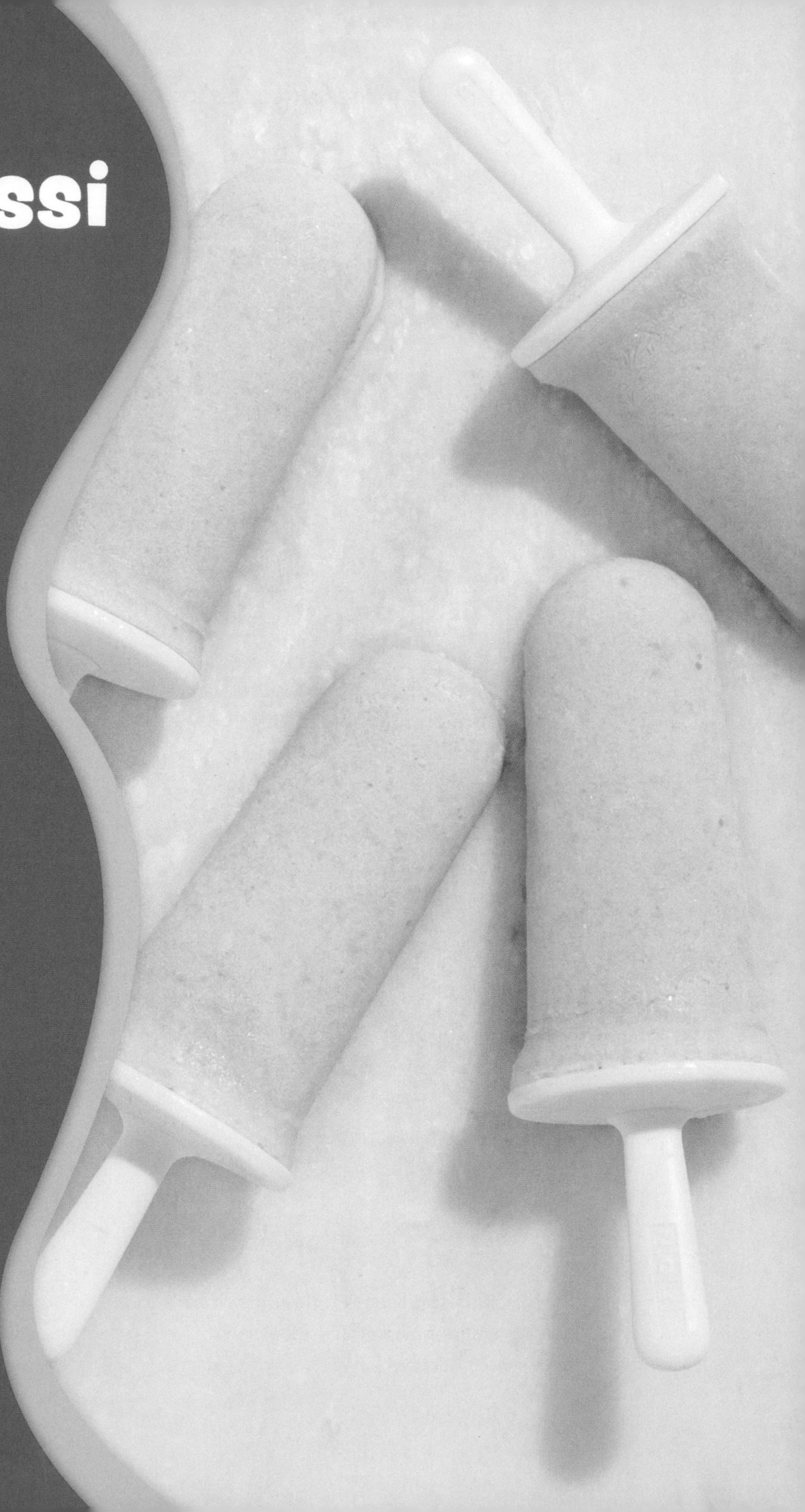

Start Cooking!

1

Process

adult help! Place all ingredients in food processor. Lock lid into place and process mixture until smooth, 30 to 40 seconds, scraping down sides of bowl halfway through. Remove processor blade.

2

Fill

Pour mixture into large liquid measuring cup, using rubber spatula to help scrape out mixture. Divide mixture evenly among ice pop molds.

3

Freeze

Insert 1 ice pop stick in center of each mold and seal with cover. Place in freezer and chill until firm, at least 6 hours or up to 5 days.

4

Unmold

Hold mold under warm running water for 30 seconds to thaw slightly. Slide popsicle out of mold.

make it YOUR way
Chocolate-Dipped Treats

Dipping fruit, cookies, or salty snacks in chocolate makes them a next-level treat.

Cookies

1 Start with MELTED CHOCOLATE

Melted Chocolate Coating

Place 1½ cups (9 ounces) **semisweet** or **white chocolate chips** and 2 teaspoons **vegetable oil** in 2-cup microwave-safe liquid measuring cup or small microwave-safe bowl. Heat in microwave at 50 percent power (see page 12) until chocolate chips are almost (but not quite!) melted, about 2 minutes, stirring with spoon every 30 seconds. Remove from microwave and stir until chocolate chips are completely melted and smooth. Let cool slightly, about 5 minutes. Add food coloring if desired.

Strawberries
Orange slices
Clementine slices

2 Then DIP

Dip your treat into the melted chocolate mixture, shake gently to let the extra chocolate drip off, and then place on a parchment paper–lined baking sheet or platter.

Marshmallows (on a treat stick or a candy cane!)

Dried fruit (such as apricot, mango, or pineapple)

Pretzels twists

Pretzels rods

3 Then ADD TOPPINGS

While the chocolate is still warm, you can sprinkle your dipped treat with things such as:

Chopped nuts

Sprinkles

Sanding sugar

Shredded coconut

Flaky salt

Crushed cookies

4 Then CHILL

Freeze until chocolate is hardened, about 5 minutes, or refrigerate for at least 15 minutes or up to 1 day.

try it THIS way

Marshmallow on a mini candy cane

Pretzel rod with sprinkles

Dried apricot with pistachios

Strawberry with sprinkles

holidays and celebrations

Around the world there are many holidays—each for different reasons, with different foods cooked to celebrate. **Travel the globe** with these holiday recipes today!

Pork Dumplings for Chinese New Year

Serves 4 to 6 (Makes 20 dumplings)
Total Time: 1 hour

Gather Equipment

Dry measuring cups

Chef's knife

Cutting board

Measuring spoons

Liquid measuring cup

Food processor

Rimmed baking sheet

Parchment paper

Paper towel

Pastry brush

12-inch nonstick skillet with lid

Oven mitts

Tongs

Serving platter

Prepare Ingredients

1½ cups shredded **green coleslaw mix**

4 ounces **ground pork**

1 **scallion**, chopped fine

2 teaspoons **toasted sesame oil**

1½ teaspoons **low-sodium soy sauce**, plus extra for dipping

1 teaspoon **hoisin sauce**

½ teaspoon **salt**

¼ teaspoon **ground ginger**

20 (3-inch) **round gyoza dumpling wrappers**

1 tablespoon **vegetable oil**

½ cup **water**, plus extra for brushing

Fun Fact! Happy New Year

Chinese New Year, also known as the Spring Festival, is one of the most important holidays in Chinese culture. It's usually celebrated in January or February, and families eat lots of food (especially dumplings!), watch fireworks, and hang up red lanterns to celebrate. Each year is also named for an animal—2020 is the Year of the Rat, and 2021 is the Year of the Ox!

turn the page!

Process

(adult help!) Add first 8 ingredients to food processor. Lock lid into place. Hold down pulse button for 1 second; release. Repeat until evenly combined, about eight 1-second pulses. Remove lid and blade.

Fill

Line baking sheet with parchment paper and set aside. Place 5 dumpling wrappers on clean counter (cover others with moist paper towel). Place heaping 1 teaspoon filling in center of each wrapper.

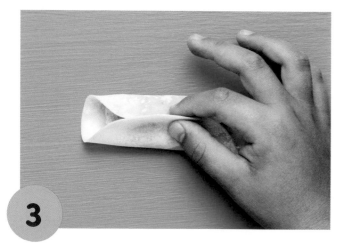

Paint and press

Use your finger to lightly paint edges of wrappers with water. Bring top and bottom edges of wrapper over filling and press together in center, leaving sides open.

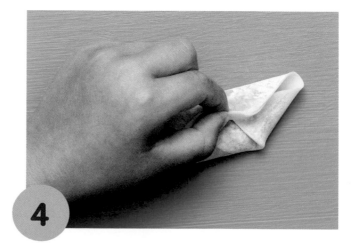

Fold and pinch

Fold 1 open side of wrapper to center and pinch together. Repeat with other side of wrapper.

"It turned out delicious!"

—KEVIN, 7

5

Seal edges

Pinch edges to seal. Place dumplings on parchment-lined baking sheet. Repeat filling and shaping with remaining filling and dumpling wrappers.

6

Oil skillet

Use pastry brush to paint 12-inch nonstick skillet evenly with vegetable oil. Place dumplings in skillet, evenly spaced, flat side down.

7

Cook

adult help! Cook over medium heat until bottoms turn spotty brown, 3 to 4 minutes. Reduce heat to low, carefully add water, and cover. Cook until most of water is absorbed, about 10 minutes.

8

Brown

adult help! Use oven mitts to remove lid. Increase heat to medium-high and cook until water has evaporated and bottoms of dumplings are browned, 2 to 4 minutes. Transfer to platter.

Chocolate-Raspberry Mug Cakes for Valentine's Day

Serves 2

Total Time: 25 minutes

These fudgy cakes must be served warm. Add whipped cream or a small scoop of ice cream for a deluxe treat. We highly recommend using Dutch-processed cocoa powder in this recipe. If you use natural cocoa powder, the mug cakes will be drier in texture and lighter in color.

Gather Equipment

Dry measuring cups

Measuring spoons

Butter knife

2 bowls (1 medium microwave-safe, 1 small)

Whisk

Spoon

2 microwave-safe coffee mugs (11 ounces each or larger)

Oven mitts

Prepare Ingredients

¼ cup (1¼ ounces) **all-purpose flour**

½ teaspoon **baking powder**

4 tablespoons **unsalted butter**, cut into 4 pieces

3 tablespoons **semisweet chocolate chips**

2 **large eggs**

¼ cup (1¾ ounces) **sugar**

2 tablespoons **Dutch-processed cocoa powder**

2 tablespoons **seedless raspberry jam**

1 teaspoon **vanilla extract**

⅛ teaspoon **salt**

10 **raspberries**

turn the page!

Start Cooking!

1

Mix

In small bowl, whisk together flour and baking powder.

2

Melt

In medium bowl, combine butter and chocolate chips. Heat in microwave at 50 percent power for 1 to 2 minutes (see page 12). Use spoon to stir mixture until smooth.

3

Whisk

Add eggs, sugar, cocoa, jam, vanilla, and salt to chocolate mixture and whisk until smooth. Add flour mixture and whisk until smooth.

4

Divide

Use spoon to divide batter evenly between 2 coffee mugs.

5

6

Cook

Place mugs on opposite sides of microwave turntable. Cook at 50 percent power for 1 minute. Stop microwave and use spoon to stir batter in each mug, making sure to reach bottom of mug.

Cook more

Cook at 50 percent power for 1 more minute (batter will rise to below rim of mug and cake will look wet around edges—if edges are not set, cook at 50 percent power for 15 to 30 seconds more).

7

Cool and top

 Use oven mitts to remove mugs from microwave, and let cool for 5 minutes. Place 5 raspberries on top of each cake.

Back to Chocolate's Roots . . . The Mug?!

Did you know that when chocolate first came to the United States, it was more common to drink it than to eat it? In the 18th century, New Yorkers were known to grate chocolate into hot water and enjoy it as a beverage, often in the morning. That chocolaty breakfast drink (yum!) evolved into the chocolate candy bar in the mid-19th century, and chocolate has been made into all sorts of sweet treats ever since—especially around Valentine's Day.

Deviled Eggs for Easter

Serves 6 (Makes 12 deviled eggs)

Total Time: 50 minutes

Gather Equipment

Measuring spoons

Medium saucepan with lid

Ruler

Steamer basket

Oven mitts

2 medium bowls

Slotted spoon

Cutting board

Chef's knife

Spoon

Plate

Fork

Rubber spatula

Small zipper-lock plastic bag

Scissors

Prepare Ingredients

Water

6 **large eggs**

3 tablespoons **mayonnaise**

¼ teaspoon **Dijon mustard**

½ teaspoon **distilled white vinegar**

⅛ teaspoon **salt**

⅛ teaspoon **pepper**

Fun Fact! The Devil in Deviled Eggs

Many families decorate hard-boiled eggs for Easter, but after the holiday, they need a way to use them up. Deviled eggs are perfect for this. When cooking, "to devil" means "to season highly" or "to cook a food with hot or spicy seasonings." The "devil" here is the Dijon mustard and the pepper in the mashed egg yolk filling. Deviled eggs are traditionally made by combining mayonnaise, mustard, and spices with egg yolks, but some recipes call for extra-spicy ingredients, too, such as hot sauce or cayenne pepper.

turn the page!

Start Cooking!

1

Boil

 adult help! Fill medium saucepan with 1 inch water. Bring water to rolling boil.

2

Cook

 adult help! Place eggs in steamer basket and use oven mitts to carefully lower basket into saucepan. Cover saucepan with lid, reduce heat to medium-low, and cook eggs for 13 minutes.

3

Cool

While eggs cook, fill bowl halfway with ice and cold water. Use slotted spoon to transfer cooked eggs to ice bath. Let eggs sit for 15 minutes. Drain eggs.

4

Peel

Crack eggs against hard surface (such as a counter) and use your hands to peel away shells. Place eggs on cutting board.

5

Slice

adult help! Slice eggs in half lengthwise (the long way). Carefully scoop out egg yolks with spoon and transfer to second bowl. Arrange egg whites on plate.

6

Mash and smear

Mash yolks with fork until no lumps remain. Add mayonnaise, mustard, vinegar, salt, and pepper to bowl. Use rubber spatula to smear mixture against bowl until smooth paste forms, 1 to 2 minutes.

7

Fill

Transfer yolk mixture to small zipper-lock plastic bag. Press mixture into 1 corner and twist top of bag. Use scissors to snip ½ inch off filled corner. Squeeze bag to fill each egg half evenly with yolk mixture.

make it YOUR way

You can eat your deviled eggs as they are or sprinkle them with your favorite toppings! Our favorite topping options include chopped cooked **bacon**, a sprinkle of **paprika**, snipped **chives**, and other chopped fresh **herbs**.

Egyptian Spice Cookies for Eid

Makes 24 cookies

Total Time: 1 hour, plus cooling time

Ghee is a type of clarified butter that's common in Indian and Middle Eastern cooking. You can find it in the international section of many grocery stores or with other cooking oils. You can also substitute butter in this recipe.

Gather Equipment

Dry measuring cups

Measuring spoons

Butter knife

Small microwave-safe bowl and plate

Liquid measuring cup

Rimmed baking sheet

Parchment paper

Large bowl

Whisk

Rubber spatula

Fork

Oven mitts

Cooling rack

Fine-mesh strainer

Prepare Ingredients

1½ cups (7½ ounces) **all-purpose flour**

½ cup (2 ounces) **confectioners' (powdered) sugar**, plus extra for dusting

2 tablespoons **sesame seeds**, toasted

1 teaspoon **ground cinnamon**

½ teaspoon **baking powder**

⅛ teaspoon **salt**

⅔ cup **ghee**, melted, or 10 tablespoons **unsalted butter**, melted (see page 10 for how to melt butter)

⅓ cup (2⅔ ounces) **milk**

1 teaspoon **vanilla extract**

turn the page!

1

Heat and line

Adjust oven rack to middle position and heat oven to 350 degrees. Line baking sheet with parchment paper.

2

Whisk

In large bowl, whisk together flour, confectioners' sugar, sesame seeds, cinnamon, baking powder, and salt.

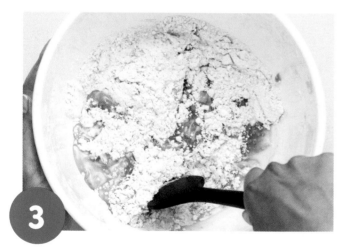

3

Mix

Add melted ghee, milk, and vanilla to flour mixture. Use rubber spatula to stir until no dry flour is visible and soft dough forms.

4

Portion

Use your hands to roll dough into 24 balls (about 1 level tablespoon each). Place dough balls on parchment-lined baking sheet, leaving space between dough balls.

Press and pattern

Gently flatten each ball. Use side of fork to firmly press diamond crosshatch pattern in each cookie.

Bake

adult help! Bake cookies until light golden brown, 20 to 24 minutes. Let cookies cool completely on baking sheet, about 30 minutes.

Dust

Add 1 to 2 tablespoons confectioners' sugar to fine-mesh strainer. Hold strainer over cookies and tap to dust lightly with sugar.

Fun Fact!
Breaking the Fast

Eid al-Fitr is a Muslim holiday that celebrates the end of the month of Ramadan. During Ramadan, Muslims fast during the day, which means they don't eat or drink. (But they do eat before dawn and after the sun sets.) *Eid al-Fitr* means "Festival of Breaking the Fast" in Arabic, and families celebrate by visiting friends and neighbors and enjoying lots of food, including treats such as these spiced, not-too-sweet cookies!

Firecracker Hot Dogs for the Fourth of July

Serves 8

Total Time: 45 minutes, plus cooling time

You can make a fun topper for your firecrackers with extra biscuit dough (see "Try It This Way," page 165). Serve with ketchup and/or mustard.

Gather Equipment

Fork

Small bowl

Measuring spoons

Rimmed baking sheet

Parchment paper

8 wooden skewers

Ruler

Chef's knife (or bench scraper)

Pastry brush

Oven mitts

Cooling rack

Prepare Ingredients

Vegetable oil spray

8 **hot dogs**

1 can **biscuit dough**

1 **large egg**, lightly beaten

1 tablespoon **sesame seeds**

Fun Fact! America's Birthday

The Fourth of July, also called Independence Day, is an American holiday celebrating the signing of the Declaration of Independence—which happened (no surprise!) on July 4, 1776. The Declaration of Independence stated that the American colonies were no longer under British rule—they were now independent states. This makes the Fourth of July like America's birthday! Today we celebrate Independence Day with fireworks, parades, and barbecues where we serve classic "American" foods such as hot dogs, burgers, and potato salad.

turn the page!

Start Cooking!

Heat and line

Adjust oven rack to middle position and heat oven to 375 degrees. Line baking sheet with parchment paper. Spray parchment lightly with vegetable oil spray.

Skewer

adult help! Carefully push 1 skewer lengthwise (the long way) through center of each hot dog.

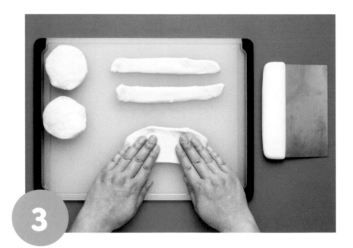

Prepare dough

Use your hands to pat and stretch 1 biscuit dough round into oval, about 8 inches long. Cut oval in half lengthwise. Repeat stretching and cutting with 3 additional biscuit dough rounds.

Wrap

Starting from top, wrap 1 dough strip around each hot dog in spiral, leaving gaps in spiral as you wrap. Place on parchment-lined baking sheet, tucking ends of dough strips underneath hot dogs.

"It's like a piggy in a blanket, but Hulk-size!"

—HILTON, 7

5

Brush

Use pastry brush to brush tops of dough strips with egg. Sprinkle sesame seeds over top.

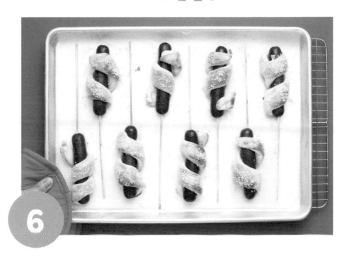

6

Bake

adult help! Bake until biscuit strips are golden brown, about 15 minutes. Let hot dogs cool on baking sheet for 10 minutes.

try it THIS way

Firecracker Topper

You can make your hot dogs extra-special by making a topper for your skewers! Pat out extra biscuit dough into 4-inch circle. Use 1½- to 2-inch star cookie cutter (use similar-size cookie cutter of another shape, if desired) to cut out dough shapes. At end of step 2, carefully push skewers all the way through hot dogs, leaving 1½ to 2 inches of skewer sticking out at top of each hot dog. At end of step 4, carefully stick 1 dough shape on end of each skewer. Continue with recipe as directed.

make it YOUR way
Spooky Halloween Treats

If you want to use your imagination to come up with your own designs, here are some helpful ingredients to try out.

Jams and jellies

Chopped fruit

Nut butter

Berries

Cookies

String cheese

Crackers

Chocolate chips

Pretzel rods

Raisins

Nuts

Candy (M&M's, candy corn)

Candy eyeballs (find these online or in the cake decorating section of a craft store)

Marshmallows

try it THIS way!

Having a Halloween party? Thrill your friends with some of these easy, spooky treats! Here are a few of our favorites.

Apple Monsters

Apple slices, peanut butter and jelly, candy corn/ slivered almonds (teeth), candy eyeballs

Clementine Pumpkins

Peeled clementines, green apple slices (stems)

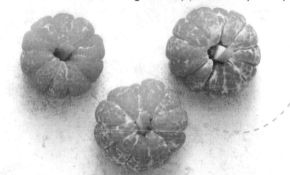

Ghost Fruit Kebabs

Skewers, melon chunks, berries, marshmallows, mini chocolate chips (use a skewer to poke holes in the marshmallows for eyes and a mouth first, and then press in the mini chocolate chips!)

Pizza Mummies

Breadsticks, pizza sauce, string cheese, sliced black olives (eyes)

Waffle Spiders

Mini waffles, Nutella, pretzel sticks (legs), raisins (eyes)

Doughnut Vampire Bats

Chocolate doughnuts, Thin Mints or Grasshopper cookies (broken in half for wings), slivered almonds (teeth), candy eyeballs

Karanji for Diwali

Makes 10 karanji
Total Time: 1 hour

Gather Equipment

Dry measuring cups

Measuring spoons

Rimmed baking sheet

Parchment paper

4-inch round cutter

Plastic wrap

Medium microwave-safe bowl

Rubber spatula

Oven mitts

Potato masher

Pastry brush

Cooling rack

Prepare Ingredients

1 package **store-bought pie dough**

1 cup **frozen peas**

2 tablespoons **water**, plus extra for brushing

½ teaspoon **garam masala**

½ teaspoon **ground cumin**

½ teaspoon **ground ginger**

½ teaspoon **garlic powder**

¼ teaspoon **salt**

2 tablespoons **vegetable oil**, plus extra for brushing

Fun Fact! What Are Karanji?

Karanji are sweet or savory dumplings that are typically fried. They are often served around Diwali, a religious festival of lights that originated in India. Diwali lasts for five days and usually occurs between October and November. *Diwali* means "row of lights" in Sanskrit, and during the festival people decorate their homes with special oil lamps called *diyas*. Our karanji are baked (not fried) and savory—they're filled with peas!

turn the page!

Start Cooking!

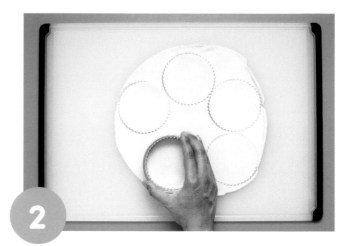

1 Heat and line

Adjust oven rack to upper-middle position and heat oven to 450 degrees. Line baking sheet with parchment paper.

2 Cut

Working with 1 pie dough round at a time, use 4-inch round cutter to cut out 10 dough rounds. Transfer dough rounds to parchment-lined baking sheet. Cover with plastic wrap and refrigerate while making filling.

3 Cook

adult help! In bowl, combine peas, water, garam masala, cumin, ginger, garlic, salt, and vegetable oil. Heat in microwave for 2 minutes. Use oven mitts to remove bowl from microwave.

4 Mash

Use potato masher to mash filling until mostly broken down and some whole peas remain. Stir with rubber spatula to combine.

"Now I like green peas!"
—BLAKE, 5

Fill

Remove baking sheet from refrigerator and discard plastic. Use 1-tablespoon measuring spoon to place 1 tablespoon filling in center of each dough round.

Shape and seal

Use your finger to lightly coat edge of each dough round with water. Fold dough over filling to create half-moon shape. Use your fingers to press edges together to seal.

Brush

Use pastry brush to brush tops of karanji with extra vegetable oil.

Bake karanji

adult help! Bake karanji until golden brown, 12 to 14 minutes. Let karanji cool on baking sheet for 10 minutes.

Mexican Hot Chocolate for Día de los Muertos

Serves 10 (Makes 3½ cups mix)

Total Time: 15 minutes

The hot chocolate mix can be stored at room temperature for up to three months.

Gather Equipment

Dry measuring cups

Measuring spoons

Liquid measuring cup

Food processor

Rubber spatula

Airtight storage container

1 large mug (per serving)

Oven mitts

Spoon

Prepare Ingredients

1½ cups (4½ ounces) **nonfat dry milk powder**

1 cup (4 ounces) **confectioners' (powdered) sugar**

¾ cup (2¼ ounces) **Dutch-processed cocoa powder**

¾ cup (4½ ounces) **semisweet chocolate chips**

1 teaspoon **vanilla extract**

1 teaspoon **ground cinnamon**

⅛ teaspoon **cayenne pepper**

⅛ teaspoon **salt**

1 cup (8 ounces) **milk** (per serving)

Start Cooking!

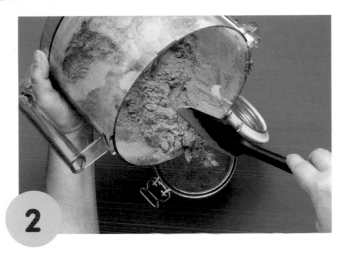

1

Mix

Add all ingredients except milk to food processor. Lock lid into place. Hold down pulse button for 1 second, then release. Repeat until chocolate chips are finely ground, about ten 1-second pulses.

2

Store

adult help! Remove lid and carefully remove processor blade. Use rubber spatula to transfer mixture to airtight storage container.

3

Make

adult help! To make 1 serving of hot chocolate, add ⅓ cup mix and 1 cup milk to large mug. Heat in microwave until hot, about 2 minutes. Use oven mitts to remove mug. Stir until well combined.

Día de los Muertos

Day of the Dead is a Mexican holiday during which people celebrate and remember loved ones who are no longer living. Celebrators often enjoy a cup of spicy hot chocolate to warm up on these chilly November nights.

Easy Biscuits for Thanksgiving

Makes 10 biscuits

Total Time: 40 minutes, plus cooling time

Gather Equipment

Dry measuring cups

Measuring spoons

Large liquid measuring cup

Rimmed baking sheet

Parchment paper

Medium bowl

Whisk

Instant-read thermometer

Rubber spatula

Oven mitts

Cooling rack

Prepare Ingredients

3 cups (15 ounces) **all-purpose flour**

4 teaspoons **sugar**

1 tablespoon **baking powder**

¼ teaspoon **baking soda**

1¼ teaspoons **salt**

2 cups (16 ounces) **heavy cream**

Vegetable oil spray

turn the page!

1

Heat and line

Adjust oven rack to upper-middle position and heat oven to 450 degrees. Line baking sheet with parchment paper.

2

Whisk

In bowl, whisk together flour, sugar, baking powder, baking soda, and salt.

3

Heat

In liquid measuring cup, heat cream in microwave until warmed and cream registers 95 to 100 degrees, 1 to 1½ minutes, stirring halfway through microwaving.

4

Mix

Add warm cream to bowl with flour mixture. Use rubber spatula to stir until soft, uniform dough forms.

"Mixing was hard at first, but it helped to use our hands to mix the dough."

—FINN, 6

5

6

Shape

Spray inside of ⅓-cup dry measuring cup with vegetable oil spray. Scoop batter (measuring cup should be full) and drop scoops onto baking sheet. Respray measuring cup after every 2 or 3 scoops.

Bake

adult help! Bake biscuits until tops are golden brown, 12 to 14 minutes. Let biscuits cool on baking sheet for 10 minutes. Serve warm.

Fun Fact! Goose, Goose . . . Fish

Thanksgiving is an American tradition that was started by Native Americans and English settlers in the 1600s. While biscuits were probably not served at the first Thanksgiving celebration (the menu was probably more like goose, fish, and cranberries), having bread or rolls alongside your turkey and stuffing has become a traditional part of the meal for many American families today.

Oven-Baked Latkes for Hanukkah

Serves 4 to 6 (Makes 12 latkes)

Total Time: 1 hour

If you don't have a food processor with a shredding disk, you can grate the potatoes and onion by hand on the large holes of a box grater. Be careful of sharp edges! Serve with applesauce and sour cream, if desired.

Gather Equipment

Liquid measuring cup

Cutting board

Chef's knife

Dry measuring cups

Measuring spoons

Rimmed baking sheet

Food processor with shredding disk

Dish towel

Large bowl

Rubber spatula

Oven mitts

Spatula

Cooling rack

Serving platter

Paper towels

Prepare Ingredients

Vegetable oil spray

½ cup **vegetable oil**

1¼ pounds **Yukon Gold potatoes**, unpeeled (if potatoes are too big to fit in feed tube, cut them in half)

1 **onion**, peeled and cut into quarters

¼ cup (1¼ ounces) **all-purpose flour**

1 **large egg**

1 teaspoon **salt**

turn the page!

1

Heat and grease

Adjust oven rack to middle position and heat oven to 400 degrees. Spray baking sheet with vegetable oil spray. Pour oil onto baking sheet and tip sheet until evenly coated.

2

Shred

adult help! Set shredding disk in food processor. Lock lid into place. Place potatoes and onion in feed tube. Turn on processor and push vegetables down with plunger. Remove lid and disk.

3

Squeeze

Transfer vegetables to center of clean dish towel. Gather ends of towel together, twist tightly, and squeeze over sink to drain as much liquid as possible from vegetables.

4

Mix

Transfer vegetables to bowl. Add flour, egg, and salt. Use your hands or rubber spatula to mix until well combined.

"These are so much better than the ones we make in the frying pan!"
—KEVIN, 7

5

Shape

Use ¼-cup dry measuring cup to scoop and drop 12 mounds of potato mixture onto greased baking sheet. Gently press each mound to flatten.

6

Bake

adult help! Bake latkes until bottoms are browned, 25 to 30 minutes. Use spatula to carefully flip latkes (oil will be hot). Bake until second side is golden brown, 5 to 10 minutes.

7

Drain

Line serving platter with paper towels. Transfer latkes to paper towels. Let latkes drain and cool for 5 minutes.

Fun Fact!

All About Oil

Hanukkah is a Jewish holiday that is celebrated for eight days and nights, often in December. It remembers a story about a temple that had only enough oil to burn a menorah (a special lamp) for one night, but the oil lasted for eight nights instead. Today, for eight nights in a row, families light their own menorahs at home and fry foods such as latkes in lots of oil.

Peppermint Bark for Christmas

Serves 12

Total Time: 25 minutes, plus 1 hour chilling time

The bark can be refrigerated in an airtight container for up to 3 days.

Gather Equipment

Dry measuring cups

Aluminum foil

13-by-9-inch metal baking pan

Large zipper-lock plastic bag

Rolling pin

2 medium microwave-safe bowls

Oven mitts

Rubber spatula

Plastic wrap

Cutting board

Chef's knife

Prepare Ingredients

18 **mini candy canes** or 6 **large candy canes** or 20 **peppermint candies**

2 cups (12 ounces) **semisweet chocolate chips**

2 cups (12 ounces) **white chocolate chips**

turn the page!

1

2

Make sling

Make aluminum foil sling for 13-by-9-inch metal baking pan (see photos, page 14).

Smash

Place candy canes in zipper-lock plastic bag. Seal bag, making sure to press out all air. Use rolling pin to gently pound candy into small pieces (you should have ½ cup pieces).

3

4

Melt

(adult help!) In bowl, heat semisweet chips in microwave at 50 percent power (see page 12) until mostly melted, 2 to 3 minutes. Stir until smooth. In second bowl, repeat with white chips.

Layer chocolate

Use rubber spatula to scrape melted semisweet chocolate into foil-lined baking pan and smooth top (make sure to get all the way to corners of pan). Pour melted white chocolate over top.

5

Swirl

Drag tip of clean rubber spatula through chocolate to create swirls. Make sure not to swirl too much!

6

Sprinkle

Sprinkle pounded candy canes on top of chocolate. Cover pan with plastic wrap and refrigerate until firm, about 1 hour.

7

Cut

(adult help!) Remove pan from refrigerator. Use foil to lift bark out of pan and transfer to cutting board. Cut bark into pieces.

Fun Fact!
How Did Candy Canes Get Their Shape?

People enjoy lots of different treats for Christmas, but one of the most popular is the candy cane. Candy canes used to be just straight sticks of candy. But when people started using them to decorate their Christmas trees, some say that the J shape was introduced to make them easier to hook onto branches. At first the candy canes were bent by hand, which led to many of them breaking. In 1919 the Keller Machine was invented—it automatically bent the straight candy sticks around a wheel into a cane shape.

Conversions & Equivalents

The recipes in this book were developed using standard U.S. measures. The charts below offer equivalents for U.S. and metric measures. All conversions are approximate and have been rounded up or down to the nearest whole number.

Volume Conversions

U.S.	Metric
1 teaspoon	5 milliliters
2 teaspoons	10 milliliters
1 tablespoon	15 milliliters
2 tablespoons	30 milliliters
¼ cup	59 milliliters
⅓ cup	79 milliliters
½ cup	118 milliliters
¾ cup	177 milliliters
1 cup	237 milliliters
2 cups (1 pint)	473 milliliters
4 cups (1 quart)	0.946 liter
4 quarts (1 gallon)	3.8 liters

Weight Conversions

Ounces	Grams
½	14
¾	21
1	28
2	57
3	85
4	113
5	142
6	170
8	227
10	283
12	340
16 (1 pound)	454

Oven Temperatures

Fahrenheit	Celsius	Gas Mark
225	105	¼
250	120	½
275	135	1
300	150	2
325	165	3
350	180	4
375	190	5
400	200	6
425	220	7
450	230	8
475	245	9

Converting Temperatures from an Instant-Read Thermometer

We include doneness temperatures in some recipes in this book. We recommend an instant-read thermometer for the job. To convert Fahrenheit degrees to Celsius:

Subtract 32 degrees from the Fahrenheit reading and then divide the result by 1.8.

Example
"Roast chicken until thighs register 175 degrees."

To Convert
175°F – 32 = 143°
143° ÷ 1.8 = 79.44°C, rounded down to 79°C

Recipe Stats

Per Serving		Calories	Fat (g)	Saturated Fat (g)	Sodium (mg)	Carbohydrates (g)	Fiber (g)	Total Sugar (g)	Added Sugar (g)	Protein (g)
Chapter 1: After-School Snacks										
Yogurt and Berry Swirl	serves 1	100	2.5	1.5	35	13	2	10	4	10
Strawberry-Mango Smoothie Bowls	serves 2	160	0.5	0	45	38	4	29	5	3
Green Smoothie Bowls	serves 2	210	8	1.5	70	35	6	23	5	5
Frozen Banana Bites	per 2 bites	120	5	3	0	20	2	14	10	1
Cranberry-Almond No-Bake Energy Bites	per bite	110	5	1	60	13	2	7	3	3
Chocolate-Raisin No-Bake Energy Bites	per bite	110	5	1.5	60	15	1	9	5	3
Blueberry-Coconut No-Bake Energy Bites	per bite	110	5	2	65	13	2	7	3	3
Smashed Cucumber Salad	serves 2	50	2	0	440	9	1	5	1	2
Creamy Yogurt Dip	serves 6	25	1	0.5	210	2	0	2	0	3
Avocado Toast	serves 2	410	23	3.5	450	45	7	3	0	10
English Muffin Pizzas	per pizza	100	3	1.5	220	14	0	1	0	5
Bean and Cheese Quesadillas	serves 2	350	23	9	750	27	2	1	0	13
Cheesy Zucchini Crisps	serves 4	80	4	2	150	7	0	1	0	5
Applesauce Mini Muffins	per muffin	80	4	2.5	100	11	0	5	4	1
Chapter 2: Breakfast, Lunch, and Dinner										
Banana-Oat Pancakes	serves 6	320	11	2	330	48	3	14	6	9
Sheet Pan French Toast	serves 4	390	13	5	530	50	0	12	3	13
Whole-Grain French Toast	serves 4	400	15	6	580	13	6	13	3	17
Cheesy Scrambled Eggs	serves 4	220	17	8	260	1	0	0	0	14
Kale Salad with Maple-Balsamic Dressing	serves 4	180	14	1.5	160	13	3	8	1	3
Oven Grilled Cheese	serves 4	470	25	13	590	44	0	6	0	15
Cheese Pupusas	per pupusa	210	11	5	410	21	2	0	0	9
Cabbage Slaw	serves 8	5	0	0	80	1	0	1	0	0

Per Serving		Calories	Fat (g)	Saturated Fat (g)	Sodium (mg)	Carbohydrates (g)	Fiber (g)	Total Sugar (g)	Added Sugar (g)	Protein (g)
Parmesan Chicken Tenders	serves 4	500	27	7	950	19	0	1	0	42
Meatballs	serves 4	450	26	9	1160	24	4	11	0	32
Baked Macaroni and Cheese	serves 6	300	12	7	590	33	1	4	0	15
Cake Pan Pizzas	serves 6	280	12	4	690	31	1	2	1	11
Pesto Cake Pan Pizzas	serves 6	360	21	6	740	30	1	3	1	12
Sheet Pan Barbecue Chicken and Broccoli	serves 4	320	12	2	470	12	3	8	0	42
Fancy Fish in Foil	serves 4	240	12	7	380	0	0	0	0	30
Rice Noodle Bowls with Peanut Sauce	serves 4	680	26	4	640	91	4	12	4	23
Couscous with Carrots and Raisins	serves 6	270	8	1	450	42	4	11	0	7
Couscous with White Beans and Feta	serves 6	250	10	3	530	31	4	2	0	8
Roasted Green Beans	serves 4	70	4	0.5	300	8	3	4	0	2

Chapter 3: Sweet Treats

		Calories	Fat (g)	Saturated Fat (g)	Sodium (mg)	Carbohydrates (g)	Fiber (g)	Total Sugar (g)	Added Sugar (g)	Protein (g)
M&M Cookies	per cookie	150	5	3	85	24	0	16	13	2
Molasses Cookies	per cookie	150	6	3.5	80	23	0	13	13	2
Trail Mix Cookies	per cookie	200	10	4.5	130	26	2	14	11	3
Chocolate Brownie Cookies	per cookie	140	7	4	75	22	1	17	17	2
Blondies	per bar	190	11	5	50	23	1	16	16	2
S'mores Rice Cereal Treats	per bar	140	4.5	2.5	85	26	0	14	14	1
Peanut Butter–Pretzel Rice Cereal Treats	per bar	130	4	2	105	23	0	11	11	1
Nutella Rice Cereal Treats	per bar	150	5	2.5	80	26	0	11	11	1
Pumpkin Snack Cake	serves 12	200	10	1	200	26	1	17	17	2
Strawberry Cream "Shortcake"	serves 12	250	14	9	130	28	0	17	15	4
Whipped Cream	per 2 tablespoons	50	5	3.5	0	1	0	1	1	0

Per Serving		Calories	Fat (g)	Saturated Fat (g)	Sodium (mg)	Carbohydrates (g)	Fiber (g)	Total Sugar (g)	Added Sugar (g)	Protein (g)
Chocolate Glazed Cupcakes	per cupcake	270	16	4.5	180	31	0	22	21	3
Ice Cream Cake	serves 16	300	16	8	150	39	0	27	0	3
Peach-Raspberry Crisp	serves 8	230	8	4.5	40	39	4	23	13	3
Key Lime Cups	serves 4	420	17	11	230	58	0	55	0	10
Mango Lassi Popsicles	per popsicle	110	2	1.5	30	22	0	14	11	2

Chapter 4: Holidays and Celebrations

Pork Dumplings for Chinese New Year	serves 6	140	8	2	390	12	0	1	0	5
Chocolate-Raspberry Mug Cakes for Valentine's Day	serves 2	570	33	19	330	63	2	47	34	10
Deviled Eggs for Easter	serves 6	120	10	2.5	170	0	0	0	0	6
Egyptian Spice Cookies for Eid	per cookie	100	7	4	25	9	0	3	3	1
Firecracker Hot Dogs for the Fourth of July	serves 8	220	17	6	610	9	0	2	0	8
Karanji for Diwali	per karanji	130	8	2.5	180	13	1	1	0	2
Mexican Hot Chocolate for Día de los Muertos	per 1 cup	280	9	6	380	39	1	35	18	13
Easy Biscuits for Thanksgiving	per biscuit	290	17	11	470	28	0	3	2	5
Oven-Baked Latkes for Hanukkah	serves 6	190	10	1	400	22	2	1	0	4
Peppermint Bark for Christmas	serves 12	240	13	8	25	32	1	28	15	2

Index

A

Almond-Cranberry No-Bake Energy Bites, 24–25
aluminum foil sling, 14
Applesauce Mini Muffins, 40–43
avocados
  Avocado Toast, 30–31
  Green Smoothie Bowls, 20
  preparing, 12

B

bananas
  Banana-Oat Pancakes, 49–51
  Frozen Banana Bites, 22–23
beans
  Bean and Cheese Quesadillas, 34–35
  Couscous with Carrots and Raisins, 86–87
  Couscous with White Beans and Feta, 87
  Roasted Green Beans, 88–89
beef
  Firecracker Hot Dogs for the Fourth of July, 163–65
  Meatballs, 69–71
Berry and Yogurt Swirl, 18–19
Biscuits, Easy, for Thanksgiving, 175–76
Blondies, 111–13
Blueberry-Coconut No-Bake Energy Bites, 25
boiling water, 7
bread. See toast
Broccoli and Barbecue Chicken, Sheet Pan, 78–79
butter, melting, 10

C

Cabbage Slaw, 65
cakes
  Chocolate-Raspberry Mug Cakes for Valentine's Day, 151–53
  Ice Cream Cake, 129–31
  lining cake pan for, 14
  Pumpkin Snack Cake, 117–19
  removing from pan, 15
Carrots and Raisins, Couscous with, 86–87
cheese
  Baked Macaroni and Cheese, 72–73
  Bean and Cheese Quesadillas, 34–35
  Cake Pan Pizzas, 75–77
  Cheese Pupusas, 63–65
  Cheesy Scrambled Eggs, 56–57
  Cheesy Zucchini Crisps, 36–39
  Couscous with White Beans and Feta, 87
  English Muffin Pizzas, 32–33
  grating or shredding, 11
  Oven Grilled Cheese, 60–61
  Parmesan Chicken Tenders, 66–67
chicken
  Parmesan Chicken Tenders, 66–67
  Sheet Pan Barbecue Chicken and Broccoli, 78–79
chocolate
  Blondies, 111–13
  Chocolate Brownie Cookies, 107–9
  chocolate-dipped treats, 142–43
  Chocolate-Glazed Cupcakes, 125–27
  Chocolate-Raisin No-Bake Energy Bites, 25
  Chocolate-Raspberry Mug Cakes for Valentine's Day, 151–53
  Frozen Banana Bites, 22–23
  Ice Cream Cake, 129–31
  Mexican Hot Chocolate for Dia de los Muertos, 172–73
  Peppermint Bark for Christmas, 183–85
  S'mores Rice Cereal Treats, 114–15
  Trail Mix Cookies, 103–5
chopping foods, 6
citrus fruit, zesting and juicing, 11
Coconut-Blueberry No-Bake Energy Bites, 25
cookies
  Chocolate Brownie Cookies, 107–9
  Egyptian Spice Cookies for Eid, 159–61
  M&M Cookies, 95–97
  Molasses Cookies, 99–101
  Trail Mix Cookies, 103–5
cooking tools, 9
cookware, 8
Couscous with Carrots and Raisins, 86–87
cranberries
  Cranberry-Almond No-Bake Energy Bites, 24–25
  Trail Mix Cookies, 103–5
Cucumber Salad, Smashed, 26–27
Cupcakes, Chocolate-Glazed, 125–27

D

Deviled Eggs for Easter, 155–57
Dip, Creamy Yogurt, 28–29
dry ingredients, 7, 13
dumplings
  Karanji for Diwali, 169–71
  Pork Dumplings for Chinese New Year, 147–49

E

eggs
  Cheesy Scrambled Eggs, 56–57
  cracking and separating, 10
  Deviled Eggs for Easter, 155–57
Energy Bites, Cranberry-Almond No-Bake, 24–25
English Muffin Pizzas, 32–33
equipment for recipes, 8–9

F

Fish in Foil, Fancy, 80–81
French Toast, Sheet Pan, 52–55

G

graham cracker pieces
  Key Lime Cups, 137–39
  S'mores Rice Cereal Treats, 114–15
Green Beans, Roasted, 88–89
Green Smoothie Bowls, 20

H

Halloween Treats, 166–67
Hot Dogs, Firecracker, for the Fourth of July, 163–65

I

Ice Cream Cake, 129–31

K

kale
  Green Smoothie Bowls, 20
  Kale Salad with Maple-Balsamic Dressing, 58–59
Karanji for Diwali, 169–71
Key Lime Cups, 137–39
kitchen basics, 8
knives, 8

L

Latkes, Oven-Baked, for Hanukkah, 179–81
Lime, Key, Cups, 137–39
liquid ingredients, 7, 13

THIS BIBLE BELONGS TO:

_____

GIVEN BY:

_____

DATE:

_____

OCCASION:

_____

"How can a young [man] live a pure life?
By obeying your word."
—Psalm 119:9

REFUEL™

THE COMPLETE NEW TESTAMENT FOR GUYS

A Nelson BibleZine™

NCV

NEW CENTURY VERSION®

TRANSIT®

www.TransitBooks.com
A Division of Thomas Nelson, Inc.
www.ThomasNelson.com

NELSON BIBLES
A Division of Thomas Nelson Publishers
Since 1798

For other life-enriching books, visit us at:
www.thomasnelson.com

REFUEL™: THE COMPLETE NEW TESTAMENT FOR GUYS

Page Design: Anderson Thomas Design, Nashville, Tennessee
Page Layout: Koechel-Peterson and Associates, Minneapolis, Minnesota
Cover Design: Anderson Thomas Design, Nashville, Tennessee

Articles written by Kevin Johnson and Christopher Soderstrom.

Travel the Road photographs appear courtesy of Travel the Road, Tim Scott, and Will Decker.
Visit www.traveltheroad.com.

For media inquiries, contact Thomas Nelson, Inc., at P.O. Box 141000,
Nashville, TN 37214-1000, 1-800-251-4000.

TABLE OF CONTENTS

INTRODUCTION

This Bible is about radical devotion and revolutionary people. It is a book that God breathed into the hearts and minds of people who were grappling with life and rising to the challenge of faith in the extreme.

The stories were written by and about dreamers and risk-takers—people who bet their lives on what they could only see through faith. They were people who took a chance on God and dared to believe that this world we live in is a virtual world compared to the reality of who God is and how he wants to connect with us.

They didn't pretty up their lives. They told the truth even when it was raw. They admitted their mistakes. God inspired a book that reveals life with all its problems and all of humankind's frailties. He gave us a picture of the out-on-a-limb life that is the life of faith.

This whole Bible is really about God connecting with us through Jesus Christ. It is about Jesus' life and the universal shock waves from his death and resurrection.

Jesus was all-the-way man and all-the-way God. He was the truest revolutionary of all time. He wasn't afraid to blast the hypocritical religious leaders or to cry when his friend died. He lived through a life just like ours, with its frustrations and hard times, to do something no one else has done: die as a sacrifice for our sins. The truth he spoke and the fact that he beat death turned the world upside down.

THIS BIBLE IS A SURVIVAL GUIDE

The Bible is a lot of books strapped together. They are all inspired by God, but written by different kinds of people in all kinds of circumstances and for different reasons. These people weren't setting out to write a book of the Bible. They were facing life and surviving as best they could. Their stories teach us to survive as well by God's power. Because God inspired them, they're one hundred percent accurate and reliable.

Some of these books are stories, listings of events. Some are letters, and some are sermons. When you read the Bible, any part of it, understand the big picture. Understand why that book was written. what that writer was trying to accomplish. What were the people involved struggling with? What were they trying to make sense of? Each book has an Introduction written specifically to help answer these kinds of questions.

There are other special features to help you get as deep inside the Bible as you can.

Experts Answer Your Questions deals with a variety of topics important to you every day. Count On It points out the commitments that God makes to us. Radical Faith notes push us to trust God in the extreme. Ways to Walk the Walk gives real-life application of tons of Bible verses. Men of the Sword tells the stories of real-life guys who lived during the Bible times. There are notes on Relationships and Issues that you deal with daily. Inside Her Head notes give you the opinion of real-life teen girls on questions you wonder about. There's just a ton of info for you to learn from.

It's all here—truth, inspiration, bottom-line *actual reality*. Are you up for the challenge?

FROM THE EDITORS
OF REFUEL™:

A note about the *New Century Version*®

God never intended the Bible to be too difficult for his people. To make sure God's message was clear, the authors of the Bible recorded God's word in familiar everyday language. These books brought a message that the original readers could understand. These first readers knew that God spoke through these books. Down through the centuries, many people wanted a Bible so badly that they copied different Bible books by hand!

Today, now that the Bible is readily available, many Christians do not regularly read it. Many feel that the Bible is too hard to understand or irrelevant to life.

The *New Century Version* captures the clear and simple message that the very first readers understood. This version presents the Bible as God intended it: clear and dynamic.

A team of scholars from the World Bible Translation Center worked together with twenty-one other experienced Bible scholars from all over the world to translate the text directly from the best available Greek and Hebrew texts. You can trust that this Bible accurately presents God's Word as it came to us in the original languages.

Translators kept sentences short and simple. They avoided difficult words and worked to make the text easier to read. They used modern terms for places and measurements. And they put figures of speech and idiomatic expressions ("he was gathered to his people") in language that even children understand ("he died").

Following the tradition of other English versions, the *New Century Version* indicates the divine name, *Yahweh*, by putting LORD, and sometimes GOD, in capital letters. This distinguishes it from *Adonai*, another Hebrew word that is translated Lord.

We acknowledge the infallibility of God's Word and yet our own frailty. We pray that God will use this Bible to help you understand his rich truth for yourself. To God be the glory.

BIBLE

THE NEW
TESTAMENT

MATTHEW

TELLS THE JEWISH PEOPLE ABOUT JESUS

Imagine this: You've just kicked back on a soft clump of grass on a Galilean hillside. The air is crisp and warm. Your day is wide open... nothing to do but soak up the wisdom of Jesus. You're there with thousands of others who have shown up to hear Jesus teach. As Jesus begins to speak, it's as if the crowd vanishes. It's just you and him. He's talking straight to you.

That's the spirit of Matthew. The book was intended for hundreds of thousands of millions of people. But it reads like it's for one person. You.

Mathew is the first of four New Testament books about Jesus. Like any collection of stories about one person, each version is different.

And there's something unique enough about Matthew's story to have inspired Christian leaders long ago to put this ahead of all others in the New Testament. So, what's so unique?

In Matthew, you won't find as much dramatic action as you'll discover in Mark, or as many spotlights on compassion as in Luke, or even as much proof that Jesus is God as you'll uncover in John. But in Matthew, you'll find the most complete record of what Jesus taught. And you'll learn how his teachings grow out of Old Testament Scriptures. Matthew's book is like an encyclopedia of Jesus. This is the total good news.

TOTALLY COMPLETE. TOTALLY TRUE.

THE FAMILY HISTORY OF JESUS

1 This is the family history of Jesus Christ. He came from the family of David, and David came from the family of Abraham.

[2]Abraham was the father[n] of Isaac.

Isaac was the father of Jacob.

Jacob was the father of Judah and his brothers.

[3]Judah was the father of Perez and Zerah. (Their mother was Tamar.)

Perez was the father of Hezron.

Hezron was the father of Ram.

[4]Ram was the father of Amminadab.

Amminadab was the father of Nahshon.

Nahshon was the father of Salmon.

[5]Salmon was the father of Boaz. (Boaz's mother was Rahab.)

Boaz was the father of Obed. (Obed's mother was Ruth.)

Obed was the father of Jesse.

[6]Jesse was the father of King David.

David was the father of Solomon. (Solomon's mother had been Uriah's wife.)

[7]Solomon was the father of Rehoboam.

Rehoboam was the father of Abijah.

Abijah was the father of Asa.

[8]Asa was the father of Jehoshaphat.

Jehoshaphat was the father of Jehoram.

Jehoram was the ancestor of Uzziah.

[9]Uzziah was the father of Jotham.

Jotham was the father of Ahaz.

Ahaz was the father of Hezekiah.

[10]Hezekiah was the father of Manasseh.

Manasseh was the father of Amon.

Amon was the father of Josiah.

[11]Josiah was the grandfather of Jehoiachin and his brothers. (This was at the time that the people were taken to Babylon.)

[12]After they were taken to Babylon:

Jehoiachin was the father of Shealtiel.

Shealtiel was the grandfather of Zerubbabel.

[13]Zerubbabel was the father of Abiud.

Abiud was the father of Eliakim.

Eliakim was the father of Azor.

[14]Azor was the father of Zadok.

Zadok was the father of Akim.

Akim was the father of Eliud.

[15]Eliud was the father of Eleazar.

Eleazar was the father of Matthan.

Matthan was the father of Jacob.

[16]Jacob was the father of Joseph.

Joseph was the husband of Mary, and Mary was the mother of Jesus.

Jesus is called the Christ.

[17]So there were fourteen generations from Abraham to David. And there were fourteen generations from David until the people were taken to Babylon. And there were fourteen generations from the time when the people were taken to Babylon until Christ was born.

THE BIRTH OF JESUS CHRIST

[18]This is how the birth of Jesus Christ came about. His mother Mary was engaged[n] to marry Joseph, but before they married, she learned she was pregnant by the power of the Holy Spirit. [19]Because Mary's husband, Joseph, was a good man, he did not want to disgrace her in public, so he planned to divorce her secretly.

[20]While Joseph thought about these things, an angel of the Lord came to him in a dream. The angel said, "Joseph, descendant of David, don't be afraid to take Mary as your wife, because the baby in her is from the Holy Spirit. [21]She will give birth to a son, and you will name him Jesus,[n] because he will save his people from their sins."

[22]All this happened to bring about what the Lord had said through the prophet: [23]"The virgin will be pregnant. She will have a son, and they will name him Immanuel,"[n] which means "God is with us."

[24]When Joseph woke up, he did what the Lord's angel had told him to do. Joseph took Mary as his wife, [25]but he did not have sexual relations with her until she gave birth to the son. And Joseph named him Jesus.

WISE MEN COME TO VISIT JESUS

2 Jesus was born in the town of Bethlehem in Judea during the time when Herod was king. When Jesus was born, some wise men from the east came to Jerusalem. [2]They asked, "Where is the baby who was born to be the king of the Jews? We saw his star in the east and have come to worship him."

[3]When King Herod heard this, he was troubled, as well as all the people in Jerusalem. [4]Herod called a meeting of all the leading priests and teachers of the law and asked them where the Christ would be born. [5]They answered, "In the town of Bethlehem in Judea. The prophet wrote about this in the Scriptures:

[6]'But you, Bethlehem, in the land of Judah,

BIBLE BASICS

The Bible is a collection of sixty-six books written by different people throughout history, but all divinely inspired by God. This means that God controlled what they wrote, writing *through* them. Christians believe that the Bible is "living and active," that it still applies to us today, and that God uses it to speak to us. They believe that everything in the Bible is absolutely true and will never change. The Word of God will last forever.

are important among the tribes of Judah.

A ruler will come from you

who will be like a shepherd

for my people Israel.' " *Micah 5:2*

[7]Then Herod had a secret meeting with the wise men and learned from them the exact time they first saw the star. [8]He sent the wise men to Bethlehem, saying, "Look carefully for

EXPERTS ANSWER YOUR QUESTIONS

Q. *My youth group is packed with girls. I like the odds, but where are the guys to hang out with?*

A. God's goal at church isn't to turn you into a wuss. Show the girls what it means to be a strong and committed Christian guy, and focus on bringing your guy friends. If those guys aren't into Bible studies or deep stuff yet, start with casual events. Brave it.

Q. *I have a beef with the Christian guys my age. Lots of them just mess around. They're intense about everything but their faith. Why won't they listen to me?*

A. Instead of telling them what a growing faith looks like, show them. Then cut them slack while they figure it out. You can also connect with older guys or mentors like college students or even the grown-up men in your church.

Q. *Church feels like a ritual my family does every Sunday. Can't I just have my own faith?*

A. Getting together with other Christians isn't about a ritual. It's about relationships, both with God and people who boost your faith. You need other believers like a coal needs the rest of the campfire to keep from going out. Don't settle for going solo.

the child. When you find him, come tell me so I can worship him too."

9After the wise men heard the king, they left. The star that they had seen in the east went before them until it stopped above the place where the child was. 10When the wise men saw the star, they were filled with joy. 11They came to the house where the child was and saw him with his mother, Mary, and they bowed down and worshiped him. They opened their gifts and gave him treasures of gold, frankincense, and myrrh. 12But God warned the wise men in a dream not to go back to Herod, so they returned to their own country by a different way.

JESUS' PARENTS TAKE HIM TO EGYPT

13After they left, an angel of the Lord came to Joseph in a dream and said, "Get up! Take the child and his mother and escape to Egypt, because Herod is starting to look for the child so he can kill him. Stay in Egypt until I tell you to return."

14So Joseph got up and left for Egypt during the night with the child and his mother. 15And Joseph stayed in Egypt until Herod died. This happened to bring about what the Lord had said through the prophet: "I called my son out of Egypt."[n]

HEROD KILLS THE BABY BOYS

16When Herod saw that the wise men had tricked him, he was furious. So he gave an order to kill all the baby boys in Bethlehem and in the surrounding area who were two years old or younger. This was in keeping with the time he learned from the wise men. 17So what God had said through the prophet Jeremiah came true:

18"A voice was heard in Ramah
　of painful crying and deep sadness:
Rachel crying for her children.
　She refused to be comforted,
　because her children are dead."

Jeremiah 31:15

JOSEPH AND MARY RETURN

19After Herod died, an angel of the Lord spoke to Joseph in a dream while he was in Egypt. 20The angel said, "Get up! Take the child and his mother and go to the land of Israel, because the people who were trying to kill the child are now dead."

21So Joseph took the child and his mother and went to Israel. 22But he heard that Archelaus was now king in Judea since his

father Herod had died. So Joseph was afraid to go there. After being warned in a dream, he went to the area of Galilee, 23to a town called Nazareth, and lived there. And so what God had said through the prophets came true: "He will be called a Nazarene."[n]

THE WORK OF JOHN THE BAPTIST

3 About that time John the Baptist began preaching in the desert area of Judea. 2John said, "Change your hearts and lives because the kingdom of heaven is near." 3John the Baptist is the one Isaiah the prophet was talking about when he said:

"This is a voice of one
　who calls out in the desert:
'Prepare the way for the Lord.
　Make the road straight for him.' " *Isaiah 40:3*

4John's clothes were made from camel's hair, and he wore a leather belt around his waist. For food, he ate locusts and wild honey. 5Many people came from Jerusalem and Judea and all the area around the Jordan River to hear John. 6They confessed their sins, and he baptized them in the Jordan River.

7Many of the Pharisees and Sadducees came to the place where John was baptizing people. When John saw them, he said, "You are all snakes! Who warned you to run away from God's coming punishment? 8Do the things that show you really have changed your hearts and lives. 9And don't think you can say to yourselves, 'Abraham is our father.' I tell you that God could make children for Abraham from these rocks. 10The ax is now ready to cut down the trees, and every tree that does not produce good fruit will be cut down and thrown into the fire.[n]

11"I baptize you with water to show that your hearts and lives have changed. But there is one coming after me who is greater than I am, whose sandals I am not good enough to carry. He will baptize you with the Holy Spirit and fire. 12He will come ready to clean the grain, separating the good grain from the chaff. He will put the good part of the grain into his barn, but he will burn the chaff with a fire that cannot be put out."[n]

JESUS IS BAPTIZED BY JOHN

13At that time Jesus came from Galilee to the Jordan River and wanted John to baptize him. 14But John tried to stop him, saying, "Why do

 2:15 "I called . . . Egypt." Quotation from Hosea 11:1.
2:23 Nazarene A person from the city of Nazareth, a name probably meaning "branch" (see Isaiah 11:1). 3:10 The ax . . . fire. This means that God is ready to punish his people who do not obey him. 3:12 He will . . . out. This means that Jesus will come to separate good people from bad people, saving the good and punishing the bad.

RADICAL FAITH:

matthew 3:16

There are two ceremonies Jesus gave for every believer to observe—communion and baptism. Why should we get baptized? Because Jesus did, and he did it publicly. Getting baptized tells the world about your faith in Jesus as your Savior. This lets people know that you mean business with God, and that you're going to live for him, with courage and excitement! Not only does God want you to profess him by being baptized in water, but he also wants you to be a witness for him by being filled daily with his Holy Spirit. Why be baptized in the Holy Spirit? Because we need the power we receive from it. Acts 1:8 says, "But when the Holy Spirit comes to you, you will receive power." We don't need to depend on our own strength and ability. God makes unlimited strength and power available to us through his Holy Spirit. As a teenager, you need that power to make a difference for him. Everyone does. Jesus is the baptizer. Let him baptize you with his power today!

you come to me to be baptized? I need to be baptized by you!"

[15]Jesus answered, "Let it be this way for now. We should do all things that are God's will." So John agreed to baptize Jesus.

[16]As soon as Jesus was baptized, he came up out of the water. Then heaven opened, and he saw God's Spirit coming down on him like a dove. [17]And a voice from heaven said, "This is my Son, whom I love, and I am very pleased with him."

THE TEMPTATION OF JESUS

4 Then the Spirit led Jesus into the desert to be tempted by the devil. [2]Jesus ate nothing for forty days and nights. After this, he was very hungry. [3]The devil came to Jesus to tempt him, saying, "If you are the Son of God, tell these rocks to become bread."

[4]Jesus answered, "It is written in the Scriptures, 'A person does not live by eating only bread, but by everything God says.' "[n]

[5]Then the devil led Jesus to the holy city of Jerusalem and put him on a high place of the Temple. [6]The devil said, "If you are the Son of God, jump down, because it is written in the Scriptures:

'He has put his angels in charge of you.

They will catch you in their hands

so that you will not hit your foot

on a rock.' "   *Psalm 91:11-12*

[7]Jesus answered him, "It also says in the Scriptures, 'Do not test the Lord your God.' "[n]

[8]Then the devil led Jesus to the top of a very high mountain and showed him all the kingdoms of the world and all their splendor. [9]The devil said, "If you will bow down and worship me, I will give you all these things."

[10]Jesus said to the devil, "Go away from me, Satan! It is written in the Scriptures, 'You must worship the Lord your God and serve only him.' "[n]

[11]So the devil left Jesus, and angels came and took care of him.

JESUS BEGINS WORK IN GALILEE

[12]When Jesus heard that John had been put in prison, he went back to Galilee. [13]He left Nazareth and went to live in Capernaum, a town near Lake Galilee, in the area near Zebulun and Naphtali. [14]Jesus did this to bring about what the prophet Isaiah had said:

[15]"Land of Zebulun and land of Naphtali
   along the sea,

RANDOM WAYS TO ASK A GIRL OUT

1. **CHALK YOUR INVITATION ON HER DRIVEWAY.**

2. **SEND HER HUNTING FOR CLUES—WITH YOUR QUESTION AT THE LAST SPOT.**

3. **PEN HER A POEM.**

4. **MOW YOUR INVITE INTO A TALL-GRASS FIELD.**

5. **E-MAIL HER OPTIONS FOR YOUR FIRST DATE.**

6. **POST THE INVITE ON YOUR WEB PAGE, THEN GIVE HER THE URL.**

7. **GET RIGHT TO THE POINT.**

8. **SEND FLOWERS WITH A CARD REQUESTING A DATE.**

9. **IM HER CELL PHONE.**

10. **ASK HER DAD'S PERMISSION.**

beyond the Jordan River.

   This is Galilee where the non-Jewish people live.

[16]These people who live in darkness
   will see a great light.

They live in a place covered with
   the shadows of death,

   but a light will shine on them." *Isaiah 9:1-2*

JESUS CHOOSES SOME FOLLOWERS

[17]From that time Jesus began to preach, saying, "Change your hearts and lives, because the kingdom of heaven is near."

[18]As Jesus was walking by Lake Galilee, he saw two brothers, Simon (called Peter) and his brother Andrew. They were throwing a net into the lake because they were fishermen. [19]Jesus said, "Come follow me, and I will make you fish

4:4 'A person . . . says.' Quotation from Deuteronomy 8:3.   4:7 'Do . . . God.' Quotation from Deuteronomy 6:16.   4:10 'You . . . him.' Quotation from Deuteronomy 6:13.

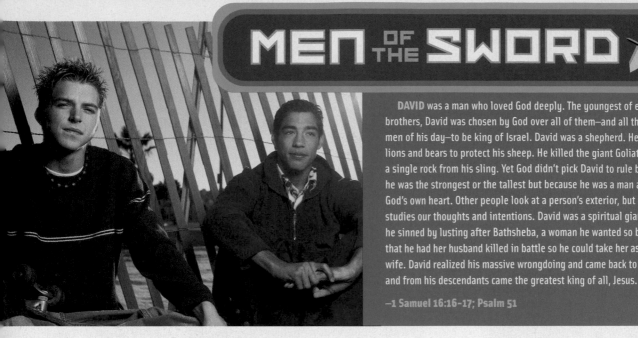

MEN OF THE SWORD

DAVID was a man who loved God deeply. The youngest of eight brothers, David was chosen by God over all of them—and all the other men of his day—to be king of Israel. David was a shepherd. He killed lions and bears to protect his sheep. He killed the giant Goliath with a single rock from his sling. Yet God didn't pick David to rule because he was the strongest or the tallest but because he was a man after God's own heart. Other people look at a person's exterior, but God studies our thoughts and intentions. David was a spiritual giant, but he sinned by lusting after Bathsheba, a woman he wanted so badly that he had her husband killed in battle so he could take her as his wife. David realized his massive wrongdoing and came back to God—and from his descendants came the greatest king of all, Jesus.

—1 Samuel 16:16–17; Psalm 51

for people." [20]So Simon and Andrew immediately left their nets and followed him.

[21]As Jesus continued walking by Lake Galilee, he saw two other brothers, James and John, the sons of Zebedee. They were in a boat with their father Zebedee, mending their nets. Jesus told them to come with him. [22]Immediately they left the boat and their father, and they followed Jesus.

JESUS TEACHES AND HEALS PEOPLE

[23]Jesus went everywhere in Galilee, teaching in the synagogues, preaching the Good News about the kingdom of heaven, and healing all the people's diseases and sicknesses. [24]The news about Jesus spread all over Syria, and people brought all the sick to him. They were suffering from different kinds of diseases. Some were in great pain, some had demons, some were epileptics,[n] and some were paralyzed. Jesus healed all of them. [25]Many people from Galilee, the Ten Towns,[n] Jerusalem, Judea, and the land across the Jordan River followed him.

JESUS TEACHES THE PEOPLE

5 When Jesus saw the crowds, he went up on a hill and sat down. His followers came to him, [2]and he began to teach them, saying:

[3]"Those people who know they have great spiritual needs are happy,
    because the kingdom of heaven belongs
        to them.

[4]Those who are sad now are happy,
    because God will comfort them.
[5]Those who are humble are happy,
    because the earth will belong to them.
[6]Those who want to do right more than
        anything else are happy,
    because God will fully satisfy them.
[7]Those who show mercy to others are happy,
    because God will show mercy to them.
[8]Those who are pure in their thinking
        are happy,
    because they will be with God.
[9]Those who work to bring peace are happy,
    because God will call them
        his children.
[10]Those who are treated badly for doing good
        are happy,
    because the kingdom of heaven belongs
        to them.

[11]"People will insult you and hurt you. They will lie and say all kinds of evil things about you because you follow me. But when they do, you will be happy. [12]Rejoice and be glad, because you have a great reward waiting for you in heaven. People did the same evil things to the prophets who lived before you.

travel the road

There's only one Christian missionary for every two million people in the northern region of Africa. If that same ratio were true of the United States and Canada, there would only be 120 full-time Christian workers spread across those two countries. And there would only be seven tiny churches for the hundreds of millions of people living between the Atlantic and Pacific, the Arctic Ocean and the Gulf of Mexico.

For more on extreme missions visit www.traveltheroad.com.

 4:24 epileptics People with a disease that causes them sometimes to lose control of their bodies and maybe faint, shake strongly, or not be able to move.   **4:25 Ten Towns** In Greek, called "Decapolis." It was an area east of Lake Galilee that once had ten main towns.

1 — ✓
New Year's Day!
Kick it back!

2
Pray for a Person of Influence:
Wish Cuba Gooding Jr.
a happy birthday.

3
Pray for a Person of Influence:
Today is Mel Gibson's birthday.

4

5
Pray for a Person of Influence:
Marilyn Manson piles
on another birthday.

6
It's Bean Day.
Live it up!

7
Pray for a Person of Influence: Today is
Jon from Delirious?'s birthday!

8
Send a card to the oldest
living member of your family.

9
Reach out to a stranger of another race.

10
Help a friend to keep a resolution.

11
Fend off Seasonal Affective Disorder:
Make time to work out today.

12
Sign up now to go
on a summer mission trip.

13
Pray for a Person of Influence:
Today is Orlando Bloom's birthday.

14
Don't miss National
Dress Up Your Pet Day!

15

16

17
Pray for a Person of Influence:
Wish Jim Carrey a happy birthday.

18
Take a little kid sledding!

19
Wash your gym clothes
this weekend.

20
Martin Luther King Jr. Day. Listen to
Pride by U2 in honor of his life.

21
Pray for a Person of Influence: Today is
Stew from Delirious?'s birthday!

22

23
Take your dog for a long walk
in the cold. Borrow a dog
if you don't have one.

24
Scrub every square inch
of a bathroom today.

25

26

27
Put gas in the family roadster.

28
Pray for a Person of Influence:
Today is Elijah Wood's birthday.

29

30
Even a guy can take advantage
of after-Christmas sales.
Go shop today.

31

issues

SPORTS SUPPLEMENTS

SOME GUYS SWEAR BY THE POWER OF PILLS ranging from performance enhancers to supposed weight-loss aids—and many more guys wonder about the benefits. While it's true that various forms of steroids, herbs, and other supplements have the potential to make you bigger, stronger, or faster, they're not worth the risk. Most are either illegal or unregulated. The most dangerous ones mimic your body's production of testosterone, but they give you too much of a good thing. They can shut down your growth spurt, leaving you undersized for life. And your shortcut to looking good for the girls can turn you into one—with results like breast growth and shrinking male parts. Honest. When it comes to putting any sort of pills into your body, get your parents' okay—and doctor's supervision. And if you eat right and stick to well-planned workouts, you'll grow at God's pace.

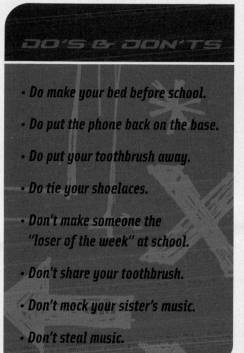

DO'S & DON'TS

- Do make your bed before school.

- Do put the phone back on the base.

- Do put your toothbrush away.

- Do tie your shoelaces.

- Don't make someone the "loser of the week" at school.

- Don't share your toothbrush.

- Don't mock your sister's music.

- Don't steal music.

MUSIC REVIEWS

AUDIO ADRENALINE: WORLDWIDE

Worldwide, Audio Adrenaline's seventh album, showcases the band's rowdy but rhythmic style, similar to the wildly popular sound heard on earlier releases such as *Underdog*. A blend of alternative and classic rock, *Worldwide* is a passionate plea for Christians to get out into the world and make a difference. Like vocalist Mark Stuart told *Christianity Today*, "Hey, I want to get serious about my faith.... [*Worldwide*] is basically a call to action." "Go and Be" urges, "Run with your life and you will find / all the things that you leave behind / don't mean that much when everything's brand new."

WHY IT ROCKS: AA BLENDS TRADEMARK ENERGY WITH A CAN'T-MISS MESSAGE.

YOU ARE LIKE SALT AND LIGHT

13"You are the salt of the earth. But if the salt loses its salty taste, it cannot be made salty again. It is good for nothing, except to be thrown out and walked on.

14"You are the light that gives light to the world. A city that is built on a hill cannot be hidden. 15And people don't hide a light under a bowl. They put it on a lampstand so the light shines for all the people in the house. 16In the same way, you should be a light for other people. Live so that they will see the good things you do and will praise your Father in heaven.

THE IMPORTANCE OF THE LAW

17"Don't think that I have come to destroy the law of Moses or the teaching of the prophets. I have not come to destroy them but to bring about what they said. 18I tell you the truth, nothing will disappear from the law until heaven and earth are gone. Not even the smallest letter or the smallest part of a letter will be lost until everything has happened. 19Whoever refuses to obey any command and teaches other people not to obey that command will be the least important in the kingdom of heaven. But whoever obeys the commands and teaches other people to obey them will be great in the kingdom of heaven. 20I tell you that if you are no more obedient than the teachers of the law and the Pharisees, you will never enter the kingdom of heaven.

JESUS TEACHES ABOUT ANGER

21"You have heard that it was said to our people long ago, 'You must not murder anyone.'[n] Anyone who murders another will be judged.' 22But I tell you, if you are angry with a brother or sister,[n] you will be judged. If you say bad things to a brother or sister, you will be judged by the council. And if you call someone a fool, you will be in danger of the fire of hell.

23"So when you offer your gift to God at the altar, and you remember that your brother or sister has something against you, 24leave your gift there at the altar. Go and make peace with that person, and then come and offer your gift.

25"If your enemy is taking you to court, become friends quickly, before you go to court. Otherwise, your enemy might turn you over to the judge, and the judge might give you to a guard to put you in jail. 26I tell you the truth, you will not leave there until you have paid everything you owe.

JESUS TEACHES ABOUT SEXUAL SIN

27"You have heard that it was said, 'You must not be guilty of adultery.'[n] 28But I tell you that if anyone looks at a woman and wants to sin sexually with her, in his mind he has already done that sin with the woman. 29If your right eye causes you to sin, take it out and throw it away. It is better to lose one part of your body than to have your whole body thrown into hell. 30If your right hand causes you to sin, cut it off and throw it away. It is better to lose one part of your body than for your whole body to go into hell.

JESUS TEACHES ABOUT DIVORCE

31"It was also said, 'Anyone who divorces his

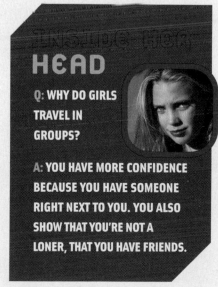

INSIDE HER HEAD

Q: WHY DO GIRLS TRAVEL IN GROUPS?

A: YOU HAVE MORE CONFIDENCE BECAUSE YOU HAVE SOMEONE RIGHT NEXT TO YOU. YOU ALSO SHOW THAT YOU'RE NOT A LONER, THAT YOU HAVE FRIENDS.

5:21 You . . . anyone. Quotation from Exodus 20:13; Deuteronomy 5:17. 5:22 brother . . . sister Although the Greek text reads "brother" here and throughout this book, Jesus' words were meant for the entire church, including men and women. 5:27 'You . . . adultery.' Quotation from Exodus 20:14; Deuteronomy 5:18.

WAYS TO WALK THE WALK

matthew 1:1-17

WORD: Family is important.

WALK IT: Find out something about your family that you never knew before.

wife must give her a written divorce paper.'[n] [32]But I tell you that anyone who divorces his wife forces her to be guilty of adultery. The only reason for a man to divorce his wife is if she has sexual relations with another man. And anyone who marries that divorced woman is guilty of adultery.

MAKE PROMISES CAREFULLY

[33]"You have heard that it was said to our people long ago, 'Don't break your promises, but keep the promises you make to the Lord.'[n] [34]But I tell you, never swear an oath. Don't swear an oath using the name of heaven, because heaven is God's throne. [35]Don't swear an oath using the name of the earth, because the earth belongs to God. Don't swear an oath using the name of Jerusalem, because that is the city of the great King. [36]Don't even swear by your own head, because you cannot make one hair on your head become white or black. [37]Say only yes if you mean yes, and no if you mean no. If you say more than yes or no, it is from the Evil One.

DON'T FIGHT BACK

[38]"You have heard that it was said, 'An eye for an eye, and a tooth for a tooth.'[n] [39]But I tell you, don't stand up against an evil person. If someone slaps you on the right cheek, turn to him the other cheek also. [40]If someone wants to sue you in court and take your shirt, let him have your coat also. [41]If someone forces you to go with him one mile, go with him two miles. [42]If a person asks you for something, give it to him. Don't refuse to give to someone who wants to borrow from you.

LOVE ALL PEOPLE

[43]"You have heard that it was said, 'Love your neighbor[n] and hate your enemies.' [44]But I say to you, love your enemies. Pray for those who hurt you. [45]If you do this, you will be true children of your Father in heaven. He causes the sun to rise on good people and on

GET OUT THERE

YOUTH VENTURE empowers young people to create and launch their own enterprises—and through these enterprises, to take greater responsibility for their lives and communities. Youth Venture is leading a growing global movement of young people committed to making a positive difference and playing an instrumental role in the welfare of their communities. They are initiating a change in the role of youth in society and are challenging traditional perceptions of young people as they take the initiative to improve their own lives and those of their communities by launching ventures of their own design.

The ventures are as diverse as the needs—ranging from tutoring services to virtual radio stations, from bike stores to dance academies, from video festivals to youth diabetes support groups. What turns these diverse activities into Youth Ventures is that the young people themselves come up with the ideas and control the projects.

Plug in by visiting www.youthventure.org

5:31 'Anyone . . . divorce paper.' Quotation from Deuteronomy 24:1.   5:33 'Don't . . . Lord.' This refers to Leviticus 19:12; Numbers 30:2; Deuteronomy 23:21.   5:38 'An eye . . . tooth.' Quotation from Exodus 21:24; Leviticus 24:20; Deuteronomy 19:21.   5:43 'Love your neighbor' Quotation from Leviticus 19:18.

evil people, and he sends rain to those who do right and to those who do wrong. ⁴⁶If you love only the people who love you, you will get no reward. Even the tax collectors do that. ⁴⁷And if you are nice only to your friends, you are no better than other people. Even those who don't know God are nice to their friends. ⁴⁸So you must be perfect, just as your Father in heaven is perfect.

JESUS TEACHES ABOUT GIVING

6 "Be careful! When you do good things, don't do them in front of people to be seen by them. If you do that, you will have no reward from your Father in heaven.

²"When you give to the poor, don't be like the hypocrites. They blow trumpets in the synagogues and on the streets so that people will see them and honor them. I tell you the truth, those hypocrites already have their full reward. ³So when you give to the poor, don't let anyone know what you are doing. ⁴Your giving should be done in secret. Your Father can see what is done in secret, and he will reward you.

JESUS TEACHES ABOUT PRAYER

⁵"When you pray, don't be like the hypocrites. They love to stand in the synagogues and on the street corners and pray so people will see them. I tell you the truth, they already have their full reward. ⁶When you pray, you should go into your room and close the door and pray to your Father who cannot be seen. Your Father can see what is done in secret, and he will reward you.

⁷"And when you pray, don't be like those people who don't know God. They continue saying things that mean nothing, thinking that God will hear them because of their many words. ⁸Don't be like them, because your Father knows the things you need before you ask him. ⁹So when you pray, you should pray like this:

'Our Father in heaven,
may your name always be kept holy.
¹⁰May your kingdom come
and what you want be done,
here on earth as it is in heaven.
¹¹Give us the food we need for each day.
¹²Forgive us for our sins,
just as we have forgiven those who
sinned against us.
¹³And do not cause us to be tempted,
but save us from the Evil One.'

¹⁴Yes, if you forgive others for their sins, your Father in heaven will also forgive you for your sins. ¹⁵But if you don't forgive others, your Father in heaven will not forgive your sins.

JESUS TEACHES ABOUT WORSHIP

¹⁶"When you give up eating," don't put on a sad face like the hypocrites. They make their faces look sad to show people they are giving up eating. I tell you the truth, those hypocrites already have their full reward. ¹⁷So when you give up eating, comb your hair and wash your face, ¹⁸Then people will not know that you are giving up eating, but your Father, whom you cannot see, will see you. Your Father sees what is done in secret, and he will reward you.

HOW TO PULL A CAR OUT OF A SKID

You're speeding along when your car slides out of control. How do you recover? Job One: *Look where you want to go.* It's normal when you're skidding toward another car, for example, to lock eyes on that car. But your body—and your car—follow where you focus. So look for an open space and aim your attention there. Job Two: *Point your front tires where you want to go.* That usually means "steering in the direction of the skid," an often-repeated phrase that sounds more confusing than helpful. Job three: *Apply the tiniest bit of gas.* That move shifts the weight of the vehicle and gives you a shot at traction with all four wheels. Job four: *Don't miss the life lesson here.* When your life hits the skids, focus on where you want to go, point your feet in the right direction, and press on.

Matthew 3:1-2

WORD: Your heart is sinful and needs to be changed.

WALK IT: Figure out one thing that's wrong about how you look at life. Ask God to help you really focus on changing it for two weeks.

Matthew 5:28

WORD: Sex outside marriage is out-of-bounds.

WALK IT: Ditch anything that makes you not want to save sex for marriage. Right now! No exceptions! No excuses!

 6:16 give up eating This is called "fasting." The people would give up eating for a special time of prayer and worship to God. It was also done to show sadness and disappointment.

RADICAL FAITH:

matthew 5:13-14

Jesus teaches in Matthew 5:13-14 that part of being a Christian is being salt and light to this world. Being salt means that a follower of Jesus creates a thirst for greater information. When you meet someone who is different and has qualities superior to your own, you want to know why that person is different. Have you ever met someone who was really cool, had a great attitude even when life was hard, did nice things for no obvious reason, and later found out that he was a Christian? That explained it! That person was being salt. He made people want to know what made him different.

How about light? A light shines and gives direction. It points people toward the right path. Do you know Christians who radiate Jesus? Others are drawn to them. Their lives are examples that many want to follow. People see their goodness and know it is Jesus who lives in them. Jesus says don't hide who you are. Don't put your light under a basket where others can't see it. Go boldly into the world and give 'em Jesus. You are bound to change the place where you are when others see Jesus in you.

GOD IS MORE IMPORTANT THAN MONEY

19"Don't store treasures for yourselves here on earth where moths and rust will destroy them and thieves can break in and steal them. 20But store your treasures in heaven where they cannot be destroyed by moths or rust and where thieves cannot break in and steal them. 21Your heart will be where your treasure is.

22"The eye is a light for the body. If your eyes are good, your whole body will be full of light. 23But if your eyes are evil, your whole body will be full of darkness. And if the only light you have is really darkness, then you have the worst darkness.

24"No one can serve two masters. The person will hate one master and love the other, or will follow one master and refuse to follow the other. You cannot serve both God and worldly riches.

DON'T WORRY

25"So I tell you, don't worry about the food or drink you need to live, or about the clothes you need for your body. Life is more than food, and the body is more than clothes. 26Look at the birds in the air. They don't plant or harvest or store food in barns, but your heavenly Father feeds them. And you know that you are worth much more than the birds. 27You cannot add any time to your life by worrying about it.

28"And why do you worry about clothes? Look at how the lilies in the field grow. They don't work or make clothes for themselves. 29But I tell you that even Solomon with his riches was not dressed as beautifully as one of these flowers. 30God clothes the grass in the field, which is alive today but tomorrow is thrown into the fire. So you can be even more sure that God will clothe you. Don't have so little faith! 31Don't worry and say, 'What will we eat?' or 'What will we drink?' or 'What will we wear?' 32The people who don't know God keep trying to get these things, and your Father in heaven knows you need them. 33The thing you should want most is God's kingdom and doing what God wants. Then all these other things you need will be given to you. 34So don't worry about tomorrow, because tomorrow will have

RANDOM FUN DATES

1. **GO BOWLING.**
2. **VOLUNTEER AT A SOUP KITCHEN.**
3. **CHEER FOR YOUR TEAM.**
4. **MAKE DINNER.**
5. **PLAY TWENTY QUESTIONS.**
6. **TAKE AN AFTERNOON PICNIC.**
7. **ANIMAL WATCH AT THE ZOO.**
8. **PLAY MINI-GOLF.**
9. **READ A NOVEL TOGETHER AND TALK ABOUT IT.**
10. **SIT BY A LAKE AND TALK.**

its own worries. Each day has enough trouble of its own.

BE CAREFUL ABOUT JUDGING OTHERS

7 "Don't judge other people, or you will be judged. 2You will be judged in the same way that you judge others, and the amount you give to others will be given to you.

3"Why do you notice the little piece of dust in your friend's eye, but you don't notice the big piece of wood in your own eye? 4How can you say to your friend, 'Let me take that little piece of dust out of your eye'? Look at yourself! You still have that big piece of wood in your own eye. 5You hypocrite! First, take the wood out of your own eye. Then you will see clearly to take the dust out of your friend's eye.

6"Don't give holy things to dogs, and don't throw your pearls before pigs. Pigs will only trample on them, and dogs will turn to attack you.

ASK GOD FOR WHAT YOU NEED

7"Ask, and God will give to you. Search, and you will find. Knock, and the door will open for you. 8Yes, everyone who asks will receive.

travel the road

You probably aren't one of the hundreds of millions of Christians around the world who face discrimination, harassment, political repression, imprisonment, rape, and torture because of their faith. Here's reality: Every three-and-a-half minutes a Christian dies for his or her faith. That means that during the average one-hour youth group meeting, 17 Christians will be martyred somewhere in the world. You can learn more about the suffering church by checking out Open Doors International at www.opendoorsusa.org.

For more on extreme missions visit www.traveltheroad.com.

Everyone who searches will find. And everyone who knocks will have the door opened.

⁹"If your children ask for bread, which of you would give them a stone? ¹⁰Or if your children ask for a fish, would you give them a snake? ¹¹Even though you are bad, you know how to give good gifts to your children. How much more your heavenly Father will give good things to those who ask him!

THE MOST IMPORTANT RULE

¹²"Do to others what you want them to do to you. This is the meaning of the law of Moses and the teaching of the prophets.

THE WAY TO HEAVEN IS HARD

¹³"Enter through the narrow gate. The gate is wide and the road is wide that leads to hell, and many people enter through that gate. ¹⁴But the gate is small and the road is narrow that leads to true life. Only a few people find that road.

PEOPLE KNOW YOU BY YOUR ACTIONS

¹⁵"Be careful of false prophets. They come to you looking gentle like sheep, but they are really dangerous like wolves. ¹⁶You will know these people by what they do. Grapes don't come from thornbushes, and figs don't come from thorny weeds. ¹⁷In the same way, every good tree produces good fruit, but a bad tree produces bad fruit. ¹⁸A good tree cannot produce bad fruit, and a bad tree cannot produce good fruit. ¹⁹Every tree that does not produce good fruit is cut down and thrown into the fire. ²⁰In the same way, you will know these false prophets by what they do.

²¹"Not all those who say that I am their Lord will enter the kingdom of heaven. The only people who will enter the kingdom of heaven are those who do what my Father in heaven wants. ²²On the last day many people will say to me, 'Lord, Lord, we spoke for you, and through you we forced out demons and did many miracles.' ²³Then I will tell them clearly, 'Get away from me, you who do evil. I never knew you.'

TWO KINDS OF PEOPLE

²⁴"Everyone who hears my words and obeys them is like a wise man who built his house on rock. ²⁵It rained hard, the floods came, and the winds blew and hit that house. But it did not fall, because it was built on rock. ²⁶Everyone who hears my words and does not obey them is like a foolish man who built his house on sand. ²⁷It rained hard, the floods came, and the winds blew and hit that house, and it fell with a big crash."

²⁸When Jesus finished saying these things, the people were amazed at his teaching, ²⁹because he did not teach like their teachers of the law. He taught like a person who had authority.

JESUS HEALS A SICK MAN

8 When Jesus came down from the hill, great crowds followed him. ²Then a man with a skin disease came to Jesus. The man bowed down before him and said, "Lord, you can heal me if you will."

³Jesus reached out his hand and touched the man and said, "I will. Be healed!" And immediately the man was healed from his disease. ⁴Then Jesus said to him, "Don't tell anyone about this. But go and show yourself to the

EXPERTS ANSWER YOUR QUESTIONS

Q. *My parents drag me to this church I hate. How can I get out of it?*

A. Prove to your parents that you want to get tight with God, not just skip out of Sunday school. Start by checking what you put into church. If the problem is truly the atmosphere at church and not your attitude, then ask to go church hunting with your parents and talk about what you see. Maybe you can switch, or maybe just go there part-time.

Q. *My parents are freaked that I'm growing up. They're scared about everything I do.*

A. Most parents are scared that their little boy suddenly has a growing-up body and brain. Not much you can do about that. But the biggest thing they want is for you to stay close even as you grow into a real live adult. Just keep making room for them in your life. Every day, not just when you feel like it.

Q. *I can't wait to leave home. How can I get my parents to ease up on me now?*

A. Well, rethink that "can't wait to leave" thing by focusing on the positives of having parents around. In the meantime, the only way to score some flexibility on the rules is by showing your parents you're not messing up your life. Are you giving them reason to worry?

matthew 6:19

WORD: Life is more than just having stuff.

WALK IT: Stash some stuff you think you can't live without—then after two weeks see how much you can gladly give away to people who really need it.

matthew 7:4-5

WORD: We need to focus on our own faults before we blame others.

WALK IT: Take a look at your most annoying relationship—and change one bad thing you do that makes the problem worse.

priest[n] and offer the gift Moses commanded[n] for people who are made well. This will show the people what I have done."

JESUS HEALS A SOLDIER'S SERVANT

[5]When Jesus entered the city of Capernaum, an army officer came to him, begging for help. [6]The officer said, "Lord, my servant is at home in bed. He can't move his body and is in much pain."

[7]Jesus said to the officer, "I will go and heal him."

[8]The officer answered, "Lord, I am not worthy for you to come into my house. You only need to command it, and my servant will be healed. [9]I, too, am a man under the authority of others, and I have soldiers under my command. I tell one soldier, 'Go,' and he goes. I tell another soldier, 'Come,' and he comes. I say to my servant, 'Do this,' and my servant does it.

[10]When Jesus heard this, he was amazed. He said to those who were following him, "I tell you the truth, this is the greatest faith I have found, even in Israel. [11]Many people will come from the east and from the west and will sit and eat with Abraham, Isaac, and Jacob in the kingdom of heaven. [12]But those people who should be in the kingdom will be thrown outside into the darkness, where people will cry and grind their teeth with pain."

[13]Then Jesus said to the officer, "Go home. Your servant will be healed just as you believed he would." And his servant was healed that same hour.

JESUS HEALS MANY PEOPLE

[14]When Jesus went to Peter's house, he saw that Peter's mother-in-law was sick in bed with a fever. [15]Jesus touched her hand, and the fever left her. Then she stood up and began to serve Jesus.

[16]That evening people brought to Jesus many who had demons. Jesus spoke and the demons left them, and he healed all the sick. [17]He did these things to bring about what Isaiah the prophet had said:

"He took our suffering on him
and carried our diseases." *Isaiah 53:4*

PEOPLE WANT TO FOLLOW JESUS

[18]When Jesus saw the crowd around him, he told his followers to go to the other side of the lake. [19]Then a teacher of the law came to Jesus and said, "Teacher, I will follow you any place you go."

[20]Jesus said to him, "The foxes have holes to live in, and the birds have nests, but the Son of Man has no place to rest his head."

[21]Another man, one of Jesus' followers, said to him, "Lord, first let me go and bury my father."

[22]But Jesus told him, "Follow me, and let the people who are dead bury their own dead."

JESUS CALMS A STORM

[23]Jesus got into a boat, and his followers went with him. [24]A great storm arose on the lake so that waves covered the boat, but Jesus was sleeping. [25]His followers went to him and woke him, saying, "Lord, save us! We will drown!"

[26]Jesus answered, "Why are you afraid? You don't have enough faith." Then Jesus got up and gave a command to the wind and the waves, and it became completely calm.

[27]The men were amazed and said, "What kind of man is this? Even the wind and the waves obey him!"

JESUS HEALS TWO MEN WITH DEMONS

[28]When Jesus arrived at the other side of the lake in the area of the Gadarene[n] people, two men who had demons in them met him. These men lived in the burial caves and were so dangerous that people could not use the road by those caves. [29]They shouted, "What do you want with us, Son of God? Did you come here to torture us before the right time?"

[30]Near that place there was a large herd of pigs feeding. [31]The demons begged Jesus, "If you make us leave these men, please send us into that herd of pigs."

[32]Jesus said to them, "Go!" So the demons left the men and went into the pigs. Then the whole herd rushed down the hill into the lake and were drowned. [33]The herdsmen ran away and went into town, where they told about all of this and what had happened to the men who had demons. [34]Then the whole town went out to see Jesus. When they saw him, they begged him to leave their area.

JESUS HEALS A PARALYZED MAN

9 Jesus got into a boat and went back across the lake to his own town. [2]Some people brought to Jesus a man who was paralyzed and lying on a mat. When Jesus saw the faith of these people, he said to the paralyzed man, "Be encouraged, young man. Your sins are forgiven."

[3]Some of the teachers of the law said to themselves, "This man speaks as if he were God. That is blasphemy!"[n]

[4]Knowing their thoughts, Jesus said, "Why are you thinking evil thoughts? [5]Which is easier: to say, 'Your sins are forgiven,' or to tell him, 'Stand up and walk'? [6]But I will prove to you that the Son of Man has authority on earth to forgive sins." Then Jesus said to the paralyzed man, "Stand up, take your mat, and go home." [7]And the man stood up and went home. [8]When the people saw this, they were amazed and praised God for giving power like this to human beings.

JESUS CHOOSES MATTHEW

[9]When Jesus was leaving, he saw a man

 8:4 show . . . priest The Law of Moses said a priest must say when a Jewish person with a skin disease was well.   **8:4 Moses commanded** Read about this in Leviticus 14:1–32.   **8:28 Gadarene** From Gadara, an area southeast of Lake Galilee.   **9:3 blasphemy** Saying things against God or not showing respect for God.

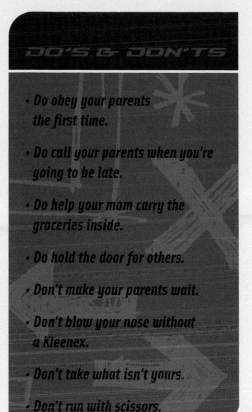

DO'S & DON'TS

- Do obey your parents the first time.

- Do call your parents when you're going to be late.

- Do help your mom carry the groceries inside.

- Do hold the door for others.

- Don't make your parents wait.

- Don't blow your nose without a Kleenex.

- Don't take what isn't yours.

- Don't run with scissors.

named Matthew sitting in the tax collector's booth. Jesus said to him, "Follow me," and he stood up and followed Jesus.

[10]As Jesus was having dinner at Matthew's house, many tax collectors and "sinners" came and ate with Jesus and his followers. [11]When the Pharisees saw this, they asked Jesus' followers, "Why does your teacher eat with tax collectors and sinners?"

[12]When Jesus heard them, he said, "It is not the healthy people who need a doctor, but the sick. [13]Go and learn what this means: 'I want kindness more than I want animal sacrifices.'[n] I did not come to invite good people but to invite sinners."

JESUS' FOLLOWERS ARE CRITICIZED

[14]Then the followers of John[n] came to Jesus and said, "Why do we and the Pharisees often give up eating for a certain time,[n] but your followers don't?"

[15]Jesus answered, "The friends of the bridegroom are not sad while he is with them. But the time will come when the bridegroom will be taken from them, and then they will give up eating.

[16]"No one sews a patch of unshrunk cloth over a hole in an old coat. If he does, the patch will shrink and pull away from the coat, making the hole worse. [17]Also, people never pour new wine into old leather bags. Otherwise, the bags will break, the wine will spill, and the wine bags will be ruined. But people always pour new wine into new wine bags. Then both will continue to be good."

JESUS GIVES LIFE TO A DEAD GIRL AND HEALS A SICK WOMAN

[18]While Jesus was saying these things, a leader of the synagogue came to him. He bowed down before Jesus and said, "My daughter has just died. But if you come and lay your hand on her, she will live again." [19]So Jesus and his followers stood up and went with the leader.

[20]Then a woman who had been bleeding for twelve years came behind Jesus and touched the edge of his coat. [21]She was thinking, "If I can just touch his clothes, I will be healed."

[22]Jesus turned and saw the woman and said, "Be encouraged, dear woman. You are made well because you believed." And the woman was healed from that moment on.

[23]Jesus continued along with the leader and went into his house. There he saw the funeral musicians and many people crying. [24]Jesus said, "Go away. The girl is not dead, only asleep." But the people laughed at him. [25]After the crowd had been thrown out of the house, Jesus went into the girl's room and took hold of her hand, and she stood up. [26]The news about this spread all around the area.

JESUS HEALS MORE PEOPLE

[27]When Jesus was leaving there, two blind men followed him. They cried out, "Have mercy on us, Son of David!"

[28]After Jesus went inside, the blind men went with him. He asked the men, "Do you believe that I can make you see again?"

They answered, "Yes, Lord."

[29]Then Jesus touched their eyes and said, "Because you believe I can make you see again, it will happen." [30]Then the men were able to see. But Jesus warned them strongly, saying, "Don't tell anyone about this." [31]But the blind men left and spread the news about Jesus all around that area.

[32]When the two men were leaving, some people brought another man to Jesus. This man could not talk because he had a demon in him. [33]After

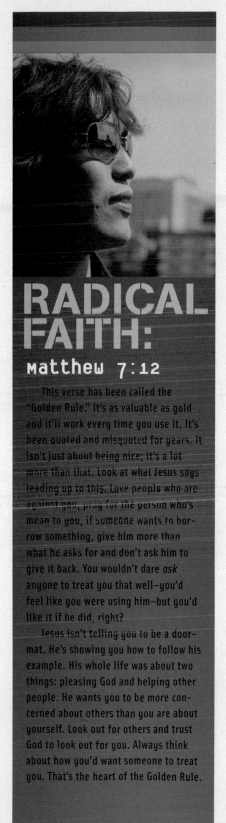

RADICAL FAITH:
matthew 7:12

This verse has been called the "Golden Rule." It's as valuable as gold and it'll work every time you use it. It's been quoted and misquoted for years. It isn't just about being nice; it's a lot more than that. Look at what Jesus says leading up to this. Love people who are against you, pray for the person who's mean to you, if someone wants to borrow something, give him more than what he asks for and don't ask him to give it back. You wouldn't dare *ask* anyone to treat you that well—you'd feel like you were using him—but you'd like it if he did, right?

Jesus isn't telling you to be a doormat. He's showing you how to follow his example. His whole life was about two things: pleasing God and helping other people. He wants you to be more concerned about others than you are about yourself. Look out for others and trust God to look out for you. Always think about how you'd want someone to treat you. That's the heart of the Golden Rule.

 9:13 'I want . . . sacrifices.' Quotation from Hosea 6:6.   9:14 John John the Baptist, who preached to people about Christ's coming (Matthew 3, Luke 3).   9:14 give up . . . time This is called "fasting." The people would give up eating for a special time of prayer and worship to God. It was also done to show sadness and disappointment.

RADICAL FAITH:

matthew 7:29

This passage of Scripture tells us that the crowds were surprised because Jesus taught with authority. We're not talking about your basic authority; we're talking about power! There is power in the words of Jesus. Look at what Hebrews 4:12 says: "God's word is alive and working and is sharper than a double-edged sword. It cuts all the way into us, where the soul and the spirit are joined, to the center of our joints and bones. And it judges the thoughts and feelings in our hearts." Start putting the Word of God in your mind and heart today, so that when troubles come against you, you can use it like a sword.

When the devil tempted Jesus in the wilderness, what did Jesus do? He spoke the Word of God. He said, "It is written . . ." (see Matthew 4:4, 6, 10). And you know what? The devil split. We need to do the same. John 1:1 tells us, "In the beginning there was the Word. The Word was with God, and the Word was God." Jesus is the Word, and he wants to teach you today. As you begin to study the Scriptures, you will begin to gain understanding of what the verses mean. This will help you live every day of the week and cause you to walk in victory! Remember, the Bible isn't meant to be difficult. You'll never know until you dive in. Let Jesus be *your* teacher!

Jesus forced the demon to leave the man, he was able to speak. The crowd was amazed and said, "We have never seen anything like this in Israel."

34But the Pharisees said, "The prince of demons is the one that gives him power to force demons out."

35Jesus traveled through all the towns and villages, teaching in their synagogues, preaching the Good News about the kingdom, and healing all kinds of diseases and sicknesses. 36When he saw the crowds, he felt sorry for them because they were hurting and helpless, like sheep without a shepherd. 37Jesus said to his followers, "There are many people to harvest but only a few workers to help harvest them. 38Pray to the Lord, who owns the harvest, that he will send more workers to gather his harvest."[n]

JESUS SENDS OUT HIS APOSTLES

10 Jesus called his twelve followers together and gave them authority to drive out evil spirits and to heal every kind of disease and sickness. 2These are the names of the twelve apostles: Simon (also called Peter) and his brother Andrew; James son of Zebedee, and his brother John; 3Philip and Bartholomew; Thomas and Matthew, the tax collector; James son of Alphaeus, and Thaddaeus; 4Simon the Zealot and Judas Iscariot, who turned against Jesus.

5Jesus sent out these twelve men with the following order: "Don't go to the non-Jewish people or to any town where the Samaritans live. 6But go to the people of Israel, who are like lost sheep. 7When you go, preach this: 'The kingdom of heaven is near.' 8Heal the sick, raise the dead to life again, heal those who have skin diseases, and force demons out of people. I give you these powers freely, so help other people freely. 9Don't carry any money with you—gold or silver or copper. 10Don't carry a bag or extra clothes or sandals or a walking stick. Workers should be given what they need.

11"When you enter a city or town, find some worthy person there and stay in that home until you leave. 12When you enter that home, say, 'Peace be with you.' 13If the people there welcome you, let your peace stay there.

But if they don't welcome you, take back the peace you wished for them. 14And if a home or town refuses to welcome you or listen to you, leave that place and shake its dust off your feet.[n] 15I tell you the truth, on the Judgment Day it will be better for the towns of Sodom and Gomorrah[n] than for the people of that town.

JESUS WARNS HIS APOSTLES

16"Listen, I am sending you out like sheep among wolves. So be as smart as snakes and as innocent as doves. 17Be careful of people, because they will arrest you and take you to court and whip you in their synagogues. 18Because of me you will be taken to stand before governors and kings, and you will tell them and the non-Jewish people about me. 19When you are arrested, don't worry about what to say or how to say it. At that time you will be given the things to say. 20It will not really be you speaking but the Spirit of your Father speaking through you.

21"Brothers will give their own brothers to be killed, and fathers will give their own children to be killed. Children will fight against

RANDOM WAYS TO IMPRESS A GIRL

1. SHOW RESPECT.

2. GET TO KNOW HER FRIENDS.

3. WORSHIP GOD FREELY.

4. OPEN DOORS FOR HER.

5. SPEND TIME WITH HER PARENTS.

6. FIND OUT HER INTERESTS.

7. PRAY FOR HER.

8. BE CONFIDENT INSTEAD OF ARROGANT.

9. THINK BEFORE YOU TALK.

10. PUT HER FIRST.

9:37-38 "There are . . . harvest." As a farmer sends workers to harvest the grain, Jesus sends his followers to bring people to God.   10:14 shake . . . feet. A warning. It showed that they had rejected these people.   10:15 Sodom and Gomorrah Two cities that God destroyed because the people were so evil.

their own parents and have them put to death. ²²All people will hate you because you follow me, but those people who keep their faith until the end will be saved. ²³When you are treated badly in one city, run to another city. I tell you the truth, you will not finish going through all the cities of Israel before the Son of Man comes.

²⁴"A student is not better than his teacher, and a servant is not better than his master. ²⁵A student should be satisfied to become like his teacher; a servant should be satisfied to become like his master. If the head of the family is called Beelzebul, then the other members of the family will be called worse names!

FEAR GOD, NOT PEOPLE

²⁶"So don't be afraid of those people, because everything that is hidden will be shown. Everything that is secret will be made known. ²⁷I tell you these things in the dark, but I want you to tell them in the light. What you hear whispered in your ear you should shout from the housetops. ²⁸Don't be afraid of people, who can kill the body but cannot kill the soul. The only one you should fear is the one who can destroy the soul and the body in hell. ²⁹Two sparrows cost only a penny, but not even one of them can die without your Father's knowing it. ³⁰God even knows how many hairs are on your head. ³¹So don't be afraid. You are worth much more than many sparrows.

TELL PEOPLE ABOUT YOUR FAITH

³²"All those who stand before others and say they believe in me, I will say before my Father in heaven that they belong to me. ³³But all who stand before others and say they do not believe in me, I will say before my Father in heaven that they do not belong to me.

³⁴"Don't think that I came to bring peace to the earth. I did not come to bring peace, but a sword. ³⁵I have come so that

'a son will be against his father,
    a daughter will be against her mother,
a daughter-in-law will be against her
        mother-in-law.
³⁶   A person's enemies will be members
        of his own family.'   *Micah 7:6*

³⁷"Those who love their father or mother more than they love me are not worthy to be my followers. Those who love their son or daughter more than they love me are not worthy to be my followers. ³⁸Whoever is not willing to carry the cross and follow me is not worthy of me. ³⁹Those who try to hold on to their lives will give up true life. Those who give up their lives

GET OUT THERE →

AMERICA'S SECOND HARVEST believes that every single person can do something to help end hunger in America. Whether you have one dollar to give or one hour to share, or more, you can make an enormous difference in the lives of the hungry women, men, and children served by our network of food banks and food-rescue organizations. You can: *Give Funds*—a little or a lot, because every dollar raised helps to distribute 28 pounds of food to hungry Americans. *Give Food*—whether it's a truckload or a partial case, they deliver your food donation to where it is needed most. *Give Time*—join more than one million volunteers nationwide. *Build Awareness*—share what you know about hunger and help build an ever stronger movement for a hunger-free America. *Advocate*—get the latest legislative updates and tell your elected officials that hunger is an issue that matters to you. Join an Event—participate in a national campaign in your local community.

Stop by www.secondharvest.org to learn about the many ways you can help end hunger in America.

MUSIC REVIEWS

CAEDMON'S CALL: BACK HOME

A group of gifted worship leaders and songwriters, Caedmon's Call often swings your focus to life's deepest stuff. *Back Home* is emotional, delivering CC's characteristic sound (acoustic, folk) with tight, smart vocals. Though their music is easy to recognize, Caedmon's Call stays clear of musical ruts by swapping songwriting and lead vocal duties among several band members. Commenting on the tune "The Emptiest Day," keyboardist Josh Moore told *CCM*, "[Often,] emptiness or 'emotional sedation' is worse than actual distress. In these times, nothing makes more sense than to acknowledge that I am loved and am empowered to love because of Christ."

WHY IT ROCKS: SOMETIMES DRIVEN, MORE OFTEN MELLOW, ALWAYS APPEALING.

for me will hold on to true life. [40]Whoever accepts you also accepts me, and whoever accepts me also accepts the One who sent me. [41]Whoever meets a prophet and accepts him will receive the reward of a prophet. And whoever accepts a good person because that person is good will receive the reward of a good person.

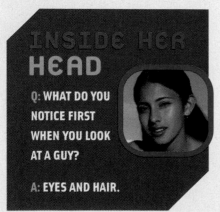

[42]Those who give one of these little ones a cup of cold water because they are my followers will truly get their reward."

JESUS AND JOHN THE BAPTIST

11 After Jesus finished telling these things to his twelve followers, he left there and went to the towns in Galilee to teach and preach.

[2]John the Baptist was in prison, but he heard about what Christ was doing. So John sent some of his followers to Jesus. [3]They asked him, "Are you the One who is to come, or should we wait for someone else?"

[4]Jesus answered them, "Go tell John what you hear and see: [5]The blind can see, the crippled can walk, and people with skin diseases are healed. The deaf can hear, the dead are raised to life, and the Good News is preached to the poor. [6]Those who do not stumble in their faith because of me are blessed."

[7]As John's followers were leaving, Jesus began talking to the people about John. Jesus said, "What did you go out into the desert to see? A reed[n] blown by the wind? [8]What did you go out to see? A man dressed in fine clothes? No, those who wear fine clothes live in kings' palaces. [9]So why did you go out? To see a prophet? Yes, and I tell you, John is more than a prophet. [10]This was written about him:

'I will send my messenger ahead of you,
who will prepare the way for you.'

Malachi 3:1

[11]I tell you the truth, John the Baptist is greater than any other person ever born, but even the least important person in the kingdom of heaven is greater than John. [12]Since the time John the Baptist came until now, the kingdom of heaven has been going forward in strength, and people have been trying to take it by force. [13]All the prophets and the law of Moses told about what

11:7 **reed** It means that John was not ordinary or weak like grass blown by the wind.

would happen until the time John came. [14]And if you will believe what they said, you will believe that John is Elijah, whom they said would come. [15]You people who can hear me, listen!

[16]"What can I say about the people of this time? What are they like? They are like children sitting in the marketplace, who call out to each other,

[17]'We played music for you, but you
    did not dance;

    we sang a sad song, but you did not cry.'
[18]John came and did not eat or drink like other people. So people say, 'He has a demon.' [19]The Son of Man came, eating and drinking, and people say, 'Look at him! He eats too much and drinks too much wine, and he is a friend of tax collectors and sinners.' But wisdom is proved to be right by what it does."

JESUS WARNS UNBELIEVERS

[20]Then Jesus criticized the cities where he did most of his miracles, because the people did not change their lives and stop sinning. [21]He said, "How terrible for you, Korazin! How terrible for you, Bethsaida! If the same miracles I did in you had happened in Tyre and Sidon,[n] those people would have changed their lives a long time ago. They would have worn rough cloth and put ashes on themselves to show they had changed. [22]But I tell you, on the Judgment Day it will be better for Tyre and Sidon than for you. [23]And you, Capernaum,[n] will you be lifted up to heaven? No, you will be thrown down to the depths. If the miracles I did in you had happened in Sodom,[n] its people would have stopped sinning, and it would still be a city today. [24]But I tell you, on the Judgment Day it will be better for Sodom than for you."

JESUS OFFERS REST TO PEOPLE

[25]At that time Jesus said, "I praise you, Father, Lord of heaven and earth, because you have hidden these things from the people who are wise and smart. But you have shown them to those who are like little children. [26]Yes, Father, this is what you really wanted.

[27]"My Father has given me all things. No one knows the Son, except the Father. And no one knows the Father, except the Son and those whom the Son chooses to tell.

[28]"Come to me, all of you who are tired and have heavy loads, and I will give you rest. [29]Accept my teachings and learn from me, because I am gentle and humble in spirit, and you will find rest for your lives. [30]The teaching that I ask you to accept is easy; the load I give you to carry is light."

JESUS IS LORD OF THE SABBATH

12 At that time Jesus was walking through some fields of grain on a Sabbath day. His followers were hungry, so they began to pick the grain and eat it. [2]When the Pharisees saw this, they said to Jesus, "Look! Your followers are doing what is unlawful to do on the Sabbath day."

[3]Jesus answered, "Have you not read what David did when he and the people with him were hungry? [4]He went into God's house, and he and those with him ate the holy bread, which was lawful only for priests to eat. [5]And have you not read in the law of Moses that on every Sabbath day the priests in the Temple break this law about the Sabbath day? But the priests are not wrong for doing that. [6]I tell you that there is something here that is greater than the Temple. [7]The Scripture says, 'I want kindness more than I want animal sacrifices.'[n] You don't really know what those words mean. If you understood them, you would not judge those who have done nothing wrong.

[8]"So the Son of Man is Lord of the Sabbath day."

JESUS HEALS A MAN'S HAND

[9]Jesus left there and went into their synagogue, [10]where there was a man with a crippled hand. They were looking for a reason to accuse Jesus, so they asked him, "Is it right to heal on the Sabbath day?"[n]

[11]Jesus answered, "If any of you has a sheep, and it falls into a ditch on the Sabbath day, you will help it out of the ditch. [12]Surely a human being is more important than a sheep. So it is lawful to do good things on the Sabbath day."

[13]Then Jesus said to the man with the crippled hand, "Hold out your hand." The man held out his hand, and it became well again, like the other hand. [14]But the Pharisees left and made plans to kill Jesus.

JESUS IS GOD'S CHOSEN SERVANT

[15]Jesus knew what the Pharisees were doing, so he left that place. Many people followed him, and he healed all who were sick. [16]But Jesus warned the people not to tell who he was. [17]He did these things to bring about what Isaiah the prophet had said:

MATTHEW 10:20

Have you ever been in a situation where you just didn't know what to say? Maybe you were "smack-dab" in the middle of witnessing to someone, and suddenly you didn't know what to do? This has happened to everybody. In this verse, Jesus was telling his followers that he was sending them out to be witnesses, and he assured them they should not be worried about what to say or how to say it. Why? Because the Holy Spirit was going to give them the words to say.

One of the cool parts of being a Christian is that you don't have to live on your own. Jesus is right there with you. He's never going to leave you or stand you up. He's always ready to speak to you and through you. So the next time you're sharing Jesus with a friend, or someone at school is drilling you about Christianity, remember *he* is the One who speaks. The Holy Spirit will give you the words to say. Just calm down, and let him do it. He always will, because his Word never fails!

 11:21 Tyre and Sidon Towns where wicked people lived. 11:21, 23 Korazin . . . Bethsaida . . . Capernaum Towns by Lake Galilee where Jesus preached to the people. 11:23 Sodom A city that God destroyed because the people were so evil. 12:7 'I . . . sacrifices.' Quotation from Hosea 6:6. 12:10 "Is it right . . . day?" It was against Jewish Law to work on the Sabbath day.

18"Here is my servant whom I have chosen.
I love him, and I am pleased with him.
I will put my Spirit upon him,
and he will tell of my justice to all people.
19He will not argue or cry out;
no one will hear his voice in the streets.
20He will not break a crushed blade of grass
or put out even a weak flame
until he makes justice win the victory.
21 In him will the non-Jewish people
find hope." *Isaiah 42:1-4*

JESUS' POWER IS FROM GOD

22Then some people brought to Jesus a man who was blind and could not talk, because he had a demon. Jesus healed the man so that he could talk and see. 23All the people were amazed and said, "Perhaps this man is the Son of David!"

24When the Pharisees heard this, they said, "Jesus uses the power of Beelzebul, the ruler of demons, to force demons out of people."

25Jesus knew what the Pharisees were thinking, so he said to them, "Every kingdom that is divided against itself will be destroyed. And any city or family that is divided against itself will not continue. 26And if Satan forces out himself, then Satan is divided against himself, and his kingdom will not continue. 27You say that I use the power of Beelzebul to force out demons. If that is true, then what power do your people use to force out demons? So they will be your judges. 28But if I use the power of God's Spirit to force out demons, then the kingdom of God has come to you.

29"If anyone wants to enter a strong person's house and steal his things, he must first tie up the strong person. Then he can steal the things from the house.

30"Whoever is not with me is against me. Whoever does not work with me is working against me. 31So I tell you, people can be forgiven for every sin and everything they say against God. But whoever speaks against the Holy Spirit will not be forgiven. 32Anyone who speaks against the Son of Man can be forgiven, but anyone who speaks against the Holy Spirit will not be forgiven, now or in the future.

PEOPLE KNOW YOU BY YOUR WORDS

33"If you want good fruit, you must make the tree good. If your tree is not good, it will have bad fruit. A tree is known by the kind of fruit it produces. 34You snakes! You are evil people, so how can you say anything good? The mouth speaks the things that are in the heart. 35Good people have good things in their hearts, and so they say good things. But evil people have evil in their hearts, so they say evil things. 36And I tell you that on the Judgment Day people will be responsible for every careless thing they have said. 37The words you have said will be used to judge you. Some of your words will prove you right, but some of your words will prove you guilty."

THE PEOPLE ASK FOR A MIRACLE

38Then some of the Pharisees and teachers of the law answered Jesus, saying, "Teacher, we want to see you work a miracle as a sign."

39Jesus answered, "Evil and sinful people are the ones who want to see a miracle for a sign.

BIBLE BASICS

Jesus is the Son of God. Even though he was God, he came to earth and lived as a man—all for the purpose of saving humans from their sins. He lived a perfect life, but was killed on a cross as a criminal because he claimed to be the Son of God. He said that he would rise from the dead three days later, and he did. He left his followers, the guys who lived and worked with him, with the Holy Spirit to guide them here on earth. Jesus is now in heaven seated next to God the Father.

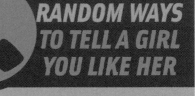

RANDOM WAYS TO TELL A GIRL YOU LIKE HER

1. ASK IF YOU CAN CALL HER.

2. HAVE SOMETHING SHE LIKES DELIVERED TO HER HOME.

3. TELL HER WHY SHE FASCINATES YOU.

4. COMPLIMENT HER FRIENDS AND FAMILY.

5. WEAR A SIGN THAT SAYS SO.

6. WRITE HER A SONG.

7. GRAB HER HAND—NOTHING MORE.

8. WRITE "I LIKE YOU" IN SILLY STRING ON HER WINDSHIELD.

9. TELL HER THAT BEING AROUND HER MAKES YOU HAPPY.

10. BUILD AN ACROSTIC "A TO Z" POEM ABOUT HER GREAT QUALITIES.

But no sign will be given to them, except the sign of the prophet Jonah. [40]Jonah was in the stomach of the big fish for three days and three nights. In the same way, the Son of Man will be in the grave three days and three nights. [41]On the Judgment Day the people from Nineveh[n] will stand up with you people who live now, and they will show that you are guilty. When Jonah preached to them, they were sorry and changed their lives. And I tell you that someone greater than Jonah is here. [42]On the Judgment Day, the Queen of the South[n] will stand up with you people who live today. She will show that you are guilty, because she came from far away to listen to Solomon's wise teaching. And I tell you that someone greater than Solomon is here.

PEOPLE TODAY ARE FULL OF EVIL

[43]"When an evil spirit comes out of a person, it travels through dry places, looking for a place to rest, but it doesn't find it. [44]So the spirit says, 'I will go back to the house I left.' When the spirit comes back, it finds the house still empty, swept clean, and made neat. [45]Then the evil spirit goes out and brings seven other spirits even more evil than it is, and they go in and live there. So the person has even more trouble than before. It is the same way with the evil people who live today."

JESUS' TRUE FAMILY

[46]While Jesus was talking to the people, his mother and brothers stood outside, trying to find a way to talk to him. [47]Someone told Jesus, "Your mother and brothers are standing outside, and they want to talk to you."

[48]He answered, "Who is my mother? Who are my brothers?" [49]Then he pointed to his followers and said, "Here are my mother and my brothers. [50]My true brother and sister and mother are those who do what my Father in heaven wants."

A STORY ABOUT PLANTING SEED

13 That same day Jesus went out of the house and sat by the lake. [2]Large crowds gathered around him, so he got into a boat and sat down, while the people stood on the shore. [3]Then Jesus used stories to teach them many things. He said: "A farmer went out to plant his seed. [4]While he was planting, some seed fell by the road, and the birds came and ate it all up. [5]Some seed fell on rocky ground, where there wasn't much dirt. That seed grew very fast, because the ground was not deep. [6]But when the sun rose, the plants dried up, because they did not have deep roots. [7]Some other seed fell among thorny weeds, which grew and choked the good plants. [8]Some other seed fell on good ground where it grew and produced a crop. Some plants made a hundred times more, some made sixty times more, and

HOW TO WRESTLE AN ALLIGATOR

One in ten Americans would wrestle an alligator for a million bucks. Here's what you need to know in case a stranger ponies up that cash—or you get caught by surprise in a swamp. Your first move is to get on the alligator's back and force its neck and jaws downward. If you're attacked from the front, punch at the alligator's eyes and snout. If you're locked in its jaws, clobber its nose. But your best plan is to not bug a gator in the first place. It's like wrestling with evil. Stay clear of the jaws that can mangle you, and you get to keep all of your body parts.

MATTHEW 11:28

Have you ever been hiking in the mountains with a huge backpack strapped to your back all day long? What's the first thing you did when you finally reached your destination—the top? You unstrapped that pack, stretched out on the ground, and rested, right? Oh, what a feeling! At that very moment, there was nothing better than removing that weight, lying down, and resting.

A lot of people carry around heavy backpacks every day of their lives. Now they don't carry a literal pack, but a backpack of sin, a suitcase full of guilt, or a huge load of worry. Jesus wants to give us rest. He wants to help us. It's not worth carrying around a bunch of heavy junk when all we have to do is come to Jesus and let him take the weight off our shoulders. He paid the price to carry it so we don't have to!

When he says that he will give you rest, he means it. If you can learn to rest in Jesus as a teenager, you'll be a step ahead of a lot of adults. The key is to really learn what Jesus has done for you—what burdens he bears for you—and then to let him have them. When you do what you're supposed to do and let him do what he's supposed to do, then you can rest in him.

12:41 **Nineveh** The city where Jonah preached to warn the people. Read Jonah 3. 12:42 **Queen of the South** The Queen of Sheba. She traveled a thousand miles to learn God's wisdom from Solomon. Read 1 Kings 10:1–13.

some made thirty times more. ⁹You people who can hear me, listen."

WHY JESUS USED STORIES TO TEACH

¹⁰The followers came to Jesus and asked, "Why do you use stories to teach the people?"

¹¹Jesus answered, "You have been chosen to know the secrets about the kingdom of heaven, but others cannot know these secrets. ¹²Those who have understanding will be given more, and they will have all they need. But those who do not have understanding, even what they have will be taken away from them. ¹³This is why I use stories to teach the people: They see, but they don't really see. They hear, but they don't really hear or understand. ¹⁴So they show that the things Isaiah said about them are true:

LOOK COOL
TIPS ON YOURSELF

Maybe you think you'd look suave showing up at a prom wearing a t-shirt printed with a tux design. Better ask your date ahead of time. She's likely to invest major effort in looking her best, so don't let her down. You can do your part to dress up even without spending a fortune. Plan early where you'll borrow or rent a tux or suit. You want to show off your own style, so you can personalize your look by picking the color, length, and cut of your coat; the style and color of your tie; and the choice of a cummerbund or vest. If you do your best, you won't disappoint. It's the same way you should approach life: Dress for the occasion, but never leave your own style behind.

'You will listen and listen, but you will not
    understand.
 You will look and look, but you will
    not learn.
¹⁵For the minds of these people have become
    stubborn.
 They do not hear with their ears,
    and they have closed their eyes.
 Otherwise they might really understand
    what they see with their eyes
    and hear with their ears.
 They might really understand in their minds
    and come back to me and be healed.'

Isaiah 6:9-10

¹⁶But you are blessed, because you see with your eyes and hear with your ears. ¹⁷I tell you the truth, many prophets and good people wanted to see the things that you now see, but they did not see them. And they wanted to hear the things that you now hear, but they did not hear them.

JESUS EXPLAINS THE SEED STORY

¹⁸"So listen to the meaning of that story about the farmer. ¹⁹What is the seed that fell by the road? That seed is like the person who hears the message about the kingdom but does not understand it. The Evil One comes and takes away what was planted in that person's heart. ²⁰And what is the seed that fell on rocky ground? That seed is like the person who hears the teaching and quickly accepts it with joy. ²¹But he does not let the teaching go deep into his life, so he keeps it only a short time. When trouble or persecution comes because of the teaching he accepted, he quickly gives up. ²²And what is the seed that fell among the thorny weeds? That seed is like the person who hears the teaching but lets worries about this life and the temptation of wealth stop that teaching from growing. So the teaching does not produce fruit*ⁿ* in that person's life. ²³But what is the seed that fell on the good ground? That seed is like the person who hears the teaching and understands it. That person grows and produces fruit, sometimes a hundred times more, sometimes sixty times more, and sometimes thirty times more."

A STORY ABOUT WHEAT AND WEEDS

²⁴Then Jesus told them another story: "The kingdom of heaven is like a man who planted good seed in his field. ²⁵That night, when everyone was asleep, his enemy came and planted weeds among the wheat and then left. ²⁶Later, the wheat sprouted and the heads of grain grew, but the weeds also grew. ²⁷Then the man's servants came to him and said, 'You planted good seed in your field. Where did the weeds come from?' ²⁸The man answered, 'An enemy planted weeds.' The servants asked, 'Do you want us to pull up the weeds?' ²⁹The man answered, 'No, because when you pull up the weeds, you might also pull up the wheat. ³⁰Let the weeds and the wheat grow together until the harvest time. At harvest time I will tell the workers, "First gather the weeds and tie them together to be burned. Then gather the wheat and bring it to my barn." ' "

STORIES OF MUSTARD SEED AND YEAST

³¹Then Jesus told another story: "The kingdom of heaven is like a mustard seed that a man planted in his field. ³²That seed is the smallest of all seeds, but when it grows, it is one of the largest garden plants. It becomes big enough for the wild birds to come and build nests in its branches."

³³Then Jesus told another story: "The kingdom of heaven is like yeast that a woman took and hid in a large tub of flour until it made all the dough rise."

³⁴Jesus used stories to tell all these things to the people; he always used stories to teach them. ³⁵This is as the prophet said:
 "I will speak using stories;
    I will tell things that have been secret
       since the world was made." *Psalm 78:2*

JESUS EXPLAINS ABOUT THE WEEDS

³⁶Then Jesus left the crowd and went into the house. His followers came to him and said, "Explain to us the meaning of the story about the weeds in the field."

³⁷Jesus answered, "The man who planted the good seed in the field is the Son of Man. ³⁸The field is the world, and the good seed are all of God's children who belong to the kingdom. The weeds are those people who belong to the Evil One. ³⁹And the enemy who planted the bad seed is the devil. The harvest time is the end of the world, and the workers who gather are God's angels.

⁴⁰"Just as the weeds are pulled up and

13:22 **produce fruit** To produce fruit means to have in your life the good things God wants.

burned in the fire, so it will be at the end of the world. [41]The Son of Man will send out his angels, and they will gather out of his kingdom all who cause sin and all who do evil. [42]The angels will throw them into the blazing furnace, where the people will cry and grind their teeth with pain. [43]Then the good people will shine like the sun in the kingdom of their Father. You people who can hear me, listen.

STORIES OF A TREASURE AND A PEARL

[44]"The kingdom of heaven is like a treasure hidden in a field. One day a man found the treasure, and then he hid it in the field again. He was so happy that he went and sold everything he owned to buy that field.

[45]"Also, the kingdom of heaven is like a man looking for fine pearls. [46]When he found a very valuable pearl, he went and sold everything he had and bought it.

A STORY OF A FISHING NET

[47]"Also, the kingdom of heaven is like a net that was put into the lake and caught many different kinds of fish. [48]When it was full, the fishermen pulled the net to the shore. They sat down and put all the good fish in baskets and threw away the bad fish. [49]It will be this way at the end of the world. The angels will come and separate the evil people from the good people. [50]The angels will throw the evil people into the blazing furnace, where people will cry and grind their teeth with pain."

[51]Jesus asked his followers, "Do you understand all these things?"

They answered, "Yes, we understand."

[52]Then Jesus said to them, "So every teacher of the law who has been taught about the kingdom of heaven is like the owner of a house. He brings out both new things and old things he has saved."

JESUS GOES TO HIS HOMETOWN

[53]When Jesus finished teaching with these stories, he left there. [54]He went to his hometown and taught the people in the synagogue, and they were amazed. They said, "Where did this man get this wisdom and this power to do miracles? [55]He is just the son of a carpenter. His mother is Mary, and his brothers are James, Joseph, Simon, and Judas. [56]And all his sisters are here with us. Where then does this man get all these things?" [57]So the people were upset with Jesus.

But Jesus said to them, "A prophet is honored everywhere except in his hometown and in his own home."

[58]So he did not do many miracles there because they had no faith.

HOW JOHN THE BAPTIST WAS KILLED

14 At that time Herod, the ruler of Galilee, heard the reports about Jesus. [2]So he said to his servants, "Jesus is John the Baptist, who has risen from the dead. That is why he can work these miracles."

[3]Sometime before this, Herod had arrested John, tied him up, and put him into prison. Herod did this because of Herodias, who had been the wife of Philip, Herod's brother. [4]John had been telling Herod, "It is not lawful for you to be married to Herodias." [5]Herod wanted to kill John, but he was afraid of the people, because they believed John was a prophet.

[6]On Herod's birthday, the daughter of Herodias danced for Herod and his guests, and she pleased him. [7]So he promised with an oath to give her anything she wanted. [8]Herodias told her daughter what to ask for, so she said to Herod, "Give me the head of John the Baptist here on a platter." [9]Although King Herod was very sad, he had made a promise, and his dinner guests had heard him. So Herod ordered that what she asked for be done. [10]He sent soldiers to the prison to cut off John's head. [11]And they brought it on a platter and gave it to the girl, and she took it to her mother. [12]John's followers came and got his body and buried it. Then they went and told Jesus.

MORE THAN FIVE THOUSAND FED

[13]When Jesus heard what had happened to John, he left in a boat and went to a lonely place by himself. But the crowds

MEN OF THE SWORD

STEPHEN was a guy whose martyrdom jump-started the spread of Christianity. When the early church got in a fight, they put Stephen in charge of looking after the practical needs of poor widows in their community. He was a "a man with great faith and full of the Holy Spirit," so skilled at defending his faith that his opponents couldn't shut him up when he argued that Jesus was the Messiah. But when Stephen accused those same religious leaders that by rejecting Jesus that they had rejected God, they hauled him away and stoned him. The apostle Paul—in the dark days before he became a Christian—stood by and held the coats of the stone-throwers. Stephen's death rocked the world because it caused most believers to flee Jerusalem, taking the Good News with them as they went.

—Acts 6:1–8:4

RELATIONSHIPS

"But I say to you, love your enemies. Pray for those who hurt you" (Matthew 5:44). Those rank near the top of the Bible's most upside-down words. And they make no sense if you think you have to purposely throw yourself in front of a guy who pummels you, or a girl who goes out of her way to be unpleasant. You don't need to go looking to get thrashed. But when you're doing life and hurts happen, you can react with the kindness you wish others would show you. It's how Christ responded to the people who killed him.

heard about it and followed him on foot from the towns. [14]When he arrived, he saw a great crowd waiting. He felt sorry for them and healed those who were sick.

[15]When it was evening, his followers came to him and said, "No one lives in this place, and it is already late. Send the people away so they can go to the towns and buy food for themselves."

[16]But Jesus answered, "They don't need to go away. You give them something to eat."

[17]They said to him, "But we have only five loaves of bread and two fish."

[18]Jesus said, "Bring the bread and the fish to me." [19]Then he told the people to sit down on the grass. He took the five loaves and the two fish and, looking to heaven, he thanked God for the food. Jesus divided the bread and gave it to his followers, who gave it to the people. [20]All the people ate and were satisfied. Then the followers filled twelve baskets with the leftover pieces of food. [21]There were about five thousand men there who ate, not counting women and children.

JESUS WALKS ON THE WATER

[22]Immediately Jesus told his followers to get into the boat and go ahead of him across the lake. He stayed there to send the people home. [23]After he had sent them away, he went by himself up into the hills to pray. It was late, and Jesus was there alone. [24]By this time, the boat was already far away from land. It was being hit by waves, because the wind was blowing against it.

[25]Between three and six o'clock in the morning, Jesus came to them, walking on the water. [26]When his followers saw him walking on the water, they were afraid. They said, "It's a ghost!" and cried out in fear.

[27]But Jesus quickly spoke to them, "Have courage! It is I. Do not be afraid."

[28]Peter said, "Lord, if it is really you, then command me to come to you on the water."

[29]Jesus said, "Come."

And Peter left the boat and walked on the water to Jesus. [30]But when Peter saw the wind and the waves, he became afraid and began to sink. He shouted, "Lord, save me!"

WAYS TO WALK THE WALK

matthew 9:37

WORD: We need more people sharing the good news of God!

WALK IT: Tell one friend or acquaintance about Christ this week—someone who doesn't know him.

matthew 10:42

WORD: We will be rewarded for helping others.

WALK IT: Buy someone a snack today—and tell them you're doing it because Christ cares about them.

[31]Immediately Jesus reached out his hand and caught Peter. Jesus said, "Your faith is small. Why did you doubt?"

[32]After they got into the boat, the wind became calm. [33]Then those who were in the boat worshiped Jesus and said, "Truly you are the Son of God!"

[34]When they had crossed the lake, they came to shore at Gennesaret. [35]When the people there recognized Jesus, they told people all around there that Jesus had come, and they brought all their sick to him. [36]They begged Jesus to let them touch just the edge of his coat, and all who touched it were healed.

OBEY GOD'S LAW

15 Then some Pharisees and teachers of the law came to Jesus from

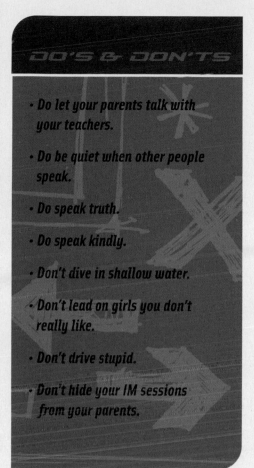

Jerusalem. They asked him, [2]"Why don't your followers obey the unwritten laws which have been handed down to us? They don't wash their hands before they eat."

[3]Jesus answered, "And why do you refuse to obey God's command so that you can follow your own teachings? [4]God said, 'Honor your father and your mother,'[n] and 'Anyone who says cruel things to his father or mother must be put to death.'[n] [5]But you say a person can tell his father or mother, 'I have something I could use to help you, but I have given it to God already.' [6]You teach that person not to honor his father or his mother. You rejected what God said for the sake of your own rules. [7]You are hypocrites! Isaiah was right when he said about you:

[8]"These people show honor to me
        with words,
    but their hearts are far from me.
[9]Their worship of me is worthless.
    The things they teach are nothing but
        human rules.' "   *Isaiah 29:13*

[10]After Jesus called the crowd to him, he said, "Listen and understand what I am saying. [11]It is not what people put into their mouths that makes them unclean. It is what comes out of their mouths that makes them unclean."

[12]Then his followers came to him and asked, "Do you know that the Pharisees are angry because of what you said?"

[13]Jesus answered, "Every plant that my Father in heaven has not planted himself will be pulled up by the roots. [14]Stay away from the Pharisees; they are blind leaders. And if a blind person leads a blind person, both will fall into a ditch."

[15]Peter said, "Explain the example to us."

[16]Jesus said, "Do you still not understand? [17]Surely you know that all the food that enters the mouth goes into the stomach and then goes out of the body. [18]But what people say with their mouths comes from the way they think; these are the things that make people unclean. [19]Out of the mind come evil thoughts, murder, adultery, sexual sins, stealing, lying, and speaking evil of others. [20]These things make people unclean; eating with unwashed hands does not make them unclean."

JESUS HELPS A NON-JEWISH WOMAN

[21]Jesus left that place and went to the area of Tyre and Sidon. [22]A Canaanite woman from that area came to Jesus and cried out, "Lord, Son of David, have mercy on me! My daughter has a demon, and she is suffering very much."

[23]But Jesus did not answer the woman. So his followers came to Jesus and begged him. "Tell the woman to go away. She is following us and shouting."

[24]Jesus answered, "God sent me only to the lost sheep, the people of Israel."

[25]Then the woman came to Jesus again and bowed before him and said, "Lord, help me!"

[26]Jesus answered, "It is not right to take the children's bread and give it to the dogs."

[27]The woman said, "Yes, Lord, but even the dogs eat the crumbs that fall from their masters' table."

[28]Then Jesus answered, "Woman, you have great faith! I will do what you asked." And at that moment the woman's daughter was healed.

JESUS HEALS MANY PEOPLE

[29]After leaving there, Jesus went along the shore of Lake Galilee. He went up on a hill and sat there.

EXPERTS ANSWER YOUR QUESTIONS

Q. *I have some major repair work to do with my parents. Where do I start?*

A. If you've made a mess of your life, you've likely been hiding a lot from them. Start by living out in the open. Communicate about where you're going, what you're doing, who you're with. Let them in on your fears and feelings. And don't get irked when they check up on you. You're on probation.

Q. *The Bible says I'm supposed to love my enemies. Does that include loving Satan?*

A. Not a chance. We aren't to love Satan. He's God's enemy. Not only is he a foe to us, he is evil itself. As children of light we cannot love darkness or have any part in it.

Q: *Can demons control people?*

A: Satan can't own a guy who's given his life to Christ. But the demons a person has let into his life can hang around, whispering stuff in his ear. If you know someone who's been deep into bondage to Satan yet hasn't broken completely free, get him to talk to a pastor.

15:4 'Honor . . . mother.' Quotation from Exodus 20:12; Deuteronomy 5:16.   15:4 'Anyone . . . death.' Quotation from Exodus 21:17.

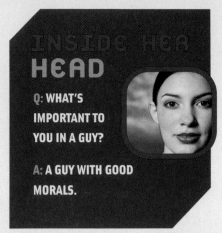

INSIDE HER HEAD

Q: WHAT'S IMPORTANT TO YOU IN A GUY?

A: A GUY WITH GOOD MORALS.

[30]Great crowds came to Jesus, bringing with them the lame, the blind, the crippled, those who could not speak, and many others. They put them at Jesus' feet, and he healed them. [31]The crowd was amazed when they saw that people who could not speak before were now able to speak. The crippled were made strong. The lame could walk, and the blind could see. And they praised the God of Israel for this.

MORE THAN FOUR THOUSAND FED

[32]Jesus called his followers to him and said, "I feel sorry for these people, because they have already been with me three days, and they have nothing to eat. I don't want to send them away hungry. They might faint while going home."

[33]His followers asked him, "How can we get enough bread to feed all these people? We are far away from any town."

[34]Jesus asked, "How many loaves of bread do you have?"

They answered, "Seven, and a few small fish."

[35]Jesus told the people to sit on the ground. [36]He took the seven loaves of bread and the fish and gave thanks to God. Then he divided the food and gave it to his followers, and they gave it to the people. [37]All the people ate and were satisfied. Then his followers filled seven baskets with the leftover pieces of food. [38]There were about four thousand men there who ate, besides women and children. [39]After sending the people home, Jesus got into the boat and went to the area of Magadan.

THE LEADERS ASK FOR A MIRACLE

16 The Pharisees and Sadducees came to Jesus, wanting to trick him. So they asked him to show them a miracle from God.

[2]Jesus answered, "At sunset you say we will have good weather, because the sky is red. [3]And in the morning you say that it will be a rainy day, because the sky is dark and red. You see these signs in the sky and know what they mean. In the same way, you see the things that I am doing now, but you don't know their meaning. [4]Evil and sinful people ask for a miracle as a sign, but they will not be given any sign, except the sign of Jonah."[n] Then Jesus left them and went away.

GUARD AGAINST WRONG TEACHINGS

[5]Jesus' followers went across the lake, but they had forgotten to bring bread. [6]Jesus said to them, "Be careful! Beware of the yeast of the Pharisees and the Sadducees."

[7]His followers discussed the meaning of this, saying, "He said this because we forgot to bring bread."

[8]Knowing what they were talking about, Jesus asked them, "Why are you talking about not having bread? Your faith is small. [9]Do you still not understand? Remember the five loaves of bread that fed the five thousand? And remember that you filled many baskets with the leftovers? [10]Or the seven loaves of bread that fed the four thousand and the many baskets you filled then also? [11]I was not talking to you about bread. Why don't you understand that? I am telling you to beware of the yeast of the Pharisees and the Sadducees." [12]Then the followers understood that Jesus was not telling them to beware of the yeast used in bread but to beware of the teaching of the Pharisees and the Sadducees.

PETER SAYS JESUS IS THE CHRIST

[13]When Jesus came to the area of Caesarea Philippi, he asked his followers, "Who do people say the Son of Man is?"

[14]They answered, "Some say you are John the Baptist. Others say you are Elijah, and still others say you are Jeremiah or one of the prophets."

[15]Then Jesus asked them, "And who do you say I am?"

[16]Simon Peter answered, "You are the Christ, the Son of the living God."

[17]Jesus answered, "You are blessed, Simon son of Jonah, because no person taught you that. My Father in heaven showed you who I am. [18]So I tell you, you are Peter.[n] On this rock I will build my church, and the power of death

will not be able to defeat it. [19]I will give you the keys of the kingdom of heaven; the things you don't allow on earth will be the things that God does not allow, and the things you allow on earth will be the things that God allows." [20]Then Jesus warned his followers not to tell anyone he was the Christ.

JESUS SAYS THAT HE MUST DIE

[21]From that time on Jesus began telling his followers that he must go to Jerusalem, where the older Jewish leaders, the leading priests, and the teachers of the law would make him suffer many things. He told them he must be killed and then be raised from the dead on the third day.

[22]Peter took Jesus aside and told him not to talk like that. He said, "God save you from those things, Lord! Those things will never happen to you!"

[23]Then Jesus said to Peter, "Go away from me, Satan![n] You are not helping me! You don't care about the things of God, but only about the things people think are important."

[24]Then Jesus said to his followers, "If people want to follow me, they must give up the things they want. They must be willing even to give up their lives to follow me. [25]Those who want to save their lives will give up true life, and those who give up their lives for me will have true life. [26]It is worth nothing for them to have the whole world if they lose their souls. They could never pay enough to buy back their souls. [27]The Son of Man will come again with his Father's glory and with his angels. At that time, he will reward them for what they have done. [28]I tell you the truth, some people standing here will see the Son of Man coming with his kingdom before they die."-

JESUS TALKS WITH MOSES AND ELIJAH

17 Six days later, Jesus took Peter, James, and John, the brother of James, up on a high mountain by themselves. [2]While they watched, Jesus' appearance was changed; his face became bright like the sun, and his clothes became white as light. [3]Then Moses and Elijah[n] appeared to them, talking with Jesus.

[4]Peter said to Jesus, "Lord, it is good that we are here. If you want, I will put up three tents here—one for you, one for Moses, and one for Elijah."

16:4 sign of Jonah Jonah's three days in the fish are like Jesus' three days in the tomb. The story about Jonah is in the Book of Jonah.   16:18 Peter The Greek name "Peter," like the Aramaic name "Cephas," means "rock."   16:23 Satan Name for the devil, meaning "the enemy." Jesus means that Peter was talking like Satan.   17:3 Moses and Elijah Two of the most important Jewish leaders in the past. God had given Moses the Law, and Elijah was an important prophet.

5While Peter was talking, a bright cloud covered them. A voice came from the cloud and said, "This is my Son, whom I love, and I am very pleased with him. Listen to him!"

6When his followers heard the voice, they were so frightened they fell to the ground. 7But Jesus went to them and touched them and said, "Stand up. Don't be afraid." 8When they looked up, they saw Jesus was now alone.

9As they were coming down the mountain, Jesus commanded them not to tell anyone about what they had seen until the Son of Man had risen from the dead.

10Then his followers asked him, "Why do the teachers of the law say that Elijah must come first?"

11Jesus answered, "They are right to say that Elijah is coming and that he will make everything the way it should be. 12But I tell you that Elijah has already come, and they did not recognize him. They did to him whatever they wanted to do. It will be the same with the Son of Man; those same people will make the Son of Man suffer." 13Then the followers understood that Jesus was talking about John the Baptist.

JESUS HEALS A SICK BOY

14When Jesus and his followers came back to the crowd, a man came to Jesus and bowed before him. 15The man said, "Lord, have mercy on my son. He has epilepsy[n] and is suffering very much, because he often falls into the fire or into the water. 16I brought him to your followers, but they could not cure him."

17Jesus answered, "You people have no faith, and your lives are all wrong. How long must I put up with you? How long must I continue to be patient with you? Bring the boy here." 18Jesus commanded the demon inside the boy. Then the demon came out, and the boy was healed from that time on.

19The followers came to Jesus when he was alone and asked, "Why couldn't we force the demon out?"

20Jesus answered, "Because your faith is too small. I tell you the truth, if your faith is as big as a mustard seed, you can say to this mountain, 'Move from here to there,' and it will move. All things will be possible for you." 21[n]

JESUS TALKS ABOUT HIS DEATH

22While Jesus' followers were gathering in Galilee, he said to them, "The Son of Man will be handed over to people, 23and they will kill him. But on the third day he will be raised from the dead." And the followers were filled with sadness.

JESUS TALKS ABOUT PAYING TAXES

24When Jesus and his followers came to Capernaum, the men who collected the Temple tax came to Peter. They asked, "Does your teacher pay the Temple tax?"

25Peter answered, "Yes, Jesus pays the tax."

Peter went into the house, but before he could speak, Jesus said to him, "What do you think? The kings of the earth collect different kinds of taxes. But who pays the taxes—the king's children or others?"

26Peter answered, "Other people pay the taxes."

Jesus said to Peter, "Then the children of the king don't have to pay taxes. 27But we don't want to upset these tax collectors. So go to the lake and fish. After you catch the first fish, open its mouth and you will find a coin. Take that coin and give it to the tax collectors for you and me."

WHO IS THE GREATEST?

18 At that time the followers came to Jesus and asked, "Who is greatest in the kingdom of heaven?"

2Jesus called a little child to him and stood the child before his followers. 3Then he said, "I tell you the truth, you must change and become like little children. Otherwise, you will never enter the kingdom of heaven. 4The greatest person in the kingdom of heaven is the one who makes himself humble like this child.

5"Whoever accepts a child in my name accepts me. 6If one of these little children

travel the road

God loves you. But he doesn't aim for you to hog that love for yourself. After Jesus rose from the grave, he told his followers to take the Good News to the world. He said, "Go and make followers of all people in the world. Baptize them in the name of the Father and the Son and the Holy Spirit. Teach them to obey everything that I have taught you" (Matthew 28:19-20). That's a command so huge it has its own name: the *Great Commission*. If you're a Christian, it's at the top of your to-do list.

For more on extreme missions visit www.traveltheroad.com.

RANDOM WAYS TO BE FRIENDS WITH A GIRL

1. BE LAB PARTNERS.

2. SHARE CHURCH ACTIVITIES.

3. LISTEN TO HER PLANS.

4. INVITE HER TO DINNER WITH YOUR FAMILY.

5. JOIN A CLUB TOGETHER.

6. READ THE BIBLE OUT LOUD TO EACH OTHER.

7. SERVE AT THE SAME CHARITY.

8. E-MAIL OR IM HER.

9. CHEER HER ON AT HER SPORTING EVENTS.

10. PRAY FOR EACH OTHER.

17:15 epilepsy A disease that causes a person sometimes to lose control of his body and maybe faint, shake strongly, or not be able to move.   17:21 Verse 21 Some Greek copies add verse 21: "That kind of spirit comes out only if you use prayer and give up eating."

believes in me, and someone causes that child to sin, it would be better for that person to have a large stone tied around the neck and be drowned in the sea. [7]How terrible for the people of the world because of the things that cause them to sin. Such things will happen, but how terrible for the one who causes them to happen! [8]If your hand or your foot causes you to sin, cut it off and throw it away. It is better for you to lose part of your body and live forever than to have two hands and two feet and be thrown into the fire that burns forever. [9]If your eye causes you to sin, take it out and throw it away. It is better for you to have only one eye and live forever than to have two eyes and be thrown into the fire of hell.

A LOST SHEEP

[10]"Be careful. Don't think these little children are worth nothing. I tell you that they have angels in heaven who are always with my Father in heaven. [11]n

[12]"If a man has a hundred sheep but one of the sheep gets lost, he will leave the other ninety-nine on the hill and go to look for the lost sheep. [13]I tell you the truth, he is happier about that one sheep than about the ninety-nine that were never lost. [14]In the same way, your Father in heaven does not want any of these little children to be lost.

WHEN A PERSON SINS AGAINST YOU

[15]"If your fellow believer sins against you, go and tell him in private what he did wrong. If he listens to you, you have helped that person to be your brother or sister again. [16]But if he refuses to listen, go to him again and take one or two other people with you. 'Every case may be proved by two or three witnesses.'n [17]If he refuses to listen to them, tell the church. If he refuses to listen to the church, then treat him like a person who does not believe in God or like a tax collector.

[18]"I tell you the truth, the things you don't allow on earth will be the things God does not allow. And the things you allow on earth will be the things that God allows.

[19]"Also, I tell you that if two of you on earth agree about something and pray for it, it will be done for you by my Father in heaven.

GET OUT THERE

For more than 20 years STUDENTS AGAINST DESTRUCTIVE DECISIONS has helped young people lead education and prevention initiatives in their schools and communities. Founded as Students Against Driving Drunk, SADD has grown to become the nation's dominant peer-to-peer youth education and prevention organization, with thousands of chapters in middle schools, high schools, and colleges. In response to requests from SADD students, SADD has expanded its mission and now sponsors chapters called Students Against Destructive Decisions. SADD now highlights prevention of all destructive behaviors and attitudes harmful to young people, including underage drinking, substance abuse, impaired driving, violence, and suicide. Projects include peer-led classes and forums, teen workshops, conferences and rallies, prevention education and leadership training, and awareness-raising activities and legislative work.

Check out www.saddonline.com to get involved.

18:11 Verse 11 Some Greek copies add verse 11: "The Son of Man came to save lost people." 18:16 'Every . . . witnesses.' Quotation from Deuteronomy 19:15.

MUSIC REVIEWS

THE NEWSBOYS: ADORATION

Originally from Australia and New Zealand, The Newsboys have become one of contemporary Christian music's strongest bands. *Adoration*, their latest, is a worship album that www.jesusfreakhideout.com calls "a collection of songs written and performed for the sole purpose of moving the heart of God." One of the best qualities of The Newsboys (a pop/rock band) is that they're no imitation—lead singer Peter Furler once told *Shout* magazine, "I'm really proud ... that we don't sound like a Christian version of something." The Newsboys are absolutely wild about Jesus, and their music reflects it.

WHY IT ROCKS: ENERGY AND PASSION MEET PRAISE AND ADORATION.

WAYS TO WALK THE WALK

matthew 11:25

WORD: God gives wisdom to people who depend on him totally.

WALK IT: Ask God to show you ways you trust too much in your own resourcefulness. Then change your attitude by telling him you want to rely on him.

[20]This is true because if two or three people come together in my name, I am there with them."

AN UNFORGIVING SERVANT

[21]Then Peter came to Jesus and asked, "Lord, when my fellow believer sins against me, how many times must I forgive him? Should I forgive him as many as seven times?"

[22]Jesus answered, "I tell you, you must forgive him more than seven times. You must forgive him even if he wrongs you seventy times seven.

[23]"The kingdom of heaven is like a king who decided to collect the money his servants owed him. [24]When the king began to collect his money, a servant who owed him several million dollars was brought to him. [25]But the servant did not have enough money to pay his master, the king. So the master ordered that everything the servant owned should be sold, even the servant's wife and children. Then the money would be used to pay the king what the servant owed.

[26]"But the servant fell on his knees and begged, 'Be patient with me, and I will pay you everything I owe.' [27]The master felt sorry for his servant and told him he did not have to pay it back. Then he let the servant go free.

[28]"Later, that same servant found another servant who owed him a few dollars. The servant grabbed him around the neck and said, 'Pay me the money you owe me!'

[29]"The other servant fell on his knees and begged him, 'Be patient with me, and I will pay you everything I owe.'

[30]"But the first servant refused to be patient. He threw the other servant into prison until he

RANDOM WAYS TO SCORE POINTS WITH YOUR DATE'S PARENTS

1. DEMONSTRATE RESPECT.

2. TREAT HER THE WAY YOU'D WANT A GUY TO TREAT YOUR OWN DAUGHTER SOMEDAY.

3. SAY THANK YOU.

4. GET HER HOME ON TIME.

5. DON'T TALK SMUT ABOUT HER. EVER. ANYWHERE.

6. LOOK THEM IN THE EYE.

7. MAKE GOD YOUR LIFE'S FIRST PRIORITY.

8. BE HUMBLE.

9. ASK ABOUT THEIR DATING RULES.

10. LAUGH AT THEIR JOKES.

could pay everything he owed. [31]When the other servants saw what had happened, they were very sorry. So they went and told their master all that had happened.

[32]"Then the master called his servant in and said, 'You evil servant! Because you begged me to forget what you owed, I told you that you did not have to pay anything. [33]You should have showed mercy to that other servant, just as I showed mercy to you.' [34]The master was very angry and put the servant in prison to be punished until he could pay everything he owed.

[35]"This king did what my heavenly Father will do to you if you do not forgive your brother or sister from your heart."

JESUS TEACHES ABOUT DIVORCE

19 After Jesus said all these things, he left Galilee and went into the area of Judea on the other side of the Jordan River. [2]Large crowds followed him, and he healed them there.

[3]Some Pharisees came to Jesus and tried to trick him. They asked, "Is it right for a man to divorce his wife for any reason he chooses?"

[4]Jesus answered, "Surely you have read in the Scriptures: When God made the world, 'he made them male and female.'[n] [5]And God said, 'So a man will leave his father and mother and be united with his wife, and the two will become one body.'[n] [6]So there are not two, but one. God has joined the two together, so no one should separate them."

[7]The Pharisees asked, "Why then did Moses give a command for a man to divorce his wife by giving her divorce papers?"

[8]Jesus answered, "Moses allowed you to divorce your wives because you refused to accept God's teaching, but divorce was not allowed in the beginning. [9]I tell you that anyone who divorces his wife and marries another woman is guilty of adultery. The only reason for a man to divorce his wife is if his wife has sexual relations with another man."

[10]The followers said to him, "If that is the only reason a man can divorce his wife, it is better not to marry."

[11]Jesus answered, "Not everyone can accept this teaching, but God has made some able to accept it. [12]There are different reasons why some men cannot marry. Some men were born without the ability to become fathers. Others were made that way later in life by other people. And some men have given up marriage because of the kingdom of heaven. But the person who can marry should accept this teaching about marriage."[n]

JESUS WELCOMES CHILDREN

[13]Then the people brought their little children to Jesus so he could put his hands on them[n] and pray for them. His followers told them to stop, [14]but Jesus said, "Let the little children come to me. Don't stop them, because the kingdom of heaven belongs to people who are like these children." [15]After Jesus put his hands on the children, he left there.

A RICH YOUNG MAN'S QUESTION

[16]A man came to Jesus and asked, "Teacher, what good thing must I do to have life forever?"

[17]Jesus answered, "Why do you ask me about what is good? Only God is good. But if you want to have life forever, obey the commands."

[18]The man asked, "Which commands?"

Jesus answered, " 'You must not murder anyone; you must not be guilty of adultery; you must not steal; you must not tell lies about your neighbor; [19]honor your father and mother;[n] and love your neighbor as you love yourself.' "[n]

[20]The young man said, "I have obeyed all these things. What else do I need to do?"

[21]Jesus answered, "If you want to be perfect, then go and sell your possessions and give the money to the poor. If you do this, you will have treasure in heaven. Then come and follow me."

[22]But when the young man heard this, he left sorrowfully, because he was rich.

[23]Then Jesus said to his followers, "I tell you the truth, it will be hard for a rich person to enter the kingdom of heaven. [24]Yes, I tell you that it is easier for a camel to go through the eye of a needle than for a rich person to enter the kingdom of God."

[25]When Jesus' followers heard this, they were very surprised and asked, "Then who can be saved?"

[26]Jesus looked at them and said, "This is something people cannot do, but God can do all things."

[27]Peter said to Jesus, "Look, we have left everything and followed you. So what will we have?"

[28]Jesus said to them, "I tell you the truth, when the age to come has arrived, the Son of Man will sit on his great throne. All of you who followed me will also sit on twelve thrones, judging the twelve tribes of Israel. [29]And all those who have left houses, brothers, sisters, father, mother, children, or farms to follow me will get much more than they left, and they will have life forever. [30]Many who have the highest place now will have the lowest place in the future. And many who have the lowest place now will have the highest place in the future.

A STORY ABOUT WORKERS

20 "The kingdom of heaven is like a person who owned some land. One morning, he went out very early to hire some people to work in his vineyard. [2]The man

19:4 'he made . . . female.' Quotation from Genesis 1:27 or 5:2.   19:5 'So . . . body.' Quotation from Genesis 2:24.   19:12 But . . . marriage. This may also mean, "The person who can accept this teaching about not marrying should accept it."   19:13 put his hands on them Showing that Jesus gave special blessings to these children.   19:18-19 'You . . . mother.' Quotation from Exodus 20:12-16; Deuteronomy 5:16-20.   19:19 'love . . . yourself.' Quotation from Leviticus 19:18.

agreed to pay the workers one coin[n] for working that day. Then he sent them into the vineyard to work. [3]About nine o'clock the man went to the marketplace and saw some other people standing there, doing nothing. [4]So he said to them, 'If you go and work in my vineyard, I will pay you what your work is worth.' [5]So they went to work in the vineyard. The man went out again about twelve o'clock and three o'clock and did the same thing. [6]About five o'clock the man went to the marketplace again and saw others standing there. He asked them, 'Why did you stand here all day doing nothing?' [7]They answered, 'No one gave us a job.' The man said to them, 'Then you can go and work in my vineyard.'

[8]"At the end of the day, the owner of the vineyard said to the boss of all the workers, 'Call the workers and pay them. Start with the last people I hired and end with those I hired first.'

[9]"When the workers who were hired at five o'clock came to get their pay, each received one coin. [10]When the workers who were hired first came to get their pay, they thought they would be paid more than the others. But each one of them also received one coin. [11]When they got their coin, they complained to the man who owned the land. [12]They said, 'Those people were hired last and worked only one hour. But you paid them the same as you paid us who worked hard all day in the hot sun.' [13]But the man who owned the vineyard said to one of those workers, 'Friend, I am being fair to you. You agreed to work for one coin. [14]So take your pay and go. I want to give the man who was hired last the same pay that I gave you. [15]I can do what I want with my own money. Are you jealous because I am good to those people?'

[16]"So those who have the last place now will have the first place in the future, and those who have the first place now will have the last place in the future."

JESUS TALKS ABOUT HIS OWN DEATH

[17]While Jesus was going to Jerusalem, he took his twelve followers aside privately and said to them, [18]"Look, we are going to Jerusalem. The Son of Man will be turned over to the leading priests and the teachers of the law, and they will say that he must die. [19]They will give the Son of Man to the non-Jewish people to laugh at him and beat him with whips and crucify him. But on the third day, he will be raised to life again."

A MOTHER ASKS JESUS A FAVOR

[20]Then the wife of Zebedee came to Jesus with her sons. She bowed before him and asked him to do something for her.

[21]Jesus asked, "What do you want?"

She said, "Promise that one of my sons will sit at your right side and the other will sit at your left side in your kingdom."

[22]But Jesus said, "You don't understand what you are asking. Can you drink the cup that I am about to drink?"[n]

The sons answered, "Yes, we can."

[23]Jesus said to them, "You will drink from my cup. But I cannot choose who will sit at my right or my left; those places belong to those for whom my Father has prepared them."

[24]When the other ten followers heard this, they were angry with the two brothers. [25]Jesus called all the followers together and said, "You know that the rulers of the non-Jewish people love to show their power over the people. And their important leaders love to use all their authority. [26]But it should not be that way among you. Whoever wants to become great among you must serve the rest of you like a servant. [27]Whoever wants to become first among you must serve the rest of you like a slave. [28]In the same way, the Son of Man did not come to be served. He came to serve others and to give his life as a ransom for many people."

JESUS HEALS TWO BLIND MEN

[29]When Jesus and his followers were leaving Jericho, a great many people followed him. [30]Two blind men sitting by the road heard that Jesus was going by, so they shouted, "Lord, Son of David, have mercy on us!"

[31]The people warned the blind men to be quiet, but they shouted even more, "Lord, Son of David, have mercy on us!"

[32]Jesus stopped and said to the blind men, "What do you want me to do for you?"

[33]They answered, "Lord, we want to see."

[34]Jesus felt sorry for the blind men and touched their eyes, and at once they could see. Then they followed Jesus.

JESUS ENTERS JERUSALEM AS A KING

21 As Jesus and his followers were coming closer to Jerusalem, they

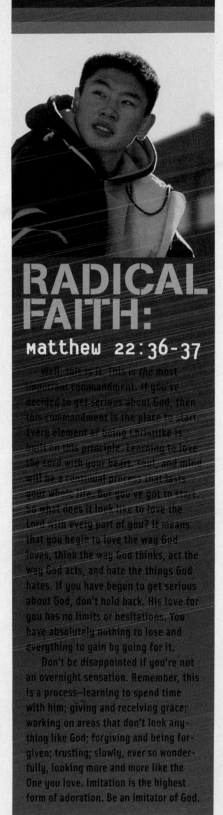

RADICAL FAITH:
matthew 22:36-37

Well, this is it. This is the most important commandment. If you've decided to get serious about God, then this commandment is the place to start. Every element of being Christlike is built on this principle. Learning to love the Lord with your heart, soul, and mind will be a continual process that lasts your whole life. But you've got to start. So what does it look like to love the Lord with every part of you? It means that you begin to love the way God loves, think the way God thinks, act the way God acts, and hate the things God hates. If you have begun to get serious about God, don't hold back. His love for you has no limits or hesitations. You have absolutely nothing to lose and everything to gain by going for it.

Don't be disappointed if you're not an overnight sensation. Remember, this is a process—learning to spend time with him; giving and receiving grace; working on areas that don't look anything like God; forgiving and being forgiven; trusting; slowly, ever so wonderfully, looking more and more like the One you love. Imitation is the highest form of adoration. Be an imitator of God.

20:2 coin A Roman denarius. One coin was the average pay for one day's work.   20:22 drink . . . drink Jesus used the idea of drinking from a cup to ask if they could accept the same terrible things that would happen to him.

HOW TO TIE A TIE

Maybe you're supposed to sport a tie for a special event, but the last tie you owned was a clip-on for your four-year-old preschool picture. Ties come down to a matter of taste, so browse and find one that shows off your personal style. But you still have to know the knot. Ask your dad to demonstrate and have some laughs together. Or if you want to learn more than the one or two knots that his dad taught him, dart over to www.neckties.com for helpful diagrams. Your first step in solving any knotty problem of life, by the way, is admitting you need help. Everyone needs it sometimes. Just ask.

stopped at Bethphage at the hill called the Mount of Olives. From there Jesus sent two of his followers [2]and said to them, "Go to the town you can see there. When you enter it, you will quickly find a donkey tied there with its colt. Untie them and bring them to me. [3]If anyone asks you why you are taking the donkeys, say that the Master needs them, and he will send them at once."

[4]This was to bring about what the prophet had said:

[5]"Tell the people of Jerusalem,
    'Your king is coming to you.
He is gentle and riding on a donkey,
    on the colt of a donkey.' " *Isaiah 62:11; Zechariah 9:9*

[6]The followers went and did what Jesus told them to do. [7]They brought the donkey and the colt to Jesus and laid their coats on them, and Jesus sat on them. [8]Many people spread their coats on the road. Others cut branches from the trees and spread them on the road. [9]The people were walking ahead of Jesus and behind him, shouting,

"Praise[n] to the Son of David!
God bless the One who comes in the name
    of the Lord!   *Psalm 118:26*
Praise to God in heaven!"

[10]When Jesus entered Jerusalem, all the city was filled with excitement. The people asked, "Who is this man?"

[11]The crowd said, "This man is Jesus, the prophet from the town of Nazareth in Galilee."

JESUS GOES TO THE TEMPLE

[12]Jesus went into the Temple and threw out all the people who were buying and selling there. He turned over the tables of those who were exchanging different kinds of money, and he upset the benches of those who were selling doves. [13]Jesus said to all the people there, "It is written in the Scriptures, 'My Temple will be called a house for prayer.'[n] But you are changing it into a 'hideout for robbers.' "[n]

[14]The blind and crippled people came to Jesus in the Temple, and he healed them. [15]The leading priests and the teachers of the law saw that Jesus was doing wonderful things and that the children were praising him in the Temple, saying, "Praise[n] to the Son of David." All these things made the priests and the teachers of the law very angry.

[16]They asked Jesus, "Do you hear the things these children are saying?"

Jesus answered, "Yes. Haven't you read in the Scriptures, 'You have taught children and babies to sing praises'?"[n]

[17]Then Jesus left and went out of the city to Bethany, where he spent the night.

THE POWER OF FAITH

[18]Early the next morning, as Jesus was going back to the city, he became hungry. [19]Seeing a fig tree beside the road, Jesus went to it, but there were no figs on the tree, only leaves. So

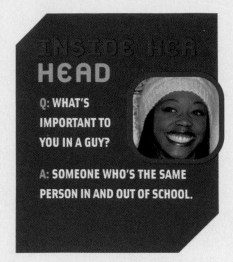
Jesus said to the tree, "You will never again have fruit." The tree immediately dried up.

[20]When his followers saw this, they were amazed. They asked, "How did the fig tree dry up so quickly?"

[21]Jesus answered, "I tell you the truth, if you have faith and do not doubt, you will be able to do what I did to this tree and even more. You will be able to say to this mountain, 'Go, fall into the sea.' And if you have faith, it will happen. [22]If you believe, you will get anything you ask for in prayer."

LEADERS DOUBT JESUS' AUTHORITY

[23]Jesus went to the Temple, and while he was teaching there, the leading priests and the older leaders of the people came to him. They said, "What authority do you have to do these things? Who gave you this authority?"

[24]Jesus answered, "I also will ask you a question. If you answer me, then I will tell you what authority I have to do these things. [25]Tell me: When John baptized people, did that come from God or just from other people?"

They argued about Jesus' question, saying, "If we answer, 'John's baptism was from God,' Jesus will say, 'Then why didn't you believe him?' [26]But if we say, 'It was from people,' we are afraid of what the crowd will do because they all believe that John was a prophet."

[27]So they answered Jesus, "We don't know."

Jesus said to them, "Then I won't tell you what authority I have to do these things.

A STORY ABOUT TWO SONS

[28]"Tell me what you think about this: A man had two sons. He went to the first son and said,

 21:9, 15 Praise Literally, "Hosanna," a Hebrew word used at first in praying to God for help. At this time it was probably a shout of joy used in praising God or his Messiah.   21:13 'My Temple . . . prayer.' Quotation from Isaiah 56:7.   21:13 'hideout for robbers.' Quotation from Jeremiah 7:11.   21:16 'You . . . praises' Quotation from the Septuagint (Greek) version of Psalm 8:2.

32

'Son, go and work today in my vineyard.' [29]The son answered, 'I will not go.' But later the son changed his mind and went. [30]Then the father went to the other son and said, 'Son, go and work today in my vineyard.' The son answered, 'Yes, sir, I will go and work,' but he did not go. [31]Which of the two sons obeyed his father?"

The priests and leaders answered, "The first son."

Jesus said to them, "I tell you the truth, the tax collectors and the prostitutes will enter the kingdom of God before you do. [32]John came to show you the right way to live. You did not believe him, but the tax collectors and prostitutes believed him. Even after seeing this, you still refused to change your ways and believe him.

A STORY ABOUT GOD'S SON

[33]"Listen to this story: There was a man who owned a vineyard. He put a wall around it and dug a hole for a winepress and built a tower. Then he leased the land to some farmers and left for a trip. [34]When it was time for the grapes to be picked, he sent his servants to the farmers to get his share of the grapes. [35]But the farmers grabbed the servants, beat one, killed another, and then killed a third servant with stones. [36]So the man sent some other servants to the farmers, even more than he sent the first time. But the farmers did the same thing to the servants that they had done before. [37]So the man decided to send his son to the farmers. He said, 'They will respect my son.' [38]But when the farmers saw the son, they said to each other, 'This son will inherit the vineyard. If we kill him, it will be ours!' [39]Then the farmers grabbed the son, threw him out of the vineyard, and killed him. [40]So what will the owner of the vineyard do to these farmers when he comes?"

[41]The priests and leaders said, "He will surely kill those evil men. Then he will lease the vineyard to some other farmers who will give him his share of the crop at harvest time."

[42]Jesus said to them, "Surely you have read this in the Scriptures:

'The stone that the builders rejected
    became the cornerstone.
The Lord did this,
    and it is wonderful to us.'
                              Psalm 118:22-23

[43]"So I tell you that the kingdom of God will be taken away from you and given to people who do the things God wants in his kingdom. [44]The person who falls on this stone will be broken, and on whomever that stone falls, that person will be crushed."[n]

[45]When the leading priests and the Pharisees heard these stories, they knew Jesus was talking about them. [46]They wanted to arrest him, but they were afraid of the people, because the people believed that Jesus was a prophet.

A STORY ABOUT A WEDDING FEAST

22 Jesus again used stories to teach the people. He said, [2]"The kingdom of heaven is like a king who prepared a wedding feast for his son. [3]The king invited some people to the feast. When the feast was ready, the king sent his servants to tell the people, but they refused to come.

[4]"Then the king sent other servants, saying, 'Tell those who have been invited that my feast is ready. I have killed my best bulls and calves for the dinner, and everything is ready. Come to the wedding feast.'

[5]"But the people refused to listen to the servants and left to do other things. One went to work in his field, and another went to his business. [6]Some of the other people grabbed the servants, beat them, and killed them. [7]The king was furious and sent his army to kill the murderers and burn their city.

[8]"After that, the king said to his servants, 'The wedding feast is ready. I invited those people, but they were not worthy to come. [9]So go to the street corners and invite everyone you find to come to my feast.' [10]So the servants went into the streets and gathered all the people they could find, both good and bad. And the wedding hall was filled with guests.

[11]"When the king came in to see the guests, he saw a man who was not dressed for a wedding. [12]The king said, 'Friend, how were you allowed to come in here? You are not dressed for a wedding.' But the man said nothing. [13]So the king told some servants, 'Tie this man's hands and feet. Throw him out into the darkness, where people will cry and grind their teeth with pain.'

[14]"Yes, many people are invited, but only a few are chosen."

IS IT RIGHT TO PAY TAXES OR NOT?

[15]Then the Pharisees left that place and

made plans to trap Jesus in saying something wrong. [16]They sent some of their own followers and some people from the group called Herodians.[n] They said, "Teacher, we know that you are an honest man and that you teach the truth about God's way. You are not afraid of what other people think about you, because you pay no attention to who they are. [17]So tell us what you think. Is it right to pay taxes to Caesar or not?"

[18]But knowing that these leaders were trying to trick him, Jesus said, "You hypocrites! Why are you trying to trap me? [19]Show me a coin used for paying the tax." So the men showed him a coin.[n] [20]Then Jesus asked, "Whose image and name are on the coin?"

[21]The men answered, "Caesar's."

Then Jesus said to them, "Give to Caesar the things that are Caesar's, and give to God the things that are God's."

[22]When the men heard what Jesus said, they were amazed and left him and went away.

SOME SADDUCEES TRY TO TRICK JESUS

[23]That same day some Sadducees came to Jesus and asked him a question. (Sadducees

21:44 Verse 44 Some copies do not have verse 44. **22:16 Herodians** A political group that followed Herod and his family.

believed that people would not rise from the dead.) [24]They said, "Teacher, Moses said if a married man dies without having children, his brother must marry the widow and have children for him. [25]Once there were seven brothers among us. The first one married and died. Since he had no children, his brother married the widow. [26]Then the second brother also died. The same thing happened to the third brother and all the other brothers. [27]Finally, the woman died. [28]Since all seven men had married her, when people rise from the dead, whose wife will she be?"

[29]Jesus answered, "You don't understand, because you don't know what the Scriptures say, and you don't know about the power of God. [30]When people rise from the dead, they will not marry, nor will they be given to someone to marry. They will be like the angels in heaven. [31]Surely you have read what God said to you about rising from the dead. [32]God said, 'I am the God of Abraham, the God of Isaac, and the God of Jacob.'[n] God is the God of the living, not the dead."

[33]When the people heard this, they were amazed at Jesus' teaching.

THE MOST IMPORTANT COMMAND

[34]When the Pharisees learned that the Sadducees could not argue with Jesus' answers to them, the Pharisees met together. [35]One Pharisee, who was an expert on the law of Moses, asked Jesus this question to test him: [36]"Teacher, which command in the law is the most important?"

[37]Jesus answered, " 'Love the Lord your God with all your heart, all your soul, and all your mind.'[n] [38]This is the first and most important command. [39]And the second command is like the first: 'Love your neighbor as you love yourself.'[n] [40]All the law and the writings of the prophets depend on these two commands."

JESUS QUESTIONS THE PHARISEES

[41]While the Pharisees were together, Jesus asked them, [42]"What do you think about the Christ? Whose son is he?"

They answered, "The Christ is the Son of David."

[43]Then Jesus said to them, "Then why did David call him 'Lord'? David, speaking by the power of the Holy Spirit, said,

[44]'The Lord said to my Lord:

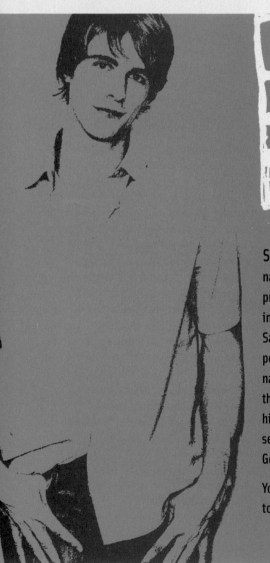

GET OUT THERE

SAMARITAN'S PURSE is a nondenominational evangelical Christian organization providing spiritual and physical aid to hurting people around the world. Since 1970, Samaritan's Purse has helped meet needs of people who are victims of war, poverty, natural disasters, disease, and famine with the purpose of sharing God's love through his Son, Jesus Christ. The organization serves the church worldwide to promote the Gospel of the Lord Jesus Christ.

You can join in Operation Christmas Child to send a message of hope to children in desperate situations around the world through gift-filled shoe boxes and Christian literature. It's a simple, hands-on missions project that reaches out to suffering children while focusing on the true meaning of Christmas—Jesus Christ, God's greatest gift. In the most recent year reported they collected over 6 million shoe boxes worldwide and distributed them to children in about 95 countries.

To get involved,
visit www.samaritanspurse.org.

 22:19 coin A Roman denarius. One coin was the average pay for one day's work.   22:32 'I am . . . Jacob.' Quotation from Exodus 3:6.   22:37 'Love . . . mind.' Quotation from Deuteronomy 6:5.   22:39 'Love . . . yourself.' Quotation from Leviticus 19:18.

RANDOM WAYS TO HAVE FUN WITH YOUR FRIENDS

1. KARAOKE!

2. HIT A WATER PARK ON A RAINY DAY.

3. DO "MORP" EVENTS ("PROM" BACKWARDS), LIKE FAST-FOOD OR BOWLING IN NICE CLOTHES.

4. PLAY FOOTBALL ON YOUR KNEES.

5. GO OUT TO EAT AFTER CHURCH.

6. FONDUE!

7. CLEAN UP ELDERLY NEIGHBORS' LAWNS TOGETHER.

8. DO A CONFERENCE CALL TO A LOCAL TALK-RADIO STATION.

9. HANG OUT AT A COOL RESTAURANT.

10. WATCH "PINKY AND THE BRAIN" RERUNS.

Sit by me at my right side,
until I put your enemies under your
control.'   *Psalm 110:1*

[45]David calls the Christ 'Lord,' so how can the Christ be his son?"

[46]None of the Pharisees could answer Jesus' question, and after that day no one was brave enough to ask him any more questions.

JESUS ACCUSES SOME LEADERS

23 Then Jesus said to the crowds and to his followers, [2]"The teachers of the law and the Pharisees have the authority to tell you what the law of Moses says. [3]So you should obey and follow whatever they tell you, but their lives are not good examples for you to follow. They tell you to do things, but they themselves don't do them. [4]They make strict rules and try to force people to obey them, but they are unwilling to help those who struggle under the weight of their rules.

[5]"They do good things so that other people will see them. They make the boxes[n] of Scriptures that they wear bigger, and they make their special prayer clothes very long. [6]Those Pharisees and teachers of the law love to have the most important seats at feasts and in the synagogues. [7]They love people to greet them with respect in the marketplaces, and they love to have people call them 'Teacher.'

[8]"But you must not be called 'Teacher,' because you have only one Teacher, and you are all brothers and sisters together. [9]And don't call any person on earth 'Father,' because you have one Father, who is in heaven. [10]And you should not be called 'Master,' because you have only one Master, the Christ. [11]Whoever is your servant is the greatest among you. [12]Whoever makes himself great will be made humble. Whoever makes himself humble will be made great.

[13]"How terrible for you, teachers of the law and Pharisees! You are hypocrites! You close the door for people to enter the kingdom of heaven. You yourselves don't enter, and you stop others who are trying to enter. [14][n]

[15]"How terrible for you, teachers of the law and Pharisees! You are hypocrites! You travel across land and sea to find one person who will change to your ways. When you find that person, you make him more fit for hell than you are.

[16]"How terrible for you! You guide the people, but you are blind. You say, 'If people swear by the Temple when they make a promise, that means nothing. But if they swear by the gold that is in the Temple, they must keep that promise.' [17]You are blind fools! Which is greater: the gold or the Temple that makes that gold holy? [18]And you say, 'If people swear by the altar when they make a promise, that means nothing. But if they swear by the gift on the altar, they must keep that promise.' [19]You are blind! Which is greater: the gift or the altar that makes the gift holy? [20]The person who swears by the altar is really using the altar and

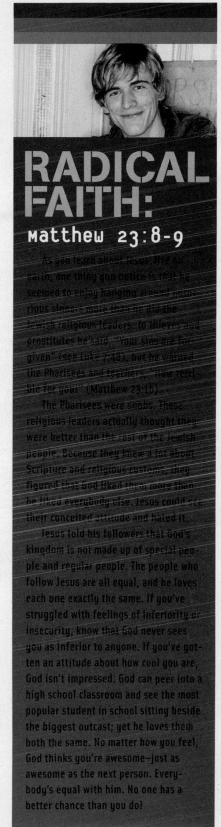

RADICAL FAITH:
matthew 23:8-9

As you learn about Jesus' life on earth, one thing you notice is that he seemed to enjoy hanging around unreligious sinners more than he did the Jewish religious leaders. To thieves and prostitutes he said, "Your sins are forgiven" (see Luke 7:48), but he warned the Pharisees and teachers, "How terrible for you" (Matthew 23:16).

The Pharisees were snobs. These religious leaders actually thought they were better than the rest of the Jewish people. Because they knew a lot about Scripture and religious customs, they figured that God liked them more than he liked everybody else. Jesus could see their conceited attitude and hated it.

Jesus told his followers that God's kingdom is not made up of special people and regular people. The people who follow Jesus are all equal, and he loves each one exactly the same. If you've struggled with feelings of inferiority or insecurity, know that God never sees you as inferior to anyone. If you've gotten an attitude about how cool you are, God isn't impressed. God can peer into a high school classroom and see the most popular student in school sitting beside the biggest outcast; yet he loves them both the same. No matter how you feel, God thinks you're awesome—just as awesome as the next person. Everybody's equal with him. No one has a better chance than you do!

23:5 **boxes** Small leather boxes containing four important Scriptures. Some Jews tied these to their foreheads and left arms, probably to show they were very religious.   23:14 **Verse 14** Some Greek copies add verse 14: "How terrible for you, teachers of the law and Pharisees. You are hypocrites. You take away widows' houses, and you say long prayers so that people will notice you. So you will have a worse punishment."

BIBLE BASICS

The Old Testament is a collection of thirty-nine books that were written before Jesus lived on the earth. They tell the story of the creation of the world and mankind, describe the early history of the nation of Israel, and predict the coming of the Messiah. These books fall into categories of History, Prophecy, and Poetry and Wisdom.

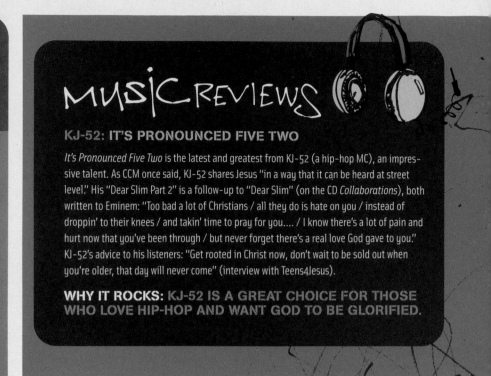

MUSIC REVIEWS

KJ-52: IT'S PRONOUNCED FIVE TWO

It's Pronounced Five Two is the latest and greatest from KJ-52 (a hip-hop MC), an impressive talent. As CCM once said, KJ-52 shares Jesus "in a way that it can be heard at street level." His "Dear Slim Part 2" is a follow-up to "Dear Slim" (on the CD *Collaborations*), both written to Eminem: "Too bad a lot of Christians / all they do is hate on you / instead of droppin' to their knees / and takin' time to pray for you.... / I know there's a lot of pain and hurt now that you've been through / but never forget there's a real love God gave to you." KJ-52's advice to his listeners: "Get rooted in Christ now, don't wait to be sold out when you're older, that day will never come" (interview with Teens4Jesus).

WHY IT ROCKS: KJ-52 IS A GREAT CHOICE FOR THOSE WHO LOVE HIP-HOP AND WANT GOD TO BE GLORIFIED.

also everything on the altar. [21]And the person who swears by the Temple is really using the Temple and also everything in the Temple. [22]The person who swears by heaven is also using God's throne and the One who sits on that throne.

[23]"How terrible for you, teachers of the law and Pharisees! You are hypocrites! You give to God one-tenth of everything you earn—even your mint, dill, and cumin.[n] But you don't obey the really important teachings of the law—justice, mercy, and being loyal. These are the things you should do, as well as those other things. [24]You guide the people, but you are blind! You are like a person who picks a fly out of a drink and then swallows a camel![n]

[25]"How terrible for you, teachers of the law and Pharisees! You are hypocrites! You wash the outside of your cups and dishes, but inside they are full of things you got by cheating others and by pleasing only yourselves. [26]Pharisees, you are blind! First make the inside of the cup clean, and then the outside of the cup can be truly clean.

[27]"How terrible for you, teachers of the law and Pharisees! You are hypocrites! You are like tombs that are painted white. Outside, those tombs look fine, but inside, they are full of the bones of dead people and all kinds of unclean things. [28]It is the same with you. People look at you and think you are good, but on the inside you are full of hypocrisy and evil.

[29]"How terrible for you, teachers of the law and Pharisees! You are hypocrites! You build tombs for the prophets, and you show honor to the graves of those who lived good lives. [30]You say, 'If we had lived during the time of our ancestors, we would not have helped them kill the prophets.' [31]But you give proof that you are children of those who murdered the prophets. [32]And you will complete the sin that your ancestors started.

[33]"You are snakes! A family of poisonous snakes! How are you going to escape God's judgment? [34]So I tell you this: I am sending to you prophets and wise men and teachers. Some of them you will kill and crucify. Some of them you will beat in your synagogues and chase from town to town. [35]So you will be guilty for the death of all the good people who have been killed on earth—from the murder of that good man Abel to the murder of Zechariah[n] son of Berakiah, whom you murdered between the Temple and the altar. [36]I tell you the truth, all of these things will happen to you people who are living now.

JESUS FEELS SORRY FOR JERUSALEM

[37]"Jerusalem, Jerusalem! You kill the prophets and stone to death those who are sent to you.

23:23 **mint, dill, and cumin** Small plants grown in gardens and used for spices. Only very religious people would be careful enough to give a tenth of these plants. 23:24 **You . . . camel!** Meaning, "You worry about the smallest mistakes but commit the biggest sin." 23:35 **Abel . . . Zechariah** In the order of the books of the Hebrew Old Testament, the first and last men to be murdered.

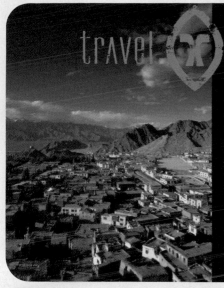

travel [X] the road

There might be days when you feel totally alone as a Christian. Don't. According to Justin Long of the *World Christian Encyclopedia*, each year 17 million people around the world become Christians and join a church. Add to that another 53 million born into Christian families. Even when you subtract Christians who die or head out the back door, the church worldwide grows by more than two jam-packed stadiums each day—some 115,000 people.

For more on extreme missions visit www.traveltheroad.com.

Many times I wanted to gather your people as a hen gathers her chicks under her wings, but you did not let me. [38]Now your house will be left completely empty. [39]I tell you, you will not see me again until that time when you will say, 'God bless the One who comes in the name of the Lord.' "[n]

THE TEMPLE WILL BE DESTROYED

24 As Jesus left the Temple and was walking away, his followers came up to show him the Temple's buildings. [2]Jesus asked, "Do you see all these buildings? I tell you the truth, not one stone will be left on another. Every stone will be thrown down to the ground."

[3]Later, as Jesus was sitting on the Mount of Olives, his followers came to be alone with him. They said, "Tell us, when will these things happen? And what will be the sign that it is time for you to come again and for this age to end?"

[4]Jesus answered, "Be careful that no one fools you. [5]Many will come in my name, saying, 'I am the Christ,' and they will fool many people. [6]You will hear about wars and stories of wars that are coming, but don't be afraid. These things must happen before the end comes. [7]Nations will fight against other nations; kingdoms will fight against other kingdoms. There will be times when there is no food for people to eat, and there will be earthquakes in different places. [8]These things are like the first pains when something new is about to be born.

[9]"Then people will arrest you, hand you over to be hurt, and kill you. They will hate you because you believe in me. [10]At that time, many will lose their faith, and they will turn against each other and hate each other. [11]Many false prophets will come and cause many people to believe lies. [12]There will be more and more evil in the world, so most people will stop showing their love for each other. [13]But those people who keep their faith until the end will be saved. [14]The Good News about God's kingdom will be preached in all the world, to every nation. Then the end will come.

[15]"Daniel the prophet spoke about 'the destroying terror.'[n] You will see this standing in the holy place." (You who read this should understand what it means.) [16]"At that time, the people in Judea should run away to the mountains. [17]If people are on the roofs[n] of their houses, they must not go down to get anything out of their houses. [18]If people are in the fields, they must not go back to get their coats. [19]At that time, how terrible it will be for women who are pregnant or have nursing babies! [20]Pray that it will not be winter or a Sabbath day when these things happen and you have to run away, [21]because at that time there will be much trouble. There will be more trouble than there has ever been since the beginning of the world until now, and nothing as bad will ever happen again. [22]God has decided to make that terrible time short. Otherwise, no one would go on living. But God will make that time short to help the

EXPERTS ANSWER YOUR QUESTIONS

Q. *How did God get there?*

A. Scripture tells us that there was never a time when God wasn't. He has always existed. If he were created, then he wouldn't be God. The one who created him would be God. It's really impossible for us humans to wrap our minds around, isn't it? That's why it takes faith.

Q. *I've heard the Bible says Jesus never sinned. I don't get that.*

A. Jesus' sinless life is part of what sets him apart from us. Jesus is fully God, but he came to be born as a man. Even though he lived a life completely unblemished by sin, he still knows what it's like to be human. The Bible says he was tempted like we are, yet didn't sin. That's why we can run to him for help when we struggle.

Q. *Why does God get so worked up about sin?*

A. It isn't hard to spot a teacher who makes rules for the sake of rules—and then a teacher just strict enough to make school go smoothly. God is like that second kind of teacher. He commands us to ditch sin for our own good. He gets upset when he sees us (1) disrespecting his perfection and (2) pounding on each other. Sin keeps us from the cool life God planned for us, and he never wants us to miss out on his best.

23:39 'God . . . Lord.' Quotation from Psalm 118:26.   24:15 'the destroying terror' Mentioned in Daniel 9:27; 12:11 (see also Daniel 11:31).   24:17 roofs In Bible times houses were built with flat roofs. The roof was used for drying things such as flax and fruit. And it was used as an extra room, as a place for worship, and as a cool place to sleep in the summer.

issues

ROAD RAGE

YOU'RE DRIVING DOWN A ROAD when some guy swerves and cuts you off. Or glues himself to your bumper. Or shines his brights in your face. How do you react? "Road rage" is when you let your angry reaction control you. Without thinking, you take revenge by slamming your horn, flipping the bird, or seeing how close you can cut to the back end of the other guys' vehicle. But the only place for road rage is a video game. The Bible says, "When you are angry, do not sin" (Ephesians 4:26), and that applies to how you drive. The next time someone wrongs you on the road, remember how many times you've done the same thing. Then back off. And decide now to keep from offending others: Use your turn signals, slow down, keep your distance, and pay attention to your driving every time you climb behind the wheel.

people he has chosen. 23At that time, someone might say to you, 'Look, there is the Christ!' Or another person might say, 'There he is!' But don't believe them. 24False Christs and false prophets will come and perform great wonders and miracles. They will try to fool even the people God has chosen, if that is possible. 25Now I have warned you about this before it happens.

26"If people tell you, 'The Christ is in the desert,' don't go there. If they say, 'The Christ is in the inner room,' don't believe it. 27When the Son of Man comes, he will be seen by everyone, like lightning flashing from the east to the west. 28Wherever the dead body is, there the vultures will gather.

29"Soon after the trouble of those days,

'the sun will grow dark,

and the moon will not give its light.

The stars will fall from the sky.

And the powers of the heavens

will be shaken.' *Isaiah 13:10; 34:4*

30"At that time, the sign of the Son of Man will appear in the sky. Then all the peoples of the world will cry. They will see the Son of Man coming on clouds in the sky with great power and glory. 31He will use a loud trumpet to send his angels all around the earth, and they will gather his chosen people from every part of the world.

32"Learn a lesson from the fig tree: When its branches become green and soft and new leaves appear, you know summer is near. 33In the same way, when you see all these things happening, you will know that the time is near, ready to come. 34I tell you the truth, all these things will happen while the people of this time are still living. 35Earth and sky will be destroyed, but the words I have said will never be destroyed.

WHEN WILL JESUS COME AGAIN?

36"No one knows when that day or time will be, not the angels in heaven, not even the Son. Only the Father knows. 37When the Son of Man comes, it will be like what happened during Noah's time. 38In those days before the flood, people were eating and drinking, marrying and giving their children to be married, until the day Noah entered the boat. 39They knew nothing about what was happening until the flood came and destroyed them. It will be the same when the Son of Man comes. 40Two men will be in the field. One will be taken, and the other will be left. 41Two women will be

grinding grain with a mill.*ⁿ* One will be taken, and the other will be left.

42"So always be ready, because you don't know the day your Lord will come. 43Remember this: If the owner of the house knew what time of night a thief was coming, the owner would watch and not let the thief break in. 44So you also must be ready, because the Son of Man will come at a time you don't expect him.

45"Who is the wise and loyal servant that the master trusts to give the other servants their food at the right time? 46When the master comes and finds the servant doing his work, the servant will be blessed. 47I tell you the truth, the master will choose that servant to take care of everything he owns. 48But suppose that evil servant thinks to himself, 'My master will not come back soon,' 49and he begins to beat the other servants and eat and get drunk with others like him? 50The master will come when that servant is not ready and is not expecting him. 51Then the master will cut him in pieces and send him away to be with the hypocrites, where people will cry and grind their teeth with pain.

A STORY ABOUT TEN BRIDESMAIDS

25 "At that time the kingdom of heaven will be like ten bridesmaids who took their lamps and went to wait for the bridegroom. 2Five of them were foolish and five were wise. 3The five foolish bridesmaids took their lamps, but they did not take more oil for the lamps to burn. 4The wise bridesmaids took their lamps and more oil in jars. 5Because the bridegroom was late, they became sleepy and went to sleep.

6"At midnight someone cried out, 'The bridegroom is coming! Come and meet him!' 7Then all the bridesmaids woke up and got their lamps ready. 8But the foolish ones said to the wise, 'Give us some of your oil, because our lamps are going out.' 9The wise bridesmaids answered, 'No, the oil we have might not be enough for all of us. Go to the people who sell oil and buy some for yourselves.'

10"So while the five foolish bridesmaids went to buy oil, the bridegroom came. The bridesmaids who were ready went in with the bridegroom to the wedding feast. Then the door was closed and locked.

11"Later the others came back and said, 'Sir,

RADICAL FAITH:
matthew 24:4

This is a great chapter in the Bible. Jesus is foretelling some of the things that are going to happen before he comes back to the earth: wars, stories of wars, famines, earthquakes, etc. He goes on to tell us not to worry or be afraid because these things must happen before he comes back. But before he goes into all of this, he says that there will be many people who claim to be Jesus and then warns us not to be fooled by them. You've seen this already.

Remember the suicide by the cult group called "Heaven's Gate"? All of the people in that compound died because they allowed themselves to be fooled. Adam and Eve were cast out of the garden because they allowed themselves to be fooled. Esau lost his inheritance because he allowed himself to be fooled. Samson lost his strength because he allowed himself to be fooled.

You don't have to allow yourself to be fooled by some false prophet who claims to be Jesus or from God. If something doesn't line up with the Word of God, then don't believe it. There are more fruitcakes around today than ever before. This is what we call *a sign of the times*.

Jesus is coming back. No one knows exactly when, so stay tight with God and don't be fooled!

 24:41 mill Two large, round, flat rocks used for grinding grain to make flour.

EXPERTS ANSWER YOUR QUESTIONS

Q. *Did Jesus really rise from the dead?*

A. Absolutely. But you don't have to accept that blindly. The Bible accounts of Jesus' death and resurrection are packed with persuasive evidence that Jesus truly rose from the dead. Not only was he undeniably dead, but scores of eyewitnesses saw him alive. Check out the facts in a book like Josh McDowell's massive The New Evidence that Demands a Verdict.

Q. *Did Jesus really heal people? Miracles like that are tough for me to swallow.*

A. If you're going to choke on something, Jesus' rising from the dead is a bigger hunk of truth to get down. But if you get to know the facts about Jesus' real-life resurrection, then other Bible miracles seem minor. The bottom line is: If Jesus really is the Son of God, it's only natural that he should be able to act in a miraculous way.

Q. *Does God really know everything?*

A. Yep. Absolutely everything.

sir, open the door to let us in.' ¹²But the bridegroom answered, 'I tell you the truth, I don't want to know you.'

¹³"So always be ready, because you don't know the day or the hour the Son of Man will come.

A STORY ABOUT THREE SERVANTS

¹⁴"The kingdom of heaven is like a man who was going to another place for a visit. Before he left, he called for his servants and told them to take care of his things while he was gone. ¹⁵He gave one servant five bags of gold, another servant two bags of gold, and a third servant one bag of gold, to each one as much as he could handle. Then he left. ¹⁶The servant who got five bags went quickly to invest the money and earned five more bags. ¹⁷In the same way, the servant who had two bags invested them and earned two more. ¹⁸But the servant who got one bag went out and dug a hole in the ground and hid the master's money.

¹⁹"After a long time the master came home and asked the servants what they did with his money. ²⁰The servant who was given five bags of gold brought five more bags to the master and said, 'Master, you trusted me to care for five bags of gold, so I used your five bags to earn five more.' ²¹The master answered, 'You did well. You are a good and loyal servant. Because you were loyal with small things, I will let you care for much greater things. Come and share my joy with me.'

²²"Then the servant who had been given two bags of gold came to the master and said, 'Master, you gave me two bags of gold to care for, so I used your two bags to earn two more.' ²³The master answered, 'You did well. You are a good and loyal servant. Because you were loyal with small things, I will let you care for much greater things. Come and share my joy with me.'

²⁴"Then the servant who had been given one bag of gold came to the master and said, 'Master, I knew that you were a hard man. You harvest things you did not plant. You gather crops where you did not sow any seed. ²⁵So I was afraid and went and hid your money in the ground. Here is your bag of gold.' ²⁶The master answered, 'You are a wicked and lazy servant! You say you knew that I harvest things I did not

plant and that I gather crops where I did not sow any seed. ²⁷So you should have put my gold in the bank. Then, when I came home, I would have received my gold back with interest.'

²⁸"So the master told his other servants, 'Take the bag of gold from that servant and give it to the servant who has ten bags of gold. ²⁹Those who have much will get more, and they will have much more than they need. But those who do not have much will have everything taken away from them.' ³⁰Then the master said, 'Throw that useless servant outside, into the darkness where people will cry and grind their teeth with pain.'

THE KING WILL JUDGE ALL PEOPLE

³¹"The Son of Man will come again in his great glory, with all his angels. He will be King and sit on his great throne. ³²All the

RANDOM COOL THINGS TO DO FOR A FRIEND

1. OFFER TO DRIVE HIM TO OR FROM SCHOOL.
2. HELP HIM WITH A TOUGH HOMEWORK.
3. BUY HIM LUNCH.
4. WASH HIS CAR.
5. BURN HIM A CD OFF A SITE LIKE ITUNES. (NOTHING'S AS UNCOOL AS ILLEGAL DOWNLOADING!)
6. PRAY FOR HIM.
7. DEFEND HIM WHEN OTHERS SLAM HIM.
8. INVITE HIM TO FAMILY FUNCTIONS.
9. HELP HIM WITH CHORES.
10. BUY HIM SOMETHING HE WOULDN'T BUY FOR HIMSELF.

WAYS TO WALK THE WALK

matthew 13:44

WORD: God's kingdom is priceless.

WALK IT: Ask yourself if anything in your life is more important than God. Change how you think and act to put that thing in its proper place.

matthew 18:20

WORD: Jesus is with you wherever two or three get together in his name.

WALK IT: Pray with some friends today. Thank Jesus that he is with you.

nations of the world will be gathered before him, and he will separate them into two groups as a shepherd separates the sheep from the goats. ³³The Son of Man will put the sheep on his right and the goats on his left.

³⁴"Then the King will say to the people on his right, 'Come, my Father has given you his blessing. Receive the kingdom God has prepared for you since the world was made. ³⁵I was hungry, and you gave me food. I was thirsty, and you gave me something to drink. I was alone and away from home, and you invited me into your house. ³⁶I was without clothes, and you gave me something to wear. I was sick, and you cared for me. I was in prison, and you visited me.'

³⁷"Then the good people will answer, 'Lord, when did we see you hungry and give you food, or thirsty and give you something to drink? ³⁸When did

we see you alone and away from home and invite you into our house? When did we see you without clothes and give you something to wear? ³⁹When did we see you sick or in prison and care for you?'

⁴⁰"Then the King will answer, 'I tell you the truth, anything you did for even the least of my people here, you also did for me.'

⁴¹"Then the King will say to those on his left, 'Go away from me. You will be punished. Go into the fire that burns forever that was prepared for the devil and his angels. ⁴²I was hungry, and you gave me nothing to eat. I was thirsty, and you gave me nothing to drink. ⁴³I was alone and away from home, and you did not invite me into your house. I was without clothes, and you gave me nothing to wear. I

was sick and in prison, and you did not care for me.'

⁴⁴"Then those people will answer, 'Lord, when did we see you hungry or thirsty or alone and away from home or without clothes or sick or in prison? When did we see these things and not help you?'

⁴⁵"Then the King will answer, 'I tell you the truth, anything you refused to do for even the least of my people here, you refused to do for me.'

⁴⁶"These people will go off to be punished forever, but the good people will go to live forever."

THE PLAN TO KILL JESUS

26 After Jesus finished saying all these things, he told his followers, ²"You know that the day after

MEN OF THE SWORD

PAUL was the ultimate Christian missionary, but he had an unlikely beginning. He grew up well trained in the Jewish faith, and he was just a young teen when his family sent him to study under the most famous rabbi of his day. Paul became a passionate defender of his faith, so radical that he persecuted fellow Jews who became Christians. When he headed out on a mission to hunt down Christians and haul them back to prison in Jerusalem, God knocked him to the ground with a blinding light from heaven. Paul heard the voice of Jesus, who he was really persecuting. After that jolt on the Damascus road, Paul became an intense Christian evangelist who spread the Good News about Christ all over the Roman Empire, despite hardship ranging from shipwrecks to beatings and more. He cared deeply for the people who believed in Jesus because of his preaching, and his letters to those churches became a large portion of the New Testament, from Romans to Philemon (and maybe Hebrews). Tradition says he was executed in Rome.

–Acts 8, 2 Corinthians 11, Philippians 3

FEBRUARY

1
Read the Book of Ephesians today.

2
Groundhog Day—Get on the net and find out about some of the creatures God made.

3

4

5
Clean out your closet and give away stuff you don't use anymore.

6

7
Pray for a Person of Influence: It's Ashton Kutcher's birthday.

8

9

10
Get some exercise; take a vitamin. February is the month most people suffer depression.

11
Pray for a Person of Influence: Jennifer Aniston gets older today.

Reach out to a stranger of another race.

13
Pray for a Person of Influence: Randy Moss catches another birthday today.

14
Watch your siblings so your parents can go out to celebrate Valentine's Day.

15

16

17
Pray for a Person of Influence: Today is Michael Jordan's birthday.

18
Chat with someone you usually ignore.

19
Round up your friends and get tickets for a Christian concert.

20

21
Eat a hot pepper to stay warm today.

22

23
It's Dog Biscuit Appreciation Day. Share one with a furry friend.

24
Pile up some pillows and blankets and take them to a homeless shelter tonight.

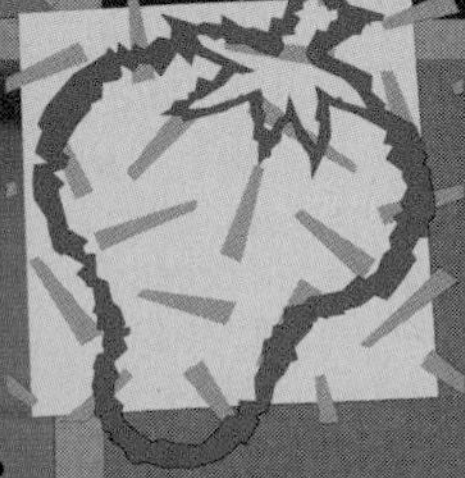

How's the semester going so far? Do you need to step back and recheck your priorities?

25

26
Check in on your New Year's resolutions today. Any you need to keep?

27

28
Have no fear—spring is almost here.

tomorrow is the day of the Passover Feast. On that day the Son of Man will be given to his enemies to be crucified."

[3]Then the leading priests and the older leaders had a meeting at the palace of the high priest, named Caiaphas. [4]At the meeting, they planned to set a trap to arrest Jesus and kill him. [5]But they said, "We must not do it during the feast, because the people might cause a riot."

PERFUME FOR JESUS' BURIAL

[6]Jesus was in Bethany at the house of Simon, who had a skin disease. [7]While Jesus was there, a woman approached him with an alabaster jar filled with expensive perfume. She poured this perfume on Jesus' head while he was eating.

[8]His followers were upset when they saw the woman do this. They asked, "Why waste that perfume? [9]It could have been sold for a great deal of money and the money given to the poor."

[10]Knowing what had happened, Jesus said, "Why are you troubling this woman? She did an excellent thing for me. [11]You will always have the poor with you, but you will not always have me. [12]This woman poured perfume on my body to prepare me for burial. [13]I tell you the truth, wherever the Good News is preached in all the world, what this woman has done will be told, and people will remember her."

JUDAS BECOMES AN ENEMY OF JESUS

[14]Then one of the twelve apostles, Judas Iscariot, went to talk to the leading priests. [15]He said, "What will you pay me for giving Jesus to you?" And they gave him thirty silver coins. [16]After that, Judas watched for the best time to turn Jesus in.

JESUS EATS THE PASSOVER MEAL

[17]On the first day of the Feast of Unleavened Bread, the followers came to Jesus. They said, "Where do you want us to prepare for you to eat the Passover meal?"

[18]Jesus answered, "Go into the city to a certain man and tell him, 'The Teacher says: The chosen time is near. I will have the Passover with my followers at your house.' " [19]The followers did what Jesus told them to do, and they prepared the Passover meal.

[20]In the evening Jesus was sitting at the table with his twelve followers. [21]As they were eating, Jesus said, "I tell you the truth, one of you will turn against me."

[22]This made the followers very sad. Each one began to say to Jesus, "Surely, Lord, I am not the one who will turn against you, am I?"

RELATIONSHIPS

"Do not try to punish others when they wrong you, but wait for God to punish them with his anger" (Romans 12:19). You got slammed—by a friend, an enemy, a family member, whoever. As soon as you're over the sting, what's the first thought that scampers through your brain? "It's payback time." Good as that sounds, God has a better way. He says to let *him* take care of evildoers. He actually tells us to *help* those who hurt us. That might be the most scorching revenge of all, because God says it's like pouring burning coals on their heads (Romans 12:20).

MUSIC REVIEWS

PASSION WORSHIP BAND: SACRED REVOLUTION

Sacred Revolution is the most recent live recording from Passion, a collection of worship leaders that hosted the OneDay '03 event in Houston (with over 20,000 youth singing along). Vocals and lyrics feature Matt Redman ("Come Let Us Return to the Lord"), Chris Tomlin ("Not to Us"), Charlie Hall ("All the Earth"), David Crowder Band ("O Praise Him"), Candi Pearson ("Sing to the King"), Steve Fee, and Christy Nockels of Watermark ("Knees to the Earth"). More than 75 minutes of new tunes, classic pieces, and an inspiring cover of Jason Wade's "Revolution Cry" (Lifehouse). The entire CD is pure worship, from anthem rock songs to soothing ballads.

WHY IT ROCKS: AN AUTHENTIC THRONG OF WORSHIPERS PRAISING THE LORD TOGETHER.

HOW TO MIND YOUR MANNERS AT PROM

Your mom may have given up long ago on trying to teach you manners. But prom is an occasion when crowds of people stare at your smoothness—or lack of it. Follow these pointers and don't act like a stooge: Bring your date a corsage, which gets pinned on her left side, flowers pointing up. Open the car door for your date, both when you get in and get out. Open other doors too. At dinner, help your date take her seat at the table. Your napkin goes on your lap, the girl orders first, and you use all those forks from the outside in. When you stroll down a sidewalk, you walk on the street side. Let your date take your arm if she likes. Remember: Special events call for special behavior. It's like going into the presence of God in worship. Yeah, God is your best friend. But he's also the King of the Universe. Don't go totally casual on him.

²³Jesus answered, "The man who has dipped his hand with me into the bowl is the one who will turn against me. ²⁴The Son of Man will die, just as the Scriptures say. But how terrible it will be for the person who hands the Son of Man over to be killed. It would be better for him if he had never been born."

²⁵Then Judas, who would give Jesus to his enemies, said to Jesus, "Teacher, surely I am not the one, am I?"

Jesus answered, "Yes, it is you."

THE LORD'S SUPPER

²⁶While they were eating, Jesus took some bread and thanked God for it and broke it. Then he gave it to his followers and said, "Take this bread and eat it; this is my body."

²⁷Then Jesus took a cup and thanked God for it and gave it to the followers. He said, "Every one of you drink this. ²⁸This is my blood which is the new agreement that God makes with his people. This blood is poured out for many to forgive their sins. ²⁹I tell you this: I will not drink of this fruit of the vine^n again until that day when I drink it new with you in my Father's kingdom."

³⁰After singing a hymn, they went out to the Mount of Olives.

JESUS' FOLLOWERS WILL LEAVE HIM

³¹Jesus told his followers, "Tonight you will all stumble in your faith on account of me, because it is written in the Scriptures:

'I will kill the shepherd,
    and the sheep will scatter.'   *Zechariah 13:7*
³²But after I rise from the dead, I will go ahead of you into Galilee."

³³Peter said, "Everyone else may stumble in their faith because of you, but I will not."

³⁴Jesus said, "I tell you the truth, tonight before the rooster crows you will say three times that you don't know me."

³⁵But Peter said, "I will never say that I don't know you! I will even die with you!" And all the other followers said the same thing.

JESUS PRAYS ALONE

³⁶Then Jesus went with his followers to a place called Gethsemane. He said to them, "Sit here while I go over there and pray." ³⁷He took Peter and the two sons of Zebedee with him, and he began to be very sad and troubled. ³⁸He

NON-GIRLY WAYS TO COMFORT A HURTING FRIEND

1. LISTEN.
2. TELL HIM YOU'LL STICK WITH HIM.
3. GIVE HIM MUSIC THAT HELPS WHEN IT HURTS.
4. ASK HIM WHAT YOU CAN DO FOR HIM. ASK AGAIN.
5. DON'T TRY TO TOP HIS STORIES WITH YOUR OWN.
6. MEAN IT WHEN YOU SAY YOU'RE PRAYING FOR HIM.
7. HELP HIM FIND A COUNSELOR.
8. LET HIM KNOW HE CAN CALL YOU ANYTIME.
9. JUST BE THERE. DON'T TRY TO FIX EVERYTHING.
10. REMIND HIM THAT GOD CARES.

INSIDE HER HEAD

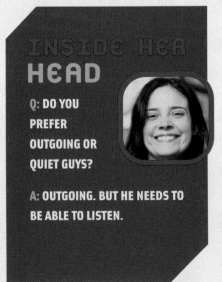

Q: DO YOU PREFER OUTGOING OR QUIET GUYS?

A: OUTGOING. BUT HE NEEDS TO BE ABLE TO LISTEN.

 26:29 **fruit of the vine** Product of the grapevine; this may also be translated "wine."

said to them, "My heart is full of sorrow, to the point of death. Stay here and watch with me."

[39]After walking a little farther away from them, Jesus fell to the ground and prayed, "My Father, if it is possible, do not give me this cup[n] of suffering. But do what you want, not what I want." [40]Then Jesus went back to his followers and found them asleep. He said to Peter, "You men could not stay awake with me for one hour? [41]Stay awake and pray for strength against temptation. The spirit wants to do what is right, but the body is weak."

[42]Then Jesus went away a second time and prayed, "My Father, if it is not possible for this painful thing to be taken from me, and if I must do it, I pray that what you want will be done."

[43]Then he went back to his followers, and again he found them asleep, because their eyes were heavy. [44]So Jesus left them and went away and prayed a third time, saying the same thing.

[45]Then Jesus went back to his followers and said, "Are you still sleeping and resting? The time has come for the Son of Man to be handed over to sinful people. [46]Get up, we must go. Look, here comes the man who has turned against me."

JESUS IS ARRESTED

[47]While Jesus was still speaking, Judas, one of the twelve apostles, came up. With him were many people carrying swords and clubs who had been sent from the leading priests and the older Jewish leaders of the people. [48]Judas had planned to give them a signal, saying, "The man I kiss is Jesus. Arrest him." [49]At once Judas went

to Jesus and said, "Greetings, Teacher!" and kissed him.

[50]Jesus answered, "Friend, do what you came to do."

Then the people came and grabbed Jesus and arrested him.. [51]When that happened, one of Jesus' followers reached for his sword and pulled it out. He struck the servant of the high priest and cut off his ear.

[52]Jesus said to the man, "Put your sword back in its place. All who use swords will be killed with swords. [53]Surely you know I could ask my Father, and he would give me more than twelve armies of angels. [54]But it must happen this way to bring about what the Scriptures say."

[55]Then Jesus said to the crowd, "You came to get me with swords and clubs as if I were a criminal. Every day I sat in the Temple teaching, and you did not arrest me there. [56]But all these things have happened so that it will come about as the prophets wrote." Then all of Jesus' followers left him and ran away.

JESUS BEFORE THE LEADERS

[57]Those people who arrested Jesus led him to the house of Caiaphas, the high priest, where the teachers of the law and the older leaders were gathered. [58]Peter followed far behind to the courtyard of the high priest's house, and he sat down with the guards to see what would happen to Jesus.

[59]The leading priests and the whole Jewish council tried to find something false against Jesus so they could kill him. [60]Many people came and

RADICAL FAITH:
matthew 27:4

When Judas found out that the Jewish leaders intended to have Jesus executed, it was like a lightbulb came on in his head. He suddenly realized what he had done—the simple kiss that had earned him thirty silver coins was going to cost Jesus his life. Judas knew that Jesus was innocent of all the charges the Jews brought against him, and they were going to kill him anyway.

But Jesus wasn't just innocent under the man-made law of the land; he was also innocent in God's eyes. He *literally* never did anything wrong. And his innocence wasn't just a natural thing because he was God's Son. He still had to make choices. Meanwhile Satan did all he could to convince Jesus not to choose God's way. Hebrews 4:15 says, "For our high priest is able to understand our weaknesses. When he lived on earth, he was tempted in every way that we are, but he did not sin."

Because Jesus is innocent, his blood is an acceptable sacrifice to God for your sins. And because he didn't give in to temptation, he paved the way for you to stand up to Satan's tricks, because his Spirit lives in you. When you do sin, confess, repent, and ask his forgiveness and Jesus will declare you innocent too.

travel ✖ the road

It's a fact that 90 percent of people unreached by the Good News about Jesus live in a rectangular block stretching from west Africa to east Asia between the 10th and 40th parallels. This "10/40 Window" covers more than four billion people in 65 countries, including a massive 1.6 billion who have never heard about Jesus—not even once. Some 80 percent of the people living in the 10/40 Window exist on less than five hundred dollars per person a year. Surf to www.win1040.org to learn more.

For more on extreme missions visit www.traveltheroad.com.

 26:39 cup Jesus is talking about the terrible things that will happen to him. Accepting these things will be very hard, like drinking a cup of something bitter.

told lies about him, but the council could find no real reason to kill him. Then two people came and said, [61]"This man said, 'I can destroy the Temple of God and build it again in three days.' "

[62]Then the high priest stood up and said to Jesus, "Aren't you going to answer? Don't you have something to say about their charges against you?" [63]But Jesus said nothing.

Again the high priest said to Jesus, "I command you by the power of the living God: Tell us if you are the Christ, the Son of God."

[64]Jesus answered, "Those are your words. But I tell you, in the future you will see the Son of Man sitting at the right hand of God, the Powerful One, and coming on clouds in the sky."

[65]When the high priest heard this, he tore his clothes and said, "This man has said things that are against God! We don't need any more witnesses; you all heard him say these things against God. [66]What do you think?"

The people answered, "He should die."

[67]Then the people there spat in Jesus' face and beat him with their fists. Others slapped him. [68]They said, "Prove to us that you are a prophet, you Christ! Tell us who hit you!"

PETER SAYS HE DOESN'T KNOW JESUS

[69]At that time, as Peter was sitting in the courtyard, a servant girl came to him and said, "You also were with Jesus of Galilee."

[70]But Peter said to all the people there that he was never with Jesus. He said, "I don't know what you are talking about."

[71]When he left the courtyard and was at the gate, another girl saw him. She said to the people there, "This man was with Jesus of Nazareth."

[72]Again, Peter said he was never with him, saying, "I swear I don't know this man Jesus!"

[73]A short time later, some people standing there went to Peter and said, "Surely you are one of those who followed Jesus. The way you talk shows it."

[74]Then Peter began to place a curse on himself and swear, "I don't know the man." At once, a rooster crowed. [75]And Peter remembered what Jesus had told him: "Before the rooster crows, you will say three times that you don't know me." Then Peter went outside and cried painfully.

JESUS IS TAKEN TO PILATE

27 Early the next morning, all the leading priests and older leaders of the people decided that Jesus should die. [2]They tied him, led him away, and turned him over to Pilate, the governor.

JUDAS KILLS HIMSELF

[3]Judas, the one who had given Jesus to his enemies, saw that they had decided to kill Jesus. Then he was very sorry for what he had done. So he took the thirty silver coins back to the priests and the leaders, [4]saying, "I sinned; I handed over to you an innocent man."

The leaders answered, "What is that to us? That's your problem, not ours."

[5]So Judas threw the money into the Temple. Then he went off and hanged himself.

[6]The leading priests picked up the silver coins in the Temple and said, "Our law does not allow us to keep this money with the Temple money, because it has paid for a man's death." [7]So they decided to use the coins to buy Potter's Field as a place to bury strangers who died in Jerusalem. [8]That is why that field is still called the Field of Blood. [9]So what Jeremiah the prophet had said came true: "They took thirty silver coins. That is how little the Israelites thought he was worth. [10]They used those thirty silver coins to buy the potter's field, as the Lord commanded me."[n]

PILATE QUESTIONS JESUS

[11]Jesus stood before Pilate the governor, and Pilate asked him, "Are you the king of the Jews?"

Jesus answered, "Those are your words."

[12]When the leading priests and the older leaders accused Jesus, he said nothing.

[13]So Pilate said to Jesus, "Don't you hear them accusing you of all these things?"

[14]But Jesus said nothing in answer to Pilate, and Pilate was very surprised at this.

PILATE TRIES TO FREE JESUS

[15]Every year at the time of Passover the governor would free one prisoner whom the people chose. [16]At that time there was a man in prison, named Barabbas, who was known to be very bad. [17]When the people gathered at Pilate's house, Pilate said, "Whom do you want me to set free: Barabbas or Jesus who is called the Christ?" [18]Pilate knew that the people turned Jesus in to him because they were jealous.

[19]While Pilate was sitting there on the

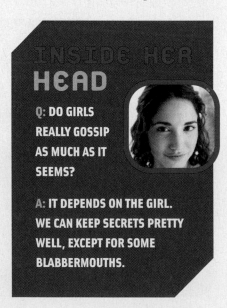

INSIDE HER HEAD

Q: DO GIRLS REALLY GOSSIP AS MUCH AS IT SEEMS?

A: IT DEPENDS ON THE GIRL. WE CAN KEEP SECRETS PRETTY WELL, EXCEPT FOR SOME BLABBERMOUTHS.

27:9-10 "They . . . commanded me." See Zechariah 11:12–13 and Jeremiah 32:6–9.

judge's seat, his wife sent this message to him: "Don't do anything to that man, because he is innocent. Today I had a dream about him, and it troubled me very much."

20But the leading priests and older leaders convinced the crowd to ask for Barabbas to be freed and for Jesus to be killed.

21Pilate said, "I have Barabbas and Jesus. Which do you want me to set free for you?"

The people answered, "Barabbas."

22Pilate asked, "So what should I do with Jesus, the one called the Christ?"

They all answered, "Crucify him!"

23Pilate asked, "Why? What wrong has he done?"

But they shouted louder, "Crucify him!"

24When Pilate saw that he could do nothing about this and that a riot was starting, he took some water and washed his hands[n] in front of the crowd. Then he said, "I am not guilty of this man's death. You are the ones who are causing it!"

25All the people answered, "We and our children will be responsible for his death."

26Then he set Barabbas free. But Jesus was beaten with whips and handed over to the soldiers to be crucified.

27The governor's soldiers took Jesus into the governor's palace, and they all gathered around him. 28They took off his clothes and put a red robe on him. 29Using thorny branches, they made a crown, put it on his head, and put a stick in his right hand. Then the soldiers bowed before Jesus and made fun of him, saying, "Hail, King of the Jews!" 30They spat on Jesus. Then they took his stick and began to beat him on the head. 31After they finished, the soldiers took off the robe and put his own clothes on him again. Then they led him away to be crucified.

JESUS IS CRUCIFIED

32As the soldiers were going out of the city with Jesus, they forced a man from Cyrene, named Simon, to carry the cross for Jesus. 33They all came to the place called Golgotha, which means the Place of the Skull. 34The soldiers gave Jesus wine mixed with gall[n] to drink. He tasted the wine but refused to drink it. 35When the soldiers had crucified him, they threw lots to decide who would get his clothes.

GET OUT THERE

THE SALVATION ARMY was founded as an evangelical organization dedicated to bringing people into a meaningful relationship with God through Christ. The word "army" indicates that the organization is a fighting force, constantly at war with the powers of evil. Battles are effectively waged through a ministry that gives attention to both body and spirit—total ministry for the total person. The Army cooperates with churches of all denominations to meet the needs of the community.

Along with 1.5 million other Americans, you can volunteer with The Salvation Army to serve the needy. From ringing the bell at Salvation Army kettles during the Christmas season to working with youth in character-building activities, you can help The Salvation Army meet far more needs than it could without your help. Whether you have a skill or just a heart to serve, The Salvation Army has a place for you.

To help, go to www.salvationarmyusa.org.

 27:24 washed his hands He did this as a sign to show that he wanted no part in what the people did. **27:34 gall** Probably a drink of wine mixed with drugs to help a person feel less pain.

RADICAL FAITH:

matthew 28:19

Notice what this verse is saying. It instructs us to go and make followers—not just converts, but followers in the same way of Jesus' first twelve. We want to do more than just see people give their hearts to the Lord. We want to help them mature and grow in him. Aren't you glad that someone helped you? When you gave your heart to Jesus, God just didn't throw you out and say, "Okay, you're on your own now."

If people are going to be developed, they have to be mentored in the growth of their faith. That's where we come in, *showing* them as well as *telling* them how to follow Christ. That's our job—to assist in spreading the Good News, to be totally devoted to God, and to stick to him like glue. We want to see people get saved and stick with it. Let's help our friends develop and grow so they can help others!

---

[36]The soldiers sat there and continued watching him. [37]They put a sign above Jesus' head with a charge against him. It said: THIS IS JESUS, THE KING OF THE JEWS. [38]Two robbers were crucified beside Jesus, one on the right and the other on the left. [39]People walked by and insulted Jesus and shook their heads, [40]saying, "You said you could destroy the Temple and build it again in three days. So save yourself! Come down from that cross if you are really the Son of God!"

[41]The leading priests, the teachers of the law, and the older Jewish leaders were also making fun of Jesus. [42]They said, "He saved others, but he can't save himself! He says he is the king of Israel! If he is the king, let him come down now from the cross. Then we will believe in him. [43]He trusts in God, so let God save him now, if God really wants him. He himself said, 'I am the Son of God.'" [44]And in the same way, the robbers who were being crucified beside Jesus also insulted him.

JESUS DIES

[45]At noon the whole country became dark, and the darkness lasted for three hours. [46]About three o'clock Jesus cried out in a loud voice, "Eli, Eli, lama sabachthani?" This means, "My God, my God, why have you rejected me?"

[47]Some of the people standing there who heard this said, "He is calling Elijah."

[48]Quickly one of them ran and got a sponge and filled it with vinegar and tied it to a stick and gave it to Jesus to drink. [49]But the others said, "Don't bother him. We want to see if Elijah will come to save him."

[50]But Jesus cried out again in a loud voice and died.

[51]Then the curtain in the Temple[n] was torn into two pieces, from the top to the bottom. Also, the earth shook and rocks broke apart. [52]The graves opened, and many of God's people who had died were raised from the dead. [53]They came out of the graves after Jesus was raised from the dead and went into the holy city, where they appeared to many people.

[54]When the army officer and the soldiers guarding Jesus saw this earthquake and everything else that happened, they were very frightened and said, "He really was the Son of God!"

[55]Many women who had followed Jesus from Galilee to help him were standing at a distance from the cross, watching. [56]Mary

Magdalene, and Mary the mother of James and Joseph, and the mother of James and John were there.

JESUS IS BURIED

[57]That evening a rich man named Joseph, a follower of Jesus from the town of Arimathea, came to Jerusalem. [58]Joseph went to Pilate and asked to have Jesus' body. So Pilate gave orders for the soldiers to give it to Joseph. [59]Then Joseph took the body and wrapped it in a clean linen cloth. [60]He put Jesus' body in a new tomb that he had cut out of a wall of rock, and he rolled a very large stone to block the entrance of the tomb. Then Joseph went away. [61]Mary Magdalene and the other woman named Mary were sitting near the tomb.

THE TOMB OF JESUS IS GUARDED

[62]The next day, the day after Preparation Day, the leading priests and the Pharisees went to Pilate. [63]They said, "Sir, we remember that while that liar was still alive he said, 'After three days I will rise from the dead.' [64]So give the

---

 27:51 curtain in the Temple A curtain divided the Most Holy Place from the other part of the Temple. That was the special building in Jerusalem where God commanded the Jewish people to worship him.

RANDOM WAYS TO LEAD YOUR PEERS

1. LIVE OUT YOUR CONVICTIONS, NO MATTER WHO DOES OR DOESN'T FOLLOW YOU.

2. HAVE FUN DOING THE RIGHT THING.

3. BE TRUE TO YOUR WORD.

4. ENCOURAGE OTHERS.

5. DON'T LOWER YOUR STANDARDS FOR POPULARITY.

6. BE ONE-FACED.

7. BE KIND TO PEOPLE WHO HAVE NOTHING TO OFFER YOU.

8. HONOR PEOPLE IN AUTHORITY.

9. ASK GOD FOR WISDOM, THEN USE IT.

10. ADMIT IT WHEN YOU'RE WRONG.

order for the tomb to be guarded closely till the third day. Otherwise, his followers might come and steal the body and tell people that he has risen from the dead. That lie would be even worse than the first one."

[65]Pilate said, "Take some soldiers and go guard the tomb the best way you know." [66]So they all went to the tomb and made it safe from thieves by sealing the stone in the entrance and putting soldiers there to guard it.

JESUS RISES FROM THE DEAD

28 The day after the Sabbath day was the first day of the week. At dawn on the first day, Mary Magdalene and another woman named Mary went to look at the tomb.

[2]At that time there was a strong earthquake. An angel of the Lord came down from heaven, went to the tomb, and rolled the stone away from the entrance. Then he sat on the stone. [3]He was shining as bright as lightning, and his clothes were white as snow. [4]The soldiers guarding the tomb shook with fear because of the angel, and they became like dead men.

[5]The angel said to the women, "Don't be afraid. I know that you are looking for Jesus, who has been crucified. [6]He is not here. He has risen from the dead as he said he would. Come and see the place where his body was. [7]And go quickly and tell his followers, 'Jesus has risen from the dead. He is going into Galilee ahead of you, and you will see him there.'" Then the angel said, "Now I have told you."

[8]The women left the tomb quickly. They were afraid, but they were also very happy. They ran to tell Jesus' followers what had happened. [9]Suddenly, Jesus met them and said, "Greetings." The women came up to him, took hold of his feet, and worshiped him. [10]Then Jesus said to them, "Don't be afraid. Go and tell my followers to go on to Galilee, and they will see me there."

THE SOLDIERS REPORT TO THE LEADERS

[11]While the women went to tell Jesus' followers, some of the soldiers who had been guarding the tomb went into the city to tell the leading priests everything that had happened. [12]Then the priests met with the older leaders and made a plan. They paid the soldiers a large amount of money [13]and said to them, "Tell the people that Jesus' followers came during the night and stole the body while you were asleep. [14]If the governor hears about this, we will satisfy him and save you from trouble." [15]So the soldiers kept the money and did as they were told. And that story is still spread among the people even today.

JESUS TALKS TO HIS FOLLOWERS

[16]The eleven followers went to Galilee to the mountain where Jesus had told them to go. [17]On the mountain they saw Jesus and worshiped him, but some of them did not believe it was really Jesus. [18]Then Jesus came to them and said, "All power in heaven and on earth is given to me. [19]So go and make followers of all people in the world. Baptize them in the name of the Father and the Son and the Holy Spirit. [20]Teach them to obey everything that I have taught you, and I will be with you always, even until the end of this age."

BIBLE BASICS

The New Testament contains the twenty-seven books that were written after Jesus' life on earth. These books talk about how he was born, explain what he taught, describe the early church, and end with the Book of Revelation, which tells about Christ's future final triumph over evil.

MARK

If you're scoping for an action-jammed account of Jesus, you've found it. Here you'll spot Jesus moving from place to place... healing to healing... miracle to miracle. Mark follows along and doesn't miss a scene.

Mark's Gospel is the shortest in the New Testament, but it packs in so much information in so few chapters, it feels a lot bigger than it is. Mark's Gospel was highly influential in the development of Matthew and Luke. When Matthew and Luke sat down to write their Gospels, they had probably already read Mark. Their books show signs of borrowing from the Book of Mark.

This story makes one thing unmistakably clear— Jesus suffered on our behalf. Almost 40 percent of this short book lays out details of the final, traumatic week of Jesus' life. And the earlier part of the book throws a spotlight on the pain Jesus endured from the very start of his ministry: confrontation with hostile spiritual forces and human beings intent on humiliating and then killing him. It even describes the suffering and rejection he endured from his family and the confusion of his closest friends.

JOHN PREPARES FOR JESUS

1 This is the beginning of the Good News about Jesus Christ, the Son of God,[n] [2]as the prophet Isaiah wrote:

"I will send my messenger ahead of you,
who will prepare your way."   *Malachi 3:1*

[3]"This is a voice of one
who calls out in the desert:
'Prepare the way for the Lord.
Make the road straight for him.'"

Isaiah 40:3

[4]John was baptizing people in the desert and preaching a baptism of changed hearts and lives for the forgiveness of sins. [5]All the people from Judea and Jerusalem were going out to him. They confessed their sins and were baptized by him in the Jordan River. [6]John wore clothes made from camel's hair, had a leather belt around his waist, and ate locusts and wild honey. [7]This is what John preached to the people: "There is one coming after me who is greater than I; I am not good enough even to kneel down and untie his sandals. [8]I baptize you with water, but he will baptize you with the Holy Spirit."

JESUS IS BAPTIZED

[9]At that time Jesus came from the town of Nazareth in Galilee and was baptized by John in the Jordan River. [10]Immediately, as Jesus was coming up out of the water, he saw heaven open. The Holy Spirit came down on him like a dove, [11]and a voice came from heaven: "You are my Son, whom I love, and I am very pleased with you."

[12]Then the Spirit sent Jesus into the desert. [13]He was in the desert forty days and was tempted by Satan. He was with the wild animals, and the angels came and took care of him.

JESUS CHOOSES SOME FOLLOWERS

[14]After John was put in prison, Jesus went into Galilee, preaching the Good News from God. [15]He said, "The right time has come. The kingdom of God is near. Change your hearts and lives and believe the Good News!"

[16]When Jesus was walking by Lake Galilee, he saw Simon[n] and his brother Andrew throwing a net into the lake because they were fishermen. [17]Jesus said to them, "Come follow me, and I will make you fish for people." [18]So Simon and Andrew immediately left their nets and followed him.

[19]Going a little farther, Jesus saw two more brothers, James and John, the sons of Zebedee. They were in a boat, mending their nets. [20]Jesus immediately called them, and they left their father in the boat with the hired workers and followed Jesus.

JESUS FORCES OUT AN EVIL SPIRIT

[21]Jesus and his followers went to Capernaum. On the Sabbath day He went to the synagogue and began to teach. [22]The people were amazed at his teaching, because he taught like a person who had authority, not like their teachers of the law. [23]Just then, a man was there in the synagogue who had an evil spirit in him. He shouted, [24]"Jesus of Nazareth! What do you want with us? Did you come to destroy us? I know who you are—God's Holy One!"

[25]Jesus commanded the evil spirit, "Be quiet! Come out of the man!" [26]The evil spirit shook the man violently, gave a loud cry, and then came out of him.

[27]The people were so amazed they asked each other, "What is happening here? This man is teaching something new, and with authority. He even gives commands to evil spirits, and they obey him." [28]And the news about Jesus spread quickly everywhere in the area of Galilee.

JESUS HEALS MANY PEOPLE

[29]As soon as Jesus and his followers left the synagogue, they went with James and John to the home of Simon[n] and Andrew. [30]Simon's mother-in-law was sick in bed with a fever, and the people told Jesus about her. [31]So Jesus went to her bed, took her hand, and helped her up. The fever left her, and she began serving them.

[32]That evening, after the sun went down, the people brought to Jesus all who were sick and had demons in them. [33]The whole town gathered at the door. [34]Jesus healed many who had different kinds of sicknesses, and he forced many demons to leave people. But he would not allow the demons to speak, because they knew who he was.

[35]Early the next morning, while it was still dark, Jesus woke and left the house. He went to a lonely place, where he prayed. [36]Simon and his friends went to look for Jesus. [37]When they found him, they said, "Everyone is looking for you!"

[38]Jesus answered, "We should go to other towns around here so I can preach there too. That is the reason I came." [39]So he went

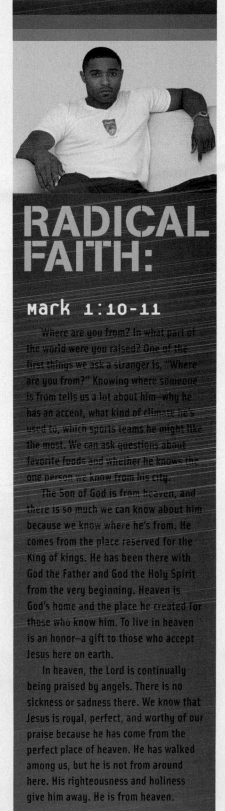

RADICAL FAITH:

mark 1:10-11

Where are you from? In what part of the world were you raised? One of the first things we ask a stranger is, "Where are you from?" Knowing where someone is from tells us a lot about him—why he has an accent, what kind of climate he's used to, which sports teams he might like the most. We can ask questions about favorite foods and whether he knows the one person we know from his city.

The Son of God is from heaven, and there is so much we can know about him because we know where he's from. He comes from the place reserved for the King of kings. He has been there with God the Father and God the Holy Spirit from the very beginning. Heaven is God's home and the place he created for those who know him. To live in heaven is an honor—a gift to those who accept Jesus here on earth.

In heaven, the Lord is continually being praised by angels. There is no sickness or sadness there. We know that Jesus is royal, perfect, and worthy of our praise because he has come from the perfect place of heaven. He has walked among us, but he is not from around here. His righteousness and holiness give him away. He is from heaven.

 1:1 the Son of God Some Greek copies omit these words.   **1:16 Simon** Simon's other name was Peter.   **1:29 Simon** Simon's other name was Peter.

everywhere in Galilee, preaching in the synagogues and forcing out demons.

JESUS HEALS A SICK MAN

⁴⁰A man with a skin disease came to Jesus. He fell to his knees and begged Jesus, "You can heal me if you will."

⁴¹Jesus felt sorry for the man, so he reached out his hand and touched him and said, "I will. Be healed!" ⁴²Immediately the disease left the man, and he was healed.

⁴³Jesus told the man to go away at once, but he warned him strongly, ⁴⁴"Don't tell anyone about this. But go and show yourself to the priest. And offer the gift Moses commanded for people who are made well.ⁿ This will show the people what I have done." ⁴⁵The man left there, but he began to tell everyone that Jesus had healed him, and so he spread the news about Jesus. As a result, Jesus could not enter a town if people saw him. He stayed in places where nobody lived, but people came to him from everywhere.

JESUS HEALS A PARALYZED MAN

2 A few days later, when Jesus came back to Capernaum, the news spread that he was at home. ²Many people gathered together so that there was no room in the house, not even outside the door. And Jesus was teaching them God's message. ³Four people came, carrying a paralyzed man. ⁴Since they could not get to Jesus because of the crowd, they dug a hole in the roof right above where he was speaking. When they got through, they lowered the mat with the paralyzed man on it. ⁵When Jesus saw the faith of these people, he said to the paralyzed man, "Young man, your sins are forgiven."

⁶Some of the teachers of the law were sitting there, thinking to themselves, ⁷"Why does this man say things like that? He is speaking as if he were God. Only God can forgive sins."

⁸Jesus knew immediately what these teachers of the law were thinking. So he said to them, "Why are you thinking these things? ⁹Which is easier: to tell this paralyzed man, 'Your sins are forgiven,' or to tell him, 'Stand up. Take your mat and walk'? ¹⁰But I will prove to you that the Son of Man has authority on earth to forgive sins." So Jesus said to the paralyzed man, ¹¹"I tell you, stand up, take your mat, and go home." ¹²Immediately the paralyzed man stood up, took his mat, and walked out while everyone was watching him.

The people were amazed and praised God. They said, "We have never seen anything like this!"

¹³Jesus went to the lake again. The whole crowd followed him there, and he taught them. ¹⁴While he was walking along, he saw a man named Levi son of Alphaeus, sitting in the tax

✓ COUNT ON IT

MARK 1:38

Not too long after Jesus started traveling around telling people about God's kingdom, he visited his hometown. On the Sabbath, he went to the local synagogue, where someone asked him to read from the Scriptures. He read from the Book of Isaiah: "The Lord has put his Spirit in me, because he appointed me to tell the Good News to the poor. He has sent me to tell the captives they are free and to tell the blind that they can see again. God sent me to free those who have been treated unfairly and to announce the time when the Lord will show his kindness." When Jesus finished reading, he said, "While you heard these words just now, they were coming true!" (Luke 4:16-21).

Jesus wanted the people to know that what seemed impossible was possible with God. When matters seemed hopeless, God was able to turn things around.

Jesus knew why he was on earth and put his whole heart into fulfilling the purpose God had given him. That's still his purpose today. What he came to earth to do then in the flesh, his Word and his Spirit continue to do today. Be serious about reading his Word. If you want to know what Jesus said when he lived on earth, read Matthew, Mark, Luke, and John. See what good news he has for you!

travel 🜨 the road

Most of the people who haven't heard the Good News about Jesus are part of five great unreached blocks: Tribals, Hindus, Chinese, Muslims, and Buddhists. (That's easy to remember: If you flip the "C" in "Chinese" sideways to make a "U," the first letters of those group names spell "THUMB.") Another way to look at it: Of 17 thousand cultural groups in the world, roughly 6,600 don't have a vibrant church. Reaching out to these "least-reached peoples" is a massive priority in missions today. Learn more at www.joshuaproject.net.

For more on extreme missions visit www.traveltheroad.com.

1:44 Moses . . . well Read about this in Leviticus 14:1–32.

WAYS TO WALK THE WALK

Mark 4:20

WORD: We need hearts that hunger for God's teaching.

WALK IT: Spend time each day digging into the black-and-white parts of this book, the all-important Word of God!

collector's booth. Jesus said to him, "Follow me," and he stood up and followed Jesus.

[15]Later, as Jesus was having dinner at Levi's house, many tax collectors and "sinners" were eating there with Jesus and his followers. Many people like this followed Jesus. [16]When the teachers of the law who were Pharisees saw Jesus eating with the tax collectors and "sinners," they asked his followers, "Why does he eat with tax collectors and sinners?"

[17]Jesus heard this and said to them, "It is not the healthy people who need a doctor, but the sick. I did not come to invite good people but to invite sinners."

JESUS' FOLLOWERS ARE CRITICIZED

[18]Now the followers of John[n] and the Pharisees often gave up eating for a certain time.[n] Some people came to Jesus and said, "Why do John's followers and the followers of the Pharisees often give up eating, but your followers don't?"

[19]Jesus answered, "The friends of the bridegroom do not give up eating while the bridegroom is still with them. As long as the bridegroom is with them, they cannot give up eating. [20]But the time will come when the bridegroom will be taken from them, and then they will give up eating.

[21]"No one sews a patch of unshrunk cloth over a hole in an old coat. Otherwise, the patch will shrink and pull away—the new patch will pull away from the old coat. Then the hole will be worse. [22]Also, no one ever pours new wine into old leather bags. Otherwise, the new wine will break the bags, and the wine will be ruined along with the bags. But new wine should be put into new leather bags."

JESUS IS LORD OF THE SABBATH

[23]One Sabbath day, as Jesus was walking through some fields of grain, his followers began to pick some grain to eat. [24]The Pharisees said to Jesus, "Why are your followers doing what is not lawful on the Sabbath day?"

[25]Jesus answered, "Have you never read what David did when he and those with him were hungry and needed food? [26]During the time of Abiathar the high priest, David went into God's house and ate the holy bread, which is lawful only for priests to eat. And David also gave some of the bread to those who were with him."

[27]Then Jesus said to the Pharisees, "The Sabbath day was made to help people; they were not made to be ruled by the Sabbath day. [28]So then, the Son of Man is Lord even of the Sabbath day."

JESUS HEALS A MAN'S HAND

3 Another time when Jesus went into a synagogue, a man with a crippled hand was there. [2]Some people watched Jesus closely to see if he would heal the man on the Sabbath day so they could accuse him.

[3]Jesus said to the man with the crippled hand, "Stand up here in the middle of everyone."

[4]Then Jesus asked the people, "Which is lawful on the Sabbath day: to do good or to do evil, to save a life or to kill?" But they said nothing to answer him.

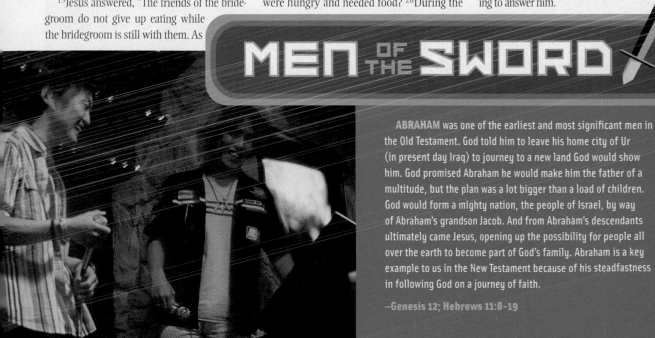

MEN OF THE SWORD

ABRAHAM was one of the earliest and most significant men in the Old Testament. God told him to leave his home city of Ur (in present day Iraq) to journey to a new land God would show him. God promised Abraham he would make him the father of a multitude, but the plan was a lot bigger than a load of children. God would form a mighty nation, the people of Israel, by way of Abraham's grandson Jacob. And from Abraham's descendants ultimately came Jesus, opening up the possibility for people all over the earth to become part of God's family. Abraham is a key example to us in the New Testament because of his steadfastness in following God on a journey of faith.

—Genesis 12; Hebrews 11:8-19

2:18 **John** John the Baptist, who preached to the Jewish people about Christ's coming (Mark 1:4–8). 2:18 **gave . . . time** This is called "fasting." The people would give up eating for a special time of prayer and worship to God. It was also done to show sadness and disappointment.

[5]Jesus was angry as he looked at the people, and he felt very sad because they were stubborn. Then he said to the man, "Hold out your hand." The man held out his hand and it was healed. [6]Then the Pharisees left and began making plans with the Herodians[n] about a way to kill Jesus.

MANY PEOPLE FOLLOW JESUS

[7]Jesus left with his followers for the lake, and a large crowd from Galilee followed him. [8]Also many people came from Judea, from Jerusalem, from Idumea, from the lands across the Jordan River, and from the area of Tyre and Sidon. When they heard what Jesus was doing, many people came to him. [9]When Jesus saw the crowds, he told his followers to get a boat ready for him to keep people from crowding against him. [10]He had healed many people, so all the sick were pushing toward him to touch him. [11]When evil spirits saw Jesus, they fell down before him and shouted, "You are the Son of God!" [12]But Jesus strongly warned them not to tell who he was.

JESUS CHOOSES HIS TWELVE APOSTLES

[13]Then Jesus went up on a mountain and called to him the men he wanted, and they came to him. [14]Jesus chose twelve men and called them apostles. He wanted them to be with him, and he wanted to send them out to preach [15]and to have the authority to force demons out of people. [16]These are the twelve men he chose: Simon (Jesus named him Peter), [17]James and John, the sons of Zebedee (Jesus named them Boanerges, which means "Sons of Thunder"), [18]Andrew, Philip, Bartholomew, Matthew, Thomas, James the son of Alphaeus, Thaddaeus, Simon the Zealot, [19]and Judas Iscariot, who later turned against Jesus.

SOME PEOPLE SAY JESUS HAS A DEVIL

[20]Then Jesus went home, but again a crowd gathered. There were so many people that Jesus and his followers could not eat. [21]When his family heard this, they went to get him because they thought he was out of his mind. [22]But the teachers of the law from Jerusalem were saying, "Beelzebul is living inside him! He uses power from the ruler of demons to force demons out of people."

[23]So Jesus called the people together and taught them with stories. He said, "Satan will not force himself out of people. [24]A kingdom that is divided cannot continue, [25]and a family that is divided cannot continue. [26]And if Satan is against himself and fights against his own people, he cannot continue; that is the end of Satan. [27]No one can enter a strong person's house and steal his things unless he first ties up the strong person. Then he can steal things from the house. [28]I tell you the truth, all sins that people do and all the things people say against God can be forgiven. [29]But anyone who speaks against the Holy Spirit will never be forgiven; he is guilty of a sin that continues forever."

[30]Jesus said this because the teachers of the law said that he had an evil spirit inside him.

JESUS' TRUE FAMILY

[31]Then Jesus' mother and brothers arrived. Standing outside, they sent someone in to tell him to come out. [32]Many people were sitting around Jesus, and they said to him, "Your mother and brothers are waiting for you outside."

[33]Jesus asked, "Who are my mother and my brothers?" [34]Then he looked at those sitting around him and said, "Here are my mother and my brothers! [35]My true brother and sister and mother are those who do what God wants."

A STORY ABOUT PLANTING SEED

4 Again Jesus began teaching by the lake. A great crowd gathered around him, so he sat down in a boat near the shore. All the people stayed on the shore close to the water. [2]Jesus taught them many things, using stories. He said, [3]"Listen! A farmer went out to plant his seed. [4]While he was planting, some seed fell by the road, and the birds came and ate it up. [5]Some seed fell on rocky ground where there wasn't much dirt. That seed grew very fast, because the ground was not deep. [6]But when the sun rose, the plants dried up because they did not have deep roots. [7]Some other seed fell among thorny weeds, which grew and choked the good plants. So those plants did not produce a crop. [8]Some other seed fell on good ground and began to grow. It got taller and produced a crop. Some plants made thirty times more, some made sixty times more, and some made a hundred times more."

[9]Then Jesus said, "You people who can hear me, listen!"

MARK 3:28

Be encouraged! It doesn't matter what you've done in the past, where you've done it, or who you've done it with. God loves you and wants to forgive you. In fact, God has more grace than you can imagine. You may *feel* like you've blown it, and then again, you may *have* blown it. It doesn't matter. Jesus is more than ready to give you a fresh start. He wants you to run to him, not away from him!

Remember when David blew it with Bathsheba? Then he blew it again by having her husband killed. David kept messing up trying to cover his sin. God sent the prophet Nathan to confront him. David's eyes were finally opened, and he repented. God forgave David, and he later was known as the kind of man God wants (Acts 13:22). If David can be forgiven, so can you. But the key is this: David repented. He didn't just apologize. He was truly sorry in his heart. To repent means to turn from sin and go the other direction. Whatever it is that you need to be forgiven for, give it to God right now. Ask for forgiveness: tell him you're sorry, repent, and move on.

Even good people may fall many times, but they will get back up! God is the One who will always forgive, no matter what you've done. He loves you!

3:6 **Herodians** A political group that followed Herod and his family.

JESUS TELLS WHY HE USED STORIES

[10]Later, when Jesus was alone, the twelve apostles and others around him asked him about the stories.

[11]Jesus said, "You can know the secret about the kingdom of God. But to other people I tell everything by using stories [12]so that:

'They will look and look,
  but they will not learn.
They will listen and listen,
  but they will not understand.
If they did learn and understand,
  they would come back to me
  and be forgiven.' "

Isaiah 6:9-10

JESUS EXPLAINS THE SEED STORY

[13]Then Jesus said to his followers, "Don't you understand this story? If you don't, how will you understand any story? [14]The farmer is like a person who plants God's message in people. [15]Sometimes the teaching falls on the road. This is like the people who hear the teaching of God, but Satan quickly comes and takes away the teaching that was planted in

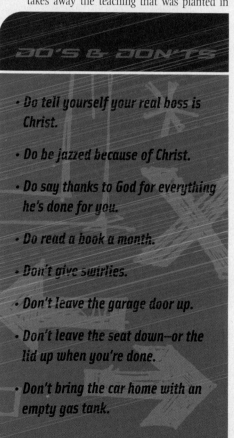

DO'S & DON'TS

- *Do tell yourself your real boss is Christ.*
- *Do be jazzed because of Christ.*
- *Do say thanks to God for everything he's done for you.*
- *Do read a book a month.*
- *Don't give swirlies.*
- *Don't leave the garage door up.*
- *Don't leave the seat down—or the lid up when you're done.*
- *Don't bring the car home with an empty gas tank.*

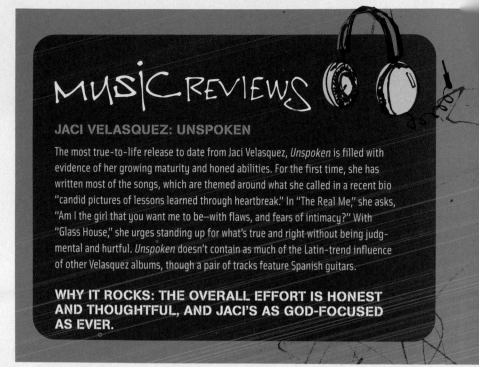

MUSIC REVIEWS

JACI VELASQUEZ: UNSPOKEN

The most true-to-life release to date from Jaci Velasquez, *Unspoken* is filled with evidence of her growing maturity and honed abilities. For the first time, she has written most of the songs, which are themed around what she called in a recent bio "candid pictures of lessons learned through heartbreak." In "The Real Me," she asks, "Am I the girl that you want me to be—with flaws, and fears of intimacy?" With "Glass House," she urges standing up for what's true and right without being judgmental and hurtful. *Unspoken* doesn't contain as much of the Latin-trend influence of other Velasquez albums, though a pair of tracks feature Spanish guitars.

WHY IT ROCKS: THE OVERALL EFFORT IS HONEST AND THOUGHTFUL, AND JACI'S AS GOD-FOCUSED AS EVER.

them. [16]Others are like the seed planted on rocky ground. They hear the teaching and quickly accept it with joy. [17]But since they don't allow the teaching to go deep into their lives, they keep it only a short time. When trouble or persecution comes because of the teaching they accepted, they quickly give up. [18]Others are like the seed planted among the thorny weeds. They hear the teaching, [19]but the worries of this life, the temptation of wealth, and many other evil desires keep the teaching from growing and producing fruit[n] in their lives. [20]Others are like the seed planted in the good ground. They hear the teaching and accept it. Then they grow and produce fruit—sometimes thirty times more, sometimes sixty times more, and sometimes a hundred times more."

USE WHAT YOU HAVE

[21]Then Jesus said to them, "Do you hide a lamp under a bowl or under a bed? No! You put the lamp on a lampstand. [22]Everything that is hidden will be made clear and every secret thing will be made known. [23]You people who can hear me, listen!

[24]"Think carefully about what you hear. The way you give to others is the way God will give to you, but God will give you even more.

[25]Those who have understanding will be given more. But those who do not have understanding, even what they have will be taken away from them."

JESUS USES A STORY ABOUT SEED

[26]Then Jesus said, "The kingdom of God is like someone who plants seed in the ground. [27]Night and day, whether the person is asleep or awake, the seed still grows, but the person does not know how it grows. [28]By itself the earth produces grain. First the plant grows, then the head, and then all the grain in the head. [29]When the grain is ready, the farmer cuts it, because this is the harvest time."

A STORY ABOUT MUSTARD SEED

[30]Then Jesus said, "How can I show you what the kingdom of God is like? What story can I use to explain it? [31]The kingdom of God is like a mustard seed, the smallest seed you plant in the ground. [32]But when planted, this seed grows and becomes the largest of all garden plants. It produces large branches, and the wild birds can make nests in its shade."

[33]Jesus used many stories like these to teach the crowd God's message—as much as they could understand. [34]He always used stories to teach them. But when he and his followers were alone, Jesus explained everything to them.

 4:19 *producing fruit* To produce fruit means to have in your life the good things God wants.

JESUS CALMS A STORM

[35]That evening, Jesus said to his followers, "Let's go across the lake." [36]Leaving the crowd behind, they took him in the boat just as he was. There were also other boats with them. [37]A very strong wind came up on the lake. The waves came over the sides and into the boat so that it was already full of water. [38]Jesus was at the back of the boat, sleeping with his head on a cushion. His followers woke him and said, "Teacher, don't you care that we are drowning!"

[39]Jesus stood up and commanded the wind and said to the waves, "Quiet! Be still!" Then the wind stopped, and it became completely calm.

[40]Jesus said to his followers, "Why are you afraid? Do you still have no faith?"

[41]The followers were very afraid and asked each other, "Who is this? Even the wind and the waves obey him!"

A MAN WITH DEMONS INSIDE HIM

5Jesus and his followers went to the other side of the lake to the area of the Gerasene people. [2]When Jesus got out of the boat, instantly a man with an evil spirit came to him from the burial caves. [3]This man lived in the caves, and no one could tie him up, not even with a chain. [4]Many times people had used chains to tie the man's hands and feet, but he always broke them off. No one was strong enough to control him. [5]Day and night he would wander around the burial caves and on the hills, screaming and cutting himself with stones. [6]While Jesus was still far away, the man saw him, ran to him, and fell down before him.

[7]The man shouted in a loud voice, "What do you want with me, Jesus, Son of the Most High God? I command you in God's name not to torture me!" [8]He said this because Jesus was saying to him, "You evil spirit, come out of the man."

[9]Then Jesus asked him, "What is your name?"

He answered, "My name is Legion,[n] because we are many spirits." [10]He begged Jesus again and again not to send them out of that area.

[11]A large herd of pigs was feeding on a hill near there. [12]The demons begged Jesus, "Send us into the pigs; let us go into them." [13]So Jesus allowed them to do this. The evil spirits left the man and went into the pigs. Then the herd of pigs—about two thousand of them—rushed down the hill into the lake and were drowned.

[14]The herdsmen ran away and went to the town and to the countryside, telling everyone about this. So people went out to see what had happened. [15]They came to Jesus and saw the man who used to have the many evil spirits, sitting, clothed, and in his right mind. And they were frightened. [16]The people who saw this told the others what had happened to the man who had the demons living in him, and they told about the pigs. [17]Then the people began to beg Jesus to leave their area.

[18]As Jesus was getting back into the boat, the man who was freed from the demons begged to go with him.

[19]But Jesus would not let him. He said, "Go home to your family and tell them how much the Lord has done for you and how he has had mercy on you." [20]So the man left and began to tell the people in the Ten Towns[n] about what Jesus had done for him. And everyone was amazed.

JESUS GIVES LIFE TO A DEAD GIRL AND HEALS A SICK WOMAN

[21]When Jesus went in the boat back to the other side of the lake, a large crowd gathered around him there. [22]A leader of the synagogue, named Jairus, came there, saw Jesus, and fell at his feet. [23]He begged Jesus, saying again and again, "My daughter is dying. Please come and put your hands on her so she will be healed and will live." [24]So Jesus went with him.

A large crowd followed Jesus and pushed very close around him. [25]Among them was a woman who had been bleeding for twelve years. [26]She had suffered very much from many doctors and had spent all the money she had, but instead of improving, she was getting worse. [27]When the woman heard about Jesus, she came up behind him in the crowd and touched his coat. [28]She thought, "If I can just touch his clothes, I will be healed." [29]Instantly her bleeding stopped, and she felt in her body that she was healed from her disease.

[30]At once Jesus felt power go out from him. So he turned around in the crowd and asked, "Who touched my clothes?"

[31]His followers said, "Look at how many people are pushing against you! And you ask, 'Who touched me?' "

[32]But Jesus continued looking around to see who had touched him. [33]The woman, knowing that she was healed, came and fell at Jesus'

RANDOM WAYS TO THROW A GREAT PARTY

1. **ERA THEMES (70S, 80S, ETC.)**

2. **ROOT BEER KEGGER**

3. **SLIP-N-SLIDES**

4. **COMEDY CLIPS NITE (BRING CHOICE MOVIES AND TAKE TURNS SHOWING THE BEST PARTS)**

5. **VIDEO-GAME CHALLENGE**

6. **GIANT TWISTER**

7. **SUMMER POOL BASH**

8. **ANIMATED VIDEO MARATHON**

9. **PROGRESSIVE DINNER (ONE COURSE EACH, AT SEVERAL HOMES)**

10. **LUAU (WITH TIKI LIGHTS)**

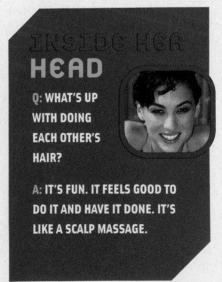

INSIDE HER HEAD

Q: WHAT'S UP WITH DOING EACH OTHER'S HAIR?

A: IT'S FUN. IT FEELS GOOD TO DO IT AND HAVE IT DONE. IT'S LIKE A SCALP MASSAGE.

5:9 **Legion** Means very many. A legion was about five thousand men in the Roman army.   5:20 **Ten Towns** In Greek, called "Decapolis." It was an area east of Lake Galilee that once had ten main towns.

feet. Shaking with fear, she told him the whole truth. [34]Jesus said to her, "Dear woman, you are made well because you believed. Go in peace; be healed of your disease."

[35]While Jesus was still speaking, some people came from the house of the synagogue leader. They said, "Your daughter is dead. There is no need to bother the teacher anymore."

[36]But Jesus paid no attention to what they said. He told the synagogue leader, "Don't be afraid; just believe."

[37]Jesus let only Peter, James, and John the brother of James go with him. [38]When they came to the house of the synagogue leader, Jesus found many people there making lots of noise and crying loudly. [39]Jesus entered the house and said to them, "Why are you crying and making so much noise? The child is not dead, only asleep." [40]But they laughed at him. So, after throwing them out of the house, Jesus took the child's father and mother and his three followers into the room where the child was. [41]Taking hold of the girl's hand, he said to her, "Talitha, koum!" (This means, "Young girl, I tell you to stand up!") [42]At once the girl stood right up and began walking. (She was twelve years old.) Everyone was completely amazed. [43]Jesus gave them strict orders not to tell people about this. Then he told them to give the girl something to eat.

JESUS GOES TO HIS HOMETOWN

6 Jesus left there and went to his hometown, and his followers went with him. [2]On the Sabbath day he taught in the synagogue. Many people heard him and were amazed, saying, "Where did this man get these teachings? What is this wisdom that has been given to him? And where did he get the power to do miracles? [3]He is just the carpenter, the son of Mary and the brother of James, Joseph, Judas, and Simon. And his sisters are here with us." So the people were upset with Jesus.

[4]Jesus said to them, "A prophet is honored everywhere except in his hometown and with his own people and in his own home." [5]So Jesus was not able to work any miracles there except to heal a few sick people by putting his hands on them. [6]He was amazed at how many people had no faith.

Then Jesus went to other villages in that area and taught. [7]He called his twelve followers together and got ready to send them out two by two and gave them authority over evil spirits. [8]This is what Jesus commanded them: "Take nothing for your trip except a walking stick. Take no bread, no bag, and no money in your pockets. [9]Wear sandals, but take only the clothes you are wearing. [10]When you enter a house, stay there until you leave that town. [11]If the people in a certain place refuse to welcome

GET OUT THERE

Every day, between 1.3 and 2.8 million runaway and homeless youth live on the streets of America, and one out of every seven children will run away before the age of 18. The NATIONAL RUNAWAY SWITCHBOARD works 24 hours a day to connect runaways with a place to stay, food, clothing, legal or medical assistance. Whether you are in a crisis, have a friend who is in trouble, need statistics for a school report, or want ideas for spreading the word about our services, the National Runaway Switchboard has over 200,000 resources that you can use, including thousands of different support groups, hotlines, and counseling centers, information about pursuing legal issues, medical questions, and drug treatment centers. The National Runaway Switchboard is confidential and free.

Find out how you can help at www.nrscrisisline.org.

RADICAL FAITH:

mark 2:17

The Pharisees didn't understand what Jesus was all about. For one thing, he hung out with people they would have crossed the street to avoid. The Pharisees thought they were way too holy to rub elbows with those people.

What Jesus said to them is like music to your ears if you think you've done such horrible things that God could never love you. He lets you know right off the bat that he's more interested in changing sinners than in recruiting good, religious people to his cause.

But does that mean that Jesus isn't interested in you if you haven't gotten messed up in sex or drugs or haven't broken the law? Not at all. When he said he wasn't inviting "the righteous," He was talking about the attitude in people's hearts. People who consider themselves "righteous" (good), like the Pharisees, don't think they need Jesus. People who know they are sinners—whether their sins are obvious to everyone or the invisible sins of the heart—know they need Jesus. He welcomes them with open arms.

you or listen to you, leave that place. Shake its dust off your feet[n] as a warning to them."

[12]So the followers went out and preached that people should change their hearts and lives. [13]They forced many demons out and put olive oil on many sick people and healed them.

HOW JOHN THE BAPTIST WAS KILLED

[14]King Herod heard about Jesus, because he was now well known. Some people said, "He is John the Baptist, who has risen from the dead. That is why he can work these miracles."

[15]Others said, "He is Elijah."[n]

Other people said, "Jesus is a prophet, like the prophets who lived long ago."

[16]When Herod heard this, he said, "I killed John by cutting off his head. Now he has risen from the dead!"

[17]Herod himself had ordered his soldiers to arrest John and put him in prison in order to please his wife, Herodias. She had been the wife of Philip, Herod's brother, but then Herod had married her. [18]John had been telling Herod, "It is not lawful for you to be married to your brother's wife." [19]So Herodias hated John and wanted to kill him. But she couldn't, [20]because Herod was afraid of John and protected him. He knew John was a good and holy man. Also, though John's preaching always bothered him, he enjoyed listening to John.

[21]Then the perfect time came for Herodias to cause John's death. On Herod's birthday, he gave a dinner party for the most important government leaders, the commanders of his army, and the most important people in Galilee. [22]When the daughter of Herodias came in and danced, she pleased Herod and the people eating with him.

So King Herod said to the girl, "Ask me for anything you want, and I will give it to you." [23]He promised her, "Anything you ask for I will give to you—up to half of my kingdom."

[24]The girl went to her mother and asked, "What should I ask for?"

Her mother answered, "Ask for the head of John the Baptist."

[25]At once the girl went back to the king and said to him, "I want the head of John the Baptist right now on a platter."

[26]Although the king was very sad, he had made a promise, and his dinner guests had heard it. So he did not want to refuse what she

HOW TO MAKE FAST CASH

Benjamin Franklin was the guy who said that "a penny saved is a penny earned," an idea so smart it scored him a picture on every $100 bill. But what good does that tidbit do you? The point is that it's far easier to *not spend* money than it is to *make* money. In fact, experts say that keeping track of each dollar you spend gives you the equivalent of a 20 percent boost in income—or more. Knowing that you have to write down where your money goes just might keep you from spending stupidly. But it also lets you look back and discover that you dropped $63 last month on lattes. Or that those downloads and extra minutes on your cell phone rang up another $40. Once you know the facts, you can get smart. God wants you to use your money to glorify him, so get a grip on where it goes.

 6:11 Shake . . . feet A warning. It showed that they were rejecting these people.   **6:15 Elijah** A great prophet who spoke for God and who lived hundreds of years before Christ. See 1 Kings 17.

LOOK COOL
TIPS ON YOURSELF

Loads of guys—especially younger teens—get radically uncool plantar warts. Caused by a virus that hijacks your foot through microscopic skin tears, they start out the size of a small pimple but can spread into painful patches if left untreated. These growths burrow into your foot without making the usual warty bump, often showing tiny dark specks within a patch of skin that looks a like you've been in the tub too long. You can get rid of plantar warts with over-the-counter wart remover in liquids or patches, or you can go to the doctor to get them frozen off. And at least one medical journal says it's even more effective to cover warts with duct tape for a week. No joke. Like a lot of ugly things in life, it's best to stop warts when they're small.

asked, [27]Immediately the king sent a soldier to bring John's head. The soldier went and cut off John's head in the prison [28]and brought it back on a platter. He gave it to the girl, and the girl gave it to her mother. [29]When John's followers heard this, they came and got John's body and put it in a tomb.

MORE THAN FIVE THOUSAND FED

[30]The apostles gathered around Jesus and told him about all the things they had done and taught. [31]Crowds of people were coming and going so that Jesus and his followers did not even have time to eat. He said to them, "Come away by yourselves, and we will go to a lonely place to get some rest."

[32]So they went in a boat by themselves to a lonely place. [33]But many people saw them leave and recognized them. So from all the towns they ran to the place where Jesus was going, and they got there before him. [34]When he arrived, he saw a great crowd waiting. He felt sorry for them, because they were like sheep without a shepherd. So he began to teach them many things.

[35]When it was late in the day, his followers came to him and said, "No one lives in this place, and it is already very late. [36]Send the people away so they can go to the countryside and towns around here to buy themselves something to eat."

[37]But Jesus answered, "You give them something to eat."

They said to him, "We would all have to work a month to earn enough money to buy that much bread!"

[38]Jesus asked them, "How many loaves of bread do you have? Go and see."

When they found out, they said, "Five loaves and two fish."

[39]Then Jesus told his followers to have the people sit in groups on the green grass. [40]So they sat in groups of fifty or a hundred. [41]Jesus took the five loaves and two fish and, looking up to heaven, he thanked God for the food. He divided the bread and gave it to his followers for them to give to the people. Then he divided the two fish among them all. [42]All the people ate and were satisfied. [43]The followers filled twelve baskets with the leftover pieces of bread and fish. [44]There were five thousand men who ate.

JESUS WALKS ON THE WATER

[45]Immediately Jesus told his followers to get into the boat and go ahead of him to Bethsaida across the lake. He stayed there to send the people home. [46]After sending them away, he went into the hills to pray.

[47]That night, the boat was in the middle of the lake, and Jesus was alone on the land. [48]He saw his followers struggling hard to row the boat, because the wind was blowing against them. Between three and six o'clock in the morning, Jesus came to them, walking on the water, and he wanted to walk past the boat. [49]But when they saw him walking on the water, they thought he was a ghost and cried out. [50]They all saw him and were afraid. But quickly Jesus spoke to

RELATIONSHIPS

"Love your neighbor as you love yourself" (Matthew 19:19). If you want to be sure you're loving someone like God wants, there's just one test to take. Do you care about that person as much as you care for yourself? And are you showing that care in concrete ways? That's what real love looks like. Don't settle for a love that's anything less.

them and said, "Have courage! It is I. Do not be afraid." [51]Then he got into the boat with them, and the wind became calm. The followers were greatly amazed. [52]They did not understand about the miracle of the five loaves, because their minds were closed.

[53]When they had crossed the lake, they came to shore at Gennesaret and tied the boat there. [54]When they got out of the boat, people immediately recognized Jesus. [55]They ran everywhere in that area and began to bring sick people on mats wherever they heard he was. [56]And everywhere he went—into towns, cities, or countryside—the people brought the sick to the marketplaces. They begged him to let them touch just the edge of his coat, and all who touched it were healed.

OBEY GOD'S LAW

7 When some Pharisees and some teachers of the law came from Jerusalem, they gathered around Jesus. [2]They saw that some of Jesus' followers ate food with hands that were not clean, that is, they hadn't washed them. [3](The Pharisees and all the Jews never eat before washing their hands in a special way according to their unwritten laws. [4]And when they buy something in the market, they never eat it until they wash themselves in a special way. They also follow many other unwritten laws, such as the washing of cups, pitchers, and pots.)

[5]The Pharisees and the teachers of the law said to Jesus, "Why don't your followers obey the unwritten laws which have been handed down to us? Why do your followers eat their food with hands that are not clean?"

[6]Jesus answered, "Isaiah was right when he spoke about you hypocrites. He wrote,

'These people show honor to me with words,
but their hearts are far from me.
[7]Their worship of me is worthless.
The things they teach are nothing but
human rules.'   *Isaiah 29:13*

[8]You have stopped following the commands of God, and you follow only human teachings."

[9]Then Jesus said to them, "You cleverly ignore the commands of God so you can follow your own teachings. [10]Moses said, 'Honor your father and your mother,'[n] and 'Anyone who says cruel things to his father or mother must be put to death.'[n] [11]But you say a person can tell his father or mother, 'I have something I could use to help you, but it is Corban—a gift to God.' [12]You no longer let that person use that money for his father or his mother. [13]By your own rules, which you teach people, you are rejecting what God said. And you do many things like that."

[14]After Jesus called the crowd to him again, he said, "Every person should listen to me and understand what I am saying. [15]There is nothing people put into their bodies that makes them unclean. People are made unclean by the things that come out of them." [16][n]

[17]When Jesus left the people and went into the house, his followers asked him about this story. [18]Jesus said, "Do you still not understand? Surely you know that nothing that enters someone from the outside can make that person unclean. [19]It does not go into the mind, but into the stomach. Then it goes out of the body." (When Jesus said this, he meant that no longer was any food unclean for people to eat.)

[20]And Jesus said, "The things that come out of people are the things that make them unclean. [21]All these evil things begin inside people, in the mind: evil thoughts, sexual sins, stealing, murder, adultery, [22]greed, evil actions, lying, doing sinful things, jealousy, speaking evil of others, pride, and foolish living. [23]All these evil things come from inside and make people unclean."

RANDOM THINGS TO DO INSTEAD OF HAZING

1. **POUND OFF THE ADRENALINE AT THE GYM.**
2. **HAVE A SLURPEE-DRINKING CONTEST (FOR A DIFFERENT KIND OF HEAD-RUSH).**
3. **COMPETE (GAMES, SPORTS).**
4. **HANG AT THE POOL HALL.**
5. **RUN FIVE MILES.**
6. **EAT CHEESE STICKS.**
7. **PLAY RISK.**
8. **HAVE THE FRESHMEN PUT ON A FASHION SHOW.**
9. **HOST A POLAROID SCAVENGER HUNT.**
10. **WATCH TELEVANGELISTS.**

WAYS TO WALK THE WALK

Mark 4:38-40

WORD: Even when you panic, Jesus is in control of your life.

WALK IT: Spend time today telling Jesus about your biggest worry—then tackle your day trusting him to take care of you.

Mark 10:31

WORD: The first will be last and the last, first.

WALK IT: Ask God to show you ways you make yourself more important than others—and spend the next week focusing on letting others go first. Notice how it changes your life.

 7:10 'Honor . . . mother' Quotation from Exodus 20:12; Deuteronomy 5:16.   7:10 'Anyone . . . death.' Quotation from Exodus 21:17.   7:16 Verse 16 Some Greek copies add verse 16: "You people who can hear me, listen!"

issues
DIVORCE

NOTHING REARRANGES a guy's life like his parents getting a divorce. He wonders if it's his fault. He's turned inside out with shock and anger. He prays for life to go back to normal, even if normal wasn't much fun. With half of the marriages in the United States ending in divorce, it's not a problem you can ignore. Even if you come from a strong family, you're likely surrounded by friends whose parents have split. It's true that God doesn't like divorce, and your aim is a marriage bond that lasts from your wedding day until death do you part. But kids and teens can't control what parents decide. If divorce hits you or a friend, your job is to weave a safety net of support. Communicate as much as you can with both parents. Hang tight with your sibs. Find peers who've endured their parents' divorce and kept their heads screwed on. And rely on God's never-ending care. Even when you feel shoved around by divorce, God has his eyes on you.

EXPERTS ANSWER YOUR QUESTIONS

Q. *My friend's older brother is off at college, and he says a bunch of people wrote the Bible. Why is the Bible any good if it's like any other human book?*

A. That guy is right that the Bible is a human book. After all, it didn't drop from heaven printed and bound in black leather. But it's also a divine book. The people who wrote the words of the Bible conveyed God's inspired message—what he wanted said, the way he wanted it said. That's what makes the Bible "God's Word," a book worth reading and obeying with your whole life.

Q. *How can the Bible matter to me when it's so old?*

A. The Bible was written to a world way worse than whatever neighborhood you live in. People in Bible times were into child sacrifice and temple prostitution. Many starved or suffered as slaves. People knew all about getting drunk and hooking up. That's reality, and the Bible's teachings still make sense. Plus—it's God eternal truth, and it goes way beyond the time it was written.

JESUS HELPS A NON-JEWISH WOMAN

24Jesus left that place and went to the area around Tyre. When he went into a house, he did not want anyone to know he was there, but he could not stay hidden. 25A woman whose daughter had an evil spirit in her heard that he was there. So she quickly came to Jesus and fell at his feet. 26She was Greek, born in Phoenicia, in Syria. She begged Jesus to force the demon out of her daughter.

27Jesus told the woman, "It is not right to take the children's bread and give it to the dogs. First let the children eat all they want."

28But she answered, "Yes, Lord, but even the dogs under the table can eat the children's crumbs."

29Then Jesus said, "Because of your answer, you may go. The demon has left your daughter."

30The woman went home and found her daughter lying in bed; the demon was gone.

JESUS HEALS A DEAF MAN

31Then Jesus left the area around Tyre and went through Sidon to Lake Galilee, to the area of the Ten Towns.[n] 32While he was there, some people brought a man to him who was deaf and could not talk plainly. The people begged Jesus to put his hand on the man to heal him.

33Jesus led the man away from the crowd, by himself. He put his fingers in the man's ears and then spit and touched the man's tongue. 34Looking up to heaven, he sighed and said to the man, "Ephphatha!" (This means, "Be opened.") 35Instantly the man was able to hear and to use his tongue so that he spoke clearly.

36Jesus commanded the people not to tell anyone about what happened. But the more he commanded them, the more they told about it. 37They were completely amazed and said, "Jesus does everything well. He makes the deaf hear! And those who can't talk he makes able to speak."

MORE THAN FOUR THOUSAND PEOPLE FED

8Another time there was a great crowd with Jesus that had nothing to eat. So Jesus called his followers and said, 2"I feel sorry for these people, because they have already been with me for three days, and they have nothing to eat. 3If I send them home hungry,

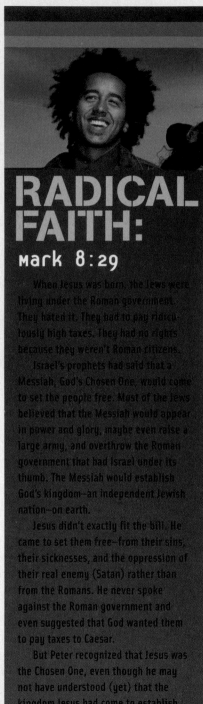

RADICAL FAITH:
mark 8:29

When Jesus was born, the Jews were living under the Roman government. They hated it. They had to pay ridiculously high taxes. They had no rights because they weren't Roman citizens.

Israel's prophets had said that a Messiah, God's Chosen One, would come to set the people free. Most of the Jews believed that the Messiah would appear in power and glory, maybe even raise a large army, and overthrow the Roman government that had Israel under its thumb. The Messiah would establish God's kingdom—an independent Jewish nation—on earth.

Jesus didn't exactly fit the bill. He came to set them free—from their sins, their sicknesses, and the oppression of their real enemy (Satan) rather than from the Romans. He never spoke against the Roman government and even suggested that God wanted them to pay taxes to Caesar.

But Peter recognized that Jesus was the Chosen One, even though he may not have understood (yet) that the kingdom Jesus had come to establish was not a political regime, but a kingdom of the heart and of the spirit.

Jesus is the Messiah. Let him be the ruler of your heart right now—not just in the easy places, but also in the places that may be hard for you to submit to him. Let him be the King of your whole life.

7:31 Ten Towns In Greek, called "Decapolis." It was an area east of Lake Galilee that once had ten main towns.

they will faint on the way. Some of them live a long way from here."

⁴Jesus' followers answered, "How can we get enough bread to feed all these people? We are far away from any town."

⁵Jesus asked, "How many loaves of bread do you have?"

They answered, "Seven."

⁶Jesus told the people to sit on the ground. Then he took the seven loaves, gave thanks to God, and divided the bread. He gave the pieces to his followers to give to the people, and they did so. ⁷The followers also had a few small fish. After Jesus gave thanks for the fish, he told his followers to give them to the people also. ⁸All the people ate and were satisfied. Then his followers filled seven baskets with the leftover pieces of food. ⁹There were about four thousand people who ate. After they had eaten, Jesus sent them home. ¹⁰Then right away he got into a boat with his followers and went to the area of Dalmanutha.

THE LEADERS ASK FOR A MIRACLE

¹¹The Pharisees came to Jesus and began to ask him questions. Hoping to trap him, they asked Jesus for a miracle from God. ¹²Jesus sighed deeply and said, "Why do you people ask for a miracle as a sign? I tell you the truth, no sign will be given to you." ¹³Then Jesus left the Pharisees and went in the boat to the other side of the lake.

GUARD AGAINST WRONG TEACHINGS

¹⁴His followers had only one loaf of bread with them in the boat; they had forgotten to bring more. ¹⁵Jesus warned them, "Be careful! Beware of the yeast of the Pharisees and the yeast of Herod."

¹⁶His followers discussed the meaning of this, saying, "He said this because we have no bread."

¹⁷Knowing what they were talking about, Jesus asked them, "Why are you talking about not having bread? Do you still not see or understand? Are your minds closed? ¹⁸You have eyes, but you don't really see. You have ears, but you don't really listen. Remember when ¹⁹I divided five loaves of bread for the five thousand? How many baskets did you fill with leftover pieces of food?"

They answered, "Twelve."

²⁰"And when I divided seven loaves of bread for the four thousand, how many baskets did you fill with leftover pieces of food?"

They answered, "Seven."

²¹Then Jesus said to them, "Don't you understand yet?"

JESUS HEALS A BLIND MAN

²²Jesus and his followers came to Bethsaida. There some people brought a blind man to Jesus and begged him to touch the man. ²³So Jesus took the blind man's hand and led him out of the village. Then he spit on the man's eyes and put his hands on the man and asked, "Can you see now?"

²⁴The man looked up and said, "Yes, I see people, but they look like trees walking around."

²⁵Again Jesus put his hands on the man's eyes. Then the man opened his eyes wide and they were healed, and he was able to see everything clearly. ²⁶Jesus told him to go home, saying, "Don't go into the town."

MUSIC REVIEWS

MXPX: EVERYTHING BEFORE AND AFTER

Even though there's less punk (and more rock/pop) than on some prior releases, *Everything Before and After* is true to MxPx form, featuring a more developed flair with upbeat drums and guitars. The kings of what listen.com calls "the seemingly paradoxical genre of Christian Punk," MxPx is both subtle and straightforward about their faith. Thematically, *Everything Before and After* covers committed relationships and staying close to God; lyrics from the "The Capitol" include, "Those that seek will surely find / Those that don't are surely blind." Many fans recognize "Well Adjusted" from a 2003 Super-Bowl commercial produced by Pepsi. "MxPx" is a unique acronym for "Magnified Plaid."

WHY IT ROCKS: MXPX IS AN INFECTIOUS BLEND OF RAVING FUN AND A SINCERE MESSAGE.

PETER SAYS JESUS IS THE CHRIST

[27] Jesus and his followers went to the towns around Caesarea Philippi. While they were traveling, Jesus asked them, "Who do people say I am?"

[28] They answered, "Some say you are John the Baptist. Others say you are Elijah,[n] and others say you are one of the prophets."

[29] Then Jesus asked, "But who do you say I am?"

Peter answered, "You are the Christ."

[30] Jesus warned his followers not to tell anyone who he was.

[31] Then Jesus began to teach them that the Son of Man must suffer many things and that he would be rejected by the older Jewish leaders, the leading priests, and the teachers of the law. He told them that the Son of Man must be killed and then rise from the dead after three days. [32] Jesus told them plainly what would happen. Then Peter took Jesus aside and began to tell him not to talk like that. [33] But Jesus turned and looked at his followers. Then he told Peter not to talk that way. He said, "Go away from me, Satan![n] You don't care about the things of God, but only about things people think are important."

[34] Then Jesus called the crowd to him, along with his followers. He said, "If people want to follow me, they must give up the things they want. They must be willing even to give up their lives to follow me. [35] Those who want to save their lives will give up true life. But those who give up their lives for me and for the Good News will have true life. [36] It is worth nothing for them to have the whole world if they lose their souls. [37] They could never pay enough to buy back their souls. [38] The people who live now are living in a sinful and evil time. If people are ashamed of me and my teaching, the Son of Man will be ashamed of them when he comes with his Father's glory and with the holy angels."

9 Then Jesus said to the people, "I tell you the truth, some people standing here will see the kingdom of God come with power before they die."

JESUS TALKS WITH MOSES AND ELIJAH

[2] Six days later, Jesus took Peter, James, and John up on a high mountain by themselves. While they watched, Jesus' appearance was changed. [3] His clothes became shining white, whiter than any person could make them. [4] Then Elijah and Moses[n] appeared to them, talking with Jesus.

[5] Peter said to Jesus, "Teacher, it is good that we are here. Let us make three tents—one for you, one for Moses, and one for Elijah." [6] Peter did not know what to say, because he and the others were so frightened.

[7] Then a cloud came and covered them, and a voice came from the cloud, saying, "This is my Son, whom I love. Listen to him!"

[8] Suddenly Peter, James, and John looked around, but they saw only Jesus there alone with them.

[9] As they were coming down the mountain, Jesus commanded them not to tell anyone

8:28 Elijah A man who spoke for God and who lived hundreds of years before Christ. See 1 Kings 17.   **8:33 Satan** Name for the devil meaning "the enemy." Jesus means that Peter was talking like Satan.   **9:4 Elijah and Moses** Two of the most important Jewish leaders in the past. God had given Moses the Law, and Elijah was an important prophet.

LOOK COOL
TIPS ON YOURSELF

You'd look cool with a beard. Well, maybe. But that fuzz thing you got going isn't going to wow anyone for a while. There's a secret to getting clean-cut without drawing blood: Start wet and stay wet. If you're using a razor, wash your face with soap and warm water and rub the shaving cream into your skin. Use a sharp blade, rinsing it with hot water and doing slow, short strokes with the grain—the direction your hair grows. Go it any other way and you're in for a rash or razor burn. It's like going against God's instructions for life. You're in for some unnecessary burns.

about what they had seen until the Son of Man had risen from the dead.

¹⁰So the followers obeyed Jesus, but they discussed what he meant about rising from the dead.

¹¹Then they asked Jesus, "Why do the teachers of the law say that Elijah must come first?"

¹²Jesus answered, "They are right to say that Elijah must come first and make everything the way it should be. But why does the Scripture say that the Son of Man will suffer much and that people will treat him as if he were nothing? ¹³I tell you that Elijah has

already come. And people did to him whatever they wanted to do, just as the Scriptures said it would happen."

JESUS HEALS A SICK BOY

¹⁴When Jesus, Peter, James, and John came back to the other followers, they saw a great crowd around them and the teachers of the law arguing with them. ¹⁵But as soon as the crowd saw Jesus, the people were surprised and ran to welcome him.

¹⁶Jesus asked, "What are you arguing about?"

¹⁷A man answered, "Teacher, I brought my son to you. He has an evil spirit in him that stops him from talking. ¹⁸When the spirit attacks him, it throws him on the ground. Then my son foams at the mouth, grinds his teeth, and becomes very stiff. I asked your followers to force the evil spirit out, but they couldn't."

¹⁹Jesus answered, "You people have no faith. How long must I stay with you? How long must I put up with you? Bring the boy to me."

²⁰So the followers brought him to Jesus. As soon as the evil spirit saw Jesus, it made the boy lose control of himself, and he fell down and rolled on the ground, foaming at the mouth.

PROVERBS 3:5 "TRUST THE LORD WITH ALL YOUR HEART, AND DON'T DEPEND ON YOUR OWN UNDERSTANDING."

²¹Jesus asked the boy's father, "How long has this been happening?"

The father answered, "Since he was very young. ²²The spirit often throws him into a fire or into water to kill him. If you can do anything for him, please have pity on us and help us."

²³Jesus said to the father, "You said, 'If you can!' All things are possible for the one who believes."

²⁴Immediately the father cried out, "I do believe! Help me to believe more!"

INSIDE HER HEAD

Q: WHAT'S THE BIGGEST DIFFERENCE BETWEEN GUYS AND GIRLS?

A: GUYS AREN'T SO EMOTIONAL, NOT AS DRAMATIC, MORE LAID BACK.

²⁵When Jesus saw that a crowd was quickly gathering, he ordered the evil spirit, saying, "You spirit that makes people unable to hear or speak, I command you to come out of this boy and never enter him again!"

²⁶The evil spirit screamed and caused the boy to fall on the ground again. Then the spirit came out. The boy looked as if he were dead, and many people said, "He is dead!" ²⁷But Jesus took hold of the boy's hand and helped him to stand up.

²⁸When Jesus went into the house, his followers began asking him privately, "Why couldn't we force that evil spirit out?"

²⁹Jesus answered, "That kind of spirit can only be forced out by prayer."

JESUS TALKS ABOUT HIS DEATH

³⁰Then Jesus and his followers left that place and went through Galilee. He didn't want anyone to know where he was, ³¹because he was teaching his followers. He said to them, "The Son of Man will be handed over to people, and they will kill him. After three days, he will rise from the dead." ³²But the followers did not understand what Jesus meant, and they were afraid to ask him.

FEWER THAN HALF OF ALL HIGH SCHOOL STUDENTS HAVE HAD SEXUAL INTERCOURSE, AND THE PERCENTAGE IS DROPPING.
—CENTERS FOR DISEASE CONTROL AND PREVENTION

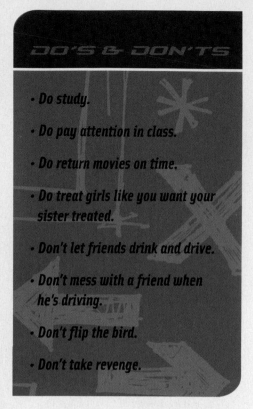

DO'S & DON'TS

- Do study.

- Do pay attention in class.

- Do return movies on time.

- Do treat girls like you want your sister treated.

- Don't let friends drink and drive.

- Don't mess with a friend when he's driving.

- Don't flip the bird.

- Don't take revenge.

WHO IS THE GREATEST?

[33]Jesus and his followers went to Capernaum. When they went into a house there, he asked them, "What were you arguing about on the road?" [34]But the followers did not answer, because their argument on the road was about which one of them was the greatest.

[35]Jesus sat down and called the twelve apostles to him. He said, "Whoever wants to be the most important must be last of all and servant of all."

[36]Then Jesus took a small child and had him stand among them. Taking the child in his arms, he said, [37]"Whoever accepts a child like this in my name accepts me. And whoever accepts me accepts the One who sent me."

ANYONE NOT AGAINST US IS FOR US

[38]Then John said, "Teacher, we saw someone using your name to force demons out of a person. We told him to stop, because he does not belong to our group."

[39]But Jesus said, "Don't stop him, because anyone who uses my name to do powerful things will not easily say evil things about me. [40]Whoever is not against us is with us. [41]I tell you the truth, whoever gives you a drink of water because you belong to the Christ will truly get his reward.

[42]"If one of these little children believes in me, and someone causes that child to sin, it would be better for that person to have a large stone tied around his neck and be drowned in the sea. [43]If your hand causes you to sin, cut it off. It is better for you to lose part of your body and live forever than to have two hands and go to hell, where the fire never goes out. [44n] [45]If your foot causes you to sin, cut it off. It is better for you to lose part of your body and to live forever than to have two feet and be thrown into hell. [46n] [47]If your eye causes you to sin, take it out. It is better for you to enter the kingdom of God with only one eye than to have two eyes and be thrown into hell. [48]In hell the worm does not die; the fire is never put out. [49]Every person will be salted with fire.

[50]"Salt is good, but if the salt loses its salty taste, you cannot make it salty again. So, be full of salt, and have peace with each other."

JESUS TEACHES ABOUT DIVORCE

10 Then Jesus left that place and went into the area of Judea and across the Jordan River. Again, crowds came to him, and he taught them as he usually did.

[2]Some Pharisees came to Jesus and tried to trick him. They asked, "Is it right for a man to divorce his wife?"

[3]Jesus answered, "What did Moses command you to do?"

[4]They said, "Moses allowed a man to write out divorce papers and send her away."[n]

[5]Jesus said, "Moses wrote that command for you because you were stubborn. [6]But when God made the world, 'he made them male and female.'[n] [7]'So a man will leave his father and mother and be united with his wife, [8]and the two will become one body.'[n] So there are not two, but one. [9]God has joined the two together, so no one should separate them."

[10]Later, in the house, his followers asked Jesus again about the question of divorce. [11]He answered, "Anyone who divorces his wife and marries another woman is guilty of adultery against her. [12]And the woman who divorces her husband and marries another man is also guilty of adultery."

JESUS ACCEPTS CHILDREN

[13]Some people brought their little children to

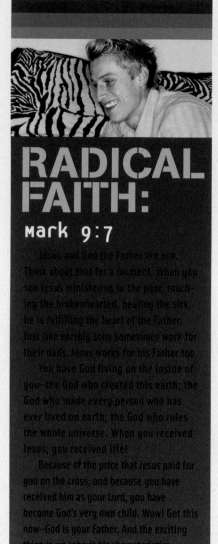

RADICAL FAITH:
mark 9:7

Jesus and God the Father are one. Think about that for a moment. When you see Jesus ministering to the poor, touching the brokenhearted, healing the sick, he is fulfilling the heart of the Father. Just like earthly sons sometimes work for their dads, Jesus works for his Father too.

You have God living on the inside of you—the God who created this earth; the God who made every person who has ever lived on earth; the God who rules the whole universe. When you received Jesus, you received life!

Because of the price that Jesus paid for you on the cross, and because you have received him as your Lord, you have become God's very own child. Wow! Get this now—God is your Father. And the exciting thing is we inherit his characteristics.

Ever notice a father and his son? Sometimes they look a whole lot like each other; in fact, they have a lot of the same mannerisms. It's that way because they are father and son. When you accepted Jesus as your Savior, you inherited some of the same mannerisms of your heavenly Father—love, joy, and peace, to name a few (see Galatians 5:22-23).

It's amazing—the more we hang around God, the more of his ways we will pick up! When we look at people from God's perspective, we see them in a completely different light! God has given us a great heritage. We are his children. Remember: "Like Father, like son!"

 9:44 Verse 44 Some Greek copies of Mark add verse 44, which is the same as verse 48. **9:46** Verse 46 Some Greek copies of Mark add verse 46, which is the same as verse 48. **10:4** "Moses . . . away." Quotation from Deuteronomy 24:1. **10:6** 'he made . . . female.' Quotation from Genesis 1:27. **10:7-8** 'So . . . body.' Quotation from Genesis 2:24.

RANDOM WAYS TO MAKE AN ENEMY INTO A FRIEND

1. SPEAK HIGHLY OF HIM TO OTHERS.

2. INVITE HIM TO HANG OUT WITH YOU AND YOUR FRIENDS.

3. PRAY FOR HIM.

4. INVITE HIM TO LUNCH, THEN PAY FOR IT.

5. FIGURE OUT THINGS YOU HAVE IN COMMON.

6. HAVE A TRUSTED FRIEND CHECK YOUR WORDS AND ACTIONS.

7. HELP HIM HOWEVER HE'S STRUGGLING.

8. GIVE HIM SOMETHING YOU'D RATHER KEEP FOR YOURSELF.

9. STAND UP FOR HIM IF HE'S GETTING RIPPED ON.

10. LOOK FOR HIS GOOD SIDE.

and fell on his knees before Jesus. The man asked, "Good teacher, what must I do to have life forever?"

[18]Jesus answered, "Why do you call me good? Only God is good. [19]You know the commands: 'You must not murder anyone. You must not be guilty of adultery. You must not steal. You must not tell lies about your neighbor. You must not cheat. Honor your father and mother.' "[n]

[20]The man said, "Teacher, I have obeyed all these things since I was a boy."

[21]Jesus, looking at the man, loved him and said, "There is one more thing you need to do. Go and sell everything you have, and give the money to the poor, and you will have treasure in heaven. Then come and follow me."

[22]He was very sad to hear Jesus say this, and he left sorrowfully, because he was rich.

[23]Then Jesus looked at his followers and said, "How hard it will be for the rich to enter the kingdom of God!"

[24]The followers were amazed at what Jesus said. But he said again, "My children, it is very hard to enter the kingdom of God! [25]It is easier for a camel to go through the eye of a needle than for a rich person to enter the kingdom of God."

[26]The followers were even more surprised and said to each other, "Then who can be saved?"

[27]Jesus looked at them and said, "This is something people cannot do, but God can. God can do all things."

[28]Peter said to Jesus, "Look, we have left everything and followed you."

[29]Jesus said, "I tell you the truth, all those who have left houses, brothers, sisters, mother, father, children, or farms for me and for the Good News [30]will get more than they left. Here in this world they will have a hundred times more homes, brothers, sisters, mothers, children, and fields. And with those things, they will also suffer for their belief. But in the age that is coming they will have life forever. [31]Many who have the highest place now will have the lowest place in the future. And many who have the lowest place now will have the highest place in the future."

JESUS TALKS ABOUT HIS DEATH

[32]As Jesus and the people with him were on

BIBLE BASICS

Sin literally means "missing the mark." It's any time you don't do something God commands or go ahead and do anything that God doesn't allow. So if he's told you to go ask your best friend for forgiveness for something you did—don't avoid it. That would be sin. Or ripping on a kid at school—that's actively doing something against what God commands.

Jesus so he could touch them, but his followers told them to stop. [14]When Jesus saw this, he was upset and said to them, "Let the little children come to me. Don't stop them, because the kingdom of God belongs to people who are like these children. [15]I tell you the truth, you must accept the kingdom of God as if you were a little child, or you will never enter it." [16]Then Jesus took the children in his arms, put his hands on them, and blessed them.

A RICH YOUNG MAN'S QUESTION

[17]As Jesus started to leave, a man ran to him

the road to Jerusalem, he was leading the way. His followers were amazed, but others in the crowd who followed were afraid. Again Jesus took the twelve apostles aside and began to tell them what was about to happen in Jerusalem. [33]He said, "Look, we are going to Jerusalem. The Son of Man will be turned over to the leading priests and the teachers of the law. They will say that he must die, and they will turn him over to the non-Jewish people, [34]who will laugh at him and spit on him. They will beat

10:19 'You . . . mother.' Quotation from Exodus 20:12–16; Deuteronomy 5:16–20.

him with whips and crucify him. But on the third day, he will rise to life again."

TWO FOLLOWERS ASK JESUS A FAVOR

[35]Then James and John, sons of Zebedee, came to Jesus and said, "Teacher, we want to ask you to do something for us."

[36]Jesus asked, "What do you want me to do for you?"

[37]They answered, "Let one of us sit at your right side and one of us sit at your left side in your glory in your kingdom."

[38]Jesus said, "You don't understand what you are asking. Can you drink the cup that I must drink? And can you be baptized with the same kind of baptism that I must go through?"[n]

[39]They answered, "Yes, we can."

Jesus said to them, "You will drink the same cup that I will drink, and you will be baptized with the same baptism that I must go through. [40]But I cannot choose who will sit at my right or my left; those places belong to those for whom they have been prepared."

[41]When the other ten followers heard this, they began to be angry with James and John.

[42]Jesus called them together and said, "The other nations have rulers. You know that those rulers love to show their power over the people, and their important leaders love to use all their authority. [43]But it should not be that way among you. Whoever wants to become great among you must serve the rest of you like a servant. [44]Whoever wants to become the first among you must serve all of you like a slave. [45]In the same way, the Son of Man did not come to be served. He came to serve others and to give his life as a ransom for many people."

JESUS HEALS A BLIND MAN

[46]Then they came to the town of Jericho. As Jesus was leaving there with his followers and a great many people, a blind beggar named Bartimaeus son of Timaeus was sitting by the road. [47]When he heard that Jesus from Nazareth was walking by, he began to shout, "Jesus, Son of David, have mercy on me!"

[48]Many people warned the blind man to be quiet, but he shouted even more, "Son of David, have mercy on me!"

[49]Jesus stopped and said, "Tell the man to come here."

So they called the blind man, saying, "Cheer up! Get to your feet. Jesus is calling you." [50]The blind man jumped up, left his coat there, and went to Jesus.

[51]Jesus asked him, "What do you want me to do for you?"

The blind man answered, "Teacher, I want to see."

[52]Jesus said, "Go, you are healed because you believed." At once the man could see, and he followed Jesus on the road.

JESUS ENTERS JERUSALEM AS A KING

11 As Jesus and his followers were coming closer to Jerusalem, they came to the towns of Bethphage and Bethany near the Mount of Olives. From there Jesus sent two of his followers [2]and said to them, "Go to the town you can see there. When you enter it, you will quickly find a colt tied, which no one has ever ridden. Untie it and bring it here to me. [3]If anyone asks you why you are doing this, tell him its Master needs the colt, and he will send it at once. "

[4]The followers went into the town, found a colt tied in the street near the door of a house, and untied it. [5]Some people were standing there and asked, "What are you doing? Why are you untying that colt?" [6]The followers answered the way Jesus told them to answer, and the people let them take the colt.

[7]They brought the colt to Jesus and put their coats on it, and Jesus sat on it. [8]Many people spread their coats on the road. Others cut branches in the fields and spread them on the road. [9]The people were walking ahead of Jesus and behind him, shouting,

"Praise God!

MEN OF THE SWORD

MOSES

The life of Moses was a wild ride. Born in early Old Testament times to Hebrew slaves in Egypt, Moses' life was threatened by an edict from the pharaoh of Egypt to kill all newborn Hebrew boys. But Moses' mother defied this edict, and floated him to safety in a basket of reeds along the Nile River. He was rescued from the river by a daughter of Pharaoh and raised in the royal house. Moses later discovered his real heritage, killed an Egyptian guard, hid from his crime in the desert, and married a woman he met there. In time God appeared to Moses in a burning bush and told him to go back to Egypt and lead his people out of slavery. God inflicted plagues upon Egypt, led the people out, parted the Red Sea, and was with Israel for forty years as they wandered in the desert. Moses received the Ten Commandments from God on Mount Sinai and led God's people to freedom, all the way to edge of the promised land of Israel. He often struggled with God, and he usually obeyed. However, because of one particular act of disobedience, Moses was not allowed to enter the Promised Land and died outside its borders.
—Exodus 3; 20; Numbers 20; Deuteronomy 34

 10:38 Can you . . . through? Jesus was asking if they could suffer the same terrible things that would happen to him.

HOW TO THROW DOWN EXTREME SNOWBOARD MOVES

Don't be stupid. You can't expect to throw down a Cork 720 your first day on the hill—not on purpose anyway. You learn the moves session by session, season by season. For starters, you strap in and spin circles on dry land or at the bottom of the hill to get a feel for your balance on the board. But the first real technique to learn is the toe turn. Step one: You start with a basic stance—legs bent, arms out, head up, body forward. Step two: Straighten your legs and lean forward more. Step three: Turn your arms where you want to go. Your torso comes with. Then you're back to your basic stance. Got the picture? Snowboarding is just like following God. Master these basic moves before you go daring for God: Read. Pray. Fellowship. Worship.

WAYS TO WALK THE WALK

mark 10:45

WORD: The greatest person is the greatest servant.

WALK IT: Offer to do the hardest chore at home, or step out and clean up after your friends after lunch at school.

God bless the One who comes in the name of the Lord! *Psalm 118:26*

[10]God bless the kingdom of our father David! That kingdom is coming! Praise[n] to God in heaven!"

[11]Jesus entered Jerusalem and went into the Temple. After he had looked at everything, since it was already late, he went out to Bethany with the twelve apostles.

[12]The next day as Jesus was leaving Bethany, he became hungry. [13]Seeing a fig tree in leaf from far away, he went to see if it had any figs on it. But he found no figs, only leaves, because it was not the right season for figs. [14]So Jesus said to the tree, "May no one ever eat fruit from you again." And Jesus' followers heard him say this.

JESUS GOES TO THE TEMPLE

[15]When Jesus returned to Jerusalem, he went into the Temple and began to throw out those who were buying and selling there. He turned over the tables of those who were exchanging different kinds of money, and he upset the benches of those who were selling doves. [16]Jesus refused to allow anyone to carry goods through the Temple courts. [17]Then he taught the people, saying, "It is written in the Scriptures, 'My Temple will be called a house for prayer for people from all nations.'[n] But you are changing God's house into a 'hideout for robbers.' "[n]

[18]The leading priests and the teachers of the law heard all this and began trying to find a way to kill Jesus. They were afraid of him, because all the people were amazed at his teaching. [19]That evening, Jesus and his followers left the city.

THE POWER OF FAITH

[20]The next morning as Jesus was passing by with his followers, they saw the fig tree dry and dead, even to the roots. [21]Peter remembered the tree and said to Jesus, "Teacher, look! The fig tree you cursed is dry and dead!"

[22]Jesus answered, "Have faith in God. [23]I tell you the truth, you can say to this mountain,

Travel the road

William Cameron Townsend was a missionary selling Spanish Bibles to the Cakchiquel Indians of Guatemala when a Cakchiquel man got in his face: "If your God is so great, why doesn't he speak in my language?" Townsend realized that all people need the Bible in their native language to fully understand Jesus. After translating the New Testament for the Cakchiquels, he founded Wycliffe Bible Translators. WBT has completed more than five hundred translations, with hundreds more in progress.
Surf to www.wycliffe.org.

For more on extreme missions visit www.traveltheroad.com.

11:10 Praise Literally, "Hosanna," a Hebrew word used at first in praying to God for help, but at this time it was probably a shout of joy used in praising God or his Messiah.   11:17 'My Temple . . . nations.' Quotation from Isaiah 56:7.   11:17 'hideout for robbers.' Quotation from Jeremiah 7:11.

MARCH

1

March is National Foot Health Month. Take care of those planter's warts today.

2

3

Help your parents clean out the most cluttered room in your pad.

4

5

Multiple Personalities Day. Give it a try.

6

7

8

Pray for a Person of Influence: Freddie Prinze Jr. celebrates a birthday today.

9

10

Read the Book of Colossians today.

11

12

Make up with a friend you've been mad at.

13

Say thanks to God for his forgiveness today.

14

15

Get a really good picture taken of you and your siblings in time for Mother's Day.

16

17

St. Patrick's Day. Do you have any idea what St. Pat did? Read up on him.

18

19

20

Treat your parents to breakfast in bed.

21

22

Pray for a Person of Influence: Today is Reese Witherspoon's birthday.

23

Ask your parents how you can stay focused for the last couple months of school.

24

25

26

27

28

Eat a corn dog to celebrate "Something on a Stick Day."

Crank up the tunes and thank God for making music.

29

Visit another denomination's church this week. Find out about your fellow Christians.

30

31

Ask your science teacher if they know it's Bunsen Burner Day.

issues

PORNOGRAPHY

PORNOGRAPHY is a $10 billion-a-year business. That's bigger than the NFL, the NBA, and Major League Baseball combined. While guys in your dad's generation had to hunt down porn to catch a glimpse of skin, now any wired computer puts you just a click away from it. Any guy's mind can come up with all kinds of excuses why pornography is no big deal. "It's a woman's choice to get naked." "It's just pictures." "It doesn't hurt anyone." But porn destroys your ability to get close to your future wife in mind and body. How? It's wildly unrealistic—it's airbrushed perfect, grossly warped, or violently evil. It aims your sexual desire at someone other than your wife-for-life. It trains you to get physical pleasure without emotional intimacy. And to your brain, it's as addictive as cocaine. If pornography is part of your life, surf to www.exxit.org or www.pureintimacy.org. And get help from an older Christian male you trust.

✓COUNT ON IT

MARK 13:10

One of these days, the world as you know it won't even exist. One glorious day, everyone on earth will hear the explosive blast of a trumpet and that will be the end. Whoa! Can you imagine what it's going to be like when Jesus Christ comes back to earth and sets up his kingdom? There won't be any more violence on the streets. There won't be any more cancer to kill the people you love. Even the deepest, most private pain in your own heart will be gone. The devil won't be able to torment you and cause devastation anywhere, because he'll be burning in a lake of fire.

But some things have to happen before Jesus returns to rule with perfect peace and justice. He says that "the Good News must be told to all people." Now that's something you can help with! You can go on a mission trip while you're a teen. That's the best time to go! Start to pray about it now. Ask God where he wants to send you and how you are to get the money to go. One of the conditions for Jesus' return is for the Good News to be preached in all nations. You can go and do it!

'Go, fall into the sea.' And if you have no doubts in your mind and believe that what you say will happen, God will do it for you. [24]So I tell you to believe that you have received the things you ask for in prayer, and God will give them to you. [25]When you are praying, if you are angry with someone, forgive him so that your Father in heaven will also forgive your sins." [26]n

LEADERS DOUBT JESUS' AUTHORITY

[27]Jesus and his followers went again to Jerusalem. As Jesus was walking in the Temple, the leading priests, the teachers of the law, and the older leaders came to him. [28]They said to him, "What authority do you have to do these things? Who gave you this authority?"

[29]Jesus answered, "I will ask you one question. If you answer me, I will tell you what authority I have to do these things. [30]Tell me: When John baptized people, was that authority from God or just from other people?"

[31]They argued about Jesus' question, saying, "If we answer, 'John's baptism was from God,' Jesus will say, 'Then why didn't you believe him?' [32]But if we say, 'It was from other people,' the crowd will be against us." (These leaders were afraid of the people, because all the people believed that John was a prophet.)

[33]So they answered Jesus, "We don't know."

Jesus said to them, "Then I won't tell you what authority I have to do these things."

A STORY ABOUT GOD'S SON

12 Jesus began to use stories to teach the people. He said, "A man planted a vineyard. He put a wall around it and dug a hole for a winepress and built a tower. Then he leased the land to some farmers and left for a trip. [2]When it was time for the grapes to be picked, he sent a servant to the farmers to get his share of the grapes. [3]But the farmers grabbed the servant and beat him and sent him away empty-handed. [4]Then the man sent another servant. They hit him on the head and showed no respect for him. [5]So the man sent another servant, whom they killed. The man sent many other servants; the farmers beat some of them and killed others.

[6]"The man had one person left to send, his son whom he loved. He sent him last of all, saying, 'They will respect my son.'

[7]"But the farmers said to each other, 'This son will inherit the vineyard. If we kill him, it will be ours.' [8]So they took the son, killed him, and threw him out of the vineyard.

[9]"So what will the owner of the vineyard do? He will come and kill those farmers and will give the vineyard to other farmers. [10]Surely you have read this Scripture:

'The stone that the builders rejected
    became the cornerstone.
[11]The Lord did this,
    and it is wonderful to us.' " *Psalm 118:22-23*

[12]The Jewish leaders knew that the story was about them. So they wanted to find a way to arrest Jesus, but they were afraid of the people. So the leaders left him and went away.

RANDOM WAYS TO SCARE OFF A GIRL WHO LIKES YOU

1. **DON'T SPEND ONE-ON-ONE TIME WITH HER.**
2. **TREAT HER THE SAME WAY YOU TREAT EVERY OTHER GIRL.**
3. **TELL HER HOW YOU HONESTLY FEEL.**
4. **TALK TO YOURSELF.**
5. **DON'T CALL HER.**
6. **STAY OUT OF CORNERS.**
7. **SHOW UP AT SCHOOL IN A MONK ROBE.**
8. **GET TOO SERIOUS TOO FAST.**
9. **SEE IF YOU CAN SET HER UP WITH A GUY WHO'S A BETTER FIT.**
10. **DYE YOUR HAIR MAUVE.**

 11:26 Verse 26 Some early Greek copies add verse 26: "But if you don't forgive other people, then your Father in heaven will not forgive your sins."

IS IT RIGHT TO PAY TAXES OR NOT?

[13]Later, the Jewish leaders sent some Pharisees and Herodians[n] to Jesus to trap him in saying something wrong. [14]They came to him and said, "Teacher, we know that you are an honest man. You are not afraid of what other people think about you, because you pay no attention to who they are. And you teach the truth about God's way. Tell us: Is it right to pay taxes to Caesar or not? [15]Should we pay them, or not?"

But knowing what these men were really trying to do, Jesus said to them, "Why are you trying to trap me? Bring me a coin to look at." [16]They gave Jesus a coin, and he asked, "Whose image and name are on the coin?"

They answered, "Caesar's."

[17]Then Jesus said to them, "Give to Caesar the things that are Caesar's, and give to God the things that are God's." The men were amazed at what Jesus said.

SOME SADDUCEES TRY TO TRICK JESUS

[18]Then some Sadducees came to Jesus and asked him a question. (Sadducees believed that people would not rise from the dead.) [19]They said, "Teacher, Moses wrote that if a man's brother dies, leaving a wife but no children, then that man must marry the widow and have children for his brother. [20]Once there were seven brothers. The first brother married and died, leaving no children. [21]So the second brother married the widow, but he also died and had no children. The same thing happened with the third brother. [22]All seven brothers married her and died, and none of the brothers had any children. Finally the woman died too. [23]Since all seven brothers had married her, when people rise from the dead, whose wife will she be?"

[24]Jesus answered, "Why don't you understand? Don't you know what the Scriptures say, and don't you know about the power of God? [25]When people rise from the dead, they will not marry, nor will they be given to someone to marry. They will be like the angels in heaven. [26]Surely you have read what God said about people rising from the dead. In the book in which Moses wrote about the burning bush,[n] it says that God told Moses, 'I am the God of Abraham, the God of Isaac, and the God of Jacob.'[n] [27]God is the God of the living, not the dead. You Sadducees are wrong!"

THE MOST IMPORTANT COMMAND

[28]One of the teachers of the law came and heard Jesus arguing with the Sadducees. Seeing

COUNT ON IT

MARK 13:31

The earth and the sky look like the strongest, most permanent things around. In fact, if there's one thing that most people will bet on, it's that—cloudy or clear—the sun will come out tomorrow. It's a lot easier to bank on the things you can see rather than on the things you can't see.

But Jesus looked at the huge, blue sky above him and the solid, dusty earth under his feet and told his followers that the things he was saying would outlast the earth and sky. He wanted them to know that even though it might not look like it, it would be better for them to invest in things they couldn't see—the kingdom of God that he was telling them about—rather than in things they could see.

It will be tempting for you to spend your time and your energy going after things that you can see—an education, a good job, a nice place to live, neat stuff to make your life comfortable, a family of your own eventually. There's certainly nothing wrong with those things. But Jesus is encouraging you, even warning you, to give the best and the most of your time and energy to the things that will last forever—his Word, his kingdom, and your relationship with him.

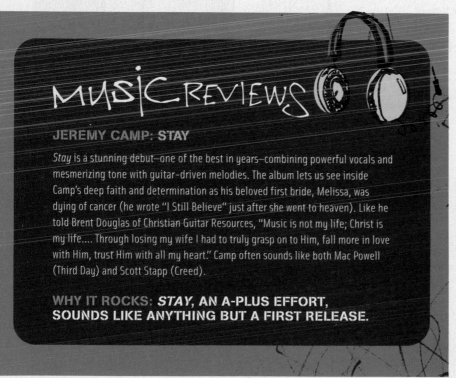

MUSIC REVIEWS

JEREMY CAMP: STAY

Stay is a stunning debut—one of the best in years—combining powerful vocals and mesmerizing tone with guitar-driven melodies. The album lets us see inside Camp's deep faith and determination as his beloved first bride, Melissa, was dying of cancer (he wrote "I Still Believe" just after she went to heaven). Like he told Brent Douglas of Christian Guitar Resources, "Music is not my life; Christ is my life.... Through losing my wife I had to truly grasp on to Him, fall more in love with Him, trust Him with all my heart." Camp often sounds like both Mac Powell (Third Day) and Scott Stapp (Creed).

WHY IT ROCKS: *STAY*, AN A-PLUS EFFORT, SOUNDS LIKE ANYTHING BUT A FIRST RELEASE.

 12:13 Herodians A political group that followed Herod and his family.   **12:26 burning bush** Read Exodus 3:1–12 in the Old Testament.   **12:26 'I am . . . Jacob.'** Quotation from Exodus 3:6.

that Jesus gave good answers to their questions, he asked Jesus, "Which of the commands is most important?"

[29]Jesus answered, "The most important command is this: 'Listen, people of Israel! The Lord our God is the only Lord. [30]Love the Lord your God with all your heart, all your soul, all your mind, and all your strength.'[n] [31]The second command is this: 'Love your neighbor as you love yourself.'[n] There are no commands more important than these."

[32]The man answered, "That was a good answer, Teacher. You were right when you said God is the only Lord and there is no other God besides him. [33]One must love God with all his heart, all his mind, and all his strength. And one must love his neighbor as he loves himself. These commands are more important than all the animals and sacrifices we offer to God."

[34]When Jesus saw that the man answered him wisely, Jesus said to him, "You are close to the kingdom of God." And after that, no one was brave enough to ask Jesus any more questions.

[35]As Jesus was teaching in the Temple, he asked, "Why do the teachers of the law say that the Christ is the son of David? [36]David himself, speaking by the Holy Spirit, said:

'The Lord said to my Lord:

  Sit by me at my right side,

  until I put your enemies

    under your control.'   *Psalm 110:1*

[37]David himself calls the Christ 'Lord,' so how can the Christ be his son?" The large crowd listened to Jesus with pleasure.

[38]Jesus continued teaching and said, "Beware of the teachers of the law. They like to walk around wearing fancy clothes, and they love for people to greet them with respect in the marketplaces. [39]They love to have the most important seats in the synagogues and at feasts. [40]But they cheat widows and steal their houses and then try to make themselves look good by saying long prayers. They will receive a greater punishment."

TRUE GIVING

[41]Jesus sat near the Temple money box and watched the people put in their money. Many rich people gave large sums of money. [42]Then

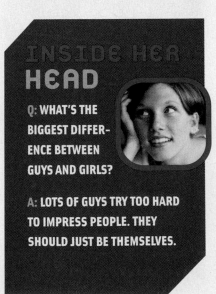

INSIDE HER HEAD

Q: WHAT'S THE BIGGEST DIFFERENCE BETWEEN GUYS AND GIRLS?

A: LOTS OF GUYS TRY TOO HARD TO IMPRESS PEOPLE. THEY SHOULD JUST BE THEMSELVES.

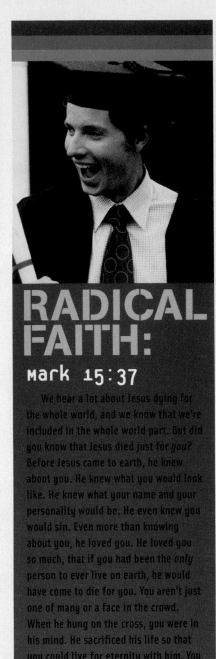

RADICAL FAITH:

Mark 15:37

We hear a lot about Jesus dying for the whole world, and we know that we're included in the whole world part. But did you know that Jesus died just for *you?* Before Jesus came to earth, he knew about you. He knew what you would look like. He knew what your name and your personality would be. He even knew you would sin. Even more than knowing about you, he loved you. He loved you so much, that if you had been the *only* person to ever live on earth, he would have come to die for you. You aren't just one of many or a face in the crowd. When he hung on the cross, you were in his mind. He sacrificed his life so that you could live for eternity with him. You are the reason Jesus came, lived, died, and rose from the grave. He paid for your sin through his own death. He knows you intimately and wants you to know him—the One who died so you could live forever with him.

12:30 'Listen . . . strength.' Quotation from Deuteronomy 6:4–5.   12:31 'Love . . . yourself.' Quotation from Leviticus 19:18.

RELATIONSHIPS

"And if you are nice only to your friends, you are no better than other people. Even those who don't know God are nice to their friends" (Matthew 5:47). Ouch! Jesus spoke straight up about the big stretch he expects our love to make. It reaches not just to one special girl. Or to two or three best friends. Not just to the people we call "close." God wants us to love everyone within our reach, friend or foe. Who right near you needs your friendship today—someone you usually ignore?

a poor widow came and put in two small copper coins, which were only worth a few cents.

43Calling his followers to him, Jesus said, "I tell you the truth, this poor widow gave more than all those rich people. 44They gave only what they did not need. This woman is very poor, but she gave all she had; she gave all she had to live on."

THE TEMPLE WILL BE DESTROYED

13 As Jesus was leaving the Temple, one of his followers said to him, "Look, Teacher! How beautiful the buildings are! How big the stones are!"

2Jesus said, "Do you see all these great buildings? Not one stone will be left on another. Every stone will be thrown down to the ground."

3Later, as Jesus was sitting on the Mount of Olives, opposite the Temple, he was alone with Peter, James, John, and Andrew. They asked Jesus, 4"Tell us, when will these things happen? And what will be the sign that they are going to happen?"

5Jesus began to answer them, "Be careful that no one fools you. 6Many people will come in my name, saying, 'I am the One,' and they will fool many people. 7When you hear about wars and stories of wars that are coming, don't

be afraid. These things must happen before the end comes. 8Nations will fight against other nations, and kingdoms against other kingdoms. There will be earthquakes in different places, and there will be times when there is no food for people to eat. These things are like the first pains when something new is about to be born.

9"You must be careful. People will arrest you and take you to court and beat you in their synagogues. You will be forced to stand before kings and governors, to tell them about me. This will happen to you because you follow me. 10But before these things happen, the Good News must be told to all people. 11When you are arrested and judged, don't worry ahead of time about what you should say. Say whatever is given you to say at that time, because it will not really be you speaking; it will be the Holy Spirit.

12"Brothers will give their own brothers to be killed, and fathers will give their own children to be killed. Children will fight against their own parents and cause them to be put to death. 13All people will hate you because you follow me, but those people who keep their faith until the end will be saved.

14"You will see 'the destroying terror'[n] standing where it should not be." (You who read this

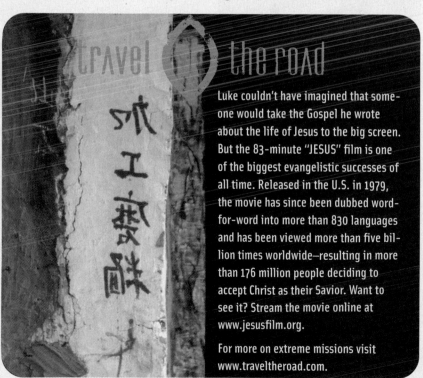

travel the road

Luke couldn't have imagined that someone would take the Gospel he wrote about the life of Jesus to the big screen. But the 83-minute "JESUS" film is one of the biggest evangelistic successes of all time. Released in the U.S. in 1979, the movie has since been dubbed word-for-word into more than 830 languages and has been viewed more than five billion times worldwide—resulting in more than 176 million people deciding to accept Christ as their Savior. Want to see it? Stream the movie online at www.jesusfilm.org.

For more on extreme missions visit www.traveltheroad.com.

 13:14 'the destroying terror' Mentioned in Daniel 9:27; 12:11 (cf. Daniel 11:31).

RADICAL FAITH:
mark 16:16

God designed the world so that there would be consequences for sin. He also required that a payment be made for sin. He knew we could never pay for all our sins. Without payment, the eternal consequence is condemnation and separation from God in hell—forever. His heart was broken by that thought. The only way to save us was to send someone to be perfect, and to die the death that we deserved. To give us a way out of eternal damnation, he sent his perfect Son, Jesus.

Jesus lived a sinless life and then died as a sacrifice for our sins. God said that Jesus' death was enough to pay for everyone's sin. Nothing else needed to be done. Nothing else could be done. The payment has been made for all of your sin.

To receive the benefit of Jesus' death, you have to believe in him. Deciding to believe that Jesus Christ died for you is called "being saved." Believing in him saves you from being condemned and separated from God forever. Heaven is reserved for those who decide to believe that Jesus Christ is who he said he was. Run to him and be saved!

should understand what it means.) "At that time, the people in Judea should run away to the mountains. [15]If people are on the roofs[n] of their houses, they must not go down or go inside to get anything out of their houses. [16]If people are in the fields, they must not go back to get their coats. [17]At that time, how terrible it will be for women who are pregnant or have nursing babies! [18]Pray that these things will not happen in winter, [19]because those days will be full of trouble. There will be more trouble than there has ever been since the beginning, when God made the world, until now, and nothing as bad will ever happen again. [20]God has decided to make that terrible time short. Otherwise, no one would go on living. But God will make that time short to help the people he has chosen. [21]At that time, someone might say to you, 'Look, there is the Christ!' Or another person might say, 'There he is!' But don't believe them. [22]False Christs and false prophets will come and perform great wonders and miracles. They will try to fool even the people God has chosen, if that is possible. [23]So be careful. I have warned you about all this before it happens.

[24]"During the days after this trouble comes,
'the sun will grow dark,
and the moon will not give its light.
[25]The stars will fall from the sky.
And the powers of the heavens
will be shaken.'   *Isaiah 13:10; 34:4*

[26]"Then people will see the Son of Man coming in clouds with great power and glory. [27]Then he will send his angels all around the earth to gather his chosen people from every part of the earth and from every part of heaven.

[28]"Learn a lesson from the fig tree: When its branches become green and soft and new leaves appear, you know summer is near. [29]In the same way, when you see these things happening, you will know that the time is near, ready to come. [30]I tell you the truth, all these things will happen while the people of this time are still living. [31]Earth and sky will be destroyed, but the words I have said will never be destroyed.

[32]"No one knows when that day or time will be, not the angels in heaven, not even the Son. Only the Father knows. [33]Be careful! Always be ready, because you don't know when that time will be. [34]It is like a man who goes on a trip. He leaves his house and lets his

EXPERTS ANSWER YOUR QUESTIONS

Q. *A teacher at school said that you can't trust the Bible because it's full of contradictions. Is that true?*

A. Maybe your teacher has honest questions about the Bible, but plenty of people who claim the Bible contradicts itself can't defend that statement. So politely ask the person to show you some contradictions. Look at the passages for yourself. If you can't figure it out, ask a parent or pastor. There's no question you will ever hear that hasn't been asked before—and adequately answered by really smart people who believe the Bible.

Q. *Does God want us to know more about himself than he put in the Bible?*

A. The Bible says we learn that God exists by looking at the world he made. It also says we get the full picture of who God is by looking at Jesus. The Bible is the one place in the world where we find that full picture. The last chapter of Revelation says that anyone who adds to it will suffer disaster.

13:15 roofs In Bible times houses were built with flat roofs. The roof was used for drying things such as flax and fruit. And it was used as an extra room, as a place for worship, and as a cool place to sleep in the summer.

servants take care of it, giving each one a special job to do. The man tells the servant guarding the door always to be watchful. ³⁵So always be ready, because you don't know when the owner of the house will come back. It might be in the evening, or at midnight, or in the morning while it is still dark, or when the sun rises. ³⁶Always be ready. Otherwise he might come back suddenly and find you sleeping. ³⁷I tell you this, and I say this to everyone: 'Be ready!' "

THE PLAN TO KILL JESUS

14 It was now only two days before the Passover and the Feast of Unleavened Bread. The leading priests and teachers of the law were trying to find a trick to arrest Jesus and kill him. ²But they said, "We must not do it during the feast, because the people might cause a riot."

A WOMAN WITH PERFUME FOR JESUS

³Jesus was in Bethany at the house of Simon, who had a skin disease. While Jesus was eating there, a woman approached him with an alabaster jar filled with very expensive perfume, made of pure nard. She opened the jar and poured the perfume on Jesus' head.

⁴Some who were there became upset and said to each other, "Why waste that perfume? ⁵It was worth a full year's work. It could have been sold and the money given to the poor." And they got very angry with the woman.

⁶Jesus said, "Leave her alone. Why are you troubling her? She did an excellent thing for me. ⁷You will always have the poor with you, and you can help them anytime you want. But you will not always have me. ⁸This woman did the only thing she could do for me; she poured perfume on my body to prepare me for burial. ⁹I tell you the truth, wherever the Good News is preached in all the world, what this woman has done will be told, and people will remember her."

JUDAS BECOMES AN ENEMY OF JESUS

¹⁰One of the twelve apostles, Judas Iscariot, went to talk to the leading priests to offer to hand Jesus over to them. ¹¹These priests were pleased about this and promised to pay Judas money. So he watched for the best time to turn Jesus in.

JESUS EATS THE PASSOVER MEAL

¹²It was now the first day of the Feast of Unleavened Bread when the Passover lamb was sacrificed. Jesus' followers said to him, "Where do you want us to go and prepare for you to eat the Passover meal?"

¹³Jesus sent two of his followers and said to them, "Go into the city and a man carrying a jar of water will meet you. Follow him. ¹⁴When he goes into a house, tell the owner of the house, 'The Teacher says: Where is my guest room in which I can eat the Passover meal with my followers?' ¹⁵The owner will show you a large room upstairs that is furnished and ready. Prepare the food for us there."

¹⁶So the followers left and went into the city. Everything happened as Jesus had said, so they prepared the Passover meal.

¹⁷In the evening, Jesus went to that house with the twelve. ¹⁸While they were all eating, Jesus said, "I tell you the truth, one of you will turn against me—one of you eating with me now."

DO'S & DON'TS

• Do treat others the way you want to be treated.

• Do act unselfishly.

• Do look people in the eye.

• Do speak up.

• Don't call in sick when you're not.

• Don't twist the truth.

• Don't swipe stuff from work.

• Don't shove stuff under your bed.

RANDOM WAYS TO SCORE GOOD GRADES

1. PLAN TIME FOR HOMEWORK.

2. TAKE NOTES.

3. ASK FOR HELP WHEN YOU NEED IT.

4. DON'T PROCRASTINATE.

5. LOG HOURS WITH A TUTOR.

6. DON'T SIT NEXT TO PEOPLE WHO DISTRACT YOU.

7. READ YOUR ASSIGNMENTS.

8. ASK FOR A WEEKLY OR MONTHLY PROGRESS REPORT.

9. PUT IMPORTANT STUFF ON FLASHCARDS.

10. BELIEVE THAT SCHOOL MATTERS.

---

¹⁹The followers were very sad to hear this. Each one began to say to Jesus, "I am not the one, am I?"

²⁰Jesus answered, "It is one of the twelve—the one who dips his bread into the bowl with me. ²¹The Son of Man will die, just as the Scriptures say. But how terrible it will be for the person who hands the Son of Man over to be killed. It would be better for him if he had never been born."

THE LORD'S SUPPER

²²While they were eating, Jesus took some bread and thanked God for it and broke it. Then he gave it to his followers and said, "Take it; this is my body."

²³Then Jesus took a cup and thanked God for it and gave it to the followers, and they all drank from the cup.

²⁴Then Jesus said, "This is my blood which is the new agreement that God makes with his people. This blood is poured out for many. ²⁵I

tell you the truth, I will not drink of this fruit of the vine[n] again until that day when I drink it new in the kingdom of God."

[26]After singing a hymn, they went out to the Mount of Olives.

JESUS' FOLLOWERS WILL LEAVE HIM

[27]Then Jesus told the followers, "You will all stumble in your faith, because it is written in the Scriptures:

'I will kill the shepherd,
    and the sheep will scatter.'   *Zechariah 13:7*
[28]But after I rise from the dead, I will go ahead of you into Galilee."

[29]Peter said, "Everyone else may stumble in their faith, but I will not."

[30]Jesus answered, "I tell you the truth, tonight before the rooster crows twice you will say three times you don't know me."

[31]But Peter insisted, "I will never say that I don't know you! I will even die with you!" And all the other followers said the same thing.

JESUS PRAYS ALONE

[32]Jesus and his followers went to a place called Gethsemane. He said to them, "Sit here while I pray." [33]Jesus took Peter, James, and John with him, and he began to be very sad and troubled. [34]He said to them, "My heart is full of sorrow, to the point of death. Stay here and watch."

[35]After walking a little farther away from them, Jesus fell to the ground and prayed that, if possible, he would not have this time of suffering. [36]He prayed, "Abba,[n] Father! You can do all things. Take away this cup[n] of suffering. But do what you want, not what I want."

[37]Then Jesus went back to his followers and found them asleep. He said to Peter, "Simon, are you sleeping? Couldn't you stay awake with me for one hour? [38]Stay awake and pray for strength against temptation. The spirit wants to do what is right, but the body is weak."

[39]Again Jesus went away and prayed the same thing. [40]Then he went back to his followers, and again he found them asleep, because their eyes were very heavy. And they did not know what to say to him.

[41]After Jesus prayed a third time, he went

More than 29,000 children die every day—and you can do something about it. **THE 30 HOUR FAMINE** puts hands and feet to your desire to live a life of Christian compassion. Each year, thousands of groups in more than 21 countries—more than a million teens—unite to help the millions of starving and hurting children in some of the world's poorest countries. Together you and your friends raise money through donors and sponsors. Then you go 30 hours without food, so that you can have a real taste of what hunger is like. During this time, you engage in activities from community service projects to lock-ins. The money raised is sent to the development agency World Vision, where it goes to work in areas like Peru, Ethiopia, and the United States.

Your work helps kids living in the most deplorable conditions on earth. It takes just $30 a month to feed and care for a child, so getting twelve people to donate $30 raises $360, enough money to feed and care for a child for a whole year.

Get a kit to hold your own 30 Hour Famine at www.30hourfamine.org.

14:25 **fruit of the vine** Product of the grapevine; this may also be translated "wine."   14:36 **Abba** Name that a Jewish child called his father.   14:36 **cup** Jesus is talking about the terrible things that will happen to him. Accepting these things will be very hard, like drinking a cup of something bitter.

back to his followers and said to them, "Are you still sleeping and resting? That's enough. The time has come for the Son of Man to be handed over to sinful people. ⁴²Get up, we must go. Look, here comes the man who has turned against me."

JESUS IS ARRESTED

⁴³At once, while Jesus was still speaking, Judas, one of the twelve apostles, came up. With him were many people carrying swords and clubs who had been sent from the leading priests, the teachers of the law, and the older Jewish leaders.

⁴⁴Judas had planned a signal for them, saying, "The man I kiss is Jesus. Arrest him and guard him while you lead him away." ⁴⁵So Judas went straight to Jesus and said, "Teacher!" and kissed him. ⁴⁶Then the people grabbed Jesus and arrested him. ⁴⁷One of his followers standing nearby pulled out his sword and struck the servant of the high priest and cut off his ear.

⁴⁸Then Jesus said, "You came to get me with swords and clubs as if I were a criminal. ⁴⁹Every day I was with you teaching in the Temple, and you did not arrest me there. But all these things have happened to make the Scriptures come true." ⁵⁰Then all of Jesus' followers left him and ran away.

⁵¹A young man, wearing only a linen cloth, was following Jesus, and the people also grabbed him. ⁵²But the cloth he was wearing came off, and he ran away naked.

JESUS BEFORE THE LEADERS

⁵³The people who arrested Jesus led him to the house of the high priest, where all the leading priests, the older leaders, and the teachers of the law were gathered. ⁵⁴Peter followed far behind and entered the courtyard of the high priest's house. There he sat with the guards, warming himself by the fire.

⁵⁵The leading priests and the whole Jewish council tried to find something that Jesus had done wrong so they could kill him. But the council could find no proof of anything. ⁵⁶Many people came and told false things about him, but all said different things—none of them agreed.

⁵⁷Then some people stood up and lied about Jesus, saying, ⁵⁸"We heard this man say, 'I will destroy this Temple that people made. And three days later, I will build another Temple not made

by people.' " ⁵⁹But even the things these people said did not agree.

⁶⁰Then the high priest stood before them and asked Jesus, "Aren't you going to answer? Don't you have something to say about their charges against you?" ⁶¹But Jesus said nothing; he did not answer.

The high priest asked Jesus another question: "Are you the Christ, the Son of the blessed God?"

⁶²Jesus answered, "I am. And in the future you will see the Son of Man sitting at the right hand of God, the Powerful One, and coming on clouds in the sky."

⁶³When the high priest heard this, he tore his clothes and said, "We don't need any more witnesses! ⁶⁴You all heard him say these things against God. What do you think?"

They all said that Jesus was guilty and should die. ⁶⁵Some of the people there began to spit at Jesus. They blindfolded him and beat him with their fists and said, "Prove you are a prophet!" Then the guards led Jesus away and beat him.

PETER SAYS HE DOESN'T KNOW JESUS

⁶⁶While Peter was in the courtyard, a servant girl of the high priest came there. ⁶⁷She saw Peter warming himself at the fire and looked closely at him.

Then she said, "You also were with Jesus, that man from Nazareth."

⁶⁸But Peter said that he was never with Jesus. He said, "I don't know or understand what you are talking about." Then Peter left and went toward the entrance of the courtyard. And the rooster crowed.ⁿ

⁶⁹The servant girl saw Peter there, and again she said to the people who were standing nearby, "This man is one of those who followed Jesus." ⁷⁰Again Peter said that it was not true.

A short time later, some people were standing near Peter saying, "Surely you are one of those who followed Jesus, because you are from Galilee, too."

⁷¹Then Peter began to place a curse on himself and swear, "I don't know this man you're talking about!"

⁷²At once, the rooster crowed the second time. Then Peter remembered what Jesus had told him: "Before the rooster crows twice, you will say three times that you don't know me." Then Peter lost control of himself and began to cry.

BIBLE BASICS

Salvation is what all humans need in order to live eternally with God. The Book of Romans says that all people have sinned and don't come anywhere close to being as good as God. But when Jesus died on the cross, he took the punishment we deserved. When we trust that Jesus died for us, God forgives all of our faults and sees us as if we had never sinned. He sees us like he sees Jesus, who is perfect. That's how Christians are allowed into heaven.

PILATE QUESTIONS JESUS

15 Very early in the morning, the leading priests, the older leaders, the teachers of the law, and all the Jewish council decided what to do with Jesus. They tied him, led him away, and turned him over to Pilate, the governor.

14:68 **And . . . crowed.** A few, early Greek copies leave out this phrase.

HOW TO SHOP FOR DIAMOND

So you're not ready to pop the question. Good thing. But that shouldn't stop you from appreciating the splendor of a diamond, one of the world's most stunning visuals. Every diamond in the world gets rated for four C's. *Color:* That's what you're paying for. Diamonds range from colorless to light yellow. The shape and skill of the *Cut* determines the sparkle, the flashing colors, and the brightness of a stone. Round remains the most popular cut. *Clarity* is all about the imperfections in the stone, ranging from flawless to embedded hunks easy to spot with 10X magnification. *Carat* refers to the size. A one-carat diamond is a sizable rock when set in a ring, 6.5mm across in a round cut. Got it? See, before you buy a diamond, you need to know how to spot quality. Keep that in mind when you're looking for a wife as well. The highest quality girl is one with a pure heart for God.

²Pilate asked Jesus, "Are you the king of the Jews?"

Jesus answered, "Those are your words."

³The leading priests accused Jesus of many things. ⁴So Pilate asked Jesus another question, "You can see that they are accusing you of many things. Aren't you going to answer?"

⁵But Jesus still said nothing, so Pilate was very surprised.

PILATE TRIES TO FREE JESUS

⁶Every year at the time of the Passover the governor would free one prisoner whom the people chose. ⁷At that time, there was a man named Barabbas in prison who was a rebel and had committed murder during a riot. ⁸The crowd came to Pilate and began to ask him to free a prisoner as he always did.

⁹So Pilate asked them, "Do you want me to free the king of the Jews?" ¹⁰Pilate knew that the leading priests had turned Jesus in to him because they were jealous. ¹¹But the leading priests had persuaded the people to ask Pilate to free Barabbas, not Jesus.

¹²Then Pilate asked the crowd again, "So what should I do with this man you call the king of the Jews?"

¹³They shouted, "Crucify him!"

¹⁴Pilate asked, "Why? What wrong has he done?"

But they shouted even louder, "Crucify him!"

¹⁵Pilate wanted to please the crowd, so he freed Barabbas for them. After having Jesus beaten with whips, he handed Jesus over to the soldiers to be crucified.

¹⁶The soldiers took Jesus into the governor's palace (called the Praetorium) and called all the other soldiers together. ¹⁷They put a purple robe on Jesus and used thorny branches to make a crown for his head. ¹⁸They began to call out to him, "Hail, King of the Jews!" ¹⁹The soldiers beat Jesus on the head many times with a stick. They spit on him and made fun of him by bowing on their knees and worshiping him. ²⁰After they finished, the soldiers took off the purple robe and put his own clothes on him again. Then they led him out of the palace to be crucified.

JESUS IS CRUCIFIED

²¹A man named Simon from Cyrene, the father of Alexander and Rufus, was coming from the fields to the city. The soldiers forced Simon to carry the cross for Jesus. ²²They led Jesus to the place called Golgotha, which means the Place of the Skull. ²³The soldiers tried to give Jesus wine mixed with myrrh to drink, but he refused. ²⁴The soldiers crucified Jesus and divided his clothes among themselves, throwing lots to decide what each soldier would get.

²⁵It was nine o'clock in the morning when they crucified Jesus. ²⁶There was a sign with this charge against Jesus written on it: THE KING OF THE JEWS. ²⁷They also put two robbers on crosses beside Jesus, one on the right, and the other on the left. ²⁸ⁿ ²⁹People walked by and insulted Jesus and shook their heads, saying, "You said you could destroy the Temple and build it again in three days. ³⁰So save yourself! Come down from that cross!"

³¹The leading priests and the teachers of the law were also making fun of Jesus. They said to each other, "He saved other people, but he can't save himself. ³²If he is really the Christ, the king of Israel, let him come down now

ACTS 4:29 "LORD, HELP US, YOUR SERVANTS, TO SPEAK YOUR WORD WITHOUT FEAR."

from the cross. When we see this, we will believe in him." The robbers who were being crucified beside Jesus also insulted him.

JESUS DIES

³³At noon the whole country became dark, and the darkness lasted for three hours. ³⁴At three o'clock Jesus cried in a loud voice, "Eloi, Eloi, lama sabachthani." This means, "My God, my God, why have you rejected me?"

³⁵When some of the people standing there heard this, they said, "Listen! He is calling Elijah."

³⁶Someone there ran and got a sponge, filled it with vinegar, tied it to a stick, and gave it to Jesus to drink. He said, "We want to see if Elijah will come to take him down from the cross."

³⁷Then Jesus cried in a loud voice and died.

³⁸The curtain in the Templeⁿ was torn into two pieces, from the top to the bottom. ³⁹When the army officer who was standing in front of the cross saw what happened when Jesus died, he said, "This man really was the Son of God!"

15:28 Verse 28 Some Greek copies add verse 28: "And the Scripture came true that says, 'They put him with criminals.'" **15:38 curtain in the Temple** A curtain divided the Most Holy Place from the other part of the Temple. That was the special building in Jerusalem where God commanded the Jewish people to worship him.

⁴⁰Some women were standing at a distance from the cross, watching; among them were Mary Magdalene, Salome, and Mary the mother of James and Joseph. (James was her youngest son.) ⁴¹These women had followed Jesus in Galilee and helped him. Many other women were also there who had come with Jesus to Jerusalem.

JESUS IS BURIED

⁴²This was Preparation Day. (That means the day before the Sabbath day.) That evening, ⁴³Joseph from Arimathea was brave enough to go to Pilate and ask for Jesus' body. Joseph, an important member of the Jewish council, was one of the people who was waiting for the kingdom of God to come. ⁴⁴Pilate was amazed that Jesus would have already died, so he called the army officer who had guarded Jesus and asked him if Jesus had already died. ⁴⁵The officer told Pilate that he was dead, so Pilate told Joseph he could have the body. ⁴⁶Joseph bought some linen cloth, took the body down from the cross, and wrapped it in the linen. He put the body in a tomb that was cut out of a wall of rock. Then he rolled a very large stone to block the entrance of the tomb. ⁴⁷And Mary Magdalene and Mary the mother of Joseph saw the place where Jesus was laid.

JESUS RISES FROM THE DEAD

16 The day after the Sabbath day, Mary Magdalene, Mary the mother of James, and Salome bought some sweet-smelling spices to put on Jesus' body. ²Very early on that day, the first day of the week, soon after sunrise, the women were on their way to the tomb. ³They said to each other, "Who will roll away for us the stone that covers the entrance of the tomb?"

⁴Then the women looked and saw that the

white robe and sitting on the right side, and they were afraid.

⁶But the man said, "Don't be afraid. You are looking for Jesus from Nazareth, who has been crucified. He has risen from the dead; he is not here. Look, here is the place they laid him. ⁷Now go and tell his followers and Peter, 'Jesus is going into Galilee ahead of you, and you will see him there as he told you before.'"

⁸The women were confused and shaking with fear, so they left the tomb and ran away. They did not tell anyone about what happened, because they were afraid.

Verses 9-20 are not included in two of the best and oldest Greek manuscripts of Mark.

SOME FOLLOWERS SEE JESUS

[⁹After Jesus rose from the dead early on the first day of the week, he showed himself first to Mary Magdalene. One time in the past, he had forced seven demons out of her. ¹⁰After Mary saw Jesus, she went and told his followers, who were very sad and were crying. ¹¹But Mary told them that Jesus was alive. She said that she had seen him, but the followers did not believe her.

¹²Later, Jesus showed himself to two of his followers while they were walking in the country, but he did not look the same as before. ¹³These followers went back to the others and told them what had happened, but again, the followers did not believe them.

JESUS TALKS TO THE APOSTLES

¹⁴Later Jesus showed himself to the eleven apostles while they were eating, and he criticized them because they had no faith. They were

where in the world, and tell the Good News to everyone. ¹⁶Anyone who believes and is baptized will be saved, but anyone who does not believe will be punished. ¹⁷And those who believe will be able to do these things as proof: They will use my name to force out demons. They will speak in new languages.ⁿ ¹⁸They will pick up snakes and drink poison without being hurt. They will touch the sick, and the sick will be healed."

¹⁹After the Lord Jesus said these things to his followers, he was carried up into heaven, and he sat at the right side of God. ²⁰The followers went everywhere in the world and told the Good News to people, and the Lord helped them. The Lord proved that the Good News they told was true by giving them power to work miracles.]

stone had already been rolled away, even though it was very large. ⁵The women entered the tomb and saw a young man wearing a

stubborn and refused to believe those who had seen him after he had risen from the dead.

¹⁵Jesus said to his followers, "Go every-

16:17 **languages** This can also be translated "tongues."

LUKE

Luke's Gospel might feel like the same old story told yet again. Why bother? Actually, the elements are the same, but Luke's account is absolutely essential. He says at the start of his book that he set out to write an orderly account of the life of Jesus. So he starts way back at the birth of Jesus as the world's most powerful baby. Luke, a physician, is the only one who reports the earliest days of Jesus in such moving detail.

There are great stories here. You get the story of the loving shepherd who leaves his ninety-nine safe sheep to look for the one lost lamb. And the story of the prodigal son, squandering his share of the family wealth, then returning home to the open arms of a loving father. And the story of the good Samaritan, a half-breed who shows compassion to an injured man after blue-blooded Jews, supposed men of God, walk on by. In fact, there are fourteen of these classic stories that are found only in Luke. Oh, yeah... there are also six miracles and ten leper healings. Lots of stories here. And all of them point us to Jesus... the most powerful baby ever born.

LUKE WRITES ABOUT JESUS' LIFE

1 Many have tried to report on the things that happened among us. [2]They have written the same things that we learned from others—the people who saw those things from the beginning and served God by telling people his message. [3]Since I myself have studied everything carefully from the beginning, most excellent[n] Theophilus, it seemed good for me to write it out for you. I arranged it in order [4]to help you know that what you have been taught is true.

ZECHARIAH AND ELIZABETH

[5]During the time Herod ruled Judea, there was a priest named Zechariah who belonged to Abijah's group.[n] Zechariah's wife, Elizabeth, came from the family of Aaron. [6]Zechariah and Elizabeth truly did what God said was good. They did everything the Lord commanded and were without fault in keeping his law. [7]But they had no children, because Elizabeth could not have a baby, and both of them were very old.

[8]One day Zechariah was serving as a priest before God, because his group was on duty. [9]According to the custom of the priests, he was chosen by lot to go into the Temple of the Lord and burn incense. [10]There were a great many people outside praying at the time the incense was offered. [11]Then an angel of the Lord appeared to Zechariah, standing on the right side of the incense table. [12]When he saw the angel, Zechariah was startled and frightened. [13]But the angel said to him, "Zechariah, don't be afraid. God has heard your prayer. Your wife, Elizabeth, will give birth to a son, and you will name him John. [14]He will bring you joy and gladness, and many people will be happy because of his birth. [15]John will be a great man for the Lord. He will never drink wine or beer, and even from birth, he will be filled with the Holy Spirit. [16]He will help many people of Israel return to the Lord their God. [17]He will go before the Lord in spirit and power like Elijah. He will make peace between parents and their children and will bring those who are not obeying God back to the right way of thinking, to make a people ready for the coming of the Lord."

[18]Zechariah said to the angel, "How can I know that what you say is true? I am an old man, and my wife is old, too."

LUKE 3:4 "THIS IS A VOICE OF ONE WHO CALLS OUT IN THE DESERT: 'PREPARE THE WAY FOR THE LORD.'"

[19]The angel answered him, "I am Gabriel. I stand before God, who sent me to talk to you and to tell you this good news. [20]Now, listen! You will not be able to speak until the day these things happen, because you did not believe what I told you. But they will really happen."

[21]Outside, the people were still waiting for Zechariah and were surprised that he was staying so long in the Temple. [22]When Zechariah came outside, he could not speak to them, and they knew he had seen a vision in the Temple. He could only make signs to them and remained unable to speak. [23]When his time of service at the Temple was finished, he went home.

[24]Later, Zechariah's wife, Elizabeth, became pregnant and did not go out of her house for five months. Elizabeth said, [25]"Look what the Lord has done for me! My people were ashamed[n] of me, but now the Lord has taken away that shame."

AN ANGEL APPEARS TO MARY

[26]During Elizabeth's sixth month of pregnancy, God sent the angel Gabriel to Nazareth, a town in Galilee, [27]to a virgin. She was engaged to marry a man named Joseph from the family of David. Her name was Mary.

INSIDE HER HEAD

Q: WHAT'S THE BIGGEST DIFFERENCE BETWEEN GUYS AND GIRLS?

A: THEY GIVE IN TO PEER PRESSURE MORE THAN GIRLS BECAUSE THEY WANT TO BE COOL.

EXPERTS ANSWER YOUR QUESTIONS

Q. *If God wants everyone to know him, then why didn't he make us all Christians so we would all love him?*

A. Love doesn't mean much when it's forced. God built humans with hearts and minds free to choose for or against him. If you don't like losing control over small things—like when your mother makes you eat broccoli—how would you feel if God took away your choice on such a huge issue?

Q. *My neighbor has a different religion, and he says that he's glad I'm a Christian—but that people of all religions worship the same God. Is he right?*

A. It's true that there's only one God, and it's a popular idea that all religious people run to the same Big Guy upstairs. But check out what the gods in other religions say, and you see that their personalities are completely different from the God of the Bible. All religions don't serve the same God.

 1:3 excellent This word was used to show respect to an important person like a king or ruler. **1:5 Abijah's group** The Jewish priests were divided into twenty-four groups. See 1 Chronicles 24. **1:25 ashamed** The Jewish people thought it was a disgrace for women not to have children.

28The angel came to her and said, "Greetings! The Lord has blessed you and is with you."

29But Mary was very startled by what the angel said and wondered what this greeting might mean.

30The angel said to her, "Don't be afraid, Mary; God has shown you his grace. 31Listen! You will become pregnant and give birth to a son, and you will name him Jesus. 32He will be great and will be called the Son of the Most High. The Lord God will give him the throne of King David, his ancestor. 33He will rule over the people of Jacob forever, and his kingdom will never end."

34Mary said to the angel, "How will this happen since I am a virgin?"

35The angel said to Mary, "The Holy Spirit will come upon you, and the power of the Most High will cover you. For this reason the baby will be holy and will be called the Son of God. 36Now Elizabeth, your relative, is also pregnant with a son though she is very old. Everyone thought she could not have a baby, but she has been pregnant for six months. 37God can do anything!"

38Mary said, "I am the servant of the Lord. Let this happen to me as you say!" Then the angel went away.

MARY VISITS ELIZABETH

39Mary got up and went quickly to a town in the hills of Judea. 40She came to Zechariah's house and greeted Elizabeth. 41When Elizabeth heard Mary's greeting, the unborn baby inside her jumped, and Elizabeth was filled with the Holy Spirit. 42She cried out in a loud voice, "God has blessed you more than any other woman, and he has blessed the baby to which you will give birth. 43Why has this good thing happened to me, that the mother of my Lord comes to me? 44When I heard your voice, the baby inside me jumped with joy. 45You are blessed because you believed that what the Lord said to you would really happen."

MARY PRAISES GOD

46Then Mary said,

"My soul praises the Lord;
47   my heart rejoices in God my Savior,
48because he has shown his concern for his
      humble servant girl.

PSALM 18:34 "HE TRAINS MY HANDS FOR BATTLE SO MY ARMS CAN BEND A BRONZE BOW."

From now on, all people will say that
      I am blessed,
49   because the Powerful One has done
      great things for me.
      His name is holy.
50God will show his mercy forever and ever
      to those who worship and serve him.
51He has done mighty deeds by his power.
      He has scattered the people who
      are proud
      and think great things about themselves.
52He has brought down rulers from their
      thrones
      and raised up the humble.
53He has filled the hungry with
      good things
      and sent the rich away with nothing.

54He has helped his servant, the people
      of Israel,
      remembering to show them mercy
55as he promised to our ancestors,
      to Abraham and to his children forever."

56Mary stayed with Elizabeth for about three months and then returned home.

THE BIRTH OF JOHN

57When it was time for Elizabeth to give birth, she had a boy. 58Her neighbors and relatives heard how good the Lord was to her, and they rejoiced with her.

59When the baby was eight days old, they came to circumcise him. They wanted to name him Zechariah because this was his father's name, 60but his mother said, "No! He will be named John."

61The people said to Elizabeth, "But no one in your family has this name." 62Then they made signs to his father to find out what he would like to name him.

63Zechariah asked for a writing tablet and wrote, "His name is John," and everyone was surprised. 64Immediately Zechariah could talk again, and he began praising God. 65All their neighbors became alarmed, and in all the mountains of Judea people continued talking about all these things. 66The people who heard about them wondered, saying, "What will this child be?" because the Lord was with him.

ZECHARIAH PRAISES GOD

67Then Zechariah, John's father, was filled with the Holy Spirit and prophesied:
68"Let us praise the Lord, the God of Israel,
      because he has come to help his people
      and has given them freedom.
69He has given us a powerful Savior
      from the family of God's servant David.
70He said that he would do this
      through his holy prophets who lived
      long ago:
71He promised he would save us
      from our enemies
      and from the power of all those
      who hate us.
72He said he would give mercy to our fathers

WAYS TO WALK THE WALK

Luke 4:1-13

WORD: Even Jesus was tempted.

WALK IT: Think about how you usually fight off temptations. Then tackle a big temptation by putting Jesus' tactics into action, defending your heart and mind with God's Word.

issues

PREMARITAL SEX

Most Christian guys feel stuck when it comes to sex. They have developed bodies hungry to get close to a girl, yet marriage is a long way off. You probably know that the Bible commands you to save sex for marriage. God created sex as his awe-inspiring wedding present to a man and woman who commit to stick together for life—and he says that sex outside of marriage is sin. So whether you're a guy who's 14 or 40, you have to manage your desires. Your best bet is to stay out of situations that tempt you to do what you shouldn't.

Beware that even little kisses can heat you up. Groping not only grabs what God says isn't yours, but it makes you want more. And if you think sexual activity that isn't actual intercourse is okay because "it's not really having sex," you're fooling yourself with a technicality. It's the kind of closeness to save for marriage.

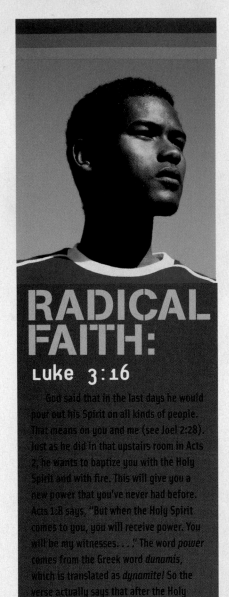

RADICAL FAITH:

Luke 3:16

God said that in the last days he would pour out his Spirit on all kinds of people. That means on you and me (see Joel 2:28). Just as he did in that upstairs room in Acts 2, he wants to baptize you with the Holy Spirit and with fire. This will give you a new power that you've never had before. Acts 1:8 says, "But when the Holy Spirit comes to you, you will receive power. You will be my witnesses. . . ." The word *power* comes from the Greek word *dunamis*, which is translated as *dynamite!* So the verse actually says that after the Holy Spirit comes upon you, you will receive dynamite power to be witnesses!

This is exactly what happened to Peter. The same Peter who denied Christ three times preached with dynamite power after he received the Holy Spirit and fire as told in Acts 2. In fact, he led 3,000 people to the Lord in one day. Now that's power! That's the same kind of power everyone needs. How do we get it? It's a gift. All we have to do is ask the Lord for it. He wants to baptize us with the Holy Spirit and fire today, so we can receive that dynamite power to be witnesses for him.

and that he would remember
  his holy promise.
73God promised Abraham, our father,
74   that he would save us from the power
      of our enemies
  so we could serve him without fear,
75being holy and good before God
  as long as we live.

76"Now you, child, will be called a prophet
      of the Most High God.
  You will go before the Lord to prepare
      his way.
77You will make his people know that they
      will be saved
  by having their sins forgiven.
78With the loving mercy of our God,
  a new day from heaven will dawn
      upon us.
79It will shine on those who live in darkness,
  in the shadow of death.
  It will guide us into the path of peace."

80And so the child grew up and became strong in spirit. John lived in the desert until the time when he came out to preach to Israel.

THE BIRTH OF JESUS

2 At that time, Augustus Caesar sent an order that all people in the countries under Roman rule must list their names in a register. 2This was the first registration;*n* it was taken while Quirinius was governor of Syria. 3And all went to their own towns to be registered.

4So Joseph left Nazareth, a town in Galilee, and went to the town of Bethlehem in Judea, known as the town of David. Joseph went there because he was from the family of David. 5Joseph registered with Mary, to whom he was engaged*n* and who was now pregnant. 6While they were in Bethlehem, the time came for Mary to have the baby, 7and she gave birth to her first son. Because there were no rooms left in the inn, she wrapped the baby with pieces of cloth and laid him in a box where animals are fed.

SHEPHERDS HEAR ABOUT JESUS

8That night, some shepherds were in the fields nearby watching their sheep. 9Then an angel of the Lord stood before them. The glory of the Lord was shining around them, and they became very frightened. 10The angel said to them, "Do not be afraid. I am bringing you good news that will be a great joy to all the people. 11Today your Savior was born in the town of David. He is Christ, the Lord. 12This is how you will know him: You will find a baby wrapped in pieces of cloth and lying in a feeding box."

travel the road

Tradition says that two thousand years ago the apostle Thomas took the Good News about Jesus to India. But in 2003 India's Supreme Court ruled that the government can restrict people from changing religions. A law already passed in several Indian states—and introduced at the national level by the ruling party—dictates that anyone who wants to become a Christian must get written permission from a government official. In addition, only people with a high-school education can convert, making it illegal for more than 350 million illiterate Indians to follow Jesus.

For more on extreme missions visit www.traveltheroad.com.

2:2 **registration** Census. A counting of all the people and the things they own. 2:5 **engaged** For the Jewish people, an engagement was a lasting agreement. It could only be broken by divorce.

¹³Then a very large group of angels from heaven joined the first angel, praising God and saying:
¹⁴"Give glory to God in heaven,
and on earth let there be peace among the people who please God."

¹⁵When the angels left them and went back to heaven, the shepherds said to each other, "Let's go to Bethlehem. Let's see this thing that has happened which the Lord has told us about."

¹⁶So the shepherds went quickly and found Mary and Joseph and the baby, who was lying in a feeding box. ¹⁷When they had seen him, they told what the angels had said about this child. ¹⁸Everyone was amazed at what the shepherds said to them. ¹⁹But Mary treasured these things and continued to think about them. ²⁰Then the shepherds went back to their sheep, praising God and thanking him for everything they had seen and heard. It had been just as the angel had told them.

²¹When the baby was eight days old, he was circumcised and was named Jesus, the name given by the angel before the baby began to grow inside Mary.

JESUS IS PRESENTED IN THE TEMPLE

²²When the time came for Mary and Joseph

PSALM 18:46 "THE LORD LIVES! MAY MY ROCK BE PRAISED. PRAISE THE GOD WHO SAVES ME!"

to do what the law of Moses taught about being made pure,ⁿ they took Jesus to Jerusalem to present him to the Lord. ²³(It is written in the law of the Lord: "Every firstborn male shall be given to the Lord.")ⁿ ²⁴Mary and Joseph also went to offer a sacrifice, as the law of the Lord says: "You must sacrifice two doves or two young pigeons."ⁿ

SIMEON SEES JESUS

²⁵In Jerusalem lived a man named Simeon who was a good man and godly. He was waiting for the time when God would take away Israel's sorrow, and the Holy Spirit was in him. ²⁶Simeon had been told by the Holy Spirit that he would not die before he saw the Christ promised by the Lord. ²⁷The Spirit led Simeon to the Temple. When Mary and Joseph brought the baby Jesus to the Temple to do what the law said they must do, ²⁸Simeon took the baby in his arms and thanked God:
²⁹"Now, Lord, you can let me, your servant, die in peace as you said.
³⁰With my own eyes I have seen your salvation,
³¹ which you prepared before all people.
³²It is a light for the non-Jewish people to see and an honor for your people, the Israelites."
³³Jesus' father and mother were amazed at what Simeon had said about him. ³⁴Then

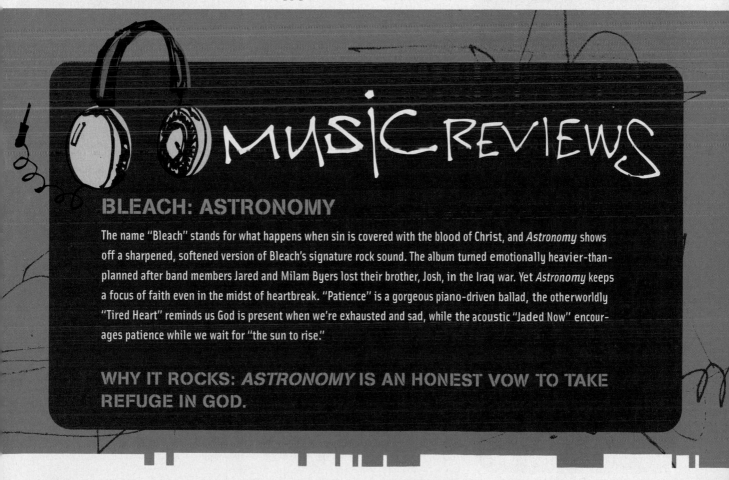

BLEACH: ASTRONOMY

The name "Bleach" stands for what happens when sin is covered with the blood of Christ, and *Astronomy* shows off a sharpened, softened version of Bleach's signature rock sound. The album turned emotionally heavier-than-planned after band members Jared and Milam Byers lost their brother, Josh, in the Iraq war. Yet *Astronomy* keeps a focus of faith even in the midst of heartbreak. "Patience" is a gorgeous piano-driven ballad, the otherworldly "Tired Heart" reminds us God is present when we're exhausted and sad, while the acoustic "Jaded Now" encourages patience while we wait for "the sun to rise."

WHY IT ROCKS: *ASTRONOMY* IS AN HONEST VOW TO TAKE REFUGE IN GOD.

 2:22 pure The Law of Moses said that forty days after a Jewish woman gave birth to a son, she must be cleansed by a ceremony at the Temple. Read Leviticus 12:2–8. 2:23 "Every . . . Lord." Quotation from Exodus 13:2. 2:24 "You . . . pigeons." Quotation from Leviticus 12:8.

HOW TO ACT LIKE A REGULAR GUY AT THE GYM

You're at the gym or the health club to get pumped up. There's no quicker way to feel deflated than getting treated like a rug rat because you broke the unspoken rules of the gym. Here's how to hang at the gym like you've been going since you were two. *Put stuff back.* Does that guy with no neck look like your mother? *Share.* Everyone wants a turn, whether on weights or cardio. Train efficiently and don't nap on the machines. Jump off cardio equipment after 30 minutes max if someone is waiting. *Be patient.* Don't ask, duh, when someone will be done. Just wait. *Shut up.* Most people don't go the gym to talk, and no one wants your advice. *Carry a towel, and wipe your sweat off the machines.* No one wants to share your slime. Note to self: It's smart to scope out the rules of any social setting. And if the norms don't go against God, go ahead and fit in as you see fit.

Simeon blessed them and said to Mary, "God has chosen this child to cause the fall and rise of many in Israel. He will be a sign from God that many people will not accept [35]so that the thoughts of many will be made known. And the things that will happen will make your heart sad, too."

ANNA SEES JESUS

[36]There was a prophetess, Anna, from the family of Phanuel in the tribe of Asher. Anna was very old. She had once been married for seven years. [37]Then her husband died, and she was a widow for eighty-four years. Anna never left the Temple but worshiped God, going without food and praying day and night. [38]Standing there at that time, she thanked God and spoke about Jesus to all who were waiting for God to free Jerusalem.

JOSEPH AND MARY RETURN HOME

[39]When Joseph and Mary had done everything the law of the Lord commanded, they went home to Nazareth, their own town in Galilee. [40]The little child grew and became strong. He was filled with wisdom, and God's goodness was upon him.

JESUS AS A BOY

[41]Every year Jesus' parents went to Jerusalem for the Passover Feast. [42]When he was twelve years old, they went to the feast as they always did. [43]After the feast days were over,

JOHN 1:1 "IN THE BEGINNING THERE WAS THE WORD. THE WORD WAS WITH GOD, AND THE WORD WAS GOD."

they started home. The boy Jesus stayed behind in Jerusalem, but his parents did not know it. [44]Thinking that Jesus was with them in the group, they traveled for a whole day. Then they began to look for him among their family and friends. [45]When they did not find him, they went back to Jerusalem to look for him there. [46]After three days they found Jesus sitting in the Temple with the teachers, listening to them and asking them questions. [47]All who heard him were amazed at his understanding and answers. [48]When Jesus' parents saw him, they were astonished. His mother said to him,

"Son, why did you do this to us? Your father and I were very worried about you and have been looking for you."

[49]Jesus said to them, "Why were you looking for me? Didn't you know that I must be in my Father's house?" [50]But they did not understand the meaning of what he said.

[51]Jesus went with them to Nazareth and was obedient to them. But his mother kept in her mind all that had happened. [52]Jesus became wiser and grew physically. People liked him, and he pleased God.

THE PREACHING OF JOHN

3 It was the fifteenth year of the rule of Tiberius Caesar. These men were under Caesar: Pontius Pilate, the ruler of Judea; Herod, the ruler of Galilee; Philip, Herod's brother, the ruler of Iturea and Traconitis; and Lysanias, the ruler of Abilene. [2]Annas and Caiaphas were the high priests. At this time, the word of God came to John son of Zechariah in the desert. [3]He went all over the area around the Jordan River preaching a baptism of changed hearts and lives for the forgiveness of sins. [4]As it is written in the book of Isaiah the prophet:

"This is a voice of one
who calls out in the desert:
'Prepare the way for the Lord.
Make the road straight for him.
⁵Every valley should be filled in,
and every mountain and hill should
be made flat.
Roads with turns should be made straight,
and rough roads should be made
smooth.
⁶And all people will know about the
salvation of God!' "   *Isaiah 40:3-5*

⁷To the crowds of people who came to be baptized by John, he said, "You are all snakes! Who warned you to run away from God's coming punishment? ⁸Do the things that show you really have changed your hearts and lives. Don't begin to say to yourselves, 'Abraham is our father.' I tell you that God could make children for Abraham from these rocks. ⁹The ax is now ready to cut down the trees, and every tree that does not produce good fruit will be cut down and thrown into the fire."[n]

¹⁰The people asked John, "Then what should we do?"

¹¹John answered, "If you have two shirts, share with the person who does not have one. If you have food, share that also."

¹²Even tax collectors came to John to be baptized. They said to him, "Teacher, what should we do?"

¹³John said to them, "Don't take more taxes from people than you have been ordered to take."

¹⁴The soldiers asked John, "What about us? What should we do?"

John said to them, "Don't force people to give you money, and don't lie about them. Be satisfied with the pay you get."

¹⁵Since the people were hoping for the Christ to come, they wondered if John might be the one.

¹⁶John answered everyone, "I baptize you with water, but there is one coming who is greater than I am. I am not good enough to untie his sandals. He will baptize you with the Holy Spirit and fire. ¹⁷He will come ready to clean the grain, separating the good grain from the chaff. He will put the good part of the grain into his barn, but he will burn the chaff with a fire that cannot be put out."[n] ¹⁸And John continued to preach the Good News, saying many other things to encourage the people.

¹⁹But John spoke against Herod, the governor, because of his sin with Herodias, the wife of Herod's brother, and because of the many other evil things Herod did. ²⁰So Herod did something even worse: He put John in prison.

JESUS IS BAPTIZED BY JOHN

²¹When all the people were being baptized by John, Jesus also was baptized. While Jesus was praying, heaven opened ²²and the Holy Spirit came down on him in the form of a dove. Then a voice came from heaven, saying, "You are my Son, whom I love, and I am very pleased with you."

THE FAMILY HISTORY OF JESUS

²³When Jesus began his ministry, he was about thirty years old. People thought that Jesus was Joseph's son.

Joseph was the son[n] of Heli.
²⁴Heli was the son of Matthat.
Matthat was the son of Levi.

RADICAL FAITH:
Luke 4:8

Jesus had been in the desert praying about how to get through to men's hearts. Satan tempted him to take the easy way out—turn stones into bread instead of fasting; serve him in return for glory and power; or jump off the Temple, let the angels miraculously save him, and immediately be accepted by the people. Jesus knew that the only way to win the souls of men was to suffer and go to the cross. It was the harder way, but it was the only right way.

You are going to face incredible temptation in your life. You must know that Jesus has been there. He knows the battles you face. You've got the same spiritual resources that Jesus had. You have prayer and the love of your heavenly Father. The power of the Holy Spirit was with Jesus (4:1), and the Holy Spirit lives in you. Jesus quoted the Word of God to Satan, and you have the complete Word in your hands. Plus, you now have Jesus in heaven, interceding on your behalf.

Do not play around with Satan. Stay on your toes. Keep alert. Serve God and flee the devil!

LOOK COOL
TIPS ON YOURSELF

Maybe somewhere in the world a unibrow is a sign of fierce intelligence. But we haven't found it yet. If you've got one eyebrow crawling like a giant caterpillar across your forehead, tweezer the hairs in the middle one by one. Just don't shave the excess hair. It will grow back thicker and faster and soon your brow bush will be wildly out of control. As a guy living for God, killer looks aren't the sum total of life. But it's okay to kill the caveman look.

3:9 **The ax . . . fire.** This means that God is ready to punish his people who do not obey him.   3:17 **He will . . . out.** This means that Jesus will come to separate good people from bad people, saving the good and punishing the bad.   3:23 **son** "Son" in Jewish lists of ancestors can sometimes mean grandson or more distant relative.

RANDOM WAYS TO IMPRESS THE BOSS

1. SHOW UP TEN MINUTES EARLY.

2. CALL HER "MA'AM" (UNLESS HE'S A GUY).

3. ASK FOR SOMETHING TO DO WHEN YOU RUN OUT OF WORK.

4. SAVE YOUR SLANG FOR YOUR FRIENDS.

5. BE HELPFUL TO CUSTOMERS.

6. TAKE CARE OF A TASK BEFORE YOU'RE ASKED.

7. PUT IN EXTRA TIME IF THERE'S A RUSH OR A DEADLINE.

8. GIVE 100 PERCENT.

9. CHOOSE TO BE POSITIVE AND ENTHUSIASTIC.

10. MAKE FRIENDS WITH THE OTHER EMPLOYEES.

Levi was the son of Melki.
Melki was the son of Jannai.
Jannai was the son of Joseph.
25Joseph was the son of Mattathias.
Mattathias was the son of Amos.
Amos was the son of Nahum.
Nahum was the son of Esli.
Esli was the son of Naggai.
26Naggai was the son of Maath.
Maath was the son of Mattathias.
Mattathias was the son of Semein.
Semein was the son of Josech.
Josech was the son of Joda.
27Joda was the son of Joanan.
Joanan was the son of Rhesa.
Rhesa was the son of Zerubbabel.

Zerubbabel was the grandson of Shealtiel.
Shealtiel was the son of Neri.
28Neri was the son of Melki.
Melki was the son of Addi.
Addi was the son of Cosam.
Cosam was the son of Elmadam.
Elmadam was the son of Er.
29Er was the son of Joshua.
Joshua was the son of Eliezer.
Eliezer was the son of Jorim.
Jorim was the son of Matthat.
Matthat was the son of Levi.
30Levi was the son of Simeon.
Simeon was the son of Judah.
Judah was the son of Joseph.
Joseph was the son of Jonam.
Jonam was the son of Eliakim.
31Eliakim was the son of Melea.
Melea was the son of Menna.
Menna was the son of Mattatha.
Mattatha was the son of Nathan.
Nathan was the son of David.
32David was the son of Jesse.
Jesse was the son of Obed.
Obed was the son of Boaz.
Boaz was the son of Salmon.
Salmon was the son of Nahshon.
33Nahshon was the son of Amminadab.
Amminadab was the son of Admin.
Admin was the son of Arni.
Arni was the son of Hezron.
Hezron was the son of Perez.
Perez was the son of Judah.
34Judah was the son of Jacob.
Jacob was the son of Isaac.
Isaac was the son of Abraham.
Abraham was the son of Terah.
Terah was the son of Nahor.
35Nahor was the son of Serug.
Serug was the son of Reu.
Reu was the son of Peleg.
Peleg was the son of Eber.
Eber was the son of Shelah.
36Shelah was the son of Cainan.
Cainan was the son of Arphaxad.
Arphaxad was the son of Shem.
Shem was the son of Noah.
Noah was the son of Lamech.
37Lamech was the son of Methuselah.
Methuselah was the son of Enoch.
Enoch was the son of Jared.

COUNT ON IT

LUKE 4:18

This is such an exciting verse! Did you know that *you* have been chosen to tell the Good News to the poor? The Lord has sent you to announce freedom. But not only have you been sent to announce freedom; you can have freedom as well! There is freedom in Jesus—freedom for everyone who struggles or suffers. What kind of needs do you have? What kind of needs do your friends have? You've been chosen by God, and you've also been equipped with the power of God to get free, stay free, and bring freedom to anyone and everyone who needs it! Now that's power—power over drugs, alcohol, cigarettes, lust, sex, bitterness, or whatever.

There was a movie about a man who gave up his life just to bring freedom to his people. He was beaten, tortured, and put on a chopping block. All he had to do was simply surrender his freedom, and he would live. His people would remain in bondage, but he could live. Instead, he let out a bloodcurdling cry, "Freeeeeedom!" He lost his life, but his people gained their freedom.

There is another story that hits home for all of us. Jesus died a horrible, shameful death on a cross so we could be free from sin and spend eternity with him. Don't allow yourself to be in bondage over some stupid sin—a sin that Jesus has already paid the price for. Choose freedom today, and watch God work a miracle in your life and in the lives of your friends! He is the One who sets you free!

Jared was the son of Mahalalel.

Mahalalel was the son of Kenan.

[38]Kenan was the son of Enosh.

Enosh was the son of Seth.

Seth was the son of Adam.

Adam was the son of God.

JESUS IS TEMPTED BY THE DEVIL

4 Jesus, filled with the Holy Spirit, returned from the Jordan River. The Spirit led Jesus into the desert [2]where the devil tempted Jesus for forty days. Jesus ate nothing during that time, and when those days were ended, he was very hungry.

[3]The devil said to Jesus, "If you are the Son of God, tell this rock to become bread."

[4]Jesus answered, "It is written in the Scriptures: 'A person does not live by eating only bread.' "[n]

[5]Then the devil took Jesus and showed him all the kingdoms of the world in an instant. [6]The devil said to Jesus, "I will give you all these king-

PSALM 18:35 "YOU SUPPORT ME WITH YOUR RIGHT HAND. YOU HAVE STOOPED TO MAKE ME GREAT."

doms and all their power and glory. It has all been given to me, and I can give it to anyone I wish. [7]If you worship me, then it will all be yours."

[8]Jesus answered, "It is written in the Scriptures: 'You must worship the Lord your God and serve only him.' "[n]

[9]Then the devil led Jesus to Jerusalem and put him on a high place of the Temple. He said to Jesus, "If you are the Son of God, jump down. [10]It is written in the Scriptures:

'He has put his angels in charge of you

to watch over you.'   *Psalm 91:11*

[11]It is also written:

'They will catch you in their hands

so that you will not hit your foot

on a rock.' "   *Psalm 91:12*

[12]Jesus answered, "But it also says in the Scriptures: 'Do not test the Lord your God.' "[n]

[13]After the devil had tempted Jesus in every way, he left him to wait until a better time.

JESUS TEACHES THE PEOPLE

[14]Jesus returned to Galilee in the power of the Holy Spirit, and stories about him spread all through the area. [15]He began to teach in their synagogues, and everyone praised him.

[16]Jesus traveled to Nazareth, where he had grown up. On the Sabbath day he went to the synagogue, as he always did, and stood up to read. [17]The book of Isaiah the prophet was given to him. He opened the book and found the place where this is written:

[18]"The Lord has put his Spirit in me,

because he appointed me to tell the

Good News to the poor.

He has sent me to tell the captives

they are free

and to tell the blind that they can

see again.   *Isaiah 61:1*

God sent me to free those who have been

treated unfairly   *Isaiah 58:6*

[19]   and to announce the time when the Lord

will show his kindness."   *Isaiah 61:2*

[20]Jesus closed the book, gave it back to the assistant, and sat down. Everyone in the synagogue was watching Jesus closely. [21]He began to say to them, "While you heard these words just now, they were coming true!"

[22]All the people spoke well of Jesus and were amazed at the words of grace he spoke. They asked, "Isn't this Joseph's son?"

[23]Jesus said to them, "I know that you will tell me the old saying: 'Doctor, heal yourself.' You want to say, 'We heard about the things you did in Capernaum. Do those things here in your own town!' " [24]Then Jesus said, "I tell you the truth, a prophet is not accepted in his hometown. [25]But I tell you the truth, there were many widows in Israel during the time of Elijah. It did not rain in Israel for three and one-half years, and there was no food anywhere in the whole country. [26]But Elijah was

sent to none of those widows, only to a widow in Zarephath, a town in Sidon. [27]And there were many with skin diseases living in Israel during the time of the prophet Elisha. But none of them were healed, only Naaman, who was from the country of Syria."

[28]When all the people in the synagogue heard these things, they became very angry. [29]They got up, forced Jesus out of town, and took him to the edge of the cliff on which the town was built. They planned to throw him off the edge, [30]but Jesus walked through the crowd and went on his way.

JESUS FORCES OUT AN EVIL SPIRIT

[31]Jesus went to Capernaum, a city in Galilee, and on the Sabbath day, he taught the people. [32]They were amazed at his teaching, because he spoke with authority. [33]In the synagogue a man who had within him an evil spirit shouted in a loud voice, [34]"Jesus of Nazareth! What do you want with us? Did you come to destroy us? I know who you are—God's Holy One!"

[35]Jesus commanded the evil spirit, "Be quiet! Come out of the man!" The evil spirit threw the man down to the ground before all the people and then left the man without hurting him.

[36]The people were amazed and said to each

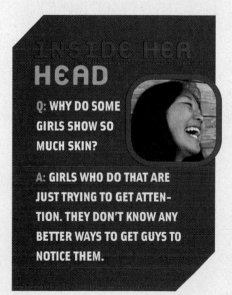

INSIDE HER HEAD

Q: WHY DO SOME GIRLS SHOW SO MUCH SKIN?

A: GIRLS WHO DO THAT ARE JUST TRYING TO GET ATTENTION. THEY DON'T KNOW ANY BETTER WAYS TO GET GUYS TO NOTICE THEM.

4:4 'A person . . . bread.' Quotation from Deuteronomy 8:3.   4:8 'You . . . him.' Quotation from Deuteronomy 6:13.   4:12 'Do . . . God.' Quotation from Deuteronomy 6:16.

other, "What does this mean? With authority and power he commands evil spirits, and they come out." [37]And so the news about Jesus spread to every place in the whole area.

JESUS HEALS MANY PEOPLE

[38]Jesus left the synagogue and went to the home of Simon.[n] Simon's mother-in-law was sick with a high fever, and they asked Jesus to help her. [39]He came to her side and commanded the fever to leave. It left her, and immediately she got up and began serving them.

[40]When the sun went down, the people brought those who were sick to Jesus. Putting his hands on each sick person, he healed every one of them. [41]Demons came out of many people, shouting, "You are the Son of God." But Jesus commanded the demons and would not allow them to speak, because they knew Jesus was the Christ.

[42]At daybreak, Jesus went to a lonely place, but the people looked for him. When they found him, they tried to keep him from leaving. [43]But Jesus said to them, "I must preach about God's kingdom to other towns, too. This is why I was sent."

[44]Then he kept on preaching in the synagogues of Judea.

JESUS' FIRST FOLLOWERS

5 One day while Jesus was standing beside Lake Galilee, many people were pressing all around him to hear the word of God. [2]Jesus saw two boats at the shore of the lake. The fishermen had left them and were washing their nets. [3]Jesus got into one of the boats, the one that belonged to Simon,[n] and asked him to push off a little from the land. Then Jesus sat down and continued to teach the people from the boat.

[4]When Jesus had finished speaking, he said to Simon, "Take the boat into deep water, and put your nets in the water to catch some fish."

[5]Simon answered, "Master, we worked hard all night trying to catch fish, and we caught nothing. But you say to put the nets in the water, so I will." [6]When the fishermen did as Jesus told them, they caught so many fish that the nets began to break. [7]They called to their partners in the other boat to come and help them. They came and filled both boats so full that they were almost sinking.

[8]When Simon Peter saw what had happened, he bowed down before Jesus and said, "Go away from me, Lord. I am a sinful man!" [9]He and the other fishermen were amazed at the many fish they caught, as were [10]James and John, the sons of Zebedee, Simon's partners.

Jesus said to Simon, "Don't be afraid. From now on you will fish for people." [11]When the men brought their boats to the shore, they left everything and followed Jesus.

JESUS HEALS A SICK MAN

[12]When Jesus was in one of the towns, there was a man covered with a skin disease. When he saw Jesus, he bowed before him and begged him, "Lord, you can heal me if you will."

[13]Jesus reached out his hand and touched

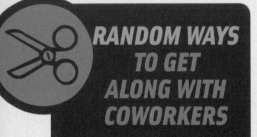

RANDOM WAYS TO GET ALONG WITH COWORKERS

1. **COMPLIMENT THEM.**

2. **DON'T HOG THE CREDIT FOR YOURSELF.**

3. **SEND THEM A FUNNY E-CARD.**

4. **COVER THEIR SHIFTS WHEN THEY NEED TIME OFF.**

5. **CHIP IN TO HELP THEM WHEN THEY'RE OVERWHELMED.**

6. **TALK TO THEM WITH FINGER PUPPETS.**

7. **OFFER TO PICK UP LUNCH IF THEY DON'T HAVE TIME TO GRAB IT.**

8. **COME TO WORK WITH A JOKE OF THE DAY.**

9. **NEVER GOSSIP.**

10. **HOST A PARTY FOR THEM AT YOUR HOUSE.**

COUNT ON IT

LUKE 5:24

Some schools have a wall in the school post office where they post the exam grades. Students sometimes affectionately refer to those places as "the wailing walls." One semester, a young man neglected to study for a particular exam and his test grade reflected it! They left the grades of that test up the entire semester. It was a continual reminder to him of how he had messed up. You can imagine what a happy day it was for him when they finally took down the grades at the end of the term. He could have tried covering up that exam with a black marker (which, by the way, he did). But every time he went into the school post office, there was that big black mark reminding him of his failure.

Jesus is the only One who has the right to forgive your sins. John 1:29 says that he takes them away—completely.

So if you've been struggling with something, confess your sins to him right now. Jesus is not only going to forgive you of your sins; he is going to see to it that they are taken away! After all, he is the One who forgives, forgets, and removes!

4:38 Simon Simon's other name was Peter.   5:3 Simon Simon's other name was Peter.

the man and said, "I will. Be healed!" Immediately the disease disappeared. [14]Then Jesus said, "Don't tell anyone about this, but go and show yourself to the priest[n] and offer a gift for your healing, as Moses commanded.[n] This will show the people what I have done."

[15]But the news about Jesus spread even more. Many people came to hear Jesus and to be healed of their sicknesses, [16]but Jesus often slipped away to be alone so he could pray.

JESUS HEALS A PARALYZED MAN

[17]One day as Jesus was teaching the people, the Pharisees and teachers of the law from every town in Galilee and Judea and from Jerusalem were there. The Lord was giving Jesus the power to heal people. [18]Just then, some men were carrying on a mat a man who was paralyzed. They tried to bring him in and put him down before Jesus. [19]But because there were so many people there, they could not find a way in. So they went up on the roof and lowered the man on his mat through the ceiling into the middle of the crowd right before Jesus. [20]Seeing their faith, Jesus said, "Friend, your sins are forgiven."

[21]The Jewish teachers of the law and the Pharisees thought to themselves, "Who is this man who is speaking as if he were God? Only God can forgive sins."

[22]But Jesus knew what they were thinking and said, "Why are you thinking these things? [23]Which is easier: to say, 'Your sins are forgiven,' or to say, 'Stand up and walk'? [24]But I will prove to you that the Son of Man has authority on earth to forgive sins." So Jesus said to the paralyzed man, "I tell you, stand up, take your mat, and go home."

[25]At once the man stood up before them, picked up his mat, and went home, praising God. [26]All the people were fully amazed and began to praise God. They were filled with much respect and said, "Today we have seen amazing things!"

LEVI FOLLOWS JESUS

[27]After this, Jesus went out and saw a tax collector named Levi sitting in the tax collector's booth. Jesus said to him, "Follow me!" [28]So Levi got up, left everything, and followed him.

[29]Then Levi gave a big dinner for Jesus at his house. Many tax collectors and other people were eating there, too. [30]But the Pharisees and the men who taught the law for the Pharisees began to complain to Jesus' followers, "Why do you eat and drink with tax collectors and sinners?"

[31]Jesus answered them, "It is not the healthy people who need a doctor, but the sick. [32]I have not come to invite good people but sinners to change their hearts and lives."

JESUS ANSWERS A QUESTION

[33]They said to Jesus, "John's followers often give up eating[n] for a certain time and pray, just as the Pharisees do. But your followers eat and drink all the time."

[34]Jesus said to them, "You cannot make the friends of the bridegroom give up eating while he is still with them. [35]But the time will come when the bridegroom will be taken away from them, and then they will give up eating."

[36]Jesus told them this story: "No one takes cloth off a new coat to cover a hole in an old coat. Otherwise, he ruins the new coat, and the cloth from the new coat will not be the same as the old cloth. [37]Also, no one ever pours new wine into old leather bags. Otherwise, the new wine will break the bags, the wine will spill out, and the leather bags will be ruined. [38]New wine must be put into new leather bags. [39]No one after drinking old wine wants new wine, because he says, 'The old wine is better.'"

JESUS IS LORD OVER THE SABBATH

6One Sabbath day Jesus was walking through some fields of grain. His followers picked the heads of grain, rubbed them in their hands, and ate them. [2]Some Pharisees said, "Why do you do what is not lawful on the Sabbath day?"

[3]Jesus answered, "Have you not read what David did when he and those with him were hungry? [4]He went into God's house and took and ate the holy bread, which is lawful only for priests to eat. And he gave some to the people who were with him." [5]Then Jesus said to the Pharisees, "The Son of Man is Lord of the Sabbath day."

JESUS HEALS A MAN'S HAND

[6]On another Sabbath day Jesus went into the synagogue and was teaching, and a man with a crippled right hand was there. [7]The teachers of the law and the Pharisees were watching closely to see if Jesus would heal on the Sabbath day so they could accuse him. [8]But he knew what they were thinking, and he said to the man with the crippled hand, "Stand up here in the middle of everyone." The man got up and stood there. [9]Then Jesus said to them, "I ask you, which is lawful on the Sabbath day: to do good or to do evil, to save a life or to destroy it?" [10]Jesus looked around at all of them and said to the man, "Hold out your hand." The man held out his hand, and it was healed.

[11]But the Pharisees and the teachers of the law were very angry and discussed with each other what they could do to Jesus.

WAYS TO WALK THE WALK

Luke 6:49

WORD: A good foundation for a house makes the house stand firm.

WALK IT: Take time to build a foundation of faith. Spend time in prayer and meditation on God's Word today.

5:14 show . . . priest The Law of Moses said a priest must say when a Jewish person with a skin disease was well. **5:14 Moses commanded** Read about this in Leviticus 14:1–32. **5:33 give up eating** This is called "fasting." The people would give up eating for a special time of prayer and worship to God. It was also done to show sadness and disappointment.

RADICAL FAITH:

Luke 6:28, 35

Luke says, "Welcome to the club." People who love God have been lied about since the beginning. He also says that God will bless those who have been mistreated because of him. Proverbs 25:18-22 gives us some wisdom about friends who tell lies about us or treat us badly. The advice is to do exactly the opposite of what your friends do. Even when you're disappointed and angry, you are supposed to be Christlike. Matthew 5:11 says, "People will insult you and hurt you. They will lie and say all kinds of evil things about you because you follow me. But when they do, you will be happy" because you love Jesus. When you love a person who hurts you, it "will be like pouring burning coals on his head" (Proverbs 25:22).

Wow—that's pretty tough advice. When people tell lies or spread rumors about you, your reputation gets shattered, your pride gets wounded, and your heart gets broken. And God wants you to do what? Yep, he says to love them anyway—even give food to them if they are hungry and pray for them too. By doing so you prove the strength of your character and you overcome evil with good. God promises to reward you for that.

JESUS CHOOSES HIS APOSTLES

¹²At that time Jesus went off to a mountain to pray, and he spent the night praying to God. ¹³The next morning, Jesus called his followers to him and chose twelve of them, whom he named apostles: ¹⁴Simon (Jesus named him Peter), his brother Andrew, James, John, Philip, Bartholomew, ¹⁵Matthew, Thomas, James son of Alphaeus, Simon (called the Zealot), ¹⁶Judas son of James, and Judas Iscariot, who later turned Jesus over to his enemies.

JESUS TEACHES AND HEALS

¹⁷Jesus and the apostles came down from the mountain, and he stood on level ground. A large group of his followers was there, as well as many people from all around Judea, Jerusalem, and the seacoast cities of Tyre and Sidon. ¹⁸They all came to hear Jesus teach and to be healed of their sicknesses, and he healed those who were troubled by evil spirits. ¹⁹All the people were trying to touch Jesus, because power was coming from him and healing them all.

²⁰Jesus looked at his followers and said,
"You people who are poor are happy,
  because the kingdom of God belongs
    to you.
²¹You people who are now hungry are happy,
  because you will be satisfied.
You people who are now crying are happy,
  because you will laugh with joy.
²²"People will hate you, shut you out, insult you, and say you are evil because you follow the Son of Man. But when they do, you will be happy. ²³Be full of joy at that time, because you have a great reward waiting for you in heaven. Their ancestors did the same things to the prophets.
²⁴"But how terrible it will be for you who
    are rich,
  because you have had your easy life.
²⁵How terrible it will be for you who are
    full now,
  because you will be hungry.
How terrible it will be for you who are
    laughing now,
  because you will be sad and cry.
²⁶"How terrible when everyone says only good things about you, because their ancestors said the same things about the false prophets.

LOVE YOUR ENEMIES

²⁷"But I say to you who are listening, love your enemies. Do good to those who hate you,

EXPERTS ANSWER YOUR QUESTIONS

Q. *Did God really make the world in six days—or did he take more like billions of years?*

A. We don't have a solid answer. First, God can do whatever he wants. Now about the days: Some believe the earth really is only about six thousand years old. Others see a huge gap between Genesis 1:1 and 1:2, so the creation days that follow could have been twenty-four hours and the earth itself could still be billions of years old. And others say that in the original language the word for "day" could have meant a longer time.

Q. *Jesus said I'm supposed to turn the other cheek. Am I really supposed to let people walk all over me?*

A. The Bible doesn't say you shouldn't stop someone from hitting you. It's wrong to start fights, and it's wrong to take matters into your own hands to get revenge.

Q. *Are some sins worse than others?*

A. Some sins are totally obvious—everyone can see them. Some sins have really ugly consequences—bad results that reach far and wide. But in another sense, all sins are equally bad. Each sin breaks God's law and steps outside his plan for us. So we can't shake our fingers at sins "worse" than our own. We're all guilty.

HALF OF TEENS SAY THEY FEEL ANGRY, AFRAID, SAD, OR DEPRESSED AFTER WATCHING, READING, OR HEARING ABOUT THE NEWS. –CHILDREN NOW

²⁸bless those who curse you, pray for those who are cruel to you. ²⁹If anyone slaps you on one cheek, offer him the other cheek, too. If someone takes your coat, do not stop him from taking your shirt. ³⁰Give to everyone who asks you, and when someone takes something that is yours, don't ask for it back. ³¹Do to others what you would want them to do to you. ³²If you love only the people who love you, what praise should you get? Even sinners love the people who love them. ³³If you do good only to those who do good to you, what praise should you get? Even sinners do that!

³⁴If you lend things to people, always hoping to get something back, what praise should you get? Even sinners lend to other sinners so that they can get back the same amount! ³⁵But love your enemies, do good to them, and lend to them without hoping to get anything back. Then you will have a great reward, and you will be children of the Most High God, because he is kind even to people who are ungrateful and full of sin. ³⁶Show mercy, just as your Father shows mercy.

LOOK AT YOURSELVES

³⁷"Don't judge other people, and you will not be judged. Don't accuse others of being guilty, and you will not be accused of being guilty. Forgive, and you will be forgiven. ³⁸Give, and you will receive. You will be given much. Pressed down, shaken together, and running over, it will spill into your lap. The way you give to others is the way God will give to you."

³⁹Jesus told them this story: "Can a blind person lead another blind person? No! Both of them will fall into a ditch. ⁴⁰A student is not better than the teacher, but the student who has been fully trained will be like the teacher.

⁴¹"Why do you notice the little piece of dust in your friend's eye, but you don't notice the big piece of wood in your own eye? ⁴²How can you say to your friend, 'Friend, let me take that little piece of dust out of your eye' when you cannot see that big piece of wood in your own eye! You hypocrite! First, take the wood out of your own eye. Then you will see clearly to take the dust out of your friend's eye.

GET OUT THERE

JOIN TOGETHER ONLINE (JTO) is a comprehensive network of free Internet services. They support community-based efforts to address substance abuse and gun violence. Thousands of visitors use JTO every day to be more informed and effective in their local efforts to reduce and prevent these devastating problems. JTO currently features over 40,000 daily news and fundraising articles, action alerts, resource listings, in-depth feature stories, and other fully searchable documents dating back nearly ten years. You'll find in-depth background information on key issues as well as hands-on tools that show you how to reduce substance abuse and gun violence on a local and national level.

Visit www.jointogetheronline.org to get involved.

TWO KINDS OF FRUIT

⁴³"A good tree does not produce bad fruit, nor does a bad tree produce good fruit. ⁴⁴Each tree is known by its own fruit. People don't gather figs from thornbushes, and they don't get grapes from bushes. ⁴⁵Good people bring good things out of the good they stored in their hearts. But evil people bring evil things out of the evil they stored in their hearts. People speak the things that are in their hearts.

TWO KINDS OF PEOPLE

⁴⁶"Why do you call me, 'Lord, Lord,' but do not do what I say? ⁴⁷I will show you what everyone is like who comes to me and hears my words and obeys. ⁴⁸That person is like a man building a house who dug deep and laid the foundation on rock. When the floods came, the water tried to wash the house away, but it could not shake it, because the house was built well. ⁴⁹But the one who hears my words and does not obey is like a man who built his house on the ground without a foundation. When the floods came, the house quickly fell and was completely destroyed."

JESUS HEALS A SOLDIER'S SERVANT

7 When Jesus finished saying all these things to the people, he went to Capernaum.

²There was an army officer who had a servant who was very important to him. The servant was so sick he was nearly dead. ³When the officer heard about Jesus, he sent some older Jewish leaders to him to ask Jesus to come and heal his servant. ⁴The men went to Jesus and begged him, saying, "This officer is worthy of your help. ⁵He loves our people, and he built us a synagogue."

⁶So Jesus went with the men. He was getting near the officer's house when the officer sent friends to say, "Lord, don't trouble yourself, because I am not worthy to have you come into my house. ⁷That is why I did not come to you myself. But you only need to command it, and my servant will be healed. ⁸I, too, am a man under the authority of others, and I have soldiers under my command. I tell one soldier, 'Go,' and he goes. I tell another soldier, 'Come,' and he comes. I say to my servant, 'Do this,' and my servant does it."

⁹When Jesus heard this, he was amazed. Turning to the crowd that was following him, he said, "I tell you, this is the greatest faith I have found anywhere, even in Israel."

¹⁰Those who had been sent to Jesus went back to the house where they found the servant in good health.

JESUS BRINGS A MAN BACK TO LIFE

¹¹Soon afterwards Jesus went to a town called Nain, and his followers and a large crowd traveled with him. ¹²When he came near the town gate, he saw a funeral. A mother, who was a widow, had lost her only son. A large crowd from the town was with the mother while her son was being carried out. ¹³When the Lord saw her, he felt very sorry for her and said, "Don't cry." ¹⁴He went up and touched the coffin, and the people who were carrying it

stopped. Jesus said, "Young man, I tell you, get up!" [15]And the son sat up and began to talk. Then Jesus gave him back to his mother.

[16]All the people were amazed and began praising God, saying, "A great prophet has come to us! God has come to help his people."

[17]This news about Jesus spread through all Judea and into all the places around there.

JOHN ASKS A QUESTION

[18]John's followers told him about all these things. He called for two of his followers [19]and sent them to the Lord to ask, "Are you the One who is to come, or should we wait for someone else?"

[20]When the men came to Jesus, they said, "John the Baptist sent us to you with this question: 'Are you the One who is to come, or should we wait for someone else?' "

[21]At that time, Jesus healed many people of their sicknesses, diseases, and evil spirits, and he gave sight to many blind people. [22]Then Jesus answered John's followers, "Go tell John what you saw and heard here. The blind can see, the crippled can walk, and people with skin diseases are healed. The deaf can hear, the dead are raised to life, and the Good News is preached to the poor. [23]Those who do not stumble in their faith because of me are blessed!"

[24]When John's followers left, Jesus began talking to the people about John: "What did you go out into the desert to see? A reed[n] blown by the wind? [25]What did you go out to see? A man dressed in fine clothes? No, people who have fine clothes and much wealth live in kings' palaces. [26]But what did you go out to see? A prophet? Yes, and I tell you, John is more than a prophet. [27]This was written about him:

'I will send my messenger ahead of you,
    who will prepare the way
        for you.'   *Malachi 3:1*

[28]I tell you, John is greater than any other person ever born, but even the least important person in the kingdom of God is greater than John."

[29](When the people, including the tax collectors, heard this, they all agreed that God's teaching was good, because they had been baptized by John. [30]But the Pharisees and experts on the law refused to accept God's plan for themselves; they did not let John baptize them.)

[31]Then Jesus said, "What shall I say about

RELATIONSHIPS

"Husbands, love your wives as Christ loved the church and gave himself for it" (Ephesians 5:25). Suppose you want to be a Navy Seal. You'd be insane to think you could go from couch potato to Seal just by signing up. You would dream about it. Plan for it. And show up for duty with six-pack abs. It's the same way with marriage. You won't go from selfish to Jesus-like unselfishness just by standing at the altar. You've got maybe five, ten, or fifteen years to practice laying down your life for the people you love. Then you'll find the right woman and get hitched. And then the real training will start.

BIBLE BASICS

Heaven is where God's throne is. The Bible describes heaven with major symbols like streets of gold and gates of rubies, sapphires, and diamonds. It's a beautiful place with no sadness, death, sin, or suffering. God's children will live there forever with God. (Hard to imagine, isn't it?) It will be over the top!

the people of this time? What are they like? [32]They are like children sitting in the marketplace, calling to one another and saying,

'We played music for you, but you did not
    dance;
    we sang a sad song, but you did not cry.'

[33]John the Baptist came and did not eat bread or drink wine, and you say, 'He has a demon in him.' [34]The Son of Man came eating and drinking, and you say, 'Look at him! He eats too much and drinks too much wine, and he is a friend of

7:24 reed It means that John was not ordinary or weak like grass blown by the wind.

tax collectors and sinners!' [35]But wisdom is proved to be right by what it does."

A WOMAN WASHES JESUS' FEET

[36]One of the Pharisees asked Jesus to eat with him, so Jesus went into the Pharisee's house and sat at the table. [37]A sinful woman in the town learned that Jesus was eating at the Pharisee's house. So she brought an alabaster jar of perfume [38]and stood behind Jesus at his feet, crying. She began to wash his feet with her tears, and she dried them with her hair, kissing them many times and rubbing them with the perfume. [39]When the Pharisee who asked Jesus to come to his house saw this, he thought to himself, "If Jesus were a prophet, he would know that the woman touching him is a sinner!"

[40]Jesus said to the Pharisee, "Simon, I have something to say to you."

Simon said, "Teacher, tell me."

[41]Jesus said, "Two people owed money to the same banker. One owed five hundred coins[n] and the other owed fifty. [42]They had no money to pay what they owed, but the banker told both of them they did not have to pay him. Which person will love the banker more?"

[43]Simon, the Pharisee, answered, "I think it would be the one who owed him the most money."

Jesus said to Simon, "You are right." [44]Then Jesus turned toward the woman and said to Simon, "Do you see this woman? When I came into your house, you gave me no water for my feet, but she washed my feet with her tears and dried them with her hair. [45]You gave me no kiss of greeting, but she has been kissing my feet since I came in. [46]You did not put oil on my head, but she poured perfume on my feet. [47]I tell you that her many sins are forgiven, so she showed great love. But the person who is forgiven only a little will love only a little."

[48]Then Jesus said to her, "Your sins are forgiven."

[49]The people sitting at the table began to say among themselves, "Who is this who even forgives sins?"

[50]Jesus said to the woman, "Because you believed, you are saved from your sins. Go in peace."

THE GROUP WITH JESUS

8 After this, while Jesus was traveling through some cities and small towns, he preached and told the Good News about God's kingdom. The twelve apostles were with him, [2]and also some women who had been healed of sicknesses and evil spirits: Mary, called Magdalene, from whom seven demons had gone out; [3]Joanna, the wife of Cuza (the manager of Herod's house); Susanna; and many others. These women used their own money to help Jesus and his apostles.

A STORY ABOUT PLANTING SEED

[4]When a great crowd was gathered, and people were coming to Jesus from every town, he told them this story:

[5]"A farmer went out to plant his seed. While he was planting, some seed fell by the road. People walked on the seed, and the birds ate it up. [6]Some seed fell on rock, and when it began to grow, it

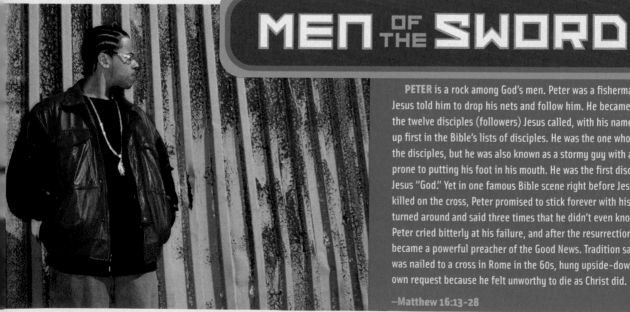

MEN OF THE SWORD

PETER is a rock among God's men. Peter was a fisherman when Jesus told him to drop his nets and follow him. He became leader of the twelve disciples (followers) Jesus called, with his name showing up first in the Bible's lists of disciples. He was the one who spoke for the disciples, but he was also known as a stormy guy with a temper, prone to putting his foot in his mouth. He was the first disciple to call Jesus "God." Yet in one famous Bible scene right before Jesus was killed on the cross, Peter promised to stick forever with his Lord—then turned around and said three times that he didn't even know Jesus. Peter cried bitterly at his failure, and after the resurrection of Jesus became a powerful preacher of the Good News. Tradition says Peter was nailed to a cross in Rome in the 60s, hung upside-down at his own request because he felt unworthy to die as Christ did.

—Matthew 16:13-28

 7:41 coins Roman denarii. One coin was the average pay for one day's work.

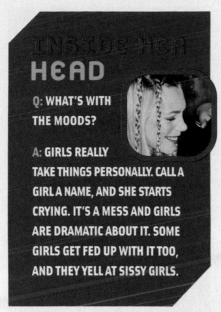
died because it had no water. [7]Some seed fell among thorny weeds, but the weeds grew up with it and choked the good plants. [8]And some seed fell on good ground and grew and made a hundred times more."

As Jesus finished the story, he called out, "You people who can hear me, listen!"

[9]Jesus' followers asked him what this story meant.

[10]Jesus said, "You have been chosen to know the secrets about the kingdom of God. But I use stories to speak to other people so that:

'They will look, but they may not see.
They will listen, but they may not
understand.'   *Isaiah 6:9*

[11]"This is what the story means: The seed is God's message. [12]The seed that fell beside the road is like the people who hear God's teaching, but the devil comes and takes it away from them so they cannot believe it and be saved. [13]The seed that fell on rock is like those who hear God's teaching and accept it gladly, but they don't allow the teaching to go deep into their lives. They believe for a while, but when trouble comes, they give up. [14]The seed that fell among the thorny weeds is like those who hear God's

teaching, but they let the worries, riches, and pleasures of this life keep them from growing and producing good fruit. [15]And the seed that fell on the good ground is like those who hear God's teaching with good, honest hearts and obey it and patiently produce good fruit.

USE WHAT YOU HAVE

[16]"No one after lighting a lamp covers it with a bowl or hides it under a bed. Instead, the person puts it on a lampstand so those who come in will see the light. [17]Everything that is hidden will become clear, and every secret thing will be made known. [18]So be careful how you listen. Those who have understanding will be given more. But those who do not have understanding, even what they think they have will be taken away from them."

JESUS' TRUE FAMILY

[19]Jesus' mother and brothers came to see him, but there was such a crowd they could not get to him. [20]Someone said to Jesus, "Your mother and your brothers are standing outside, wanting to see you."

[21]Jesus answered them, "My mother and my brothers are those who listen to God's teaching and obey it!"

JESUS CALMS A STORM

[22]One day Jesus and his followers got into a boat, and he said to them, "Let's go across the lake." And so they started across. [23]While they were sailing, Jesus fell asleep. A very strong wind blew up on the lake, causing the boat to fill with water, and they were in danger.

[24]The followers went to Jesus and woke him, saying, "Master! Master! We will drown!"

Jesus got up and gave a command to the wind and the waves. They stopped, and it became calm. [25]Jesus said to his followers, "Where is your faith?"

The followers were afraid and amazed and said to each other, "Who is this that commands even the wind and the water, and they obey him?"

A MAN WITH DEMONS INSIDE HIM

[26]Jesus and his followers sailed across the lake from Galilee to the area of the Gerasene people. [27]When Jesus got out on the land, a man from the town who had demons inside him came to Jesus. For a long time he had worn no clothes and had lived in the burial caves, not in a house. [28]When he saw Jesus, he cried out and fell down before him. He said with a loud voice, "What do you want with me, Jesus, Son of the Most High God? I beg you, don't torture me!" [29]He said this because Jesus was commanding the evil spirit to come out of the man. Many times it had taken hold of him. Though he had been kept under guard and chained hand and foot, he had broken his chains and had been forced by the demon out into a lonely place.

FOUR IN TEN TEENS LIVE IN A HOME WHERE THE TV SET IS ON IN THE BACKGROUND MOST OF THE TIME—EVEN WHEN NO ONE IS WATCHING. –KAISER FAMILY FOUNDATION

HOW TO SUCK A LEMON WITHOUT SCREWING UP YOUR FACE

Your tastebuds that sense sour foods reside on the sides of your tongue, about halfway back. So if you're in lemon-sucking contest of who-can-last-the-longest-without-making-a-face, keep the lemon slice at the tip of your tongue (the part that senses sweet) or way at the back (the part for tasting bitter). Then you just have to tough out whatever juice slurps over to the side of your tongue. It's like life. There's nothing wrong with avoiding sour stuff. But there's always some sourness that will seep in. You just have to deal with it. Still, there's good news. While no one can take a lemon on the tongue for you, in the tough stuff of life God is with you always.

[30]Jesus asked him, "What is your name?"

He answered, "Legion,"[n] because many demons were in him. [31]The demons begged Jesus not to send them into eternal darkness.[n]

[32]A large herd of pigs was feeding on a hill, and the demons begged Jesus to allow them to go into the pigs. So Jesus allowed them to do this. [33]When the demons came out of the man, they went into the pigs, and the herd ran down the hill into the lake and was drowned.

[34]When the herdsmen saw what had happened, they ran away and told about this in the town and the countryside. [35]And people went to see what had happened. When they came to Jesus, they found the man sitting at Jesus' feet, clothed and in his right mind, because the demons were gone. But the people were frightened. [36]The people who saw this happen told the others how Jesus had made the man well. [37]All the people of the Gerasene country asked Jesus to leave, because they were all very afraid. So Jesus got into the boat and went back to Galilee.

[38]The man whom Jesus had healed begged to go with him, but Jesus sent him away, saying, [39]"Go back home and tell people how much God has done for you." So the man went all over town telling how much Jesus had done for him.

JESUS GIVES LIFE TO A DEAD GIRL AND HEALS A SICK WOMAN

[40]When Jesus got back to Galilee, a crowd welcomed him, because everyone was waiting for him. [41]A man named Jairus, a leader of the synagogue, came to Jesus and fell at his feet, begging him to come to his house. [42]Jairus' only daughter, about twelve years old, was dying.

While Jesus was on his way to Jairus' house, the people were crowding all around him. [43]A woman was in the crowd who had been bleeding for twelve years, but no one was able to heal her. [44]She came up behind Jesus and touched the edge of his coat, and instantly her bleeding stopped. [45]Then Jesus said, "Who touched me?"

When all the people said they had not touched him, Peter said, "Master, the people are all around you and are pushing against you."

[46]But Jesus said, "Someone did touch me, because I felt power go out from me." [47]When the woman saw she could not hide, she came forward, shaking, and fell down before Jesus. While all the people listened, she told why she had touched him and how she had been instantly healed. [48]Jesus said to her, "Dear woman, you are made well because you believed. Go in peace."

RADICAL FAITH:
Luke 9:32

Can you imagine waking up and seeing Jesus in his glory? Wow! That would be something—to see the all-powerful and majestic One right there beside you when you wake up!

The fact is, we do serve a glorious God and we have the opportunity to wake up every morning and see "his glory." That's why it's so important to reach over, grab the Word of God, and meditate on it every morning. It gets our thinking headed in the right direction. If we aren't reminded of the glory and power of God every morning, it can be so easy to get caught up in our everyday affairs to the point that we forget that the "all-powerful One" is right beside us!

One thing that will bring us into the presence of his glory is to simply praise the Lord for who he is.

He's our safe place and our strong place. He's a tower in which we can hide from our enemy. In him we are more than winners. He's the glorious God who is more than enough.

Take time to think about the Lord's glory every day. He is the One who is glorious!

 8:30 "Legion" Means very many. A legion was about five thousand men in the Roman army. 8:31 eternal darkness Literally, "the abyss," something like a pit or a hole that has no end.

Easter falls on the first Sunday following the first full moon that occurs on or after March 21—the vernal equinox. No wonder no one ever knows when it falls. Note that it can never today happen before March 22 or after April 25.

APRIL

1

April is National Anxiety Month. Cast all your cares on God, because he cares for you.

2

Eat like a little kid. It's Peanut Butter and Jelly Day.

3

4

Pray for a Person of Influence: Dave Mirra cranks out another birthday today.

5

Pray for a Person of Influence: Colin Powell celebrates his birthday today.

6

7

Pray for a Person of Influence: Russell Crowe gets older today.

8

Yesterday was No Housework Day. Sorry you missed it.

9

10

Resolve today not to blow off the end of the school year.

11

12 ✓

It's National Stress Awareness Day. It's also National Eggs Benedict Day. Take your pick.

13

Go for a walk with your parents to celebrate spring.

14

15

16

17

18

19

Shock your parents by cleaning out the garage.

20

Read the Book of Galatians today and thank God that getting right with him is a gift.

21

Talk to your parents about how they want you to spend your summer.

22

23

Today is World Laboratory Animal Day. Read the back of your shampoo bottle to see if it says, "Not tested on animals."

24

25

26

27

Talk to your parents about your future.

28

Do something really nice today for a girl—like your sister.

29

The weather is heating up—put powder in your shoes today.

30

Daylight Saving Time is the first weekend in April. Turn your clocks forward one hour!

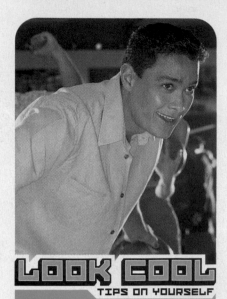

LOOK COOL
TIPS ON YOURSELF

Want a cheap and easy way to a cool smile? Yeah, brush at least twice a day. But don't forget to floss. Doing both rids your mouth of millions of acid-producing bacteria that attack your teeth and eat into tooth enamel. More importantly, they spew the sulfur compounds that cause bad breath. Brushing gets rid of 65% of these nasties, but you need to floss to take care of the other 35%. Some researchers say that flossing even lowers your risk of heart disease. Like the dentist says: You should only floss the teeth you want to keep. It's like lots of areas of life: A little effort yields big results. Go all out.

49While Jesus was still speaking, someone came from the house of the synagogue leader and said to him, "Your daughter is dead. Don't bother the teacher anymore."

50When Jesus heard this, he said to Jairus, "Don't be afraid. Just believe, and your daughter will be well."

51When Jesus went to the house, he let only Peter, John, James, and the girl's father and mother go inside with him. 52All the people were crying and feeling sad because the girl was dead, but Jesus said, "Stop crying. She is not dead, only asleep."

53The people laughed at Jesus because they knew the girl was dead. 54But Jesus took hold of her hand and called to her, "My child, stand up!" 55Her spirit came back into her, and she stood up at once. Then Jesus ordered that she be given something to eat. 56The girl's parents were amazed, but Jesus told them not to tell anyone what had happened.

JESUS SENDS OUT THE APOSTLES

9 Jesus called the twelve apostles together and gave them power and authority over all demons and the ability to heal sicknesses. 2He sent the apostles out to tell about God's kingdom and to heal the sick. 3He said to them, "Take nothing for your trip, neither a walking stick, bag, bread, money, or extra clothes. 4When you enter a house, stay there until it is time to leave. 5If people do not welcome you, shake the dust off of your feet[n] as you leave the town, as a warning to them."

6So the apostles went out and traveled through all the towns, preaching the Good News and healing people everywhere.

HEROD IS CONFUSED ABOUT JESUS

7Herod, the governor, heard about all the things that were happening and was confused, because some people said, "John the Baptist has risen from the dead." 8Others said, "Elijah has come to us." And still others said, "One of the prophets who lived long ago has risen from the dead." 9Herod said, "I cut off John's head, so who is this man I hear such things about?" And Herod kept trying to see Jesus.

MORE THAN FIVE THOUSAND FED

10When the apostles returned, they told Jesus everything they had done. Then Jesus took them with him to a town called Bethsaida where they could be alone together. 11But the people learned where Jesus went and followed him. He welcomed them and talked with them about God's kingdom and healed those who needed to be healed.

12Late in the afternoon, the twelve apostles came to Jesus and said, "Send the people away. They need to go to the towns and countryside around here and find places to sleep and something to eat, because no one lives in this place."

13But Jesus said to them, "You give them something to eat."

They said, "We have only five loaves of bread and two fish, unless we go buy food for all these people." 14(There were about five thousand men there.)

Jesus said to his followers, "Tell the people to sit in groups of about fifty people."

15So the followers did this, and all the people sat down. 16Then Jesus took the five loaves of bread and two fish, and looking up to heaven, he thanked God for the food. Then he divided the food and gave it to the followers to give to the people. 17They all ate and were satisfied, and what was left over was gathered up, filling twelve baskets.

JESUS IS THE CHRIST

18One time when Jesus was praying alone, his followers were with him, and he asked them, "Who do the people say I am?"

19They answered, "Some say you are John the Baptist. Others say you are Elijah.[n] And others say you are one of the prophets from long ago who has come back to life."

20Then Jesus asked, "But who do you say I am?"

Peter answered, "You are the Christ from God."

21Jesus warned them not to tell anyone, saying, 22"The Son of Man must suffer many things. He will be rejected by the older Jewish leaders, the leading priests, and the teachers of the law. He will be killed and after three days will be raised from the dead."

23Jesus said to all of them, "If people want to follow me, they must give up the things

WAYS TO WALK THE WALK

Luke 12:31

WORD: God will take care of you when you put him first.

WALK IT: Challenge yourself to get your homework done so you can go to church and hang with your friends without worry.

9:5 shake . . . feet A warning. It showed that they had rejected these people.   9:19 Elijah A man who spoke for God and who lived hundreds of years before Christ. See 1 Kings 17.

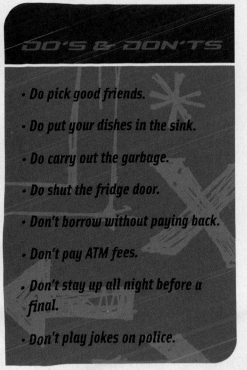
they want. They must be willing to give up their lives daily to follow me. [24]Those who want to save their lives will give up true life. But those who give up their lives for me will have true life. [25]It is worth nothing for them to have the whole world if they themselves are destroyed or lost. [26]If people are ashamed of me and my teaching, then the Son of Man will be ashamed of them when he comes in his glory and with the glory of the Father and the holy angels. [27]I tell you the truth, some people standing here will see the kingdom of God before they die."

JESUS TALKS WITH MOSES AND ELIJAH

[28]About eight days after Jesus said these things, he took Peter, John, and James and went up on a mountain to pray. [29]While Jesus was praying, the appearance of his face changed, and his clothes became shining white. [30]Then two men, Moses and Elijah,[n] were talking with Jesus. [31]They appeared in heavenly glory, talking about his departure which he would soon bring about in Jerusalem. [32]Peter and the others were very sleepy, but when they awoke fully, they saw the glory of Jesus and the two men standing with him. [33]When Moses and Elijah were about to leave, Peter said to Jesus, "Master, it is good that

we are here. Let us make three tents—one for you, one for Moses, and one for Elijah." (Peter did not know what he was talking about.)

[34]While he was saying these things, a cloud came and covered them, and they became afraid as the cloud covered them. [35]A voice came from the cloud, saying, "This is my Son, whom I have chosen. Listen to him!"

[36]When the voice finished speaking, only Jesus was there. Peter, John, and James said nothing and told no one at that time what they had seen.

JESUS HEALS A SICK BOY

[37]The next day, when they came down from the mountain, a large crowd met Jesus. [38]A man in the crowd shouted to him, "Teacher, please come and look at my son, because he is my only child. [39]An evil spirit seizes my son, and suddenly he screams. It causes him to lose control of himself and foam at the mouth. The evil spirit keeps on hurting him and almost never leaves him. [40]I begged your followers to force the evil spirit out, but they could not do it."

[41]Jesus answered, "You people have no faith, and your lives are all wrong. How long must I stay with you and put up with you? Bring your son here."

[42]While the boy was coming, the demon threw him on the ground and made him lose

control of himself. But Jesus gave a strong command to the evil spirit and healed the boy and gave him back to his father. [43]All the people were amazed at the great power of God.

JESUS TALKS ABOUT HIS DEATH

While everyone was wondering about all that Jesus did, he said to his followers, [44]"Don't forget what I tell you now: The Son of Man will be handed over to people." [45]But the followers did not understand what this meant; the meaning was hidden from them so they could not understand. But they were afraid to ask Jesus about it.

WHO IS THE GREATEST?

[46]Jesus' followers began to have an argument about which one of them was the greatest. [47]Jesus knew what they were thinking, so he took a little child and stood the child beside him. [48]Then Jesus said, "Whoever accepts this little child in my name accepts me. And whoever accepts me accepts the One who sent me, because whoever is least among you all is really the greatest."

ANYONE NOT AGAINST US IS FOR US

[49]John answered, "Master, we saw someone using your name to force demons out of people. We told him to stop, because he does not belong to our group."

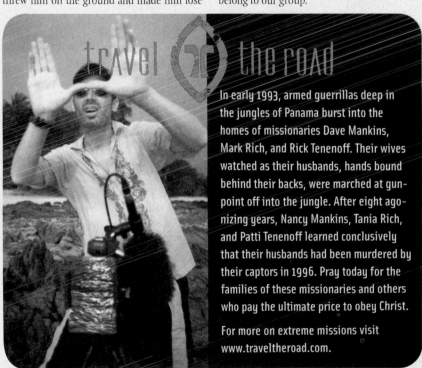

travel the road

In early 1993, armed guerrillas deep in the jungles of Panama burst into the homes of missionaries Dave Mankins, Mark Rich, and Rick Tenenoff. Their wives watched as their husbands, hands bound behind their backs, were marched at gunpoint off into the jungle. After eight agonizing years, Nancy Mankins, Tania Rich, and Patti Tenenoff learned conclusively that their husbands had been murdered by their captors in 1996. Pray today for the families of these missionaries and others who pay the ultimate price to obey Christ.

For more on extreme missions visit www.traveltheroad.com.

 9:30 **Moses and Elijah** Two of the most important Jewish leaders in the past. God had given Moses the Law, and Elijah was an important prophet.

HOW TO CARE FOR SPRAINED ANKLE

Sprains happen when you torque a joint, stretching or tearing the ligaments that hold your bones together. The sprain causes pain, tenderness, swelling, and bruising. While a coach might yell at you to walk it off, a real sprain will keep you off your feet for at least 24 hours. Care for your sprain the right way: Reduce swelling by elevating your ankle and icing it for 15 minutes an hour the first day or two. Use crutches until you can put weight on your ankle without pain. Apply mild heat after a couple days to ease the ache. Don't dodge the doctor if there's any question of a break—and call right away if the pain or swelling gets worse, your toes feel numb or cold, or those toesies turn blue or gray. Nursing a sprain is like other pains in life. You need the right kind of care to mend.

[50]But Jesus said to him, "Don't stop him, because whoever is not against you is for you."

A TOWN REJECTS JESUS

[51]When the time was coming near for Jesus to depart, he was determined to go to Jerusalem. [52]He sent some men ahead of him, who went into a town in Samaria to make everything ready for him. [53]But the people there would not welcome him, because he was set on going to Jerusalem. [54]When James and John, followers of Jesus, saw this, they said, "Lord, do you want us to call fire down from heaven and destroy those people?"[n]

[55]But Jesus turned and scolded them. [56]Then[n] they went to another town.

FOLLOWING JESUS

[57]As they were going along the road, someone said to Jesus, "I will follow you any place you go."

[58]Jesus said to them, "The foxes have holes to live in, and the birds have nests, but the Son of Man has no place to rest his head."

[59]Jesus said to another man, "Follow me!"

But he said, "Lord, first let me go and bury my father."

[60]But Jesus said to him, "Let the people who are dead bury their own dead. You must go and tell about the kingdom of God."

[61]Another man said, "I will follow you, Lord, but first let me go and say good-bye to my family."

[62]Jesus said, "Anyone who begins to plow a field but keeps looking back is of no use in the kingdom of God."

JESUS SENDS OUT THE SEVENTY-TWO

10 After this, the Lord chose seventy-two[n] others and sent them out in pairs ahead of him into every town and place where he planned to go. [2]He said to them, "There are a great many people to harvest, but there are only a few workers. So pray to God, who owns the harvest, that he will send more workers to help gather his harvest. [3]Go now, but listen! I am sending you out like sheep among wolves. [4]Don't carry a purse, a bag, or sandals, and don't waste time talking with people on the road. [5]Before you go into a house, say, 'Peace be with this house.' [6]If peaceful people live there, your blessing of peace will stay with them, but if not, then your blessing will come back to you. [7]Stay in the peaceful house, eating and drinking what the people there give you. A worker should be given his pay. Don't move from house to house. [8]If you go into a town and the people welcome you, eat what they give you. [9]Heal the sick who live there, and tell them, 'The kingdom of God is near you.' [10]But if you go into a town, and the people don't welcome you, then go into the streets and say, [11]'Even the dirt from your town that sticks to our feet we wipe off against you.'[n] But remember that the kingdom of God is near.' [12]I tell you, on the Judgment Day it will be better for the people of Sodom[n] than for the people of that town.

2 TIMOTHY 4:17 "THE LORD STAYED WITH ME AND GAVE ME STRENGTH SO I COULD FULLY TELL THE GOOD NEWS."

JESUS WARNS UNBELIEVERS

[13]"How terrible for you, Korazin! How terrible for you, Bethsaida! If the miracles I did in you had happened in Tyre and Sidon,[n] those people would have changed their lives long ago. They would have worn rough cloth and put ashes on themselves to show they had changed. [14]But on the Judgment Day it will be better for Tyre and Sidon than for you. [15]And you, Capernaum,[n] will you be lifted up to heaven? No! You will be thrown down to the depths!

[16]"Whoever listens to you listens to me, and whoever refuses to accept you refuses to accept me. And whoever refuses to accept me refuses to accept the One who sent me."

SATAN FALLS

[17]When the seventy-two[n] came back, they were very happy and said, "Lord, even the demons obeyed us when we used your name!"

[18]Jesus said, "I saw Satan fall like lightning from heaven. [19]Listen, I have given you power to walk on snakes and scorpions, power that is greater than the enemy has. So nothing will hurt you. [20]But you should not be happy because the spirits obey you but because your names are written in heaven."

JESUS PRAYS TO THE FATHER

[21]Then Jesus rejoiced in the Holy Spirit and said, "I praise you, Father, Lord of heaven and earth, because you have hidden these things

9:54 Verse 54 Here, some Greek copies add: ". . . as Elijah did." **9:55-56 Verses 55-56** Some copies read: "But Jesus turned and scolded them. And Jesus said, 'You don't know what kind of spirit you belong to. [56]The Son of Man did not come to destroy the souls of people but to save them.' Then. . . ." **10:1 seventy-two** Many Greek copies read seventy. **10:11 dirt . . . you** A warning. It showed that they had rejected these people. **10:12 Sodom** City that God destroyed because the people were so evil. **10:13 Tyre and Sidon** Towns where wicked people lived. **10:13, 15 Korazin, Bethsaida, Capernaum** Towns by Lake Galilee where Jesus preached to the people. **10:17 seventy-two** Many Greek copies read seventy.

104

EXPERTS ANSWER YOUR QUESTIONS

Q. *What does God think of the Internet?*

A. Doubtless the same thing he thinks about knives, guns, and drugs, all things that can be used for good or evil. On one hand, Internet porn has become a business worth an untidy $10 billion a year. On the other, people can use the Net for work and fun, to stay tight with friends and family, and even spread the Good News to places missionaries aren't allowed to go to.

Q. *I've had a foul mouth since second grade. I want to stop. What can I do?*

A. Cussing is a habit, so it can help to engage your brain by stopping to count to three before you speak. But it's also a heart problem. Your mouth usually gushes what's going on inside you. So you have to deal with your core issues. Are you angry? Trying too hard to be funny? Aiming to be cool? Whatever causes you to cuss, talk to God about it.

---

from the people who are wise and smart. But you have shown them to those who are like little children. Yes, Father, this is what you really wanted.

²²"My Father has given me all things. No one knows who the Son is, except the Father. And no one knows who the Father is, except the Son and those whom the Son chooses to tell."

²³Then Jesus turned to his followers and said privately, "You are blessed to see what you now see. ²⁴I tell you, many prophets and kings wanted to see what you now see, but they did not, and they wanted to hear what you now hear, but they did not."

THE GOOD SAMARITAN

²⁵Then an expert on the law stood up to test Jesus, saying, "Teacher, what must I do to get life forever?"

²⁶Jesus said, "What is written in the law? What do you read there?"

²⁷The man answered, "Love the Lord your God with all your heart, all your soul, all your strength, and all your mind."ⁿ Also, "Love your neighbor as you love yourself."ⁿ

²⁸Jesus said to him, "Your answer is right. Do this and you will live."

²⁹But the man, wanting to show the importance of his question, said to Jesus, "And who is my neighbor?"

³⁰Jesus answered, "As a man was going down from Jerusalem to Jericho, some robbers attacked him. They tore off his clothes, beat him, and left him lying there, almost dead. ³¹It happened that a priest was going down that road. When he saw the man, he walked by on the other side. ³²Next, a Leviteⁿ came there, and after he went over and looked at the man, he walked by on the other side of the road. ³³Then a Samaritanⁿ traveling down the road came to where the hurt man was. When he saw the man, he felt very sorry for him. ³⁴The Samaritan went to him, poured olive oil and wineⁿ on his wounds, and bandaged them. Then he put the hurt man on his own donkey and took him to an inn where he cared for him. ³⁵The next day, the Samaritan brought out two coins,ⁿ gave them to the innkeeper, and said, 'Take care of this man. If you spend more money on him, I will pay it back to you when I come again.' "

RANDOM PSYCHE-UP SONGS

1. "ADONAI" (O.C. SUPERTONES)
2. "IRENE" (TOBY MAC)
3. "LIQUID" (JARS OF CLAY)
4. "DIVE" (STEVEN CURTIS CHAPMAN)
5. "BASIC INSTRUCTIONS" (BURLAP TO CASHMERE)
6. "ALIVE" (P.O.D.)
7. "HANGING BY A MOMENT" (LIGHTHOUSE)
8. "PRESSING ON" (RELIENT K)
9. "THE DEVIL IS BAD" (THE W'S)
10. "CONSUMING FIRE" (THIRD DAY)

---

³⁶Then Jesus said, "Which one of these three men do you think was a neighbor to the man who was attacked by the robbers?"

³⁷The expert on the law answered, "The one who showed him mercy."

Jesus said to him, "Then go and do what he did."

MARY AND MARTHA

³⁸While Jesus and his followers were traveling, Jesus went into a town. A woman named Martha let Jesus stay at her house. ³⁹Martha had a sister named Mary, who was sitting at Jesus' feet and listening to him teach. ⁴⁰But Martha was busy with all the work to be done. She went in and said, "Lord, don't you care that my sister has left me alone to do all the work? Tell her to help me."

⁴¹But the Lord answered her, "Martha, Martha, you are worried and upset about

---

10:27 "Love . . . mind." Quotation from Deuteronomy 6:5.   10:27 "Love . . . yourself." Quotation from Leviticus 19:18.   10:32 Levite Levites were members of the tribe of Levi who helped the Jewish priests with their work in the Temple. Read 1 Chronicles 23:24-32.   10:33 Samaritan Samaritans were people from Samaria. These people were part Jewish, but the Jews did not accept them as true Jews. Samaritans and Jews disliked each other.   10:34 olive oil and wine Oil and wine were used like medicine to soften and clean wounds.   10:35 coins Roman denarii. One coin was the average pay for one day's work.

issues
SEXUALLY TRANSMITTED DISEASES

IF YOUR BRAIN AND BODY need a good reason to stay sexually pure, ponder the explosion of sexually transmitted diseases. STDs spread person-to-person through close sexual touching, by intercourse as well as other kinds of sexual contact. The Centers for Disease Control and Prevention say that 12 million Americans get a new STD each year. That's 33,000 people a day, some 22,000 of them between 15 and 24 years old! In fact, a whopping 25 percent of high-school students will be infected with an STD before graduation. So get these facts:

(1) STDs spread easily. (2) STDs can catch anyone, because you can't spot them just by looking. (3) STDs can be impossible to treat. (4) STDs can kill you—or worse. While AIDS/HIV can end your life other STDs can leave you infertile or permanently disabled. Herpes creates sores that live on your mouth or way down in your boxers. And you don't even want to know where cauliflower-like genital warts can grow.

many things. [42]Only one thing is important. Mary has chosen the better thing, and it will never be taken away from her."

JESUS TEACHES ABOUT PRAYER

11 One time Jesus was praying in a certain place. When he finished, one of his followers said to him, "Lord, teach us to pray as John taught his followers."

[2]Jesus said to them, "When you pray, say:
'Father, may your name always be kept holy.
May your kingdom come.

[3] Give us the food we need for each day.

[4] Forgive us for our sins,
because we forgive everyone who has done wrong to us.
And do not cause us to be tempted.' "

CONTINUE TO ASK

[5]Then Jesus said to them, "Suppose one of you went to your friend's house at midnight and said to him, 'Friend, loan me three loaves of bread. [6]A friend of mine has come into town to visit me, but I have nothing for him to eat.' [7]Your friend inside the house answers, 'Don't bother me! The door is already locked, and my children and I are in bed. I cannot get up and give you anything.' [8]I tell you, if friendship is not enough to make him get up to give you the bread, your boldness will make him get up and give you whatever you need. [9]So I tell you, ask, and God will give to you. Search, and you will find. Knock, and the door will open for you. [10]Yes, everyone who asks will receive. The one who searches will find. And everyone who knocks will have the door opened. [11]If

the man who had been unable to speak, then spoke. The people were amazed. [15]But some of them said, "Jesus uses the power of Beelzebul, the ruler of demons, to force demons out of people."

[16]Other people, wanting to test Jesus, asked him to give them a sign from heaven. [17]But knowing their thoughts, he said to them, "Every kingdom that is divided against itself will be destroyed. And a family that is divided against itself will not continue. [18]So if Satan is divided against himself, his kingdom will not continue. You say that I use the power of Beelzebul to force out demons. [19]But if I use the power of Beelzebul to force out demons, what power do your people use to force demons out? So they will be your judges. [20]But if I use the power of God to force out demons, then the kingdom of God has come to you.

[21]"When a strong person with many weapons guards his own house, his possessions are safe. [22]But when someone stronger comes and defeats him, the stronger one will take away the weapons the first man trusted and will give away the possessions.

[23]"Anyone who is not with me is against me, and anyone who does not work with me is working against me.

THE EMPTY PERSON

[24]"When an evil spirit comes out of a person, it travels through dry places, looking for a place to rest. But when it finds no place, it says, 'I will go back to the house I left.' [25]And when it comes back, it finds that house swept clean and made neat. [26]Then the evil spirit

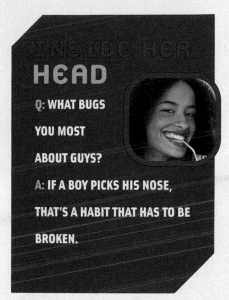

THE PEOPLE WANT A MIRACLE

[29]As the crowd grew larger, Jesus said, "The people who live today are evil. They want to see a miracle for a sign, but no sign will be given them, except the sign of Jonah.[n] [30]As Jonah was a sign for those people who lived in Nineveh, the Son of Man will be a sign for the people of this time. [31]On the Judgment Day the Queen of the South[n] will stand up with the people who live now. She will show they are guilty, because she came from far away to listen to Solomon's wise teaching. And I tell you that someone greater than Solomon is here. [32]On the Judgment Day the people of Nineveh will stand up with the people who live now, and they will show that you are guilty. When

your children ask for a fish, which of you would give them a snake instead? [12]Or, if your children ask for an egg, would you give them a scorpion? [13]Even though you are bad, you know how to give good things to your children. How much more your heavenly Father will give the Holy Spirit to those who ask him!"

JESUS' POWER IS FROM GOD

[14]One time Jesus was sending out a demon that could not talk. When the demon came out,

goes out and brings seven other spirits more evil than it is, and they go in and live there. So the person has even more trouble than before."

PEOPLE WHO ARE TRULY HAPPY

[27]As Jesus was saying these things, a woman in the crowd called out to Jesus, "Happy is the mother who gave birth to you and nursed you."

[28]But Jesus said, "No, happy are those who hear the teaching of God and obey it."

Jonah preached to them, they were sorry and changed their lives. And I tell you that someone greater than Jonah is here.

BE A LIGHT FOR THE WORLD

[33]"No one lights a lamp and puts it in a secret place or under a bowl, but on a lampstand so the people who come in can see. [34]Your eye is a light for the body. When your eyes are good, your whole body will be full of light. But when your eyes are evil, your whole body will be full of darkness. [35]So be careful

11:29 **sign of Jonah** Jonah's three days in the fish are like Jesus' three days in the tomb. See Matthew 12:40.   11:31 **Queen of the South** The Queen of Sheba. She traveled a thousand miles to learn God's wisdom from Solomon. Read 1 Kings 10:1–3.

not to let the light in you become darkness. [36]If your whole body is full of light, and none of it is dark, then you will shine bright, as when a lamp shines on you."

JESUS ACCUSES THE PHARISEES

[37]After Jesus had finished speaking, a Pharisee asked Jesus to eat with him. So Jesus went in and sat at the table. [38]But the Pharisee was surprised when he saw that Jesus did not wash

PSALM 33:18 "BUT THE LORD LOOKS AFTER THOSE WHO FEAR HIM, THOSE WHO PUT THEIR HOPE IN HIS LOVE."

his hands[n] before the meal. [39]The Lord said to him, "You Pharisees clean the outside of the cup and the dish, but inside you are full of greed and evil. [40]You foolish people! The same one who made what is outside also made what is inside. [41]So give what is in your dishes to the poor, and then you will be fully clean. [42]How terrible for you Pharisees! You give God one-tenth of even your mint, your rue, and every other plant in your garden. But you fail to be fair to others and to love God. These are the things you should do while continuing to do those other things. [43]How terrible for you Pharisees, because you love to have the most important seats in the synagogues, and you love to be greeted with respect in the marketplaces. [44]How terrible for you, because you are like hidden graves, which people walk on without knowing."

JESUS TALKS TO EXPERTS ON THE LAW

[45]One of the experts on the law said to Jesus, "Teacher, when you say these things, you are insulting us, too."

[46]Jesus answered, "How terrible for you, you experts on the law! You make strict rules

that are very hard for people to obey, but you yourselves don't even try to follow those rules. [47]How terrible for you, because you build tombs for the prophets whom your ancestors killed! [48]And now you show that you approve of what your ancestors did. They killed the prophets, and you build tombs for them! [49]This is why in his wisdom God said, 'I will send prophets and apostles to them. They will kill some, and they will treat others cruelly.' [50]So you who live now will be punished for the deaths of all the prophets who were killed since the beginning of the world— [51]from the killing of Abel to the killing of Zechariah,[n] who died between the altar and the Temple. Yes, I tell you that you who are alive now will be punished for them all.

[52]"How terrible for you, you experts on the law. You have taken away the key to learning about God. You yourselves would not learn, and you stopped others from learning, too."

[53]When Jesus left, the teachers of the law and the Pharisees began to give him trouble, asking him questions about many things, [54]trying to catch him saying something wrong.

DON'T BE LIKE THE PHARISEES

12 So many thousands of people had gathered that they were stepping on each other. Jesus spoke first to his followers, saying, "Beware of the yeast of the Pharisees, because they are hypocrites. [2]Everything that is hidden will be shown, and everything that is secret will be made known. [3]What you have said in the dark will be heard in the light, and what you have whispered in an inner room will be shouted from the housetops.

[4]"I tell you, my friends, don't be afraid of people who can kill the body but after that can do nothing more to hurt you. [5]I will show you

MELLOW AFTERSCHOOL TUNES

1. "PATIENCE" (BLEACH)

2. "HOLINESS" (SONICFLOOD)

3. "OCEAN FLOOR" (AUDIO ADRENALINE)

4. "TWO SETS OF JONESES" (BIG TENT REVIVAL)

5. "INVESTIGATE" (DELIRIOUS?)

6. "HYMN" (DAN HASELTINE)

7. "I CAN ONLY IMAGINE" (MERCYME)

8. "THIS WORLD" (CAEDMON'S CALL)

9. "HOLY ONE" (MARK SCHULTZ/CHRIS RICE)

10. "AGNUS DEI" (MICHAEL W. SMITH)

the one to fear. Fear the one who has the power to kill you and also to throw you into hell. Yes, this is the one you should fear.

[6]"Five sparrows are sold for only two pennies, and God does not forget any of them. [7]But God even knows how many hairs you have on your head. Don't be afraid. You are worth much more than many sparrows.

DON'T BE ASHAMED OF JESUS

[8]"I tell you, all those who stand before others and say they believe in me, I, the Son of Man, will say before the angels of God that they belong to me. [9]But all who stand before others and say they do not believe in me, I will say before the angels of God that they do not belong to me.

[10]"Anyone who speaks against the Son of

Luke 12:48

WORD: From everyone who has been given much, much will be demanded.

WALK IT: Ask yourself what has been given to you. Talents? Money? Brains? Brawn? Use what God has given you according to his good will.

11:38 wash his hands This was a Jewish religious custom that the Pharisees thought was very important.   11:51 Abel . . . Zechariah In the Hebrew Old Testament, the first and last men to be murdered.

Man can be forgiven, but anyone who speaks against the Holy Spirit will not be forgiven.

[11]"When you are brought into the synagogues before the leaders and other powerful people, don't worry about how to defend yourself or what to say. [12]At that time the Holy Spirit will teach you what you must say."

JESUS WARNS AGAINST SELFISHNESS

[13]Someone in the crowd said to Jesus, "Teacher, tell my brother to divide with me the property our father left us."

[14]But Jesus said to him, "Who said I should judge or decide between you?" [15]Then Jesus said to them, "Be careful and guard against all kinds of greed. Life is not measured by how much one owns."

[16]Then Jesus told this story: "There was a rich man who had some land, which grew a good crop. [17]He thought to himself, 'What will I do? I have no place to keep all my crops.' [18]Then he said, 'This is what I will do: I will tear down my barns and build bigger ones, and there I will store all my grain and other goods. [19]Then I can say to myself, "I have enough good things stored to last for many years. Rest, eat, drink, and enjoy life!" '

[20]"But God said to him, 'Foolish man! Tonight your life will be taken from you. So who will get those things you have prepared for yourself?'

[21]"This is how it will be for those who store up things for themselves and are not rich toward God."

DON'T WORRY

[22]Jesus said to his followers, "So I tell you, don't worry about the food you need to live, or about the clothes you need for your body. [23]Life is more than food, and the body is more than clothes. [24]Look at the birds. They don't plant or harvest, they don't have storerooms or barns, but God feeds them. And you are worth much more than birds. [25]You cannot add any time to your life by worrying about it. [26]If you cannot do even the little things, then why worry about the big things? [27]Consider how the lilies grow; they don't work or make clothes for themselves. But I tell you that even Solomon with his riches was not dressed as beautifully as one of these flowers. [28]God clothes the grass in the field, which is alive today but tomorrow is thrown into the fire. So how much more will God clothe you? Don't have so little faith! [29]Don't always think about what you will eat or what you will drink, and don't keep worrying. [30]All the people in the world are trying to

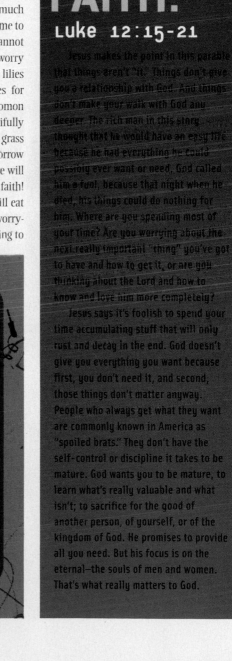

RADICAL FAITH:
Luke 12:15-21

Jesus makes the point in this parable that things aren't "it." Things don't give you a relationship with God. And things don't make your walk with God any deeper. The rich man in this story thought that he would have an easy life because he had everything he could possibly ever want or need. God called him a fool, because that night when he died, his things could do nothing for him. Where are you spending most of your time? Are you worrying about the next really important "thing" you've got to have and how to get it, or are you thinking about the Lord and how to know and love him more completely?

Jesus says it's foolish to spend your time accumulating stuff that will only rust and decay in the end. God doesn't give you everything you want because first, you don't need it, and second, those things don't matter anyway. People who always get what they want are commonly known in America as "spoiled brats." They don't have the self-control or discipline it takes to be mature. God wants you to be mature, to learn what's really valuable and what isn't; to sacrifice for the good of another person, of yourself, or of the kingdom of God. He promises to provide all you need. But his focus is on the eternal—the souls of men and women. That's what really matters to God.

MUSIC REVIEWS

THIRD DAY: OFFERINGS II

Offerings II: All I Have to Give exalts the Creator with an alternative/Southern rock style, leading listeners step-by-step into intense communion with God. Fronted by Mac Powell, one of the most gripping voices in music today, Third Day gets more polished with each release. *Offering II* is a class example of why real worshipers outshine mere performers. It's half live tracks and half studio cuts, as well as about half new tracks and half classic tunes. "God of Wonders" showcases Mike Tait; the disc also contains a impressive version of Rich Mullins' "Creed."

WHY IT ROCKS: IT'S DIFFICULT TO OVERPROP THIRD DAY—SOUND, LYRICS, AND MESSAGE, THEY'RE THE WHOLE PACKAGE.

MOTOR VEHICLE ACCIDENTS ARE THE LEADING CAUSE OF DEATH FOR PEOPLE AGES 4 TO 24. – CHILD TRENDS DATABANK

get these things, and your Father knows you need them. [31]But seek God's kingdom, and all the other things you need will be given to you.

DON'T TRUST IN MONEY

[32]"Don't fear, little flock, because your Father wants to give you the kingdom. [33]Sell your possessions and give to the poor. Get for yourselves purses that will not wear out, the treasure in heaven that never runs out, where thieves can't steal and moths can't destroy. [34]Your heart will be where your treasure is.

ALWAYS BE READY

[35]"Be dressed, ready for service, and have your lamps shining. [36]Be like servants who are waiting for their master to come home from a wedding party. When he comes and knocks, the servants immediately open the door for him. [37]They will be blessed when their master comes home, because he sees that they were watching for him. I tell you the truth, the master will dress himself to serve and tell the servants to sit at the table, and he will serve them. [38]Those servants will be happy when he comes in and finds them still waiting, even if it is midnight or later.

[39]"Remember this: If the owner of the house knew what time a thief was coming, he would not allow the thief to enter his house. [40]So you also must be ready, because the Son of Man will come at a time when you don't expect him!"

WHO IS THE TRUSTED SERVANT?

[41]Peter said, "Lord, did you tell this story to us or to all people?"

[42]The Lord said, "Who is the wise and trusted servant that the master trusts to give the other servants their food at the right time? [43]When the master comes and finds the servant doing his work, the servant will be blessed. [44]I tell you the truth, the master will choose that servant to

HABITAT FOR HUMANITY INTERNATIONAL is a nonprofit, non-denominational Christian housing organization. They welcome all people to join as they build simple, decent, affordable houses in partnership with those in need of adequate shelter. Since 1976, Habitat has built more than 150,000 houses in more than 89 countries, including some 50,000 houses across the United States.

Thousands of students are putting their love into action through Habitat's Campus Chapters and Youth Programs. To volunteer in your local area, use their search engine to find contact information for a Habitat affiliate near you. Or you can make your vacation matter with opportunities like The Summer Youth Blitz, a unique service experience for youth ages 16 and up. Along with 15 to 20 other youth participants and adult leaders from around the United States, you'll "blitz build" an entire Habitat house in two weeks!

To get involved, go to www.habitat.org.

take care of everything he owns. [45]But suppose the servant thinks to himself, 'My master will not come back soon,' and he begins to beat the other servants, men and women, and to eat and drink and get drunk. [46]The master will come when that servant is not ready and is not expecting him. Then the master will cut him in pieces and send him away to be with the others who don't obey.

[47]"The servant who knows what his master wants but is not ready, or who does not do what the master wants, will be beaten with many blows! [48]But the servant who does not know what his master wants and does things that should be punished will be beaten with few blows. From everyone who has been given much, much will be demanded. And from the one trusted with much, much more will be expected.

JESUS CAUSES DIVISION

[49]"I came to set fire to the world, and I wish it were already burning! [50]I have a baptism[n] to suffer through, and I feel very troubled until it is over. [51]Do you think I came to give peace to the earth? No, I tell you, I came to divide it. [52]From now on, a family with five people will be divided, three against two, and two against

three. [53]They will be divided: father against son and son against father, mother against daughter and daughter against mother, mother-in-law against daughter-in-law and daughter-in-law against mother-in-law."

UNDERSTANDING THE TIMES

[54]Then Jesus said to the people, "When you see clouds coming up in the west, you say, 'It's going to rain,' and it happens. [55]When you feel the wind begin to blow from the south, you say, 'It will be a hot day,' and it happens. [56]Hypocrites! You know how to understand the appearance of the earth and sky. Why don't you understand what is happening now?

SETTLE YOUR PROBLEMS

[57]"Why can't you decide for yourselves what is right? [58]If your enemy is taking you to court, try hard to settle it on the way. If you don't, your enemy might take you to the judge, and the judge might turn you over to the officer, and the officer might throw you into jail. [59]I tell you, you will not get out of there until you have paid everything you owe."

CHANGE YOUR HEARTS

13 At that time some people were there who told Jesus that Pilate[n] had killed some people from Galilee while they were worshiping. He mixed their blood with the blood of the animals they were sacrificing to God. [2]Jesus answered, "Do you think this happened to them because they were more sinful than all others

from Galilee? [3]No, I tell you. But unless you change your hearts and lives, you will be destroyed as they were! [4]What about those eighteen people who died when the tower of Siloam fell on them? Do you think they were more sinful than all the others who live in Jerusalem? [5]No, I tell you. But unless you change your hearts and lives, you will all be destroyed too!"

HEBREWS 1:2 "GOD HAS CHOSEN HIS SON TO OWN ALL THINGS, AND THROUGH HIM HE MADE THE WORLD."

THE USELESS TREE

[6]Jesus told this story: "A man had a fig tree planted in his vineyard. He came looking for some fruit on the tree, but he found none. [7]So the man said to his gardener, 'I have been looking for fruit on this tree for three years, but I never find any. Cut it down. Why should it waste the ground?' [8]But the servant answered, 'Master, let the tree have one more year to produce fruit. Let me dig up the dirt around it and put on some fertilizer. [9]If the tree produces fruit next year, good. But if not, you can cut it down.' "

JESUS HEALS ON THE SABBATH

[10]Jesus was teaching in one of the synagogues on the Sabbath day. [11]A woman was there who, for eighteen years, had an evil spirit

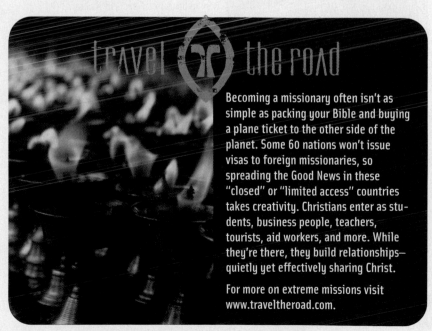

Becoming a missionary often isn't as simple as packing your Bible and buying a plane ticket to the other side of the planet. Some 60 nations won't issue visas to foreign missionaries, so spreading the Good News in these "closed" or "limited access" countries takes creativity. Christians enter as students, business people, teachers, tourists, aid workers, and more. While they're there, they build relationships—quietly yet effectively sharing Christ.

For more on extreme missions visit www.traveltheroad.com.

12:50 | . . . **baptism** Jesus was talking about the suffering he would soon go through.   13:1 **Pilate** Pontius Pilate was the Roman governor of Judea from A.D. 26 to A.D. 36.

111

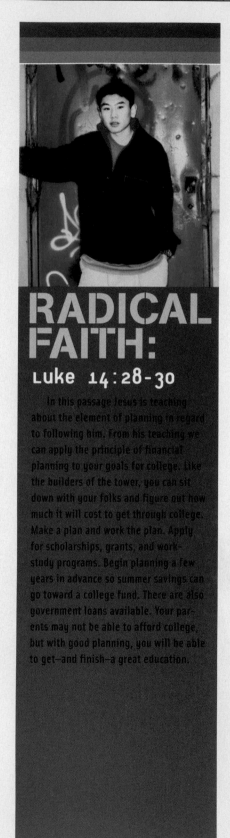

RADICAL FAITH:
Luke 14:28-30

In this passage Jesus is teaching about the element of planning in regard to following him. From his teaching we can apply the principle of financial planning to your goals for college. Like the builders of the tower, you can sit down with your folks and figure out how much it will cost to get through college. Make a plan and work the plan. Apply for scholarships, grants, and work-study programs. Begin planning a few years in advance so summer savings can go toward a college fund. There are also government loans available. Your parents may not be able to afford college, but with good planning, you will be able to get—and finish—a great education.

in her that made her crippled. Her back was always bent; she could not stand up straight. [12]When Jesus saw her, he called her over and said, "Woman, you are free from your sickness." [13]Jesus put his hands on her, and immediately she was able to stand up straight and began praising God.

[14]The synagogue leader was angry because Jesus healed on the Sabbath day. He said to the people, "There are six days when one has to work. So come to be healed on one of those days, and not on the Sabbath day."

[15]The Lord answered, "You hypocrites! Doesn't each of you untie your work animals and lead them to drink water every day—even on the Sabbath day? [16]This woman that I healed, a daughter of Abraham, has been held by Satan for eighteen years. Surely it is not wrong for her to be freed from her sickness on a Sabbath day!" [17]When Jesus said this, all of those who were criticizing him were ashamed, but the entire crowd rejoiced at all the wonderful things Jesus was doing.

STORIES OF MUSTARD SEED AND YEAST

[18]Then Jesus said, "What is God's kingdom like? What can I compare it with? [19]It is like a mustard seed that a man plants in his garden. The seed grows and becomes a tree, and the wild birds build nests in its branches."

[20]Jesus said again, "What can I compare God's kingdom with? [21]It is like yeast that a woman took and hid in a large tub of flour until it made all the dough rise."

THE NARROW DOOR

[22]Jesus was teaching in every town and village as he traveled toward Jerusalem. [23]Someone said to Jesus, "Lord, will only a few people be saved?"

Jesus said, [24]"Try hard to enter through the narrow door, because many people will try to enter there, but they will not be able. [25]When the owner of the house gets up and closes the door, you can stand outside and knock on the door and say, 'Sir, open the door for us.' But he will answer, 'I don't know you or where you come from.' [26]Then you will say, 'We ate and drank with you, and you taught in the streets of our town.' [27]But he will say to you, 'I don't

RANDOM CHRISTIAN CDS WORTH OWNING

1. P.O.D.—*SATELLITE*
2. TOBYMAC—*MOMENTUM*
3. SWITCHFOOT—*THE BEAUTIFUL LETDOWN*
4. JARS OF CLAY—*WE WHO ARE INSTEAD*
5. RELIENT K–*TWO LEFTS DON'T MAKE A RIGHT, BUT THREE DO*
6. KUTLESS—*KUTLESS*
7. THE BENJAMIN GATE–*UNTITLED*
8. DELIRIOUS?—*WORLD SERVICE*
9. PLUS ONE—*EXODUS*
10. PILLAR—*FIREPROOF*

know you or where you come from. Go away from me, all you who do evil!' [28]You will cry and grind your teeth with pain when you see Abraham, Isaac, Jacob, and all the prophets in God's kingdom, but you yourselves thrown outside. [29]People will come from the east, west, north, and south and will sit down at the table in the kingdom of God. [30]There are those who have the lowest place in life now who will have the highest place in the future. And there are those who have the highest place now who will have the lowest place in the future."

JESUS WILL DIE IN JERUSALEM

[31]At that time some Pharisees came to Jesus and said, "Go away from here! Herod wants to kill you!"

[32]Jesus said to them, "Go tell that fox Herod, 'Today and tomorrow I am forcing demons out and healing people. Then, on the third day, I will reach my goal.' [33]Yet I must be on my way today and tomorrow and the next

RELATIONSHIPS

"Husbands should love their wives as they love their own bodies" (Ephesians 5:28). Do you want someday to have an outstanding physical relationship with your wife? Then ditch the attitude of sexual selfishness that infects many Christian guys. We think, "If I just save myself for marriage, it'll be a free-for-all. I'll get what I want whenever I want it." Sorry, guys. Marriage means you put your wife's needs and wants right up there with your own. Including when she doesn't want what you want. Or when you want it. Too much information for a teen guy? Nope. Get your thinking straight right now: No part of a relationship is ever all about you.

day. Surely it cannot be right for a prophet to be killed anywhere except in Jerusalem.

[34] "Jerusalem, Jerusalem! You kill the prophets and stone to death those who are sent to you. Many times I wanted to gather your people as a hen gathers her chicks under her wings, but you would not let me. [35] Now your house is left completely empty. I tell you, you will not see me until that time when you will say, 'God bless the One who comes in the name of the Lord.' "[n]

HEALING ON THE SABBATH

14 On a Sabbath day, when Jesus went to eat at the home of a leading Pharisee, the people were watching Jesus very closely. [2] And in front of him was a man with dropsy.[n] [3] Jesus said to the Pharisees and experts on the law, "Is it right or wrong to heal on the Sabbath day?" [4] But they would not answer his question. So Jesus took the man, healed him, and sent him away. [5] Jesus said to the Pharisees and teachers of the law, "If your child or ox falls into a well on the Sabbath day, will you not pull him out quickly?" [6] And they could not answer him.

DON'T MAKE YOURSELF IMPORTANT

[7] When Jesus noticed that some of the guests were choosing the best places to sit, he told this story: [8] "When someone invites you to a wedding feast, don't take the most important seat, because someone more important than you may have been invited. [9] The host, who invited both of you, will come to you and say, 'Give this person your seat.' Then you will be embarrassed and will have to move to the last place. [10] So when you are invited, go sit in a seat that is not important. When the host comes to you, he may say, 'Friend, move up here to a more important place.' Then all the other guests will respect you. [11] All who make themselves great will be made humble, but those who make themselves humble will be made great."

YOU WILL BE REWARDED

[12] Then Jesus said to the man who had invited him, "When you give a lunch or a dinner, don't invite only your friends, your family, your other relatives, and your rich neighbors. At another time they will invite you to eat with them, and you will be repaid. [13] Instead, when you give a feast, invite the poor, the crippled, the lame, and the blind. [14] Then you will be

blessed, because they have nothing and cannot pay you back. But you will be repaid when the good people rise from the dead."

A STORY ABOUT A BIG BANQUET

[15] One of those at the table with Jesus heard these things and said to him, "Happy are the people who will share in the meal in God's kingdom."

 13:35 'God . . . Lord.' Quotation from Psalm 118:26.　14:2 dropsy A sickness that causes the body to swell larger and larger.

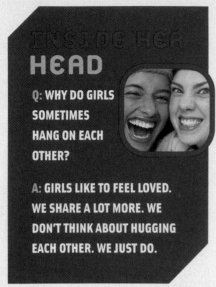

INSIDE HER HEAD

Q: WHY DO GIRLS SOMETIMES HANG ON EACH OTHER?

A: GIRLS LIKE TO FEEL LOVED. WE SHARE A LOT MORE. WE DON'T THINK ABOUT HUGGING EACH OTHER. WE JUST DO.

[16]Jesus said to him, "A man gave a big banquet and invited many people. [17]When it was time to eat, the man sent his servant to tell the guests, 'Come. Everything is ready.'

[18]"But all the guests made excuses. The first one said, 'I have just bought a field, and I must go look at it. Please excuse me.' [19]Another said, 'I have just bought five pairs of oxen; I must go and try them. Please excuse me.' [20]A third person said, 'I just got married; I can't come.' [21]So the servant returned and told his master what had happened. Then the master became angry and said, 'Go at once into the streets and alleys of the town, and bring in the poor, the crippled, the blind, and the lame.' [22]Later the servant said to him, 'Master, I did what you commanded, but we still have room.' [23]The master said to the servant, 'Go out to the roads and country lanes, and urge the people there to come so my house will be full. [24]I tell you, none of those whom I invited first will eat with me.' "

THE COST OF BEING JESUS' FOLLOWER

[25]Large crowds were traveling with Jesus, and he turned and said to them, [26]"If anyone comes to me but loves his father, mother, wife, children, brothers, or sisters—or even life—more than me, he cannot be my follower. [27]Whoever is not willing to carry the cross and follow me cannot be my follower. [28]If you want to build a tower, you first sit down and decide how much it will cost, to see if you have enough money to finish the job. [29]If you don't, you might lay the foundation, but you would not be able to finish. Then all who would see it would make fun of you, [30]saying, 'This person began to build but was not able to finish.'

[31]"If a king is going to fight another king, first he will sit down and plan. He will decide if he and his ten thousand soldiers can defeat the other king who has twenty thousand soldiers. [32]If he can't, then while the other king is still far away, he will send some people to speak to him and ask for peace. [33]In the same way, you must give up everything you have to be my follower.

DON'T LOSE YOUR INFLUENCE

[34]"Salt is good, but if it loses its salty taste, you cannot make it salty again. [35]It is no good for the soil or for manure; it is thrown away.

"You people who can hear me, listen."

A LOST SHEEP, A LOST COIN

15 The tax collectors and sinners all came to listen to Jesus. [2]But the Pharisees and the teachers of the law began to complain: "Look, this man welcomes sinners and even eats with them."

[3]Then Jesus told them this story: [4]"Suppose one of you has a hundred sheep but loses one of them. Then he will leave the other ninety-nine sheep in the open field and go out and look for the lost sheep until he finds it. [5]And when he finds it, he happily puts it on his shoulders [6]and goes home. He calls to his friends and neighbors and says, 'Be happy with me because I found my lost sheep.' [7]In the same way, I tell you there is more joy in heaven over one sinner who changes his heart and life, than over ninety-nine good people who don't need to change.

[8]"Suppose a woman has ten silver coins,[n] but loses one. She will light a lamp, sweep the house, and look carefully for the coin until she finds it. [9]And when she finds it, she will call her friends and neighbors

MEN OF THE SWORD

JAMES was one of three guys—along with Peter and John—in Jesus' tightest circle of friends. These three men were present when Jesus shone with brilliant light in a mountaintop experience called the "Transfiguration," and Jesus asked the three to support him when he agonized about dying on the cross. Jesus called James and his brother John "Sons of Thunder," maybe because they tried to call fire down from heaven on a village that rejected Jesus. The mom of James and John once tried to score them seats at the right and left of Jesus in heaven, but Jesus instead promised the brothers they would share in his suffering. James became the first disciple killed for his faith.

—Matthew 17:1-11; 20:20-21; Mark 3:17; Acts 12:2

15:8 **silver coins** Roman denarii. One coin was the average pay for one day's work.

and say, 'Be happy with me because I have found the coin that I lost.' [10]In the same way, there is joy in the presence of the angels of God when one sinner changes his heart and life."

THE SON WHO LEFT HOME

[11]Then Jesus said, "A man had two sons. [12]The younger son said to his father, 'Give me my share of the property.' So the father divided the property between his two sons. [13]Then the younger son gathered up all that was his and traveled far away to another country. There he wasted his money in foolish living. [14]After he had spent everything, a time came when there was no food anywhere in the country, and the son was poor and hungry. [15]So he got a job with one of the citizens there who sent the son into the fields to feed pigs. [16]The son was so hungry that he wanted to eat the pods the pigs were eating, but no one gave him anything. [17]When he realized what he was doing, he thought, 'All of my father's servants have plenty of food. But I am here, almost dying with hunger. [18]I will leave and return to my father and say to him, "Father, I have sinned against God and have done wrong to you. [19]I am no longer worthy to be called your son, but let me be like one of your servants."' [20]So the son left and went to his father.

"While the son was still a long way off, his father saw him and felt sorry for his son. So the father ran to him and hugged and kissed him. [21]The son said, 'Father, I have sinned against God and have done wrong to you. I am no longer worthy to be called your son.' [22]But the father said to his servants, 'Hurry! Bring the best clothes and put them on him. Also, put a ring on his finger and sandals on his feet. [23]And get our fat calf and kill it so we can have a feast and celebrate. [24]My son was dead, but now he is alive again! He was lost, but now he is found!' So they began to celebrate.

[25]"The older son was in the field, and as he came closer to the house, he heard the sound of music and dancing. [26]So he called to one of the servants and asked what all this meant. [27]The servant said, 'Your brother has come back, and your father killed the fat calf, because your brother came home safely.' [28]The older son was angry and would not go in to the feast. So his father went out and begged him to come in. [29]But the older son said to his father, 'I have served you like a slave for many years and have always obeyed your commands. But you never gave me even a young goat to have at a feast with my friends. [30]But your other son, who wasted all your money on prostitutes,

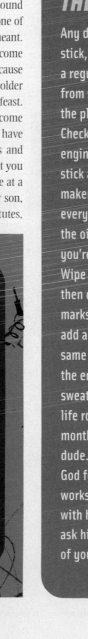

HOW TO CHECK THE OIL

Any dipstick can find the dipstick, but eyeing your car's oil on a regular basis saves your engine from serious damage. So here's the plan. Park in a level spot. Check the oil level when the engine is cool. Pull out the dipstick and study the oil. Most carmakers recommend an oil change every 3,000 to 7,500 miles, but if the oil looks grainy before that, you're due for an early change. Wipe the stick clean, reinsert it, then check the level against marks on the stick. If you're low, add a bit at a time. Stick with the same brand and weight already in the engine. Checking the oil is no sweat, but make it part of your life routine at least once a month. It's not about the skill, dude. It's the schedule. Coming to God for a serious heartcheck works the same way. Get quiet with him at least once a week and ask him to measure up the state of your heart.

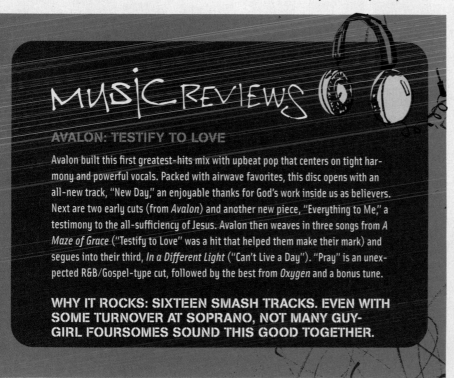

MUSIC REVIEWS

AVALON: TESTIFY TO LOVE

Avalon built this first greatest-hits mix with upbeat pop that centers on tight harmony and powerful vocals. Packed with airwave favorites, this disc opens with an all-new track, "New Day," an enjoyable thanks for God's work inside us as believers. Next are two early cuts (from *Avalon*) and another new piece, "Everything to Me," a testimony to the all-sufficiency of Jesus. Avalon then weaves in three songs from *A Maze of Grace* ("Testify to Love" was a hit that helped them make their mark) and segues into their third, *In a Different Light* ("Can't Live a Day"). "Pray" is an unexpected R&B/Gospel-type cut, followed by the best from *Oxygen* and a bonus tune.

WHY IT ROCKS: SIXTEEN SMASH TRACKS. EVEN WITH SOME TURNOVER AT SOPRANO, NOT MANY GUY-GIRL FOURSOMES SOUND THIS GOOD TOGETHER.

comes home, and you kill the fat calf for him!' [31]The father said to him, 'Son, you are always with me, and all that I have is yours. [32]We had to celebrate and be happy because your brother was dead, but now he is alive. He was lost, but now he is found.' "

TRUE WEALTH

16 Jesus also said to his followers, "Once there was a rich man who had a manager to take care of his business. This manager was accused of cheating him. [2]So he called the manager in and said to him, 'What is this I hear about you? Give me a report of what you have done with my money, because you can't be my manager any longer.' [3]The manager thought to himself, 'What will I do since my master is taking my job away from me? I am not strong enough to dig ditches, and I am ashamed to beg. [4]I know what I'll do so that when I lose my job people will welcome me into their homes.'

[5]"So the manager called in everyone who owed the master any money. He asked the first one, 'How much do you owe?' [6]He answered, 'Eight hundred gallons of olive oil.' The manager said to him, 'Take your bill, sit down quickly, and write four hundred gallons.' [7]Then the manager asked another one, 'How much do you owe?' He answered, 'One thousand bushels of wheat.' Then the manager said to him, 'Take your bill and write eight hundred bushels.' [8]So, the master praised the dishonest manager for being smart. Yes, worldly people are smarter with their own kind than spiritual people are.

[9]"I tell you, make friends for yourselves using worldly riches so that when those riches are gone, you will be welcomed in those homes that continue forever. [10]Whoever can be trusted with a little can also be trusted with a lot, and whoever is dishonest with a little is dishonest with a lot. [11]If you cannot be trusted with worldly riches, then who will trust you with true riches? [12]And if you cannot be trusted with things that belong to someone else, who will give you things of your own?

[13]"No servant can serve two masters. The servant will hate one master and love the other, or will follow one master and refuse to follow the other. You cannot serve both God and worldly riches."

GOD'S LAW CANNOT BE CHANGED

[14]The Pharisees, who loved money, were listening to all these things and made fun of Jesus. [15]He said to them, "You make yourselves look good in front of people, but God knows what is really in your hearts. What is important to people is hateful in God's sight.

[16]"The law of Moses and the writings of the prophets were preached until John[n] came. Since then the Good News about the kingdom

YOUTHNOISE is about maximum volume. It's about the racket young people can generate when they get together to make their voices heard. It's about being heard over the negative stereotypes about teens. It's a place where you can take action and make a difference in issues that affect you—like school violence, teen pregnancy, and more. YouthNOISE is young people—from all 50 states, the District of Columbia and more than 118 countries—working together with adults to spark youth action. YouthNOISE is an initiative of Save the Children Federation, Inc., a group that has worked for nearly 70 years to improve the lives of children and youth. They empower you to take action to make change in your lives and the lives of other young people locally and globally.

Stop by www.youthnoise.org to learn more.

16:16 **John** John the Baptist, who preached to people about Christ's coming (Matthew 3, Luke 3).

of God is being told, and everyone tries to enter it by force. [17]It would be easier for heaven and earth to pass away than for the smallest part of a letter in the law to be changed.

DIVORCE AND REMARRIAGE

[18]"If a man divorces his wife and marries another woman, he is guilty of adultery, and the man who marries a divorced woman is also guilty of adultery."

THE RICH MAN AND LAZARUS

[19]Jesus said, "There was a rich man who always dressed in the finest clothes and lived in luxury every day. [20]And a very poor man named Lazarus, whose body was covered with sores, was laid at the rich man's gate. [21]He wanted to eat only the small pieces of food that fell from the rich man's table. And the dogs would come and lick his sores. [22]Later, Lazarus died, and the angels carried him to the arms of Abraham. The rich man died, too, and was buried. [23]In the place of the dead, he was in much pain. The rich man saw Abraham far away with Lazarus at his side. [24]He called, 'Father Abraham, have mercy on me! Send Lazarus to dip his finger in water and cool my tongue, because I am suffering in this fire!' [25]But Abraham said, 'Child, remember when you were alive you had the good things in life, but bad things happened to Lazarus. Now he is comforted here, and you are suffering. [26]Besides, there is a big pit between you and us, so no one can cross over to you, and no one can leave there and come here.' [27]The rich man said, 'Father, then please send Lazarus to my father's house. [28]I have five brothers, and Lazarus could warn them so that they will not

come to this place of pain.' [29]But Abraham said, 'They have the law of Moses and the writings of the prophets; let them learn from them.' [30]The rich man said, 'No, father Abraham! If someone goes to them from the dead, they would believe and change their

hearts and lives.' [31]But Abraham said to him, 'If they will not listen to Moses and the prophets, they will not listen to someone who comes back from the dead.' "

SIN AND FORGIVENESS

17 Jesus said to his followers, "Things that cause people to sin will happen, but how terrible for the person who causes them to happen! [2]It would be better for you to be thrown into the sea with a large stone around your neck than to cause one of these little ones to sin. [3]So be careful!

"If another follower sins, warn him, and if he is sorry and stops sinning, forgive him. [4]If he sins against you seven times in one day and says that he is sorry each time, forgive him."

HOW BIG IS YOUR FAITH?

[5]The apostles said to the Lord, "Give us more faith!"

[6]The Lord said, "If your faith were the size of a mustard seed, you could say to this mulberry tree, 'Dig yourself up and plant yourself in the sea,' and it would obey you.

BE GOOD SERVANTS

[7]"Suppose one of you has a servant who has been plowing the ground or caring for the sheep. When the servant comes in from working in the field, would you say, 'Come in and sit down to eat'? [8]No, you would say to him, 'Prepare something for me to eat. Then get yourself ready and serve me. After I finish eating and drinking, you can eat.' [9]The servant does not get any special thanks for doing what his master commanded. [10]It is the same with you. When you have done everything you are told to

do, you should say, 'We are unworthy servants; we have only done the work we should do.' "

BE THANKFUL

[11]While Jesus was on his way to Jerusalem, he was going through the area between Samaria and Galilee. [12]As he came into a small town,

NTA (NOT THAT AWFUL) CHICK FLICKS

1. *THE PRINCESS BRIDE*
2. *A WALK TO REMEMBER*
3. *PRIDE AND PREJUDICE*
4. *THE MAN FROM SNOWY RIVER*
5. *SENSE AND SENSIBILITY*
6. *LEGALLY BLONDE*
7. *FATHER OF THE BRIDE*
8. *EVER AFTER*
9. *SABRINA*
10. *RETURN TO ME*

ten men who had a skin disease met him there. They did not come close to Jesus [13]but called to him, "Jesus! Master! Have mercy on us!"

[14]When Jesus saw the men, he said, "Go and show yourselves to the priests."[n]

As the ten men were going, they were healed. [15]When one of them saw that he was healed, he went back to Jesus, praising God in a loud voice. [16]Then he bowed down at Jesus' feet and thanked him. (And this man was a Samaritan.) [17]Jesus said, "Weren't ten men healed? Where are the other nine? [18]Is this Samaritan the only one who came back to thank God?" [19]Then Jesus said to him, "Stand up and go on your way. You were healed because you believed."

GOD'S KINGDOM IS WITHIN YOU

[20]Some of the Pharisees asked Jesus, "When will the kingdom of God come?"

Jesus answered, "God's kingdom is coming, but not in a way that you will be able to see with your eyes. [21]People will not say, 'Look, here it is!' or, 'There it is!' because God's kingdom is within[n] you."

[22]Then Jesus said to his followers, "The time will come when you will want very much to see one of the days of the Son of Man. But

WAYS TO WALK THE WALK

Luke 15:31

WORD: As God's child, all that God has is yours.

WALK IT: Celebrate that you are and always will be God's treasured son.

17:14 **show . . . priests** The Law of Moses said a priest must say when a person with a skin disease became well.   17:21 **within** Or "among."

issues
DATE RAPE

IT'S REPORTED THAT ONE-QUARTER of all college women are victims of some form of rape or attempted rape, and acquaintances commit more than four out of five campus rapes. Date rape is forced sex between two people who already know each other—as in boyfriends and girlfriends, dates, friends, or classmates. Force isn't always physical. Pressuring a girl by threatening to break up or ruin her reputation is just as coercive. And you don't have to go all the way to leave a girl wounded and distrustful of guys for life. So when a girl says "No!" she means "No!" No matter how in love you claim to be... no matter what you think you deserve... no matter how willing she appears... you never have a right to force sexual contact.

you will not see it. [23]People will say to you, 'Look, there he is!' or, 'Look, here he is!' Stay where you are; don't go away and search.

WHEN JESUS COMES AGAIN

[24]"When the Son of Man comes again, he will shine like lightning, which flashes across the sky and lights it up from one side to the other. [25]But first he must suffer many things and be rejected by the people of this time. [26]When the Son of Man comes again, it will be as it was when Noah lived. [27]People were eating, drinking, marrying, and giving their children to be married until the day Noah entered the boat. Then the flood came and killed them all. [28]It will be the same as during the time of Lot. People were eating, drinking, buying, selling,

planting, and building. [29]But the day Lot left Sodom,*n* fire and sulfur rained down from the sky and killed them all. [30]This is how it will be when the Son of Man comes again.

[31]"On that day, a person who is on the roof and whose belongings are in the house should not go inside to get them. A person who is in the field should not go back home. [32]Remember Lot's wife.*n* [33]Those who try to keep their lives will lose them. But those who give up their lives will save them. [34]I tell you, on that night two people will be sleeping in one bed; one will be taken and the other will be left. [35]There will be two women grinding grain together; one will be taken, and the other will be left." [36]*n*

[37]The followers asked Jesus, "Where will this be, Lord?"

Jesus answered, "Where there is a dead body, there the vultures will gather."

GOD WILL ANSWER HIS PEOPLE

18 Then Jesus used this story to teach his followers that they should always pray and never lose hope. [2]"In a certain town there was a judge who did not respect God or care about people. [3]In that same town there was a widow who kept coming to this judge, saying, 'Give me my rights against my enemy.' [4]For a while the judge refused to help her. But afterwards, he thought to himself, 'Even though I don't respect God or care about people, [5]I will see that she gets her rights. Otherwise she will continue to bother me until I am worn out.' "

[6]The Lord said, "Listen to what the unfair judge said. [7]God will always give what is right to his people who cry to him night and day, and he will not be slow to answer them. [8]I tell you, God will help his people quickly. But when the Son of Man comes again, will he find those on earth who believe in him?"

BEING RIGHT WITH GOD

[9]Jesus told this story to some people who thought they were very good and looked down on everyone else: [10]"A Pharisee and a tax collector both went to the Temple to pray. [11]The Pharisee stood alone and prayed, 'God, I thank you that I am not like other people who steal, cheat, or take part in adultery, or even like this tax collector. [12]I give up eating*n* twice a week, and I give one-tenth of everything I get!'

[13]"The tax collector, standing at a distance, would not even look up to heaven. But he beat on his chest because he was so sad. He said, 'God, have mercy on me, a sinner.' [14]I tell you, when this man went home, he was right with God, but the Pharisee was not. All who make themselves great will be made humble, but all who make themselves humble will be made great."

WHO WILL ENTER GOD'S KINGDOM?

[15]Some people brought even their babies to Jesus so he could touch them. When the followers saw this, they told them to stop. [16]But Jesus called for the children, saying, "Let the little children come to me. Don't stop them, because the kingdom of God belongs to people who are like these children. [17]I tell you the truth, you must accept the kingdom of God as if you were a child, or you will never enter it."

A RICH MAN'S QUESTION

[18]A certain leader asked Jesus, "Good Teacher, what must I do to have life forever?"

EXPERTS ANSWER YOUR QUESTIONS

Q. Am I breaking the Sabbath when I miss church to play soccer on Sundays? I can't help it when they schedule games!

A. The "Sabbath" is a day dedicated to God, not just an hour on Sunday mornings but a whole day set aside for rest and worship. In the Old Testament, God commanded the Israelites not to do work on the Sabbath—no cooking, cleaning, or mountain climbing. While most Christians today recognize Sunday as a Sabbath, most of us miss out on the refreshment God plans for us. If your Sunday schedule won't budge, you have a choice: Either quit, or make ample time for rest and worship elsewhere in your week.

Q. My mom said I'm sinning when I "covet" other people's stuff. I know what she means, but what exactly is coveting?

A. It's when you sit around thinking about what other people have, wishing you could have it. It might be drooling on the hood of the nice car parked next to yours at school. Or plotting how to steal your buddy's girlfriend. Or wasting your whole life looking at catalogs, browsing to buy online, or staring at the Sunday ads.

 17:29 Sodom City that God destroyed because the people were so evil.   **17:32 Lot's wife** A story about what happened to Lot's wife is found in Genesis 19:15-17, 26.   **17:36 Verse 36** A few Greek copies add verse 36: "Two people will be in the field. One will be taken, and the other will be left."   **18:12 give up eating** This is called "fasting." The people would give up eating for a special time of prayer and worship to God. It was also done to show sadness and disappointment.

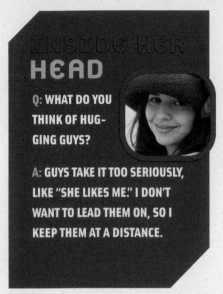

[19]Jesus said to him, "Why do you call me good? Only God is good. [20]You know the commands: 'You must not be guilty of adultery. You must not murder anyone. You must not steal. You must not tell lies about your neighbor. Honor your father and mother.'"[n]

[21]But the leader said, "I have obeyed all these commands since I was a boy."

[22]When Jesus heard this, he said to him, "There is still one more thing you need to do. Sell everything you have and give it to the poor, and you will have treasure in heaven. Then come and follow me." [23]But when the man heard this, he became very sad, because he was very rich.

[24]Jesus looked at him and said, "It is very hard for rich people to enter the kingdom of God. [25]It is easier for a camel to go through the eye of a needle than for a rich person to enter the kingdom of God."

WHO CAN BE SAVED?

[26]When the people heard this, they asked, "Then who can be saved?"

[27]Jesus answered, "God can do things that are not possible for people to do."

[28]Peter said, "Look, we have left everything and followed you."

[29]Jesus said, "I tell you the truth, all those who have left houses, wives, brothers, parents, or children for the kingdom of God [30]will get much more in this life. And in the age that is coming, they will have life forever."

JESUS WILL RISE FROM THE DEAD

[31]Then Jesus took the twelve apostles aside and said to them, "We are going to Jerusalem. Everything the prophets wrote about the Son of Man will happen. [32]He will be turned over to those who are evil. They will laugh at him, insult him, spit on him, [33]beat him with whips, and kill him. But on the third day, he will rise to life again." [34]The apostles did not understand this; the meaning was hidden from them, and they did not realize what was said.

JESUS HEALS A BLIND MAN

[35]As Jesus came near the city of Jericho, a blind man was sitting beside the road, begging. [36]When he heard the people coming down the road, he asked, "What is happening?"

[37]They told him, "Jesus, from Nazareth, is going by."

[38]The blind man cried out, "Jesus, Son of David, have mercy on me!"

[39]The people leading the group warned the blind man to be quiet. But the blind man shouted even more, "Son of David, have mercy on me!"

[40]Jesus stopped and ordered the blind man to be brought to him. When he came near, Jesus asked him, [41]"What do you want me to do for you?"

He said, "Lord, I want to see."

[42]Jesus said to him, "Then see. You are healed because you believed."

[43]At once the man was able to see, and he followed Jesus, thanking God. All the people who saw this praised God.

ZACCHAEUS MEETS JESUS

19 Jesus was going through the city of Jericho. [2]A man was there named Zacchaeus, who was a very important tax collector, and he was wealthy. [3]He wanted to see who Jesus was, but he was not able because he was too short to see above the crowd. [4]He ran ahead to a place where Jesus would come, and he climbed a sycamore tree so he could see him. [5]When Jesus came to that place, he looked up and said to him, "Zacchaeus, hurry and come down! I must stay at your house today."

[6]Zacchaeus came down quickly and welcomed him gladly. [7]All the people saw this and began to complain, "Jesus is staying with a sinner!"

[8]But Zacchaeus stood and said to the Lord, "I will give half of my possessions to the poor. And if I have cheated anyone, I will pay back four times more."

[9]Jesus said to him, "Salvation has come to this house today, because this man also belongs to the family of Abraham. [10]The Son of Man came to find lost people and save them."

A STORY ABOUT THREE SERVANTS

[11]As the people were listening to this, Jesus told them a story because he was near Jerusalem and they thought God's kingdom would appear immediately. [12]He said: "A very important man went to a country far away to be made a king and then to return home. [13]So he called ten of his servants and gave a coin[n] to each servant. He said, 'Do business with this

money until I get back.' [14]But the people in the kingdom hated the man. So they sent a group to follow him and say, 'We don't want this man to be our king.'

[15]"But the man became king. When he returned home, he said, 'Call those servants who have my money so I can know how much they earned with it.'

[16]"The first servant came and said, 'Sir, I earned ten coins with the one you gave me.' [17]The king said to the servant, 'Excellent! You are a good servant. Since I can trust you with small things, I will let you rule over ten of my cities.'

[18]"The second servant said, 'Sir, I earned five coins with your one.' [19]The king said to this servant, 'You can rule over five cities.'

[20]"Then another servant came in and said to the king, 'Sir, here is your coin which I wrapped in a piece of cloth and hid. [21]I was afraid of you, because you are a hard man. You even take money that you didn't earn and

18:20 'You . . . mother.' Quotation from Exodus 20:12–16; Deuteronomy 5:16–20.   19:13 coin A Greek "mina." One mina was enough money to pay a person for working three months.

gather food that you didn't plant.' ²²Then the king said to the servant, 'I will condemn you by your own words, you evil servant. You knew that I am a hard man, taking money that I didn't earn and gathering food that I didn't plant. ²³Why then didn't you put my money in the bank? Then when I came back, my money would have earned some interest.'

²⁴"The king said to the men who were standing by, 'Take the coin away from this servant and give it to the servant who earned ten coins.' ²⁵They said, 'But sir, that servant already has ten coins.' ²⁶The king said, 'Those who

PSALM 136:3 "GIVE THANKS TO THE LORD OF LORDS. HIS LOVE CONTINUES FOREVER."

have will be given more, but those who do not have anything will have everything taken away from them. ²⁷Now where are my enemies who didn't want me to be king? Bring them here and kill them before me.' "

JESUS ENTERS JERUSALEM AS A KING

²⁸After Jesus said this, he went on toward Jerusalem. ²⁹As Jesus came near Bethphage and Bethany, towns near the hill called the Mount of Olives, he sent out two of his followers. ³⁰He said, "Go to the town you can see there. When you enter it, you will find a colt tied there, which no one has ever ridden. Untie it and bring it here to me. ³¹If anyone asks you why you are untying it, say that the Master needs it."

³²The two followers went into town and found the colt just as Jesus had told them. ³³As they were untying it, its owners came out and asked the followers, "Why are you untying our colt?"

³⁴The followers answered, "The Master

needs it." ³⁵So they brought it to Jesus, threw their coats on the colt's back, and put Jesus on it. ³⁶As Jesus rode toward Jerusalem, others spread their coats on the road before him.

³⁷As he was coming close to Jerusalem, on the way down the Mount of Olives, the whole crowd of followers began joyfully shouting praise to God for all the miracles they had seen. ³⁸They said,

"God bless the king who comes in the name of the Lord! *Psalm 118:26*
There is peace in heaven and glory to God!"

³⁹Some of the Pharisees in the crowd said to Jesus, "Teacher, tell your followers not to say these things."

⁴⁰But Jesus answered, "I tell you, if my followers didn't say these things, then the stones would cry out."

JESUS CRIES FOR JERUSALEM

⁴¹As Jesus came near Jerusalem, he saw the city and cried for it. ⁴²saying, "I wish you knew today what would bring you peace. But now it is hidden from you. ⁴³The time is coming when your enemies will build a wall around you and will hold you in on all sides. ⁴⁴They will destroy you and all your people, and not one stone will be left on another. All this will happen because you did not recognize the time when God came to save you."

JESUS GOES TO THE TEMPLE

⁴⁵Jesus went into the Temple and began to throw out the people who were selling things there. ⁴⁶He said, "It is written in the Scriptures, 'My Temple will be a house for prayer.'ⁿ But you have changed it into a 'hideout for robbers'!"ⁿ

⁴⁷Jesus taught in the Temple every day. The leading priests, the experts on the law, and some of the leaders of the people wanted to kill Jesus. ⁴⁸But they did not know how they could do it, because all the people were listening closely to him.

RANDOM WAYS TO SPEND $10

1. TITHE.
2. BUY FLOWERS FOR YOUR MOM.
3. GO TO A LOCAL ARTIST'S CONCERT.
4. PICK OUT A GIFT FOR A FRIEND.
5. CALL SOMEONE IN ARGENTINA.
6. TREAT YOUR DAD TO BREAKFAST.
7. FUEL UP YOUR SISTER'S CAR.
8. GET FOUR SHIRTS AT A THRIFT SHOP.
9. BAKE DOZENS OF COOKIES AND GIVE THEM TO YOUR NEIGHBORS.
10. BUY UP EVERYTHING AT A LITTLE KID'S LEMONADE STAND.

JEWISH LEADERS QUESTION JESUS

20 One day Jesus was in the Temple, teaching the people and telling them the Good News. The leading priests, teachers of the law, and older leaders came up to talk with him, ²saying, "Tell us what authority you have to do these things? Who gave you this authority?"

³Jesus answered, "I will also ask you a question. Tell me: ⁴When John baptized people, was that authority from God or just from other people?"

⁵They argued about this, saying, "If we answer, 'John's baptism was from God,' Jesus will say, 'Then why did you not believe him?' ⁶But if we say, 'It was from other people,' all the

Luke 17:6

WORD: Faith the size of a tiny mustard seed can move mountains.

WALK IT: Set a supersized goal for yourself. Work hard and believe Christ will give you strength to achieve it.

19:46 'My Temple . . . prayer.' Quotation from Isaiah 56:7.   19:46 'hideout for robbers' Quotation from Jeremiah 7:11.

people will stone us to death, because they believe John was a prophet." [7]So they answered that they didn't know where it came from.

[8]Jesus said to them, "Then I won't tell you what authority I have to do these things."

A STORY ABOUT GOD'S SON

[9]Then Jesus told the people this story: "A man planted a vineyard and leased it to some farmers. Then he went away for a long time. [10]When it was time for the grapes to be picked, he sent a servant to the farmers to get some of the grapes. But they beat the servant and sent him away empty-handed. [11]Then he sent another servant. They beat this servant also, and showed no respect for him, and sent him away empty-handed. [12]So the man sent a third servant. The farmers wounded him and threw him out. [13]The owner of the vineyard said, 'What will I do now? I will send my son whom I love. Maybe they will respect him.' [14]But when the farmers saw the son, they said to each other, 'This son will inherit the vineyard. If we kill him, it will be ours.' [15]So the farmers threw the son out of the vineyard and killed him.

"What will the owner of this vineyard do to them? [16]He will come and kill those farmers and will give the vineyard to other farmers."

When the people heard this story, they said, "Let this never happen!"

[17]But Jesus looked at them and said, "Then what does this verse mean:

'The stone that the builders rejected
became the cornerstone'? *Psalm 118:22*

[18]Everyone who falls on that stone will be broken, and the person on whom it falls, that person will be crushed!"

[19]The teachers of the law and the leading priests wanted to arrest Jesus at once, because they knew the story was about them. But they were afraid of what the people would do.

IS IT RIGHT TO PAY TAXES OR NOT?

[20]So they watched Jesus and sent some spies who acted as if they were sincere. They wanted to trap Jesus in saying something wrong so they could hand him over to the authority and power of the governor. [21]So the spies asked Jesus, "Teacher, we know that what you say and teach is true. You pay no attention to who people are, and you always teach the truth about God's way. [22]Tell us, is it right for us to pay taxes to Caesar or not?"

[23]But Jesus, knowing they were trying to trick him, said, [24]"Show me a coin. Whose image and name are on it?"

They said, "Caesar's."

[25]Jesus said to them, "Then give to Caesar

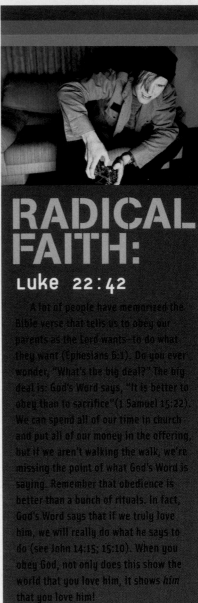

RADICAL FAITH:
Luke 22:42

A lot of people have memorized the Bible verse that tells us to obey our parents as the Lord wants—to do what they want (Ephesians 6:1). Do you ever wonder, "What's the big deal?" The big deal is: God's Word says, "It is better to obey than to sacrifice"(1 Samuel 15:22). We can spend all of our time in church and put all of our money in the offering, but if we aren't walking the walk, we're missing the point of what God's Word is saying. Remember that obedience is better than a bunch of rituals. In fact, God's Word says that if we truly love him, we will really do what he says to do (see John 14:15; 15:10). When you obey God, not only does this show the world that you love him, it shows *him* that you love him!

You can study the whole Bible looking at the lives of those who obeyed God and those who didn't. You'll find that the ones who were obedient were the ones who got blessed! Abraham obeyed God. Noah obeyed God. Joseph obeyed God. Daniel obeyed God. Jesus obeyed his Father, God. Paul obeyed God. Every one of those folks reaped the benefits of obedience. Obey God today, and reap the blessings of God tomorrow!

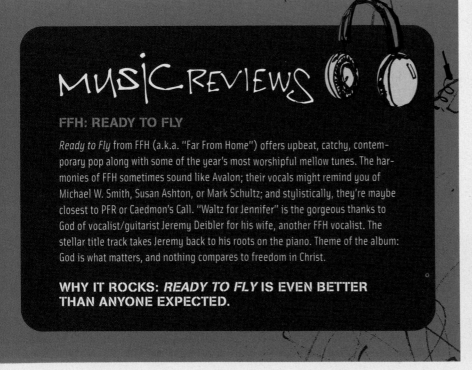

MUSIC REVIEWS

FFH: READY TO FLY

Ready to Fly from FFH (a.k.a. "Far From Home") offers upbeat, catchy, contemporary pop along with some of the year's most worshipful mellow tunes. The harmonies of FFH sometimes sound like Avalon; their vocals might remind you of Michael W. Smith, Susan Ashton, or Mark Schultz; and stylistically, they're maybe closest to PFR or Caedmon's Call. "Waltz for Jennifer" is the gorgeous thanks to God of vocalist/guitarist Jeremy Deibler for his wife, another FFH vocalist. The stellar title track takes Jeremy back to his roots on the piano. Theme of the album: God is what matters, and nothing compares to freedom in Christ.

WHY IT ROCKS: *READY TO FLY* IS EVEN BETTER THAN ANYONE EXPECTED.

the things that are Caesar's, and give to God the things that are God's."

[26]So they were not able to trap Jesus in anything he said in the presence of the people. And being amazed at his answer, they became silent.

SOME SADDUCEES TRY TO TRICK JESUS

[27]Some Sadducees, who believed people would not rise from the dead, came to Jesus. [28]They asked, "Teacher, Moses wrote that if a man's brother dies and leaves a wife but no children, then that man must marry the widow and have children for his brother. [29]Once there were seven brothers. The first brother married and died, but had no children. [30]Then the second brother married the widow, and he died. [31]And the third brother married the widow, and he died. The same thing happened with all seven brothers; they died and had no children. [32]Finally, the woman died also. [33]Since all seven brothers had married her, whose wife will she be when people rise from the dead?"

[34]Jesus said to them, "On earth, people marry and are given to someone to marry. [35]But those who will be worthy to be raised from the dead and live again will not marry, nor will they be given to someone to marry. [36]In that life they are like angels and cannot die. They are children of God, because they have been raised from the dead. [37]Even Moses clearly showed

HEBREWS 13:1 "KEEP ON LOVING EACH OTHER AS BROTHERS AND SISTERS."

that the dead are raised to life. When he wrote about the burning bush,[n] he said that the Lord is 'the God of Abraham, the God of Isaac, and the God of Jacob.'[n] [38]God is the God of the living, not the dead, because all people are alive to him."

[39]Some of the teachers of the law said, "Teacher, your answer was good." [40]No one was brave enough to ask him another question.

IS THE CHRIST THE SON OF DAVID?

[41]Then Jesus said, "Why do people say that the Christ is the Son of David? [42]In the book of Psalms, David himself says:

'The Lord said to my Lord:
Sit by me at my right side,
[43] until I put your enemies under
your control.'[n]   *Psalm 110:1*

[44]David calls the Christ 'Lord,' so how can the Christ be his son?"

JESUS ACCUSES SOME LEADERS

[45]While all the people were listening, Jesus said to his followers, [46]"Beware of the teachers of the law. They like to walk around wearing fancy clothes, and they love for people to greet them with respect in the marketplaces. They love to have the most important seats in the synagogues and at feasts. [47]But they cheat widows and steal their houses and then try to make themselves look good by saying long prayers. They will receive a greater punishment."

TRUE GIVING

21 As Jesus looked up, he saw some rich people putting their gifts into the Temple money box.[n] [2]Then he saw a poor widow putting two small copper coins into the box.

USAONWATCH (UOW) was created by the National Sheriffs' Association together with federal agencies to keep the USA and its neighborhoods safer and more secure. USAonwatch revamps and revitalizes Neighborhood Watch programs throughout the country. One of the oldest and best-known crime prevention concepts in history,

Neighborhood Watch was created as a massive effort to reduce residential crime. USAonwatch can show you how to start a Neighborhood Watch group and beef up safety in your hometown.

To learn more, go to
www.usaonwatch.org.

20:37 **burning bush** Read Exodus 3:1–12 in the Old Testament.   20:37 **'the God of . . . Jacob'** These words are taken from Exodus 3:6.   20:43 **until . . . control** Literally, "until I make your enemies a footstool for your feet."   21:1 **money box** A special box in the Jewish place of worship where people put their gifts to God.

[3]He said, "I tell you the truth, this poor widow gave more than all those rich people. [4]They gave only what they did not need. This woman is very poor, but she gave all she had to live on."

THE TEMPLE WILL BE DESTROYED

[5]Some people were talking about the Temple and how it was decorated with beautiful stones and gifts offered to God.

But Jesus said, [6]"As for these things you are looking at, the time will come when not one stone will be left on another. Every stone will be thrown down."

ISAIAH 54:10 "THE MOUNTAINS MAY DISAPPEAR, AND THE HILLS MAY COME TO AN END, BUT MY LOVE WILL NEVER DISAPPEAR; MY PROMISE OF PEACE WILL NOT COME TO AN END."

[7]They asked Jesus, "Teacher, when will these things happen? What will be the sign that they are about to take place?"

[8]Jesus said, "Be careful so you are not fooled. Many people will come in my name, saying, 'I am the One' and, 'The time has come!' But don't follow them. [9]When you hear about wars and riots, don't be afraid, because these things must happen first, but the end will come later."

[10]Then he said to them, "Nations will fight against other nations, and kingdoms against other kingdoms. [11]In various places there will be great earthquakes, sicknesses, and a lack of food. Fearful events and great signs will come from heaven.

[12]"But before all these things happen, people will arrest you and treat you cruelly. They will judge you in their synagogues and put you in jail and force you to stand before kings and governors, because you follow me. [13]But this will give you an opportunity to tell about me. [14]Make up your minds not to worry ahead of time about what you will say. [15]I will give you the wisdom to say things that none of your enemies will be able to stand against or prove wrong. [16]Even your parents, brothers, rela-

tives, and friends will turn against you, and they will kill some of you. [17]All people will hate you because you follow me. [18]But none of these things can really harm you. [19]By continuing to have faith you will save your lives.

JERUSALEM WILL BE DESTROYED

[20]"When you see armies all around Jerusalem, you will know it will soon be destroyed. [21]At that time, the people in Judea should run away to the mountains. The people in Jerusalem must get out, and those who are near the city should not go in. [22]These are the days of punishment to bring about all that is written in the Scriptures. [23]How terrible it will be for women who are pregnant or have nursing babies! Great trouble will come upon this land, and God will be angry with these people. [24]They will be killed by the sword and taken as prisoners to all nations. Jerusalem will be crushed by non-Jewish people until their time is over.

DON'T FEAR

[25]"There will be signs in the sun, moon, and stars. On earth, nations will be afraid and confused because of the roar and fury of the sea. [26]People will be so afraid they will faint, wondering what is happening to the world, because the powers of the heavens will be shaken. [27]Then people will see the Son of Man

coming in a cloud with power and great glory. [28]When these things begin to happen, look up and hold your heads high, because the time when God will free you is near!"

JESUS' WORDS WILL LIVE FOREVER

[29]Then Jesus told this story: "Look at the fig tree and all the other trees. [30]When their leaves appear, you know that summer is near. [31]In the same way, when you see these things happening, you will know that God's kingdom is near.

[32]"I tell you the truth, all these things will happen while the people of this time are still living. [33]Earth and sky will be destroyed, but the words I have spoken will never be destroyed.

BE READY ALL THE TIME

[34]"Be careful not to spend your time feasting, drinking, or worrying about worldly things. If you do, that day might come on you suddenly, [35]like a trap on all people on earth. [36]So be ready all the time. Pray that you will be strong enough to escape all these things that will happen and that you will be able to stand before the Son of Man."

[37]During the day, Jesus taught the people in the Temple, and at night he went out of the city and stayed on the Mount of Olives. [38]Every morning all the people got up early to go to the Temple to listen to him.

travel the road

In the days before planes, trains, and automobiles, missionaries sailed off with their belongings packed in coffins, knowing a wooden box was likely their only ride home. John Leonard Dober and David Nitschman were willing to pay a price even greater than death when they sailed from the port of Copenhagen in October 1732. Intent on selling themselves into slavery to share Jesus with the slaves of the West Indies, the two young men cried out that Christ was worth whatever they would suffer: "May the Lamb that was slain receive the reward of his suffering!"

For more on extreme missions visit www.traveltheroad.com

JUDAS BECOMES AN ENEMY OF JESUS

22 It was almost time for the Feast of Unleavened Bread, called the Passover Feast. [2] The leading priests and teachers of the law were trying to find a way to kill Jesus, because they were afraid of the people.

[3] Satan entered Judas Iscariot, one of Jesus' twelve apostles. [4] Judas went to the leading priests and some of the soldiers who guarded the Temple and talked to them about a way to hand Jesus over to them. [5] They were pleased and agreed to give Judas money. [6] He agreed and watched for the best time to hand Jesus over to them when he was away from the crowd.

JESUS EATS THE PASSOVER MEAL

[7] The Day of Unleavened Bread came when the Passover lambs had to be sacrificed. [8] Jesus said to Peter and John, "Go and prepare the Passover meal for us to eat."

[9] They asked, "Where do you want us to prepare it?" [10] Jesus said to them, "After you go into the city, a man carrying a jar of water will meet you. Follow him into the house that he enters, [11] and tell the owner of the house, 'The Teacher says: Where is the guest room in which I may eat the Passover meal with my followers?' [12] Then he will show you a large, furnished room upstairs. Prepare the Passover meal there."

[13] So Peter and John left and found everything as Jesus had said. And they prepared the Passover meal.

THE LORD'S SUPPER

[14] When the time came, Jesus and the apostles were sitting at the table. [15] He said to them, "I wanted very much to eat this Passover meal with you before I suffer. [16] I will not eat another Passover meal until it is given its true meaning in the kingdom of God."

[17] Then Jesus took a cup, gave thanks, and said, "Take this cup and share it among yourselves. [18] I will not drink again from the fruit of the vine" until God's kingdom comes."

[19] Then Jesus took some bread, gave thanks, broke it, and gave it to the apostles, saying, "This is my body, which I am giving for you. Do this to remember me." [20] In the same way, after supper, Jesus took the cup and said, "This cup is the new agreement that God makes with his people. This new agreement begins with my blood which is poured out for you.

WHO WILL TURN AGAINST JESUS?

[21] "But one of you will turn against me, and his hand is with mine on the table. [22] What God has planned for the Son of Man will happen, but how terrible it will be for that one who turns against the Son of Man."

[23] Then the apostles asked each other which one of them would do that.

BE LIKE A SERVANT

[24] The apostles also began to argue about which one of them was the most important. [25] But Jesus said to them, "The kings of the non-Jewish people rule over them, and those who have authority over others like to be called 'friends of the people.' [26] But you must not be like that. Instead, the greatest among you should be like the youngest, and the leader should be like the servant. [27] Who is more important: the one sitting at the table or the one serving? You think the one at the table is more important, but I am like a servant among you.

[28] "You have stayed with me through my struggles. [29] Just as my Father has given me a kingdom, I also give you a kingdom [30] so you may eat and drink at my table in my kingdom. And you will sit on thrones, judging the twelve tribes of Israel.

DON'T LOSE YOUR FAITH!

[31] "Simon, Simon, Satan has asked to test all of you as a farmer sifts his wheat. [32] I have prayed that you will not lose your faith! Help

22:18 **fruit of the vine** Product of the grapevine; this may also be translated "wine."

HOW TO EXTINGUISH A RAGING INFERNO

Guys like to play with fire, and smart ones channel that fascination into backyard barbecues and safely contained bonfires. Yet there comes a time in every man's life when he has to stop a fire gone bad. You can't extinguish the flames without knowing what you're fighting. You can put out wood, paper, and cloth fires with water. But water actually makes an oil fire worse. You need to smother an oil fire, for example, using a lid to put out a flaming pan on the stove. And the first step to stopping an electrical fire is pulling the plug or switching off the power at the fuse box. Want to give your family a manly gift that screams, "I CARE!"? Buy an extinguisher with a label that says "ABC" for each floor of your home. Only an ABC extinguisher will put out all three types of fire.

your brothers be stronger when you come back to me."

[33]But Peter said to Jesus, "Lord, I am ready to go with you to prison and even to die with you!"

[34]But Jesus said, "Peter, before the rooster crows this day, you will say three times that you don't know me."

BE READY FOR TROUBLE

[35]Then Jesus said to the apostles, "When I sent you out without a purse, a bag, or sandals, did you need anything?"

They said, "No."

[36]He said to them, "But now if you have a purse or a bag, carry that with you. If you don't have a sword, sell your coat and buy one. [37]The Scripture says, 'He was treated like a criminal,'[n] and I tell you this scripture must have its full meaning. It was written about me, and it is happening now."

[38]His followers said, "Look, Lord, here are two swords."

He said to them, "That is enough."

JESUS PRAYS ALONE

[39]Jesus left the city and went to the Mount of Olives, as he often did, and his followers went with him. [40]When he reached the place, he said to them, "Pray for strength against temptation."

[41]Then Jesus went about a stone's throw away from them. He kneeled down and prayed, [42]"Father, if you are willing, take away this cup[n] of suffering. But do what you want, not what I want." [43]Then an angel from heaven appeared to him to strengthen him. [44]Being full of pain, Jesus prayed even harder. His sweat was like drops of blood falling to the ground. [45]When he finished praying, he went to his followers and found them asleep because of their sadness. [46]Jesus said to them, "Why are you sleeping? Get up and pray for strength against temptation."

JESUS IS ARRESTED

[47]While Jesus was speaking, a crowd came up, and Judas, one of the twelve apostles, was leading them. He came close to Jesus so he could kiss him.

[48]But Jesus said to him, "Judas, are you using the kiss to give the Son of Man to his enemies?"

RANDOM CAUSES WORTH STANDING FOR

1. THE RIGHTS OF THE UNBORN
2. FOOD FOR THE HUNGRY
3. A BIBLE FOR EVERYONE WHO WANTS ONE
4. UNIVERSAL LITERACY
5. GOOD SCHOOLS IN THE CITY
6. PREMARITAL ABSTINENCE
7. RACIAL EQUALITY
8. HELP FOR THE HOMELESS
9. WOMEN'S RIGHTS IN OPPRESSIVE NATIONS
10. FREEDOM OF WORSHIP

[49]When those who were standing around him saw what was happening, they said, "Lord, should we strike them with our swords?" [50]And one of them struck the servant of the high priest and cut off his right ear.

[51]Jesus said, "Stop! No more of this." Then he touched the servant's ear and healed him.

[52]Those who came to arrest Jesus were the leading priests, the soldiers who guarded the Temple, and the older leaders. Jesus said to them, "You came out here with swords and clubs as though I were a criminal. [53]I was with you every day in the Temple, and you didn't arrest me there. But this is your time—the time when darkness rules."

PETER SAYS HE DOESN'T KNOW JESUS

[54]They arrested Jesus, and led him away, and brought him into the house of the high priest. Peter followed far behind them. [55]After the soldiers started a fire in the middle of the courtyard and sat together, Peter sat with them. [56]A servant girl saw Peter sitting there

 22:37 'He . . . criminal' Quotation from Isaiah 53:12.   22:42 cup Jesus is talking about the painful things that will happen to him. Accepting these things will be hard, like drinking a cup of something bitter.

in the firelight, and looking closely at him, she said, "This man was also with him."

⁵⁷But Peter said this was not true; he said, "Woman, I don't know him."

⁵⁸A short time later, another person saw Peter and said, "You are also one of them."

But Peter said, "Man, I am not!"

⁵⁹About an hour later, another man insisted, "Certainly this man was with him, because he is from Galilee, too."

⁶⁰But Peter said, "Man, I don't know what you are talking about!"

At once, while Peter was still speaking, a rooster crowed. ⁶¹Then the Lord turned and looked straight at Peter. And Peter remembered what the Lord had said: "Before the rooster crows this day, you will say three times that you don't know me." ⁶²Then Peter went outside and cried painfully.

THE PEOPLE MAKE FUN OF JESUS

⁶³The men who were guarding Jesus began making fun of him and beating him.

⁶⁴They blindfolded him and said, "Prove that you are a prophet, and tell us who hit you." ⁶⁵They said many cruel things to Jesus.

JESUS BEFORE THE LEADERS

⁶⁶When day came, the council of the older leaders of the people, both the leading priests and the teachers of the law, came together and led Jesus to their highest court. ⁶⁷They said, "If you are the Christ, tell us."

Jesus said to them, "If I tell you, you will not believe me. ⁶⁸And if I ask you, you will not answer. ⁶⁹But from now on, the Son of Man will sit at the right hand of the powerful God."

⁷⁰They all said, "Then are you the Son of God?"

Jesus said to them, "You say that I am."

⁷¹They said, "Why do we need witnesses now? We ourselves heard him say this."

PILATE QUESTIONS JESUS

23 Then the whole group stood up and led Jesus to Pilate.[n] ²They began to accuse Jesus, saying, "We caught this man telling things that mislead our people. He says that we should not pay taxes to Caesar, and he calls himself the Christ, a king."

³Pilate asked Jesus, "Are you the king of the Jews?"

Jesus answered, "Those are your words."

⁴Pilate said to the leading priests and the people, "I find nothing against this man."

⁵They were insisting, saying, "But Jesus makes trouble with the people, teaching all around Judea. He began in Galilee, and now he is here."

PILATE SENDS JESUS TO HEROD

⁶Pilate heard this and asked if Jesus was from Galilee. ⁷Since Jesus was under Herod's authority, Pilate sent Jesus to Herod, who was in Jerusalem at that time. ⁸When Herod saw Jesus, he was very glad, because he had heard about Jesus and had wanted to meet him for a long time. He was hoping to see Jesus work a miracle. ⁹Herod asked Jesus many questions, but Jesus said nothing. ¹⁰The leading priests and teachers of the law were standing there, strongly accusing Jesus. ¹¹After Herod and his soldiers had made fun of Jesus, they dressed him in a kingly robe and sent him back to Pilate. ¹²In the past, Pilate and Herod had always been enemies, but on that day they became friends.

JESUS MUST DIE

¹³Pilate called the people together with the leading priests and the rulers. ¹⁴He said to them, "You brought this man to me, saying he makes trouble among the people. But I have questioned him before you all, and I have not found him guilty of

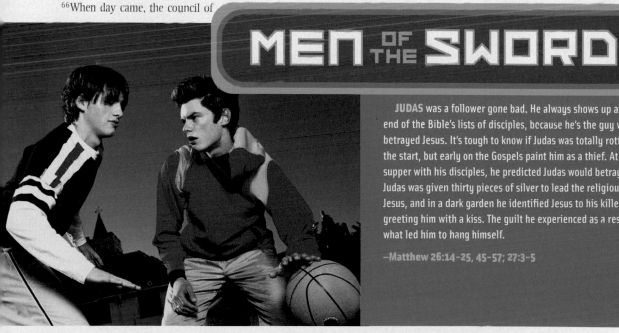

MEN OF THE SWORD

JUDAS was a follower gone bad. He always shows up at the tail end of the Bible's lists of disciples, because he's the guy who betrayed Jesus. It's tough to know if Judas was totally rotten from the start, but early on the Gospels paint him as a thief. At Jesus' last supper with his disciples, he predicted Judas would betray him. Judas was given thirty pieces of silver to lead the religious leaders to Jesus, and in a dark garden he identified Jesus to his killers by greeting him with a kiss. The guilt he experienced as a result is likely what led him to hang himself.

—Matthew 26:14-25, 45-57; 27:3-5

23:1 **Pilate** Pontius Pilate was the Roman governor of Judea from A.D. 26 to A.D. 36.

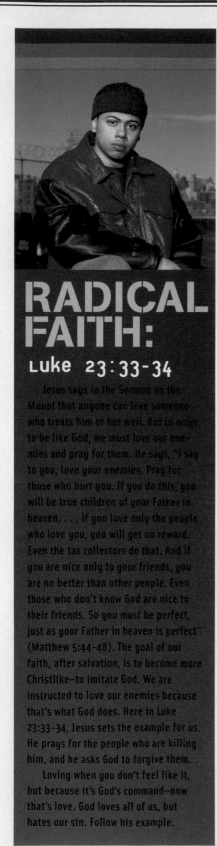

RADICAL FAITH:

Luke 23:33-34

Jesus says in the Sermon on the Mount that anyone can love someone who treats him or her well. But in order to be like God, we must love our enemies and pray for them. He says, "I say to you, love your enemies. Pray for those who hurt you. If you do this, you will be true children of your Father in heaven. . . . If you love only the people who love you, you will get no reward. Even the tax collectors do that. And if you are nice only to your friends, you are no better than other people. Even those who don't know God are nice to their friends. So you must be perfect, just as your Father in heaven is perfect" (Matthew 5:44-48). The goal of our faith, after salvation, is to become more Christlike—to imitate God. We are instructed to love our enemies because that's what God does. Here in Luke 23:33-34, Jesus sets the example for us. He prays for the people who are killing him, and he asks God to forgive them.

Loving when you don't feel like it, but because it's God's command—now that's love. God loves all of us, but hates our sin. Follow his example.

what you say. [15]Also, Herod found nothing wrong with him; he sent him back to us. Look, he has done nothing for which he should die. [16]So, after I punish him, I will let him go free." [17n]

[18]But the people shouted together, "Take this man away! Let Barabbas go free!" [19](Barabbas was a man who was in prison for his part in a riot in the city and for murder.)

[20]Pilate wanted to let Jesus go free and told this to the crowd. [21]But they shouted again, "Crucify him! Crucify him!"

[22]A third time Pilate said to them, "Why? What wrong has he done? I can find no reason to kill him. So I will have him punished and set him free."

[23]But they continued to shout, demanding that Jesus be crucified. Their yelling became so loud that [24]Pilate decided to give them what they wanted. [25]He set free the man who was in jail for rioting and murder, and he handed Jesus over to them to do with him as they wished.

JESUS IS CRUCIFIED

[26]As they led Jesus away, Simon, a man from Cyrene, was coming in from the fields. They forced him to carry Jesus' cross and to walk behind him.

[27]A large crowd of people was following Jesus, including some women who were sad and crying for him. [28]But Jesus turned and said to them, "Women of Jerusalem, don't cry for me. Cry for yourselves and for your children. [29]The time is coming when people will say, 'Happy are the women who cannot have children and who have no babies to nurse.' [30]Then people will say to the mountains, 'Fall on us!' And they will say to the hills, 'Cover us!' [31]If they act like this now when life is good, what will happen when bad times come?"[n]

[32]There were also two criminals led out with Jesus to be put to death. [33]When they came to a place called the Skull, the soldiers crucified Jesus and the criminals—one on his right and the other on his left. [34]Jesus said, "Father, forgive them, because they don't know what they are doing."[n]

The soldiers threw lots to decide who would get his clothes. [35]The people stood there watching. And the leaders made fun of Jesus, saying, "He saved others. Let him save himself if he is God's Chosen One, the Christ."

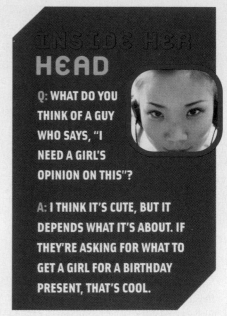

INSIDE HER HEAD

Q: WHAT DO YOU THINK OF A GUY WHO SAYS, "I NEED A GIRL'S OPINION ON THIS"?

A: I THINK IT'S CUTE, BUT IT DEPENDS WHAT IT'S ABOUT. IF THEY'RE ASKING FOR WHAT TO GET A GIRL FOR A BIRTHDAY PRESENT, THAT'S COOL.

[36]The soldiers also made fun of him, coming to Jesus and offering him some vinegar. [37]They said, "If you are the king of the Jews, save yourself!" [38]At the top of the cross these words were written: THIS IS THE KING OF THE JEWS.

[39]One of the criminals on a cross began to shout insults at Jesus: "Aren't you the Christ? Then save yourself and us."

[40]But the other criminal stopped him and said, "You should fear God! You are getting the same punishment he is. [41]We are punished justly, getting what we deserve for what we did. But this man has done nothing wrong." [42]Then he said, "Jesus, remember me when you come into your kingdom."

[43]Jesus said to him, "I tell you the truth, today you will be with me in paradise."[n]

JESUS DIES

[44]It was about noon, and the whole land became dark until three o'clock in the afternoon, [45]because the sun did not shine. The curtain in the Temple[n] was torn in two. [46]Jesus cried out in a loud voice, "Father, I give you my life." After Jesus said this, he died.

[47]When the army officer there saw what happened, he praised God, saying, "Surely this was a good man!"

[48]When all the people who had gathered there to watch saw what happened, they returned home, beating their chests because they were so sad. [49]But those who were close

23:17 Verse 17 A few Greek copies add verse 17: "Every year at the Passover Feast, Pilate had to release one prisoner to the people." 23:31 If . . . come? Literally, "If they do these things in the green tree, what will happen in the dry?" 23:34 Verse 34 Some early Greek copies do not have this first part of the verse. 23:43 paradise Another word for heaven. 23:45 curtain in the Temple A curtain divided the Most Holy Place from the other part of the Temple, the special building in Jerusalem where God commanded the Jewish people to worship him.

friends of Jesus, including the women who had followed him from Galilee, stood at a distance and watched.

JOSEPH TAKES JESUS' BODY

[50]There was a good and religious man named Joseph who was a member of the council. [51]But he had not agreed to the other leaders' plans and actions against Jesus. He was from the town of Arimathea and was waiting for the kingdom of God to come. [52]Joseph went to Pilate to ask for the body of Jesus. [53]He took the body down from the cross, wrapped it in

ACTS 4:12 "JESUS IS THE ONLY ONE WHO CAN SAVE PEOPLE. HIS NAME IS THE ONLY POWER IN THE WORLD THAT HAS BEEN GIVEN TO SAVE PEOPLE."

cloth, and put it in a tomb that was cut out of a wall of rock. This tomb had never been used before. [54]This was late on Preparation Day, and when the sun went down, the Sabbath day would begin.

[55]The women who had come from Galilee with Jesus followed Joseph and saw the tomb and how Jesus' body was laid. [56]Then the women left to prepare spices and perfumes.

On the Sabbath day they rested, as the law of Moses commanded.

JESUS RISES FROM THE DEAD

24 Very early on the first day of the week, at dawn, the women came to the tomb, bringing the spices they had prepared. [2]They found the stone rolled away from the entrance of the tomb, [3]but when they went in, they did not find the body of the Lord Jesus. [4]While they were wondering about this, two men in shining clothes suddenly stood beside them. [5]The women were very afraid and bowed their heads to the ground. The men said to them, "Why are you looking for a living person in this place for the dead? [6]He is not here; he has risen from the dead. Do you remember what he told you in Galilee? [7]He said the Son of Man must be handed over to sinful people, be crucified, and rise from the dead on the third day." [8]Then the women remembered what Jesus had said.

[9]The women left the tomb and told all these things to the eleven apostles and the other followers. [10]It was Mary Magdalene, Joanna, Mary the mother of James, and some other women who told the apostles everything that had happened at the tomb. [11]But they did not believe the women, because it sounded like nonsense. [12]But Peter got up and ran to the tomb. Bending down and looking in, he saw only the cloth that Jesus' body had been wrapped in. Peter went away to his home, wondering about what had happened.

JESUS ON THE ROAD TO EMMAUS

[13]That same day two of Jesus' followers were going to a town named Emmaus, about seven miles from Jerusalem. [14]They were talking about everything that had happened. [15]While they were talking and discussing, Jesus himself came near and began walking with them, [16]but they were kept from recognizing him. [17]Then he said, "What are these things you are talking about while you walk?"

The two followers stopped, looking very sad. [18]The one named Cleopas answered, "Are you the only visitor in Jerusalem who does not know what just happened there?"

[19]Jesus said to them, "What are you talking about?"

They said, "About Jesus of Nazareth. He was a prophet who said and did many powerful things before God and all the people. [20]Our leaders and the leading priests handed him over to be sentenced to death, and they crucified him. [21]But we were hoping that he would free Israel. Besides this, it is now the third day since this happened. [22]And today some women among us amazed us. Early this morning they went to the tomb, [23]but they did not find his body there. They came and told us that they had seen a vision of angels who said that Jesus was alive! [24]So some of our group went to the tomb, too. They found it just as the women said, but they did not see Jesus."

[25]Then Jesus said to them, "You are foolish and slow to believe everything the prophets said. [26]They said that the Christ must suffer these things before he enters his glory." [27]Then starting with what Moses and all the prophets had said about him, Jesus began to explain everything that had been written about himself in the Scriptures.

EXPERTS ANSWER YOUR QUESTIONS

Q. *How much beer can I drink before it's a sin?*

A. There's no easy answer. It's hard to make the case that the Bible forbids all drinking; after all, even Jesus turned water into wine at a wedding party. But it's clear that getting drunk is another story. So is underage drinking. If you never start, you'll never have to stop.

Q. *Did Jesus sport any tattoos?*

A. In Leviticus 19:28, the Israelites are told not to get tattoos, which the heathen used in their religion. If you're wondering what God thinks about your latest plan to accessorize, he'd no doubt ask, "Why do you want one?" God built you an awesome body, and you need to think hard about a mark that will show when you get a sponge bath in the nursing home. It's not something you want to decide without your parents' input.

Q. *How can a person say something is wrong when they've never tried it?*

A. That makes no sense at all. You don't have to jump off a 20-story building to know it will do more than wrinkle your clothes. You likewise don't have to sin to be sure of the damage it causes.

²⁸They came near the town of Emmaus, and Jesus acted as if he were going farther. ²⁹But they begged him, "Stay with us, because it is late; it is almost night." So he went in to stay with them.

³⁰When Jesus was at the table with them, he took some bread, gave thanks, divided it, and gave it to them. ³¹And then, they were allowed to recognize Jesus. But when they saw who he was, he disappeared. ³²They said to each other, "It felt like a fire burning in us when Jesus talked to us on the road and explained the Scriptures to us."

because a ghost does not have a living body as you see I have."

⁴⁰After Jesus said this, he showed them his hands and feet. ⁴¹While they still could not believe it because they were amazed and happy, Jesus said to them, "Do you have any food here?" ⁴²They gave him a piece of broiled fish. ⁴³While the followers watched, Jesus took the fish and ate it.

⁴⁴He said to them, "Remember when I was with you before? I said that everything written

RANDOM WAYS TO TAKE A STAND

1. **WRITE A LETTER TO YOUR SCHOOL PAPER.**

2. **PUT YOUR TIME TOWARD BRINGING ABOUT CHANGE.**

3. **COMPLAIN INTELLIGENTLY TO POWERFUL PEOPLE.**

4. **DO WHAT YOU SAY YOU BELIEVE.**

5. **COURTEOUSLY INFORM OTHERS OF YOUR CONVICTIONS.**

6. **BUILD A WEBSITE.**

7. **START A SPECIAL-INTEREST GROUP AND TAKE ACTION.**

8. **ORGANIZE YOUR FRIENDS.**

9. **DISTRIBUTE FLIERS.**

10. **PUT YOUR MONEY WHERE YOUR MOUTH IS.**

WAYS TO WALK THE WALK

Luke 18:14

WORD: All who humble themselves will be made great.

WALK IT: Eat lunch today with somebody who might typically eat alone—someone labeled "uncool." Treat that person with the same importance God gives to you.

³³So the two followers got up at once and went back to Jerusalem. There they found the eleven apostles and others gathered. ³⁴They were saying, "The Lord really has risen from the dead! He showed himself to Simon."

³⁵Then the two followers told what had happened on the road and how they recognized Jesus when he divided the bread.

JESUS APPEARS TO HIS FOLLOWERS

³⁶While the two followers were telling this, Jesus himself stood right in the middle of them and said, "Peace be with you."

³⁷They were fearful and terrified and thought they were seeing a ghost. ³⁸But Jesus said, "Why are you troubled? Why do you doubt what you see? ³⁹Look at my hands and my feet. It is I myself! Touch me and see,

about me must happen—everything in the law of Moses, the books of the prophets, and the Psalms."

⁴⁵Then Jesus opened their minds so they could understand the Scriptures. ⁴⁶He said to them, "It is written that the Christ would suffer and rise from the dead on the third day ⁴⁷and that a change of hearts and lives and forgiveness of sins would be preached in his name to all nations, starting at Jerusalem. ⁴⁸You are witnesses of these things. ⁴⁹I will send you what my Father has promised, but you must stay in Jerusalem until you have received that power from heaven."

JESUS GOES BACK TO HEAVEN

⁵⁰Jesus led his followers as far as Bethany, and he raised his hands and blessed them.

⁵¹While he was blessing them, he was separated from them and carried into heaven. ⁵²They worshiped him and returned to Jerusalem very happy. ⁵³They stayed in the Temple all the time, praising God.

Mother's Day is always the second Sunday in May. Dedicate your whole day to making Mom feel appreciated!

1
May is Better Sleep Month. Don't miss it.

2
Engelbert Humperdinck's birthday. Figure out who he was.

3

4
Empty every garbage can in your home every Saturday this month. Can you make it a habit?

5

6

7
International Tuba Day. If you don't own one, borrow one and blatt a note.

8
Check the tire inflation on the family car today.

9

10
Pray for a Person of Influence. Today is Bono's birthday.

11

12
Pray for a Person of Influence: Tony Hawk racks up other birthday today.

13
Read the Book of 1 John today.

14
Visit a nursing home this weekend.

15

16

17

18
Pray for a Person of Influence: Today is Tait's birthday.

19
Do your part to reduce third world debt! Visit www.datadata.org for information.

20
Pray for a Person of Influence: It's Tony Stewart's birthday.

21

22
Plan a cookout for Memorial Day. Invite someone who needs a friend.

23
Pray for a Person of Influence: P Diddy gets older today.

24
National Escargot Day. Maybe you want to pass.

25
Pray for a Person of Influence: Mike Myers has a birthday today.

26

27
Avoid summer school: Start pulling together stuff to help you study for finals.

28

29

31
It's National Book Month. Ask your English teacher for three books you should read over the summer.

JOHN

JOHN STATES WHY WE SHOULD BELIEVE IN JESUS

This is the Gospel for guys with big brains. It's for thinkers who want to take all the facts about Jesus and give them a spin to get a good look. If the action-packed Gospel of Mark seems aimed at shorter attention spans, John has a different kind of person in mind. This book is for people who like to peel off layer after layer of dramatic, insightful symbolism, and people who want extensive, detailed teaching sessions led by the Master Teacher. It's a tour inside the mind of Jesus told by his tightest friend.

John wrote this with one purpose in mind: to convince us to have faith in what he couldn't possibly explain. The unexplainable is that Jesus and God are one, and that when Jesus lived on earth, he was both truly God and truly human. That's a thought that almost doesn't even fit inside your head. John doesn't even try to explain how this could be. He simply reports that it is. He provides testimony from a ton of eyewitnesses, including Jesus himself. He tosses us a convincing set of miracles that prove who Jesus is. And John writes so we can believe—and, by believing, enjoy the same kind of close friendship with Jesus that he does.

CHRIST COMES TO THE WORLD

1 In the beginning there was the Word.[n] The Word was with God, and the Word was God. [2]He was with God in the beginning. [3]All things were made by him, and nothing was made without him. [4]In him there was life, and that life was the light of all people. [5]The Light shines in the darkness, and the darkness has not overpowered it.

[6]There was a man named John[n] who was sent by God. [7]He came to tell people the truth about the Light so that through him all people could hear about the Light and believe. [8]John was not the Light, but he came to tell people the truth about the Light. [9]The true Light that gives light to all was coming into the world!

[10]The Word was in the world, and the world was made by him, but the world did not know him. [11]He came to the world that was his own, but his own people did not accept him. [12]But to all who did accept him and believe in him he gave the right to become children of God. [13]They did not become his children in any human way—by any human parents or human desire. They were born of God.

[14]The Word became a human and lived among us. We saw his glory—the glory that belongs to the only Son of the Father—and he was full of grace and truth. [15]John tells the truth about him and cries out, saying, "This is the One I told you about: 'The One who comes after me is greater than I am, because he was living before me.'"

[16]Because he was full of grace and truth, from him we all received one gift after another. [17]The law was given through Moses, but grace and truth came through Jesus Christ. [18]No one has ever seen God. But God the only Son is very close to the Father,[n] and he has shown us what God is like.

JOHN TELLS PEOPLE ABOUT JESUS

[19]Here is the truth John[n] told when the leaders in Jerusalem sent priests and Levites to ask him, "Who are you?"

[20]John spoke freely and did not refuse to answer. He said, "I am not the Christ."

[21]So they asked him, "Then who are you? Are you Elijah?"[n]

He answered, "No, I am not."

"Are you the Prophet?"[n] they asked.

He answered, "No."

[22]Then they said, "Who are you? Give us an answer to tell those who sent us. What do you say about yourself?"

[23]John told them in the words of the prophet Isaiah:

"I am the voice of one
    calling out in the desert:
'Make the road straight for the Lord.'" *Isaiah 40:3*

[24]Some Pharisees who had been sent asked John: [25]"If you are not the Christ or Elijah or the Prophet, why do you baptize people?"

[26]John answered, "I baptize with water, but there is one here with you that you don't know about. [27]He is the One who comes after me. I am not good enough to untie the strings of his sandals."

[28]This all happened at Bethany on the other side of the Jordan River, where John was baptizing people.

[29]The next day John saw Jesus coming toward him. John said, "Look, the Lamb of God,[n] who takes away the sin of the world! [30]This is the One I was talking about when I said, 'A man will come after me, but he is greater than I am, because he was living before me.' [31]Even I did not know who he was, although I came baptizing with water so that the people of Israel would know who he is."

[32-33]Then John said, "I saw the Spirit come down from heaven in the form of a dove and rest on him. Until then I did not know who the Christ was. But the God who sent me to baptize with water told me, 'You will see the Spirit come down and rest on a man; he is the One who will baptize with the Holy Spirit.' [34]I have seen this happen, and I tell you the truth: This man is the Son of God."

THE FIRST FOLLOWERS OF JESUS

[35]The next day John[n] was there again with two of his followers. [36]When he saw Jesus walking by, he said, "Look, the Lamb of God!"[n]

[37]The two followers heard John say this, so they followed Jesus. [38]When Jesus turned and saw them following him, he asked, "What are you looking for?"

They said, "Rabbi, where are you staying?" ("Rabbi" means "Teacher.")

[39]He answered, "Come and see." So the two men went with Jesus and saw where he was staying and stayed there with him that day. It was about four o'clock in the afternoon.

RELATIONSHIPS

"So there are not two, but one. God has joined the two together, so no one should separate them" (Mark 10:8). Some guys figure that sex is so incredible they should get whatever they can, whenever they can, from whomever they can. Idiots. They haven't even scratched the surface of God's grand design. Sex is more than two strangers encountering each other's bodies. It's getting glued together in heart, mind, and body. That's a bond not meant to be broken. If you give yourself to someone before marriage, you break God's command. But you're also setting yourself up to get shredded.

 1:1 **Word** The Greek word is "logos," meaning any kind of communication; it could be translated "message." Here, it means Christ, because Christ was the way God told people about himself. 1:6, 19, 35 **John** John the Baptist, who preached to people about Christ's coming (Matthew 3, Luke 3). 1:18 **But . . . Father** This could be translated, "But the only God is very close to the Father." Also, some Greek copies say, "But the only Son is very close to the Father." 1:21 **Elijah** A prophet who spoke for God. He lived hundreds of years before Christ and was expected to return before Christ (Malachi 4:5–6). 1:21 **Prophet** They probably meant the prophet that God told Moses he would send (Deuteronomy 18:15–19). 1:29, 36 **Lamb of God** Name for Jesus. Jesus is like the lambs that were offered for a sacrifice to God.

EXPERTS ANSWER YOUR QUESTIONS

Q. *Why did God make weed if he didn't want people to smoke it?*

A. God created lots of things that are subject to *abuse*. He gave us water to drink, but he's not keen on us drowning people in it. And smoking weed is illegal, right? So don't use hemp for a smoke; save it for making soap on a rope.

Q. *I've done some really bad stuff I'm not proud of. Can I ever get rid of the guilt I feel?*

A. You've probably told yourself a thousand times that God can't forgive you. But start telling yourself this truth: that if you admit your sins to God, he forgives and cleanses you (1 John 1:8-9). You might have to think that thought a thousand times before you believe it, but it's true. Start now!

Q. *My mom has cancer. Can God do miracles now?*

A. God cares deeply for your mom and sees what's going on in every cell of her body. It would be easy to say, "God always heals." Or even "God never heals." But the truth is "God sometimes heals." We have every right to ask him for a miracle until he says no. And even then we can rely on his strength to help us through it all.

[40]One of the two men who followed Jesus after they heard John speak about him was Andrew, Simon Peter's brother. [41]The first thing Andrew did was to find his brother Simon and say to him, "We have found the Messiah." ("Messiah" means "Christ.")

[42]Then Andrew took Simon to Jesus. Jesus looked at him and said, "You are Simon son of John. You will be called Cephas." ("Cephas" means "Peter."[n])

[43]The next day Jesus decided to go to Galilee. He found Philip and said to him, "Follow me."

[44]Philip was from the town of Bethsaida, where Andrew and Peter lived. [45]Philip found Nathanael and told him, "We have found the man that Moses wrote about in the law, and the prophets also wrote about him. He is Jesus, the son of Joseph, from Nazareth."

[46]But Nathanael said to Philip, "Can anything good come from Nazareth?"

Philip answered, "Come and see."

[47]As Jesus saw Nathanael coming toward him, he said, "Here is truly an Israelite. There is nothing false in him."

[48]Nathanael asked, "How do you know me?"

Jesus answered, "I saw you when you were under the fig tree, before Philip told you about me."

[49]Then Nathanael said to Jesus, "Teacher, you are the Son of God; you are the King of Israel."

[50]Jesus said to Nathanael, "Do you believe simply because I told you I saw you under the fig tree? You will see greater things than that." [51]And Jesus said to them, "I tell you the truth, you will all see heaven open and 'angels of God going up and coming down'[n] on the Son of Man."

THE WEDDING AT CANA

2 Two days later there was a wedding in the town of Cana in Galilee. Jesus' mother was there, [2]and Jesus and his followers were also invited to the wedding. [3]When all the wine was gone, Jesus' mother said to him, "They have no more wine."

[4]Jesus answered, "Dear woman, why come to me? My time has not yet come."

[5]His mother said to the servants, "Do whatever he tells you to do."

[6]In that place there were six stone water jars that the Jews used in their washing ceremony.[n] Each jar held about twenty or thirty gallons.

[7]Jesus said to the servants, "Fill the jars

RADICAL FAITH:

john 1:1

This verse will knock anyone who doesn't believe in the Trinity—that God the Father, God the Son (Jesus), and the Holy Spirit are all three in one—right in the head. Verse 14 says, "The Word became a human and lived among us. We saw his glory—the glory that belongs to the only Son of the Father—and he was full of grace and truth." Jesus is the Word! That's why Hebrews 4:12 says that the Word of God is "alive and working."

If you want to get closer to God, start by spending time in his Word. Not only will you learn about him, but you'll hear from him. Jesus speaks to us through his Word more than any other way. That's why it's so important to read the Bible, study it, and memorize verses.

Did you know that as you spend time in this Book, the Word of God, your faith is being increased? It's vital that you put the Word of God in you when things are going great and you don't think you need it, so it will be there when you do need it. Remember, "Faith comes from hearing the Good News" (Romans 10:17). That message is in the Word of God. Jesus is the Word!

 1:42 Peter The Greek name "Peter," like the Aramaic name "Cephas," means "rock." **1:51 'angels . . . down'** These words are from Genesis 28:12. **2:6 washing ceremony** The Jewish people washed themselves in special ways before eating, before worshiping in the Temple, and at other special times.

with water." So they filled the jars to the top.

[8]Then he said to them, "Now take some out and give it to the master of the feast."

So they took the water to the master. [9]When he tasted it, the water had become wine. He did not know where the wine came from, but the servants who had brought the water knew. The master of the wedding called the bridegroom [10]and said to him, "People always serve the best wine first. Later, after the guests have been drinking awhile, they serve the cheaper wine. But you have saved the best wine till now."

[11]So in Cana of Galilee Jesus did his first miracle. There he showed his glory, and his followers believed in him.

JESUS IN THE TEMPLE

[12]After this, Jesus went to the town of Capernaum with his mother, brothers, and followers. They stayed there for just a few days. [13]When it was almost time for the Jewish Passover Feast, Jesus went to Jerusalem. [14]In the Temple he found people selling cattle, sheep, and doves. He saw others sitting at tables, exchanging different kinds of money. [15]Jesus made a whip out of cords and forced all of them, both the sheep and cattle, to leave the Temple. He turned over the tables and scattered the money of those who were exchanging it. [16]Then he said to those who were selling pigeons, "Take these things out of here! Don't make my Father's house a place for buying and selling!"

[17]When this happened, the followers remembered what was written in the Scriptures: "My strong love for your Temple completely controls me."[n]

[18]Some of his people said to Jesus, "Show us a miracle to prove you have the right to do these things."

[19]Jesus answered them, "Destroy this temple, and I will build it again in three days."

[20]They answered, "It took forty-six years to build this Temple! Do you really believe you can build it again in three days?"

[21](But the temple Jesus meant was his own body. [22]After Jesus was raised from the dead, his followers remembered that Jesus had said this. Then they believed the Scripture and the words Jesus had said.)

[23]When Jesus was in Jerusalem for the Passover Feast, many people believed in him because they saw the miracles he did. [24]But Jesus did not trust himself to them because he knew them all. [25]He did not need anyone to

GET OUT THERE

MS is a chronic, unpredictable neurological disease that affects the central nervous system. MS is not contagious and is not directly inherited. MS is not considered a fatal disease. The majority of people with MS do not become severely disabled.

The mission of the NATIONAL MULTIPLE SCLEROSIS SOCIETY is to end the devastating effects of MS. Volunteers at the National Multiple Sclerosis Society are integral partners in the fight against MS. Throughout the United States, volunteers contribute valuable resources (time, knowledge, skills, and leadership), infusing the organization with the energy and passion necessary to end the devastating effects of MS.

The National Multiple Sclerosis Society welcomes volunteers to work in leadership, education, and administration, as well as cool fundraising events like the MS Walk, the MS Bike Tour, or the MS Challenge Walk. Join in!

For more info, check out www.nmss.org.

 2:17 "My . . . me." Quotation from Psalm 69:9.

✓ COUNT ON IT

JOHN 1:16

Check out what this verse is saying. God has given us "grace and truth." This means he's given us one blessing after another. He is the One who blesses. Notice that the verse doesn't say he *takes* from us.

A lot of people have the idea that God is out to take everything away from them, but that's not true. In fact, his Word says that he has come that we might have life "in all its fullness" (John 10:10). God isn't a taker. He's a giver, and he *wants* to give you the desires of your heart (see Psalm 37:4). So what are you going to do? Make God the joy and the delight of your life—and really mean it—and he will bring to pass your heart's desires.

What's your heart's desire? Tell God! He also says that if we will put him first and do what he wants, he will also add other things to us. What kind of things? Whatever we need. Romans 8:32 sums all of this up: "He did not spare his own Son but gave him for us all. So with Jesus, God will surely give us all things." Don't forget it: he is the One who blesses!

travel the road

Hudson Taylor was only seventeen when he committed his life to missions, and just twenty-one when he sailed from England to China, where he learned Chinese and adopted Chinese dress, hairstyle, and culture. Older missionaries ridiculed him, but he refused to impose his English way of life on the Chinese—a principle that has radically changed how Christians reach out. In 1865 Taylor founded the China Inland Mission, a group that sent thousands of men and women deep into China carrying God's Good News. The work continues today as Overseas Missionary Fellowship (OMF) International.

For more on extreme missions visit www.traveltheroad.com.

tell him about people, because he knew what was in people's minds.

NICODEMUS COMES TO JESUS

3 There was a man named Nicodemus who was one of the Pharisees and an important Jewish leader. ²One night Nicodemus came to Jesus and said, "Teacher, we know you are a teacher sent from God, because no one can do the miracles you do unless God is with him."

³Jesus answered, "I tell you the truth, unless one is born again, he cannot be in God's kingdom."

⁴Nicodemus said, "But if a person is already old, how can he be born again? He cannot enter his mother's body again. So how can a person be born a second time?"

⁵But Jesus answered, "I tell you the truth, unless one is born from water and the Spirit, he cannot enter God's kingdom. ⁶Human life comes from human parents, but spiritual life comes from the Spirit. ⁷Don't be surprised when I tell you, 'You must all be born again.' ⁸The wind blows where it wants to and you hear the sound of it, but you don't know where the wind comes from or where it is going. It is the same with every person who is born from the Spirit."

⁹Nicodemus asked, "How can this happen?"

¹⁰Jesus said, "You are an important teacher in Israel, and you don't understand these things? ¹¹I tell you the truth, we talk about what we know, and we tell about what we have seen, but you don't accept what we tell you. ¹²I have told you about things here on earth, and you do not believe me. So you will not believe me if I tell you about things of heaven. ¹³The only one who has ever gone up to heaven is the One who came down from heaven—the Son of Man.

¹⁴"Just as Moses lifted up the snake in the desert,*ⁿ* the Son of Man must also be lifted up. ¹⁵So that everyone who believes can have eternal life in him.

¹⁶"God loved the world so much that he gave his one and only Son so that whoever believes in him may not be lost, but have eternal life. ¹⁷God did not send his Son into the world to judge the world guilty, but to save the world through him. ¹⁸People who believe in God's Son are not judged guilty. Those who do not believe have already been judged guilty, because they have not believed in God's one and only Son. ¹⁹They are judged by this fact:

 3:14 Moses . . . desert When the Israelites were dying from snakebites, God told Moses to put a brass snake on a pole. The people who looked at the snake were healed (Numbers 21:4–9).

The Light has come into the world, but they did not want light. They wanted darkness, because they were doing evil things. [20]All who do evil hate the light and will not come to the light, because it will show all the evil things they do. [21]But those who follow the true way come to the light, and it shows that the things they do were done through God."

JESUS AND JOHN THE BAPTIST

[22]After this, Jesus and his followers went into the area of Judea, where he stayed with his followers and baptized people. [23]John was also baptizing in Aenon, near Salim, because there was plenty of water there. People were going there to be baptized. [24](This was before John was put into prison.)

[25]Some of John's followers had an argument with a Jew about religious washing.[n] [26]So they came to John and said, "Teacher, remember the man who was with you on the other side of the Jordan River, the one you spoke about so much? He is baptizing, and everyone is going to him."

[27]John answered, "A man can get only what God gives him. [28]You yourselves heard me say, 'I am not the Christ, but I am the one sent to prepare the way for him.' [29]The bride belongs only to the bridegroom. But the friend who helps the bridegroom stands by and listens to him. He is thrilled that he gets to hear the bridegroom's voice. In the same way, I am really happy. [30]He must become greater, and I must become less important.

THE ONE WHO COMES FROM HEAVEN

[31]"The One who comes from above is greater than all. The one who is from the earth belongs to the earth and talks about things on the earth. But the One who comes from heaven is greater than all. [32]He tells what he has seen and heard, but no one accepts what he says. [33]Whoever accepts what he says has proven that God is true. [34]The One whom God sent speaks the words of God, because God gives him the Spirit fully. [35]The Father loves the Son and has given him power over everything. [36]Those who believe in the Son have eternal life, but those who do not obey the Son will never have life. God's anger stays on them."

JESUS AND A SAMARITAN WOMAN

4 The Pharisees heard that Jesus was making and baptizing more followers than John, [2]although Jesus himself did not baptize people, but his followers did. [3]Jesus knew that the Pharisees had heard about him, so he left Judea and went back to Galilee. [4]But on the way he had to go through the country of Samaria.

[5]In Samaria Jesus came to the town called Sychar, which is near the field Jacob gave to his son Joseph. [6]Jacob's well was there. Jesus was tired from his long trip, so he sat down beside the well. It was about twelve o'clock noon. [7]When a Samaritan woman came to the well to get some water, Jesus said to her, "Please give me a drink." [8](This happened while Jesus' followers were in town buying some food.)

[9]The woman said, "I am surprised that you ask me for a drink, since you are a Jewish man and I am a Samaritan woman." (Jewish people are not friends with Samaritans.[n])

[10]Jesus said, "If you only knew the free gift of God and who it is that is asking you for water, you would have asked him, and he would have given you living water."

[11]The woman said, "Sir, where will you get this living water? The well is very deep, and you have nothing to get water with. [12]Are you greater than Jacob, our father, who gave us this well and drank from it himself along with his sons and flocks?"

[13]Jesus answered, "Everyone who drinks this water will be thirsty again, [14]but whoever drinks the water I give will never be thirsty. The water I give will become a spring of water gushing up inside that person, giving eternal life."

[15]The woman said to him, "Sir, give me this water so I will never be thirsty again and will not have to come back here to get more water."

[16]Jesus told her, "Go get your husband and come back here."

[17]The woman answered, "I have no husband."

Jesus said to her, "You are right to say you have no husband. [18]Really you have had five husbands, and the man you live with now is not your husband. You told the truth."

[19]The woman said, "Sir, I can see that you are a prophet. [20]Our ancestors worshiped on this mountain, but you say that Jerusalem is the place where people must worship."

[21]Jesus said, "Believe me, woman. The time is coming when neither in Jerusalem nor on this mountain will you actually worship the Father. [22]You Samaritans worship something you don't understand. We understand what we worship, because salvation comes from the Jews. [23]The time is coming when the true worshipers will worship the Father in spirit and truth, and that time is here already. You see, the Father too is actively seeking such people to worship him. [24]God is spirit, and those who worship him must worship in spirit and truth."

[25]The woman said, "I know that the Messiah is coming." (Messiah is the One called Christ.) "When the Messiah comes, he will explain everything to us."

RANDOM REASONS NOT TO USE (alcohol or drugs)

1. DRUNK PEOPLE DO DUMB THINGS.
2. REGRETS.
3. YOU CAN'T REMEMBER WHAT YOU CAN'T REMEMBER.
4. HIGH GUYS TALK STUPID.
5. PHYSICAL AND PSYCHOLOGICAL ADDICTION.
6. DETOX.
7. LONG-TERM DAMAGE OUTWEIGHS ANY SHORT-TERM FEELING.
8. YOU MIGHT AS WELL FLUSH YOUR CASH.
9. NEEDING MORE AND MORE TO GET THE SAME FEELING.
10. A SHORTENED LIFE SPAN.

3:25 **religious washing** The Jewish people washed themselves in special ways before eating, before worshiping in the Temple, and at other special times.   4:9 **Jewish people . . . Samaritans** This can also be translated "Jewish people don't use things that Samaritans have used."

issues

IT'S FRIDAY NIGHT and you're glad to get an invite to a party. Problem is, you know that most people present will be sloshing beers. What do you do? Drinking might feel cool. It might calm your social jitters. It might make you forget about life's most hideous problems. But for now, drinking is illegal. And drinking too much can undo your life. Ephesians 5:18 says, "Do not be drunk with wine, which will ruin you." (That goes for beer, pot, illicit drugs, inhalants, or whatever else gets passed around your school.) Talk with your parents right now about what you can say to invitations to the wrong kind of party. Figure out how you can signal them that you need a ride home right now to exit a bad scene.

²⁶Then Jesus said, "I am he—I, the one talking to you."

²⁷Just then his followers came back from town and were surprised to see him talking with a woman. But none of them asked, "What do you want?" or "Why are you talking with her?"

²⁸Then the woman left her water jar and went back to town. She said to the people, ²⁹"Come and see a man who told me everything I ever did. Do you think he might be the Christ?" ³⁰So the people left the town and went to see Jesus.

³¹Meanwhile, his followers were begging him, "Teacher, eat something."

³²But Jesus answered, "I have food to eat that you know nothing about."

³³So the followers asked themselves, "Did somebody already bring him food?"

³⁴Jesus said, "My food is to do what the One who sent me wants me to do and to finish his work. ³⁵You have a saying, 'Four more months till harvest.' But I tell you, open your eyes and look at the fields ready for harvest now. ³⁶Already, the one who harvests is being paid and is gathering crops for eternal life. So the one who plants and the one who harvests celebrate at the same time. ³⁷Here the saying is true, 'One person plants, and another harvests.' ³⁸I sent you to harvest a crop that you did not work on. Others did the work, and you get to finish up their work."ⁿ

³⁹Many of the Samaritans in that town believed in Jesus because of what the woman said: "He told me everything I ever did." ⁴⁰When the Samaritans came to Jesus, they begged him to stay with them, so he stayed there two more days. ⁴¹And many more believed because of the things he said.

⁴²They said to the woman, "First we believed in Jesus because of your speech, but now we believe because we heard him ourselves. We know that this man really is the Savior of the world."

JESUS HEALS AN OFFICER'S SON

⁴³Two days later, Jesus left and went to Galilee. ⁴⁴(Jesus had said before that a prophet is not respected in his own country.) ⁴⁵When Jesus arrived in Galilee, the people there welcomed him. They had seen all the things he did at the Passover Feast in Jerusalem, because they had been there, too.

⁴⁶Jesus went again to visit Cana in Galilee where he had changed the water into wine.

One of the king's important officers lived in the city of Capernaum, and his son was sick. ⁴⁷When he heard that Jesus had come from Judea to Galilee, he went to Jesus and begged him to come to Capernaum and heal his son, because his son was almost dead. ⁴⁸Jesus said to him, "You people must see signs and miracles before you will believe in me."

⁴⁹The officer said, "Sir, come before my child dies."

⁵⁰Jesus answered, "Go. Your son will live."

The man believed what Jesus told him and went home. ⁵¹On the way the man's servants came and met him and told him, "Your son is alive."

⁵²The man asked, "What time did my son begin to get well?"

They answered, "Yesterday at one o'clock the fever left him."

⁵³The father knew that one o'clock was the exact time that Jesus had said, "Your son will live." So the man and all the people who lived in his house believed in Jesus.

⁵⁴That was the second miracle Jesus did after coming from Judea to Galilee.

JESUS HEALS A MAN AT A POOL

5 Later Jesus went to Jerusalem for a special feast. ²In Jerusalem there is a pool with five covered porches, which is called Bethzathaⁿ in the Hebrew language.ⁿ This pool is near the Sheep Gate. ³Many sick people were lying on the porches beside the pool. Some were blind, some were crippled, and some were paralyzed.ⁿ ⁵A man was lying there who had been sick for thirty-eight years. ⁶When Jesus saw the man and knew that he had been sick for such a long time, Jesus asked him, "Do you want to be well?"

⁷The sick man answered, "Sir, there is no one to help me get into the pool when the water starts moving. While I am coming to the water, someone else always gets in before me."

⁸Then Jesus said, "Stand up. Pick up your mat and walk." ⁹And immediately the man was well; he picked up his mat and began to walk.

The day this happened was a Sabbath day.

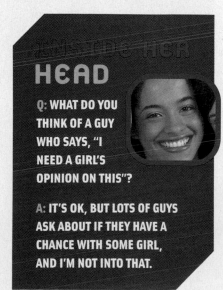

INSIDE HER

HEAD

Q: WHAT DO YOU THINK OF A GUY WHO SAYS, "I NEED A GIRL'S OPINION ON THIS"?

A: IT'S OK, BUT LOTS OF GUYS ASK ABOUT IF THEY HAVE A CHANCE WITH SOME GIRL, AND I'M NOT INTO THAT.

 4:38 I . . . **their work.** As a farmer sends workers to harvest grain, Jesus sends his followers out to bring people to God. **5:2 Bethzatha** Also called Bethsaida or Bethesda, it is a pool of water north of the Temple in Jerusalem. **5:2 Hebrew language** Hebrew or Aramaic, the languages of many people in this region in the first century. **5:3 Verse 3** Some Greek copies add "and they waited for the water to move." A few later copies add verse 4: "Sometimes an angel of the Lord came down to the pool and stirred up the water. After the angel did this, the first person to go into the pool was healed from any sickness he had."

MUSIC REVIEWS

RELIENT K: TWO LEFTS DON'T MAKE A RIGHT

Two Lefts Don't Make a Right, But Three Do is Relient K's 2003 pop-punk presentation, relying on near-ska beats and signature riffs to carry tunes about God ("I Am Understood?"), girls ("Mood Rings"), and growing up ("Forward Motion"). Somehow, after three big releases from Relient K, they're *still* college-age. *Two Lefts* demonstrates that while they remain one of the industry's most hilarious bands, their clowning ("Gibberish") paves the way for them to share their conviction ("Getting Into You"). Soundwise, Relient K is a loose counterpart to MxPx. The group was named for Matt Hoopes' Plymouth bomb, which they say took over fifteen seconds to go from 0 to 60 mph.

WHY IT ROCKS: IT'S RELIENT K'S BEST—SO FAR.

YOUNG PEOPLE'S PRESS is a non-profit organization that works to give youth the power to express themselves in the media. Their mission is to create a fresh and intelligent news source for youth. They want to showcase the stuff young people care about, be it pop culture, politics, or social issues.

YPP is a free national news service for youth. As well as their online publication, they also publish some pieces in major Canadian newspapers. YPP accepts nonfiction submissions from youth 14-24. They can be opinion pieces, soft or hard news stories, or features. An editor will work on-line with you to get you published—it's that easy. Either send them something you have written already, or think of an article or articles you would like to write. E-mail a summary of the piece to them and they'll get back to you. Let your voice be heard.

Visit www.ypp.net for more information.

¹⁰So the Jews said to the man who had been healed, "Today is the Sabbath. It is against our law for you to carry your mat on the Sabbath day."

¹¹But he answered, "The man who made me well told me, 'Pick up your mat and walk.' "

¹²Then they asked him, "Who is the man who told you to pick up your mat and walk?"

¹³But the man who had been healed did not know who it was, because there were many people in that place, and Jesus had left.

¹⁴Later, Jesus found the man at the Temple and said to him, "See, you are well now. Stop sinning so that something worse does not happen to you."

¹⁵Then the man left and told his people that Jesus was the one who had made him well.

¹⁶Because Jesus was doing this on the Sabbath day, some evil people began to persecute him. ¹⁷But Jesus said to them, "My Father never stops working, and so I keep working, too."

¹⁸This made them try still harder to kill him. They said, "First Jesus was breaking the law about the Sabbath day. Now he says that God is his own Father, making himself equal with God!"

JESUS HAS GOD'S AUTHORITY

¹⁹But Jesus said, "I tell you the truth, the Son can do nothing alone. The Son does only what he sees the Father doing, because the Son does whatever the Father does. ²⁰The Father loves the Son and shows the Son all the things he himself does. But the Father will show the Son even greater things than this so that you can all be amazed. ²¹Just as the Father raises the dead and gives them life, so also the Son gives life to those he wants to. ²²In fact, the Father judges no one, but he has given the Son power to do all the judging ²³so that all people will honor the Son as much as they honor the Father. Anyone who does not honor the Son does not honor the Father who sent him.

²⁴"I tell you the truth, whoever hears what I say and believes in the One who sent me has eternal life. That person will not be judged guilty but has already left death and entered life. ²⁵I tell you the truth, the time is coming and is already here when the dead will hear the voice of the Son of God, and those who hear will have life. ²⁶Life comes from the Father himself, and he has allowed the Son to have life in himself as well. ²⁷And the Father has given the Son the power to judge, because he is the Son of Man. ²⁸Don't be surprised at this: A time is coming when all who are dead and in their graves will hear his voice. ²⁹Then they will come out of their graves. Those who did good will rise and have life forever, but those who did evil will rise to be judged guilty.

JESUS IS GOD'S SON

³⁰"I can do nothing alone. I judge only the way I am told, so my judgment is fair. I don't try to please myself, but I try to please the One who sent me.

³¹"If only I tell people about myself, what I say is not true. ³²But there is another who tells about me, and I know that the things he says about me are true.

³³"You have sent people to John, and he has told you the truth. ³⁴It is not that I accept such human telling; I tell you this so you can be saved. ³⁵John was like a burning and shining lamp, and you were happy to enjoy his light for a while.

³⁶"But I have a proof about myself that is greater than that of John. The things I do, which are the things my Father gave me to do, prove that the Father sent me. ³⁷And the Father himself who sent me has given proof about me. You have never heard his voice or seen what he looks like. ³⁸His teaching does not live in you, because you don't believe in the One the Father sent. ³⁹You carefully study the Scriptures because you think they give you eternal life. They do in fact tell about me, ⁴⁰but you refuse to come to me to have that life.

⁴¹"I don't need praise from people. ⁴²But I know you—I know that you don't have God's love in you. ⁴³I have come from my Father and speak for him, but you don't accept me. But when another person comes, speaking only for himself, you will accept him. ⁴⁴You try to get praise from each other, but you do not try to get the praise that comes from the only God. So how can you believe? ⁴⁵Don't think that I will stand before the Father and say you are wrong. The one who says you are wrong is Moses, the one you hoped would save you. ⁴⁶If you really believed Moses, you would believe me, because Moses wrote about me. ⁴⁷But if you don't believe what Moses wrote, how can you believe what I say?"

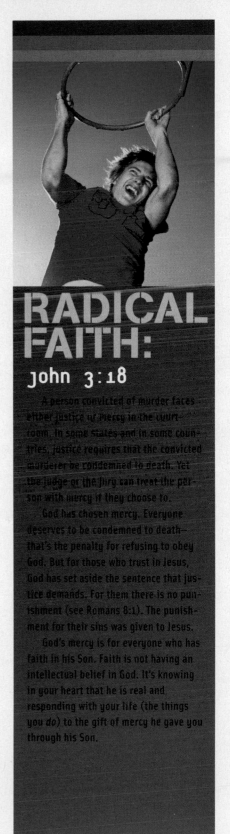

RADICAL FAITH:
john 3:18

A person convicted of murder faces either justice or mercy in the courtroom. In some states and in some countries, justice requires that the convicted murderer be condemned to death. Yet the judge or the jury can treat the person with mercy if they choose to.

God has chosen mercy. Everyone deserves to be condemned to death—that's the penalty for refusing to obey God. But for those who trust in Jesus, God has set aside the sentence that justice demands. For them there is no punishment (see Romans 8:1). The punishment for their sins was given to Jesus.

God's mercy is for everyone who has faith in his Son. Faith is not having an intellectual belief in God. It's knowing in your heart that he is real and responding with your life (the things you *do*) to the gift of mercy he gave you through his Son.

RADICAL FAITH:

john 4:24

Those who worship God must be led by the Spirit. This verse isn't talking about being led by a spirit like the ghosts you see floating around old houses on TV. It's talking about being led by the *Holy Spirit*. The Holy Spirit is part of the Trinity: God the Father, God the Son (Jesus), and God the Holy Spirit. The Holy Spirit has been sent to guide you into all truth (see John 16:13). You are free to make your own choices, but if you're going to be successful in life, you must submit to the Holy Spirit and allow him to guide you.

That's why it's so important to listen to that still, small voice. The next time you're making an important decision or stepping out in a certain direction and you don't feel at peace about it, don't ignore it! That's the Holy Spirit. He wants to lead you. He wants to help you. He wants to see you successful in everything you do. God has given us, as his children, the opportunity and the right to be led by the Holy Spirit. Start being led by the Spirit today, and watch what God will do tomorrow!

MORE THAN FIVE THOUSAND FED

6 After this, Jesus went across Lake Galilee (or, Lake Tiberias). [2]Many people followed him because they saw the miracles he did to heal the sick. [3]Jesus went up on a hill and sat down there with his followers. [4]It was almost the time for the Jewish Passover Feast.

[5]When Jesus looked up and saw a large crowd coming toward him, he said to Philip, "Where can we buy enough bread for all these people to eat?" [6](Jesus asked Philip this question to test him, because Jesus already knew what he planned to do.)

[7]Philip answered, "We would all have to work a month to buy enough bread for each person to have only a little piece."

[8]Another one of his followers, Andrew, Simon Peter's brother, said, [9]"Here is a boy with five loaves of barley bread and two little fish, but that is not enough for so many people."

[10]Jesus said, "Tell the people to sit down." This was a very grassy place, and about five thousand men sat down there. [11]Then Jesus took the loaves of bread, thanked God for them, and gave them to the people who were sitting there. He did the same with the fish, giving as much as the people wanted.

[12]When they had all had enough to eat, Jesus said to his followers, "Gather the leftover pieces of fish and bread so that nothing is wasted." [13]So they gathered up the pieces and filled twelve baskets with the pieces left from the five barley loaves.

[14]When the people saw this miracle that Jesus did, they said, "He must truly be the Prophet[n] who is coming into the world."

[15]Jesus knew that the people planned to come and take him by force and make him their king, so he left and went into the hills alone.

JESUS WALKS ON THE WATER

[16]That evening Jesus' followers went down to Lake Galilee. [17]It was dark now, and Jesus had not yet come to them. The followers got into a boat and started across the lake to Capernaum. [18]By now a strong wind was blowing, and the waves on the lake were getting bigger. [19]When they had rowed the boat about three or four miles, they saw Jesus walking on the water, coming toward the boat. The followers were afraid, [20]but Jesus said to them, "It is I. Do not be afraid." [21]Then they were glad to take him

into the boat. At once the boat came to land at the place where they wanted to go.

THE PEOPLE SEEK JESUS

[22]The next day the people who had stayed on the other side of the lake knew that Jesus had not gone in the boat with his followers but

 6:14 **Prophet** They probably meant the prophet that God told Moses he would send (Deuteronomy 18:15–19).

RANDOM WAYS TO SAY NO — 10

1. "GOT SOMETHIN' BETTER."

2. "NAH. I'M NOT INTO THAT."

3. "I'VE ALREADY GOT PLANS."

4. "NO."

5. "SORRY, IT'S NOT WORTH GETTING GROUNDED."

6. "NO—BUT WANNA DO _____ INSTEAD?"

7. "SORRY, MY LIFE'S TOO VALUABLE TO WASTE ON THIS STUFF."

8. "NOT MY THING, THANKS."

9. "DO I LOOK THAT STUPID?"

10. "ABSOLUTELY NOT."

that they had left without him. And they knew that only one boat had been there. [23]But then some boats came from Tiberias and landed near the place where the people had eaten the bread after the Lord had given thanks. [24]When the people saw that Jesus and his followers were not there now, they got into boats and went to Capernaum to find Jesus.

JESUS, THE BREAD OF LIFE

[25]When the people found Jesus on the other side of the lake, they asked him, "Teacher, when did you come here?"

[26]Jesus answered, "I tell you the truth, you aren't looking for me because you saw me do miracles. You are looking for me because you ate the bread and were satisfied. [27]Don't work for the food that spoils. Work for the food that stays good always and gives eternal life. The Son of Man will give you this food, because on him God the Father has put his power."

[28]The people asked Jesus, "What are the things God wants us to do?"

[29]Jesus answered, "The work God wants you to do is this: Believe the One he sent."

[30]So the people asked, "What miracle will you do? If we see a miracle, we will believe you. What will you do? [31]Our fathers ate the manna in the desert. This is written in the Scriptures: 'He gave them bread from heaven to eat.' "[n]

[32]Jesus said, "I tell you the truth, it was not Moses who gave you bread from heaven; it is my Father who is giving you the true bread from heaven. [33]God's bread is the One who comes down from heaven and gives life to the world."

[34]The people said, "Sir, give us this bread always."

[35]Then Jesus said, "I am the bread that gives life. Whoever comes to me will never be hungry, and whoever believes in me will never be thirsty. [36]But as I told you before, you have seen me and still don't believe. [37]The Father gives me my people. Every one of them will come to me, and I will always accept them. [38]I came down from heaven to do what God wants me to do, not what I want to do. [39]Here is what the One who sent me wants me to do: I must not lose even one whom God gave me, but I must raise them all on the last day. [40]Those who see the Son and believe in him have eternal life, and I will raise them on the last day. This is what my Father wants."

[41]Some people began to complain about Jesus because he said, "I am the bread that comes down from heaven." [42]They said, "This is Jesus, the son of Joseph. We know his father and mother. How can he say, 'I came down from heaven'?"

[43]But Jesus answered, "Stop complaining to each other. [44]The Father is the One who sent me. No one can come to me unless the Father draws him to me, and I will raise that person up on the last day. [45]It is written in the prophets, 'They will all be taught by God.'[n] Everyone who listens to the Father and learns from him comes to me. [46]No one has seen the Father except the One who is from God; only he has seen the Father. [47]I tell you the truth, whoever believes has eternal life. [48]I am the bread that gives life. [49]Your ancestors ate the manna in the desert, but still they died. [50]Here

is the bread that comes down from heaven. Anyone who eats this bread will never die. [51]I am the living bread that came down from heaven. Anyone who eats this bread will live forever. This bread is my flesh, which I will give up so that the world may have life."

[52]Then the evil people began to argue among themselves, saying, "How can this man give us his flesh to eat?"

[53]Jesus said, "I tell you the truth, you must eat the flesh of the Son of Man and drink his blood. Otherwise, you won't have real life in you. [54]Those who eat my flesh and drink my blood have eternal life, and I will raise them up on the last day. [55]My flesh is true food, and my blood is true drink. [56]Those who eat my flesh and drink my blood live in me, and I live in them. [57]The living Father sent me, and I live because of the Father. So whoever eats me will live because of me. [58]I am not like the bread your ancestors ate. They ate that bread and still died. I am the bread that came down from heaven, and whoever eats this bread will live forever." [59]Jesus said all these things while he was teaching in the synagogue in Capernaum.

THE WORDS OF ETERNAL LIFE

[60]When the followers of Jesus heard this, many of them said, "This teaching is hard. Who can accept it?"

[61]Knowing that his followers were complaining about this, Jesus said, "Does this teaching bother you? [62]Then will it also bother you to see the Son of Man going back to the place where he came from? [63]It is the Spirit that gives life. The flesh doesn't give life. The words I told you are spirit, and they give life. [64]But some of you don't believe." (Jesus knew from the beginning who did not believe and who would turn against him.) [65]Jesus said, "That is the reason I said, 'If the Father does not bring a person to me, that one cannot come.' "

[66]After Jesus said this, many of his followers left him and stopped following him.

[67]Jesus asked the twelve followers, "Do you want to leave, too?"

[68]Simon Peter answered him, "Lord, where would we go? You have the words that give eternal life. [69]We believe and know that you are the Holy One from God."

[70]Then Jesus answered, "I chose all twelve of you, but one of you is a devil."

6:31 'He gave . . . eat.' Quotation from Psalm 78:24.   6:45 'They . . . God.' Quotation from Isaiah 54:13.

MEN OF THE SWORD

JOSHUA

Born in Egypt into slavery, Joshua became a general under Moses. He was at Mount Sinai when Moses received the Ten Commandments. When God commanded the Israelites to scout out the Promised Land, only he and Caleb brought back a good report. All the other men said they would be slaughtered if they tried to conquer the land. Of all the Israelite adults alive at that time, only Joshua and Caleb were allowed to live long enough to enter the land. Joshua became Moses' successor, and he called Israel to total faithfulness to God until his death.

—Numbers 13; Joshua 24

[71]Jesus was talking about Judas, the son of Simon Iscariot. Judas was one of the twelve, but later he was going to turn against Jesus.

JESUS' BROTHERS DON'T BELIEVE

7 After this, Jesus traveled around Galilee. He did not want to travel in Judea, because some evil people there wanted to kill him. [2]It was time for the Feast of Shelters. [3]So Jesus' brothers said to him, "You should leave here and go to Judea so your followers there can see the miracles you do. [4]Anyone who wants to be well known does not hide what he does. If you are doing these things, show yourself to the world." [5](Even Jesus' brothers did not believe in him.)

[6]Jesus said to his brothers, "The right time for me has not yet come, but any time is right for you. [7]The world cannot hate you, but it hates me, because I tell it the evil things it does. [8]So you go to the feast. I will not go yet to this feast, because the right time for me has not yet come." [9]After saying this, Jesus stayed in Galilee.

[10]But after Jesus' brothers had gone to the feast, Jesus went also. But he did not let people see him. [11]At the feast some people were looking for him and saying, "Where is that man?"

[12]Within the large crowd there, many people were whispering to each other about Jesus. Some said, "He is a good man."

Others said, "No, he fools the people." [13]But no one was brave enough to talk about Jesus openly, because they were afraid of the older leaders.

JESUS TEACHES AT THE FEAST

[14]When the feast was about half over, Jesus went to the Temple and began to teach. [15]The people were amazed and said, "This man has never studied in school. How did he learn so much?"

[16]Jesus answered, "The things I teach are not my own, but they come from him who sent me. [17]If people choose to do what God wants, they will know that my teaching comes from God and not from me. [18]Those who teach their own ideas are trying to get honor for themselves. But those who try to bring honor to the one who sent him speak the truth, and there is nothing false in them. [19]Moses gave you the law,[n] but none of you obeys that law. Why are you trying to kill me?"

[20]The people answered, "A demon has come into you. We are not trying to kill you."

[21]Jesus said to them, "I did one miracle, and you are all amazed. [22]Moses gave you the law about circumcision. (But really Moses did not give you circumcision; it came from our ancestors.) And yet you circumcise a baby on a Sabbath day. [23]If a baby can be circumcised on a Sabbath day to obey the law of Moses, why are you angry at me for healing a person's whole body on the Sabbath day? [24]Stop judging by the way things look, but judge by what is really right."

IS JESUS THE CHRIST?

[25]Then some of the people who lived in Jerusalem said, "This is the man they are trying to kill. [26]But he is teaching where everyone can see and hear him, and no one is trying to stop him. Maybe the leaders have decided he really is the Christ. [27]But we know where this

WAYS TO WALK THE WALK

john 6:35

WORD: When you fill up on Jesus, you don't crave bad things.

WALK IT: The next time you feel tempted to do wrong, tell Jesus you want more of him. Spend time thanking him for meeting your every need.

7:19 law Moses gave God's people the Law that God gave him on Mount Sinai (Exodus 34:29–32).

travel  the road

Don't miss this party: "Urbana" is InterVarsity's one-of-a-kind missions event for students college-age and up. Every three years, nearly twenty thousand students gather on the campus of the University of Illinois at Urbana-Champaign to seek their place in God's mission to the world by listening to world-class speakers, attending seminars, and interacting with representatives from more than 350 mission agencies, seminaries, and Christian colleges. Find out more at www.urbana.org and get ready to go!

For more on extreme missions visit www.traveltheroad.com.

man is from. And when the real Christ comes, no one will know where he comes from."

28Jesus, teaching in the Temple, cried out, "Yes, you know me, and you know where I am from. But I have not come by my own authority. I was sent by the One who is true, whom you don't know. 29But I know him, because I am from him, and he sent me."

30When Jesus said this, the people tried to take him. But no one was able to touch him, because it was not yet the right time. 31But many of the people believed in Jesus. They said, "When the Christ comes, will he do more miracles than this man has done?"

THE LEADERS TRY TO ARREST JESUS

32The Pharisees heard the crowd whispering these things about Jesus. So the leading priests and the Pharisees sent some Temple guards to arrest him. 33Jesus said, "I will be with you a little while longer. Then I will go back to the One who sent me. 34You will look for me, but you will not find me. And you cannot come where I am."

35Some people said to each other, "Where will this man go so we cannot find him? Will he go to the Greek cities where our people live and teach the Greek people there? 36What did he mean when he said, 'You will look for me, but you will not find me,' and 'You cannot come where I am'?"

JESUS TALKS ABOUT THE SPIRIT

37On the last and most important day of the feast Jesus stood up and said in a loud voice, "Let anyone who is thirsty come to me and drink. 38If anyone believes in me, rivers of living water will flow out from that person's heart, as the Scripture says." 39Jesus was talking about the Holy Spirit. The Spirit had not yet been given, because Jesus had not yet been raised to glory. But later, those who believed in Jesus would receive the Spirit.

THE PEOPLE ARGUE ABOUT JESUS

40When the people heard Jesus' words, some of them said, "This man really is the Prophet."[n]

41Others said, "He is the Christ."

Still others said, "The Christ will not come from Galilee. 42The Scripture says that the Christ will come from David's family and from Bethlehem, the town where David lived." 43So the people did not agree with each other about Jesus. 44Some of them wanted to arrest him, but no one was able to touch him.

SOME LEADERS WON'T BELIEVE

45The Temple guards went back to the leading priests and the Pharisees, who asked, "Why didn't you bring Jesus?"

46The guards answered, "The words he says are greater than the words of any other person who has ever spoken!"

47The Pharisees answered, "So Jesus has fooled you also! 48Have any of the leaders or

✓ COUNT ON IT

JOHN 6:37

Some people think that they have to have their lives totally together before they turn to God. They think they need to make themselves worthy of Jesus' friendship. This is a lie that suits Satan's purposes pretty well. The problem is that *nobody* will ever be worthy of what God is offering him or her. That's a part of God's truth that's hard to swallow. And if Satan can keep people believing that they have to somehow earn God's favor—that it's even possible—he can keep them from taking the first step toward God's kingdom.

The truth is that God doesn't ask anyone to be worthy of him. If you come to him—without excuses, without trying to justify yourself, just putting your complete trust in him (like putting all of your weight in a chair)—then Jesus promises not to turn you away. He accepts you because he loves you, not because you've earned his friendship.

 7:40 Prophet They probably meant the prophet God told Moses he would send (Deuteronomy 18:15–19).

INSIDE HER HEAD

Q: WHAT IS THE BEST GIFT A GUY CAN GIVE A GIRL?

A: SOMETHING HE THOUGHT OF HIMSELF, EVEN A HOMEMADE CARD. I'D BE HAPPY WITH THAT.

the Pharisees believed in him? No! [49]But these people, who know nothing about the law, are under God's curse."

[50]Nicodemus, who had gone to see Jesus before, was in that group.[n] He said, [51]"Our law does not judge a man without hearing him and knowing what he has done."

[52]They answered, "Are you from Galilee, too? Study the Scriptures, and you will learn that no prophet comes from Galilee."

———————————

Some early Greek manuscripts do not contain 7:53—8:11.

[[53]And everyone left and went home.

THE WOMAN CAUGHT IN ADULTERY

8 Jesus went to the Mount of Olives. [2]But early in the morning he went back to the Temple, and all the people came to him, and he sat and taught them. [3]The teachers of the law and the Pharisees brought a woman who had been caught in adultery. They forced her to stand before the people. [4]They said to Jesus, "Teacher, this woman was caught having sexual relations with a man who is not her husband. [5]The law of Moses commands that we stone to death every woman who does this. What do you say we should do?" [6]They were asking this to trick Jesus so that they could have some charge against him.

But Jesus bent over and started writing on the ground with his finger. [7]When they continued to ask Jesus their question, he raised up and said, "Anyone here who has never sinned can throw the first stone at her." [8]Then Jesus bent over again and wrote on the ground.

GET OUT THERE →

WORLD VISION is an international partnership of Christians whose mission is to follow our Lord and Savior Jesus Christ in working with the poor and oppressed to promote human transformation, seek justice, and bear witness to the good news of the kingdom of God. World Vision provides community development, disaster relief, food and clean water, education, and health care.

World Vision helps transform the lives of the world 's poorest children and families in nearly 100 countries, including the United States. Driven by faith and in partnership with people like you, World Vision seeks to enable the world's children to realize their God-given potential by tackling the root causes of poverty. Working on six continents, World Vision is one of the largest Christian development and relief organizations in the world. You can help make a difference in your world right now through ongoing sponsorship and other giving, serving, and advocacy opportunities.

Get involved by visiting www.worldvision.org.

 7:50 Nicodemus . . . group. The story about Nicodemus going and talking to Jesus is in John 3:1–21.

RANDOM PLACES TO WEAR A TIE

1. TACO BELL
2. ROLLERBLADING
3. LIBRARY
4. MOVIE THEATER
5. FOOTBALL GAME
6. SUPPER
7. CAMPING
8. GYM CLASS
9. BATHROOM
10. AMUSEMENT PARK

⁹Those who heard Jesus began to leave one by one, first the older men and then the others. Jesus was left there alone with the woman standing before him. ¹⁰Jesus raised up again and asked her, "Woman, where are they? Has no one judged you guilty?"

¹¹She answered, "No one, sir."

Then Jesus said, "I also don't judge you guilty. You may go now, but don't sin anymore."]

JESUS IS THE LIGHT OF THE WORLD

¹²Later, Jesus talked to the people again, saying, "I am the light of the world. The person who follows me will never live in darkness but will have the light that gives life."

¹³The Pharisees said to Jesus, "When you talk about yourself, you are the only one to say these things are true. We cannot accept what you say."

¹⁴Jesus answered, "Yes, I am saying these things about myself, but they are true. I know where I came from and where I am going. But you don't know where I came from or where I am going. ¹⁵You judge by human standards. I am not judging anyone. ¹⁶But when I do judge, my judging is true, because I am not alone. The Father who sent me is with me.

¹⁷Your own law says that when two witnesses say the same thing, you must accept what they say. ¹⁸I am one of the witnesses who speaks about myself, and the Father who sent me is the other witness."

¹⁹They asked, "Where is your father?"

Jesus answered, "You don't know me or my Father. If you knew me, you would know my Father, too." ²⁰Jesus said these things while he was teaching in the Temple, near where the money is kept. But no one arrested him, because the right time for him had not yet come.

THE PEOPLE MISUNDERSTAND JESUS

²¹Again, Jesus said to the people, "I will leave you, and you will look for me, but you will die in your sins. You cannot come where I am going."

²²So the Jews asked, "Will Jesus kill himself? Is that why he said, 'You cannot come where I am going'?"

²³Jesus said, "You people are from here below, but I am from above. You belong to this world, but I don't belong to this world. ²⁴So I told you that you would die in your sins. Yes, you will die in your sins if you don't believe that I am he."

²⁵They asked, "Then who are you?"

Jesus answered, "I am what I have told you from the beginning. ²⁶I have many things to say and decide about you. But I tell people only the things I have heard from the One who sent me, and he speaks the truth."

²⁷The people did not understand that he was talking to them about the Father. ²⁸So Jesus said to them, "When you lift up the Son of Man, you will know that I am he. You will know that these things I do are not by my own authority but that I say only what the Father has taught me. ²⁹The One who sent me is with me. I always do what is pleasing to him, so he has not left me alone." ³⁰While Jesus was saying these things, many people believed in him.

FREEDOM FROM SIN

³¹So Jesus said to the Jews who believed in him, "If you continue to obey my teaching, you are truly my followers. ³²Then you will know the truth, and the truth will make you free."

³³They answered, "We are Abraham's children, and we have never been anyone's slaves. So why do you say we will be free?"

³⁴Jesus answered, "I tell you the truth, everyone who lives in sin is a slave to sin. ³⁵A

EXPERTS ANSWER YOUR QUESTIONS

Q. *My mom says I should "figure out God's will" about what college I go to. What does she mean by that?*

A. "God's will" is Christianese for "what God wants you to do." God has a universal will, the right-and-wrong commands that apply to everyone. He also has a specific will, stuff that applies just to you. If you start by obeying his universal will—listening to your parents, staying pure sexually, working hard at school—then you're ready to find his specific will through prayer, Scripture, and getting wise advice.

Q. *I just came home from a mission trip and I'm already starting to get sucked into bad old stuff. How can I keep going strong?*

A. God is just as close to you right here and right now as he was two days ago back on your trip. But that's a fact, not a feeling. Trust it. Then do what you can to keep your soul fed. Stay close to Christian friends. Keep digging into your Bible. And moment by moment, decide that you want to keep following Jesus.

JOHN 7:38

Have you ever been really thirsty—like "walking-across-the-desert-in-search-of-water" thirsty? Then you know that when you get that thirsty, there's nothing better than a nice, long drink of cool, refreshing water! That's the kind of water you need. When you gave your heart to Jesus, you received that refreshing, living water. The question is, What are you going to do with that water? Jesus said it flows from you, not just to you!

Have you ever been for a ride on a scalding hot summer's day and thought you saw a shimmering image that looked like water on the street up ahead? This is called a mirage, and it happens all of the time in the desert. We've all seen it on TV—a person in need of water, crawling across the desert, spots one. Their hopes are dashed as they realize what they had thought was an oasis is really a mirage. Nothing!

That's the question: Are you going to be a mirage or an oasis of life? You have the living water that this world is searching for. Release it today!

slave does not stay with a family forever, but a son belongs to the family forever. [36]So if the Son makes you free, you will be truly free. [37]I know you are Abraham's children, but you want to kill me because you don't accept my teaching. [38]I am telling you what my Father has shown me, but you do what your father has told you."

[39]They answered, "Our father is Abraham."

Jesus said, "If you were really Abraham's children, you would do the things Abraham did. [40]I am a man who has told you the truth which I heard from God, but you are trying to kill me. Abraham did nothing like that. [41]So you are doing the things your own father did."

But they said, "We are not like children who never knew who their father was. God is our Father; he is the only Father we have."

[42]Jesus said to them, "If God were really your Father, you would love me, because I came from God and now I am here. I did not come by my own authority; God sent me. [43]You don't understand what I say, because you cannot accept my teaching. [44]You belong to your father the devil, and you want to do what he wants. He was a murderer from the beginning and was against the truth, because there is no truth in him. When he tells a lie, he shows what he is really like, because he is a liar and the father of lies. [45]But because I speak the truth, you don't believe me. [46]Can any of you prove that I am guilty of sin? If I am telling the truth, why don't you believe me? [47]The person who belongs to God accepts what God says. But you don't accept what God says, because you don't belong to God."

JESUS IS GREATER THAN ABRAHAM

[48]They answered, "We say you are a Samaritan and have a demon in you. Are we not right?"

[49]Jesus answered, "I have no demon in me. I give honor to my Father, but you dishonor me. [50]I am not trying to get honor for myself. There is One who wants this honor for me, and he is the judge. [51]I tell you the truth, whoever obeys my teaching will never die."

[52]They said to Jesus, "Now we know that you have a demon in you! Even Abraham and the prophets died. But you say, 'Whoever obeys my teaching will never die.' [53]Do you think you are greater than our father Abraham, who died? And the prophets died, too. Who do you think you are?"

[54]Jesus answered, "If I give honor to myself, that honor is worth nothing. The One who gives me honor is my Father, and you say he is your God. [55]You don't really know him, but I know him. If I said I did not know him, I would be a liar like you. But I do know him, and I obey what he says. [56]Your father Abraham was very happy that he would see my day. He saw that day and was glad."

[57]They said to him, "You have never seen Abraham! You are not even fifty years old."

[58]Jesus answered, "I tell you the truth, before Abraham was even born, I am!" [59]When Jesus said this, the people picked up stones to throw at him. But Jesus hid himself, and then he left the Temple.

JESUS HEALS A MAN BORN BLIND

9 As Jesus was walking along, he saw a man who had been born blind. [2]His followers asked him, "Teacher, whose sin caused this man to be born blind—his own sin or his parents' sin?"

[3]Jesus answered, "It is not this man's sin or his parents' sin that made him be blind. This man was born blind so that God's power could be shown in him. [4]While it is daytime, we must continue doing the work of the One who sent me. Night is coming, when no one can work. [5]While I am in the world, I am the light of the world."

[6]After Jesus said this, he spit on the ground and made some mud with it and put the mud on the man's eyes. [7]Then he told the man, "Go and wash in the Pool of Siloam." (Siloam means Sent.) So the man went, washed, and came back seeing.

[8]The neighbors and some people who had earlier seen this man begging said, "Isn't this the same man who used to sit and beg?"

[9]Some said, "He is the one," but others said, "No, he only looks like him."

The man himself said, "I am the man."

[10]They asked, "How did you get your sight?"

[11]He answered, "The man named Jesus made some mud and put it on my eyes. Then he told me to go to Siloam and wash. So I went and washed, and then I could see."

[12]They asked him, "Where is this man?"

"I don't know," he answered.

PHARISEES QUESTION THE HEALING

[13]Then the people took to the Pharisees the man who had been blind. [14]The day Jesus had

made mud and healed his eyes was a Sabbath day. [15]So now the Pharisees asked the man, "How did you get your sight?"

He answered, "He put mud on my eyes, I washed, and now I see."

[16]So some of the Pharisees were saying, "This man does not keep the Sabbath day, so he is not from God."

But others said, "A man who is a sinner can't do miracles like these." So they could not agree with each other.

[17]They asked the man again, "What do you say about him since it was your eyes he opened?"

The man answered, "He is a prophet."

[18]These leaders did not believe that he had been blind and could now see again. So they sent for the man's parents [19]and asked them, "Is this your son who you say was born blind? Then how does he now see?"

[20]His parents answered, "We know that this is our son and that he was born blind. [21]But we don't know how he can now see. We don't know who opened his eyes. Ask him. He is old enough to speak for himself." [22]His parents said this because they were afraid of the older leaders, who had already decided that anyone who said Jesus was the Christ would be avoided. [23]That is why his parents said, "He is old enough. Ask him."

[24]So for the second time, they called the man who had been blind. They said, "You should give God the glory by telling the truth. We know that this man is a sinner."

[25]He answered, "I don't know if he is a sinner. One thing I do know: I was blind, and now I see."

[26]They asked, "What did he do to you? How did he make you see again?"

[27]He answered, "I already told you, and you didn't listen. Why do you want to hear it again? Do you want to become his followers, too?"

[28]Then they insulted him and said, "You are his follower, but we are followers of Moses. [29]We know that God spoke to Moses, but we don't even know where this man comes from."

[30]The man answered, "This is a very strange thing. You don't know where he comes from, and yet he opened my eyes. [31]We all know that God does not listen to sinners, but he listens to anyone who worships and obeys him. [32]Nobody has ever heard of anyone giving sight to a man born blind. [33]If this man were not from God, he could do nothing."

[34]They answered, "You were born full of sin! Are you trying to teach us?" And they threw him out.

SPIRITUAL BLINDNESS

[35]When Jesus heard that they had thrown him out, Jesus found him and said, "Do you believe in the Son of Man?"

[36]He asked, "Who is the Son of Man, sir, so that I can believe in him?"

[37]Jesus said to him, "You have seen him. The Son of Man is the one talking with you."

[38]He said, "Lord, I believe!" Then the man worshiped Jesus.

[39]Jesus said, "I came into this world so that the world could be judged. I came so that the blind[n] would see and so that those who see will become blind."

[40]Some of the Pharisees who were nearby heard Jesus say this and asked, "Are you saying we are blind, too?"

[41]Jesus said, "If you were blind, you would not be guilty of sin. But since you keep saying you see, your guilt remains."

MUSIC REVIEWS

MICHAEL W. SMITH: THE SECOND DECADE

The Second Decade is Smith's second compilation, son of the 1993 release *First Decade*. Like the first, this disc is more a collection of great tunes both famous and not-as-known rather than a mix of true greatest hits. *Second Decade* contains two new studio tracks ("Raging Sea" and "Signs," co-written with his son, Ryan) and thirteen cuts from Smith's previous six releases. One of the most gifted composers of our time, MWS wrote his first song at about the same age Mozart wrote his first concerto. He's been redefining musical excellence for the past twenty years. The limited edition of *Second Decade* is packaged with extended notes and a bonus DVD, containing interview excerpts, videos, and an unexpected family tribute.

WHY IT ROCKS: *SECOND DECADE* IS A MASTERPIECE OF VOCALS, INSTRUMENTATION, LYRICS, AND ARRANGEMENT.

DO'S & DON'TS

- Do call your grandparents just to talk.
- Do make birthday cards for your parents.
- Do the time if you did the crime.
- Do learn how to spell.
- Don't beat up your brother.
- Don't raise your voice at your mom.
- Don't diss your dad.
- Don't blame others for your bads.

9:39 **blind** Jesus is talking about people who are spiritually blind, not physically blind.

HOW (NOT) TO GAMBLE AWAY YOUR LIFE'S SAVINGS

You're turning 18 and you're determined: Not even your parents can keep you out of the casino right down the road. Okay, some Christians see casual gambling as a form of entertainment. If that's where you're at, lower your odds of losing every penny in your piggy bank by setting a personal limit—the $10 or $20 or $50 you're willing to toss on an evening of fun. And like Kenny Rogers sang, "You've got to know when to fold 'em." Get help fast when you see any of these warning signs of gambling addiction in you or a friend: failing to keep that spending limit, money problems, debt, secrecy, family and friends expressing concern, preoccupation with gambling, increasing amounts of time and money spent gambling, failed attempts to quit or cut back, gambling with borrowed money, or gambling to win back losses.

THE SHEPHERD AND HIS SHEEP

10 Jesus said, "I tell you the truth, the person who does not enter the sheepfold by the door, but climbs in some other way, is a thief and a robber. ²The one who enters by the door is the shepherd of the sheep. ³The one who guards the door opens it for him. And the sheep listen to the voice of the shepherd. He calls his own sheep by name and leads them out. ⁴When he brings all his sheep out, he goes ahead of them, and they follow him because they know his voice. ⁵But they will never follow a stranger. They will run away from him because they don't know his voice." ⁶Jesus told the people this story, but they did not understand what it meant.

JESUS IS THE GOOD SHEPHERD

⁷So Jesus said again, "I tell you the truth, I am the door for the sheep. ⁸All the people who came before me were thieves and robbers. The sheep did not listen to them. ⁹I am the door, and the person who enters through me will be saved and will be able to come in and go out and find pasture. ¹⁰A thief comes to steal and kill and destroy, but I came to give life—life in all its fullness.

¹¹"I am the good shepherd. The good shepherd gives his life for the sheep. ¹²The worker who is paid to keep the sheep is different from the shepherd who owns them. When the worker sees a wolf coming, he runs away and leaves the sheep alone. Then the wolf attacks the sheep and scatters them. ¹³The man runs away because he is only a paid worker and does not really care about the sheep.

¹⁴⁻¹⁵"I am the good shepherd. I know my sheep, as the Father knows me. And my sheep know me, as I know the Father. I give my life for the sheep. ¹⁶I have other sheep that are not in this flock, and I must bring them also. They will listen to my voice, and there will be one flock and one shepherd. ¹⁷The Father loves me because I give my life so that I can take it back again. ¹⁸No one takes it away from me; I give my own life freely. I have the right to give my life, and I have the right to take it back. This is what my Father commanded me to do."

¹⁹Again the leaders did not agree with each other because of these words of Jesus. ²⁰Many of them said, "A demon has come into him and made him crazy. Why listen to him?"

RELATIONSHIPS

"Love is not rude, is not selfish, and does not get upset with others" (1 Corinthians 13:5). That's part of a passage you'll likely hear at your wedding. Yep, we said *your* wedding. And those verses are a simple test to see if you're growing in love. Flip to 1 Corinthians 13:4-8 and substitute your name every time the word "love" appears. As in, "Mike is not rude. Mike is not selfish. Mike does not get upset with others." How did you do? How do you want to do?

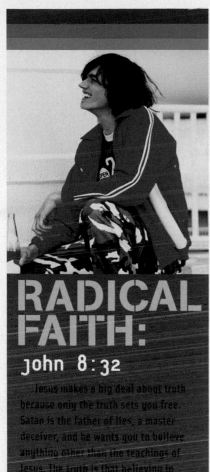

RADICAL FAITH:

John 8:32

Jesus makes a big deal about truth because only the truth sets you free. Satan is the father of lies, a master deceiver, and he wants you to believe anything other than the teachings of Jesus. The truth is that believing in Jesus saves you from your sin and saves you for eternal life. In this verse Jesus says that the truth will set you free because Jesus frees you from your bondage to sin. Satan will whisper lies to you over and over, hoping you'll believe his tricks and get confused. Remember that confusion is not from God (see 1 Corinthians 14:33).

When you feel confused or over-whelmed, return to Scripture and read the truth of the words of God. From him you will find direction and clear guidance. Meditate on those words. Let his truth come alive in your mind and in your heart.

The Bible makes a big deal about truth because lies will lead you astray. Stay focused on the truth of God's Word. Know the truth, follow the truth, tell the truth. It "will make you free"!

21But others said, "A man who is crazy with a demon does not say things like this. Can a demon open the eyes of the blind?"

JESUS IS REJECTED

22The time came for the Feast of Dedication at Jerusalem. It was winter, 23and Jesus was walking in the Temple in Solomon's Porch. 24Some people gathered around him and said, "How long will you make us wonder about you? If you are the Christ, tell us plainly."

25Jesus answered, "I told you already, but you did not believe. The miracles I do in my Father's name show who I am. 26But you don't believe, because you are not my sheep. 27My sheep listen to my voice; I know them, and they follow me. 28I give them eternal life, and they will never die, and no one can steal them out of my hand. 29My Father gave my sheep to me. He is greater than all, and no person can steal my sheep out of my Father's hand. 30The Father and I are one."

31Again some of the people picked up stones to kill Jesus. 32But he said to them, "I have done many good works from the Father. Which of these good works are you killing me for?"

33They answered, "We are not killing you because of any good work you did, but because you speak against God. You are only a human, but you say you are the same as God!"

34Jesus answered, "It is written in your law that God said, 'I said, you are gods.'[n] 35This Scripture called those people gods who received God's message, and Scripture is always true. 36So why do you say that I speak against God because I said, 'I am God's Son'? I am the one God chose and sent into the world. 37If I don't do what my Father does, then don't believe me. 38But if I do what my Father does, even though you don't believe in me, believe what I do. Then you will know and understand that the Father is in me and I am in the Father."

39They tried to take Jesus again, but he escaped from them.

40Then he went back across the Jordan River to the place where John had first baptized. Jesus stayed there, 41and many people came to him and said, "John never did a miracle, but everything John said about this man is true." 42And in that place many believed in Jesus.

---

10 AMAZING PROPHECIES ABOUT JESUS— AND THEIR FULFILLMENTS

1. BORN OF A VIRGIN (ISAIAH 7:14; MATTHEW 1:18-25)

2. BORN IN BETHLEHEM (MICAH 5:2; MATTHEW 2:1)

3. BORN TO THE LINE OF DAVID (JEREMIAH 23:5; LUKE 3:23, 31)

4. CALLED IMMANUEL, "GOD IS WITH US" (ISAIAH 7:14; MATTHEW 1:23)

5. ENTERED JERUSALEM ON A DONKEY (ZECHARIAH 9:9; LUKE 19:35-37)

6. BETRAYED BY A FRIEND (PSALM 41:9; MATTHEW 10:4)

7. SOLD FOR THIRTY PIECES OF SILVER (ZECHARIAH 11:12; MATTHEW 26:15)

8. PIERCED IN HIS HANDS AND FEET (PSALM 22:16; JOHN 20:27)

9. BURIED IN A RICH MAN'S TOMB (ISAIAH 53:9; MATTHEW 27:57-60)

10. ROSE FROM THE DEAD (PSALM 16:10; ACTS 2:31)

THE DEATH OF LAZARUS

11 A man named Lazarus was sick. He lived in the town of Bethany, where Mary and her sister Martha lived. 2Mary was the woman who later put perfume on the Lord

---

10:34 'I . . . gods.' Quotation from Psalm 82:6.

and wiped his feet with her hair. Mary's brother was Lazarus, the man who was now sick. [3]So Mary and Martha sent someone to tell Jesus, "Lord, the one you love is sick."

[4]When Jesus heard this, he said, "This sickness will not end in death. It is for the glory of God, to bring glory to the Son of God." [5]Jesus loved Martha and her sister and Lazarus. [6]But when he heard that Lazarus was sick, he stayed where he was for two more days. [7]Then Jesus said to his followers, "Let's go back to Judea."

[8]The followers said, "But Teacher, some people there tried to stone you to death only a short time ago. Now you want to go back there?"

[9]Jesus answered, "Are there not twelve hours in the day? If anyone walks in the daylight, he will not stumble, because he can see by this world's light. [10]But if anyone walks at night, he stumbles because there is no light to help him see."

[11]After Jesus said this, he added, "Our friend Lazarus has fallen asleep, but I am going there to wake him."

[12]The followers said, "But Lord, if he is only asleep, he will be all right."

[13]Jesus meant that Lazarus was dead, but his followers thought he meant Lazarus was really sleeping. [14]So then Jesus said plainly, "Lazarus is dead. [15]And I am glad for your sakes I was not there so that you may believe. But let's go to him now."

[16]Then Thomas (the one called Didymus) said to the other followers, "Let us also go so that we can die with him."

JESUS IN BETHANY

[17]When Jesus arrived, he learned that Lazarus had already been dead and in the tomb for four days. [18]Bethany was about two miles from Jerusalem. [19]Many of the Jews had come there to comfort Martha and Mary about their brother.

[20]When Martha heard that Jesus was coming, she went out to meet him, but Mary stayed home. [21]Martha said to Jesus, "Lord, if you had been here, my brother would not have died. [22]But I know that even now God will give you anything you ask."

[23]Jesus said, "Your brother will rise and live again."

[24]Martha answered, "I know that he will rise and live again in the resurrection[n] on the last day."

[25]Jesus said to her, "I am the resurrection and the life. Those who believe in me will have life even if they die. [26]And everyone who lives and believes in me will never die. Martha, do you believe this?"

[27]Martha answered, "Yes, Lord. I believe that you are the Christ, the Son of God, the One coming to the world."

JESUS CRIES

[28]After Martha said this, she went back and talked to her sister Mary alone. Martha said, "The Teacher is here and he is asking for you." [29]When Mary heard this, she got up quickly and went to Jesus. [30]Jesus had not yet come into the town but was still at the place where Martha had met him. [31]The Jews were with Mary in the house, comforting her. When they saw her stand and leave quickly, they followed her, thinking she was going to the tomb to cry there.

[32]But Mary went to the place where Jesus was. When she saw him, she fell at his feet and said, "Lord, if you had been here, my brother would not have died."

[33]When Jesus saw Mary crying and the Jews who came with her also crying, he was upset and was deeply troubled. [34]He asked, "Where did you bury him?"

"Come and see, Lord," they said.

[35]Jesus cried.

[36]So the Jews said, "See how much he loved him."

[37]But some of them said, "If Jesus opened the eyes of the blind man, why couldn't he keep Lazarus from dying?"

JESUS RAISES LAZARUS

[38]Again feeling very upset, Jesus came to the tomb. It was a cave with a large stone covering the entrance. [39]Jesus said, "Move the stone away."

Martha, the sister of the dead man, said, "But, Lord, it has been four days since he died. There will be a bad smell."

[40]Then Jesus said to her, "Didn't I tell you that if you believed you would see the glory of God?"

[41]So they moved the stone away from the entrance. Then Jesus looked up and said, "Father, I thank you that you heard me. [42]I know that you always hear me, but I said these things because of the people here around me. I want them to believe that you sent me." [43]After Jesus said this, he cried out in a loud voice, "Lazarus, come out!" [44]The dead man came out, his hands and feet wrapped with pieces of cloth, and a cloth around his face.

Jesus said to them, "Take the cloth off of him and let him go."

THE PLAN TO KILL JESUS

[45]Many of the people, who had come to visit Mary and saw what Jesus did, believed in him. [46]But some of them went to the Pharisees and told them what Jesus had done. [47]Then the leading priests and Pharisees called a meeting of the council. They asked, "What should we do? This man is doing many miracles. [48]If we let him continue doing these things, everyone will believe in him. Then the Romans will come and take away our Temple and our nation."

 11:24 resurrection Being raised from the dead to live again.

You don't have to be an adult to be a missionary. And you don't have to look far to get plugged in. In the United States alone, almost 40 thousand groups sponsor short-term mission teams—that's 35 thousand churches, 3,700 agencies, and more than one thousand schools. Together they send a staggering one million short-term missionaries each year. If you want to have a spiritual experience that will impact you and others forever, check with your youth pastor—or hunt for mission group listings at www.youthspecialties.com.

For more on extreme missions visit www.traveltheroad.com.

[49]One of the men there was Caiaphas, the high priest that year. He said, "You people know nothing! [50]You don't realize that it is better for one man to die for the people than for the whole nation to be destroyed."

[51]Caiaphas did not think of this himself. As high priest that year, he was really prophesying that Jesus would die for their nation [52]and for God's scattered children to bring them all together and make them one.

[53]That day they started planning to kill Jesus. [54]So Jesus no longer traveled openly among the people. He left there and went to a place near the desert, to a town called Ephraim and stayed there with his followers.

[55]It was almost time for the Passover Feast. Many from the country went up to Jerusalem before the Passover to do the special things to make themselves pure. [56]The people looked for Jesus and stood in the Temple asking each other, "Is he coming to the Feast? What do you think?" [57]But the leading priests and the Pharisees had given orders that if anyone knew where Jesus was, he must tell them. Then they could arrest him.

JESUS WITH FRIENDS IN BETHANY

12 Six days before the Passover Feast, Jesus went to Bethany, where Lazarus lived. (Lazarus is the man Jesus raised from the dead.) [2]There they had a dinner for Jesus. Martha served the food, and Lazarus was one of the people eating with Jesus. [3]Mary brought in a pint of very expensive perfume made from pure nard. She poured the perfume on Jesus' feet, and then she wiped his feet with her hair. And the sweet smell from the perfume filled the whole house.

[4]Judas Iscariot, one of Jesus' followers who would later turn against him, was there. Judas said, [5]"This perfume was worth three hundred coins.[n] Why wasn't it sold and the money given to the poor?" [6]But Judas did not really care about the poor; he said this because he was a thief. He was the one who kept the money box, and he often stole from it.

[7]Jesus answered, "Leave her alone. It was right for her to save this perfume for today, the day for me to be prepared for burial. [8]You will always have the poor with you, but you will not always have me."

THE PLOT AGAINST LAZARUS

[9]A large crowd of people heard that Jesus was in Bethany. So they went there to see not only Jesus but Lazarus, whom Jesus raised from the dead. [10]So the leading priests made plans to kill Lazarus, too. [11]Because of Lazarus

 12:5 coins One coin, a denarius, was the average pay for one day's work.

Q. *Can people know they're Christians for sure?*

A. Most definitely. God's Word makes it ultra clear. "If you use your mouth to say, 'Jesus is Lord,' and if you believe in your heart that God raised Jesus from the dead, you will be saved" (Romans 10:9). In order to do those two things, people have to know they are doing them. And after they've done them, they can know they are Christians.

Q. *I'm a new Christian. Am I supposed to ditch my old non-Christian friends?*

A. Picture this. Ten minutes ago you were hanging over a cliff, but someone came along and rescued you. Now you're reaching your hand down to help up another friend. It's far harder to pull your friend up than for your old friend to pull you back over the cliff. The point? Your friends need your help, so don't ditch them. But get help for yourself to stay anchored up top.

many of the Jews were leaving them and believing in Jesus.

JESUS ENTERS JERUSALEM

[12]The next day a great crowd who had come to Jerusalem for the Passover Feast heard that Jesus was coming there. [13]So they took branches of palm trees and went out to meet Jesus, shouting,

"Praise[n] God!
God bless the One who comes in the name of the Lord!
God bless the King of Israel!" *Psalm 118:25-26*

[14]Jesus found a colt and sat on it. This was as the Scripture says,

[15]"Don't be afraid, people of Jerusalem!
Your king is coming,
sitting on the colt of a donkey." *Zechariah 9:9*

[16]The followers of Jesus did not understand this at first. But after Jesus was raised to glory, they remembered that this had been written about him and that they had done these things to him.

PEOPLE TELL ABOUT JESUS

[17]There had been many people with Jesus when he raised Lazarus from the dead and told him to come out of the tomb. Now they were telling others about what Jesus did. [18]Many people went out to meet Jesus, because they had heard about this miracle. [19]So the Pharisees said to each other, "You can see that nothing is going right for us. Look! The whole world is following him."

JESUS TALKS ABOUT HIS DEATH

[20]There were some Greek people, too, who came to Jerusalem to worship at the Passover Feast. [21]They went to Philip, who was from Bethsaida in Galilee, and said, "Sir, we would like to see Jesus." [22]Philip told Andrew, and then Andrew and Philip told Jesus.

[23]Jesus said to them, "The time has come for the Son of Man to receive his glory. [24]I tell you the truth, a grain of wheat must fall to the ground and die to make many seeds. But if it never dies, it remains only a single seed. [2] Those who love their lives will lose them, but those who hate their lives in this world will keep true life forever. [26]Whoever serves me must follow me. Then my servant will be with me everywhere I am. My Father will honor anyone who serves me.

[27]"Now I am very troubled. Should I say, 'Father, save me from this time'? No, I came to this time so I could suffer. [28]Father, bring glory to your name!"

Then a voice came from heaven, "I have brought glory to it, and I will do it again."

[29]The crowd standing there, who heard the voice, said it was thunder.

GET OUT THERE →

COMPASSION INTERNATIONAL exists for one simple reason: to break the cycle of poverty for children everywhere.

This vision stems from Rev. Everett Swanson who, in the early 1950s, developed a system for caring people to sponsor Korean children for just a few dollars a month. This provided Korean children with food, shelter, and clothing, as needed; education and healthcare; and Christian training and personal attention. That work has continued, and grown, for over 50 years. Today, they're helping over 500,000 children in over 20 countries.

You can share your love, prayers, and financial support with a boy or girl who lives in poverty. Children are waiting now. When you sponsor a child, you change the life of a child...forever!

To get involved, visit www.compassion.com.

 12:13 Praise Literally, "Hosanna," a Hebrew word used at first in praying to God for help, but at this time it was probably a shout of joy used in praising God or his Messiah.

But others said, "An angel has spoken to him."

³⁰Jesus said, "That voice was for your sake, not mine. ³¹Now is the time for the world to be judged; now the ruler of this world will be thrown down. ³²If I am lifted up from the earth, I will draw all people toward me." ³³Jesus said this to show how he would die.

³⁴The crowd said, "We have heard from the law that the Christ will live forever. So why do you say, 'The Son of Man must be lifted up'? Who is this 'Son of Man'?"

³⁵Then Jesus said, "The light will be with you for a little longer, so walk while you have the light. Then the darkness will not catch you. If you walk in the darkness, you will not know where you are going. ³⁶Believe in the light while you still have it so that you will become children of light." When Jesus had said this, he left and hid himself from them.

SOME PEOPLE WON'T BELIEVE IN JESUS

³⁷Though Jesus had done many miracles in front of the people, they still did not believe in him. ³⁸This was to bring about what Isaiah the prophet had said:

"Lord, who believed what we told them?
Who saw the Lord's power in this?"

Isaiah 53:1

³⁹This is why the people could not believe: Isaiah also had said,

⁴⁰"He has blinded their eyes,
and he has closed their minds.
Otherwise they would see with their eyes
and understand in their minds
and come back to me and be healed."

Isaiah 6:10

⁴¹Isaiah said this because he saw Jesus' glory and spoke about him.

⁴²But many believed in Jesus, even many of the leaders. But because of the Pharisees, they did not say they believed in him for fear they would be put out of the synagogue. ⁴³They loved praise from people more than praise from God.

⁴⁴Then Jesus cried out, "Whoever believes in me is really believing in the One who sent me. ⁴⁵Whoever sees me sees the One who sent me. ⁴⁶I have come as light into the world so that whoever believes in me would not stay in darkness.

⁴⁷"Anyone who hears my words and does not obey them, I do not judge, because I did not come to judge the world, but to save the world. ⁴⁸There is a judge for those who refuse to believe in me and do not accept my words. The word I have taught will be their judge on the last day. ⁴⁹The things I taught were not from myself. The Father who sent me told me what to say and what to teach. ⁵⁰And I know that eternal life comes from what the Father commands. So whatever I say is what the Father told me to say."

JESUS WASHES HIS FOLLOWERS' FEET

13 It was almost time for the Passover Feast. Jesus knew that it was time for him to leave this world and go back to the Father. He had always loved those who were his own in the world, and he loved them all the way to the end.

²Jesus and his followers were at the evening meal. The devil had already persuaded Judas Iscariot, the son of Simon, to turn against Jesus. ³Jesus knew that the Father had given him power over everything and that he had come from God and was going back to God. ⁴So during the meal Jesus stood up and took off his outer clothing. Taking a towel, he wrapped it around his waist. ⁵Then he poured water into a bowl and began to wash the followers' feet, drying them with the towel that was wrapped around him.

⁶Jesus came to Simon Peter, who said to him, "Lord, are you going to wash my feet?"

⁷Jesus answered, "You don't understand now what I am doing, but you will understand later."

⁸Peter said, "No, you will never wash my feet."

Jesus answered, "If I don't wash your feet, you are not one of my people."

⁹Simon Peter answered, "Lord, then wash not only my feet, but wash my hands and my head, too!"

¹⁰Jesus said, "After a person has had a bath, his whole body is clean. He needs only to wash his feet. And you men are clean, but not all of you." ¹¹Jesus knew who would turn against him, and that is why he said, "Not all of you are clean."

¹²When he had finished washing their feet, he put on his clothes and sat down again. He asked, "Do you understand what I have just done for you? ¹³You call me 'Teacher' and 'Lord,' and you are right, because that is what I am. ¹⁴If I, your Lord and Teacher, have washed

MONUMENTAL MEN IN CHURCH HISTORY

1. **AUGUSTINE (354-430)**
2. **JEROME (C. 340-420)**
3. **FRANCIS OF ASSISI (1182-1226)**
4. **THOMAS AQUINAS (1225-1274)**
5. **MARTIN LUTHER (1483-1546)**
6. **JOHN CALVIN (1509-1564)**
7. **JOHN WESLEY (1703-1791)**
8. **JONATHAN EDWARDS (1703-1758)**
9. **BILLY GRAHAM (1918-)**
10. **LUIS PALAU (1934-)**

your feet, you also should wash each other's feet. ¹⁵I did this as an example so that you should do as I have done for you. ¹⁶I tell you the truth, a servant is not greater than his master. A messenger is not greater than the one who sent him. ¹⁷If you know these things, you will be happy if you do them.

¹⁸"I am not talking about all of you. I know those I have chosen. But this is to bring about what the Scripture said: 'The man who ate at my table has turned against me.'ⁿ ¹⁹I am telling you this now before it happens so that when it happens, you will believe that I am he. ²⁰I tell you the truth, whoever accepts anyone I send also accepts me. And whoever accepts me also accepts the One who sent me."

JESUS TALKS ABOUT HIS DEATH

²¹After Jesus said this, he was very troubled. He said openly, "I tell you the truth, one of you will turn against me."

13:18 'The man . . . me.' Quotation from Psalm 41:9.

[22]The followers all looked at each other, because they did not know whom Jesus was talking about. [23]One of the followers sitting[n] next to Jesus was the follower Jesus loved. [24]Simon Peter motioned to him to ask Jesus whom he was talking about.

[25]That follower leaned closer to Jesus and asked, "Lord, who is it?"

[26]Jesus answered, "I will dip this bread into the dish. The man I give it to is the man who will turn against me." So Jesus took a piece of bread, dipped it, and gave it to Judas Iscariot, the son of Simon. [27]As soon as Judas took the bread, Satan entered him. Jesus said to him, "The thing that you will do—do it quickly." [28]No one at the table understood why Jesus said this to Judas. [29]Since he was the one who kept the money box, some of the followers thought Jesus was telling him to buy what was needed for the feast or to give something to the poor.

[30]Judas took the bread Jesus gave him and immediately went out. It was night.

[31]When Judas was gone, Jesus said, "Now the Son of Man receives his glory, and God receives glory through him. [32]If God receives glory through him, then God will give glory to the Son through himself. And God will give him glory quickly."

[33]Jesus said, "My children, I will be with you only a little longer. You will look for me, and what I told the Jews, I tell you now: Where I am going you cannot come.

[34]"I give you a new command: Love each other. You must love each other as I have loved you. [35]All people will know that you are my followers if you love each other."

PETER WILL SAY HE DOESN'T KNOW JESUS

[36]Simon Peter asked Jesus, "Lord, where are you going?"

Jesus answered, "Where I am going you cannot follow now, but you will follow later."

[37]Peter asked, "Lord, why can't I follow you now? I am ready to die for you!"

[38]Jesus answered, "Are you ready to die for me? I tell you the truth, before the rooster crows, you will say three times that you don't know me."

JESUS COMFORTS HIS FOLLOWERS

14 Jesus said, "Don't let your hearts be troubled. Trust in God, and trust in me. [2]There are many rooms in my Father's house; I would not tell you this if it were not true. I am going there to prepare a place for you. [3]After I go and prepare a place for you, I will come back and take you to be with me so that you may be where I am. [4]You know the way to the place where I am going."

[5]Thomas said to Jesus, "Lord, we don't know where you are going. So how can we know the way?"

[6]Jesus answered, "I am the way, and the truth, and the life. The only way to the Father is through me. [7]If you really knew me, you would know my Father, too. But now you do know him, and you have seen him."

[8]Philip said to him, "Lord, show us the Father. That is all we need."

[9]Jesus answered, "I have been with you a long time now. Do you still not know me, Philip? Whoever has seen me has seen the Father. So why do you say, 'Show us the Father'? [10]Don't you believe that I am in the Father and the Father is in me? The words I say to you don't come from me, but the Father lives in me and does his own work. [11]Believe me when I say that I am in the Father and the Father is in me. Or believe because of the miracles I have done.

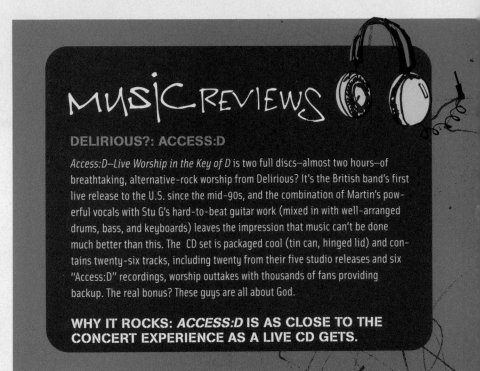

MUSIC REVIEWS

DELIRIOUS?: ACCESS:D

Access:D—Live Worship in the Key of D is two full discs—almost two hours—of breathtaking, alternative-rock worship from Delirious? It's the British band's first live release to the U.S. since the mid-90s, and the combination of Martin's powerful vocals with Stu G's hard-to-beat guitar work (mixed in with well-arranged drums, bass, and keyboards) leaves the impression that music can't be done much better than this. The CD set is packaged cool (tin can, hinged lid) and contains twenty-six tracks, including twenty from their five studio releases and six "Access:D" recordings, worship outtakes with thousands of fans providing backup. The real bonus? These guys are all about God.

WHY IT ROCKS: *ACCESS:D* IS AS CLOSE TO THE CONCERT EXPERIENCE AS A LIVE CD GETS.

DO'S & DON'TS

- Do wash your hands after using the restroom.

- Do cover your mouth and nose when you sneeze.

- Do look for the exits when you board a plane.

- Do say ma'am and sir.

- Don't blow off homework.

- Don't make your mother shop for your gifts to others.

- Don't sneak out at night.

- Don't go nuts when you turn eighteen.

13:23 **sitting** Literally, "lying." The people of that time ate lying down and leaning on one arm.

[12]I tell you the truth, whoever believes in me will do the same things that I do. Those who believe will do even greater things than these, because I am going to the Father. [13]And if you ask for anything in my name, I will do it for you so that the Father's glory will be shown through the Son. [14]If you ask me for anything in my name, I will do it.

THE PROMISE OF THE HOLY SPIRIT

[15]"If you love me, you will obey my commands. [16]I will ask the Father, and he will give you another Helper[n] to be with you forever— [17]the Spirit of truth. The world cannot accept him, because it does not see him or know him. But you know him, because he lives with you and he will be in you.

[18]"I will not leave you all alone like orphans; I will come back to you. [19]In a little while the world will not see me anymore, but you will see me. Because I live, you will live, too. [20]On that day you will know that I am in my Father, and that you are in me and I am in you. [21]Those who know my commands and obey them are the ones who love me, and my Father will love those who love me. I will love them and will show myself to them."

[22]Then Judas (not Judas Iscariot) said, "But, Lord, why do you plan to show yourself to us and not to the rest of the world?"

[23]Jesus answered, "If people love me, they will obey my teaching. My Father will love them, and we will come to them and make our home with them. [24]Those who do not love me do not obey my teaching. This teaching that you hear is not really mine; it is from my Father, who sent me.

[25]"I have told you all these things while I am with you. [26]But the Helper will teach you everything and will cause you to remember all that I told you. This Helper is the Holy Spirit whom the Father will send in my name.

[27]"I leave you peace; my peace I give you. I do not give it to you as the world does. So don't let your hearts be troubled or afraid. [28]You heard me say to you, 'I am going, but I am coming back to you.' If you loved me, you should be happy that I am going back to the Father, because he is greater than I am. [29]I have told you this now, before it happens, so that when it happens, you will believe. [30]I will not talk with you much longer, because the ruler of this world is coming. He has no power over me, [31]but the world must know that I love the Father, so I do exactly what the Father told me to do.

"Come now, let us go.

JESUS IS LIKE A VINE

15 "I am the true vine; my Father is the gardener. [2]He cuts off every branch of mine that does not produce fruit. And he trims and cleans every branch that produces fruit so that it will produce even more fruit. [3]You are already clean because of the words I have spoken to you. [4]Remain in me, and I will remain in you. A branch cannot produce fruit alone but must remain in the vine. In the same way, you cannot produce fruit alone but must remain in me.

[5]"I am the vine, and you are the branches. If any remain in me and I remain in them, they produce much fruit. But without me they can do nothing. [6]If any do not remain in me, they are like a branch that is thrown away and then dies. People pick up dead branches, throw them into the fire, and burn them. [7]If you remain in me and follow my teachings, you can ask anything you want, and it will be given to you. [8]You should produce much fruit and show that you are my followers, which brings glory to my Father. [9]I loved you as the Father loved me. Now remain in my love. [10]I have obeyed my Father's commands, and I remain in his love. In the same way, if you obey my commands, you will remain in my love. [11]I have told you these things so that you can have the same joy I have and so that your joy will be the fullest possible joy.

[12]"This is my command: Love each other as I have loved you. [13]The greatest love a person can show is to die for his friends. [14]You are my friends if you do what I command you. [15]I no longer call you servants, because a servant does not know what his master is doing. But I call you friends, because I have made known to you everything I heard from my Father. [16]You did not choose me; I chose you. And I gave you this work: to go and produce fruit, fruit that will last. Then the Father will give you anything you ask for in my name. [17]This is my command: Love each other.

JESUS WARNS HIS FOLLOWERS

[18]"If the world hates you, remember that it hated me first. [19]If you belonged to the world, it

BIBLE BASICS

The **Trinity** is the union of God the Father, God the Son (Jesus), and God the Holy Spirit. This is the Christian God. The three Persons of the Trinity are equal, but have different roles and purposes. They are all one God, but they have distinct qualities. (See notes on God the Father, Jesus, and the Holy Spirit.)

would love you as it loves its own. But I have chosen you out of the world, so you don't belong to it. That is why the world hates you. [20]Remember what I told you: A servant is not greater than his master. If people did wrong to me, they will do wrong to you, too. And if they

14:16 **Helper** "Counselor" or "Comforter." Jesus is talking about the Holy Spirit.

RANDOM SIGNS THAT YOU'RE FOLLOWING GOD

1. **YOU LET GOD RULE IN MORE AND MORE OF YOUR LIFE.**

2. **YOU BELIEVE BECAUSE YOU WANT TO, NOT BECAUSE YOU HAVE TO.**

3. **YOU KNOW GOD LISTENS WHEN YOU TALK TO HIM.**

4. **YOU DIG INTO THE BIBLE TO FIND OUT HOW GOD WANTS YOU TO LIVE.**

5. **YOU AIM TO FOLLOW JESUS, NOT JUST A BUNCH OF RULES.**

6. **YOU GET UP AFTER YOU FALL DOWN.**

7. **YOU SPILL ONTO OTHERS THE GREAT LOVE YOU GET FROM GOD.**

8. **YOU FORGIVE PEOPLE WHO WRONG YOU.**

9. **YOU FOCUS ON YOUR OWN SINS, NOT THE SINS OF OTHERS.**

10. **YOU GET IT THAT GOD'S LOVE IS A TOTALLY FREE GIFT—AND YOU DON'T TRY TO EARN IT.**

WAYS TO WALK THE WALK — john 14:1

WORD: Don't let your heart be troubled.

WALK IT: Don't worry. Be happy. When you get stressed today over a problem with peers or parents, remember that Jesus is right with you in the thick of life.

obeyed my teaching, they will obey yours, too. [21]They will do all this to you on account of me, because they do not know the One who sent me. [22]If I had not come and spoken to them, they would not be guilty of sin, but now they have no excuse for their sin. [23]Whoever hates me also hates my Father. [24]I did works among them that no one else has ever done. If I had not done these works, they would not be guilty of sin. But now they have seen what I have done, and yet they have hated both me and my Father. [25]But this happened so that what is written in their law would be true: 'They hated me for no reason.'[n]

[26]"I will send you the Helper[n] from the Father; he is the Spirit of truth who comes from the Father. When he comes, he will tell about me, [27]and you also must tell people about me, because you have been with me from the beginning.

16 "I have told you these things to keep you from giving up. [2]People will put you out of their synagogues. Yes, the time is coming when those who kill you will think they are offering service to God. [3]They will do this because they have not known the Father and they have not known me. [4]I have told you these things now so that when the time comes you will remember that I warned you.

THE WORK OF THE HOLY SPIRIT

"I did not tell you these things at the beginning, because I was with you then. [5]Now I am going back to the One who sent me. But none of you asks me, 'Where are you going?' [6]Your hearts are filled with sadness because I have told you these things. [7]But I tell you the truth, it is better for you that I go away. When I go away, I will send the Helper[n] to you. If I do not go away, the Helper will not come. [8]When the Helper comes, he will prove to the people of the world the truth about sin, about being right with God, and about judgment. [9]He will prove to them that sin is not believing in me. [10]He will prove to them that being right with God comes from my going to the Father and not being seen anymore. [11]And the Helper will prove to them that judgment happened when the ruler of this world was judged.

[12]"I have many more things to say to you, but they are too much for you now. [13]But when the Spirit of truth comes, he will lead you into all truth. He will not speak his own words, but he will speak only what he hears, and he will tell you what is to come. [14]The Spirit of truth will bring glory to me, because he will take what I have to say and tell it to you. [15]All that the Father has is mine. That is why I said that the Spirit will take what I have to say and tell it to you.

SADNESS WILL BECOME HAPPINESS

[16]"After a little while you will not see me, and then after a little while you will see me again."

[17]Some of the followers said to each other, "What does Jesus mean when he says, 'After a little while you will not see me, and then after a little while you will see me again'? And what does he mean when he says, 'Because I am going to the Father'?" [18]They also asked, "What does he mean by 'a little while'? We don't understand what he is saying."

[19]Jesus saw that the followers wanted to ask him about this, so he said to them, "Are you asking each other what I meant when I said, 'After a little while you will not see me, and then after a little while you will see me again'? [20]I tell you the truth, you will cry and be sad, but the world will be happy. You will be sad, but your sadness will become joy. [21]When a woman gives birth to a baby, she has pain, because her time has come. But when her baby is born, she forgets the pain, because she is so happy that a child has been born into the world. [22]It is the same with you. Now you are sad, but I will see you again and you will be happy, and no one will take away your joy. [23]In that day you will not ask me for anything. I tell you the truth, my Father will give you anything you ask for in my name. [24]Until now you have not asked for anything in my name. Ask and you will receive, so that your joy will be the fullest possible joy.

 15:25 'They . . . reason.' These words could be from Psalm 35:19 or Psalm 69:4.   15:26; 16:7 Helper "Counselor" or "Comforter." Jesus is talking about the Holy Spirit.

VICTORY OVER THE WORLD

²⁵"I have told you these things, using stories that hide the meaning. But the time will come when I will not use stories like that to tell you things; I will speak to you in plain words about the Father. ²⁶In that day you will ask the Father for things in my name. I mean, I will not need to ask the Father for you. ²⁷The Father himself loves you. He loves you because you loved me and believed that I came from God. ²⁸I came from the Father into the world. Now I am leaving the world and going back to the Father."

²⁹Then the followers of Jesus said, "You are speaking clearly to us now and are not using stories that are hard to understand. ³⁰We can see now that you know all things. You can answer a person's question even before it is asked. This makes us believe you came from God."

³¹Jesus answered, "So now you believe? ³²Listen to me; a time is coming when you will be scattered, each to his own home. That time is now here. You will leave me alone, but I am never really alone, because the Father is with me.

³³"I told you these things so that you can have peace in me. In this world you will have trouble, but be brave! I have defeated the world."

JESUS PRAYS FOR HIS FOLLOWERS

17 After Jesus said these things, he looked toward heaven and prayed, "Father, the time has come. Give glory to your Son so that the Son can give glory to you. ²You gave the Son power over all people so that the Son could give eternal life to all those you gave him. ³And this is eternal life: that people know you, the only true God, and that they know Jesus Christ, the One you sent. ⁴Having finished the work you gave me to do, I brought you glory on earth. ⁵And now, Father, give me glory with you; give me the glory I had with you before the world was made.

⁶"I showed what you are like to those you gave me from the world. They belonged to you, and you gave them to me, and they have obeyed your teaching. ⁷Now they know that everything you gave me comes from you. ⁸I gave them the teachings you gave me, and they accepted them. They knew that I truly came from you, and they believed that you sent me. ⁹I am praying for them. I am not praying for people in the world but for those you gave me, because they are yours. ¹⁰All I have is yours, and all you have is mine. And my glory is shown through them. ¹¹I am coming to you; I will not stay in the world any longer. But they are still in the world. Holy Father, keep them safe by the power of your name, the name you gave me, so that they will be one, just as you and I are one. ¹²While I was with them, I kept them safe by the power of your name, the name you gave me. I protected them, and only one of them, the one worthy of destruction, was lost so that the Scripture would come true.

¹³"I am coming to you now. But I pray these things while I am still in the world so that these followers can have all of my joy in them. ¹⁴I have given them your teaching. And the world has hated them, because they don't belong to the world, just as I don't belong to the world. ¹⁵I am not asking you to take them out of the world but to keep them safe from the Evil One. ¹⁶They don't belong to the world, just as I don't belong to the world. ¹⁷Make them ready for your service through your truth; your teaching is truth. ¹⁸I have sent them into the world, just as you sent me into the world. ¹⁹For their sake, I am making myself ready to serve so that they can be ready for their service of the truth.

²⁰"I pray for these followers, but I am also praying for all those who will believe in me because of their teaching. ²¹Father, I pray that they can be one. As you are in me and I am in you, I pray that they can also be one in us. Then the world will believe that you sent me. ²²I have given these people the glory that you gave me so that they can be one, just as you and I are one. ²³I will be in them and you will be in me so that they will be completely one. Then the world will know that you sent me and that you loved them just as much as you loved me.

MEN OF THE SWORD

LUKE was a doctor who aimed to assemble an orderly account of the life of Jesus. A close friend of Paul, he wrote the third Gospel—the Bible book with his name—as well as the Book of Acts. Many Bible experts believe Luke wrote these books while sticking close to Paul during Paul's first imprisonment in Rome. He also stuck with Paul during Paul's second Roman term. In the period before Paul's martyrdom, Paul wrote to Timothy that "Luke is the only one still with me."

—2 Timothy 4:11

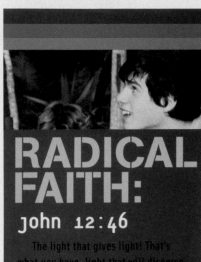

RADICAL FAITH:

john 12:46

The light that gives light! That's what you have—light that will disperse darkness. In other words, you're like a flashlight chasing out the darkness of this world. Don't let your batteries run out, and you'd better check your bulb. The light that Christians give because of Jesus is the only light this world has.

Have you ever been in a room that was pitch black—no light, no windows, totally dark? What happened when you turned on a flashlight or struck a match? The entire room lit up. You couldn't believe how much light that one match or flashlight gave off. That's exactly the kind of effect you can have in your school and everywhere else you go. We live in a dark world, but the good news is that you are the light!

What would you do if you had a friend who was trapped in a cave with a group of people, and they couldn't get out because they couldn't find their way? Let's say that they all died and when their bodies were found, it was discovered that one of the victims had a perfectly good flashlight in his backpack that would have saved all of their lives if it had been used. Wouldn't that upset you?

You know what? You are like that same flashlight that could have saved those lives. Every day you come across the paths of people who desperately need the light of Jesus. Don't hide the light. Use it to impact someone's life forever!

24"Father, I want these people that you gave me to be with me where I am. I want them to see my glory, which you gave me because you loved me before the world was made. 25Father, you are the One who is good. The world does not know you, but I know you, and these people know you sent me. 26I showed them what you are like, and I will show them again. Then they will have the same love that you have for me, and I will live in them."

JESUS IS ARRESTED

18 When Jesus finished praying, he went with his followers across the Kidron Valley. On the other side there was a garden, and Jesus and his followers went into it.

2Judas knew where this place was, because Jesus met there often with his followers. Judas was the one who turned against Jesus. 3So Judas came there with a group of soldiers and some guards from the leading priests and the Pharisees. They were carrying torches, lanterns, and weapons.

4Knowing everything that would happen to him, Jesus went out and asked, "Who is it you are looking for?"

5They answered, "Jesus from Nazareth."

"I am he," Jesus said. (Judas, the one who turned against Jesus, was standing there with them.) 6When Jesus said, "I am he," they moved back and fell to the ground.

7Jesus asked them again, "Who is it you are looking for?"

They said, "Jesus of Nazareth."

8"I told you that I am he," Jesus said. "So if you are looking for me, let the others go." 9This happened so that the words Jesus said before would come true: "I have not lost any of the ones you gave me."

10Simon Peter, who had a sword, pulled it out and struck the servant of the high priest, cutting off his right ear. (The servant's name was Malchus.) 11Jesus said to Peter, "Put your sword back. Shouldn't I drink the cup[n] the Father gave me?"

JESUS IS BROUGHT BEFORE ANNAS

12Then the soldiers with their commander and the guards arrested Jesus. They tied him 13and led him first to Annas, the father-in-law of Caiaphas, the high priest that year. 14Caiaphas was the one who told the Jews that it would be better if one man died for all the people.

LOOK COOL
TIPS ON YOURSELF

You're bound to snore in some classes, but that sliding down and slouching thing you do where your nose is pretty much level with the top of your desk isn't helping. Sit up straight before that pose becomes a habit you can't break. Scoot your posterior back into the seat and stretch like you're trying to touch your shoulder blades together. Then settle into a relaxed but upright position. You'll breathe easier, which feeds your brain the oxygen it needs to stay alert. Sometimes what seems comfortable is just what you've gotten used to. But it's not necessarily the best.

PETER SAYS HE DOESN'T KNOW JESUS

15Simon Peter and another one of Jesus' followers went along after Jesus. This follower knew the high priest, so he went with Jesus into the high priest's courtyard. 16But Peter waited outside near the door. The follower who knew the high priest came back outside, spoke to the girl at the door, and brought Peter inside. 17The girl at the door said to Peter, "Aren't you also one of that man's followers?"

Peter answered, "No, I am not!"

18It was cold, so the servants and guards had built a fire and were standing around it, warming themselves. Peter also was standing with them, warming himself.

THE HIGH PRIEST QUESTIONS JESUS

19The high priest asked Jesus questions about his followers and his teaching. 20Jesus answered, "I have spoken openly to everyone.

 18:11 cup Jesus is talking about the painful things that will happen to him. Accepting these things will be very hard, like drinking a cup of something bitter.

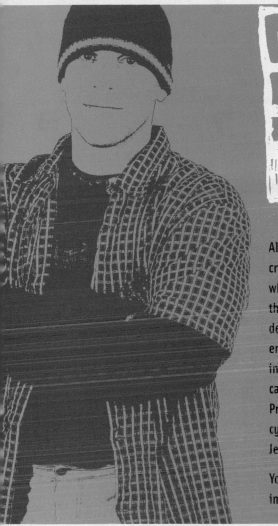

GET OUT THERE

All too often, the forgotten victims of crime are the little children of inmates, who are left without a father or mother through no fault of their own. The evidence is clear that children with a parent in prison are more likely to end up in prison themselves someday. Now you can join **ANGEL TREE**, a ministry of Prison Fellowship, and help break this cycle of crime by sharing the love of Jesus Christ with the children of inmates.

You and your church can make a dramatic impact in the lives of needy, at-risk children right in your own community by hosting Angel Tree's Christmas outreach. You can help with activities including contacting caregivers, enlisting congregation members to purchase gifts, coordinating home delivery of gifts, and holding an evangelism presentation or Angel Tree party at your church. They need you and thousands of others to meet the needs of the 500,000 children they serve each year.

Plug into this opportunity and more at www.angeltree.org.

I have always taught in synagogues and in the Temple, where all the Jews come together. I never said anything in secret. [21]So why do you question me? Ask the people who heard my teaching. They know what I said."

[22]When Jesus said this, one of the guards standing there hit him. The guard said, "Is that the way you answer the high priest?"

[23]Jesus answered him, "If I said something wrong, then show what it was. But if what I said is true, why do you hit me?"

[24]Then Annas sent Jesus, who was still tied, to Caiaphas the high priest.

PETER SAYS AGAIN HE DOESN'T KNOW JESUS

[25]As Simon Peter was standing and warming himself, they said to him, "Aren't you one of that man's followers?"

Peter said it was not true; he said, "No, I am not."

[26]One of the servants of the high priest was there. This servant was a relative of the man whose ear Peter had cut off. The servant said, "Didn't I see you with him in the garden?"

[27]Again Peter said it wasn't true. At once a rooster crowed.

JESUS IS BROUGHT BEFORE PILATE

[28]Early in the morning they led Jesus from Caiaphas's house to the Roman governor's palace. They would not go inside the palace, because they did not want to make themselves unclean;[n] they wanted to eat the Passover meal. [29]So Pilate went outside to them and asked, "What charges do you bring against this man?"

[30]They answered, "If he were not a criminal, we wouldn't have brought him to you."

[31]Pilate said to them, "Take him yourselves and judge him by your own law."

"But we are not allowed to put anyone to death," the Jews answered, [32](This happened so that what Jesus said about how he would die would come true.)

[33]Then Pilate went back inside the palace and called Jesus to him and asked, "Are you the king of the Jews?"

[34]Jesus said, "Is that your own question, or did others tell you about me?"

[35]Pilate answered, "I am not one of you. It was your own people and their leading priests who handed you over to me. What have you done wrong?"

[36]Jesus answered, "My kingdom does not belong to this world. If it belonged to this world, my servants would fight so that I would

18:28 **unclean** Going into the Roman palace would make them unfit to eat the Passover Feast, according to their Law.

JUNE

Father's Day is the third Sunday in June. Dedicate your whole day to celebrating Dad!

1 Pray for a Person of Influence: Today is Tim from Delirious?'s birthday.

2

3 Read the Gospel of John this week.

4

5

6

7 Pray for a Person of Influence: Allen Iverson celebrates a birthday today.

8

9 Pray for a Person of Influence: It's Johnny Depp's birthday.

10

11 Plan a weekend camping trip with your family.

12 Pray for a Man of Power: George Bush celebrates his birthday today.

13 Thank God for the end of school.

14 National E-mail Week! Write someone you haven't talked to for a while.

15

16

17 Pray for a Person of Influence: Venus Williams has a birthday today.

18 National Panic Day. Don't.

19

20

21

22

23 Take the family roadster in for an oil change.

24 Get ready for an uncluttered summer by radically cleaning your room without being asked.

25

26 Pray for a Person of Influence: Today is Derek Jeter's birthday.

27

June is National Accordion Awareness Month. Stay ignorant.

28 Paul Bunyan Day. Dress up like a real man.

29

30 Pray for a Person of Influence: Today is Mike Tyson's birthday.

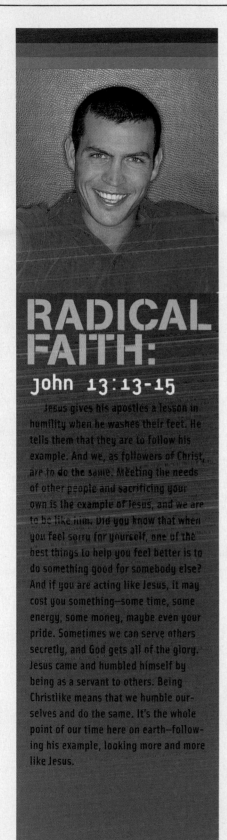

RADICAL FAITH:

john 13:13-15

Jesus gives his apostles a lesson in humility when he washes their feet. He tells them that they are to follow his example. And we, as followers of Christ, are to do the same. Meeting the needs of other people and sacrificing your own is the example of Jesus, and we are to be like him. Did you know that when you feel sorry for yourself, one of the best things to help you feel better is to do something good for somebody else? And if you are acting like Jesus, it may cost you something—some time, some energy, some money, maybe even your pride. Sometimes we can serve others secretly, and God gets all of the glory. Jesus came and humbled himself by being as a servant to others. Being Christlike means that we humble ourselves and do the same. It's the whole point of our time here on earth—following his example, looking more and more like Jesus.

not be given over to the Jews. But my kingdom is from another place."

37Pilate said, "So you are a king!"

Jesus answered, "You are the one saying I am a king. This is why I was born and came into the world: to tell people the truth. And everyone who belongs to the truth listens to me."

38Pilate said, "What is truth?" After he said this, he went out to the crowd again and said to them, "I find nothing against this man. 39But it is your custom that I free one prisoner to you at Passover time. Do you want me to free the 'king of the Jews'?"

40They shouted back, "No, not him! Let Barabbas go free!" (Barabbas was a robber.)

19 Then Pilate ordered that Jesus be taken away and whipped. 2The soldiers made a crown from some thorny branches and put it on Jesus' head and put a purple robe around him. 3Then they came to him many times and said, "Hail, King of the Jews!" and hit him in the face.

4Again Pilate came out and said to them, "Look, I am bringing Jesus out to you. I want you to know that I find nothing against him." 5So Jesus came out, wearing the crown of thorns and the purple robe. Pilate said to them, "Here is the man!"

6When the leading priests and the guards saw Jesus, they shouted, "Crucify him! Crucify him!"

But Pilate answered, "Crucify him yourselves, because I find nothing against him."

7The leaders answered, "We have a law that says he should die, because he said he is the Son of God."

8When Pilate heard this, he was even more afraid. 9He went back inside the palace and asked Jesus, "Where do you come from?" But Jesus did not answer him. 10Pilate said, "You refuse to speak to me? Don't you know I have power to set you free and power to have you crucified?"

11Jesus answered, "The only power you have over me is the power given to you by God. The man who turned me in to you is guilty of a greater sin."

12After this, Pilate tried to let Jesus go. But some in the crowd cried out, "Anyone who makes himself king is against Caesar. If you let this man go, you are no friend of Caesar."

COUNT ON IT

JOHN 14:2-4

This is one of the most awesome promises in all of Scripture. Jesus has gone to heaven to prepare our home—our forever home. A room in our Father's house waits for each one of us. And then, when it is time, Jesus will return to take us there. It's the home your heart has been longing for since the day you were born. It's the place where all your wounds will be healed. All your hopes will be fulfilled. Joy will be complete. Laughter will bounce off the walls. Tears will be banned. Worry won't even be a word. Home. Home at last with Jesus. Everything you've ever thought a home should be, and more than you ever dreamed it could be. Not a day too early, but just in time, Jesus will take us home.

EXPERTS ANSWER YOUR QUESTIONS

Q. *I trusted Christ at a Bible study last summer, but all during the school year I got back into a bad scene. Am I still a Christian?*

A. The Bible says that being saved isn't because of what you *do,* but what you *believe,* that is, in Christ. But it also says you should make him Lord of your life. If you claim to be saved but act like you're God's enemy, disobeying him on purpose, then maybe you never really trusted him. But here's the point. Get right and tight with him *now.*

Q. *My youth pastor really ripped me for saying I wasn't sure about Jesus. He said I should just accept it.*

A. Your youth pastor is probably really concerned for you, and maybe he overheated. It's normal to doubt. But remember you are a believer, not a doubter. So by definition you must say "no" to the doubt and determine in your mind to believe in him. Act on what you know to be true even if it seems way out. Remember, faith is believing in things you can't see.

Q. *Will God always love me?*

A. Doubtless. Read more in Ephesians 3, 1 John 3, Romans 5, and Psalm 36.

13When Pilate heard what they were saying, he brought Jesus out and sat down on the judge's seat at the place called The Stone Pavement. (In the Hebrew language[n] the name is Gabbatha.) 14It was about noon on Preparation Day of Passover week. Pilate said to the crowd, "Here is your king!"

15They shouted, "Take him away! Take him away! Crucify him!"

Pilate asked them, "Do you want me to crucify your king?"

The leading priests answered, "The only king we have is Caesar."

16So Pilate handed Jesus over to them to be crucified.

JESUS IS CRUCIFIED

The soldiers took charge of Jesus. 17Carrying his own cross, Jesus went out to a place called The Place of the Skull, which in the Hebrew language[n] is called Golgotha. 18There they crucified Jesus. They also crucified two other men, one on each side, with Jesus in the middle. 19Pilate wrote a sign and put it on the cross. It read: JESUS OF NAZARETH, THE KING OF THE JEWS. 20The sign was written in Hebrew, in Latin, and in Greek. Many of the people read the sign, because the place where Jesus was crucified was near the city. 21The leading priests said to Pilate, "Don't write, 'The King of the Jews.' But write, 'This man said, "I am the King of the Jews." ' "

22Pilate answered, "What I have written, I have written."

23After the soldiers crucified Jesus, they took his clothes and divided them into four parts, with each soldier getting one part. They also took his long shirt, which was all one piece of cloth, woven from top to bottom. 24So the soldiers said to each other, "We should not tear this into parts. Let's throw lots to see who will get it." This happened so that this Scripture would come true:

"They divided my clothes among them,
    and they threw lots for my clothing."
                                    Psalm 22:18

So the soldiers did this.

25Standing near his cross were Jesus' mother, his mother's sister, Mary the wife of Clopas, and Mary Magdalene. 26When Jesus saw his mother and the follower he loved standing nearby, he said to his mother, "Dear woman, here is your son." 27Then he said to the follower, "Here is your mother." From that time on, the follower took her to live in his home.

JESUS DIES

28After this, Jesus knew that everything had been done. So that the Scripture would come true, he said, "I am thirsty."[n] 29There was a jar full of vinegar there, so the soldiers soaked a sponge in it, put the sponge on a branch of a hyssop plant, and lifted it to Jesus' mouth. 30When Jesus tasted the vinegar, he said, "It is finished." Then he bowed his head and died.

31This day was Preparation Day, and the next day was a special Sabbath day. Since the religious leaders did not want the bodies to stay on the cross on the Sabbath day, they asked Pilate to order that the legs of the men be broken[n] and the bodies be taken away. 32So the soldiers came and broke the legs of the first man on the cross beside Jesus. Then they broke the legs of the man on the other cross beside Jesus. 33But when the soldiers came to Jesus and saw that he was already dead, they did not break his

19:13, 17 **Hebrew language** Or Aramaic, the languages of many people in this region in the first century.   19:28 **"I am thirsty."** Read Psalms 22:15; 69:21.   19:31 **broken** The breaking of their bones would make them die sooner.

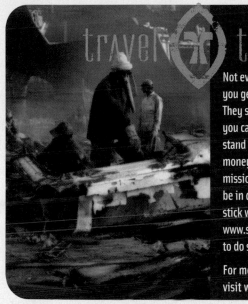

travel the road

Not everyone loves the idea of students like you getting involved in short-term missions. They say you aren't a real missionary. But you can be coached by people who understand the job. They say you cost too much money. But a taste of missions can make you mission-crazed for life. And they say you'll be in danger you can't handle. But you can stick with people who do missions right. Visit www.stmstandards.org for standards on how to do short-term missions well.

For more on extreme missions visit www.traveltheroad.com.

legs. [34]But one of the soldiers stuck his spear into Jesus' side, and at once blood and water came out. [35](The one who saw this happen is the one who told us this, and whatever he says is true. And he knows that he tells the truth, and he tells it so that you might believe.) [36]These things happened to make the Scripture come true: "Not one of his bones will be broken."[n] [37]And another Scripture says, "They will look at the one they stabbed."[n]

JESUS IS BURIED

[38]Later, Joseph from Arimathea asked Pilate if he could take the body of Jesus. (Joseph was a secret follower of Jesus, because he was afraid of some of the leaders.) Pilate gave his permission, so Joseph came and took Jesus' body away. [39]Nicodemus, who earlier had come to Jesus at night, went with Joseph. He brought about seventy-five pounds of myrrh and aloes. [40]These two men took Jesus' body and wrapped it with the spices in pieces of linen cloth, which is how they bury the dead. [41]In the place where Jesus was crucified, there was a garden. In the garden was a new tomb that had never been used before. [42]The men laid Jesus in that tomb because it was nearby, and they were preparing to start their Sabbath day.

JESUS' TOMB IS EMPTY

20 Early on the first day of the week, Mary Magdalene went to the tomb while it was still dark. When she saw that the large stone had been moved away from the tomb, [2]she ran to Simon Peter and the follower whom Jesus loved. Mary said, "They have taken the Lord out of the tomb, and we don't know where they have put him."

[3]So Peter and the other follower started for the tomb. [4]They were both running, but the other follower ran faster than Peter and reached the tomb first. [5]He bent down and looked in and saw the strips of linen cloth lying there, but he did not go in. [6]Then following him, Simon Peter arrived and went into the tomb and saw the strips of linen lying there. [7]He also saw the cloth that had been around Jesus' head, which was folded up and laid in a different place from the strips of linen. [8]Then the other follower, who had reached the tomb first, also went in. He saw and believed. [9](They did not yet understand from the Scriptures that Jesus must rise from the dead.)

JESUS APPEARS TO MARY MAGDALENE

[10]Then the followers went back home. [11]But Mary stood outside the tomb, crying. As she was crying, she bent down and looked inside the tomb. [12]She saw two angels dressed in white, sitting where Jesus' body had been, one at the head and one at the feet.

[13]They asked her, "Woman, why are you crying?"

She answered, "They have taken away my Lord, and I don't know where they have put him." [14]When Mary said this, she turned around

✓COUNT ON IT

JOHN 14:16

Have you ever needed help? Of course you have. You may need help right now. All of us need help at some time or another. None of us is immune to the storms of life, but the good news is God sent the Holy Spirit to go with us through these storms. Not only did he come to fill us with power, but he was also sent to help us with every trial, every temptation, and every circumstance.

You may be going through something at this very moment, but you know what? The Holy Spirit is there right now ready and willing to help, even as you read this. In fact, if we will become aware of God's presence in us there isn't anything that the devil can throw at us that we can't handle. Jesus, the greater One, lives on the inside! Nothing can stop us now! We have victory! He'll help you!

 19:36 "Not one . . . broken." Quotation from Psalm 34:20. The idea is from Exodus 12:46; Numbers 9:12. 19:37 "They . . . stabbed." Quotation from Zechariah 12:10.

JOHN 15:14-15

Jesus called the apostles his *friends*. That word applies to everyone who would ever become his follower. In verse 15, Jesus says, "I no longer call you servants. . . . But I call you friends."

You've probably heard a lot about being Jesus' servant. He's done so much for you! Because of him you're loved more than you can imagine. Because of him you can be strong and confident. Because of him you'll spend eternity with God. So a good response to him is, "Jesus, what can I do for you?" Of course, Jesus wants you to do your best to be a servant who pleases him. But more than that, he wants you to treat him like your friend. Jesus is a Person, and like any person, he wants a friend who loves him more than anyone or anything else. What counts is not wearing yourself out with good deeds, but turning yourself toward him and loving him with your whole heart.

Be careful not to take his friendship for granted. He isn't like your friends at school, just as imperfect as you are. He is God. While you're learning to love him as your best friend, don't ever lose sight of how awesome he is and of all the incredible gifts he gives you. Start to think of yourself as a friend of Jesus.

and saw Jesus standing there, but she did not know it was Jesus.

[15]Jesus asked her, "Woman, why are you crying? Whom are you looking for?"

Thinking he was the gardener, she said to him, "Did you take him away, sir? Tell me where you put him, and I will get him."

[16]Jesus said to her, "Mary."

Mary turned toward Jesus and said in Hebrew,[n] "Rabboni." (This means Teacher.)

[17]Jesus said to her, "Don't hold on to me, because I have not yet gone up to the Father. But go to my brothers and tell them, 'I am going back to my Father and your Father, to my God and your God.' "

[18]Mary Magdalene went and said to the followers, "I saw the Lord!" And she told them what Jesus had said to her.

JESUS APPEARS TO HIS FOLLOWERS

[19]When it was evening on the first day of the week, the followers were together. The doors were locked, because they were afraid of the older leaders. Then Jesus came and stood right in the middle of them and said, "Peace be with you." [20]After he said this, he showed them his hands and his side. The followers were thrilled when they saw the Lord.

[21]Then Jesus said again, "Peace be with you. As the Father sent me, I now send you." [22]After he said this, he breathed on them and said, "Receive the Holy Spirit. [23]If you forgive

PHILIPPIANS 4:6 "DO NOT WORRY ABOUT ANYTHING, BUT PRAY AND ASK GOD FOR EVERYTHING YOU NEED, ALWAYS GIVING THANKS."

anyone his sins, they are forgiven. If you don't forgive them, they are not forgiven."

JESUS APPEARS TO THOMAS

[24]Thomas (called Didymus), who was one of the twelve, was not with them when Jesus came. [25]The other followers kept telling Thomas, "We saw the Lord."

But Thomas said, "I will not believe it until I see the nail marks in his hands and put my finger where the nails were and put my hand into his side."

[26]A week later the followers were in the house again, and Thomas was with them. The doors were locked, but Jesus came in and stood right in the middle of them. He said, "Peace be with you." [27]Then he said to Thomas, "Put your finger here, and look at my hands. Put your hand here in my side. Stop being an unbeliever and believe."

[28]Thomas said to him, "My Lord and my God!"

[29]Then Jesus told him, "You believe because

WAYS TO WALK THE WALK

John 16:33

WORD: Life is guaranteed to give you pain, but God will help you overcome.

WALK IT: Study like you've never studied for that next big test. When you get the results, think how pain brought you gain. How else has pain brought you good results?

John 17:3

WORD: Eternal life is all about knowing God.

WALK IT: Get a head start on heaven by making your relationship with God your biggest priority in life. Invite God to show you what gets in the way of your following him.

 20:16 Hebrew language Or Aramaic, the languages of many people in this region in the first century.

RANDOM WAYS TO EARN YOUR PARENTS' TRUST

1. COME HOME BY CURFEW.

2. TELL THEM WHERE YOU'RE GOING.

3. LET THEM GET TO KNOW YOUR FRIENDS.

4. SAY WHAT YOU MEAN.

5. MEAN WHAT YOU SAY.

6. TELL THE TRUTH EVEN WHEN YOU'RE GUILTY.

7. DEMONSTRATE RESPONSIBILITY WITH YOUR SCHOOLWORK.

8. PAY ATTENTION WHEN YOU DRIVE.

9. TAKE YOUR MISTAKES SERIOUSLY AND FIX WHAT YOU CAN.

10. CALL HOME AT 10 P.M. TO CHECK IN.

you see me. Those who believe without seeing me will be truly happy."

WHY JOHN WROTE THIS BOOK

[30]Jesus did many other miracles in the presence of his followers that are not written in this book. [31]But these are written so that you may believe that Jesus is the Christ, the Son of God. Then, by believing, you may have life through his name.

JESUS APPEARS TO SEVEN FOLLOWERS

21 Later, Jesus showed himself to his followers again—this time at Lake Galilee." This is how he showed himself: [2]Some of the followers were together: Simon Peter, Thomas (called Didymus), Nathanael from Cana in Galilee, the two sons of Zebedee, and

two other followers. [3]Simon Peter said, "I am going out to fish."

The others said, "We will go with you." So they went out and got into the boat. They fished that night but caught nothing.

[4]Early the next morning Jesus stood on the shore, but the followers did not know it was Jesus. [5]Then he said to them, "Friends, did you catch any fish?"

They answered, "No."

[6]He said, "Throw your net on the right side of the boat, and you will find some." So they did, and they caught so many fish they could not pull the net back into the boat.

[7]The follower whom Jesus loved said to Peter, "It is the Lord!" When Peter heard him say this, he wrapped his coat around himself. (Peter had taken his clothes off.) Then he jumped into the water. [8]The other followers went to shore in the boat, dragging the net full of fish. They were not very far from shore, only about a hundred yards. [9]When the followers stepped out of the boat and onto the shore, they saw a fire of hot coals. There were fish on the fire, and there was bread.

[10]Then Jesus said, "Bring some of the fish you just caught."

[11]Simon Peter went into the boat and pulled the net to the shore. It was full of big fish, one hundred fifty-three in all, but even though there were so many, the net did not tear. [12]Jesus said to them, "Come and eat." None of the followers dared ask him, "Who are you?" because they knew it was the Lord. [13]Jesus came and took the bread and gave it to them, along with the fish.

[14]This was now the third time Jesus showed himself to his followers after he was raised from the dead.

JESUS TALKS TO PETER

[15]When they finished eating, Jesus said to Simon Peter, "Simon son of John do you love me more than these?"

He answered, "Yes, Lord, you know that I love you."

Jesus said, "Feed my lambs."

[16]Again Jesus said, "Simon son of John do you love me?"

He answered, "Yes, Lord, you know that I love you."

Jesus said, "Take care of my sheep."

✓ COUNT ON IT

JOHN 16:13

Have you ever had a tough time making a decision? Everybody has. Well, the Holy Spirit has been sent to speak to you at those very moments. And this verse assures you that he will not just spout off on his own, but will only say what God says. In other words, when the Holy Spirit speaks to your heart, you can take it to the bank. You'd better go with it! He will speak to you and he's going to show you what is true. That's his job. So make sure you're listening and not ignoring him.

How do you hear the Holy Spirit speak? Second Timothy 2:15 says, "Make every effort to give yourself to God as the kind of person he will accept. Be a worker who is not ashamed and who uses the true teaching in the right way." So what do you do? Begin doing your best and studying the Bible—not just reading words, but really getting into the Word of God. Start out by just reviewing a few verses in your mind- over and over. Begin putting the Word of God inside you by memorizing a verse or two. Read Psalm 119:1-24. Notice how the psalmist felt about God's Word. Whenever you read the words *teachings, demands, rules, orders, commands,* or *word,* you can think of them as the Bible. As you begin to "feed" yourself the Word of God, you'll begin to notice that you are hearing God speak to you in ways and about things you've never heard before. Start doing it now, and let the Holy Spirit lead you "into all truth"!

 21:1 Lake Galilee Literally, "Sea of Tiberias."

RELATIONSHIPS

"We love because God first loved us" (1 John 4:19). Picture yourself as a big, yellow, 30-gallon water jug. Everyone in your life comes to you for a drink. Some just bring little cups. Others want buckets of your time and energy. A few stab a spigot in your side and leave the water running full blast. When difficult people drain you dry, you have to get refilled. The only way you can keep loving is to keep getting filled by God himself. Dive into his Word. Picture what he did for you on the cross. Remind yourself he is an endless source of love for you.

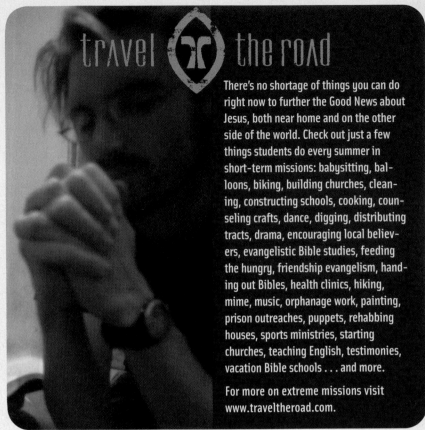

travel the road

There's no shortage of things you can do right now to further the Good News about Jesus, both near home and on the other side of the world. Check out just a few things students do every summer in short-term missions: babysitting, balloons, biking, building churches, cleaning, constructing schools, cooking, counseling crafts, dance, digging, distributing tracts, drama, encouraging local believers, evangelistic Bible studies, feeding the hungry, friendship evangelism, handing out Bibles, health clinics, hiking, mime, music, orphanage work, painting, prison outreaches, puppets, rehabbing houses, sports ministries, starting churches, teaching English, testimonies, vacation Bible schools . . . and more.

For more on extreme missions visit www.traveltheroad.com.

¹⁷A third time he said, "Simon son of John do you love me?"

Peter was hurt because Jesus asked him the third time, "Do you love me?" Peter said, "Lord, you know everything; you know that I love you!"

He said to him, "Feed my sheep. ¹⁸I tell you the truth, when you were younger, you tied against you?") ²¹When Peter saw him behind them, he asked Jesus, "Lord, what about him?"

²²Jesus answered, "If I want him to live until I come back, that is not your business. You follow me."

²³So a story spread among the followers that this one would not die. But Jesus did not

> **EVERY MINUTE OF EVERY DAY OF EVERY YEAR A BABY IS BORN TO A TEEN MOTHER IN THE UNITED STATES.** –CHILDREN'S DEFENSE FUND

your own belt and went where you wanted. But when you are old, you will put out your hands and someone else will tie you and take you where you don't want to go." ¹⁹(Jesus said this to show how Peter would die to give glory to God.) Then Jesus said to Peter, "Follow me!"

²⁰Peter turned and saw that the follower Jesus loved was walking behind them. (This was the follower who had leaned against Jesus at the supper and had said, "Lord, who will turn say he would not die. He only said, "If I want him to live until I come back, that is not your business."

²⁴That follower is the one who is telling these things and who has now written them down. We know that what he says is true.

²⁵There are many other things Jesus did. If every one of them were written down, I suppose the whole world would not be big enough for all the books that would be written.

ACTS

Acts: The extraordinary acts of ordinary people

Once you're done flipping through the Gospels—the first four books of the New Testament that tell about Jesus' birth, life, death, and resurrection—you might assume that Acts starts a whole new story. Yet it's actually the well-known sequel to the Book of Luke, penned by the same physician with the same careful precision.

Acts starts with Jesus' disappearing into heaven, then gives us some really cool snapshots of what happens next. There's the first sermon by a follower. Then the first miracle by a follower. All this is followed by the first major steps toward organizing a Christian movement. Acts also reports on the persecution of the Christians, the first Christian martyr, the first non-Jewish convert, and the first missionary trip. You could call it an important book of firsts.

And there's more stuff here. Remember the twelve apostles? In the Gospels they were important figures. Well, in Acts they're almost invisible. The Twelve are still respected, but other leaders take the stage as the news about Jesus spreads. Acts introduces these key leaders, like Paul. It also introduces us to the miracles believers can do through the Holy Spirit. God's Spirit making bold witnesses out of ordinary people is the reason behind the phenomenal success of the first-generation church. And, hey, don't forget that this same God who did all this in Acts does it for us today. He's behind our success. He's with us, just like he was with the baby church.

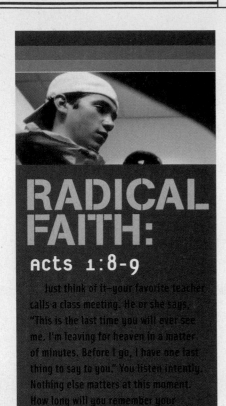

RADICAL FAITH:

Acts 1:8-9

Just think of it—your favorite teacher calls a class meeting. He or she says, "This is the last time you will ever see me. I'm leaving for heaven in a matter of minutes. Before I go, I have one last thing to say to you." You listen intently. Nothing else matters at this moment. How long will you remember your teacher's last words to you? Probably until the day you die.

That's what's happening here. Jesus leaves his followers with this final word. He tells them that the Holy Spirit is coming after him. The Holy Spirit is going to give them power. He'll give them the strength they need to do everything Jesus wants them to do.

As a Christian, you have that same power. The Holy Spirit lives inside of you to give you the power you need to do everything Jesus wants you to do. One thing you know is that he wants you to go out and spread the Good News about his love and forgiveness. He's the power for shaky voices, weak knees, butterflies in your stomach. He's the giver of abundant life, the supplier of words, the revealer of truth, and the protector of courageous hearts. He's the One who always loves you and will never leave you. He gives you comfort and good advice. He gives you the power to know what to do in every situation. That's power!

LUKE WRITES ANOTHER BOOK

1 To Theophilus.
The first book I wrote was about everything Jesus began to do and teach [2]until the day he was taken up into heaven. Before this, with the help of the Holy Spirit, Jesus told the apostles he had chosen what they should do. [3]After his death, he showed himself to them and proved in many ways that he was alive. The apostles saw Jesus during the forty days after he was raised from the dead, and he spoke to them about the kingdom of God. [4]Once when he was eating with them, he told them not to leave Jerusalem. He said, "Wait here to receive the promise from the Father which I told you about. [5]John baptized people with water, but in a few days you will be baptized with the Holy Spirit."

JESUS IS TAKEN UP INTO HEAVEN

[6]When the apostles were all together, they asked Jesus, "Lord, are you now going to give the kingdom back to Israel?"

[7]Jesus said to them, "The Father is the only One who has the authority to decide dates and times. These things are not for you to know. [8]But when the Holy Spirit comes to you, you will receive power. You will be my witnesses—in Jerusalem, in all of Judea, in Samaria, and in every part of the world."

[9]After he said this, as they were watching, he was lifted up, and a cloud hid him from their sight. [10]As he was going, they were looking into the sky. Suddenly, two men wearing white clothes stood beside them. [11]They said, "Men of Galilee, why are you standing here looking into the sky? Jesus, whom you saw taken up from you into heaven, will come back in the same way you saw him go."

A NEW APOSTLE IS CHOSEN

[12]Then they went back to Jerusalem from the Mount of Olives. (This mountain is about half a mile from Jerusalem.) [13]When they entered the city, they went to the upstairs room where they were staying. Peter, John, James, Andrew, Philip, Thomas, Bartholomew, Matthew, James son of Alphaeus, Simon (known as the Zealot), and Judas son of James were there. [14]They all continued praying together with some women, including Mary the mother of Jesus, and Jesus' brothers.

[15]During this time there was a meeting of the believers (about one hundred twenty of them). Peter stood up and said, [16-17]"Brothers and sisters,[n] in the Scriptures the Holy Spirit said through David something that must happen involving Judas. He was one of our own group and served together with us. He led those who arrested Jesus." [18](Judas bought a field with the money he got for his evil act. But he fell to his death, his body burst open, and all his intestines poured out. [19]Everyone in Jerusalem learned about this so they named this place Akeldama. In their language Akeldama means "Field of Blood.") [20]"In the Book of Psalms," Peter said, "this is written:

'May his place be empty;
    leave no one to live in it.'   *Psalm 69:25*

And it is also written:

'Let another man replace him as leader.'

                                    Psalm 109:8

[21-22]"So now a man must become a witness with us of Jesus' being raised from the dead. He must be one of the men who were part of our group during all the time the Lord Jesus was among us—from the time John was baptizing people until the day Jesus was taken up from us to heaven."

[23]They put the names of two men before the group. One was Joseph Barsabbas, who was also called Justus. The other was Matthias. [24-25]The apostles prayed, "Lord, you know the thoughts of everyone. Show us which one of these two you have chosen to do this work. Show us who should be an apostle in place of Judas,

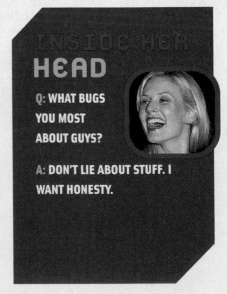
 1:16-17 Brothers and sisters Although the Greek text says "Brothers" here and throughout this book, the words of the speakers were meant for the entire church, including men and women.

who turned away and went where he belongs." [26]Then they used lots to choose between them, and the lots showed that Matthias was the one. So he became an apostle with the other eleven.

PSALM 23:4 "I WILL NOT BE AFRAID, BECAUSE YOU ARE WITH ME."

THE COMING OF THE HOLY SPIRIT

2 When the day of Pentecost came, they were all together in one place. [2]Suddenly a noise like a strong, blowing wind came from heaven and filled the whole house where they were sitting. [3]They saw something like flames of fire that were separated and stood over each person there. [4]They were all filled with the Holy Spirit, and they began to speak different languages[n] by the power the Holy Spirit was giving them.

[5]There were some religious Jews staying in Jerusalem who were from every country in the world. [6]When they heard this noise, a crowd came together. They were all surprised, because each one heard them speaking in his own language. [7]They were completely amazed at this. They said, "Look! Aren't all these people that we hear speaking from Galilee? [8]Then how is it possible that we each hear them in our own lan-

guages? We are from different places: [9]Parthia, Media, Elam, Mesopotamia, Judea, Cappadocia, Pontus, Asia, [10]Phrygia, Pamphylia, Egypt, the areas of Libya near Cyrene, Rome [11](both Jews and those who had become Jews), Crete, and Arabia. But we hear them telling in our own languages about the great things God has done!" [12]They were all amazed and confused, asking each other, "What does this mean?"

[13]But others were making fun of them, saying, "They have had too much wine."

PETER SPEAKS TO THE PEOPLE

[14]But Peter stood up with the eleven apostles, and in a loud voice he spoke to the crowd: "My fellow Jews, and all of you who are in Jerusalem, listen to me. Pay attention to what

 2:4 languages This can also be translated "tongues."

HOW TO RIP A PHONE BOOK IN HALF

You can rip a three-inch monster in two if you know the right trick. Sit with the phone book in your lap. Face the long open edge away from you. Grab the book with both hands and fan the edges so you have a thin place to start. Then keep tearing into the thicker part. Well, that's the theory. Like lot of things in life, shredding a phone book is easier said than done. Just because you can't do it right away doesn't make you a wuss. When life throws you an impossible task, keep trying. You'll figure out a way to get the job done. Even if it takes a chain saw to hack a phone book in two.

I have to say. [15]These people are not drunk, as you think; it is only nine o'clock in the morning! [16]But Joel the prophet wrote about what is happening here today:

[17]'God says: In the last days
I will pour out my Spirit on all kinds
of people.
Your sons and daughters will prophesy.
Your young men will see visions,
and your old men will dream dreams.
[18]At that time I will pour out my Spirit
also on my male slaves and female slaves,
and they will prophesy.
[19]I will show miracles
in the sky and on the earth:
blood, fire, and thick smoke.
[20]The sun will become dark,
the moon red as blood,
before the overwhelming and glorious
day of the Lord will come.
[21]Then anyone who calls on the Lord
will be saved.'   *Joel 2:28-32*

[22]"People of Israel, listen to these words: Jesus from Nazareth was a very special man. God clearly showed this to you by the miracles, wonders, and signs he did through Jesus. You all know this, because it happened right here among you. [23]Jesus was given to you, and with the help of those who don't know the law, you put him to death by nailing him to a cross. But this was God's plan which he had made long ago; he knew all this would happen. [24]God raised Jesus from the dead and set him free from the pain of death, because death could not hold him. [25]For David said this about him:

'I keep the Lord before me always.
Because he is close by my side,
I will not be hurt.
[26]So I am glad, and I rejoice.
Even my body has hope,
[27]because you will not leave me in
the grave.
You will not let your Holy One rot.
[28]You will teach me how to live a holy life.
Being with you will fill me with joy.'
          Psalm 16:8-11

[29]"Brothers and sisters, I can tell you truly that David, our ancestor, died and was buried. His grave is still here with us today. [30]He was a prophet and knew God had promised him that he would make a person from David's family a king just as he was.[n] [31]Knowing this before it happened, David talked about the Christ rising from the dead. He said:

'He was not left in the grave.
His body did not rot.'
[32]So Jesus is the One whom God raised from the dead. And we are all witnesses to this. [33]Jesus was lifted up to heaven and is now at God's right side. The Father has given the Holy Spirit to Jesus as he promised. So Jesus has poured out that Spirit, and this is what you now see and hear. [34]David was not the one who was lifted up to heaven, but he said:

'The Lord said to my Lord,
"Sit by me at my right side,
[35]until I put your enemies under your
control." '[n]   *Psalm 110:1*
[36]"So, all the people of Israel should know this truly: God has made Jesus—the man you nailed to the cross—both Lord and Christ."

[37]When the people heard this, they felt guilty and asked Peter and the other apostles, "What shall we do?"

[38]Peter said to them, "Change your hearts and lives and be baptized, each one of you, in the name of Jesus Christ for the forgiveness of your sins. And you will receive the gift of the Holy Spirit. [39]This promise is for you, for your children, and for all who are far away. It is for everyone the Lord our God calls to himself."

[40]Peter warned them with many other words. He begged them, "Save yourselves from the evil of today's people!" [41]Then those people who accepted what Peter said were baptized. About three thousand people were added to the number of believers that day. [42]They spent their time learning the apostles' teaching, sharing, breaking bread,[n] and praying together.

THE BELIEVERS SHARE

[43]The apostles were doing many miracles and signs, and everyone felt great respect for God. [44]All the believers were together and shared everything. [45]They would sell their land and the things they owned and then divide the money and give it to anyone who needed it. [46]The believers met together in the Temple every day. They ate together in their homes, happy to share their food with joyful hearts. [47]They praised God and were liked by all the people. Every day the Lord added those who were being saved to the group of believers.

PETER HEALS A CRIPPLED MAN

3 One day Peter and John went to the Temple at three o'clock, the time set each day for the afternoon prayer service. [2]There, at the Temple gate called Beautiful Gate, was a man who had been crippled all his

 2:30 God . . . was See 2 Samuel 7:13; Psalm 132:11.   2:35 until . . . control Literally, "until I make your enemies a footstool for your feet."   2:42 breaking bread This may mean a meal as in verse 46, or the Lord's Supper, the special meal Jesus told his followers to eat to remember him (Luke 22:14–20).

172

RANDOM WAYS TO STAY PSYCHED ABOUT A TOUGH TASK

1. REMEMBER WHAT YOU'RE WORKING TOWARD.

2. PLAN YOUR WORK, THEN WORK YOUR PLAN.

3. TACKLE A TOUGH JOB FIRST.

4. WORK WITH A FRIEND.

5. BREAK WORK INTO BITE-SIZED PIECES.

6. SPIN UP YOUR FAVORITE CD.

7. SEARCH FOR A QUIET SPOT TO CONCENTRATE.

8. LEARN TO GET BACK TO WORK AFTER BREAKS.

9. ASK YOUR PARENTS TO PRAY FOR YOU.

10. FEEL GOOD FROM WORKING HARD.

---

life. Every day he was carried to this gate to beg for money from the people going into the Temple. [3]The man saw Peter and John going into the Temple and asked them for money. [4]Peter and John looked straight at him and said, "Look at us!" [5]The man looked at them, thinking they were going to give him some money. [6]But Peter said, "I don't have any silver or gold, but I do have something else I can give you. By the power of Jesus Christ from Nazareth, stand up and walk!" [7]Then Peter took the man's right hand and lifted him up.

Immediately the man's feet and ankles became strong. [8]He jumped up, stood on his feet, and began to walk. He went into the Temple with them, walking and jumping and praising God. [9-10]All the people recognized him as the crippled man who always sat by the Beautiful Gate begging for money. Now they saw this same man walking and praising God, and they were amazed. They wondered how this could happen.

PETER SPEAKS TO THE PEOPLE

[11]While the man was holding on to Peter and John, all the people were amazed and ran to them at Solomon's Porch. [12]When Peter saw this, he said to them, "People of Israel, why are you surprised? You are looking at us as if it were our own power or goodness that made this man walk. [13]The God of Abraham, Isaac, and Jacob, the God of our ancestors, gave glory to Jesus, his servant. But you handed him over to be killed. Pilate decided to let him go free, but you told Pilate you did not want Jesus. [14]You did not want the One who is holy and good but asked Pilate to give you a murderer[n] instead. [15]And so you killed the One who gives life, but God raised him from the dead. We are witnesses to this. [16]It was faith in Jesus that made this crippled man well. You can see this man, and you know him. He was made completely well because of trust in Jesus, and you all saw it happen!

[17]"Brothers and sisters, I know you did those things to Jesus because neither you nor your leaders understood what you were doing. [18]God said through the prophets that his Christ would suffer and die. And now God has made these things come true in this way. [19]So you must change your hearts and lives! Come back to God, and he will forgive your sins. Then the Lord will send the time of rest. [20]And he will send Jesus, the One he chose to be the Christ. [21]But Jesus must stay in heaven until the time comes when all things will be made right again. God told about this time long ago when he spoke through his holy prophets. [22]Moses said, 'The Lord your God will give you a prophet like me, who is one of your own people. You must listen to everything he tells you. [23]Anyone who does not listen to that prophet will die, cut off from God's people.'[n] [24]Samuel, and all the other prophets who

---

BIBLE BASICS

Reading the Bible isn't as scary as it seems. The Bible is God's message to us, an instruction manual, and an answer book for life. So you should read it with the enthusiasm you feel when you read a letter from a girl you like—only this is infinitely bigger. Start anywhere you want and read as much or as little as you choose. The Gospels (Matthew, Mark, Luke, and John) are a great place to start if you feel lost. They tell the story of Jesus' life. Ephesians and Philippians tell a lot about God's love and how to live. And the Book of Romans gives a deep view of what faith is all about.

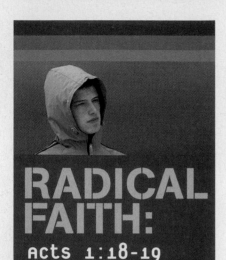

RADICAL FAITH:

Acts 1:18-19

Mike started telling his friends that he didn't have anything to live for. Nothing was fun to him anymore. He wanted to stay in bed all day. He talked a lot about a girl from school who had killed herself. He was so serious all the time. He began to give some of his clothes and stuff away. He withdrew from everybody. He didn't want to go out or to ball games. He seemed depressed. His family thought it was a phase and overlooked it. His friends thought he needed some space and left him alone. He died in his parents' car in their garage one afternoon after school. The note he left said he was just too lonely. Life was too hard. No one seemed to care.

If your friend mentions suicide, talks about not having anything to live for, distances himself/herself from everyone, or shows any other suspicious behavior, take that person seriously. Always take suicide threats seriously. Your friend needs help—quick. Talk to his or her parents, your pastor, a teacher, or counselor until you find someone who cares about your friend and is willing to help. Your job as a friend is to get qualified help. Don't try to handle this one alone. Whatever you do, believe that your friend is hurting, pray for him or her and for wisdom, and get help immediately.

spoke for God after Samuel, told about this time now. [25]You are descendants of the prophets. You have received the agreement God made with your ancestors. He said to your father Abraham, 'Through your descendants all the nations on the earth will be blessed.'[n] [26]God has raised up his servant Jesus and sent him to you first to bless you by turning each of you away from doing evil."

PETER AND JOHN AT THE COUNCIL

4 While Peter and John were speaking to the people, priests, the captain of the soldiers that guarded the Temple, and Sadducees came up to them. [2]They were upset because the two apostles were teaching the people and were preaching that people will rise from the dead through the power of Jesus. [3]The older leaders grabbed Peter and John and put them in jail. Since it was already night, they kept them in jail until the next day. [4]But many of those who had heard Peter and John preach believed the things they said. There were now about five thousand in the group of believers.

[5]The next day the rulers, the older leaders, and the teachers of the law met in Jerusalem. [6]Annas the high priest, Caiaphas, John, and Alexander were there, as well as everyone from the high priest's family. [7]They made Peter and John stand before them and then asked them, "By what power or authority did you do this?"

[8]Then Peter, filled with the Holy Spirit, said to them, "Rulers of the people and you older leaders, [9]are you questioning us about a good thing that was done to a crippled man? Are you asking us who made him well? [10]We want all of you and all the people to know that this man was made well by the power of Jesus Christ from Nazareth. You crucified him, but God raised him from the dead. This man was crippled, but he is now well and able to stand here before you because of the power of Jesus. [11]Jesus is

'the stone[n] that you builders rejected,
    which has become the cornerstone.'

Psalm 118:22

[12]Jesus is the only One who can save people. His name is the only power in the world that has been given to save people. We must be saved through him."

COUNT ON IT

ACTS 2:21

Salvation is a one-time thing. You make the decision to *become* a Christian one time. You make decisions to *live* like a Christian daily—sometimes even moment by moment. Sometimes people are insecure about their salvation. They keep wondering if they "did it right" the first time. So they wind up raising their hand to accept Christ every time the offer is made.

Jesus promises that when you call out to him and ask him to save you, he does. It's that simple. You give your heart to him, ask him to forgive your sins, and make him the Lord and Savior of your life. You are saved from that moment until forever. So nail it down. If you've accepted Jesus Christ as your Savior, then you are saved. It's time to move on and grow up in Christ. If you are still unsure, then turn to Acts 16:30-31 and find out what you need to do in order to be saved. Salvation isn't a tricky thing. The Lord sees your heart and knows your sincerity. The right attitude is more important than the right words. Jesus' promise is strong—call out to him, and you will be saved.

3:25 'Through . . . blessed.' Quotation from Genesis 22:18; 26:4. 4:11 stone A symbol meaning Jesus.

EXPERTS ANSWER YOUR QUESTIONS

Q. *Why doesn't God do everything I ask him to do?*

A. Because he isn't your slave. And he knows that some of your requests aren't best for you. Think of this. When you pray, you're asking the God of the universe to meet your needs. He is not only all-power-ful, but he is all-wise and all-loving. Part of prayer is saying, "God, you love me so much that I want what you want."

Q. *A guy I know is so tight with God. I wish I had half of his closeness.*

A. Newlyweds are all gushy about each other and that's cool. People who've been married a little while sometimes look like they're struggling. But the people who have really sweet relationships are like in their seventies or eighties. They really know each other. You have an eternity to get to know God. Don't be frustrated if others know him better. Just start now!

13The leaders saw that Peter and John were not afraid to speak, and they understood that these men had no special training or educa-tion. So they were amazed. Then they realized that Peter and John had been with Jesus. 14Because they saw the healed man standing there beside the two apostles, they could say nothing against them. 15After the leaders ordered them to leave the meeting, they began to talk to each other. 16They said, "What shall we do with these men? Everyone in Jerusalem knows they have done a great miracle, and we cannot say it is not true. 17But to keep it from spreading among the people, we must warn them not to talk to people anymore using that name."

18So they called Peter and John in again and told them not to speak or to teach at all in the name of Jesus. 19But Peter and John answered them, "You decide what God would want. Should we obey you or God? 20We cannot keep quiet. We must speak about what we have seen and heard." 21The leaders warned the apostles again and let them go free. They could not find a way to punish them, because all the people were praising God for what had been done. 22The man who received the mira-cle of healing was more than forty years old.

THE BELIEVERS PRAY

23After Peter and John left the meeting of leaders, they went to their own group and told them everything the leading priests and the older leaders had said to them. 24When the believers heard this, they prayed to God together, "Lord, you are the One who made the sky, the earth, the sea, and everything in them. 25By the Holy Spirit, through our father David your servant, you said:

> 'Why are the nations so angry?
> Why are the people making useless plans?
> 26The kings of the earth prepare to fight,
> and their leaders make plans together
> against the Lord
> and his Christ.' *Psalm 2:1-2*

27These things really happened when Herod, Pontius Pilate, and some of the people all came together against Jesus here in Jerusalem. Jesus is your holy servant, the One you made to be the Christ. 28These people made your plan happen because of your power and your will. 29And now, Lord, listen to their threats. Lord, help us, your servants, to speak your word without fear. 30Help us to be brave by showing us your power to heal. Give proofs and make miracles happen by the power of Jesus, your holy servant."

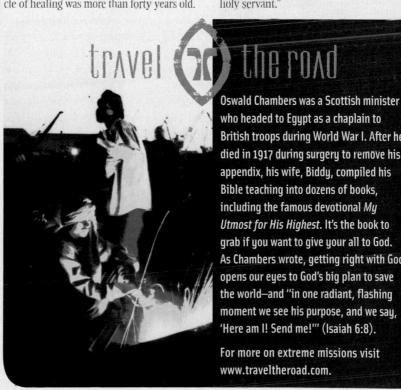

travel the road

Oswald Chambers was a Scottish minister who headed to Egypt as a chaplain to British troops during World War I. After he died in 1917 during surgery to remove his appendix, his wife, Biddy, compiled his Bible teaching into dozens of books, including the famous devotional *My Utmost for His Highest*. It's the book to grab if you want to give your all to God. As Chambers wrote, getting right with God opens our eyes to God's big plan to save the world—and "in one radiant, flashing moment we see his purpose, and we say, 'Here am I! Send me!'" (Isaiah 6:8).

For more on extreme missions visit www.traveltheroad.com.

[31] After they had prayed, the place where they were meeting was shaken. They were all filled with the Holy Spirit, and they spoke God's word without fear.

THE BELIEVERS SHARE

[32] The group of believers were united in their hearts and spirit. All those in the group acted as though their private property belonged to everyone in the group. In fact, they shared everything. [33] With great power the apostles were telling people that the Lord Jesus was truly raised from the dead. And God blessed all the believers very much. [34] No one in the group needed anything. From time to time those who owned fields or houses sold them, brought the money, [35] and gave it to the apostles. Then the money was given to anyone who needed it.

[36] One of the believers was named Joseph, a Levite born in Cyprus. The apostles called him Barnabas (which means "one who encourages"). [37] Joseph owned a field, sold it, brought the money, and gave it to the apostles.

ANANIAS AND SAPPHIRA DIE

5 But a man named Ananias and his wife Sapphira sold some land. [2] He kept back part of the money for himself; his wife knew about this and agreed to it. But he brought the rest of the money and gave it to the apostles. [3] Peter said, "Ananias, why did you let Satan rule your thoughts to lie to the Holy Spirit and to keep for yourself part of the money you received for the land? [4] Before you sold the land, it belonged to you. And even after you sold it, you could have used the money any way you wanted. Why did you think of doing this? You lied to God, not to us!" [5-6] When Ananias heard this, he fell down and died. Some young men came in, wrapped up his body, carried it out, and buried it. And everyone who heard about this was filled with fear.

[7] About three hours later his wife came in, but she did not know what had happened. [8] Peter said to her, "Tell me, was the money you got for your field this much?"

Sapphira answered, "Yes, that was the price."

[9] Peter said to her, "Why did you and your husband agree to test the Spirit of the Lord? Look! The men who buried your husband are at the door, and they will carry you out." [10] At that moment Sapphira fell down by his feet and died. When the young men came in and saw that she was dead, they carried her out and buried her beside her husband. [11] The whole church and all the others who heard about these things were filled with fear.

THE APOSTLES HEAL MANY

[12] The apostles did many signs and miracles among the people. And they would all meet together on Solomon's Porch. [13] None of the others dared to join them, but all the people respected them. [14] More and more men and women believed in the Lord and were added to the group of believers. [15] The people placed their sick on beds and mats in the streets, hoping that when Peter passed by at least his shadow might fall on them. [16] Crowds came from all the towns around Jerusalem, bringing their sick and those who were bothered by evil spirits, and all of them were healed.

DO'S & DON'TS

- *Do wipe your feet at the door.*

- *Do help your siblings with homework.*

- *Do let your parents pick the radio station in the car.*

- *Do brake for ducks.*

- *Don't ditch your date.*

- *Don't go barefoot in snow.*

- *Don't drive with bad wipers.*

- *Don't drive friends' cars.*

RANDOM WAYS TO BE A SAFE DRIVER

1. BUCKLE UP.

2. KEEP YOUR EYES ON THE ROAD.

3. HANG ON TO THE WHEEL WITH BOTH HANDS.

4. DON'T MESS WITH THE STEREO.

5. PARK TO MAKE PHONE CALLS.

6. DON'T BE DISTRACTED BY FRIENDS.

7. PUT A LID ON ROAD RAGE.

8. SLOW DOWN AND ENJOY THE VIEW.

9. KEEP AWAKE.

10. STAY SOBER.

LEADERS TRY TO STOP THE APOSTLES

[17] The high priest and all his friends (a group called the Sadducees) became very jealous. [18] They took the apostles and put them in jail. [19] But during the night, an angel of the Lord opened the doors of the jail and led the apostles outside. The angel said, [20] "Go stand in the Temple and tell the people everything about this new life." [21] When the apostles heard this, they obeyed and went into the Temple early in the morning and continued teaching.

When the high priest and his friends arrived, they called a meeting of the leaders and all the important older men. They sent some men to the jail to bring the apostles to them. [22] But, upon arriving, the officers could not find the apostles. So they went back and reported to the leaders. [23] They said, "The jail was closed and locked, and the guards were standing at the doors. But when we opened the doors, the jail was empty!" [24]Hearing this, the captain of the Temple guards and the leading priests were confused and wondered what was happening.

[25]Then someone came and told them, "Listen! The men you put in jail are standing in the Temple teaching the people." [26]Then the captain and his men went out and brought the apostles back. But the soldiers did not use force, because they were afraid the people would stone them to death.

[27]The soldiers brought the apostles to the meeting and made them stand before the leaders. The high priest questioned them, [28]saying, "We gave you strict orders not to continue teaching in that name. But look, you have filled Jerusalem with your teaching and are trying to make us responsible for this man's death."

[29]Peter and the other apostles answered, "We must obey God, not human authority! [30]You killed Jesus by hanging him on a cross. But God, the God of our ancestors, raised Jesus up from the dead! [31]Jesus is the One whom God raised to be on his right side, as Leader and Savior. Through him, all people could change their hearts and lives and have their sins forgiven. [32]We saw all these things happen. The Holy Spirit, whom God has given to all who obey him, also proves these things are true."

[33]When the leaders heard this, they became angry and wanted to kill them. [34]But a Pharisee named Gamaliel stood up in the meeting. He was a teacher of the law, and all the people respected him. He ordered the apostles to leave the meeting for a little while. [35]Then he said, "People of Israel, be careful what you are planning to do to these men. [36]Remember when Theudas appeared? He said he was a great

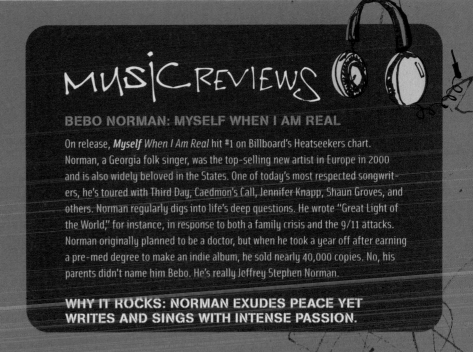

MUSIC REVIEWS

BEBO NORMAN: MYSELF WHEN I AM REAL

On release, *Myself When I Am Real* hit #1 on Billboard's Heatseekers chart. Norman, a Georgia folk singer, was the top-selling new artist in Europe in 2000 and is also widely beloved in the States. One of today's most respected songwriters, he's toured with Third Day, Caedmon's Call, Jennifer Knapp, Shaun Groves, and others. Norman regularly digs into life's deep questions. He wrote "Great Light of the World," for instance, in response to both a family crisis and the 9/11 attacks. Norman originally planned to be a doctor, but when he took a year off after earning a pre-med degree to make an indie album, he sold nearly 40,000 copies. No, his parents didn't name him Bebo. He's really Jeffrey Stephen Norman.

WHY IT ROCKS: NORMAN EXUDES PEACE YET WRITES AND SINGS WITH INTENSE PASSION.

man, and about four hundred men joined him. But he was killed, and all his followers were scattered; they were able to do nothing. [37]Later, a man named Judas came from Galilee at the time of the registration.[n] He also led a group of followers and was killed, and all his followers were scattered. [38]And so now I tell you. Stay away from these men, and leave them alone. If their plan comes from human authority, it will fail. [39]But if it is from God, you will not be able to stop them. You might even be fighting against God himself!"

The leaders agreed with what Gamaliel said. [40]They called the apostles in, beat them, and told them not to speak in the name of Jesus again. Then they let them go free. [41]The apostles left the meeting full of joy because they were given the honor of suffering disgrace for Jesus. [42]Every day in the Temple and in people's

homes they continued teaching the people and telling the Good News—that Jesus is the Christ.

SEVEN LEADERS ARE CHOSEN

6 The number of followers was growing. But during this same time, the Greek-speaking followers had an argument with the other followers. The Greek-speaking widows were not getting their share of the food that was given out every day. [2]The twelve apostles called the whole group of followers together and said, "It is not right for us to stop our work of teaching God's word in order to serve tables. [3]So, brothers and sisters, choose seven of your own men who are good, full of the Spirit and full of wisdom. We will put them in charge of this work. [4]Then we can continue to pray and to teach the word of God."

[5]The whole group liked the idea, so they chose these seven men: Stephen (a man with

5:37 **registration** Census. A counting of all the people and the things they own.

MEN OF THE SWORD

JEREMIAH was an Old Testament guy shy at first to speak up about God—but who later boldly rattled kings and religious leaders with some of the Bible's toughest words. Jeremiah served as a prophet through the reigns of several kings, and when Babylonian armies destroyed Jerusalem in 587 B.C., he moved to Babylon before being deported to Egypt. Jeremiah is an awesome model of someone God made strong to do great work. In Jeremiah 1:5, God said, "Before I made you in your mother's womb, I chose you. Before you were born, I set you apart for a special work." Jeremiah was unafraid to get gut-level honest with God, and the Bible book that wears his name is jammed with both challenging and encouraging words.

—Jeremiah 29:10-14

great faith and full of the Holy Spirit), Philip,[n] Procorus, Nicanor, Timon, Parmenas, and Nicolas (a man from Antioch who had become a follower of the Jewish religion). [6]Then they put these men before the apostles, who prayed and laid their hands[n] on them.

[7]The word of God was continuing to spread. The group of followers in Jerusalem increased, and a great number of the Jewish priests believed and obeyed.

STEPHEN IS ACCUSED

[8]Stephen was richly blessed by God who gave him the power to do great miracles and signs among the people. [9]But some people were against him. They belonged to the synagogue of Free Men[n] (as it was called), which included people from Cyrene, Alexandria, Cilicia, and Asia. They all came and argued with Stephen.

[10]But the Spirit was helping him to speak with wisdom, and his words were so strong that they could not argue with him. [11]So they secretly urged some men to say, "We heard Stephen speak against Moses and against God."

[12]This upset the people, the older leaders, and the teachers of the law. They came and grabbed Stephen and brought him to a meeting of the leaders. [13]They brought in some people to tell lies about Stephen, saying, "This man is always speaking against this holy place and the law of Moses. [14]We heard him say that Jesus from Nazareth will destroy this place and that Jesus will change the customs Moses gave us." [15]All the people in the meeting were watching Stephen closely and saw that his face looked like the face of an angel.

STEPHEN'S SPEECH

7 The high priest said to Stephen, "Are these things true?"

[2]Stephen answered, "Brothers and fathers, listen to me. Our glorious God appeared to Abraham, our ancestor, in Mesopotamia before he lived in Haran. [3]God said to Abraham, 'Leave your country and your relatives, and go to the land I will show you.'[n] [4]So Abraham left the country of Chaldea and went to live in Haran. After Abraham's father died, God sent him to this place where you now live. [5]God did not give Abraham any of this land, not even a foot of it. But God promised that he would give this land to him and his descendants, even before Abraham had a child. [6]This is what God said to him: 'Your descendants will be strangers in a land they don't own. The

PHILIPPIANS 4:13 "I CAN DO ALL THINGS THROUGH CHRIST, BECAUSE HE GIVES ME STRENGTH."

people there will make them slaves and will mistreat them for four hundred years. [7]But I will punish the nation where they are slaves. Then your descendants will leave that land and will worship me in this place.'[n] [8]God made an agreement with Abraham, the sign of which was circumcision. And so when Abraham had his son Isaac, Abraham circumcised him when he was eight days old. Isaac also circumcised his son Jacob, and Jacob did the same for his sons, the twelve ancestors[n] of our people.

[9]"Jacob's sons became jealous of Joseph and sold him to be a slave in Egypt. But God was with him [10]and saved him from all his troubles.

INSIDE HER HEAD

Q: WHAT BUGS YOU MOST ABOUT GUYS?

A: WHEN THEY TRY TO ACT COOL—ACTING DIFFERENT WHEN THERE ARE OTHER PEOPLE AROUND.

 6:5 Philip Not the apostle named Philip. 6:6 laid their hands The laying on of hands had many purposes, including the giving of a blessing, power, or authority. 6:9 Free Men Jewish people who had been slaves or whose fathers had been slaves, but were now free. 7:3 'Leave . . . you.' Quotation from Genesis 12:1. 7:6-7 'Your descendants . . . place.' Quotation from Genesis 15:13-14 and Exodus 3:12. 7:8 twelve ancestors Important ancestors of the people of Israel; the leaders of the twelve tribes of Israel.

The king of Egypt liked Joseph and respected him because of the wisdom God gave him. The king made him governor of Egypt and put him in charge of all the people in his palace.

[11]"Then all the land of Egypt and Canaan became so dry that nothing would grow, and the people suffered very much. Jacob's sons, our ancestors, could not find anything to eat. [12]But when Jacob heard there was grain in Egypt, he sent his sons there. This was their first trip to Egypt. [13]When they went there a second time, Joseph told his brothers who he was, and the king learned about Joseph's family. [14]Then Joseph sent messengers to invite Jacob, his father, to come to Egypt along with all his relatives (seventy-five persons altogether). [15]So Jacob went down to Egypt, where he and his sons died. [16]Later their bodies were moved to Shechem and put in a grave there. (It was the same grave Abraham had bought for a sum of money from the sons of Hamor in Shechem.)

[17]"The promise God made to Abraham was soon to come true, and the number of people in Egypt grew large. [18]Then a new king, who did not know who Joseph was, began to rule Egypt. [19]This king tricked our people and was cruel to our ancestors, forcing them to leave their babies outside to die. [20]At this time Moses was born, and he was very beautiful. For three months Moses was cared for in his

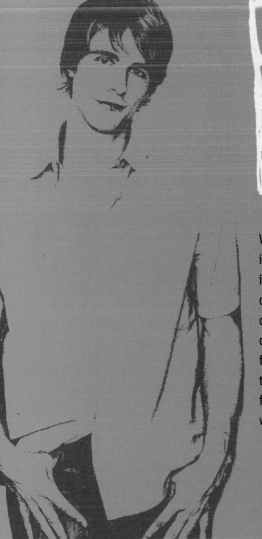

GET OUT THERE

With 16 million young Americans wanting or needing mentors, no one mentoring organization can possibly answer the demand. But MENTORING.ORG can connect you with local groups where you can provide kids with support, counsel, friendship, reinforcement, and constructive example. Whether you are looking for a mentoring opportunity or exploring ways to become a better mentor, their online training can help. You will get step-by-step advice on strengthening your mentoring skills—learning how to become a mentor, developing a strong relationship, and participating in activities that are fun and educational.

Go to www.mentoring.org to connect with needs right near your home.

HOW TO MAKE YOUR NEXT RIDE A ROCKET SHIP

Back in the old days before the turn of the century you needed to spend ten or fifteen years training to become an astronaut. But someday soon you might just need a tidy wad of cash to grab a spot. Startups all over the globe are promising to make space tourism real. Or so they say. For now you can buy time to hang out in a weightless environment or get whirled till you hurl in a g-force machine. Check out www.canadianarrow.com for a sample of this stuff. And like all extreme adventures, you need to ask your mother's permission and weigh the risks vs. the rewards. Sure, it would make a great story to tell your grandkids you were a space tourism pioneer. But you gotta make sure you live to see them.

father's house. 21When they put Moses outside, the king's daughter adopted him and raised him as if he were her own son. 22The Egyptians taught Moses everything they knew, and he was a powerful man in what he said and did.

23"When Moses was about forty years old, he thought it would be good to visit his own people, the people of Israel. 24Moses saw an Egyptian mistreating one of his people, so he defended the Israelite and punished the Egyptian by killing him. 25Moses thought his own people would understand that God was using him to save them, but they did not. 26The next day when Moses saw two men of Israel fighting, he tried to make peace between them. He said, 'Men, you are brothers. Why are you hurting each other?' 27The man who was hurting the other pushed Moses away and said, 'Who made you our ruler and judge? 28Are you going to kill me as you killed the Egyptian yesterday?'[n] 29When Moses heard him say this, he left Egypt and went to live in the land of Midian where he was a stranger. While Moses lived in Midian, he had two sons.

30"Forty years later an angel appeared to Moses in the flames of a burning bush as he was in the desert near Mount Sinai. 31When Moses saw this, he was amazed and went near to look closer. Moses heard the Lord's voice say, 32'I am the God of your ancestors, the God of Abraham, Isaac, and Jacob.'[n] Moses began to shake with fear and was afraid to look. 33The Lord said to him, 'Take off your sandals, because you are standing on holy ground. 34I have seen the troubles my people have suffered in Egypt. I have heard their cries and have come down to save them. And now, Moses, I am sending you back to Egypt.'[n]

35"This Moses was the same man the two men of Israel rejected, saying, 'Who made you a ruler and judge?'[n] Moses is the same man God sent to be a ruler and savior, with the help of the angel that Moses saw in the burning bush. 36So Moses led the people out of Egypt. He worked miracles and signs in Egypt, at the Red Sea, and then in the desert for forty years. 37This is the same Moses that said to the people of Israel, 'God will give you a prophet like me, who is one of your own people.'[n] 38This is the Moses who was with the gathering of the Israelites in the desert. He was with the angel that spoke to him

LOOK COOL
TIPS ON YOURSELF

Acne makes a guy feel anything but cool, but you're not alone. 85 percent of teens grow crops of the whiteheads, blackheads, and fifty other facial bumps that dermatologists have named. Current research says that genetics and hormones are the real cause of acne. Bacteria can make pimples worse, so keep your face clean without scrubbing it endlessly. Stress can rev up your hormones, so chill. Over-the-counter concoctions really do control most moderate acne if you use them faithfully, and a skin specialist can prescribe drugs that help more severe cases. But experts say no guy will ever control every pimple, no matter what you use. When a breakout happens that you can't bust up, remember that the real you is under the skin.

at Mount Sinai, and he was with our ancestors. He received commands from God that give life, and he gave those commands to us.

39"But our ancestors did not want to obey Moses. They rejected him and wanted to go back to Egypt. 40They said to Aaron, 'Make us gods who will lead us. Moses led us out of Egypt, but we don't know what has happened to him.'[n] 41So the people made an idol that looked like a calf. Then they brought sacrifices to it and were proud of what they had made with their own hands. 42But God turned against them and did not try to stop them from worshiping the sun, moon, and stars. This is what is

 7:27-28 'Who . . . yesterday?' Quotation from Exodus 2:14. **7:32** 'I am . . . Jacob.' Quotation from Exodus 3:6. **7:33-34** 'Take . . . Egypt.' Quotation from Exodus 3:5-10. **7:35** 'Who . . . judge?' Quotation from Exodus 2:14. **7:37** 'God . . . people.' Quotation from Deuteronomy 18:15. **7:40** 'Make . . . him.' Quotation from Exodus 32:1.

written in the book of the prophets: God says,

'People of Israel, you did not bring me
> sacrifices and offerings
> while you traveled in the desert for
> > forty years.
⁴³You have carried with you
> the tent to worship Molech
> and the idols of the star god Rephan that
> > you made to worship.
So I will send you away beyond Babylon.'

Amos 5:25-27

⁴⁴"The Holy Tent where God spoke to our ancestors was with them in the desert. God told Moses how to make this Tent, and he made it like the plan God showed him. ⁴⁵Later, Joshua led our ancestors to capture the lands of the other nations. Our people went in, and God forced the other people out. When our people went into this new land, they took with them this same Tent they had received from their ancestors. They kept it until the time of David, ⁴⁶who pleased God and asked God to let him build a house for him, the God of Jacob. ⁴⁷But Solomon was the one who built the Temple.

⁴⁸"But the Most High does not live in houses that people build with their hands. As the prophet says:

⁴⁹'Heaven is my throne,
> and the earth is my footstool.
So do you think you can build a house for
> me? says the Lord.
> Do I need a place to rest?
⁵⁰Remember, my hand made all these
> things!' "

Isaiah 66:1-2

⁵¹Stephen continued speaking: "You stubborn people! You have not given your hearts to God, nor will you listen to him! You are always against what the Holy Spirit is trying to tell you, just as your ancestors were. ⁵²Your ancestors tried to hurt every prophet who ever lived. Those prophets said long ago that the One who is good would come, but your ancestors killed them. And now you have turned against and killed the One who is good. ⁵³You received the law of Moses, which God gave you through his angels, but you haven't obeyed it."

STEPHEN IS KILLED

⁵⁴When the leaders heard this, they became furious. They were so mad they were grinding their teeth at Stephen. ⁵⁵But Stephen was full of the Holy Spirit. He looked up to heaven and saw the glory of God and Jesus standing at God's right side. ⁵⁶He said, "Look! I see heaven open and the Son of Man standing at God's right side."

⁵⁷Then they shouted loudly and covered their ears and all ran at Stephen. ⁵⁸They took him out of the city and began to throw stones at him to kill him. And those who told lies against Stephen left their coats with a young man named Saul. ⁵⁹While they were throwing stones, Stephen prayed, "Lord Jesus, receive my spirit." ⁶⁰He fell on his knees and cried in a loud voice, "Lord, do not hold this sin against them." After Stephen said this, he died.

8 Saul agreed that the killing of Stephen was good.

TROUBLES FOR THE BELIEVERS

On that day the church of Jerusalem began to be persecuted, and all the believers, except the apostles, were scattered throughout Judea and Samaria. ²And some religious people buried Stephen and cried loudly for him. ³Saul was also trying to destroy the church, going from house to house, dragging out men and women and putting them in jail. ⁴And wherever they were scattered, they told people the Good News.

PHILIP PREACHES IN SAMARIA

⁵Philip went to the city of Samaria and preached about the Christ. ⁶When the people there heard Philip and saw the miracles he was doing, they all listened carefully to what he said. ⁷Many of these people had evil spirits in them, but Philip made the evil spirits leave. The spirits made a loud noise when they came out. Philip also healed many weak and crippled people there. ⁸So the people in that city were very happy.

⁹But there was a man named Simon in that city. Before Philip came there, Simon had practiced magic and amazed all the people of Samaria. He bragged and called himself a great man. ¹⁰All the people—the least important and the most important—paid attention to Simon, saying, "This man has the power of God, called 'the Great Power'!" ¹¹Simon had amazed them with his magic so long that the people became his followers. ¹²But when Philip

RANDOM WAYS TO SAVE MONEY

1. **STASH A CHUNK OF EVERY DOLLAR YOU EARN.**

2. **WAIT SEVEN DAYS BEFORE YOU SPEND A DIME OF ANY PAYCHECK.**

3. **LET YOUR PARENTS HANG ON TO YOUR ALLOWANCE—AND KEEP A DETAILED RECORD ON PAPER.**

4. **OPEN AN INVESTMENT ACCOUNT—AND LINK IT TO YOUR CHECKING ACCOUNT FOR AUTO-DEPOSITS.**

5. **USE SOFTWARE OR A NOTEBOOK TO TRACK WHERE YOUR MONEY GOES FOR A MONTH—AND EVALUATE YOUR SPENDING.**

6. **BARGAIN SHOP ONLINE AND HUNT FOR SALES IN THE SUNDAY PAPER.**

7. **DON'T BUY NEW WHEN USED WILL DO.**

8. **DON'T BUY ON CREDIT.**

9. **LISTEN TO A WHOLE CD BEFORE YOU PLUNK DOWN YOUR CASH.**

10. **LISTEN TO YOUR PARENTS OR FRIENDS WHEN THEY SAY A PURCHASE IS STUPID.**

EXPERTS ANSWER YOUR QUESTIONS

Q. *Why did God put me on earth?*

A. Get into the Bible if you want to expand your ideas about God's great plans for you. He wants you to know him, become like him, and make him known.

Q. *Is there only one right way to pray?*

A. No, people pray different ways. If you're a believer, God is your loving Father, so talk to him that way. And remember that it's his will that counts, not yours. Check out the very simple prayer Jesus taught his disciples. It's in Matthew 6.

Q. *You can't be serious that hell is real. How can a loving God send people to hell?*

A. The Bible says hell is a real place. And like someone says, the door to hell is locked from the inside. Here's another way to look at it. How could a loving God force people to spend eternity in his presence in heaven when they don't want to be there?

told them the Good News about the kingdom of God and the power of Jesus Christ, men and women believed Philip and were baptized. [13]Simon himself believed, and after he was baptized, he stayed very close to Philip. When he saw the miracles and the powerful things Philip did, Simon was amazed.

[14]When the apostles who were still in Jerusalem heard that the people of Samaria had accepted the word of God, they sent Peter and John to them. [15]When Peter and John arrived, they prayed that the Samaritan believers might receive the Holy Spirit. [16]These people had been baptized in the name of the Lord Jesus, but the Holy Spirit had not yet come upon any of them. [17]Then, when the two apostles began laying their hands on the people, they received the Holy Spirit.

[18]Simon saw that the Spirit was given to people when the apostles laid their hands on them. So he offered the apostles money, [19]saying, "Give me also this power so that anyone on whom I lay my hands will receive the Holy Spirit."

[20]Peter said to him, "You and your money should both be destroyed, because you thought you could buy God's gift with money. [21]You cannot share with us in this work since your heart is not right before God. [22]Change your heart! Turn away from this evil thing you have done, and pray to the Lord. Maybe he will forgive you for thinking this. [23]I see that you are full of bitter jealousy and ruled by sin."

[24]Simon answered, "Both of you pray for me to the Lord so the things you have said will not happen to me."

[25]After Peter and John told the people what they had seen Jesus do and after they had spoken the message of the Lord, they went back to Jerusalem. On the way, they went through many Samaritan towns and preached the Good News to the people.

PHILIP TEACHES AN ETHIOPIAN

[26]An angel of the Lord said to Philip, "Get ready and go south to the road that leads down to Gaza from Jerusalem—the desert road." [27]So Philip got ready and went. On the road he saw a man from Ethiopia, a eunuch. He was an important officer in the service of Candace, the queen of the Ethiopians; he was responsible for taking care of all her money. He had

gone to Jerusalem to worship. [28]Now, as he was on his way home, he was sitting in his chariot reading from the Book of Isaiah, the prophet. [29]The Spirit said to Philip, "Go to that chariot and stay near it."

[30]So when Philip ran toward the chariot, he heard the man reading from Isaiah the prophet. Philip asked, "Do you understand what you are reading?"

[31]He answered, "How can I understand unless someone explains it to me?" Then he invited Philip to climb in and sit with him. [32]The portion of Scripture he was reading was this:

"He was like a sheep being led to be killed.
   He was quiet, as a lamb is quiet while
      its wool is being cut;
he never opened his mouth.
[33]   He was shamed and was treated unfairly.
   He died without children to continue
      his family.
      His life on earth has ended."   *Isaiah 53:7-8*

[34]The officer said to Philip, "Please tell me, who is the prophet talking about—himself or someone else?" [35]Philip began to speak, and starting with this same Scripture, he told the man the Good News about Jesus.

[36]While they were traveling down the road, they came to some water. The officer said, "Look, here is water. What is stopping me from being baptized?" [37n] [38]Then the officer commanded the chariot to stop. Both Philip and the officer went down into the water, and Philip baptized him. [39]When they came up out of the water, the Spirit of the Lord took Philip away; the officer never saw him again. And the officer continued on his way home, full of joy. [40]But Philip appeared in a city called Azotus and preached the Good News in all the towns on the way from Azotus to Caesarea.

SAUL IS CONVERTED

9 In Jerusalem Saul was still threatening the followers of the Lord by saying he would kill them. So he went to the high priest [2]and asked him to write letters to the synagogues in the city of Damascus. Then if Saul found any followers of Christ's Way, men or women, he would arrest them and bring them back to Jerusalem.

[3]So Saul headed toward Damascus. As he came near the city, a bright light from heaven suddenly flashed around him. [4]Saul fell to the

 8:37 Verse 37 Some late copies of Acts add verse 37: "Philip answered, 'If you believe with all your heart, you can.' The officer said, 'I believe that Jesus Christ is the Son of God.' "

ground and heard a voice saying to him, "Saul, Saul! Why are you persecuting me?"

[5]Saul said, "Who are you, Lord?"

The voice answered, "I am Jesus, whom you are persecuting. [6]Get up now and go into the city. Someone there will tell you what you must do."

[7]The people traveling with Saul stood there but said nothing. They heard the voice, but they saw no one. [8]Saul got up from the ground and opened his eyes, but he could not see. So those with Saul took his hand and led him into Damascus. [9]For three days Saul could not see and did not eat or drink.

[10]There was a follower of Jesus in Damascus named Ananias. The Lord spoke to Ananias in a vision, "Ananias!"

Ananias answered, "Here I am, Lord."

[11]The Lord said to him, "Get up and go to Straight Street. Find the house of Judas,[n] and ask for a man named Saul from the city of Tarsus. He is there now, praying. [12]Saul has seen a vision in which a man named Ananias comes to him and lays his hands on him. Then he is able to see again."

[13]But Ananias answered, "Lord, many people have told me about this man and the terrible things he did to your holy people in Jerusalem. [14]Now he has come here to Damascus, and the leading priests have given him the power to arrest everyone who worships you."

[15]But the Lord said to Ananias, "Go! I have chosen Saul for an important work. He must

GET OUT THERE

So you're cleaning out your closet and finding great stuff to unload on eBay. Did you know that you can share a portion (or all) of the proceeds from every item you sell? Through eBay and **MISSIONFISH**, you have an innovative new way to support good causes. Here's how it works: You pick a group from a list of registered charities to receive your donation and set a percentage of your sale price to share for each item you list. Charity items appear on eBay with a unique "charity" icon in the view item page. When the listing ends, winning bidders pay you as usual, and you ship your item. MissionFish receives the donation you specify, distributes the cash to your chosen nonprofit, and even provides you with a tax receipt. It's cool cash for your favorite cause.

Get the details on giving at www.missionfish.org.

 9:11 Judas This is not either of the apostles named Judas.

BIBLE BASICS

Witnessing means sharing the truth about God with other people. In the Bible, Jesus tells his followers to share the news about him with the entire world. Today, the church sends missionaries who go all over the place sharing the Good News. Some Christians preach to crowds. You can witness where you are right now through the relationships you already have, sitting down and telling someone exactly what you believe and why.

tell about me to those who are not Jews, to kings, and to the people of Israel. [16]I will show him how much he must suffer for my name."

[17]So Ananias went to the house of Judas. He laid his hands on Saul and said, "Brother Saul, the Lord Jesus sent me. He is the one you saw on the road on your way here. He sent me so that you can see again and be filled with the Holy Spirit." [18]Immediately, something that looked like fish scales fell from Saul's eyes, and he was able to see again! Then Saul got up and was baptized. [19]After he ate some food, his strength returned.

SAUL PREACHES IN DAMASCUS

Saul stayed with the followers of Jesus in Damascus for a few days. [20]Soon he began to preach about Jesus in the synagogues, saying, "Jesus is the Son of God."

[21]All the people who heard him were amazed. They said, "This is the man who was in Jerusalem trying to destroy those who trust in this name! He came here to arrest the followers of Jesus and take them back to the leading priests."

[22]But Saul grew more powerful. His proofs that Jesus is the Christ were so strong that his own people in Damascus could not argue with him.

[23]After many days, they made plans to kill Saul. [24]They were watching the city gates day and night, but Saul learned about their plan. [25]One night some followers of Saul helped him leave the city by lowering him in a basket through an opening in the city wall.

SAUL PREACHES IN JERUSALEM

[26]When Saul went to Jerusalem, he tried to join the group of followers, but they were all afraid of him. They did not believe he was really a follower. [27]But Barnabas accepted Saul and took him to the apostles. Barnabas explained to them that Saul had seen the Lord on the road and the Lord had spoken to Saul. Then he told them how boldly Saul had preached in the name of Jesus in Damascus.

[28]And so Saul stayed with the followers, going everywhere in Jerusalem, preaching boldly in the name of the Lord. [29]He would often talk and argue with the Jewish people who spoke Greek, but they were trying to kill him. [30]When the followers learned about this, they took Saul to Caesarea and from there sent him to Tarsus.

[31]The church everywhere in Judea, Galilee, and Samaria had a time of peace and became stronger. Respecting the Lord by the way they lived, and being encouraged by the Holy Spirit, the group of believers continued to grow.

PETER HEALS AENEAS

[32]As Peter was traveling through all the area, he visited God's people who lived in Lydda. [33]There he met a man named Aeneas, who was paralyzed and had not been able to leave his bed for the past eight years. [34]Peter said to him, "Aeneas, Jesus Christ heals you. Stand up and make your bed." Aeneas stood up immediately. [35]All the people living in Lydda and on the Plain of Sharon saw him and turned to the Lord.

PETER HEALS TABITHA

[36]In the city of Joppa there was a follower named Tabitha (whose Greek name was Dorcas). She was always doing good deeds and kind acts. [37]While Peter was in Lydda, Tabitha became sick and died. Her body was washed and put in a room upstairs. [38]Since Lydda is near Joppa and the followers in Joppa heard that Peter was in Lydda, they sent two messengers to Peter. They begged him, "Hurry, please come to us!" [39]So Peter got ready and went with them. When he arrived, they took him to the upstairs room

DO'S & DON'TS

- Do stay awake in boring classes.

- Do protect girls.

- Do let Jesus sit between you on dates.

- Do let your parents know where you're going.

- Don't drive on bald tires.

- Don't swim in riptides.

- Don't be lured offside.

- Don't slide headfirst to show off.

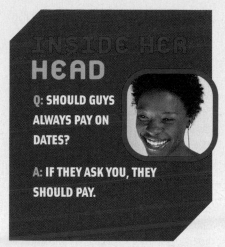

where all the widows stood around Peter, crying. They showed him the shirts and coats Tabitha had made when she was still alive. [40]Peter sent everyone out of the room and kneeled and prayed. Then he turned to the body and said, "Tabitha, stand up." She opened her eyes, and when she saw Peter, she sat up. [41]He gave her his hand and helped her up. Then he called the saints and the widows into the room and showed them that Tabitha was alive. [42]People everywhere in Joppa learned about this, and many believed in the Lord. [43]Peter stayed in Joppa for many days with a man named Simon who was a tanner.

PETER TEACHES CORNELIUS

10 At Caesarea there was a man named Cornelius, an officer in the Italian group of the Roman army. [2]Cornelius was a religious man. He and all the other people who lived in his house worshiped the true God. He gave much of his money to the poor and prayed to God often. [3]One afternoon about three o'clock, Cornelius clearly saw a vision. An angel of God came to him and said, "Cornelius!"

[4]Cornelius stared at the angel. He became afraid and said, "What do you want, Lord?"

The angel said, "God has heard your prayers. He has seen that you give to the poor, and he remembers you. [5]Send some men now to Joppa to bring back a man named Simon who is also called Peter. [6]He is staying with a man, also named Simon, who is a tanner and has a house beside the sea." [7]When the angel who spoke to Cornelius left, Cornelius called two of his servants and a soldier, a religious man who worked for him. [8]Cornelius explained

everything to them and sent them to Joppa.

[9]About noon the next day as they came near Joppa, Peter was going up to the roof[n] to pray. [10]He was hungry and wanted to eat, but while the food was being prepared, he had a vision. [11]He saw heaven opened and something coming down that looked like a big sheet being lowered to earth by its four corners. [12]In it were all kinds of animals, reptiles, and birds. [13]Then a voice said to Peter, "Get up, Peter; kill and eat."

[14]But Peter said, "No, Lord! I have never eaten food that is unholy or unclean."

[15]But the voice said to him again, "God has made these things clean so don't call them 'unholy'!" [16]This happened three times, and at once the sheet was taken back to heaven.

[17]While Peter was wondering what this vision meant, the men Cornelius sent had found Simon's house and were standing at the gate. [18]They asked, "Is Simon Peter staying here?"

[19]While Peter was still thinking about the vision, the Spirit said to him, "Listen, three men are looking for you. [20]Get up and go downstairs. Go with them without doubting, because I have sent them to you."

[21]So Peter went down to the men and said, "I am the one you are looking for. Why did you come here?"

[22]They said, "A holy angel spoke to Cornelius, an army officer and a good man; he worships God. All the people respect him. The angel told Cornelius to ask you to come to his house so that he can hear what you have to say." [23]So Peter asked the men to come in and spend the night.

The next day Peter got ready and went with them, and some of the followers from Joppa joined him. [24]On the following day they came to Caesarea. Cornelius was waiting for them and had called together his relatives and close friends. [25]When Peter entered, Cornelius met him, fell at his feet, and worshiped him. [26]But Peter helped him up, saying, "Stand up. I too am only a human." [27]As he talked with Cornelius, Peter went inside where he saw many people gathered. [28]He said, "You people understand that it is against our law for Jewish people to associate with or visit anyone who is not Jewish. But God has shown me that I should not call any person 'unholy' or 'unclean.' [29]That is why I did not argue when I

RELATIONSHIPS

"Speaking the truth with love, we will grow up in every way into Christ" (Ephesians 4:15). Suppose a friend has a wart the size of a basketball growing out the backside of his head. It's there. Everyone knows it. Your friend just can't see it. Get this: You would never let your friend be a warthead. You'd speak up. It's the same way with spotting sin in a friend. Sometimes your saying something is the only way for that friend to figure out he has a problem and get it fixed. Yet don't confuse being honest with being harsh. God wants each word you speak to build others up. Got a truth to say to someone? Say it with love.

10:9 **roof** In Bible times houses were built with flat roofs. The roof was used for drying things such as flax and fruit. And it was used as an extra room, as a place for worship, and as a cool place to sleep in the summer.

WAYS TO WALK THE WALK

Acts 4:13

WORD: Being tight with Jesus gives you abilities and insights far beyond what you have naturally.

WALK IT: Want to make a dent in your world? Then take time each day to "be with Jesus," hearing from his Word and talking to him through prayer.

was asked to come here. Now, please tell me why you sent for me."

[30]Cornelius said, "Four days ago, I was praying in my house at this same time—three o'clock in the afternoon. Suddenly, there was a man standing before me wearing shining clothes. [31]He said, 'Cornelius, God has heard your prayer and has seen that you give to the poor and remembers you. [32]So send some men to Joppa and ask Simon Peter to come. Peter is staying in the house of a man, also named Simon, who is a tanner and has a house beside the sea.' [33]So I sent for you immediately, and it was very good of you to come. Now we are all here before God to hear everything the Lord has commanded you to tell us."

[34]Peter began to speak: "I really understand now that to God every person is the same. [35]In every country God accepts anyone who worships him and does what is right. [36]You know the message that God has sent to the people of Israel is the Good News that peace has come through Jesus Christ. Jesus is the Lord of all people! [37]You know what has happened all over Judea, beginning in Galilee after John[n] preached to the people about baptism. [38]You know about Jesus from Nazareth, that God gave him the Holy Spirit and power. You know how Jesus went everywhere doing good and healing those who were ruled by the devil, because God was with him. [39]We saw what Jesus did in Judea and in Jerusalem, but the Jews in Jerusalem killed him by hanging him on a cross. [40]Yet, on the third day, God raised Jesus to life and caused him to be seen, [41]not by all the people, but only by the witnesses God had already chosen. And we are those witnesses who ate and drank with him after he was raised from the dead. [42]He told us to

preach to the people and to tell them that he is the one whom God chose to be the judge of the living and the dead. [43]All the prophets say it is true that all who believe in Jesus will be forgiven of their sins through Jesus' name."

[44]While Peter was still saying this, the Holy Spirit came down on all those who were listening. [45]The Jewish believers who came with Peter were amazed that the gift of the Holy Spirit had been given even to the nations. [46]These believers heard them speaking in different languages[n] and praising God. Then Peter said, [47]"Can anyone keep these people from being baptized with water? They have received the Holy Spirit just as we did!" [48]So Peter ordered that they be baptized in the name of Jesus Christ. Then they asked Peter to stay with them for a few days.

PETER RETURNS TO JERUSALEM

11 The apostles and the believers in Judea heard that some who were not Jewish had accepted God's teaching too. [2]But when Peter came to Jerusalem, some people argued with him. [3]They said, "You went into the homes of people who are not circumcised and ate with them!"

[4]So Peter explained the whole story to them. [5]He said, "I was in the city of Joppa, and while I was praying, I had a vision. I saw something that looked like a big sheet being lowered from heaven by its four corners. It came very close to me. [6]I looked inside it and saw animals, wild beasts, reptiles, and birds. [7]I heard a voice say to me, 'Get up, Peter. Kill and eat.' [8]But I said, 'No, Lord! I have never eaten anything that is unholy or unclean.' [9]But the voice from heaven spoke again, 'God has made these things

clean, so don't call them unholy.' [10]This happened three times. Then the whole thing was taken back to heaven. [11]Right then three men who were sent to me from Caesarea came to the house where I was staying. [12]The Spirit told me to go with them without doubting. These six believers here also went with me, and we entered the house of Cornelius. [13]He told us about the angel he saw standing in his house. The angel said to him, 'Send some men to Joppa and invite Simon Peter to come. [14]By the words he will say to you, you and all your family will be saved.' [15]When I began my speech, the Holy Spirit came on them just as he came on us at the beginning. [16]Then I remembered the words of the Lord. He said, 'John baptized with water, but you will be baptized with the Holy

RANDOM WAYS TO STAND OUT FROM A CROWD

1. **DON'T SHOP FOR CLOTHES WHERE EVERYONE ELSE DOES.**

2. **ROOT FOR THE UNDERDOG.**

3. **START A CLUB AT SCHOOL.**

4. **SAY WHAT YOU REALLY THINK.**

5. **FOLLOW THE EXAMPLES OF ACCOMPLISHED PEOPLE, NOT YOUR PEERS.**

6. **DON'T LET OTHERS TELL YOU WHAT TO LIKE—OR NOT LIKE.**

7. **PUT OTHER PEOPLE FIRST . . .**

8. **. . . LIKE YOUR FAMILY.**

9. **FORM YOUR OWN OPINIONS—AND HAVE REASONS TO BACK THEM UP.**

10. **BE UNIQUE WITHOUT BEING OBNOXIOUS.**

 10:37 John John the Baptist, who preached to people about Christ's coming (Luke 3). **10:46 languages** This can also be translated "tongues."

Spirit.' [17]Since God gave them the same gift he gave us who believed in the Lord Jesus Christ, how could I stop the work of God?"

[18]When the believers heard this, they stopped arguing. They praised God and said, "So God is allowing even other nations to turn to him and live."

THE GOOD NEWS COMES TO ANTIOCH

[19]Many of the believers were scattered when they were persecuted after Stephen was killed. Some of them went as far as Phoenicia, Cyprus, and Antioch telling the message to others, but only to Jews. [20]Some of these believers were people from Cyprus and Cyrene. When they came to Antioch, they spoke also to Greeks, telling them the Good News about the Lord Jesus. [21]The Lord was helping the believers, and a large group of people believed and turned to the Lord.

[22]The church in Jerusalem heard about all of this, so they sent Barnabas to Antioch. [23-24]Barnabas was a good man, full of the Holy Spirit and full of faith. When he reached Antioch and saw how God had blessed the people, he was glad. He encouraged all the believers in Antioch always to obey the Lord with all their hearts, and many people became followers of the Lord.

[25]Then Barnabas went to the city of Tarsus to look for Saul, [26]and when he found Saul, he brought him to Antioch. For a whole year Saul and Barnabas met with the church and taught many people there. In Antioch the followers were called Christians for the first time.

[27]About that time some prophets came from Jerusalem to Antioch. [28]One of them, named Agabus, stood up and spoke with the help of the Holy Spirit. He said, "A very hard time is coming to the whole world. There will be no food to eat." (This happened when Claudius ruled.) [29]The believers all decided to help the followers who lived in Judea, as much as each one could. [30]They gathered the money and gave it to Barnabas and Saul, who brought it to the elders in Judea.

HEROD AGRIPPA HURTS THE CHURCH

12 During that same time King Herod began to mistreat some who belonged to the church. [2]He ordered James, the brother of John, to be killed by the sword. [3]Herod saw that some of the people liked this, so he decided to arrest Peter, too. (This happened during the time of the Feast of Unleavened Bread.)

[4]After Herod arrested Peter, he put him in jail and handed him over to be guarded by sixteen soldiers. Herod planned to bring Peter before the people for trial after the Passover Feast. [5]So Peter was kept in jail, but the church prayed earnestly to God for him.

PETER LEAVES THE JAIL

[6]The night before Herod was to bring him to trial, Peter was sleeping between two soldiers, bound with two chains. Other soldiers were guarding the door of the jail. [7]Suddenly, an angel of the Lord stood there, and a light shined in the cell. The angel struck Peter on the side and woke him up. "Hurry! Get up!" the angel said. And the chains fell off Peter's hands. [8]Then the angel told him, "Get dressed and put on your sandals." And Peter did. Then the angel said, "Put on your coat and follow me." [9]So Peter followed him out, but he did not know if what the angel was doing was real; he thought he might be seeing a vision. [10]They went past the first and second guards and came to the iron gate that separated them from the city. The gate opened by itself for them, and they went through it. When they had walked

MEN OF THE SWORD

SHADRACH, MESHACH, and **ABEDNEGO** are Old Testament heroes. Friends of Daniel, they refused to bow to a golden idol cast to look like King Nebuchadnezzar. The king responded with a threat to toss them into a blazing fire, but they stood firm: "If you throw us into the blazing furnace, the God we serve is able to save us from the furnace. He will save us from your power, O king. But even if God does not save us, we want you, O king, to know this: We will not serve your gods or worship the gold statue you have set up." Nebuchadnezzar ordered the furnace to burn seven times hotter than usual, tied them up, and tossed them in. But when the king looked into the furnace, they were walking free—along with a *fourth* man, the God who saved them. You can make Shadrach, Meshach, and Abednego your role models for life.

–Daniel 3

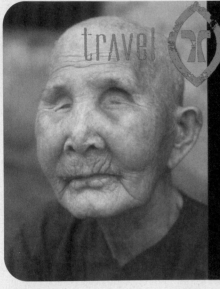

travel ☸ the road

"In my mind's eye," says Loren Cunningham, "I could see a world map, alive and moving! Waves crashed onto the continents, advancing inland until all the nations were covered. As I watched, the waves became young people of all races. They were my own age and even younger, talking to people on street corners and outside bars. Going from house to house. Helping the lonely and the hungry. Caring for people everywhere they went." When Cunningham founded Youth With A Mission (YWAM) in 1960, the idea that young people could contribute anything to missions was seen as radical and totally irresponsible. But Cunningham's persistence opened the door for teens like you to serve all over the world via hundreds of organizations.

For more on extreme missions visit www.traveltheroad.com.

down one street, the angel suddenly left him.

[11]Then Peter realized what had happened. He thought, "Now I know that the Lord really sent his angel to me. He rescued me from Herod and from all the things the people thought would happen."

[12]When he considered this, he went to the home of Mary, the mother of John Mark. Many people were gathered there, praying. [13]Peter knocked on the outside door, and a servant girl named Rhoda came to answer it. [14]When she recognized Peter's voice, she was so happy she forgot to open the door. Instead, she ran inside and told the group, "Peter is at the door!"

PSALM 29:11 "THE LORD GIVES STRENGTH TO HIS PEOPLE."

[15]They said to her, "You are crazy!" But she kept on saying it was true, so they said, "It must be Peter's angel."

[16]Peter continued to knock, and when they opened the door, they saw him and were amazed. [17]Peter made a sign with his hand to tell them to be quiet. He explained how the Lord led him out of the jail, and he said, "Tell James and the other believers what happened." Then he left to go to another place.

[18]The next day the soldiers were very upset and wondered what had happened to Peter. [19]Herod looked everywhere for him but could not find him. So he questioned the guards and ordered that they be killed.

THE DEATH OF HEROD AGRIPPA

Later Herod moved from Judea and went to the city of Caesarea, where he stayed. [20]Herod was very angry with the people of Tyre and Sidon, but the people of those cities all came in a group to him. After convincing Blastus, the king's personal servant, to be on their side, they asked Herod for peace, because their country got its food from his country.

[21]On a chosen day Herod put on his royal robes, sat on his throne, and made a speech to the people. [22]They shouted, "This is the voice of a god, not a human!" [23]Because Herod did not give the glory to God, an angel of the Lord immediately caused him to become sick, and he was eaten by worms and died.

[24]God's message continued to spread and reach people.

[25]After Barnabas and Saul finished their task in Jerusalem, they returned to Antioch, taking John Mark with them.

BARNABAS AND SAUL ARE CHOSEN

13 In the church at Antioch there were these prophets and teachers: Barnabas, Simeon (also called Niger), Lucius (from the city of Cyrene), Manaen (who had grown up with Herod, the ruler), and Saul. [2]They were all worshiping the Lord and giving up eating for a certain time.[n] During this time the Holy Spirit said to them, "Set apart for me Barnabas and Saul to do a special work for which I have chosen them."

[3]So after they gave up eating and prayed, they laid their hands on[n] Barnabas and Saul and sent them out.

BARNABAS AND SAUL IN CYPRUS

[4]Barnabas and Saul, sent out by the Holy Spirit, went to the city of Seleucia. From there they sailed to the island of Cyprus. [5]When they came to Salamis, they preached the Good News of God in the synagogues. John Mark was with them to help.

[6]They went across the whole island to Paphos where they met a magician named Bar-Jesus. He was a false prophet [7]who always stayed close to Sergius Paulus, the governor and a smart man. He asked Barnabas and Saul to come to him, because he wanted to hear the message of God. [8]But Elymas, the magician, was against them. (Elymas is the name for Bar-Jesus in the Greek language.) He tried to stop the governor from believing in Jesus. [9]But Saul, who was also called Paul, was filled with the Holy Spirit. He looked straight at Elymas [10]and said, "You son of the devil! You are an enemy of everything that is right! You are full of evil tricks and lies, always trying to change the Lord's truths into lies. [11]Now the Lord will touch you, and you will be blind. For a time you will not be able to see anything—not even the light from the sun."

Then everything became dark for Elymas,

and he walked around, trying to find someone to lead him by the hand. [12]When the governor saw this, he believed because he was amazed at the teaching about the Lord.

PAUL AND BARNABAS LEAVE CYPRUS

[13]Paul and those with him sailed from Paphos and came to Perga, in Pamphylia. There John Mark left them to return to Jerusalem. [14]They continued their trip from Perga and went to Antioch, a city in Pisidia. On the Sabbath day they went into the synagogue and sat down. [15]After the law of Moses and the writings of the prophets were read, the leaders of the synagogue sent a message to Paul and Barnabas: "Brothers, if you have any message that will encourage the people, please speak."

PHILIPPIANS 4:8 "BROTHERS AND SISTERS, THINK ABOUT THE THINGS THAT ARE GOOD AND WORTHY OF PRAISE."

[16]Paul stood up, raised his hand, and said, "You Israelites and you who worship God, please listen! [17]The God of the Israelites chose our ancestors. He made the people great during the time they lived in Egypt, and he brought them out of that country with great power. [18]And he was patient with them for forty years in the desert. [19]God destroyed seven nations in the land of Canaan and gave the land to his people. [20]All this happened in about four hundred fifty years.

"After this, God gave them judges until the time of Samuel the prophet. [21]Then the people asked for a king, so God gave them Saul son of Kish. Saul was from the tribe of Benjamin and was king for forty years. [22]After God took him away, God made David their king. God said about him: 'I have found in David son of Jesse the kind of man I want. He will do all I want him to do.' [23]So God has brought Jesus, one of David's descendants, to Israel to be its Savior,

as he promised. [24]Before Jesus came, John[n] preached to all the people of Israel about a baptism of changed hearts and lives. [25]When he was finishing his work, he said, 'Who do you think I am? I am not the Christ. He is coming later, and I am not worthy to untie his sandals.'

[26]"Brothers, sons of the family of Abraham, and others who worship God, listen! The news about this salvation has been sent to us. [27]Those who live in Jerusalem and their leaders did not realize that Jesus was the Savior. They did not understand the words that the prophets wrote, which are read every Sabbath day. But they made them come true when they said Jesus was guilty. [28]They could not find any real reason for Jesus to be put to death, but they asked Pilate to have him killed. [29]When they had done to him all that the Scriptures had said, they took him down from the cross and laid him in a tomb. [30]But God raised him up from the dead! [31]After this, for many days, those who had gone with Jesus from Galilee to Jerusalem saw him. They are now his witnesses to the people. [32]We tell you the Good News about the promise God made to our ancestors. [33]God has made this promise come true for us, his children, by raising Jesus from the dead. We read about this also in Psalm 2:

'You are my Son.

Today I have become your Father.' *Psalm 2:7*
[34]God raised Jesus from the dead, and he will never go back to the grave and become dust. So God said:

'I will give you the holy and sure blessings
that I promised to David.' *Isaiah 55:3*
[35]But in another place God says:

'You will not let your Holy One rot.' *Psalm 16:10*
[36]David did God's will during his lifetime. Then he died and was buried beside his ancestors, and his body did rot in the grave. [37]But the One God raised from the dead did not rot in the grave. [38-39]Brothers, understand what we are telling you: You can have forgiveness of your sins through Jesus. The law of Moses could not free you from your sins. But through Jesus everyone who believes is free from all

HOW TO HANDLE A JALAPEÑO

You're out on a date at an ethnic restaurant when you bite a pepper. A hot one. Your mouth is ablaze. Your nostrils flare, your forehead sweats, and you whimper like a little girl. Help, please? Your best bet is to extinguish the flames with a dairy product like milk, sour cream, or ice cream—the more fat the better. Starchy foods also absorb heat, so gulp down some rice, provided that isn't where the peppers live. By the way, peppers get their hotness from capsaicin, a compound that doesn't dissolve in water. That's why slamming pop or ice water doesn't do much good. Man, it's like dealing with the burning problem of sin. You need to grab the right solution. Get Jesus.

SIX OUT OF EVERY 100 TEEN GUYS WILL BE VICTIMS OF A VIOLENT CRIME THIS YEAR. –CHILD TRENDS DATABANK

 13:24 John John the Baptist, who preached to people about Christ's coming (Luke 3).

MUSIC REVIEWS

SIXPENCE NONE THE RICHER: DIVINE DISCONTENT

With *Divine Discontent*, Sixpence subtly shifts from their well-known alternative sound to a smoother pop style. The writing, done mostly by guitarist Matt Slocum, manages to up the ante on what you expect from Sixpence—both deep and catchy. Lead singer Leigh (Bingham) Nash, the wife of PFR's Mark Nash, wrote "Eyes Wide Open" (about fear of flying) and "Down and Out of Time" (about wanting to be needed). The album's title is all about the struggle of seeking God while not getting the answers as fast as you want. "Sixpence None the Richer" is named for an illustration from the classic book *Mere Christianity* by C. S. Lewis.

WHY IT ROCKS: LEIGH NASH'S VOICE IS ANGELIC, ENCOURAGING CHILDLIKE WONDER ABOUT LIFE'S BEAUTY.

sins. [40]Be careful! Don't let what the prophets said happen to you:

[41]'Listen, you people who doubt!
You can wonder, and then die.
I will do something in your lifetime
that you won't believe even when you
are told about it!' "   *Habakkuk 1:5*

[42]While Paul and Barnabas were leaving the synagogue, the people asked them to tell them more about these things on the next Sabbath. [43]When the meeting was over, many people with those who had changed to worship God followed Paul and Barnabas from that place. Paul and Barnabas were persuading them to continue trusting in God's grace.

must speak the message of God to you first. But you refuse to listen. You are judging yourselves not worthy of having eternal life! So we will now go to the people of other nations. [47]This is what the Lord told us to do, saying:

'I have made you a light for the nations;
you will show people all over the world
the way to be saved.' "   *Isaiah 49:6*

[48]When those who were not Jewish heard Paul say this, they were happy and gave honor to the message of the Lord. And the people who were chosen to have life forever believed the message.

[49]So the message of the Lord was spreading through the whole country. [50]But the Jewish people stirred up some of the important reli-

PAUL AND BARNABAS IN ICONIUM

14 In Iconium, Paul and Barnabas went as usual to the synagogue. They spoke so well that a great many Jews and Greeks believed. [2]But some people who did not believe excited the others and turned them against the believers. [3]Paul and Barnabas stayed in Iconium a long time and spoke bravely for the Lord. He showed that their message about his grace was true by giving them the power to work miracles and signs. [4]But the city was divided. Some of the people agreed with the Jews, and others believed the apostles.

[5]Some who were not Jews, some Jews, and some of their rulers wanted to mistreat Paul and Barnabas and to stone them to death. [6]When Paul and Barnabas learned about this, they ran away to Lystra and Derbe, cities in Lycaonia, and to the areas around those cities. [7]They announced the Good News there, too.

PAUL IN LYSTRA AND DERBE

[8]In Lystra there sat a man who had been born crippled; he had never walked. [9]As this man was listening to Paul speak, Paul looked straight at him and saw that he believed God could heal him. [10]So he cried out, "Stand up on your feet!" The man jumped up and began walking around. [11]When the crowds saw what Paul did, they shouted in the Lycaonian language, "The gods have become like humans and have come down to us!" [12]Then the people began to call Barnabas "Zeus"[n] and Paul "Hermes,"[n] because he was the main speaker. [13]The priest in the temple of Zeus, which was near the city, brought some bulls and flowers to the city gates. He and the people wanted to offer a sacrifice to Paul and Barnabas. [14]But

---

THE NUMBER OF YOUTH WHO GOT INTO PHYSICAL FIGHTS DROPPED FROM 42 PERCENT TO 33 PERCENT IN THE PAST TEN YEARS. –CHILD TRENDS DATABANK

---

[44]On the next Sabbath day, almost everyone in the city came to hear the word of the Lord. [45]Seeing the crowd, the Jewish people became very jealous and said insulting things and argued against what Paul said. [46]But Paul and Barnabas spoke very boldly, saying, "We

gious women and the leaders of the city. They started trouble against Paul and Barnabas and forced them out of their area. [51]So Paul and Barnabas shook the dust off their feet[n] and went to Iconium. [52]But the followers were filled with joy and the Holy Spirit.

when the apostles, Barnabas and Paul, heard about it, they tore their clothes. They ran in among the people, shouting, [15]"Friends, why are you doing these things? We are only human beings like you. We are bringing you the Good News and are telling you to turn away

---

13:51 **shook . . . feet** A warning. It showed that they had rejected these people.   14:12 **"Zeus"** The Greeks believed in many false gods, of whom Zeus was most important.   14:12 **"Hermes"** The Greeks believed he was a messenger for the other gods.

from these worthless things and turn to the living God. He is the One who made the sky, the earth, the sea, and everything in them. [16]In the past, God let all the nations do what they wanted. [17]Yet he proved he is real by showing kindness, by giving you rain from heaven and crops at the right times, by giving you food and filling your hearts with joy." [18]Even with these words, they were barely able to keep the crowd from offering sacrifices to them.

PSALM 31:24 "ALL YOU WHO PUT YOUR HOPE IN THE LORD BE STRONG AND BRAVE."

[19]Then some evil people came from Antioch and Iconium and persuaded the people to turn against Paul. So they threw stones at him and dragged him out of town, thinking they had killed him. [20]But the followers gathered around him, and he got up and went back into the town. The next day he and Barnabas left and went to the city of Derbe.

THE RETURN TO ANTIOCH IN SYRIA

[21]Paul and Barnabas told the Good News in Derbe, and many became followers. Paul and Barnabas returned to Lystra, Iconium, and Antioch, [22]making the followers of Jesus stronger and helping them stay in the faith. They said, "We must suffer many things to enter God's kingdom." [23]They chose elders for each church, by praying and giving up eating for a certain time.[n] These elders had trusted the Lord, so Paul and Barnabas put them in the Lord's care.

[24]Then they went through Pisidia and came to Pamphylia. [25]When they had preached the message in Perga, they went down to Attalia. [26]And from there they sailed away to Antioch where the believers had put them into God's care and had sent them out to do this work. Now they had finished.

[27]When they arrived in Antioch, Paul and Barnabas gathered the church together. They told the church all about what God had done with them and how God had made it possible for those who were not Jewish to believe. [28]And they stayed there a long time with the followers.

THE MEETING AT JERUSALEM

15 Then some people came to Antioch from Judea and began teaching the non-Jewish believers: "You cannot be saved if you are not circumcised as Moses taught us." [2]Paul and Barnabas were against this teaching and argued with them about it. So the church decided to send Paul, Barnabas, and some others to Jerusalem where they could talk more about this with the apostles and elders.

[3]The church helped them leave on the trip, and they went through the countries of Phoenicia and Samaria, telling all about how the other nations had turned to God. This made all the believers very happy. [4]When they arrived in Jerusalem, they were welcomed by the apostles, the elders, and the church. Paul, Barnabas, and the others told about everything God had done with them. [5]But some of the believers who belonged to the Pharisee group came forward and said, "The non-Jewish believers must be circumcised. They must be told to obey the law of Moses."

[6]The apostles and the elders gathered to consider this problem. [7]After a long debate, Peter stood up and said to them, "Brothers, you know that in the early days God chose me from among you to preach the Good News to the nations. They heard the Good News from me, and they believed. [8]God, who knows the thoughts of everyone, accepted them. He showed this to us by giving them the Holy Spirit, just as he did to us. [9]To God, those people are not different from us. When they believed, he made their hearts pure. [10]So now why are you testing God by putting a heavy load around the necks of the non-Jewish believers? It is a load that neither we nor our ancestors were able to carry. [11]But we believe that we and they too will be saved by the grace of the Lord Jesus."

[12]Then the whole group became quiet. They listened to Paul and Barnabas tell about all the miracles and signs that God did through them among the people. [13]After they finished speaking, James said, "Brothers, listen to me. [14]Simon has told us how God showed his love for those people. For the first time he is accepting from

RANDOM WAYS TO RECOVER WHEN YOU'VE DONE SOMETHING STUPID

1. **CONFESS YOUR GOOF TO GOD.**
2. **APOLOGIZE TO THE PEOPLE YOU HURT.**
3. **PAY FOR IT.**
4. **ASK HOW YOU CAN MAKE IT UP.**
5. **SHOW GENUINE SORROW.**
6. **FORGIVE YOURSELF AS GOD FORGIVES YOU.**
7. **GLUE IT BACK TOGETHER.**
8. **MOVE ON.**
9. **SAY FIVE COMPLIMENTS FOR EVERY PUT-DOWN.**
10. **DUCT TAPE IT.**

among them a people to be his own. [15]The words of the prophets agree with this too:
[16]'After these things I will return.

The kingdom of David is like a fallen tent.
But I will rebuild its ruins,
and I will set it up.
[17]Then those people who are left alive may
ask the Lord for help,
and the other nations that belong to me,
says the Lord,
who will make it happen.
[18]And these things have been known for a
long time.'   *Amos 9:11-12*

[19]"So I think we should not bother the other people who are turning to God. [20]Instead, we should write a letter to them telling them these things: Stay away from food

issues

SOCIAL ACTIVISM

HOW MUCH DOES IT MATTER that you're socially active? How big should it be in your life? Well, there are over 2,300 verses in Scripture that command us to take care of the poor, feed the hungry, and clothe the naked. So look for a way to live that out day-to-day. Get on www.volunteermatch.org, and see what opportunities are available in your neighborhood. Or check out the newspaper, magazine, website, or other media outlet you use most, and find out what's going on with an issue you care about. Stuff envelopes, raise cash, volunteer your time, do whatever it takes to make a difference in the lives of those less fortunate than you.

WAYS TO WALK THE WALK

ACTS 10:34

WORD: God doesn't play favorites.

WALK IT: In your next class, choose to sit by someone who may be different from you by race, class, or gender. Get to know them, to understand them.

that has been offered to idols (which makes it unclean), any kind of sexual sin, eating animals that have been strangled, and blood. [21]They should do these things, because for a long time in every city the law of Moses has been taught. And it is still read in the synagogue every Sabbath day."

LETTER TO NON-JEWISH BELIEVERS

[22]The apostles, the elders, and the whole church decided to send some of their men with Paul and Barnabas to Antioch. They chose Judas Barsabbas and Silas, who were respected by the believers. [23]They sent the following letter with them:

From the apostles and elders, your brothers.

To all the non-Jewish believers in Antioch, Syria, and Cilicia:

Greetings!

[24]We have heard that some of our group have come to you and said things that trouble and upset you. But we did not tell them to do this. [25]We have all agreed to choose some messengers and send them to you with our dear friends Barnabas and Paul—[26]people who have given their lives to serve our Lord Jesus Christ. [27]So we are sending Judas and Silas, who will tell you the same things. [28]It has pleased the Holy Spirit that you should not have a heavy load to carry, and we agree. You

need to do only these things: [29]Stay away from any food that has been offered to idols, eating any animals that have been strangled, and blood, and any kind of sexual sin. If you stay away from these things, you will do well.

Good-bye.

[30]So they left Jerusalem and went to Antioch where they gathered the church and gave them the letter. [31]When they read it, they were very happy because of the encouraging message. [32]Judas and Silas, who were also prophets, said many things to encourage the believers and make them stronger. [33]After some time Judas and Silas were sent off in peace by the believers, and they went back to those who had sent them. [34]n

[35]But Paul and Barnabas stayed in Antioch and, along with many others, preached the Good News and taught the people the message of the Lord.

PAUL AND BARNABAS SEPARATE

[36]After some time, Paul said to Barnabas, "We should go back to all those towns where we preached the message of the Lord. Let's visit the believers and see how they are doing."

[37]Barnabas wanted to take John Mark with them, [38]but he had left them at Pamphylia; he did not continue with them in the work. So Paul did not think it was a good idea to take him. [39]Paul and Barnabas had such a serious argument about this that they separated and went different ways. Barnabas took Mark and sailed to Cyprus, [40]but Paul chose Silas and left. The believers in Antioch put Paul into the Lord's care, [41]and he went through Syria and Cilicia, giving strength to the churches.

HEBREWS 13:4 "MARRIAGE SHOULD BE HONORED BY EVERYONE, AND HUSBAND AND WIFE SHOULD KEEP THEIR MARRIAGE PURE."

TIMOTHY GOES WITH PAUL

16 Paul came to Derbe and Lystra, where a follower named Timothy lived. Timothy's mother was Jewish and a believer, but his father was a Greek. [2]The believers in Lystra and Iconium respected Timothy and said good things about

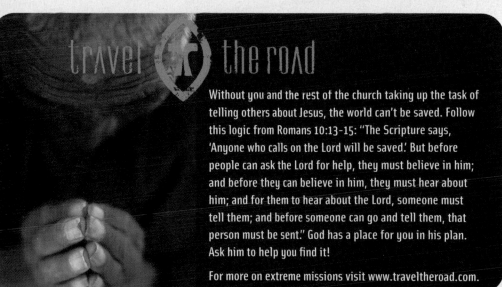

travel the road

Without you and the rest of the church taking up the task of telling others about Jesus, the world can't be saved. Follow this logic from Romans 10:13-15: "The Scripture says, 'Anyone who calls on the Lord will be saved.' But before people can ask the Lord for help, they must believe in him; and before they can believe in him, they must hear about him; and for them to hear about the Lord, someone must tell them; and before someone can go and tell them, that person must be sent." God has a place for you in his plan. Ask him to help you find it!

For more on extreme missions visit www.traveltheroad.com.

 15:34 Verse 34 Some Greek copies add verse 34: ". . . but Silas decided to remain there."

JULY

1 July is Baked Beans Month. Celebrate, come on!

2

3 July is Anti-Boredom Month. Got a plan?

4

5 Workaholics Day. Don't feel obligated.

6 Read the Book of Romans chapter-by-chapter this month.

7 Ask God to fill your dreams tonight.

8 Keep your brain from rotting by watching an educational TV show today.

9 Pray for a Person of Influence: Tom Hanks has a birthday today.

10 Don't let another day slide by. Take time to do something really important today.

11 Eric Liddell—see *Chariots of Fire*—won the Olympic gold for the 400-meter race in 1924.

12

13

14 Talk with your parents about your plans for the fall.

15

16 Pray for a Person of Influence: It's Will Ferrell's birthday.

17 Call someone you're sure is bored and lonely.

18 Pray for a Person of Influence: Vin Diesel racks up a birthday today.

19 Catch a firefly tonight. Ask God to make you a light for him.

20 First moon landing—ask your grandfather where he was.

21

22 Pray for a Person of Influence: David Spade is way older than you think today.

23

24 Pray for a Person of Influence: Barry Bonds hits another birthday today.

25

26 Pray for a Person of Influence: Sandra Bullock celebrates a birthday today.

27 Plan a weekend with your grandparents. Ask them what life was like when they were your age.

28

29

30 Pray for a Person of Influence: Arnold Schwarzenegger bulks up another birthday today.

31 Take a sibling out for ice cream today to show you care.

him. [3]Paul wanted Timothy to travel with him, but all the people living in that area knew that Timothy's father was Greek. So Paul circumcised Timothy to please his mother's people. [4]Paul and those with him traveled from town to town and gave the decisions made by the apostles and elders in Jerusalem for the people to obey. [5]So the churches became stronger in the faith and grew larger every day.

PAUL IS CALLED OUT OF ASIA

[6]Paul and those with him went through the areas of Phrygia and Galatia since the Holy Spirit did not let them preach the Good News in the country of Asia. [7]When they came near the country of Mysia, they tried to go into Bithynia, but the Spirit of Jesus did not let them. [8]So they passed by Mysia and went to Troas. [9]That night Paul saw in a vision a man from Macedonia. The man stood and begged, "Come over to Macedonia and help us." [10]After Paul had seen the vision, we immediately prepared to leave for Macedonia, under-

PAUL AND SILAS IN JAIL

[16]Once, while we were going to the place for prayer, a servant girl met us. She had a special spirit[n] in her, and she earned a lot of money for her owners by telling fortunes. [17]This girl followed Paul and us, shouting, "These men are servants of the Most High God. They are telling you how you can be saved."

[18]She kept this up for many days. This bothered Paul, so he turned and said to the spirit, "By the power of Jesus Christ, I command you to come out of her!" Immediately, the spirit came out.

[19]When the owners of the servant girl saw this, they knew that now they could not use her to make money. So they grabbed Paul and Silas and dragged them before the city rulers in the marketplace. [20]They brought Paul and Silas to the Roman rulers and said, "These men are Jews and are making trouble in our city. [21]They are teaching things that are not right for us as Romans to do."

INSIDE HER HEAD

Q: SHOULD GUYS ALWAYS PAY ON DATES?

A: GOING DUTCH IS FINE IF YOU'RE GOING OUT A LOT. GIRLS SHOULD PAY SOMETIMES.

them outside and said, "Men, what must I do to be saved?"

[31]They said to him, "Believe in the Lord Jesus and you will be saved—you and all the

---

HIGH SCHOOL MALES ARE MORE THAN FOUR TIMES MORE LIKELY THAN FEMALES TO CARRY A WEAPON—29 PERCENT TO 6 PERCENT.

—CHILD TRENDS DATABANK

---

standing that God had called us to tell the Good News to those people.

LYDIA BECOMES A CHRISTIAN

[11]We left Troas and sailed straight to the island of Samothrace. The next day we sailed to Neapolis.[n] [12]Then we went by land to Philippi, a Roman colony[n] and the leading city in that part of Macedonia. We stayed there for several days.

[13]On the Sabbath day we went outside the city gate to the river where we thought we would find a special place for prayer. Some women had gathered there, so we sat down and talked with them. [14]One of the listeners was a woman named Lydia from the city of Thyatira whose job was selling purple cloth. She worshiped God, and he opened her mind to pay attention to what Paul was saying. [15]She and all the people in her house were baptized. Then she invited us to her home, saying, "If you think I am truly a believer in the Lord, then come stay in my house." And she persuaded us to stay with her.

[22]The crowd joined the attack against them. The Roman officers tore the clothes of Paul and Silas and had them beaten with rods. [23]Then Paul and Silas were thrown into jail, and the jailer was ordered to guard them carefully. [24]When he heard this order, he put them far inside the jail and pinned their feet down between large blocks of wood.

[25]About midnight Paul and Silas were praying and singing songs to God as the other prisoners listened. [26]Suddenly, there was a strong earthquake that shook the foundation of the jail. Then all the doors of the jail broke open, and all the prisoners were freed from their chains. [27]The jailer woke up and saw that the jail doors were open. Thinking that the prisoners had already escaped, he got his sword and was about to kill himself.[n] [28]But Paul shouted, "Don't hurt yourself! We are all here."

[29]The jailer told someone to bring a light. Then he ran inside and, shaking with fear, fell down before Paul and Silas. [30]He brought

people in your house." [32]So Paul and Silas told the message of the Lord to the jailer and all the people in his house. [33]At that hour of the night the jailer took Paul and Silas and washed their wounds. Then he and all his people were baptized immediately. [34]After this the jailer took Paul and Silas home and gave them food. He and his family were very happy because they now believed in God.

[35]The next morning, the Roman officers sent the police to tell the jailer, "Let these men go free."

[36]The jailer said to Paul, "The officers have sent an order to let you go free. You can leave now. Go in peace."

[37]But Paul said to the police, "They beat us in public without a trial, even though we are Roman citizens.[n] And they threw us in jail. Now they want to make us go away quietly. No! Let them come themselves and bring us out."

[38]The police told the Roman officers what Paul said. When the officers heard that Paul

---

 16:11 Neapolis City in Macedonia. It was the first city Paul visited on the continent of Europe. **16:12 Roman colony** A town begun by Romans with Roman laws, customs, and privileges. **16:16 spirit** This was a spirit from the devil, which caused her to say she had special knowledge. **16:27 kill himself** He thought the leaders would kill him for letting the prisoners escape. **16:37 Roman citizens** Roman law said that Roman citizens must not be beaten before they had a trial.

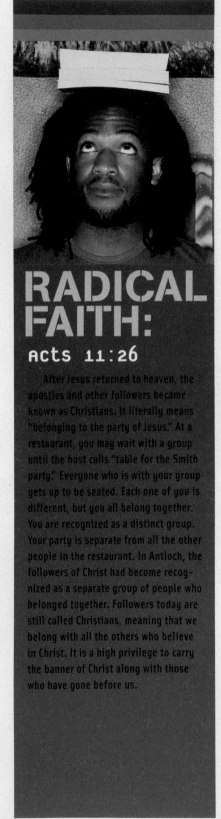

RADICAL FAITH:
ACTS 11:26

After Jesus returned to heaven, the apostles and other followers became known as Christians. It literally means "belonging to the party of Jesus." At a restaurant, you may wait with a group until the host calls "table for the Smith party." Everyone who is with your group gets up to be seated. Each one of you is different, but you all belong together. You are recognized as a distinct group. Your party is separate from all the other people in the restaurant. In Antioch, the followers of Christ had become recognized as a separate group of people who belonged together. Followers today are still called Christians, meaning that we belong with all the others who believe in Christ. It is a high privilege to carry the banner of Christ along with those who have gone before us.

and Silas were Roman citizens, they were afraid. [39]So they came and told Paul and Silas they were sorry and took them out of jail and asked them to leave the city. [40]So when they came out of the jail, they went to Lydia's house where they saw some of the believers and encouraged them. Then they left.

PAUL AND SILAS IN THESSALONICA

17 Paul and Silas traveled through Amphipolis and Apollonia and came to Thessalonica where there was a synagogue. [2]Paul went into the synagogue as he always did, and on each Sabbath day for three weeks, he talked with his fellow Jews about the Scriptures. [3]He explained and proved that the Christ must die and then rise from the dead. He said, "This Jesus I am telling you about is the Christ." [4]Some of them were convinced and joined Paul and Silas, along with many of the Greeks who worshiped God and many of the important women.

[5]But some others became jealous. So they got some evil men from the marketplace, formed a mob, and started a riot. They ran to Jason's house, looking for Paul and Silas, wanting to bring them out to the people. [6]But when they did not find them, they dragged Jason and some other believers to the leaders of the city. The people were yelling, "These people have made trouble everywhere in the world, and now they have come here too! [7]Jason is keeping them in his house. All of them do things against the laws of Caesar, saying there is another king, called Jesus."

[8]When the people and the leaders of the city heard these things, they became very upset. [9]They made Jason and the others put up a sum of money. Then they let the believers go free.

PAUL AND SILAS GO TO BEREA

[10]That same night the believers sent Paul and Silas to Berea where they went to the synagogue. [11]These people were more willing to listen than the people in Thessalonica. The Bereans were eager to hear what Paul and Silas said and studied the Scriptures every day to find out if these things were true. [12]So, many of them believed, as well as many important Greek women and men. [13]But the people in Thessalonica learned that Paul was preaching the word of God in Berea, too. So they came there, upsetting the people and making trou-

ble. [14]The believers quickly sent Paul away to the coast, but Silas and Timothy stayed in Berea. [15]The people leading Paul went with him to Athens. Then they carried a message from Paul back to Silas and Timothy for them to come to him as soon as they could.

PAUL PREACHES IN ATHENS

[16]While Paul was waiting for Silas and Timothy in Athens, he was troubled because he saw that the city was full of idols. [17]In the synagogue, he talked with the Jews and the Greeks who worshiped God. He also talked every day with people in the marketplace.

[18]Some of the Epicurean and Stoic philosophers[n] argued with him, saying, "This man doesn't know what he is talking about. What is he trying to say?" Others said, "He seems to be telling us about some other gods," because Paul was telling them about Jesus and his rising from the dead. [19]They got Paul and took him to a meeting of the Areopagus,[n] where they said, "Please explain to us this new idea

 17:18 Epicurean and Stoic philosophers Philosophers were those who searched for truth. Epicureans believed that pleasure, especially pleasures of the mind, were the goal of life. Stoics believed that life should be without feelings of joy or grief. **17:19 Areopagus** A council or group of important leaders in Athens. They were like judges.

you have been teaching. [20]The things you are saying are new to us, and we want to know what this teaching means." [21](All the people of Athens and those from other countries who lived there always used their time to talk about the newest ideas.)

[22]Then Paul stood before the meeting of the Areopagus and said, "People of Athens, I can see you are very religious in all things. [23]As I was going through your city, I saw the objects you worship. I found an altar that had these words written on it: TO A GOD WHO IS NOT KNOWN. You worship a god that you don't know, and this is the God I am telling you about! [24]The God who made the whole world and everything in it is the Lord of the land and the sky. He does not live in temples built by human hands. [25]This God is the One who gives life, breath, and everything else to people. He does not need any help from them; he has everything he needs. [26]God began by making one person, and from him came all the different people who live everywhere in the world. God decided exactly when and where they must live. [27]God wanted them to look for him and perhaps search all around for him and find him, though he is not far from any of us: [28]'We live in him. We walk in him. We are in him.' Some of your own poets have said: 'For we are his children.' [29]Since we are God's children, you must not think that God is like something that people imagine or make from gold, silver, or rock. [30]In the past, people did not understand God, and he ignored this. But now, God tells all people in the world to change their hearts and lives. [31]God has set a day that he will judge all the world with fairness, by the man he chose long ago. And God has proved this

to everyone by raising that man from the dead!"

[32]When the people heard about Jesus being raised from the dead, some of them laughed. But others said, "We will hear more about this

from you later." [33]So Paul went away from them. [34]But some of the people believed Paul and joined him. Among those who believed was Dionysius, a member of the Areopagus, a woman named Damaris, and some others.

PAUL IN CORINTH

18 Later Paul left Athens and went to Corinth. [2]Here he met a Jew named Aquila who had been born in the country of Pontus. But Aquila and his wife, Priscilla, had recently moved to Corinth from Italy, because Claudius[n] commanded that all Jews must leave Rome. Paul went to visit Aquila and Priscilla. [3]Because they were tentmakers, just as he was, he stayed with them and worked with them. [4]Every Sabbath day he talked with the Jews and Greeks in the synagogue, trying to persuade them to believe in Jesus.

[5]Silas and Timothy came from Macedonia and joined Paul in Corinth. After this, Paul spent all his time telling people the Good News, showing them that Jesus is the Christ. [6]But they would not accept Paul's teaching and said some evil things. So he shook off the dust from his clothes[n] and said to them, "If you are not saved, it will be your own fault! I have done all I can do! After this, I will go only to other nations." [7]Paul left the synagogue and moved into the home of Titius Justus, next to the synagogue. This man worshiped God. [8]Crispus was the leader of that synagogue, and he and all the people living in his house believed in the Lord. Many others in Corinth also listened to Paul and believed and were baptized.

[9]During the night, the Lord told Paul in a vision: "Don't be afraid. Continue talking to people and don't be quiet. [10]I am with you, and no one will hurt you because many of my people are in this city." [11]Paul stayed there for a year and a half, teaching God's word to the people.

RANDOM BIBLE PASSAGES ON SEX

1. **EXODUS 20:14**

2. **HEBREWS 13:4**

3. **PROVERBS 5:15-19**

4. **1 CORINTHIANS 6:12-20**

5. **1 THESSALONIANS 4:3**

6. **PROVERBS 5:1-6**

7. **REVELATION 21:6-8**

8. **ROMANS 1:26-27**

9. **SONG OF SOLOMON 7:1-9**

10. **PROVERBS 7:1-27**

PAUL IS BROUGHT BEFORE GALLIO

[12]When Gallio was the governor of the country of Southern Greece, some people came together against Paul and took him to the court. [13]They said, "This man is teaching people to worship God in a way that is against our law."

[14]Paul was about to say something, but Gallio spoke, saying, "I would listen to you if you were complaining about a crime or some wrong. [15]But the things you are saying are only questions about words and names—arguments about your own law. So you must solve this problem yourselves. I don't want to be a judge of these things." [16]And Gallio made them leave the court.

[17]Then they all grabbed Sosthenes, the leader of the synagogue, and beat him there before the court. But this did not bother Gallio.

PAUL RETURNS TO ANTIOCH

[18]Paul stayed with the believers for many more days. Then he left and sailed for Syria, with Priscilla and Aquila. At Cenchrea Paul cut

18:2 **Claudius** The emperor (ruler) of Rome, A.D. 41–54.   18:6 **shook . . . clothes** This was a warning to show that Paul was finished talking to the people in that city.

EXPERTS ANSWER YOUR QUESTIONS

Q. *Are there skate parks in heaven?*

A. Um, the Bible doesn't speak to that directly. But it is pictured as a mind-boggling happiness. You won't find a better description of heaven than in Revelation 21. No more death, crying, sadness, or pain. And God himself takes center stage. Cool.

Q. *If God created everything, why did he create evil?*

A. Actually, that was our invention. Sin entered the world in the Garden of Eden when Adam and Eve chose to disobey God. And by the way, we each make the same stupid choice. Let's not go blaming God.

Q. *What will the end of the world be like?*

A. You won't want to miss it. The Bible says that lightning will flash across the sky from the east to the west. Jesus will show up in dazzling splendor. Read more in Matthew 24 and 25.

off his hair,[n] because he had made a promise to God. [19]Then they went to Ephesus, where Paul left Priscilla and Aquila. While Paul was there, he went into the synagogue and talked with the people. [20]When they asked him to stay with them longer, he refused. [21]But as he left, he said, "I will come back to you again if God wants me to." And so he sailed away from Ephesus.

[22]When Paul landed at Caesarea, he went and gave greetings to the church in Jerusalem. After that, Paul went to Antioch. [23]He stayed there for a while and then left and went through the regions of Galatia and Phrygia. He traveled from town to town in these regions, giving strength to all the followers.

APOLLOS IN EPHESUS AND CORINTH

[24]A Jew named Apollos came to Ephesus. He was born in the city of Alexandria and was a good speaker who knew the Scriptures well. [25]He had been taught about the way of the Lord and was always very excited when he spoke and taught the truth about Jesus. But the only baptism Apollos knew about was the baptism that John[n] taught. [26]Apollos began to speak very boldly in the synagogue, and when Priscilla and Aquila heard him, they took him to their home and helped him better understand the way of God. [27]Now Apollos wanted to go to the country of Southern Greece. So the believers helped him and wrote a letter to the followers there, asking them to accept him. These followers had believed in Jesus because of God's grace, and when Apollos arrived, he helped them very much. [28]He argued very strongly with the Jews before all the people, clearly proving with the Scriptures that Jesus is the Christ.

PAUL IN EPHESUS

19 While Apollos was in Corinth, Paul was visiting some places on the way to Ephesus. There he found some followers [2]and asked them, "Did you receive the Holy Spirit when you believed?"

They said, "We have never even heard of a Holy Spirit."

[3]So he asked, "What kind of baptism did you have?"

They said, "It was the baptism that John taught."

[4]Paul said, "John's baptism was a baptism of changed hearts and lives. He told people to believe in the one who would come after him, and that one is Jesus."

[5]When they heard this, they were baptized in the name of the Lord Jesus. [6]Then Paul laid his hands on them,[n] and the Holy Spirit came upon them. They began speaking different languages[n] and prophesying. [7]There were about twelve people in this group.

[8]Paul went into the synagogue and spoke out boldly for three months. He talked with the people and persuaded them to accept the things he said about the kingdom of God. [9]But some of them became stubborn. They refused to believe and said evil things about the Way of Jesus before all the people. So Paul left them, and taking the followers with him, he went to the school of a man named Tyrannus. There Paul talked with people every day [10]for

PSALM 36:5 "LORD, YOUR LOVE REACHES TO THE HEAVENS, YOUR LOYALTY TO THE SKIES."

two years. Because of his work, every Jew and Greek in the country of Asia heard the word of the Lord.

THE SONS OF SCEVA

[11]God used Paul to do some very special miracles. [12]Some people took handkerchiefs and clothes that Paul had used and put them on the sick. When they did this, the sick were healed and evil spirits left them.

[13]But some people also were traveling around and making evil spirits go out of people. They tried to use the name of the Lord Jesus to force the evil spirits out. They would say, "By the same Jesus that Paul talks about, I order you to come out!" [14]Seven sons of Sceva, a leading priest, were doing this.

[15]But one time an evil spirit said to them, "I know Jesus, and I know about Paul, but who are you?"

[16]Then the man who had the evil spirit jumped on them. Because he was so much stronger than all of them, they ran away from the house naked and hurt. [17]All the people in Ephesus—Jews and Greeks—learned about this and were filled with fear and gave great

18:18 cut . . . hair Jews did this to show that the time of a special promise to God was finished. **18:25 John** John the Baptist, who preached to people about Christ's coming (Luke 3). **19:6 laid his hands on them** The laying on of hands had many purposes, including the giving of a blessing, power, or authority. **19:6 languages** This can also be translated "tongues."

HOW TO TEACH YOUR DOG A TRICK

You can't teach a pooch a trick in one fell swoop. You need to teach and reward in little steps, what animal trainers call "successive approximation." To teach your pup to sit, for example, try this: Looking the dog in the eye, say, "Sit!" and gently push his back end down. Repeat that half a dozen times. Then try it without the push. The minute that dog butt hits the floor, reward him with praise and a small treat. Repeat that practice until he sits still. If he forgets, back up and review; once he remembers, review at least once a week. Now, that's how God works with you, too. He doesn't expect you to learn everything at once or be totally mature overnight. He helps you look like Jesus little by little.

honor to the Lord Jesus. [18]Many of the believers began to confess openly and tell all the evil things they had done. [19]Some of them who had used magic brought their magic books and burned them before everyone. Those books

were worth about fifty thousand silver coins.[n]

[20]So in a powerful way the word of the Lord kept spreading and growing.

[21]After these things, Paul decided to go to Jerusalem, planning to go through the countries of Macedonia and Southern Greece and then on to Jerusalem. He said, "After I have been to Jerusalem, I must also visit Rome." [22]Paul sent Timothy and Erastus, two of his helpers, ahead to Macedonia, but he himself stayed in Asia for a while.

TROUBLE IN EPHESUS

[23]And during that time, there was some serious trouble in Ephesus about the Way of Jesus. [24]A man named Demetrius, who worked with silver, made little silver models that looked like the temple of the goddess Artemis.[n] Those who did this work made much money. [25]Demetrius had a meeting with them and some others who did the same kind of work. He told them, "Men, you know that we make a lot of money from our business. [26]But look at what this man Paul is doing. He has convinced and turned away many people in Ephesus and in almost all of Asia! He says the gods made by human hands are not real. [27]There is a danger that our business will lose its good name, but there is also another danger: People will begin to think that the temple of the great goddess Artemis is not important. Her greatness will be destroyed, and Artemis is the goddess that everyone in Asia and the whole world worships."

[28]When the others heard this, they became very angry and shouted, "Artemis, the goddess of Ephesus, is great!" [29]The whole city became confused. The people grabbed Gaius and Aristarchus, who were from Macedonia and were traveling with Paul, and ran to the theater. [30]Paul wanted to go in and talk to the crowd, but the followers did not let him. [31]Also, some leaders of Asia who were friends of Paul sent him a message, begging him not to go into the theater. [32]Some people were shouting one thing, and some were shouting another. The meeting was completely confused; most of them did not know why they had come together. [33]They put a man named Alexander in front of the people, and some of them told him what to do. Alexander waved his hand so he could explain things to the people. [34]But when they saw that Alexander was a Jew, they

RELATIONSHIPS

"You don't marry the girl. You marry the girl's whole family." Okay, so that's not in the Bible. Yet they're some of the world's smartest words. Can you picture yourself sitting down with your girl's family over Thanksgiving turkey—for the next thirty or forty years? That's reality. Not only that, but the good and bad traits you see in your wife's parents are likely the same qualities that will surface in her as she gets older. You want to hunt for a great girl. But keep an eye on those potential in-laws.

 19:19 **fifty thousand silver coins** Probably drachmas. One coin was enough to pay a worker for one day's labor.   19:24 **Artemis** A Greek goddess that the people of Asia Minor worshiped.

RANDOM REASONS TO SAVE SEX FOR MARRIAGE

1. **YOUR BODY IS YOUR BEST WEDDING PRESENT TO YOUR WIFE.**

2. **HERPES**

3. **YOUR BODY MIGHT FEEL READY, BUT YOUR BRAIN ISN'T.**

4. **YOU WANT TO GIVE YOUR HEART AND THEN RIP IT APART?**

5. **GENITAL WARTS**

6. **YOU WON'T SPEND YOUR LIFE COMPARING YOUR WIFE TO OTHER GIRLS YOU'VE BEEN WITH.**

7. **EVERY BABY DESERVES MARRIED PARENTS READY TO RAISE THEM.**

8. **YOU CAN LIVE WITHOUT REGRETS BEFORE GOD AND YOUR WIFE-FOR-LIFE.**

9. **PURITY IS PRICELESS.**

10. **BECAUSE GOD OWNS YOUR BODY, AND HE SAYS SO.**

all shouted the same thing for two hours: "Great is Artemis of Ephesus!"

[35]Then the city clerk made the crowd be quiet. He said, "People of Ephesus, everyone knows that Ephesus is the city that keeps the temple of the great goddess Artemis and her holy stone[n] that fell from heaven. [36]Since no one can say this is not true, you should be

quiet. Stop and think before you do anything. [37]You brought these men here, but they have not said anything evil against our goddess or stolen anything from her temple. [38]If Demetrius and those who work with him have a charge against anyone they should go to the courts and judges where they can argue with each other. [39]If there is something else you want to talk about, it can be decided at the regular town meeting of the people. [40]I say this because some people might see this trouble today and say that we are rioting. We could not explain this, because there is no real reason for this meeting." [41]After the city clerk said these things, he told the people to go home.

PAUL IN MACEDONIA AND GREECE

20 When the trouble stopped, Paul sent for the followers to come to him. After he encouraged them and then told them good-bye, he left and went to the country of Macedonia. [2]He said many things to strengthen the followers in the different places on his way through Macedonia. Then he went to Greece, [3]where he stayed for three months. He was ready to sail for Syria, but some evil people were planning something against him. So Paul decided to go back through Macedonia to Syria. [4]The men who went with him were Sopater son of Pyrrhus, from the city of Berea; Aristarchus and Secundus, from the city of Thessalonica; Gaius, from Derbe; Timothy; and Tychicus and Trophimus, two men from the country of Asia. [5]These men went on ahead and waited for us at Troas. [6]We sailed from Philippi after the Feast of Unleavened Bread. Five days later we met them in Troas, where we stayed for seven days.

PAUL'S LAST VISIT TO TROAS

[7]On the first day of the week,[n] we all met together to break bread,[n] and Paul spoke to the group. Because he was planning to leave the next day, he kept on talking until midnight. [8]We were all together in a room upstairs, and there were many lamps in the room. [9]A young man named Eutychus was sitting in the window. As Paul continued talking, Eutychus was falling into a deep sleep. Finally, he went sound asleep and fell to the ground from the third floor. When they picked him up, he was dead. [10]Paul went down to Eutychus, knelt down, and put his arms around him. He said, "Don't

worry. He is alive now." [11]Then Paul went upstairs again, broke bread, and ate. He spoke to them a long time, until it was early morning, and then he left. [12]They took the young man home alive and were greatly comforted.

THE TRIP FROM TROAS TO MILETUS

[13]We went on ahead of Paul and sailed for the city of Assos, where he wanted to join us on the ship. Paul planned it this way because he wanted to go to Assos by land. [14]When he met us there, we took him aboard and went to Mitylene. [15]We sailed from Mitylene and the next day came to a place near Kios. The following day we sailed to Samos, and the next day we reached Miletus. [16]Paul had already decided not to stop at Ephesus, because he did not want to stay too long in the country of Asia. He was hurrying to be in Jerusalem on the day of Pentecost, if that were possible.

THE ELDERS FROM EPHESUS

[17]Now from Miletus Paul sent to Ephesus and called for the elders of the church. [18]When they came to him, he said, "You know about my life from the first day I came to Asia. You know the way I lived all the time I was with you. [19]The evil people made plans against me, which troubled me very much. But you know I always served the Lord unselfishly, and I often cried. [20]You know I preached to you and did not hold back anything that would help you. You know that I taught you in public and in your homes. [21]I warned both Jews and Greeks to change their lives and turn to God and believe in our Lord Jesus. [22]But now I must obey the Holy Spirit and go to Jerusalem. I don't know what will happen to me there. [23]I know only that in every city the Holy Spirit tells me that troubles and even jail wait for me. [24]I don't care about my own life. The most important thing is that I complete my mission, the work that the Lord Jesus gave me—to tell people the Good News about God's grace.

[25]"And now, I know that none of you among whom I was preaching the kingdom of God will ever see me again. [26]So today I tell you that if any of you should be lost, I am not responsible, [27]because I have told you everything God wants you to know. [28]Be careful for yourselves and for all the people the Holy Spirit has given to you to care for. You must be like shepherds

19:35 holy stone Probably a meteorite or stone that the people thought looked like Artemis. **20:7 first day of the week** Sunday, which for Jews began at sunset on our Saturday. But if in this part of Asia a different system of time was used, then the meeting was on our Sunday night. **20:7 break bread** Probably the Lord's Supper, the special meal that Jesus told his followers to eat to remember him (Luke 22:14–20).

to the church of God,[n] which he bought with the death of his own son. [29]I know that after I leave, some people will come like wild wolves and try to destroy the flock. [30]Also, some from your own group will rise up and twist the truth and will lead away followers after them. [31]So be careful! Always remember that for three years, day and night, I never stopped warning each of you, and I often cried over you.

[32]"Now I am putting you in the care of God and the message about his grace. It is able to give you strength, and it will give you the blessings God has for all his holy people. [33]When I was with you, I never wanted anyone's money or fine clothes. [34]You know I always worked to take care of my own needs and the needs of those who were with me. [35]I showed you in all things that you should work as I did and help the weak. I taught you to remember the words Jesus said: 'It is more blessed to give than to receive.' "

[36]When Paul had said this, he knelt down with all of them and prayed. [37-38]And they all cried because Paul had said they would never see him again. They put their arms around him and kissed him. Then they went with him to the ship.

PAUL GOES TO JERUSALEM

21 After we all said good-bye to them, we sailed straight to the island of Cos. The next day we reached Rhodes, and from there we went to Patara. [2]There we found a ship going to Phoenicia, so we went aboard and sailed away. [3]We sailed near the island of Cyprus, seeing it to the north, but we sailed on to Syria. We stopped at Tyre because the ship needed to unload its cargo there. [4]We found some followers in Tyre and stayed with them for seven days. Through the Holy Spirit they warned Paul not to go to Jerusalem. [5]When we finished our visit, we left and continued our trip.

All the followers, even the women and children, came outside the city with us. After we all knelt on the beach and prayed, [6]we said good-bye and got on the ship, and the followers went back home.

[7]We continued our trip from Tyre and arrived at Ptolemais, where we greeted the believers and stayed with them for a day. [8]The next day we left Ptolemais and went to the city of Caesarea. There we went into the home of Philip the preacher, one of the seven helpers,[n] and stayed with him. [9]He had four unmarried daughters who had the gift of prophesying. [10]After we had been there for some time, a prophet named Agabus arrived from Judea. [11]He came to us and borrowed Paul's belt and used it to tie his own hands and feet. He said, "The Holy Spirit says, 'This is how evil people in Jerusalem will tie up the man who wears this belt. Then they will give him to the older leaders.' "

[12]When we all heard this, we and the people there begged Paul not to go to Jerusalem. [13]But he said, "Why are you crying and making me so sad? I am not only ready to be tied up in Jerusalem, I am ready to die for the Lord Jesus!"

[14]We could not persuade him to stay away from Jerusalem. So we stopped begging him and said, "We pray that what the Lord wants will be done."

[15]After this, we got ready and started on our way to Jerusalem. [16]Some of the followers from Caesarea went with us and took us to the home of Mnason, where we would stay. He was from Cyprus and was one of the first followers.

PAUL VISITS JAMES

[17]In Jerusalem the believers were glad to see us. [18]The next day Paul went with us to visit James, and all the elders were there. [19]Paul greeted them and told them everything God had done among the other nations through him. [20]When they heard this, they praised God. Then they said to Paul, "Brother, you can see that many thousands of our people have become believers. And they think it is very

20:28 **of God** Some Greek copies say, "of the Lord." 21:8 **helpers** The seven men chosen for a special work described in Acts 6:1–6. Sometimes they are called "deacons."

important to obey the law of Moses. [21]They have heard about your teaching, that you tell our people who live among the nations to leave the law of Moses. They have heard that you tell them not to circumcise their children and not to obey customs. [22]What should we do? They will learn that you have come. [23]So we will tell you what to do: Four of our men have made a promise to God. [24]Take these men with you and share in their cleansing ceremony.[n] Pay their expenses so they can shave their heads.[n] Then it will prove to everyone that what they have heard about you is not true and that you follow the law of Moses in your own life. [25]We have already sent a letter to the non-Jewish believers. The letter said: 'Do not eat food that has been offered to idols, or blood, or animals that have been strangled. Do not take part in sexual sin.' "

[26]The next day Paul took the four men and shared in the cleansing ceremony with them. Then he went to the Temple and announced the time when the days of the cleansing ceremony would be finished. On the last day an offering would be given for each of the men.

[27]When the seven days were almost over, some of his people from Asia saw Paul at the Temple. They caused all the people to be upset and grabbed Paul. [28]They shouted, "People of Israel, help us! This is the man who goes everywhere teaching against the law of Moses, against our people, and against this Temple. Now he has brought some Greeks into the Temple and has

GET OUT THERE

The **NATIONAL VOLUNTEER FIRE COUNCIL** (NVFC) is a nonprofit membership association representing the interests of the volunteer fire, EMS, and rescue services. The NVFC serves as the information source regarding legislation, standards, and regulatory issues.

The NVFC mission is to provide a unified voice for volunteer Fire/EMS organizations.

This Mission will be accomplished by: representing the interests of the volunteer Fire/EMS organizations at the U.S. congress and federal agencies; promoting the interests of the state and local organizations at the national level; promoting and providing education and training for the volunteer Fire/EMS organizations; providing representation on national standards setting committees and projects; and gathering information from and disseminating information to the volunteer Fire/EMS organizations.

To become a volunteer firefighter, go to www.nvfc.org.

21:24 **cleansing ceremony** The special things Jews did to end the Nazirite promise.   21:24 **shave their heads** Jews did this to show that their promise was finished.

travel the road

BIBLE BASICS

Gospel means "Good News." It's what we call the story of Jesus coming to earth to save people from their sins and to give them an abundant life in him instead. The Bible also has four books called "the Gospels"—Matthew, Mark, Luke, and John—that tell the life of Jesus.

made this holy place unclean!" [29](They said this because they had seen Trophimus, a man from Ephesus, with Paul in Jerusalem. They thought that Paul had brought him into the Temple.)

[30]All the people in Jerusalem became upset. Together they ran, took Paul, and dragged him out of the Temple. The Temple doors were closed immediately. [31]While they were trying to kill Paul, the commander of the Roman army in Jerusalem learned that there was trouble in the whole city. [32]Immediately he took some officers and soldiers and ran to the place

1 PETER 1:17 "SO WHILE YOU ARE HERE ON EARTH, YOU SHOULD LIVE WITH RESPECT FOR GOD."

where the crowd was gathered. When the people saw them, they stopped beating Paul. [33]The commander went to Paul and arrested him. He told his soldiers to tie Paul with two chains. Then he asked who he was and what he had done wrong. [34]Some in the crowd were yelling one thing, and some were yelling another. Because of all this confusion and

shouting, the commander could not learn what had happened. So he ordered the soldiers to take Paul to the army building. [35]When Paul came to the steps, the soldiers had to carry him because the people were ready to hurt him. [36]The whole mob was following them, shouting, "Kill him!"

[37]As the soldiers were about to take Paul into the army building, he spoke to the commander, "May I say something to you?"

The commander said, "Do you speak Greek? [38]I thought you were the Egyptian who started some trouble against the government not long ago and led four thousand killers out to the desert."

[39]Paul said, "No, I am a Jew from Tarsus in the country of Cilicia. I am a citizen of that important city. Please, let me speak to the people."

[40]The commander gave permission, so Paul stood on the steps and waved his hand to quiet the people. When there was silence, he spoke to them in the Hebrew language.

PAUL SPEAKS TO THE PEOPLE

22 Paul said, "Friends, fellow Jews, listen to my defense to you." [2]When they heard him speaking the Hebrew language,[n] they became very quiet. Paul said, [3]"I am a Jew, born in Tarsus in the country of

Cilicia, but I grew up in this city. I was a student of Gamaliel,[n] who carefully taught me everything about the law of our ancestors. I was very serious about serving God, just as are all of you here today. [4]I persecuted the people who followed the Way of Jesus, and some of

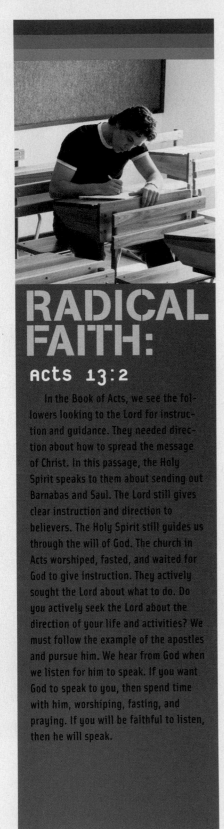

RADICAL FAITH:

Acts 13:2

In the Book of Acts, we see the followers looking to the Lord for instruction and guidance. They needed direction about how to spread the message of Christ. In this passage, the Holy Spirit speaks to them about sending out Barnabas and Saul. The Lord still gives clear instruction and direction to believers. The Holy Spirit still guides us through the will of God. The church in Acts worshiped, fasted, and waited for God to give instruction. They actively sought the Lord about what to do. Do you actively seek the Lord about the direction of your life and activities? We must follow the example of the apostles and pursue him. We hear from God when we listen for him to speak. If you want God to speak to you, then spend time with him, worshiping, fasting, and praying. If you will be faithful to listen, then he will speak.

them were even killed. I arrested men and women and put them in jail. [5]The high priest and the whole council of older leaders can tell you this is true. They gave me letters to the brothers in Damascus. So I was going there to arrest these people and bring them back to Jerusalem to be punished.

[6]"About noon when I came near Damascus, a bright light from heaven suddenly flashed all around me. [7]I fell to the ground and heard a voice saying, 'Saul, Saul, why are you persecuting me?' [8]I asked, 'Who are you, Lord?' The voice said, 'I am Jesus from Nazareth whom you are persecuting.' [9]Those who were with me did not hear the voice, but they saw the light. [10]I said, 'What shall I do, Lord?' The Lord answered, 'Get up and go to Damascus. There you will be told about all the things I have planned for you to do.' [11]I could not see, because the bright light had made me blind. So my companions led me into Damascus.

[12]"There a man named Ananias came to me. He was a religious man; he obeyed the law of Moses, and all the Jews who lived there respected him. [13]He stood by me and said, 'Brother Saul, see again!' Immediately I was able to see him. [14]He said, 'The God of our ancestors chose you long ago to know his plan, to see the Righteous One, and to hear words from him. [15]You will be his witness to all people, telling them about what you have seen and heard. [16]Now, why wait any longer? Get up, be baptized, and wash your sins away, trusting in him to save you.'

[17]"Later, when I returned to Jerusalem, I was praying in the Temple, and I saw a vision. [18]I saw the Lord saying to me, 'Hurry! Leave Jerusalem now! The people here will not accept the truth about me.' [19]But I said, 'Lord, they know that in every synagogue I put the believers in jail and beat them. [20]They also know I was there when Stephen, your witness, was killed. I stood there agreeing and holding the coats of those who were killing him!' [21]But the Lord said to me, 'Leave now. I will send you far away to the other nations.' "

[22]The crowd listened to Paul until he said this. Then they began shouting, "Kill him! Get him out of the world! He should not be allowed to live!" [23]They shouted, threw off their coats,[n] and threw dust into the air.[n]

[24]Then the commander ordered the soldiers to take Paul into the army building and beat him. He wanted to make Paul tell why the people were shouting against him like this. [25]But as the soldiers were tying him up, preparing to beat him, Paul said to an officer nearby, "Do you have the right to beat a Roman citizen[n] who has not been proven guilty?"

[26]When the officer heard this, he went to the commander and reported it. The officer said, "Do you know what you are doing? This man is a Roman citizen."

[27]The commander came to Paul and said, "Tell me, are you really a Roman citizen?"

He answered, "Yes."

[28]The commander said, "I paid a lot of money to become a Roman citizen."

But Paul said, "I was born a citizen."

[29]The men who were preparing to question Paul moved away from him immediately. The commander was frightened because he had already tied Paul, and Paul was a Roman citizen.

PAUL SPEAKS TO LEADERS

[30]The next day the commander decided to learn why the Jews were accusing Paul. So he ordered the leading priests and the council to meet. The commander took Paul's chains off. Then he brought Paul out and stood him before their meeting.

23 Paul looked at the council and said, "Brothers, I have lived my life without guilt feelings before God up to this day." [2]Ananias,[n] the high priest, heard this and

 22:23 threw off their coats This showed that the people were very angry with Paul. **22:23 threw dust into the air** This showed even greater anger. **22:25 Roman citizen** Roman law said that Roman citizens must not be beaten before they had a trial. **23:2 Ananias** This is not the same man named Ananias in Acts 22:12.

told the men who were standing near Paul to hit him on the mouth. [3]Paul said to Ananias, "God will hit you, too! You are like a wall that has been painted white. You sit there and judge me, using the law of Moses, but you are telling them to hit me, and that is against the law."

[4]The men standing near Paul said to him, "You cannot insult God's high priest like that!"

[5]Paul said, "Brothers, I did not know this

PSALM 37:7 "WAIT AND TRUST THE LORD."

man was the high priest. It is written in the Scriptures, 'You must not curse a leader of your people.' "[n]

[6]Some of the men in the meeting were Sadducees, and others were Pharisees. Knowing this, Paul shouted to them, "My brothers, I am a Pharisee, and my father was a Pharisee. I am on trial here because I believe that people will rise from the dead."

[7]When Paul said this, there was an argument between the Pharisees and the Sadducees, and the group was divided. [8](The Sadducees do not believe in angels or spirits or that people will rise from the dead. But the Pharisees believe in them all.) [9]So there was a great uproar. Some of the teachers of the law, who were Pharisees, stood up and argued,

"We find nothing wrong with this man. Maybe an angel or a spirit did speak to him."

[10]The argument was beginning to turn into such a fight that the commander was afraid some evil people would tear Paul to pieces. So he told the soldiers to go down and take Paul away and put him in the army building.

[11]The next night the Lord came and stood by Paul. He said, "Be brave! You have told people in Jerusalem about me. You must do the same in Rome."

[12]In the morning some evil people made a plan to kill Paul, and they took an oath not to eat or drink anything until they had killed him. [13]There were more than forty men who made this plan. [14]They went to the leading priests and the older leaders and said, "We have taken an oath not to eat or drink until we have killed Paul. [15]So this is what we want you to do: Send a message to the commander to bring Paul out to you as though you want to ask him more questions. We will be waiting to kill him while he is on the way here."

[16]But Paul's nephew heard about this plan and went to the army building and told Paul. [17]Then Paul called one of the officers and said, "Take this young man to the commander. He has a message for him."

[18]So the officer brought Paul's nephew to

RANDOM THINGS TO DO DURING CHURCH IF YOU CAN'T SING

1. SING ANYWAY.
2. STUDY THE SONG LYRICS.
3. TELL JESUS YOU WANT TO FOLLOW HIM.
4. PRAY FOR THE PASTOR.
5. HUM.
6. ASK GOD TO SPOTLIGHT ANYTHING YOU NEED TO GET RIGHT WITH HIM.
7. READ THE SCRIPTURE LESSONS.
8. HELP WITH THE SOUND SYSTEM.
9. DANCE.
10. REMEMBER THAT WORSHIP IS NOT ABOUT YOU.

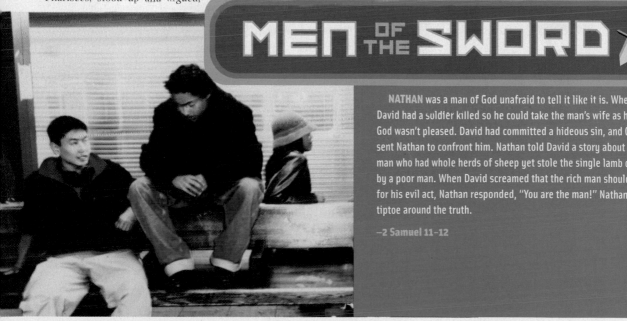

MEN OF THE SWORD

NATHAN was a man of God unafraid to tell it like it is. When King David had a soldier killed so he could take the man's wife as his own, God wasn't pleased. David had committed a hideous sin, and God sent Nathan to confront him. Nathan told David a story about a rich man who had whole herds of sheep yet stole the single lamb owned by a poor man. When David screamed that the rich man should die for his evil act, Nathan responded, "You are the man!" Nathan didn't tiptoe around the truth.

—2 Samuel 11–12

 23:5 'You . . . people.' Quotation from Exodus 22:28.

ACTS 16:23

WORD: Speaking out for Jesus sometimes brings harsh suffering.

WALK IT: Find out more about Christian brothers and sisters suffering all over the world today. Surf to www.opendoorsusa.org and learn what you can do to help!

the commander and said, "The prisoner, Paul, asked me to bring this young man to you. He wants to tell you something."

¹⁹The commander took the young man's hand and led him to a place where they could be alone. He asked, "What do you want to tell me?"

²⁰The young man said, "The Jews have decided to ask you to bring Paul down to their council meeting tomorrow. They want you to think they are going to ask him more questions. ²¹But don't believe them! More than forty men are hiding and waiting to kill Paul. They have all taken an oath not to eat or drink until they have killed him. Now they are waiting for you to agree."

²²The commander sent the young man away, ordering him, "Don't tell anyone that you have told me about their plan."

PAUL IS SENT TO CAESAREA

²³Then the commander called two officers and said, "I need some men to go to Caesarea. Get two hundred soldiers, seventy horsemen, and two hundred men with spears ready to leave at nine o'clock tonight. ²⁴Get some

SPECIAL OLYMPICS is an international organization dedicated to empowering individuals with mental retardation to become physically fit, productive, and respected members of society through sports training and competition. Special Olympics offers children and adults with mental retardation year-round training and competition in twenty-six Olympic-type summer and winter sports. There is no charge to participate in Special Olympics.

Special Olympics currently serves more than 1 million persons with mental retardation in more than 200 programs in more than 150 countries. Special Olympics relies on more than 500,000 volunteers at all levels of the movement to ensure that every athlete is offered a quality sports training and competition experience. Volunteers include civic and fraternal groups, high school and college students, amateur and professional athletes, corporate employees, sports officials, coaches, teachers, parents, and retired persons.

To get involved, go to www.specialolympics.org.

COUNT ON IT

ACTS 17:28

Ever feel like you're expected to be somebody you're not? Straight-A student? Club president? Perfect little gentleman? Sure, there are times when you need to venture out of your comfort zone and expect more of yourself than what comes easily for you. And God has given you natural, inborn abilities that (as you begin to spot them) will shape the person you are. He didn't just bundle up a bunch of leftovers and throw them in your direction. He knew what he wanted to do in you, what he wanted you to accomplish, what he wanted you to be good at. And he knew exactly what you'd need in order to pull it off.

He's placed spiritual gifts in you, unique and powerful tools that shape the way you serve him and relate to others—as a peacemaker, an encourager, a leader.

You're not an afterthought, but a complete package of Christlike potential, waiting to be discovered and put into practice. And you can start living it today right where you are, with the people right around you. You'll be miserable being anybody else.

horses for Paul to ride so he can be taken to Governor Felix safely." [25]And he wrote a letter that said:

[26]From Claudius Lysias.

To the Most Excellent Governor Felix: Greetings.

[27]Some of the Jews had taken this man and planned to kill him. But I learned that he is a Roman citizen, so I went with my soldiers and saved him. [28]I wanted to know why they were accusing him, so I brought him before their council meeting. [29]I learned that these people said Paul did some things that were wrong by their own laws, but no charge was worthy of jail or death. [30]When I was told that some of them were planning to kill Paul, I sent him to you at once. I also told them to tell you what they have against him.

[31]So the soldiers did what they were told and took Paul and brought him to the city of Antipatris that night. [32]The next day the horsemen went with Paul to Caesarea, but the other soldiers went back to the army building in Jerusalem. [33]When the horsemen came to Caesarea and gave the letter to the governor, they turned Paul over to him. [34]The governor read the letter and asked Paul, "What area are you from?" When he learned that Paul was from Cilicia, [35]he said, "I will hear your case when those who are against you come here, too." Then the governor gave orders for Paul to be kept under guard in Herod's palace.

PAUL IS ACCUSED

24 Five days later Ananias, the high priest, went to the city of Caesarea with some of the older leaders and a lawyer named Tertullus. They had come to make charges against Paul before the governor. [2]Paul was called into the meeting, and Tertullus began to accuse him, saying, "Most Excellent Felix! Our people enjoy much peace because of you, and many wrong things in our country are being made right through your wise help. [3]We accept these things always and in every place, and we are thankful for them. [4]But not wanting to take any more of your time, I beg you to be kind and listen to our few words. [5]We have found this man to be a trouble-maker, stirring up his people everywhere in the world. He is a leader of the Nazarene group. [6]Also, he was trying to make the Temple unclean, but we stopped him." [8]By asking him questions yourself, you can decide if all these things are true." [9]The others agreed and said that all of this was true.

[10]When the governor made a sign for Paul to speak, Paul said, "Governor Felix, I know you have been a judge over this nation for a long time. So I am happy to defend myself before you. [11]You can learn for yourself that I went to worship in Jerusalem only twelve days ago. [12]Those who are accusing me did not find me arguing with anyone in the Temple or stirring up the people in the synagogues or in the city. [13]They cannot prove the things they are saying against me now. [14]But I will tell you this: I worship the God of our ancestors as a follower of the Way of Jesus. The others say that the Way of Jesus is not the right way. But I believe everything that is taught in the law of

24:6 Verse 6 Some Greek copies add 6b-8a: "And we wanted to judge him by our own law. [7]But the officer Lysias came and used much force to take him from us. [8]And Lysias commanded those who wanted to accuse Paul to come to you."

INSIDE HER HEAD

Q: WHY DO GIRLS LIKE FLOWERS AND JUNK? WHAT'S THE BIG DEAL?

A: THEY SMELL BETTER THAN BOYS. IT'S NOT LIKE I WANT SOCKS, AS IN "HERE ARE SOME SOCKS—IT'S MY SPECIAL PRESENT TO YOU."

Moses and that is written in the books of the Prophets. ¹⁵I have the same hope in God that they have—the hope that all people, good and bad, will surely be raised from the dead. ¹⁶This is why I always try to do what I believe is right before God and people.

¹⁷"After being away from Jerusalem for several years, I went back to bring money to my people and to offer sacrifices. ¹⁸I was doing this when they found me in the Temple. I had finished the cleansing ceremony and had not made any trouble; no people were gathering around me. ¹⁹But there were some people from the country of Asia who should be here, standing before you. If I have really done anything wrong, they are the ones who should accuse me. ²⁰Or ask these people here if they found any wrong in me when I stood before the council in Jerusalem. ²¹But I did shout one thing when I stood before them: 'You are judging me today because I believe that people will rise from the dead!' "

²²Felix already understood much about the Way of Jesus. He stopped the trial and said, "When commander Lysias comes here, I will decide your case." ²³Felix told the officer to keep Paul guarded but to give him some freedom and to let his friends bring what he needed.

PAUL SPEAKS TO FELIX AND HIS WIFE

²⁴After some days Felix came with his wife, Drusilla, who was Jewish, and asked for Paul to be brought to him. He listened to Paul talk about believing in Christ Jesus. ²⁵But Felix became afraid when Paul spoke about living right, self-control, and the time when God will judge the world. He said, "Go away now. When I have more time, I will call for you." ²⁶At the same time Felix hoped that Paul would give him some money, so he often sent for Paul and talked with him.

²⁷But after two years, Felix was replaced by Porcius Festus as governor. But Felix had left Paul in prison to please the Jews.

PAUL ASKS TO SEE CAESAR

25 Three days after Festus became governor, he went from Caesarea to Jerusalem. ²There the leading priests and the important leaders made charges against Paul before Festus. ³They asked Festus to do them a favor. They wanted him to send Paul back to Jerusalem, because they had a plan to kill him on the way. ⁴But Festus answered that Paul would be kept in Caesarea and that he himself was returning there soon. ⁵He said, "Some of your leaders should go with me. They can accuse the man there in Caesarea, if he has really done something wrong."

⁶Festus stayed in Jerusalem another eight or ten days and then went back to Caesarea. The next day he told the soldiers to bring Paul before him. Festus was seated on the judge's seat ⁷when Paul came into the room. The people who had come from Jerusalem stood around him, making serious charges against him, which they could not prove. ⁸This is what Paul said to defend himself: "I have done nothing wrong against the law, against the Temple, or against Caesar."

⁹But Festus wanted to please the people. So he asked Paul, "Do you want to go to Jerusalem for me to judge you there on these charges?"

RANDOM WAYS TO REMEMBER PEOPLE'S NAMES

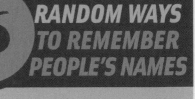

1. REPEAT THEIR NAME RIGHT AWAY.

2. THINK OF SOMEONE ELSE YOU KNOW WITH THAT NAME.

3. CONNECT THEIR NAME TO SOME UNUSUAL FEATURE—HAIR, HEIGHT, EYES, NOSE, MOUTH.

4. WRITE THEIR NAME DOWN.

5. MAKE A RHYME OUT OF THEIR NAME.

6. ASK HOW TO SPELL A NAME THAT ISN'T OBVIOUS.

7. SAY, "TELL ME YOUR NAME AGAIN" IF YOU FORGET BY THE END OF THE CONVERSATION.

8. ASK A FRIEND FOR THAT NAME YOU FORGOT.

9. GLANCE AROUND A ROOM AND DRILL YOURSELF ON EVERYONE'S NAME.

10. DECIDE IT'S IMPORTANT TO REMEMBER THE NAME OF EVERYONE YOU MEET.

¹⁰Paul said, "I am standing at Caesar's judgment seat now, where I should be judged. I have done nothing wrong to them; you know

39 PERCENT OF TENTH GRADERS SAY THEY'VE USED MARIJUANA AT LEAST ONCE. –CHILD TRENDS DATABANK

issues

RACE

SO WHEN WAS THE LAST TIME you told a joke laced with humor about people of another country or color? Or have you ever stayed away from a mall or a theater or a concert because people different from you hang out there? Maybe you're surprised to see an affluent African-American or Hispanic person. Or you automatically think all white guys are dumb jocks. You might brush off these "little things," but this is racism. The New Testament says there is neither slave nor free, Jew nor Greek. This means that God doesn't see race—he sees souls. Start looking for people's souls when you see them, not the color of their skin. You might be surprised to find out who you become friends with.

EXPERTS ANSWER YOUR QUESTIONS

Q. *Why doesn't Jesus come back right now and take us to a better place?*

A. First of all, this is a human question no man knows the answer to. But suppose you're a Christian, but you accepted Jesus just yesterday. Do you still wish Jesus had come back last week? Jesus isn't slow about coming back. He's just giving people time to turn to him. See for yourself in 2 Peter 3:9.

Q. *I'm disgusted when I see Christians littering. Don't they care about the environment?*

A. There's not a variety of stupidity Christians haven't displayed. But don't assume all Christians are like that. Many believers realize God made the planet, and they do at least as well as their neighbors in reducing, reusing, and recycling. Help us do better.

Q. *Can a Christian go to war and kill?*

A. Some believers are out-and-out pacifists who believe that any war is so wrong it shouldn't be fought. Many others believe the Bible puts the governments in charge of protecting people. To the extent that a person has the task of carrying out that job, they are obeying God.

this is true. [11]If I have done something wrong and the law says I must die, I do not ask to be saved from death. But if these charges are not true, then no one can give me to them. I want Caesar to hear my case!"

[12]Festus talked about this with his advisers. Then he said, "You have asked to see Caesar, so you will go to Caesar!"

PAUL BEFORE KING AGRIPPA

[13]A few days later King Agrippa and Bernice came to Caesarea to visit Festus. [14]They stayed there for some time, and Festus told the king about Paul's case. Festus said, "There is a man that Felix left in prison. [15]When I went to Jerusalem, the leading priests and the older leaders there made charges against him, asking me to sentence him to death. [16]But I answered, 'When a man is accused of a crime, Romans do not hand him over until he has been allowed to face his accusers and defend himself against their charges.' [17]So when these people came here to Caesarea for the trial, I did not waste time. The next day I sat on the judge's seat and commanded that the man be brought in. [18]They stood up and accused him, but not of any serious crime as I thought they would. [19]The

things they said were about their own religion and about a man named Jesus who died. But Paul said that he is still alive. [20]Not knowing how to find out about these questions, I asked Paul, 'Do you want to go to Jerusalem and be judged there?' [21]But he asked to be kept in Caesarea. He wants a decision from the emperor.[n] So I ordered that he be held until I could send him to Caesar."

[22]Agrippa said to Festus, "I would also like to hear this man myself."

Festus said, "Tomorrow you will hear him."

[23]The next day Agrippa and Bernice appeared with great show, acting like very important people. They went into the judgment room with the army leaders and the important men of Caesarea. Then Festus ordered the soldiers to bring Paul in. [24]Festus said, "King Agrippa and all who are gathered here with us, you see this man.

All the people, here and in Jerusalem, have complained to me about him, shouting that he should not live any longer. [25]When I judged him, I found no reason to order his death. But since he asked to be judged by Caesar, I decided to send him. [26]But I have nothing definite to

ROMANS 8:31 "IF GOD IS WITH US, NO ONE CAN DEFEAT US."

write the emperor about him. So I have brought him before all of you—especially you, King Agrippa. I hope you can question him and give me something to write. [27]I think it is foolish to send a prisoner to Caesar without telling what charges are against him."

PAUL DEFENDS HIMSELF

26 Agrippa said to Paul, "You may now speak to defend yourself."

Then Paul raised his hand and began to speak. [2]He said, "King Agrippa, I am very happy to stand before you and will answer all the charges the evil people make against me. [3]You know so

much about all the customs and the things they argue about, so please listen to me patiently.

[4]"All my people know about my whole life, how I lived from the beginning in my own country and later in Jerusalem. [5]They have known me for a long time. If they want to, they can tell you that I was a good Pharisee. And the Pharisees obey the laws of my tradition more carefully than any other group. [6]Now I am on trial because I hope for the promise that God made to our ancestors. [7]This is the promise that the twelve tribes of our people hope to receive as they serve God day and night. My king, they have accused me because I hope for this same promise! [8]Why do any of you people think it is impossible for God to raise people from the dead?

[9]"I, too, thought I ought to do many things against Jesus from Nazareth. [10]And that is

25:21 emperor The ruler of the Roman Empire, which was almost all the known world.

> **FEWER THAN THREE OUT OF FIVE TEENS LIVE IN THE SAME HOME WITH BOTH OF THEIR NATURAL PARENTS.** –BARNA RESEARCH GROUP

what I did in Jerusalem. The leading priests gave me the power to put many of God's people in jail, and when they were being killed, I agreed it was a good thing. [11]In every synagogue, I often punished them and tried to make them speak against Jesus. I was so angry against them I even went to other cities to find them and punish them.

[12]"One time the leading priests gave me permission and the power to go to Damascus. [13]On the way there, at noon, I saw a light from heaven. It was brighter than the sun and flashed all around me and those who were traveling with me. [14]We all fell to the ground. Then I heard a voice speaking to me in the Hebrew language,[n] saying, 'Saul, Saul, why are you persecuting me? You are only hurting yourself

> **PSALM 40:11 "LORD, DO NOT HOLD BACK YOUR MERCY FROM ME; LET YOUR LOVE AND TRUTH ALWAYS PROTECT ME."**

by fighting me.' [15]I said, 'Who are you, Lord?' The Lord said, 'I am Jesus, the one you are persecuting. [16]Stand up! I have chosen you to be my servant and my witness—you will tell people the things that you have seen and the things that I will show you. This is why I have come to you today. [17]I will keep you safe from your own people and also from the others. I am sending you to them [18]to open their eyes so that they may turn away from darkness to the light, away from the power of Satan and to God. Then their sins can be forgiven, and they can have a place with those people who have been made holy by believing in me.'

[19]"King Agrippa, after I had this vision from heaven, I obeyed it. [20]I began telling people that they should change their hearts and lives and turn to God and do things to show they

really had changed. I told this first to those in Damascus, then in Jerusalem, and in every part of Judea, and also to the other people. [21]This is why the Jews took me and were trying to kill me in the Temple. [22]But God has helped me, and so I stand here today, telling all people, small and great, what I have seen. But I am saying only what Moses and the prophets said would happen— [23]that the Christ would die, and as the first to rise from the dead, he would bring light to all people."

PAUL TRIES TO PERSUADE AGRIPPA

[24]While Paul was saying these things to defend himself, Festus said loudly, "Paul, you are out of your mind! Too much study has driven you crazy!"

[25]Paul said, "Most excellent Festus, I am not crazy. My words are true and sensible. [26]King Agrippa knows about these things, and I can speak freely to him. I know he has heard about all of these things, because they did not happen off in a corner. [27]King Agrippa, do you believe what the prophets wrote? I know you believe."

[28]King Agrippa said to Paul, "Do you think you can persuade me to become a Christian in such a short time?"

[29]Paul said, "Whether it is a short or a long time, I pray to God that not only you but every person listening to me today would be saved and be like me—except for these chains I have."

[30]Then King Agrippa, Governor Festus, Bernice, and all the people sitting with them stood up [31]and left the room. Talking to each other, they said, "There is no reason why this man should die or be put in jail." [32]And Agrippa said to Festus, "We could let this man go free, but he has asked Caesar to hear his case."

PAUL SAILS FOR ROME

27 It was decided that we would sail for Italy. An officer named Julius, who served in the emperor's[n] army, guarded Paul and some other prisoners. [2]We got on a ship that was from the city of Adramyttium and was

about to sail to different ports in the country of Asia. Aristarchus, a man from the city of Thessalonica in Macedonia, went with us. [3]The next day we came to Sidon. Julius was very good to Paul and gave him freedom to go visit his friends, who took care of his needs. [4]We left Sidon and sailed close to the island of Cyprus, because the wind was blowing against us. [5]We went across the sea by Cilicia and Pamphylia and landed at the city of Myra, in Lycia. [6]There the officer found a ship from Alexandria that was going to Italy, so he put us on it.

[7]We sailed slowly for many days. We had a hard time reaching Cnidus because the wind was blowing against us, and we could not go any farther. So we sailed by the south side of the island of Crete near Salmone. [8]Sailing past it was hard. Then we came to a place called Fair Havens, near the city of Lasea.

[9]We had lost much time, and it was now dangerous to sail, because it was already after the Day of Cleansing.[n] So Paul warned them, [10]"Men, I can see there will be a lot of trouble on this trip. The ship, the cargo, and even our lives may be lost." [11]But the captain and the owner of the ship did not agree with Paul, and the officer believed what the captain and owner of the ship said. [12]Since that harbor was not a good place for the ship to stay for the winter, most of the men decided that the ship should leave. They hoped we could go to Phoenix and stay there for the winter. Phoenix, a city on the island of Crete, had a harbor which faced southwest and northwest.

THE STORM

[13]When a good wind began to blow from the south, the men on the ship thought, "This is the wind we wanted, and now we have it." So they pulled up the anchor, and we sailed very close to the island of Crete. [14]But then a very strong wind named the "northeaster" came from the island. [15]The ship was caught in it and could not sail against it. So we stopped trying and let the wind carry us. [16]When we went below a small island named Cauda, we were barely able to bring in the lifeboat. [17]After the men took the lifeboat in, they tied ropes around the ship to hold it together. The men were afraid that the ship would hit the sandbanks of Syrtis,[n] so they lowered the sail and let the wind carry the ship. [18]The next day the

RADICAL FAITH:

Acts 16:30-31

Tommy thought that since his family went to church every Sunday and he knew the words to the hymns that he must be saved. Alexa goes to a church where they don't talk about being saved. She's heard other people talk about it, but she's confused. Every night she begs God to take her to heaven if she dies in her sleep. Every time she thinks about this "saved" thing, she gets scared. No one has ever explained it to her, and she's too proud to ask. Joey heard from a friend that God loves everybody, and that God would let everyone into heaven. Sounds great.

Tommy, Alexa, and Joey aren't saved. Here's the answer for them and for you: "Believe in the Lord Jesus and you will be saved." When you decide that you believe in God and in his Son, Jesus, and in the fact that Jesus died on a cross for you, then you are saved from an eternity away from God. That's salvation. Your faith in Jesus saves you.

Are you unsure of your salvation? Then nail it down once and for all. Tell the Lord that you love him, that you believe that Jesus died for you, and that you want him to be in charge of your life.

storm was blowing us so hard that the men threw out some of the cargo. [19]A day later with their own hands they threw out the ship's equipment. [20]When we could not see the sun or the stars for many days, and the storm was very bad, we lost all hope of being saved.

[21]After the men had gone without food for a long time, Paul stood up before them and said, "Men, you should have listened to me. You should not have sailed from Crete. Then you would not have all this trouble and loss. [22]But now I tell you to cheer up because none of you will die. Only the ship will be lost. [23]Last night an angel came to me from the God I belong to and worship. [24]The angel said, 'Paul, do not be afraid. You must stand before Caesar. And God has promised you that he will save the lives of everyone sailing with you.' [25]So men, have courage. I trust in God that everything will happen as his angel told me. [26]But we will crash on an island."

[27]On the fourteenth night we were still being carried around in the Adriatic Sea.[n] About midnight the sailors thought we were close to land, [28]so they lowered a rope with a weight on the end of it into the water. They found that the water was one hundred twenty feet deep. They went a little farther and lowered the rope again. It was ninety feet deep. [29]The sailors were afraid that we would hit the rocks, so they threw four anchors into the water and prayed for daylight to come. [30]Some of the sailors wanted to leave the ship, and they lowered the lifeboat, pretending they were throwing more anchors from the front of the ship. [31]But Paul told the officer and the other soldiers, "If these men do not stay in the ship, your lives cannot be saved." [32]So the soldiers cut the ropes and let the lifeboat fall into the water.

[33]Just before dawn Paul began persuading all the people to eat something. He said, "For the past fourteen days you have been waiting and watching and not eating. [34]Now I beg you to eat something. You need it to stay alive. None of you will lose even one hair off your heads." [35]After he said this, Paul took some bread and thanked God for it before all of them. He broke off a piece and began eating. [36]They all felt better and started eating, too. [37]There were two hundred seventy-six people

on the ship. [38]When they had eaten all they wanted, they began making the ship lighter by throwing the grain into the sea.

THE SHIP IS DESTROYED

[39]When daylight came, the sailors saw land. They did not know what land it was, but they saw a bay with a beach and wanted to sail the ship to the beach if they could. [40]So they cut the ropes to the anchors and left the anchors in the sea. At the same time, they untied the ropes that were holding the rudders. Then they raised the front sail into the wind and sailed toward the beach. [41]But the ship hit a sandbank. The front of the ship stuck there and could not move, but the back of the ship began to break up from the big waves.

[42]The soldiers decided to kill the prisoners so none of them could swim away and escape. [43]But Julius, the officer, wanted to let Paul live and did not allow the soldiers to kill the prisoners. Instead he ordered everyone who could swim to jump into the water first and swim to land. [44]The rest were to follow using wooden boards or pieces of the ship. And this is how all the people made it safely to land.

PAUL ON THE ISLAND OF MALTA

28 When we were safe on land, we learned that the island was called Malta. [2]The people who lived there were very good to us. Because it was raining and very cold, they made a fire and welcomed all of us. [3]Paul gathered a pile of sticks and was putting them on the fire when a poisonous snake came out because of the heat and bit him on the hand. [4]The people living on the island saw the snake hanging from Paul's hand and said to each other, "This man must be a murderer! He did not die in the sea, but Justice[n] does not want him to live." [5]But Paul shook the snake off into the fire and was not hurt. [6]The people thought that Paul would swell up or fall down dead. They waited and watched him for a long time, but nothing bad happened to him. So they changed their minds and said, "He is a god!"

[7]There were some fields around there owned by Publius, an important man on the island. He welcomed us into his home and was very good to us for three days. [8]Publius' father was sick with a fever and dysentery.[n] Paul went to him, prayed, and put his hands on the man and healed him. [9]After this, all the other

---

27:27 Adriatic Sea The sea between Greece and Italy, including the central Mediterranean.   28:4 Justice The people thought there was a god named Justice who would punish bad people.   28:8 dysentery A sickness like diarrhea.

sick people on the island came to Paul, and he healed them, too. [10-11]The people on the island gave us many honors. When we were ready to leave, three months later, they gave us the things we needed.

PAUL GOES TO ROME

We got on a ship from Alexandria that had stayed on the island during the winter. On the front of the ship was the sign of the twin gods.[n] [12]We stopped at Syracuse for three days. [13]From there we sailed to Rhegium. The next day a wind began to blow from the south, and a day later we came to Puteoli. [14]We found some believers there who asked us to stay with them for a week. Finally, we came to Rome. [15]The believers in Rome heard that we were there and came out as far as the Market of Appius[n] and the Three Inns[n] to meet us. When Paul saw them, he was encouraged and thanked God.

PAUL IN ROME

[16]When we arrived at Rome, Paul was allowed to live alone, with the soldier who guarded him.

[17]Three days later Paul sent for the leaders there. When they came together, he said, "Brothers, I have done nothing against our people or the customs of our ancestors. But I was arrested in Jerusalem and given to the Romans. [18]After they asked me many questions, they could find no reason why I should be killed. They wanted to let me go free, [19]but the evil people there argued against that. So I had to ask to come to Rome to have my trial before Caesar. But I have no charge to bring against my own people. [20]That is why I wanted to see you and talk with you. I am bound with this chain because I believe in the hope of Israel."

[21]They answered Paul, "We have received no letters from Judea about you. None of our Jewish brothers who have come from there brought news or told us anything bad about you. [22]But we want to hear your ideas, because we know that people everywhere are speaking against this religious group."

[23]Paul and the people chose a day for a meeting and on that day many more of the Jews met with Paul at the place he was staying. He spoke to them all day long. Using the law of Moses and the prophets' writings, he explained the kingdom of God, and he tried to persuade them to believe these things about Jesus. [24]Some believed what Paul said, but others did not. [25]So they argued and began leaving after Paul said one more thing to them: "The Holy Spirit spoke the truth to your ancestors through Isaiah the prophet, saying,

[26]'Go to this people and say:
You will listen and listen, but you will
not understand.
You will look and look, but you will
not learn,
[27]because these people have become
stubborn.
They don't hear with their ears,
and they have closed their eyes.
Otherwise, they might really understand
what they see with their eyes
and hear with their ears.
They might really understand in their minds
and come back to me and be healed.'

Isaiah 6:9-10

[28]"I want you to know that God has also sent his salvation to all nations, and they will listen!" [29][n]

[30]Paul stayed two full years in his own rented house and welcomed all people who came to visit him. [31]He boldly preached about the kingdom of God and taught about the Lord Jesus Christ, and no one tried to stop him.

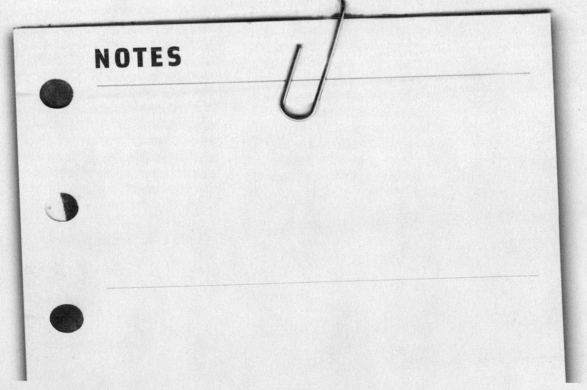

NOTES

28:10–11 twin gods Statues of Castor and Pollux, gods in old Greek tales. **28:15 Market of Appius** A town about twenty-seven miles from Rome. **28:15 Three Inns** A town about thirty miles from Rome. **28:29 Verse 29** Some late Greek copies add verse 29: "After Paul said this, the Jews left. They were arguing very much with each other."

ROMANS

THE BASICS OF THE CHRISTIAN FAITH

If you're looking for an easy read, the Book of Romans might not fit the bill. But if you really want to get into the meat of what it means to be a Christian, well, you won't find a better place to start. This letter to believers living in Rome is Paul's masterpiece, a well-crafted introduction to the basics of the Christian faith. It's written after a lifetime of ministry and devotion to being a *real* Christian. Paul didn't just talk the talk; he walked the walk. Here are some key lessons he learned along the way:

Everyone has sinned and needs God's forgiveness (3:23).

God makes forgiveness available to everyone through his Son, Jesus Christ. If we simply have faith in Jesus, Paul explains, God makes us "free from sin" (3:24).

We should live like we're taking our cues from God, not from the devil. God is good. We should do everything that is good and pleasing to him (12:1-2).

Romans ends with a few chapters of easy-reading, practical advice about daily living. But a good chunk of the book is filled with Godspeak, or theology. Paul tosses around massive concepts like justification and sanctification, but these early chapters are critical to explaining why Christians believe and behave the way they do. They unlock why we often struggle with sin and tell us how we can find freedom through Christ's work on the cross and the presence of the Holy Spirit in our lives today. Study this message and you will be a better motivated and more effective servant of God. Romans is a must-read if you want to take your faith seriously.

COUNT ON IT

ROMANS 1:17

Most people want to do something so that God will like them. They think that if they're really good, if they do every-thing—or most things—right, then God will accept them. It makes people feel really good to think there's something so neat about them that they can earn a spot in heaven.

The truth is that no one can be *that* good. There's something special about every single person on earth, but there's some junk in everyone too. God doesn't accept anyone's goodness as good enough to get into heaven. But that's not the end of the story. "The Good News shows how God makes people right with himself—that it begins and ends with faith." In other words, God accepts those who come to him in faith. Now *that's* good news. It's not being good that gets God to accept you; it's having faith in his Son. You don't have to settle for some mealy-mouthed, lip service faith. You can have a faith so strong, so alive that you can't wait to commit your whole life to Jesus. Then, as Romans 1:17 says, you will live—not just physically, but live with strength and power because you're trusting in him.

Keep renewing your mind with God's Word. That's how you build faith. Do your best to live the way God wants you to just because you love him and you want to please him. Faith sets you free from the vicious cycle of constantly trying to work your way into God's good graces.

1 From Paul, a servant of Christ Jesus. God called me to be an apostle and chose me to tell the Good News.

²God promised this Good News long ago through his prophets, as it is written in the Holy Scriptures. ³⁻⁴The Good News is about God's Son, Jesus Christ our Lord. As a man, he was born from the family of David. But through the Spirit of holiness he was appointed to be God's Son with great power by rising from the dead. ⁵Through Christ, God gave me the special work of an apostle, which was to lead people of all nations to believe and obey. I do this work for him. ⁶And you who are in Rome are also called to belong to Jesus Christ.

⁷To all of you in Rome whom God loves and has called to be his holy people:

Grace and peace to you from God our Father and the Lord Jesus Christ.

A PRAYER OF THANKS

⁸First I want to say that I thank my God through Jesus Christ for all of you, because people everywhere in the world are talking about your faith. ⁹God, whom I serve with my whole heart by telling the Good News about his Son, knows that I always mention you ¹⁰every time I pray. I pray that I will be allowed to come to you, and this will happen if God wants it. ¹¹I want very much to see you, to give you some spiritual gift to make you strong. ¹²I mean that I want us to help each other with the faith we have. Your faith will help me, and my faith will help you. ¹³Brothers and sisters,ⁿ I want you to know that I planned many times to come to you, but this has not been possible. I wanted to come so that I could help you grow spiritually as I have helped the other non-Jewish people.

¹⁴I have a duty to all people—Greeks and those who are not Greeks, the wise and the foolish. ¹⁵That is why I want so much to preach the Good News to you in Rome.

¹⁶I am proud of the Good News, because it is the power God uses to save everyone who believes—to save the Jews first, and also to save those who are not Jews. ¹⁷The Good News shows how God makes people right with him-self—that it begins and ends with faith. As the Scripture says, "But those who are right with God will live by trusting in him."ⁿ

ALL PEOPLE HAVE DONE WRONG

¹⁸God's anger is shown from heaven against all the evil and wrong things people do. By their own evil lives they hide the truth. ¹⁹God shows his anger because some knowledge of him has been made clear to them. Yes, God has shown himself to them. ²⁰There are things about him that people cannot see—his eternal

BIBLE BASICS

Disciples are people who follow Christ. The Gospels tell about twelve men who followed Jesus, lived with him, and were all about his ministry. Today there are millions of people who are disciples of Christ. It just means that they listen to his teach-ings (through the Bible) and want to follow them.

1:13 Brothers and sisters Although the Greek text says "Brothers" here and throughout this book, Paul's words were meant for the entire church, including men and women.   1:17 "But those . . . him." Quotation from Habakkuk 2:4.

power and all the things that make him God. But since the beginning of the world those things have been easy to understand by what God has made. So people have no excuse for the bad things they do. 21They knew God, but they did not give glory to God or thank him. Their thinking became useless. Their foolish minds were filled with darkness. 22They said they were wise, but they became fools. 23They traded the glory of God who lives forever for the worship of idols made to look like earthly people, birds, animals, and snakes.

24Because they did these things, God left them and let them go their sinful way, wanting only to do evil. As a result, they became full of sexual sin, using their bodies wrongly with each other. 25They traded the truth of God for a lie. They worshiped and served what had been created instead of the God who created those things, who should be praised forever. Amen.

26Because people did those things, God left them and let them do the shameful things they wanted to do. Women stopped having natural sex and started having sex with other women. 27In the same way, men stopped having natural sex and began wanting each other. Men did shameful things with other men, and in their bodies they received the punishment for those wrongs.

28People did not think it was important to have a true knowledge of God. So God left them and allowed them to have their own worthless thinking and to do things they should not do. 29They are filled with every kind of sin, evil, selfishness, and hatred. They are full of jealousy, murder, fighting, lying, and thinking the worst about each other. They gossip 30and say evil things about each other. They hate God. They are rude and conceited and brag about themselves. They invent ways of doing evil. They do not obey their parents. 31They are foolish, they do not keep their promises, and they show no kindness or mercy to others. 32They know God's law says that those who live like this should die. But they themselves not only continue to do these evil things, they applaud others who do them.

GET OUT THERE

The mission of the NATIONAL COALITION FOR THE HOMELESS is to end homelessness. Toward this end, the NCH engages in public education, policy advocacy, and grassroots organizing. They focus their work in the following four areas: housing justice, economic justice, health care justice, and civil rights.

Volunteering your time to work directly with people experiencing homelessness is one of the best ways to learn about homelessness and help to meet immediate needs at the same time. There is a lot of "behind the scenes" work (filing, sorting clothes, cutting vegetables, etc.) to be done at shelters and other direct service agencies. Think about what you do best and the kind of setting in which you work most effectively—with individuals or groups, with men, women, or children, and so on. Then call a few places, ask what help they need, and arrange for a visit.

To join in helping the homeless, check out www.nationalhomeless.org.

YOU PEOPLE ALSO ARE SINFUL

2 If you think you can judge others, you are wrong. When you judge them, you are really judging yourself guilty, because you do the same things they do. [2]God judges those who do wrong things, and we know that his judging is right. [3]You judge those who do wrong, but you do wrong yourselves. Do you think you will be able to escape the judgment of God? [4]He has been very kind and patient, waiting for you to change, but you think nothing of his kindness. Perhaps you do not understand that God is kind to you so you will change your hearts and lives. [5]But you are stubborn and refuse to change, so you are making your own punishment even greater on the day he shows his anger. On that day everyone will see God's right judgments. [6]God will reward or punish every person for what that person has done. [7]Some people, by always continuing to do good, live for God's glory, for honor, and for life that has no end. God will give them life forever. [8]But other people are selfish. They refuse to follow truth and, instead, follow evil. God will give them his punishment and anger. [9]He will give trouble and suffering to everyone who does evil—to the Jews first and also to those who are not Jews. [10]But he will give glory, honor, and peace to everyone who does good—to the Jews first and also to those who are not Jews. [11]For God judges all people in the same way.

[12]People who do not have the law and who are sinners will be lost, although they do not have the law. And, in the same way, those who have the law and are sinners will be judged by the law. [13]Hearing the law does not make people right with God. It is those who obey the law who will be right with him. [14](Those who are not Jews do not have the law, but when they freely do what the law commands, they are the law for themselves. This is true even though they do not have the law. [15]They show that in their hearts they know what is right and wrong, just as the law commands. And they show this by their consciences. Sometimes their thoughts tell them they did wrong, and sometimes their thoughts tell them they did right.) [16]All these things will happen on the day when God, through Christ Jesus, will judge people's secret thoughts. The Good News that I preach says this.

WAYS TO WALK THE WALK

ROMANS 1:12

WORD: We can help each other's faith grow.

WALK IT: Encourage a friend today by writing a note or email with a cool Bible verse. How does your friend react?

ROMANS 2:4

WORD: God's kindness is meant to lead you to change your life.

WALK IT: Think of one area of life where you know God wants you to change, but you've been holding out. Get honest with God about it today, and ask him for his help to ditch that sin.

THE JEWS AND THE LAW

[17]What about you? You call yourself a Jew. You trust in the law of Moses and brag that you are close to God. [18]You know what he wants you to do and what is important, because you have learned the law. [19]You think you are a guide for the blind and a light for those who are in darkness. [20]You think you can show foolish people what is right and teach those who know nothing. You have the law; so you think you know everything and have all truth. [21]You teach others, so why don't you teach yourself? You tell others not to steal, but you steal. [22]You say that others must not take part in adultery, but you are guilty of that sin. You hate idols, but you steal from temples. [23]You brag about having God's law, but you bring shame to God by breaking his law, [24]just as the Scriptures say: "Those who are not Jews speak against God's name because of you."[n]

[25]If you follow the law, your circumcision has meaning. But if you break the law, it is as if you were never circumcised. [26]People who are not Jews are not circumcised, but if they do what the law says, it is as if they were circumcised. [27]You Jews have the written law and circumcision, but you break the law. So those who are not circumcised in their bodies, but still obey the law, will show that you are guilty. [28]They can do this because a person is not a true Jew if he is only a Jew in his physical body; true circumcision is not only on the outside of the body. [29]A person is a Jew only if he is a Jew inside; true circumcision is done in the heart by the Spirit, not by the written law. Such a person gets praise from God rather than from people.

3 So, do Jews have anything that other people do not have? Is there anything special about being circumcised? [2]Yes, of course, there is in every way. The most important thing is this: God trusted the Jews with his teachings. [3]If some Jews were not faithful to him, will that stop God from doing what he promised? [4]No! God will continue to be true even when every person is false. As the Scriptures say:

"So you will be shown to be right
　　when you speak,
　　and you will win your case."　　*Psalm 51:4*

[5]When we do wrong, that shows more clearly that God is right. So can we say that God is wrong to punish us? (I am talking as people might talk.) [6]No! If God could not punish us, he could not judge the world.

[7]A person might say, "When I lie, it really gives him glory, because my lie shows God's truth. So why am I judged a sinner?" [8]It would be the same to say, "We should do evil so that good will come." Some people find fault with us and say we teach this, but they are wrong and deserve the punishment they will receive.

ALL PEOPLE ARE GUILTY

[9]So are we Jews better than others? No! We have already said that Jews and those who are

2:24 "Those . . . you." Quotation from Isaiah 52:5; Ezekiel 36:20.

travel the road

It's cool to be tolerant of people different from you, learning to understand their beliefs and work to love them no matter what. But it's also cool to stand rock-solid on the total truth, being sure that the whole world needs Jesus. The next time someone says "all religions are the same" or "all roads lead to God," ponder the clear-cut words of Acts 4:12: "Jesus is the only One who can save people. His name is the only power in the world that has been given to save people. We must be saved through him."

For more on extreme missions visit www.traveltheroad.com.

not Jews are all guilty of sin. ¹⁰As the Scriptures say:

"There is no one who always does
what is right,
not even one.
¹¹There is no one who understands.
There is no one who looks to God
for help.
¹²All have turned away.
Together, everyone has become useless.
There is no one who does anything good;
there is not even one." *Psalm 14:1-3*
¹³"Their throats are like open graves;
they use their tongues for
telling lies." *Psalm 5:9*
"Their words are like snake poison."
Psalm 140:3
¹⁴ "Their mouths are full of cursing
and hate." *Psalm 10:7*
¹⁵"They are always ready to kill people.
¹⁶ Everywhere they go they cause ruin
and misery.
¹⁷They don't know how to live in peace."
Isaiah 59:7-8
¹⁸ "They have no fear of God." *Psalm 36:1*

¹⁹We know that the law's commands are for those who have the law. This stops all excuses and brings the whole world under God's judgment, ²⁰because no one can be made right with God by following the law. The law only shows us our sin.

HOW GOD MAKES PEOPLE RIGHT

²¹But God has a way to make people right with him without the law, and he has now shown us that way which the law and the prophets told us about. ²²God makes people right with himself through their faith in Jesus Christ. This is true for all who believe in Christ, because all people are the same: ²³All have sinned and are not good enough for God's glory, ²⁴and all need to be made right with God by his grace, which is a free gift. They need to be made free from sin through Jesus Christ. ²⁵God gave him as a way to forgive sin through faith in the blood of Jesus' death. This showed that God always does what is right and fair, as in the past when he was patient and did not punish people for their sins. ²⁶And God gave Jesus to show today that he does what is right. God did this so he could judge rightly and so he could make right any person who has faith in Jesus.

²⁷So do we have a reason to brag about ourselves? No! And why not? It is the way of faith that stops all bragging, not the way of trying to obey the law. ²⁸A person is made right with God through faith, not through obeying the law. ²⁹Is God only the God of the Jews? Is he not also the God of those who are not Jews? ³⁰Of course he is, because there is only one God. He will make Jews right with him by their faith, and he will also make those who are not Jews right with him through their faith. ³¹So do we destroy the law by following the way of faith? No! Faith causes us to be what the law truly wants.

THE EXAMPLE OF ABRAHAM

4 So what can we say that Abraham,[n] the father of our people, learned about faith? ²If Abraham was made right by the things he did, he had a reason to brag. But this is not God's view, ³because the Scripture says, "Abraham believed God, and God accepted Abraham's faith, and that faith made him right with God."[n]

⁴When people work, their pay is not given as a gift, but as something earned. ⁵But people cannot do any work that will make them right with God. So they must trust in him, who makes even evil people right in his sight. Then God accepts their faith, and that makes them right with him. ⁶David said the same thing. He said that people are truly blessed when God, without paying attention to good deeds, makes people right with himself.

⁷"Happy are they
whose sins are forgiven,
whose wrongs are pardoned.
⁸Happy is the person
whom the Lord does not consider
guilty." *Psalm 32:1-2*

⁹Is this blessing only for those who are circumcised or also for those who are not circumcised? We have already said that God accepted Abraham's faith and that faith made him right with God. ¹⁰So how did this happen? Did God accept Abraham before or after he was circumcised? It was before his circumcision. ¹¹Abraham was circumcised to show that he was right with God through faith before he was circumcised. So Abraham is the father of all those who believe but are not circumcised; he is the father of all believers who are accepted as being right with God. ¹²And Abraham is also the father of those who have been circumcised and who live following the faith that our father Abraham had before he was circumcised.

GOD KEEPS HIS PROMISE

¹³Abraham[n] and his descendants received the promise that they would get the whole world. He did not receive that promise through

4:1 **Abraham** Most respected ancestor of the Jews. Every Jew hoped to see Abraham.　4:3 **"Abraham . . . God."** Quotation from Genesis 15:6.　4:13 **Abraham** Most respected ancestor of the Jews. Every Jew hoped to see Abraham.

the law, but through being right with God by his faith. [14]If people could receive what God promised by following the law, then faith is worthless. And God's promise to Abraham is worthless, [15]because the law can only bring God's anger. But if there is no law, there is nothing to disobey.

[16]So people receive God's promise by having faith. This happens so the promise can be a free gift. Then all of Abraham's children can have that promise. It is not only for those who live under the law of Moses but for anyone who lives with faith like that of Abraham, who is the father of us all. [17]As it is written in the Scriptures: "I am making you a father of many nations."[n] This is true before God, the God Abraham believed, the God who gives life to the dead and who creates something out of nothing.

[18]There was no hope that Abraham would have children. But Abraham believed God and continued hoping, and so he became the father of many nations. As God told him, "Your descendants also will be too many to count."[n] [19]Abraham was almost a hundred years old, much past the age for having children, and Sarah could not have children. Abraham thought about all this, but his faith in God did not become weak. [20]He never doubted that God would keep his promise, and he never stopped believing. He grew stronger in his faith and gave praise to God. [21]Abraham felt sure that God was able to do what he had promised. [22]So, "God accepted Abraham's faith, and that faith made him right with God."[n] [23]Those words ("God accepted Abraham's faith") were written not only for Abraham [24]but also for us. God will accept us also because we believe in the One who raised Jesus our Lord from the dead. [25]Jesus was given to die for our sins, and he was raised from the dead to make us right with God.

RIGHT WITH GOD

5 Since we have been made right with God by our faith, we have peace with God. This happened through our Lord Jesus Christ, [2]who has brought us into that blessing of God's grace that we now enjoy. And we are happy because of the hope we have of sharing God's glory. [3]We also have joy with our troubles, because we know that these troubles produce patience. [4]And patience produces character, and character produces hope. [5]And this hope

will never disappoint us, because God has poured out his love to fill our hearts. He gave us his love through the Holy Spirit, whom God has given to us.

[6]When we were unable to help ourselves, at the moment of our need, Christ died for us, although we were living against God. [7]Very few people will die to save the life of someone else. Although perhaps for a good person someone might possibly die. [8]But God shows his great love for us in this way: Christ died for us while we were still sinners.

[9]So through Christ we will surely be saved from God's anger, because we have been made right with God by the blood of Christ's death. [10]While we were God's enemies, he made friends with us through the death of his Son. Surely, now that we are his friends, he will save us through his Son's life. [11]And not only that, but now we are also very happy in God through our Lord Jesus Christ. Through him we are now God's friends again.

ADAM AND CHRIST COMPARED

[12]Sin came into the world because of what one man did, and with sin came death. This is why everyone must die—because everyone sinned. [13]Sin was in the world before the law of Moses, but sin is not counted against us as breaking a command when there is no law. [14]But from the time of Adam to the time of Moses, everyone had to die, even those who had not sinned by breaking a command, as Adam had.

Adam was like the One who was coming in the future. [15]But God's free gift is not like Adam's sin. Many people died because of the sin of that one man. But the grace from God was much greater; many people received God's gift of life by the grace of the one man, Jesus Christ. [16]After Adam sinned once, he was judged guilty. But the gift of God is different. God's free gift came after many sins, and it makes people right with God. [17]One man sinned, and so death ruled all people because of that one man. But now those people who accept God's full grace and the great gift of being made right with him will surely have true life and rule through the one man, Jesus Christ.

[18]So as one sin of Adam brought the punishment of death to all people, one good act that Christ did makes all people right with God. And that brings true life for all. [19]One

ROMANS 3:24

Hate to break it to you this way. You're a pretty good kid and all. But unfortunately, your situation leaves no other choice. Pockets of sin have been discovered in numerous places on your body—some leading all the way down to your heart—and your track record certainly bears out the fact that you do indeed have a serious problem.

So . . . your file's being turned over to the justice department. Been nice knowing you.

However, if it will make you feel better, you should know that you're in good company. In fact, in all the time that God's been handling this, only one Person has ever been cleared of the death sentence on the first try. Just one. Fellow from Nazareth by the name of Jesus. But ever since then, before these cases can be properly executed, convicted lawbreakers like you have the right to pursue one final route of appeal.

It goes something like this. If you'll deliver an honest confession to God that your personal performance has been a dismal failure, and that you are willing to let Jesus' innocence stand in the place of all your hard work and effort at passing the grade . . . well, let's just say no one has ever been turned down yet.

Are you ready to exercise your option? Go for it!

4:17 "I . . . nations." Quotation from Genesis 17:5.   4:18 "Your . . . count." Quotation from Genesis 15:5.   4:22 "God . . . God." Quotation from Genesis 15:6.

219

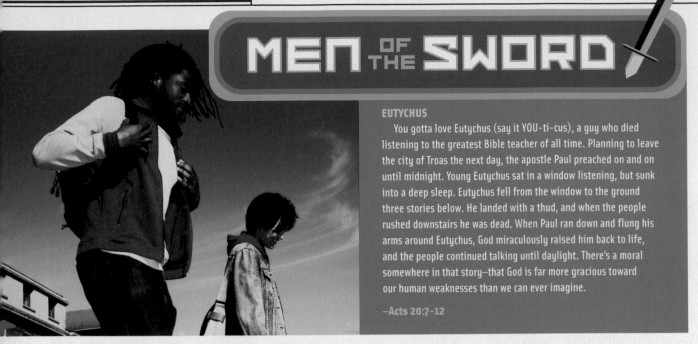

MEN OF THE SWORD

EUTYCHUS

You gotta love Eutychus (say it YOU-ti-cus), a guy who died listening to the greatest Bible teacher of all time. Planning to leave the city of Troas the next day, the apostle Paul preached on and on until midnight. Young Eutychus sat in a window listening, but sunk into a deep sleep. Eutychus fell from the window to the ground three stories below. He landed with a thud, and when the people rushed downstairs he was dead. When Paul ran down and flung his arms around Eutychus, God miraculously raised him back to life, and the people continued talking until daylight. There's a moral somewhere in that story—that God is far more gracious toward our human weaknesses than we can ever imagine.

—Acts 20:7-12

man disobeyed God, and many became sinners. In the same way, one man obeyed God, and many will be made right. [20]The law came to make sin worse. But when sin grew worse, God's grace increased. [21]Sin once used death to rule us, but God gave people more of his grace so that grace could rule by making people right with him. And this brings life forever through Jesus Christ our Lord.

DEAD TO SIN BUT ALIVE IN CHRIST

6 So do you think we should continue sinning so that God will give us even more grace? [2]No! We died to our old sinful lives, so how can we continue living with sin? [3]Did you forget that all of us became part of Christ when we were baptized? We shared his death in our baptism. [4]When we were baptized, we were buried with Christ and shared his death. So, just as Christ was raised from the dead by the wonderful power of the Father, we also can live a new life.

[5]Christ died, and we have been joined with him by dying too. So we will also be joined with him by rising from the dead as he did. [6]We know that our old life died with Christ on the cross so that our sinful selves would have no power over us and we would not be slaves to sin. [7]Anyone who has died is made free from sin's control.

[8]If we died with Christ, we know we will also live with him. [9]Christ was raised from the dead, and we know that he cannot die again. Death has no power over him now. [10]Yes, when Christ died, he died to defeat the power of sin one time—enough for all time. He now has a new life, and his new life is with God. [11]In the same way, you should see yourselves as being dead to the power of sin and alive with God through Christ Jesus.

[12]So, do not let sin control your life here on earth so that you do what your sinful self wants to do. [13]Do not offer the parts of your body to serve sin, as things to be used in doing evil. Instead, offer yourselves to God as people who have died and now live. Offer the parts of your body to God to be used in doing good. [14]Sin will not be your master, because you are not under law but under God's grace.

BE SLAVES OF RIGHTEOUSNESS

[15]So what should we do? Should we sin because we are under grace and not under law? No! [16]Surely you know that when you give yourselves like slaves to obey someone, then you are really slaves of that person. The person you obey is your master. You can follow sin, which brings spiritual death, or you can obey God, which makes you right with him. [17]In the past you were slaves to sin—sin controlled you. But thank God, you fully obeyed the things that you were taught. [18]You were made free from sin, and now you are slaves to goodness. [19]I use this example because this is hard for you to understand. In the past you offered the parts of your body to be slaves to sin and evil; you lived only for evil. In the same way now you must give yourselves to be slaves of goodness. Then you will live only for God.

[20]In the past you were slaves to sin, and goodness did not control you. [21]You did evil things, and now you are ashamed of them. Those things only bring death. [22]But now you are free from sin and have become slaves of God. This brings you a life that is only for God, and this gives you life forever. [23]When people sin, they earn what sin pays—death. But God gives us a free gift—life forever in Christ Jesus our Lord.

AN EXAMPLE FROM MARRIAGE

7 Brothers and sisters, all of you understand the law of Moses. So surely you know that the law rules over people only while they are alive. [2]For example, a woman must stay married to her husband as long as he is alive. But if her husband dies, she is free from the law of marriage. [3]But if she marries another man while her husband is still alive, the law says she is guilty of adultery. But if her husband dies, she is free from the law of marriage. Then if she marries another man, she is not guilty of adultery.

[4]In the same way, my brothers and sisters, your old selves died, and you became free from the law through the body of Christ. This happened so that you might belong to someone

EXPERTS ANSWER YOUR QUESTIONS

Q. *My neighbors have a cabinet full of guns. My family doesn't have any. Is it wrong to own weapons?*

A. Why do they have them? Are they responsible hunters who kill to eat? Or maybe target shooters? Or do they think guns are necessary to defend themselves? The flipside of the Bible's command "do not murder anyone" implies the right to defend yourself, although many Christians think that job is better left to the police. Believers can have debates about all those things, but we agree on one thing. It's not okay to have guns if you're looking to pick a fight.

Q. *My mom died in a car accident when I was three. Everyone says she was the nicest person they ever met. Why did that happen to her?*

A. Maybe the freakiest reality of life is that bad things happen to good people. No one can explain why a three-year-old kid should lose his mom. It feels anything but fair, but it's inescapably real. God isn't the one who causes evil in the world. Sometimes it's obvious that people's bad choices cause our pain, but other times we're never sure why we suffer. Either way, God wants to comfort you in your loss. Get close to him and his people.

else—the One who was raised from the dead—and so that we might be used in service to God. [5]In the past, we were ruled by our sinful selves. The law made us want to do sinful things that controlled our bodies, so the things we did were bringing us death. [6]In the past, the law held us like prisoners, but our old selves died, and we were made free from the law. So now we serve God in a new way with the Spirit, and not in the old way with written rules.

OUR FIGHT AGAINST SIN

[7]You might think I am saying that sin and the law are the same thing. That is not true. But the law was the only way I could learn what sin meant. I would never have known what it means to want to take something belonging to someone else if the law had not said, "You must not want to take your neighbor's things."[n] [8]And sin found a way to use that command and cause me to want all kinds of things I should not want. But without the law, sin has no power. [9]I was alive before I knew the law. But when the law's command came to me, then sin began to live, [10]and I died. The command was meant to bring life, but for me it brought death. [11]Sin found a way to fool me by using the command to make me die.

[12]So the law is holy, and the command is holy and right and good. [13]Does this mean that something that is good brought death to me? No! Sin used something that is good to bring death to me. This happened so that I could see what sin is really like; the command was used to show that sin is very evil.

THE WAR WITHIN US

[14]We know that the law is spiritual, but I am not spiritual since sin rules me as if I were its slave. [15]I do not understand the things I do. I do not do what I want to do, and I do the things I hate. [16]And if I do not want to do the hated things I do, that means I agree that the law is good. [17]But I am not really the one who is doing these hated things; it is sin living in me that does them. [18]Yes, I know that nothing good lives in me—I mean nothing good lives in the part of me that is earthly and sinful. I want to do the things that are good, but I do not do them. [19]I do not do the good things I want to do, but I do the bad things I do not want to do. [20]So if I do things I do not want to do, then I am not the one doing them. It is sin living in me that does those things.

[21]So I have learned this rule: When I want to do good, evil is there with me. [22]In my mind, I am happy with God's law. [23]But I see another law working in my body, which makes war against the law that my mind accepts. That other law working in my body is the law of sin, and it makes me its prisoner. [24]What a miserable man I am! Who will save me from this body that brings me death? [25]I thank God for saving me through Jesus Christ our Lord!

So in my mind I am a slave to God's law, but in my sinful self I am a slave to the law of sin.

BE RULED BY THE SPIRIT

8 So now, those who are in Christ Jesus are not judged guilty. [2]Through Christ

 7:7 "You . . . things." Quotation from Exodus 20:17.

RADICAL FAITH:

ROMANS 5:1

Now that you are a believer, the battle for your spirit is over. You chose the path of victory when you chose Jesus. When you trusted him, God gave you peace. Are you enjoying the peace you have, or are you trying to fight a battle that's already been won? God wants to come into your life and bring calm to the chaos. He wants you to let him be the light that shatters your darkest storm. A lot of people give their hearts to Jesus and then keep on fighting the same old way they used to. With the peace of God, you can let go of some of your anxiety about grades, college, finances, family, whatever. Do everything you know to do and trust God. You don't have to manipulate decisions and worry about things you can't see. You don't have to go through life by yourself anymore. Rest in the peace God brings. Maybe, if we could hear him, he would be saying, "Stop fighting that battle. I've already done that for you. Be still. Rest. Open your eyes. My love for you has cast out all fear. Look at what I've done. Stop wringing your hands in worry. I love you. I want you to experience the peace I've given you."

Jesus the law of the Spirit that brings life made me free from the law that brings sin and death. [3]The law was without power, because the law was made weak by our sinful selves. But God did what the law could not do. He sent his own Son to earth with the same human life that others use for sin. By sending his Son to be an offering for sin, God used a human life to destroy sin. [4]He did this so that we could be the kind of people the law correctly wants us to be. Now we do not live following our sinful selves, but we live following the Spirit.

[5]Those who live following their sinful selves think only about things that their sinful selves want. But those who live following the Spirit are thinking about the things the Spirit wants them to do. [6]If people's thinking is controlled by the sinful self, there is death. But if their thinking is controlled by the Spirit, there is life and peace. [7]When people's thinking is controlled by the sinful self, they are against God, because they refuse to obey God's law and really are not even able to obey God's law. [8]Those people who are ruled by their sinful selves cannot please God.

[9]But you are not ruled by your sinful selves. You are ruled by the Spirit, if that Spirit of God really lives in you. But the person who does not have the Spirit of Christ does not belong to Christ. [10]Your body will always be dead because of sin. But if Christ is in you, then the Spirit gives you life, because Christ made you right with God. [11]God raised Jesus from the dead, and if God's Spirit is living in you, he will also give life to your bodies that die. God is the One who raised Christ from the dead, and he will give life through his Spirit that lives in you.

[12]So, my brothers and sisters, we must not be ruled by our sinful selves or live the way our sinful selves want. [13]If you use your lives to do the wrong things your sinful selves want, you will die spiritually. But if you use the Spirit's help to stop doing the wrong things you do with your body, you will have true life.

[14]The true children of God are those who let God's Spirit lead them. [15]The Spirit we received does not make us slaves again to fear; it makes us children of God. With that Spirit we cry out, "Father."[n] [16]And the Spirit himself joins with our spirits to say we are God's children. [17]If we are God's children, we will receive

blessings from God together with Christ. But we must suffer as Christ suffered so that we will have glory as Christ has glory.

OUR FUTURE GLORY

[18]The sufferings we have now are nothing compared to the great glory that will be shown to us. [19]Everything God made is waiting with excitement for God to show his children's glory completely. [20]Everything God made was changed to become useless, not by its own wish but because God wanted it and because all along there was this hope: [21]that everything God made would be set free from ruin to have the freedom and glory that belong to God's children.

[22]We know that everything God made has been waiting until now in pain, like a woman ready to give birth. [23]Not only the world, but we also have been waiting with pain inside us. We have the Spirit as the first part of God's promise. So we are waiting for God to finish making us his own children, which means our bodies will be made free. [24]We were saved, and we have this hope. If we see what we are waiting for, that is not really hope. People do not hope for something they already have. [25]But we are hoping for something we do not have yet, and we are waiting for it patiently.

[26]Also, the Spirit helps us with our weakness. We do not know how to pray as we should. But the Spirit himself speaks to God for us, even begs God for us with deep feelings that words cannot explain. [27]God can see what is in people's hearts. And he knows what is in the mind of the Spirit, because the Spirit speaks to God for his people in the way God wants.

[28]We know that in everything God works for the good of those who love him. They are the people he called, because that was his plan. [29]God knew them before he made the world, and he decided that they would be like his Son so that Jesus would be the firstborn[n] of many brothers. [30]God planned for them to be like his Son; and those he planned to be like his Son, he also called; and those he called, he also made right with him; and those he made right, he also glorified.

GOD'S LOVE IN CHRIST JESUS

[31]So what should we say about this? If God is with us, no one can defeat us. [32]He did not spare his own Son but gave him for us all. So

8:15 "Father" Literally, "Abba, Father." Jewish children called their fathers "Abba." **8:29 firstborn** Here this probably means that Christ was the first in God's family to share God's glory.

with Jesus, God will surely give us all things. [33]Who can accuse the people God has chosen? No one, because God is the One who makes them right. [34]Who can say God's people are guilty? No one, because Christ Jesus died, but he was also raised from the dead, and now he is on God's right side, begging God for us. [35]Can anything separate us from the love Christ has for us? Can troubles or problems or sufferings or hunger or nakedness or danger or violent death? [36]As it is written in the Scriptures:

"For you we are in danger of death
    all the time.
  People think we are worth no more than
    sheep to be killed." *Psalm 44:22*

[37]But in all these things we have full victory through God who showed his love for us. [38]Yes, I am sure that neither death, nor life, nor angels, nor ruling spirits, nothing now, nothing in the future, no powers, [39]nothing above us, nothing below us, nor anything else in the whole world will ever be able to separate us from the love of God that is in Christ Jesus our Lord.

GOD AND THE JEWISH PEOPLE

9 I am in Christ, and I am telling you the truth; I do not lie. My conscience is ruled by the Holy Spirit, and it tells me I am not lying. [2]I have great sorrow and always feel much sadness. [3]I wish I could help my Jewish brothers and sisters, my people. I would even wish that I were cursed and cut off from Christ if that would help them. [4]They are the people of Israel, God's chosen children. They have seen the glory of God, and they have the agreements that God made between himself and his people. God gave them the law of Moses and the right way of worship and his promises. [5]They are the descendants of our great ancestors, and they are the earthly family into which Christ was born, who is God over all. Praise him forever![n] Amen.

[6]It is not that God failed to keep his promise to them. But only some of the people of Israel are truly God's people,[n] [7]and only some of Abraham's[n] descendants are true children of Abraham. But God said to Abraham: "The descendants I promised you will be from Isaac."[n] [8]This means that not all of Abraham's descendants are God's true children. Abraham's true children are those who become God's children because of the promise God made to Abraham. [9]God's promise to Abraham was this: "At the right time I will return, and Sarah will have a son."[n] [10]And that is not all. Rebekah's sons had the same father, our father Isaac. [11-12]But before the two boys were born, God told Rebekah, "The older will serve the younger."[n] This was before the boys had done anything good or bad. God said this so that the one chosen would be chosen because of God's own plan. He was chosen because he was the one God wanted to call, not because of anything

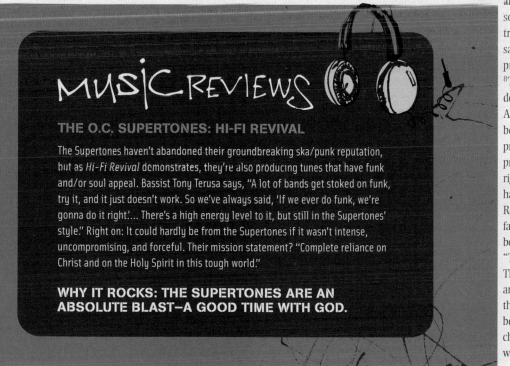
 9:5 born . . . forever! This can also mean "born. May God, who rules over all things, be praised forever!" **9:6 God's people** Literally, "Israel," the people God chose to bring his blessings to the world. **9:7 Abraham** Most respected ancestor of the Jews. Every Jew hoped to see Abraham. **9:7 "The descendants . . . Isaac."** Quotation from Genesis 21:12. **9:9 "At . . . son."** Quotation from Genesis 18:10, 14. **9:11-12 "The older . . . younger."** Quotation from Genesis 25:23.

RADICAL FAITH:
ROMANS 8:14

When you put your faith in God's Son, his Spirit became part of your life. God knew that you would need his Spirit to help you live the way he wants you to live. People who haven't trusted Jesus don't have God's Spirit. They have no choice but to live life to please themselves or to get on the good side of other people. But you don't have to live that way. You can let God's Spirit choose the road you're going to take. Living that way pleases God. And it has a fringe benefit for you too. "If people's thinking is controlled by the sinful self, there is death. But if their thinking is controlled by the Spirit, there is life and peace" (8:6).

In order for your mind to be ruled by his Spirit, you've got to stay tight with God. Spend time in prayer, in worship, and in his Word. Really work these things into your life—so much that they become a part of you. Then you'll know when the Spirit is leading you, and you'll be able to follow.

he did. [13]As the Scripture says, "I loved Jacob, but I hated Esau."[n]

[14]So what should we say about this? Is God unfair? In no way. [15]God said to Moses, "I will show kindness to anyone to whom I want to show kindness, and I will show mercy to anyone to whom I want to show mercy."[n] [16]So God will choose the one to whom he decides to show mercy; his choice does not depend on what people want or try to do. [17]The Scripture says to the king of Egypt: "I made you king for this reason: to show my power in you so that my name will be talked about in all the earth."[n] [18]So God shows mercy where he wants to show mercy, and he makes stubborn the people he wants to make stubborn.

[19]So one of you will ask me: "Then why does God blame us for our sins? Who can fight his will?" [20]You are only human, and human beings have no right to question God. An object should not ask the person who made it, "Why did you make me like this?" [21]The potter can make anything he wants to make. He can use the same clay to make one thing for special use and another thing for daily use.

[22]It is the same way with God. He wanted to show his anger and to let people see his power. But he patiently stayed with those people he was angry with—people who were made ready to be destroyed. [23]He waited with patience so that he could make known his rich glory to the people who receive his mercy. He has prepared these people to have his glory, [24]and we are those people whom God called. He called us not from the Jews only but also from those who are not Jews. [25]As the Scripture says in Hosea:

"I will say, 'You are my people'
　to those I had called 'not my people.'
And I will show my love
　to those people I did not love." *Hosea 2:1, 23*
[26]"They were called,
　'You are not my people,'
but later they will be called
　'children of the living God.'" *Hosea 1:10*
[27]And Isaiah cries out about Israel:
"The people of Israel are many,
　like the grains of sand by the sea.
But only a few of them will be saved,
[28]　because the Lord will quickly and
　　completely punish the people
　　on the earth." *Isaiah 10:22-23*

[29]It is as Isaiah said:
"The Lord All-Powerful
　allowed a few of our descendants to live.
Otherwise we would have been completely
　　destroyed
　like the cities of Sodom and
　　Gomorrah."[n] *Isaiah 1:9*
[30]So what does all this mean? Those who are not Jews were not trying to make themselves right with God, but they were made right with God because of their faith. [31]The people of Israel tried to follow a law to make themselves right with God. But they did not succeed, [32]because they tried to make themselves right by the things they did instead of trusting in God to make them right. They stumbled over the stone that causes people to stumble. [33]As it is written in the Scripture:

"I will put in Jerusalem a stone that causes
　　people to stumble,
　a rock that makes them fall.
Anyone who trusts in him will never be
　　disappointed." *Isaiah 8:14; 28:16*

10 Brothers and sisters, the thing I want most is for all the Jews to be saved. That is my prayer to God. [2]I can say this about them: They really try to follow God, but they do not know the right way. [3]Because they did not know the way that God makes people right with him, they tried to make themselves right in their own way. So they did not accept God's way of making people right. [4]Christ ended the law so that everyone who believes in him may be right with God.

[5]Moses writes about being made right by following the law. He says, "A person who obeys these things will live because of them."[n] [6]But this is what the Scripture says about being made right through faith: "Don't say to yourself, 'Who will go up into heaven?'" (That means, "Who will go up to heaven and bring Christ down to earth?") [7]"And do not say, 'Who will go down into the world below?'" (That means, "Who will go down and bring Christ up from the dead?") [8]This is what the Scripture says: "The word is near you; it is in your mouth and in your heart."[n] That is the teaching of faith that we are telling. [9]If you use your mouth to say, "Jesus is Lord," and if you believe in your heart that God raised Jesus from the dead, you will be saved. [10]We believe

---

9:13 "I . . . Esau." Quotation from Malachi 1:2–3.　**9:15** "I . . . mercy." Quotation from Exodus 33:19.　**9:17** "I . . . earth." Quotation from Exodus 9:16.　**9:29 Sodom and Gomorrah** Two cities that God destroyed because the people were so evil.　**10:5** "A person . . . them." Quotation from Leviticus 18:5.　**10:6–8** Verses 6–8 Quotations from Deuteronomy 9:4; 30:12–14; Psalm 107:26.

224

WAYS TO WALK THE WALK

ROMANS 6:15

WORD: Just because God forgives us doesn't mean we should keep sinning.

WALK IT: Talk with your best friend about being accountability partners. Holding each other "accountable" means that you guys confess your sins to each other, challenge each other to obey God, and encourage each other in faith.

ROMANS 6:23

WORD: Eternal life is a free gift from God.

WALK IT: You didn't do a thing to earn your salvation. God gave it to you. Talk with God today and say thanks for saving you despite everything you've done.

with our hearts, and so we are made right with God. And we use our mouths to say that we believe, and so we are saved. [11]As the Scripture says, "Anyone who trusts in him will never be disappointed."[n] [12]That Scripture says "anyone" because there is no difference between those who are Jews and those who are not. The same Lord is the Lord of all and gives many blessings to all who trust in him, [13]as the Scripture says, "Anyone who calls on the Lord will be saved."[n]

[14]But before people can ask the Lord for help, they must believe in him; and before they can believe in him, they must hear about him; and for them to hear about the Lord, someone must tell them; [15]and before someone can go and tell them, that person must be sent. It is written, "How beautiful is the person who comes to bring good news."[n] [16]But not all the Jews accepted the good news. Isaiah said, "Lord, who believed what we told them?"[n] [17]So faith comes from hearing the Good News, and people hear the Good News when someone tells them about Christ.

[18]But I ask: Didn't people hear the Good News? Yes, they heard—as the Scripture says:

"Their message went out
    through all the world;
    their words go everywhere
    on earth."
                        Psalm 19:4

[19]Again I ask: Didn't the people of Israel understand? Yes, they did understand. First, Moses says:

"I will use those who are not a nation to
    make you jealous.
I will use a nation that does not
    understand to make you angry."
                        Deuteronomy 32:21

[20]Then Isaiah is bold enough to say:

"I was found by those who were not asking
    me for help.
I made myself known to people who
    were not looking for me." *Isaiah 65:1*

[21]But about Israel God says,

"All day long I stood ready to accept
    people who disobey and are
    stubborn."
                        Isaiah 65:2

GOD SHOWS MERCY TO ALL PEOPLE

11 So I ask: Did God throw out his people? No! I myself am an Israelite from the family of Abraham, from the tribe of Benjamin. [2]God chose the Israelites to be his people before they were born, and he has not thrown his people out. Surely you know what the Scripture says about Elijah, how he prayed to God against the people of Israel. [3]"Lord," he said, "they have killed your prophets, and they have destroyed your altars. I am the only

travel ⨂ the road

When the work of two missions teams in the Dominican Republic ground to a halt, teens from a church in Marysville, Washington, stepped in to help. By delivering two sets of equipment for showing the "JESUS" film, they enabled the teams to continue their ministry of starting new churches. After delivering the equipment, the teens stayed in the Dominican Republic and took part in "JESUS" film showings. During their one-week stay, twenty-nine people became Christians. Do the math: twenty-nine new Christians times fifty-two weeks times two teams means that upwards of three thousand people might become Christians... just because a group of teens pitched in.

For more on extreme missions visit www.traveltheroad.com.

10:11 "Anyone . . . disappointed." Quotation from Isaiah 28:16.   10:13 "Anyone . . . saved." Quotation from Joel 2:32.   10:15 "How . . . news." Quotation from Isaiah 52:7.   10:16 "Lord, . . . them?" Quotation from Isaiah 53:1.

AUGUST

1

August is National Romance Awareness Month. Ask your mom how you can treat girls right—and try out one of her ideas.

2

3

Tell a sib you love them today—no matter how they act.

4

Pray for a Person of Influence: Today is Jeff Gordon's birthday.

5

Read your favorite Psalm today.

6

7

8

Tell yourself that whatever you do today, you do for the Lord.

9

National Polka Festival— Take someone for a twirl.

10

Read your favorite verse today and search for new meaning.

11

12

13

International Lefthanders Day— shake hands the lefty way.

14

Pray for a Person of Influence: Today is Ben from Audio Adrenaline's birthday.

15

16

Spend the day outside soaking up God's creation.

17

Pray for a Person of Influence: Today is Kevin Max's birthday.

18

Do your part to make Bad Poetry Day special.

19

Pray for a Person of Influence: It's Bill Clinton's birthday.

20

21

22

23

Martin Luther King delivered his "I have a dream" speech—pray for unity in our country.

24

25

Pray for a Person of Influence: It's Sean Connery's birthday.

26

Help a little sibling pick out back-to-school clothes and supplies.

27

28

Write yourself a letter that you'll open five years from now.

29

30

Pray for a Person of Influence: Wish Cameron Diaz a Happy Birthday.

31

Mow an elderly neighbor's lawn today.

prophet left, and now they are trying to kill me, too."[n] [4]But what answer did God give Elijah? He said, "But I have left seven thousand people in Israel who have never bowed down before Baal."[n] [5]It is the same now. There are a few people that God has chosen by his grace. [6]And if he chose them by grace, it is not for the things they have done. If they could be made God's people by what they did, God's gift of grace would not really be a gift.

[7]So this is what has happened: Although the Israelites tried to be right with God, they did not succeed, but the ones God chose did become right with him. The others were made stubborn and refused to listen to God. [8]As it is written in the Scriptures:

"God gave the people a dull mind so they
    could not understand." *Isaiah 29:10*
"He closed their eyes so they could not see
    and their ears so they could not hear.
This continues until today." *Deuteronomy 29:4*

[9]And David says:

"Let their own feasts trap them and cause
    their ruin;
let their feasts cause them to stumble
    and be paid back.
[10]Let their eyes be closed so they cannot see
    and their backs be forever weak from
    troubles." *Psalm 69:22-23*

[11]So I ask: When the Jews fell, did that fall destroy them? No! But their mistake brought salvation to those who are not Jews, in order to make the Jews jealous. [12]The Jews' mistake brought rich blessings for the world, and the Jews' loss brought rich blessings for the non-Jewish people. So surely the world will receive much richer blessings when enough Jews become the kind of people God wants.

[13]Now I am speaking to you who are not Jews. I am an apostle to those who are not Jews, and since I have that work, I will make the most of it. [14]I hope I can make my own people jealous and, in that way, help some of them to be saved. [15]When God turned away from the Jews, he became friends with other people in the world. So when God accepts the Jews, surely that will bring them life after death.

[16]If the first piece of bread is offered to God, then the whole loaf is made holy. If the roots of a tree are holy, then the tree's branches are holy too.

[17]It is as if some of the branches from an olive tree have been broken off. You non-Jewish people are like the branch of a wild olive tree that has been joined to that first tree. You now share the strength and life of the first tree, the Jews. [18]So do not brag about those branches that were broken off. If you brag, remember that you do not support the root, but the root supports you. [19]You will say, "Branches were broken off so that I could be joined to their tree." [20]That is true. But those branches were broken off because they did not believe, and you continue to be part of the tree only because you believe. Do not be proud, but be afraid. [21]If God did not let the natural

RELATIONSHIPS

"You are not the same as those who do not believe. So do not join yourselves to them" (2 Corinthians 6:14). Whenever you hear Christians say, "Don't date or marry someone who isn't a believer," that's a key verse they're thinking of. The words actually picture two animals of different breeds lashed together, yanking each other to plow in different directions. That's what happens when you let a non-Christian friend rule you. To be a well-matched guy-girl couple or even really tight same-sex friends, you've got to be going the same direction. Or you get your heads ripped off.

WAYS TO WALK THE WALK

ROMANS 8:28

WORD: In everything God works for the good of those who love him.

WALK IT: Think about the toughest situation in your life right now. How can it turn out for good in the short term? In five years?

ROMANS 8:31

WORD: If God is with you, nothing can defeat you.

WALK IT: Next time you feel fear edging on, tell yourself this truth—ten times if you need to. It's like a pregame warmup against fear. Do you feel calmer?

 11:3 "They . . . too." Quotation from 1 Kings 19:10, 14. 11:4 "But . . . Baal." Quotation from 1 Kings 19:18.

EXPERTS ANSWER YOUR QUESTIONS

Q. *Last week in school a few of the kids in my math class handed around the answers to a test. They all got A's. I studied hard and got a B-minus.*

A. People not only do bad things, but they often thrive because of their evil. Most of us wonder when God will rise up and smoke the bad guys for good. Problem is, we all do wrong. When we get honest about our sins, we're not so sure we want God to punish evil quickly. But God promises that sinners who don't turn from evil ultimately will get what they have coming.

Q. *How can I trust that the Bible isn't a messed-up copy of what God said?*

A. When you flip open a book at school from ancient Greece or Rome, you don't question whether you have the words penned by a way-old writer. Yet our texts of many ancient books are based on a handful of copies that date to many centuries after the books were written. In the case of the New Testament, we have thousands of manuscript pieces much nearer to the time those books were written. Comparing all of those copies shows that the Bible has been handed down accurately.

branches of that tree stay, then he will not let you stay if you don't believe.

[22]So you see that God is kind and also very strict. He punishes those who stop following him. But God is kind to you, if you continue following in his kindness. If you do not, you will be cut off from the tree. [23]And if the Jews will believe in God again, he will accept them back. God is able to put them back where they were. [24]It is not natural for a wild branch to be part of a good tree. And you who are not Jews are like a branch cut from a wild olive tree and joined to a good olive tree. But since those Jews are like a branch that grew from the good tree, surely they can be joined to their own tree again.

[25]I want you to understand this secret, brothers and sisters, so you will understand that you do not know everything: Part of Israel has been made stubborn, but that will change when many who are not Jews have come to God. [26]And that is how all Israel will be saved. It is written in the Scriptures:

"The Savior will come from Jerusalem;
he will take away all evil from the
family of Jacob.[n]
[27]And I will make this agreement with
those people
when I take away their sins."

Isaiah 59:20-21; 27:9

[28]The Jews refuse to accept the Good News, so they are God's enemies. This has happened to help you who are not Jews. But the Jews are still God's chosen people, and he loves them very much because of the promises he made to their ancestors. [29]God never changes his mind about the people he calls and the things he gives them. [30]At one time you refused to obey God. But now you have received mercy, because those people refused to obey. [31]And now the Jews refuse to obey, because God showed mercy to you. But this happened so that they also can receive mercy from him. [32]God has given all people over to their stubborn ways so that he can show mercy to all.

PRAISE TO GOD

[33]Yes, God's riches are very great, and his wisdom and knowledge have no end! No one can explain the things God decides or understand his ways. [34]As the Scripture says,

"Who has known the mind of the Lord,
or who has been able to give him
advice?" *Isaiah 40:13*
[35]"No one has ever given God anything
that he must pay back." *Job 41:11*
[36]Yes, God made all things, and everything continues through him and for him. To him be the glory forever! Amen.

GIVE YOUR LIVES TO GOD

12 So brothers and sisters, since God has shown us great mercy, I beg you to offer your lives as a living sacrifice to him. Your offering must be only for God and pleasing to him, which is the spiritual way for you to worship. [2]Do not change yourselves to be like the people of this world, but be changed within by a new way of thinking. Then you will be able to decide what God wants for you; you will know what is good and pleasing to him and what is perfect. [3]Because God has given me a special gift, I have something to say to everyone among you. Do not think you are better than you are. You must decide what you really are by the amount of faith God has given you. [4]Each one of us has a body with many parts, and these parts all have different uses.

 11:26 **Jacob** Father of the twelve family groups of Israel, the people God chose to be his people.

MUSIC REVIEWS

SWITCHFOOT: BEAUTIFUL LETDOWN

Switchfoot's *Beautiful Letdown* is a progressive follow-up to their excellent work on the *Walk to Remember* soundtrack. Switchfoot has become so influential that Columbia Records co-released this fourth album with Sparrow, giving the SoCal foursome an opportunity for even bigger impact. Explosive guitars and edgy vocals give Switchfoot their unique sound. Singer Jon Foreman says, "We've never fit in any of the genre boxes ... diversity [of styles] is our strength." *Beautiful Letdown* offers a mixture of tempos and probing lyrics—"I've got my hands in redemption's side / Whose scars are bigger than these doubts of mine / I'll fit all of these monstrosities inside / And I'll come alive" ("Redemption").

WHY IT ROCKS: SWITCHFOOT IS THE BEST IN THEIR BUSINESS.

GET OUT THERE

You've got your first real job. You could ask your coworkers to toss a few coins into a coffee can for a good cause. Or you could think far bigger and make significant giving easy and efficient. GLOBAL IMPACT is a not-for-profit organization dedicated to helping the poorest people on earth. Connecting with Global Impact allows you and your coworkers to contribute straight from your paycheck to 50 of the most respected U.S.-based international charities. Your giving will build pride, hope, and trust in lives affected by poverty, disaster and neglect. Pooling $60, for example, can provide enough Vitamin A to prevent blindness in 850 children for one year. Or every $200 can provide safe water to 84 poor Mozambicans through the construction of wells, sewers, and other clean water systems.

Learn how to give as an individual or a group at www.charity.org.

ROMANS 10:9-13

Know any people who think they're too far gone for Jesus? Maybe they think their sins are too big or their lives too ugly. They think God couldn't possibly save them. They think God's probably mad or that he's given up on them by now or that he's too holy to want them around.

Well, this passage is for the hopeless. God delights in saving the unlovable and the lost and the ones who think they could never be saved. To think that God couldn't save you because you're too far gone is to say, "I'm bigger than God. I can do something so evil that he can't forgive me. I have more power than God." The truth is that *everyone* is hopelessly lost without him and every sin is repulsive to him. But Jesus died for everybody—no exceptions. Anyone who calls out to him will be saved.

⁵In the same way, we are many, but in Christ we are all one body. Each one is a part of that body, and each part belongs to all the other parts. ⁶We all have different gifts, each of which came because of the grace God gave us. The person who has the gift of prophecy should use that gift in agreement with the faith. ⁷Anyone who has the gift of serving should serve. Anyone who has the gift of teaching should teach. ⁸Whoever has the gift of encouraging others should encourage. Whoever has the gift of giving to others should give freely. Anyone who has the gift of being a leader should try hard when he leads. Whoever has the gift of showing mercy to others should do so with joy.

⁹Your love must be real. Hate what is evil, and hold on to what is good. ¹⁰Love each other like brothers and sisters. Give each other more honor than you want for yourselves. ¹¹Do not be lazy but work hard, serving the Lord with all your heart. ¹²Be joyful because you have hope. Be patient when trouble comes, and pray at all times. ¹³Share with God's people who need help. Bring strangers in need into your homes.

¹⁴Wish good for those who harm you; wish them well and do not curse them. ¹⁵Be happy with those who are happy, and be sad with those who are sad. ¹⁶Live in peace with each other. Do not be proud, but make friends with those who seem unimportant. Do not think how smart you are.

¹⁷If someone does wrong to you, do not pay him back by doing wrong to him. Try to do what everyone thinks is right. ¹⁸Do your best to live in peace with everyone. ¹⁹My friends, do not try to punish others when they wrong you, but wait for God to punish them with his anger. It is written: "I will punish those who do wrong; I will repay them,"[n] says the Lord. ²⁰But you should do this:

"If your enemy is hungry, feed him;
    if he is thirsty, give him a drink.
Doing this will be like pouring burning
        coals on his head." *Proverbs 25:21-22*

²¹Do not let evil defeat you, but defeat evil by doing good.

CHRISTIANS SHOULD OBEY THE LAW

13 All of you must yield to the government rulers. No one rules unless God has given him the power to rule, and no one rules now without that power from God. ²So those who are against the government are really against what God has commanded. And they will bring punishment on themselves. ³Those who do right do not have to fear the rulers; only those who do wrong fear them. Do you want to be unafraid of the rulers? Then do what is right, and they will praise you. ⁴The ruler is God's servant to help you. But if you do wrong, then be afraid. He has the power to punish; he is God's servant to punish those who do wrong. ⁵So you must yield to the government, not only because you might be punished, but because you know it is right.

⁶This is also why you pay taxes. Rulers are working for God and give their time to their work. ⁷Pay everyone, then, what you owe. If you owe any kind of tax, pay it. Show respect and honor to them all.

LOVING OTHERS

⁸Do not owe people anything, except always owe love to each other, because the person who loves others has obeyed all the law. ⁹The law says, "You must not be guilty of adultery. You must not murder anyone. You must not

RANDOM THINGS NOT FOUND IN NATURE

1. **FACE LIFTS**
2. **POLYESTER**
3. **HOT DOGS**
4. **OFFICE CUBICLES**
5. **JOCKSTRAPS**
6. **LIPOSUCTION**
7. **SQUEAKY HELIUM VOICES**
8. **CONTACT LENSES**
9. **SHREK**
10. **SPORKS**

12:19 "I . . . them" Quotation from Deuteronomy 32:35.

steal. You must not want to take your neighbor's things."[n] All these commands and all others are really only one rule: "Love your neighbor as you love yourself."[n] [10]Love never hurts a neighbor, so loving is obeying all the law.

[11]Do this because we live in an important time. It is now time for you to wake up from your sleep, because our salvation is nearer now than when we first believed. [12]The "night"[n] is almost finished, and the "day"[n] is almost here. So we should stop doing things that belong to darkness and take up the weapons used for fighting in the light. [13]Let us live in a right way, like people who belong to the day. We should not have wild parties or get drunk. There should be no sexual sins of any kind, no fighting or jealousy. [14]But clothe yourselves with the Lord Jesus Christ and forget about satisfying your sinful self.

DO NOT CRITICIZE OTHER PEOPLE

14 Accept into your group someone who is weak in faith, and do not argue about opinions. [2]One person believes it is right to eat all kinds of food.[n] But another, who is weak, believes it is right to eat only vegetables. [3]The one who knows that it is right to eat any kind of food must not reject the one who eats only vegetables. And the person who eats only vegetables must not think that the one who eats all foods is wrong, because God has accepted that person. [4]You cannot judge another person's servant. The master decides if the servant is doing well or not. And the Lord's servant will do well because the Lord helps him do well.

[5]Some think that one day is more important than another, and others think that every day is the same. Let all be sure in their own mind. [6]Those who think one day is more important than other days are doing that for the Lord. And those who eat all kinds of food are doing that for the Lord, and they give thanks to God. Others who refuse to eat some foods do that for the Lord, and they give thanks to God. [7]We do not live or die for ourselves. [8]If we live, we are living for the Lord, and if we die, we are dying for the Lord. So living or dying, we belong to the Lord. [9]The reason Christ died and rose from the dead to live again was so he would be Lord over both the dead and the living. [10]So why do you judge your brothers or sisters in Christ?

And why do you think you are better than they are? We will all stand before God to be judged, [11]because it is written in the Scriptures:

"'As surely as I live,' says the Lord,
'Everyone will bow before me;
everyone will say that I am God.'"

Isaiah 45:23

[12]So each of us will have to answer to God.

DO NOT CAUSE OTHERS TO SIN

[13]For that reason we should stop judging each other. We must make up our minds not to do anything that will make another Christian sin. [14]I am in the Lord Jesus, and I know that there is no food that is wrong to eat. But if a person believes something is wrong, that thing is wrong for him. [15]If you hurt your brother's or sister's faith because of something you eat, you are not really following the way of love. Do not destroy someone's faith by eating food he thinks is wrong, because Christ died for him. [16]Do not allow what you think is good to become what others say is evil. [17]In the kingdom of God, eating and drinking are not important. The important things are living right with God, peace, and joy in the Holy Spirit. [18]Anyone who serves Christ by living this way is pleasing God and will be accepted by other people.

[19]So let us try to do what makes peace and helps one another. [20]Do not let the eating of food destroy the work of God. All foods are all right to eat, but it is wrong to eat food that causes someone else to sin. [21]It is better not to eat meat or drink wine or do anything that will cause your brother or sister to sin.

[22]Your beliefs about these things should be kept secret between you and God. People are happy if they can do what they think is right without feeling guilty. [23]But those who eat something without being sure it is right are wrong because they did not believe it was right. Anything that is done without believing it is right is a sin.

15 We who are strong in faith should help the weak with their weaknesses, and not please only ourselves. [2]Let each of us please our neighbors for their good, to help them be stronger in faith. [3]Even Christ did not live to please himself. It was as the Scriptures said: "When people insult you, it hurts me."[n] [4]Everything that was written in the past was written to teach us. The

Scriptures give us patience and encouragement so that we can have hope. [5]Patience and encouragement come from God. And I pray that God will help you all agree with each other the way Christ Jesus wants. [6]Then you will all be joined together, and you will give

BIBLE BASICS

The term **Christian** refers to someone who believes and places their faith in Christ. It actually means "related to Christ." Followers of Christ were first called Christians in the ancient city of Antioch. It's a name that has stuck over the years.

13:9 "You . . . things." Quotation from Exodus 20:13-15, 17.   13:9 "Love . . . yourself." Quotation from Leviticus 19:18.   13:12 "night" This is used as a symbol of the sinful world we live in. This world will soon end.   13:12 "day" This is used as a symbol of the good time that is coming, when we will be with God.   14:2 all . . . food The Jewish law said there were some foods Jews should not eat. When Jews became Christians, some of them did not understand they could now eat all foods.   15:3 "When . . . me." Quotation from Psalm 69:9.

ROMANS 10:17

WORD: Faith comes from hearing the Good News of Christ.

WALK IT: The next time you feel like your spiritual growth is at a dead end, ask yourself if you're feeding on God's Word. You've got to get the Bible in your ears and eyes if you want it in your life.

ROMANS 12:2

WORD: Transformation happens when you rearrange your thoughts.

WALK IT: Every time you sin, write it down. Ask yourself, "What was I thinking?" And then write God's way of looking at the situation. Let that good thought change how you think.

---

glory to God the Father of our Lord Jesus Christ. [7]Christ accepted you, so you should accept each other, which will bring glory to God. [8]I tell you that Christ became a servant of the Jews to show that God's promises to the Jewish ancestors are true. [9]And he also did this so that those who are not Jews could give glory to God for the mercy he gives to them. It is written in the Scriptures:

"So I will praise you among the non-Jewish people.
I will sing praises to your name."

Psalm 18:49

[10]The Scripture also says,

"Be happy, you who are not Jews, together with his people." *Deuteronomy 32:43*

[11]Again the Scripture says,

"All you who are not Jews, praise the Lord.
All you people, sing praises to him." *Psalm 117:1*

[12]And Isaiah says,

"A new king will come from the family of Jesse.[n]
He will come to rule over the non-Jewish people,
and they will have hope because of him." *Isaiah 11:10*

[13]I pray that the God who gives hope will fill you with much joy and peace while you trust in him. Then your hope will overflow by the power of the Holy Spirit.

PAUL TALKS ABOUT HIS WORK

[14]My brothers and sisters, I am sure that you are full of goodness. I know that you have all the knowledge you need and that you are able to teach each other. [15]But I have written to you very openly about some things I wanted you to remember. I did this because God gave me this special gift: [16]to be a minister of Christ Jesus to those who are not Jews. I served God by teaching his Good News, so that the non-Jewish people could be an offering that God would accept—an offering made holy by the Holy Spirit.

[17]So I am proud of what I have done for God in Christ Jesus. [18]I will not talk about anything except what Christ has done through me in leading those who are not Jews to obey God. They have obeyed God because of what I have said and done, [19]because of the power of miracles and the great things they saw, and because of the power of the Holy Spirit. I preached the Good News from Jerusalem all the way around to Illyricum, and so I have finished that part of my work. [20]I always want to preach the Good News in places where people have never heard of Christ, because I do not want to build on the work someone else has already started. [21]But it is written in the Scriptures:

"Those who were not told about him will see,
and those who have not heard about him will understand." *Isaiah 52:15*

PAUL'S PLAN TO VISIT ROME

[22]This is the reason I was stopped many times from coming to you. [23]Now I have finished my work here. Since for many years I have wanted to come to you, [24]I hope to visit you on my way to Spain. After I enjoy being with you for a while, I hope you can help me on my trip. [25]Now I am going to Jerusalem to help God's people. [26]The believers in Macedonia and Southern Greece were happy to give their money to help the poor among God's people at Jerusalem. [27]They were happy to do this, and really they owe it to them. These who are not Jews have shared in the Jews' spiritual blessings, so they should use their material possessions to help the Jews. [28]After I am sure the poor in Jerusalem get the money that has been given for them, I will leave for Spain and stop and visit you. [29]I know that when I come to you I will bring Christ's full blessing.

[30]Brothers and sisters, I beg you to help me in my work by praying to God for me. Do this because of our Lord Jesus and the love that the Holy Spirit gives us. [31]Pray that I will be saved from the nonbelievers in Judea and that this help I bring to Jerusalem will please God's people there. [32]Then, if God wants me to, I will come to you with joy, and together you and I will have a time of rest. [33]The God who gives peace be with you all. Amen.

GREETINGS TO THE CHRISTIANS

16 I recommend to you our sister Phoebe, who is a helper[n] in the church in Cenchrea. [2]I ask you to accept her in the Lord in the way God's people should. Help her with anything she needs, because she has helped me and many other people also.

[3]Give my greetings to Priscilla and Aquila, who work together with me in Christ Jesus [4]and who risked their own lives to save my life. I am thankful to them, and all the non-Jewish churches are thankful as well. [5]Also, greet for me the church that meets at their house.

Greetings to my dear friend Epenetus, who was the first person in the country of Asia to follow Christ. [6]Greetings to Mary, who worked very hard for you. [7]Greetings to Andronicus

---

15:12 **Jesse** Jesse was the father of David, king of Israel. Jesus was from their family.   16:1 **helper** Literally, "deaconess." This might mean the same as one of the special women helpers in 1 Timothy 3:11.

travel the road

Maybe you're into reading Christian books about the end of the world as we know it. But something big has to happen before Jesus shows up. Jesus said, "The Good News about God's kingdom will be preached in all the world, to every nation. Then the end will come" (Matthew 24:14). No one can put a date or time on Christ's return (Matthew 24:36), but we can be sure he will return only when the job of telling the world about him is complete. Maybe—just maybe—you will be part of the generation that finishes the task and ushers in Christ's return.

For more on extreme missions visit www.traveltheroad.com.

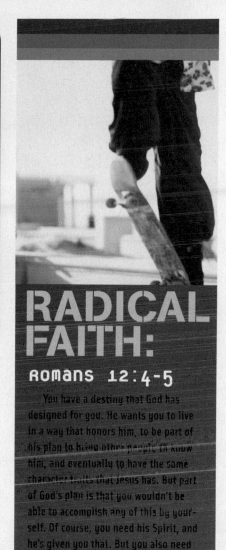

and Junia, my relatives, who were in prison with me. They are very important apostles. They were believers in Christ before I was. ⁸Greetings to Ampliatus, my dear friend in the Lord. ⁹Greetings to Urbanus, a worker together with me for Christ. And greetings to my dear friend Stachys, ¹⁰Greetings to Apelles, who was tested and proved that he truly loves Christ. Greetings to all those who are in the family of Aristobulus. ¹¹Greetings to Herodion, my fellow citizen. Greetings to all those in the family of Narcissus who belong to the Lord. ¹²Greetings to Tryphena and Tryphosa, women who work very hard for the Lord. Greetings to my dear friend Persis, who also has worked very hard for the Lord. ¹³Greetings to Rufus, who is a special person in the Lord, and to his mother, who has been

RADICAL FAITH:
ROMANS 12:4-5

You have a destiny that God has designed for you. He wants you to live in a way that honors him, to be part of his plan to bring other people to know him, and eventually to have the same character traits that Jesus has. But part of God's plan is that you wouldn't be able to accomplish any of this by yourself. Of course, you need his Spirit, and he's given you that. But you also need other people.

God wants his people to care about each other and to be able to depend on each other. Your strengths and weaknesses are different from another person's. That person may be able to help you with an area of your life that gives you a lot of trouble. Or you may be able to help someone else see clearly in a situation that is really confusing to him.

Everyone has to trust Jesus as an individual. But once you become a Christian, your life and your relationship with God is connected to other people. You need other Christians! And they need you.

WAYS TO WALK THE WALK

ROMANS 12:18-20

WORD: Do your part to call a truce—and don't take revenge.

WALK IT: Who is the most awful or annoying person in your life? Think of two things you can do today to improve your relationship. What happens when you do them?

ROMANS 13:1-7

WORD: We owe respect and obedience to authorities in our lives.

WALK IT: Today when you want to rebel against a rule, come up with a few reasons why God has put authorities in your life. Write them down. Remind yourself of them until they stick.

WORST SMELLS ON GOD'S GREEN EARTH

1. DOG BREATH
2. DIESEL EXHAUST
3. CHEAP PINK BUBBLE GUM
4. UNWASHED ARMPIT
5. SKUNK ROADKILL
6. PIG FARMS
7. FISH GUTS
8. PHYS ED LOCKERS
9. SULFURIC ACID
10. LITTLE BROTHER

like a mother to me also. [14]Greetings to Asyncritus, Phlegon, Hermes, Patrobas, Hermas, and all the brothers who are with them. [15]Greetings to Philologus and Julia, Nereus and his sister, and Olympas, and to all God's people with them. [16]Greet each other with a holy kiss. All of Christ's churches send greetings to you.

[17]Brothers and sisters, I ask you to look out for those who cause people to be against each other and who upset other people's faith. They are against the true teaching you learned, so stay away from them. [18]Such people are not serving our Lord Christ but are only doing what pleases themselves. They use fancy talk and fine words to fool the minds of those who do not know about evil. [19]All the believers have heard that you obey, so I am very happy because of you. But I want you to be wise in what is good and innocent in what is evil.

[20]The God who brings peace will soon defeat Satan and give you power over him.

The grace of our Lord Jesus be with you.

[21]Timothy, a worker together with me, sends greetings, as well as Lucius, Jason, and Sosipater, my relatives.

[22]I am Tertius, and I am writing this letter from Paul. I send greetings to you in the Lord.

[23]Gaius is letting me and the whole church here use his home. He also sends greetings to you, as do Erastus, the city treasurer, and our brother Quartus. [24][n]

[25]Glory to God who can make you strong in faith by the Good News that I tell people and by the message about Jesus Christ. The message about Christ is the secret that was hidden for long ages past but is now made known. [26]It has been made clear through the writings of the prophets. And by the command of the eternal God it is made known to all nations that they might believe and obey.

[27]To the only wise God be glory forever through Jesus Christ! Amen.

EXTRAS:

HOW TO SCALE A ROCK WALL

Sure, you can go rock climbing where you get your pants in a bunch with a safety harness. But that takes money and expert trainers. An easier option is to go bouldering with a friend—climbing rope-free while staying close enough to the ground so you can safely jump down. Instead of going up, or "ascending," you practice "traversing," or going across. You follow the same big rule of ascents: Your legs far outpower your arms, so focus on finding footholds and using your leg muscles to move around instead of pulling yourself up or across with your arms. It's a smart rule for life: You have to know where your real power comes from.

16:24 Verse 24 Some Greek copies add verse 24: "The grace of our Lord Jesus Christ be with all of you. Amen."

1 CORINTHIANS

HOW TO BUILD A BETTER CHURCH

There's no such thing as the perfect church. Period. End of story. As long as human beings are involved in running the show, there will be sins and mistakes in how we do church. Consider a congregation founded by the most notable, influential, successful Christian minister of the first generation of believers. Paul didn't stay in Corinth for just a few days or weeks as he did in most cities he visited. He settled down there for two years, training and nurturing these spiritual infants. It didn't take long after Paul left for the Corinthians to start behaving like disobedient, rebellious kids who didn't know any better.

Take a look at what was going on: They were arguing over who in the church was most important... suing each other in court... turning a blind eye to incest among the congregation... mishandling spiritual gifts... and showing they were thoroughly confused about key Christian beliefs like the Resurrection. In this blunt but loving letter, Paul replies to an array of practical questions the Corinthians had raised in a letter to him. But he also confronts issues they were apparently too embarrassed to mention.

This isn't a boring letter. First Corinthians cuts to the heart of these issues. And it's timely because, unfortunately, there's a little bit of Corinth in every church—and a lot of Corinth in some.

1 From Paul. God called me to be an apostle of Christ Jesus because that is what God wanted. Also from Sosthenes, our brother in Christ.

²To the church of God in Corinth, to you who have been made holy in Christ Jesus. You were called to be God's holy people with all people everywhere who pray in the name of the Lord Jesus Christ—their Lord and ours:

³Grace and peace to you from God our Father and the Lord Jesus Christ.

PAUL GIVES THANKS TO GOD

⁴I always thank my God for you because of the grace God has given you in Christ Jesus. ⁵I thank God because in Christ you have been made rich in every way, in all your speaking and in all your knowledge. ⁶Just as our witness about Christ has been guaranteed to you, ⁷so you have every gift from God while you wait for our Lord Jesus Christ to come again. ⁸Jesus will keep you strong until the end so that there will be no wrong in you on the day our Lord Jesus Christ comes again. ⁹God, who has called you to share everything with his Son, Jesus Christ our Lord, is faithful.

PROBLEMS IN THE CHURCH

¹⁰I beg you, brothers and sisters,ⁿ by the name of our Lord Jesus Christ that all of you agree with each other and not be split into groups. I beg that you be completely joined together by having the same kind of thinking and the same purpose. ¹¹My brothers and sisters, some people from Chloe's family have told me quite plainly that there are quarrels among you. ¹²This is what I mean: One of you says, "I follow Paul"; another says, "I follow Apollos"; another says, "I follow Peter"; and another says, "I follow Christ." ¹³Christ has been divided up into different groups! Did Paul die on the cross for you? No! Were you baptized in the name of Paul? No! ¹⁴I thank God I did not baptize any of you except Crispus and Gaius ¹⁵so that now no one can say you were baptized in my name. ¹⁶(I also baptized the family of Stephanas, but I do not remember that I baptized anyone else.) ¹⁷Christ did not send me to baptize people but to preach the Good News. And he sent me to preach the Good News without using words of human wisdom so that the crossⁿ of Christ would not lose its power.

CHRIST IS GOD'S POWER AND WISDOM

¹⁸The teaching about the cross is foolishness to those who are being lost, but to us who are being saved it is the power of God. ¹⁹It is written in the Scriptures:

> "I will cause the wise men to lose their
>   wisdom;
> I will make the wise men unable to
>   understand." *Isaiah 29:14*

²⁰Where is the wise person? Where is the educated person? Where is the skilled talker of this world? God has made the wisdom of the world foolish. ²¹In the wisdom of God the world did not know God through its own wisdom. So

RADICAL FAITH:
1 corinthians 1:9

Paul says that God chose you to "share everything" with Jesus, to be his partner. Being his partner is an honor you don't deserve, but neither does anyone else. But God, because of his kindness and love, chose you for the job even though you aren't qualified for it.

What does it mean to be Jesus' partner? Partners work together toward a common goal. Think about what that goal might be for you and Jesus. Don't just think about your own life—Jesus isn't your genie-in-a-bottle helping you get the things you want. Instead, think about other people. Ask yourself, What does Jesus want to do in my sister's life, my dad's life? What does he want to do for my friends? Ask Jesus those questions too, and ask him what you can do to make that happen. He'll answer you.

It's an awesome privilege to be chosen as Jesus' partner, to work with him to change the lives of people you care about—and maybe even some people you haven't met yet. Make up your mind to be the kind of partner Jesus can be proud of.

WAYS TO WALK THE WALK

1 corinthians 1:9

WORD: God is faithful.

WALK IT: Look closely at your life and spot an area where you're a control freak—things have to go your way. Let go of that issue and see where God takes you.

1 corinthians 2:15

WORD: Those who are spiritual discern all things.

WALK IT: Spend at least 30 minutes today praying about a big decision or something that really bugs you. Ask God to give you wisdom and look for his answers.

 1:10 brothers and sisters Although the Greek text says "brothers" here and throughout this book, Paul's words were meant for the entire church, including men and women. **1:17 cross** Paul uses the cross as a picture of the Good News, the story of Christ's death and rising from the dead for people's sins. The cross, or Christ's death, was God's way to save people.

God chose to use the message that sounds foolish to save those who believe. ²²The Jews ask for miracles, and the Greeks want wisdom. ²³But we preach a crucified Christ. This is a big problem to the Jews, and it is foolishness to those who are not Jews. ²⁴But Christ is the power of God and the wisdom of God to those people God has called—Jews and Greeks. ²⁵Even the foolishness of God is wiser than human wisdom, and the weakness of God is stronger than human strength.

MATTHEW 18:3 "YOU MUST CHANGE AND BECOME LIKE LITTLE CHILDREN."

²⁶Brothers and sisters, look at what you were when God called you. Not many of you were wise in the way the world judges wisdom. Not many of you had great influence. Not many of you came from important families. ²⁷But God chose the foolish things of the world to shame the wise, and he chose the weak things of the world to shame the strong. ²⁸He chose what the world thinks is unimportant and what the world looks down on and thinks is nothing in order to destroy what the world thinks is important. ²⁹God did this so that no one can brag in his presence. ³⁰Because of God you are in Christ Jesus, who has become for us wisdom from God. In Christ we are put right with God, and have been made holy, and have been set free from sin. ³¹So, as the Scripture says, "If someone wants to brag, he should brag only about the Lord."ⁿ

THE MESSAGE OF CHRIST'S DEATH

2 Dear brothers and sisters, when I came to you, I did not come preaching God's secret with fancy words or a show of human wisdom. ²I decided that while I was with you I would forget about everything except Jesus Christ and his death on the cross. ³So when I came to you, I was weak and fearful and trembling. ⁴My teaching and preaching were not with words of human wisdom that persuade people but with proof of the power that the Spirit gives. ⁵This was so that your faith would be in God's power and not in human wisdom.

GOD'S WISDOM

⁶However, I speak a wisdom to those who are mature. But this wisdom is not from this world or from the rulers of this world, who are losing their power. ⁷I speak God's secret wisdom, which he has kept hidden. Before the world began, God planned this wisdom for our glory. ⁸None of the rulers of this world understood it. If they had, they would not have crucified the Lord of glory. ⁹But as it is written in the Scriptures:

"No one has ever seen this,
and no one has ever heard about it.
No one has ever imagined
what God has prepared for those
who love him." *Isaiah 64:4*

¹⁰But God has shown us these things through the Spirit.

The Spirit searches out all things, even the deep secrets of God. ¹¹Who knows the thoughts that another person has? Only a person's spirit that lives within him knows his thoughts. It is the same with God. No one knows the thoughts of God except the Spirit of God. ¹²Now we did not receive the spirit of the world, but we received the Spirit that is from God so that we can know all that God has given us. ¹³And we speak about these things, not with words taught us by human wisdom but with words taught us by the Spirit. And so we explain spiritual truths to spiritual people. ¹⁴A person who does not have the Spirit does not accept the truths that come from the Spirit of God. That person thinks they are foolish and cannot understand them, because they can only be judged to be true by the Spirit. ¹⁵The spiritual person is able to judge all things, but no one can judge him. The Scripture says:

¹⁶"Who has known the mind of the Lord?
Who has been able to teach him?"
Isaiah 40:13

But we have the mind of Christ.

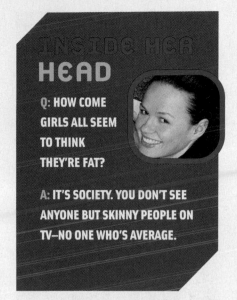

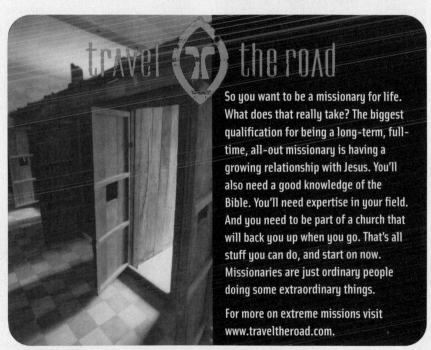

 1:31 "If . . . Lord." Quotation from Jeremiah 9:24.

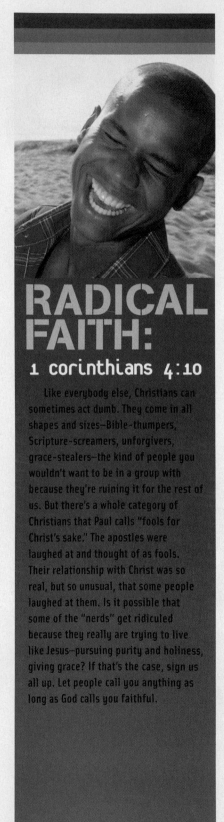

RADICAL FAITH:

1 corinthians 4:10

Like everybody else, Christians can sometimes act dumb. They come in all shapes and sizes—Bible-thumpers, Scripture-screamers, unforgivers, grace-stealers—the kind of people you wouldn't want to be in a group with because they're ruining it for the rest of us. But there's a whole category of Christians that Paul calls "fools for Christ's sake." The apostles were laughed at and thought of as fools. Their relationship with Christ was so real, but so unusual, that some people laughed at them. Is it possible that some of the "nerds" get ridiculed because they really are trying to live like Jesus—pursuing purity and holiness, giving grace? If that's the case, sign us all up. Let people call you anything as long as God calls you faithful.

FOLLOWING PEOPLE IS WRONG

3 Brothers and sisters, in the past I could not talk to you as I talk to spiritual people. I had to talk to you as I would to people without the Spirit—babies in Christ. [2]The teaching I gave you was like milk, not solid food, because you were not able to take solid food. And even now you are not ready. [3]You are still not spiritual, because there is jealousy and quarreling among you, and this shows that you are not spiritual. You are acting like people of the world. [4]One of you says, "I belong to Paul," and another says, "I belong to Apollos." When you say things like this, you are acting like people of the world.

[5]Is Apollos important? No! Is Paul important? No! We are only servants of God who helped you believe. Each one of us did the work God gave us to do. [6]I planted the seed, and Apollos watered it. But God is the One who made it grow. [7]So the one who plants is not important, and the one who waters is not important. Only God, who makes things grow, is important. [8]The one who plants and the one who waters have the same purpose, and each will be rewarded for his own work. [9]We are God's workers, working together; you are like God's farm, God's house.

[10]Using the gift God gave me, I laid the foundation of that house like an expert builder. Others are building on that foundation, but all people should be careful how they build on it. [11]The foundation that has already been laid is Jesus Christ, and no one can lay down any other foundation. [12]But if people build on that foundation, using gold, silver, jewels, wood, grass, or straw, [13]their work will be clearly seen, because the Day of Judgment[n] will make it visible. That Day will appear with fire, and the fire will test everyone's work to show what sort of work it was. [14]If the building that has been put on the foundation still stands, the builder will get a reward. [15]But if the building is burned up, the builder will suffer loss. The builder will be saved, but it will be as one who escaped from a fire.

[16]Don't you know that you are God's temple and that God's Spirit lives in you? [17]If anyone destroys God's temple, God will destroy

COOLEST THINGS GOD HAS MADE

1. GIRLS
2. JAGGED MOUNTAIN PEAKS
3. DOGS
4. TROPICAL ISLANDS
5. PTERODACTYLS
6. FACIAL HAIR
7. THE MOON
8. RHINOCEROSES
9. BLIZZARDS
10. OCEAN WAVES

that person, because God's temple is holy and you are that temple.

[18]Do not fool yourselves. If you think you are wise in this world, you should become a fool so that you can become truly wise, [19]because the wisdom of this world is foolishness with God. It is written in the Scriptures, "He catches those who are wise in their own clever traps."[n] [20]It is also written in the Scriptures, "The Lord knows what wise people think. He knows their thoughts are just a puff of wind."[n] [21]So you should not brag about human leaders. All things belong to you: [22]Paul, Apollos, and Peter; the world, life, death, the present, and the future—all these belong to you. [23]And you belong to Christ, and Christ belongs to God.

APOSTLES ARE SERVANTS OF CHRIST

4 People should think of us as servants of Christ, the ones God has trusted with his secrets. [2]Now in this way those who are trusted with something valuable must show they are worthy of that trust. [3]As for myself, I do not care if I am judged by you or by any human court. I do not even judge myself. [4]I know of no wrong I have done, but this does not make me

3:13 **Day of Judgment** The day Christ will come to judge all people and take his people home to live with him.   3:19 "He . . . traps." Quotation from Job 5:13.   3:20 "The Lord . . . wind." Quotation from Psalm 94:11.

right before the Lord. The Lord is the One who judges me. [5]So do not judge before the right time; wait until the Lord comes. He will bring to light things that are now hidden in darkness, and will make known the secret purposes of people's hearts. Then God will praise each one of them.

[6]Brothers and sisters, I have used Apollos and myself as examples so you could learn through us the meaning of the saying, "Follow only what is written in the Scriptures." Then you will not be more proud of one person than another. [7]Who says you are better than others? What do you have that was not given to you? And if it was given to you, why do you brag as if you did not receive it as a gift?

[8]You think you already have everything you need. You think you are rich. You think you have become kings without us. I wish you really were kings so we could be kings together with you. [9]But it seems to me that God has put us apostles in last place, like those sentenced to die. We are like a show for the whole world to see—angels and people. [10]We are fools for Christ's sake, but you are very wise in Christ. We are weak, but you are strong. You receive honor, but we are shamed. [11]Even to this very hour we do not have enough to eat or drink or to wear. We are often beaten, and we have no homes in which to live. [12]We work hard with our own hands for our food. When people curse us, we bless them. When they hurt us, we put up with it. [13]When they tell evil lies about us, we speak nice words about them. Even today, we are treated as though we were the garbage of the world—the filth of the earth.

[14]I am not trying to make you feel ashamed. I am writing this to give you a warning as my own dear children. [15]For though you may have ten thousand teachers in Christ, you do not have many fathers. Through the Good News I became your father in Christ Jesus, [16]so I beg you, please follow my example. [17]That is why I am sending to you Timothy, my son in the Lord. I love Timothy, and he is faithful. He will help you remember my way of life in Christ Jesus, just as I teach it in all the churches everywhere.

[18]Some of you have become proud, thinking that I will not come to you again. [19]But I will come to you very soon if the Lord wishes. Then I will know what the proud ones do, not what they say, [20]because the kingdom of God is present not in talk but in power. [21]Which do you want: that I come to you with punishment or with love and gentleness?

WICKEDNESS IN THE CHURCH

5 It is actually being said that there is sexual sin among you. And it is a kind that does not happen even among people who do not know God. A man there has his father's wife. [2]And you are proud! You should have been filled with sadness so that the man who did this should be put out of your group. [3]I am not there with you in person, but I am with you in spirit. And I have already judged the man who did that sin as if I were really there. [4]When you meet together in the name of our Lord Jesus, and I meet with you in spirit with the power of our Lord Jesus, [5]then hand this

man over to Satan. So his sinful self[n] will be destroyed, and his spirit will be saved on the day of the Lord.

[6]Your bragging is not good. You know the saying, "Just a little yeast makes the whole batch of dough rise." [7]Take out all the old yeast so that you will be a new batch of dough without yeast, which you really are. For Christ, our Passover lamb, has been sacrificed. [8]So let us celebrate this feast, but not with the bread that has the old yeast—the yeast of sin and wickedness. Let us celebrate this feast with the bread that has no yeast—the bread of goodness and truth.

92 PERCENT OF PEOPLE UNDER 18 PLAY VIDEO GAMES. –NATIONAL INSTITUTE ON MEDIA AND THE FAMILY

[9]I wrote you in my earlier letter not to associate with those who sin sexually. [10]But I did not mean you should not associate with those of this world who sin sexually, or with the greedy, or robbers, or those who worship idols. To get away from them you would have to leave this world. [11]I am writing to tell you that you must not associate with those who call themselves believers in Christ but who sin sexually, or are greedy, or worship idols, or abuse others with words, or get drunk, or cheat people. Do not even eat with people like that.

[12-13]It is not my business to judge those who are not part of the church. God will judge them. But you must judge the people who are part of the church. The Scripture says, "You must get rid of the evil person among you."[n]

JUDGING PROBLEMS AMONG CHRISTIANS

6 When you have something against another Christian, how can you bring yourself to go before judges who are not right with God? Why do you not let God's people decide who is right? [2]Surely you know that God's people will judge the world. So if you are to judge the world, are you not able to judge small cases as well? [3]You know that in the future we will judge angels, so surely we can judge the ordinary things of this life. [4]If you have ordinary cases that must be judged, are you going to appoint people as judges who mean nothing to the

church? [5]I say this to shame you. Surely there is someone among you wise enough to judge a complaint between believers. [6]But now one believer goes to court against another believer—and you do this in front of unbelievers!

[7]The fact that you have lawsuits against each other shows that you are already defeated. Why not let yourselves be wronged? Why not let yourselves be cheated? [8]But you yourselves do wrong and cheat, and you do this to other believers!

[9-10]Surely you know that the people who do wrong will not inherit God's kingdom. Do not be fooled. Those who sin sexually, worship idols, take part in adultery, those who are male prostitutes, or men who have sexual relations with other men, those who steal, are greedy, get drunk, lie about others, or rob—these people will not inherit God's kingdom. [11]In the past, some of you were like that, but you were washed clean. You were made holy, and you were made right with God in the name of the Lord Jesus Christ and in the Spirit of our God.

USE YOUR BODIES FOR GOD'S GLORY

[12]"I am allowed to do all things," but all things are not good for me to do. "I am allowed to do all things," but I will not let anything make me its slave. [13]"Food is for the stomach, and the stomach for food," but God will destroy them both. The body is not for sexual sin but for the Lord, and the Lord is for the body. [14]By his power God has raised the Lord from the dead and will also raise us from the dead. [15]Surely you know that your bodies are parts of Christ himself. So I must never take the parts of Christ and join them to a prostitute! [16]It is written in the Scriptures, "The two will become one body."[n] So you should know that anyone who joins with a prostitute becomes one body with the prostitute. [17]But the one who joins with the Lord is one spirit with the Lord.

[18]So run away from sexual sin. Every other sin people do is outside their bodies, but those who sin sexually sin against their own bodies. [19]You should know that your body is a temple for the Holy Spirit who is in you. You have received the Holy Spirit from God. So you do not belong to yourselves, [20]because you were bought by God for a price. So honor God with your bodies.

ABOUT MARRIAGE

7 Now I will discuss the things you wrote me about. It is good for a man not to

5:5 **sinful self** Literally, "flesh." This could also mean his body.   5:12-13 **"You . . . you."** Quotation from Deuteronomy 17:7; 19:19; 22:21, 24; 24:7.   6:16 **"The two . . . body."** Quotation from Genesis 2:24.

EXPERTS ANSWER YOUR QUESTIONS

Q. *I want to get my friends to church. Where do I start?*

A. Some teens know they need something deep—even if they don't quite know they need God. They might be interested in joining you for something like a Bible study or up-to-date worship service. Just ask. Others will do better if they get to know your Christian friends in a more casual setting. You can start by inviting those people to parties and non-threatening outings.

Q. *I hear all the time at church that I'm supposed to stick up for my faith. I'm not sure I can take on the teachers in a debate. Is that what I'm supposed to do?*

A. Your way of sharing about Jesus will reflect who you are. Some people are better sharing with words. Others are better with actions. You might not be able to hold your own in a debate, but you can witness by showing up, paying attention, and pulling the best grades you can. When you sense your teacher or classmates are ready to talk, take the opportunity to speak up.

have sexual relations with a woman. ²But because sexual sin is a danger, each man should have his own wife, and each woman should have her own husband. ³The husband should give his wife all that he owes her as his wife. And the wife should give her husband all that she owes him as her husband. ⁴The wife does not have full rights over her own body; her husband shares them. And the husband does not have full rights over his own body; his wife shares them. ⁵Do not refuse to give your bodies to each other, unless you both agree to stay away from sexual relations for a time so you can give your time to prayer. Then come together again so Satan cannot tempt you because of a lack of self-control. ⁶I say this to give you permission to stay away from sexual relations for a time. It is not a command to do so. ⁷I wish that everyone were like me, but each person has his own gift from God. One has one gift, another has another gift.

⁸Now for those who are not married and for the widows I say this: It is good for them to stay unmarried as I am. ⁹But if they cannot control themselves, they should marry. It is better to marry than to burn with sexual desire.

¹⁰Now I give this command for the married people. (The command is not from me; it is from the Lord.) A wife should not leave her husband. ¹¹But if she does leave, she must not marry again, or she should make up with her husband. Also the husband should not divorce his wife.

¹²For all the others I say this (I am saying this, not the Lord): If a Christian man has a wife who is not a believer, and she is happy to live with him, he must not divorce her. ¹³And if a Christian woman has a husband who is not a believer, and he is happy to live with her, she must not divorce him. ¹⁴The husband who is not a believer is made holy through his believing wife. And the wife who is not a believer is made holy through her believing husband. If this were not true, your children would not be clean, but now your children are holy.

¹⁵But if those who are not believers decide to leave, let them leave. When this happens, the Christian man or woman is free. But God called us to live in peace. ¹⁶Wife, you don't know; maybe you will save your husband. And husband, you don't know; maybe you will save your wife.

LIVE AS GOD CALLED YOU

¹⁷But in any case each one of you should continue to live the way God has given you to live—the way you were when God called you.

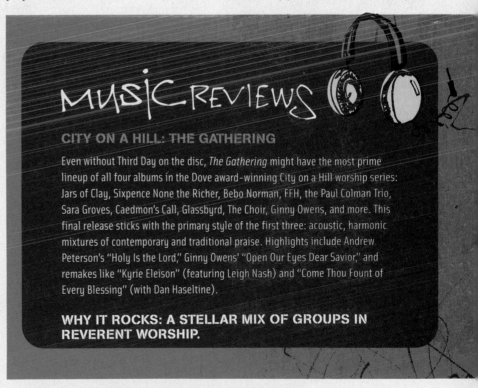

MUSIC REVIEWS

CITY ON A HILL: THE GATHERING

Even without Third Day on the disc, *The Gathering* might have the most prime lineup of all four albums in the Dove award-winning City on a Hill worship series: Jars of Clay, Sixpence None the Richer, Bebo Norman, FFH, the Paul Colman Trio, Sara Groves, Caedmon's Call, Glassbyrd, The Choir, Ginny Owens, and more. This final release sticks with the primary style of the first three: acoustic, harmonic mixtures of contemporary and traditional praise. Highlights include Andrew Peterson's "Holy Is the Lord," Ginny Owens' "Open Our Eyes Dear Savior," and remakes like "Kyrie Eleison" (featuring Leigh Nash) and "Come Thou Fount of Every Blessing" (with Dan Haseltine).

WHY IT ROCKS: A STELLAR MIX OF GROUPS IN REVERENT WORSHIP.

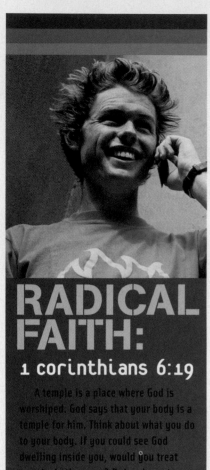

RADICAL FAITH:

1 corinthians 6:19

A temple is a place where God is worshiped. God says that your body is a temple for him. Think about what you do to your body. If you could see God dwelling inside you, would you treat your body the same? Doing drugs turns the temple into a haunted house. Not only are you tearing down the place God lives, you're making a mockery of his home and his creation. Would you go to an actual temple and mess it all up? No. Neither should you throw trash into your own temple, turn it into a house of prostitution, or cover it with graffiti.

The God who loves you deserves better than a crack house for a temple. He wants to glorify himself in you. Drugs are stupid and kill. You already know that. But did you know that Satan uses drugs to destroy as many temples as possible? Don't do drugs. Practice self-control and keep your temple pure and holy and healthy. Ask God to dwell richly in you and commit to being a good temple for him.

This is a rule I make in all the churches. 18If a man was already circumcised when he was called, he should not undo his circumcision. If a man was without circumcision when he was called, he should not be circumcised. 19It is not important if a man is circumcised or not. The important thing is obeying God's commands. 20Each one of you should stay the way you were when God called you. 21If you were a slave when God called you, do not let that bother you. But if you can be free, then make good use of your freedom. 22Those who were slaves when the Lord called them are free persons who belong to the Lord. In the same way, those who were free when they were called are now Christ's slaves. 23You all were bought at a great price, so do not become slaves of people. 24Brothers and sisters, each of you should stay as you were when you were called, and stay there with God.

QUESTIONS ABOUT GETTING MARRIED

25Now I write about people who are not married. I have no command from the Lord about this; I give my opinion. But I can be trusted, because the Lord has shown me mercy. 26The present time is a time of trouble, so I think it is good for you to stay the way you are. 27If you have a wife, do not try to become free from her. If you are not married, do not try to find a wife. 28But if you decide to marry, you have not sinned. And if a girl who has never married decides to marry, she has not sinned. But those who marry will have trouble in this life, and I want you to be free from trouble.

29Brothers and sisters, this is what I mean: We do not have much time left. So starting now, those who have wives should live as if they had no wives. 30Those who are crying should live as if they were not crying. Those who are happy should live as if they were not happy. Those who buy things should live as if they own nothing. 31Those who use the things of the world should live as if they were not using them, because this world in its present form will soon be gone.

32I want you to be free from worry. A man who is not married is busy with the Lord's work, trying to please the Lord. 33But a man who is married is busy with things of the world, trying to please his wife. 34He must think about two things—pleasing his wife and pleasing the Lord. A woman who is not married or a girl who has never married is busy with the Lord's work. She wants to be holy in body and spirit. But a married woman is busy with things of the world, as to how she can please her husband. 35I am saying this to help you, not to limit you. But I want you to live in the right way, to give yourselves fully to the Lord without concern for other things.

36If a man thinks he is not doing the right thing with the girl he is engaged to, if she is almost past the best age to marry and he feels he should marry her, he should do what he wants. They should get married. It is no sin. 37But if a man is sure in his mind that there is no need for marriage, and has his own desires under control, and has decided not to marry the one to whom he is engaged, he is doing the right thing. 38So the man who marries his girl does right, but the man who does not marry will do better.

39A woman must stay with her husband as long as he lives. But if her husband dies, she is free to marry any man she wants, but she must marry in the Lord. 40The woman is happier if she does not marry again. This is my opinion, but I believe I also have God's Spirit.

ABOUT FOOD OFFERED TO IDOLS

8 Now I will write about meat that is sacrificed to idols. We know that "we all have knowledge." Knowledge puffs you up with pride, but love builds up. 2If you think you know something, you do not yet know anything as you should. 3But if any person loves God, that person is known by God.

4So this is what I say about eating meat sacrificed to idols: We know that an idol is really nothing in the world, and we know there is only one God. 5Even though there are things called gods, in heaven or on earth (and there are many "gods" and "lords"), 6for us there is only one God—our Father. All things came from him, and we live for him. And there is only one Lord—Jesus Christ. All things were made through him, and we also were made through him.

7But not all people know this. Some people are still so used to idols that when they eat meat, they still think of it as being sacrificed to an idol. Because their conscience is weak, when they eat it, they feel guilty. 8But food will not bring us closer to God. Refusing to eat does not make us less pleasing to God, and eating does not make us better in God's sight.

[9]But be careful that your freedom does not cause those who are weak in faith to fall into sin. [10]You have "knowledge," so you eat in an idol's temple.[n] But someone who is weak in faith might see you eating there and be encouraged to eat meat sacrificed to idols while thinking it is wrong to do so. [11]This weak believer for whom Christ died is ruined because of your "knowledge." [12]When you sin against your brothers and sisters in Christ like this and cause them to do what they feel is wrong, you are also sinning against Christ. [13]So if the food I eat causes them to fall into sin, I will never eat meat again so that I will not cause any of them to sin.

PAUL IS LIKE THE OTHER APOSTLES

9 I am a free man. I am an apostle. I have seen Jesus our Lord. You people are all an example of my work in the Lord. [2]If others do not accept me as an apostle, surely you do, because you are proof that I am an apostle in the Lord.

[3]This is the answer I give people who want to judge me: [4]Do we not have the right to eat and drink? [5]Do we not have the right to bring a believing wife with us when we travel as do the other apostles and the Lord's brothers and Peter? [6]Are Barnabas and I the only ones who must work to earn our living? [7]No soldier ever serves in the army and pays his own salary. No one ever plants a vineyard without eating some of the grapes. No person takes care of a flock without drinking some of the milk.

[8]I do not say this by human authority; God's law also says the same thing. [9]It is written in the law of Moses: "When an ox is working in the grain, do not cover its mouth to keep it from eating."[n] When God said this, was he thinking only about oxen? No. [10]He was really talking about us. Yes, that Scripture was written for us, because it goes on to say: "The one who plows and the one who works in the grain should hope to get some of the grain for their work." [11]Since we planted spiritual seed among you, is it too much if we should harvest from you some things for this life? [12]If others have the right to get something from you, surely we have this right, too. But we do not use it. No, we put up with everything ourselves so that we will not keep anyone from believing the Good News of Christ. [13]Surely you know that those who work at the Temple get their food from the Temple, and those who serve at the altar get part of what is offered at the altar. [14]In the same way, the Lord has commanded that those who tell the Good News should get their living from this work.

[15]But I have not used any of these rights. And I am not writing this now to get anything from you. I would rather die than to have my reason for bragging taken away. [16]Telling the Good News does not give me any reason for bragging. Telling the Good News is my duty—something I must do. And how terrible it will be for me if I do not tell the Good News. [17]If I preach because it is my own choice, I have a reward. But if I preach and it is not my choice to do so, I am only doing the duty that was given to me. [18]So what reward do I get? This is my reward: that when I tell the Good News I can offer it freely. I do not use my full rights in my work of preaching the Good News.

[19]I am free and belong to no one. But I make myself a slave to all people to win as many as I can. [20]To the Jews I became like a Jew to win the Jews. I myself am not ruled by the law. But to those who are ruled by the law I became like a person who is ruled by the law. I did this to win those who are ruled by the law. [21]To those who are without the law I became like a person who is without the law. I did this to win those people who are without the law. (But really, I am not without God's law—I am ruled by Christ's law.) [22]To those who are weak, I became weak so I could win the weak. I have become all things to all people so I could save some of them in any way possible. [23]I do all this because of the Good News and so I can share in its blessings.

[24]You know that in a race all the runners run, but only one gets the prize. So run to win! [25]All those who compete in the games use self-control so they can win a crown. That crown is an earthly thing that lasts only a short time, but our crown will never be destroyed. [26]So I do not run without a goal. I fight like a boxer

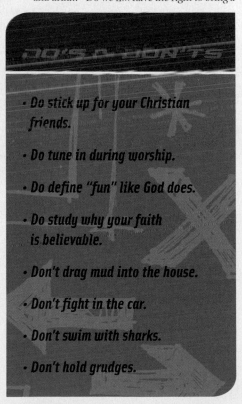

- *Do stick up for your Christian friends.*
- *Do tune in during worship.*
- *Do define "fun" like God does.*
- *Do study why your faith is believable.*
- *Don't drag mud into the house.*
- *Don't fight in the car.*
- *Don't swim with sharks.*
- *Don't hold grudges.*

COOLEST THINGS GOD GAVE PEOPLE BRAINS TO MAKE

1. SURFBOARDS
2. MICROPROCESSORS
3. SWISS ARMY KNIVES
4. ENGINES
5. ROLLERCOASTERS
6. CHEMOTHERAPY
7. GLASS
8. KAYAKS
9. CHALUPAS
10. INSTANT REPLAY

8:10 idol's temple Building where a god is worshiped. 9:9 "When an ox . . . eating." Quotation from Deuteronomy 25:4.

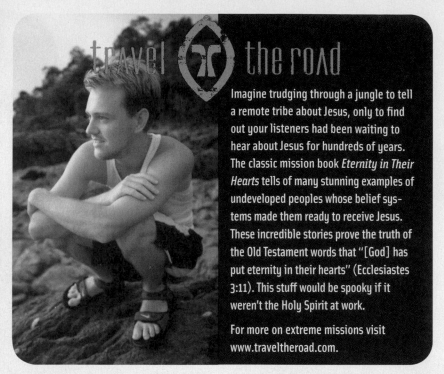

travel the ROAD

Imagine trudging through a jungle to tell a remote tribe about Jesus, only to find out your listeners had been waiting to hear about Jesus for hundreds of years. The classic mission book *Eternity in Their Hearts* tells of many stunning examples of undeveloped peoples whose belief systems made them ready to receive Jesus. These incredible stories prove the truth of the Old Testament words that "[God] has put eternity in their hearts" (Ecclesiastes 3:11). This stuff would be spooky if it weren't the Holy Spirit at work.

For more on extreme missions visit www.traveltheroad.com.

RELATIONSHIPS

"Children, obey your parents as the Lord wants, because this is the right thing to do" (Ephesians 6:1). God doesn't tell you to obey your parents because he wants to squash you under your parents' heavy thumb. He puts them in your life to bless you. God knows parents have been around the block, even not-so-hot parents. They know where you need to go in life. So he gives them the power to steer you for a while. Ever wonder about how God wants you to please him? Obeying your parents is at the top of his list for you.

who is hitting something—not just the air. ²⁷I treat my body hard and make it my slave so that I myself will not be disqualified after I have preached to others.

WARNINGS FROM ISRAEL'S PAST

10 Brothers and sisters, I want you to know what happened to our ancestors who followed Moses. They were all under the cloud and all went through the sea. [2]They were all baptized as followers of Moses in the cloud and in the sea. [3]They all ate the same spiritual food, [4]and all drank the same spiritual drink. They drank from that spiritual rock that followed them, and that rock was Christ. [5]But God was not pleased with most of them, so they died in the desert.

[6]And these things happened as examples for us, to stop us from wanting evil things as those people did. [7]Do not worship idols, as some of them did. Just as it is written in the Scriptures: "They sat down to eat and drink, and then they got up and sinned sexually."*n* [8]We must not take part in sexual sins, as some of them did. In one day twenty-three thousand of them died because of their sins. [9]We must not test Christ as some of them did; they were killed by snakes. [10]Do not complain as some of them did; they were killed by the angel that destroys.

[11]The things that happened to those people are examples. They were written down to teach us, because we live in a time when all these things of the past have reached their goal. [12]If you think you are strong, you should be careful not to fall. [13]The only temptation that has come to you is that which everyone has. But you can trust God, who will not permit you to be tempted more than you can stand. But when you are tempted, he will also give you a way to escape so that you will be able to stand it.

[14]So, my dear friends, run away from the worship of idols. [15]I am speaking to you as to intelligent people; judge for yourselves what I say. [16]We give thanks for the cup of blessing,*n* which is a sharing in the blood of Christ. And the bread that we break is a sharing in the body of Christ. [17]Because there is one loaf of bread, we who are many are one body, because we all share that one loaf.

[18]Think about the Israelites: Do not those who eat the sacrifices share in the altar? [19]I do not mean that the food sacrificed to an idol is important. I do not mean that an idol is anything at all. [20]But I say that what is sacrificed to idols is offered to demons, not to God. And I do not want you to share anything with demons.

10:7 "They . . . sexually." Quotation from Exodus 32:6.   10:16 cup of blessing The cup of the fruit of the vine that Christians thank God for and drink at the Lord's Supper.

244

21You cannot drink the cup of the Lord and the cup of demons also. You cannot share in the Lord's table and the table of demons. 22Are we trying to make the Lord jealous? We are not stronger than he is, are we?

HOW TO USE CHRISTIAN FREEDOM

23"We are allowed to do all things," but all things are not good for us to do. "We are allowed to do all things," but not all things help others grow stronger. 24Do not look out only for yourselves. Look out for the good of others also.

25Eat any meat that is sold in the meat market. Do not ask questions to see if it is meat you think is wrong to eat. 26You may eat it, "because the earth belongs to the Lord, and everything in it."[n]

27Those who are not believers may invite you to eat with them. If you want to go, eat anything that is put before you. Do not ask questions to see if you think it might be wrong to eat. 28But if anyone says to you, "That food was offered to idols," do not eat it. Do not eat it because of that person who told you and because eating it might be thought to be wrong. 29I don't mean you think it is wrong, but the other person might. But why, you ask, should my freedom be judged by someone else's conscience? 30If I eat the meal with thankfulness, why am I criticized because of something for which I thank God?

31The answer is, if you eat or drink, or if you do anything, do it all for the glory of God. 32Never do anything that might hurt others— Jews, Greeks, or God's church— 33just as I, also,

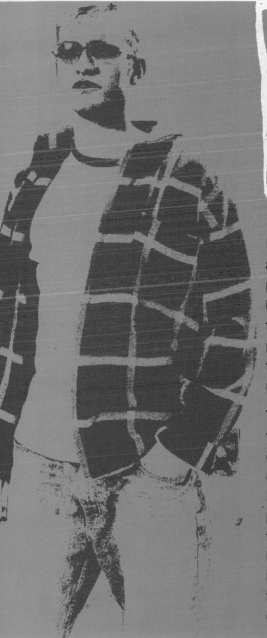

GET OUT THERE

HEAD START and **EARLY HEAD START** are comprehensive child development programs which serve children from birth to age 5, pregnant women, and their families. They are child-focused programs and have the overall goal of increasing the school readiness of young children in low-income families.

The Head Start program has a long tradition of delivering comprehensive and high quality services designed to foster healthy development in low-income children. Head Start grantee and delegate agencies provide a range of individualized services in the areas of education and early childhood development; medical, dental, and mental health; nutrition; and parent involvement. In addition, the entire range of Head Start services is responsive and appropriate to each child's and family's developmental, ethnic, cultural, and linguistic heritage and experience.

Volunteers are critical to the success of Head Start. In one recent year, approximately 1,345,000 individuals volunteered to work at Head Start centers. Head Start volunteers can assist with classroom activities, transportation, upkeep and renovation of centers, playground supervision, parent education, and other similar tasks. Head Start volunteers may choose to give a few hours of time or may volunteer every week.

To locate the Head Start program in your area, go to:
http://www.acf.hhs.gov/programs/hsb/hsweb/index.jsp.

 10:26 "because . . . it" Quotation from Psalms 24:1; 50:12; 89:11.

INSIDE HER HEAD

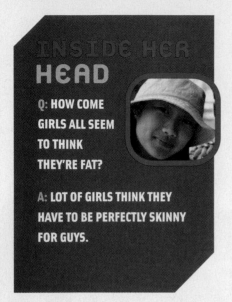

Q: HOW COME GIRLS ALL SEEM TO THINK THEY'RE FAT?

A: LOT OF GIRLS THINK THEY HAVE TO BE PERFECTLY SKINNY FOR GUYS.

try to please everybody in every way. I am not trying to do what is good for me but what is good for most people so they can be saved.

11 Follow my example, as I follow the example of Christ.

BEING UNDER AUTHORITY

[2]I praise you because you remember me in everything, and you follow closely the teachings just as I gave them to you. [3]But I want you to understand this: The head of every man is Christ, the head of a woman is the man,[n] and the head of Christ is God. [4]Every man who prays or prophesies with his head covered brings shame to his head. [5]But every woman who prays or prophesies with her head uncovered brings shame to her head. She is the same as a woman who has her head shaved. [6]If a woman does not cover her head, she should have her hair cut off. But since it is shameful for a woman to cut off her hair or to shave her head, she should cover her head. [7]But a man should not cover his head, because he is the likeness and glory of God. But woman is man's glory. [8]Man did not come from woman, but woman came from man. [9]And man was not made for woman, but woman was made for man. [10]So that is why a woman should have a symbol of authority on her head, because of the angels.

[11]But in the Lord women are not independent of men, and men are not independent of women. [12]This is true because woman came from man, but also man is born from woman. But everything comes from God. [13]Decide this for yourselves: Is it right for a woman to pray to God with her head uncovered? [14]Even nature itself teaches you that wearing long hair is shameful for a man. [15]But long hair is a woman's glory. Long hair is given to her as a covering. [16]Some people may still want to argue about this, but I would add that neither we nor the churches of God have any other practice.

THE LORD'S SUPPER

[17]In the things I tell you now I do not praise you, because when you come together you do more harm than good. [18]First, I hear that when you meet together as a church you are divided, and I believe some of this. [19](It is necessary to have differences among you so that it may be clear which of you really have God's approval.) [20]When you come together, you are not really eating the Lord's Supper.[n] [21]This is because when you eat, each person eats without waiting for the others. Some people do not get enough to eat, while others have too much to drink. [22]You can eat and drink in your own homes! You seem to think God's church is not important, and you embarrass those who are poor. What should I tell you? Should I praise you? I do not praise you for doing this.

[23]The teaching I gave you is the same teaching I received from the Lord: On the night when the Lord Jesus was handed over to be killed, he took bread [24]and gave thanks for it. Then he broke the bread and said, "This is my body; it is for you. Do this to remember me." [25]In the same way, after they ate, Jesus took the cup. He said, "This cup is the new agreement that is sealed with the blood of my death. When you drink this, do it to remember me." [26]Every time you eat this bread and drink this cup you are telling others about the Lord's death until he comes.

[27]So a person who eats the bread or drinks the cup of the Lord in a way that is not worthy of it will be guilty of sinning against the body and the blood of the Lord. [28]Look into your own hearts before you eat the bread and drink the cup, [29]because all who eat the bread and drink the cup without recognizing the body eat and drink judgment against themselves. [30]That is why many in your group are sick and weak, and many have died. [31]But if we judged ourselves in the right way, God would not judge us. [32]But when the Lord judges us, he

✓ COUNT ON IT

1 CORINTHIANS 10:12

Before there's heavy breathing and a backseat, there's a door. A way out. Before there's a friend's test paper to cheat off of, there's a window to study by.

Temptations can sometimes get too hot for you to handle on your own, but only because you've passed up a long line of escape hatches along the way—places where God was warning you to turn back, to trust him, to bail out with his parachute of protection.

If you can learn to avoid temptation when it's just a sprinkle, before it builds into a driving rain that hits you from all sides, you'll find life a lot easier, guilt a lot rarer, and the warm, safe feeling of living under God's umbrella.

He always gives you a way out, over and over again, far in advance of the 40-foot drop-off at the end. And even up there, when you're hanging on by your fingernails—if you'll call on him to help you and if you'll stop trying to grit your teeth and fight the battle in your own strength, he'll be right there to put you back on solid ground.

 11:3 **the man** This could also mean "her husband." 11:20 **Lord's Supper** The meal Jesus told his followers to eat to remember him (Luke 22:14–20).

TIPS ON YOURSELF

Being a head-to-toe billboard is no way to look cool. If a corporation wants to rent your body to sell their stuff, then they should hand you an envelope stuffed with cash. But as it is, you pay big bucks to let them sticker you with logos from your hat to your shoes. It sorta screams "I can't think for myself." Not a statement a guy wants to make.

punishes us so that we will not be destroyed along with the world.

[33]So my brothers and sisters, when you come together to eat, wait for each other. [34]Anyone who is too hungry should eat at home so that in meeting together you will not bring God's judgment on yourselves. I will tell you what to do about the other things when I come.

GIFTS FROM THE HOLY SPIRIT

12 Now, brothers and sisters, I want you to understand about spiritual gifts. [2]You know the way you lived before you were believers. You let yourselves be influenced and led away to worship idols—things that could not speak. [3]So I want you to understand that no one who is speaking with the help of God's Spirit says, "Jesus be cursed." And no one can say, "Jesus is Lord," without the help of the Holy Spirit.

[4]There are different kinds of gifts, but they are all from the same Spirit. [5]There are different ways to serve but the same Lord to serve. [6]And there are different ways that God works

through people but the same God. God works in all of us in everything we do. [7]Something from the Spirit can be seen in each person, for the common good. [8]The Spirit gives one person the ability to speak with wisdom, and the same Spirit gives another the ability to speak with knowledge. [9]The same Spirit gives faith to one person. And, to another, that one Spirit gives gifts of healing. [10]The Spirit gives to another person the power to do miracles, to another the ability to prophesy. And he gives to another the ability to know the difference between good and evil spirits. The Spirit gives one person the ability to speak in different kinds of languages[n] and to another the ability to interpret those languages. [11]One Spirit, the same Spirit, does all these things, and the Spirit decides what to give each person.

THE BODY OF CHRIST WORKS TOGETHER

[12]A person's body is only one thing, but it has many parts. Though there are many parts to a body, all those parts make only one body. Christ is like that also. [13]Some of us are Jews, and some are Greeks. Some of us are slaves, and some are free. But we were all baptized into one body through one Spirit. And we were all made to share in the one Spirit.

[14]The human body has many parts. [15]The foot might say, "Because I am not a hand, I am not part of the body." But saying this would not stop the foot from being a part of the body. [16]The ear might say, "Because I am not an eye, I am not part of the body." But saying this would not stop the ear from being a part of the body. [17]If the whole body were an eye, it would not be able to hear. If the whole body were an ear, it would not be able to smell. [18-19]If each part of the body were the same part, there would be no body. But truly God put all the parts, each one of them, in the body as he wanted them. [20]So then there are many parts, but only one body.

[21]The eye cannot say to the hand, "I don't need you!" And the head cannot say to the foot, "I don't need you!" [22]No! Those parts of the body that seem to be the weaker are really necessary. [23]And the parts of the body we think are less deserving are the parts to which we give the most honor. We give special respect to the parts we want to hide. [24]The

BIBLE BASICS

Communion is one of the sacraments (sometimes called *ordinances*) of the Christian church. In the Bible, the Gospels talk about the Last Supper that Jesus had with his followers. During that meal, he told his followers to eat bread and drink wine to remember him. So, in church today, Christians will eat a piece of bread (or cracker; churches do it differently) and drink some wine (or grape juice) to recall that Jesus' body was broken and his blood shed so that we might have eternal life.

more respectable parts of our body need no special care. But God put the body together and gave more honor to the parts that need it [25]so our body would not be divided. God wanted the different parts to care the same for each other.

12:10 languages This can also be translated "tongues."

RANDOM WAYS TO MAKE A DIFFERENCE IN YOUR COMMUNITY

1. **PICK UP SOMEONE ELSE'S LITTER.**

2. **DROP CASH IN CHARITY BOXES.**

3. **WATCH THE NEIGHBOR KIDS FOR FREE.**

4. **PLANT A TREE. OR TEN.**

5. **RECYCLE CANS AND BOTTLES.**

6. **DONATE YOUR OLD STUFF TO NEEDY FAMILIES.**

7. **DO YARD WORK FOR THE ELDERLY AND SICK.**

8. **COACH.**

9. **SHOW UP AT A SCHOOL BOARD MEETING AND SPEAK UP.**

10. **MENTOR.**

[26]If one part of the body suffers, all the other parts suffer with it. Or if one part of our body is honored, all the other parts share its honor.

[27]Together you are the body of Christ, and each one of you is a part of that body. [28]In the church God has given a place first to apostles, second to prophets, and third to teachers. Then God has given a place to those who do miracles, those who have gifts of healing, those who can help others, those who are able to govern, and those who can speak in different languages.[n] [29]Not all are apostles. Not all are prophets. Not all are teachers. Not all do miracles. [30]Not all have gifts of healing. Not all speak in different languages. Not all interpret those languages. [31]But you should truly want to have the greater gifts.

LOVE IS THE GREATEST GIFT

And now I will show you the best way of all.

13 I may speak in different languages[n] of people or even angels. But if I do not have love, I am only a noisy bell or a crashing cymbal. [2]I may have the gift of prophecy. I may understand all the secret things of God and have all knowledge, and I may have faith so great I can move mountains. But even with all these things, if I do not have love, then I am nothing. [3]I may give away everything I have, and I may even give my body as an offering to be burned.[n] But I gain nothing if I do not have love.

[4]Love is patient and kind. Love is not jealous, it does not brag, and it is not proud. [5]Love is not rude, is not selfish, and does not get upset with others. Love does not count up wrongs that have been done. [6]Love is not happy with evil but is happy with the truth. [7]Love patiently accepts all things. It always trusts, always hopes, and always remains strong.

[8]Love never ends. There are gifts of prophecy, but they will be ended. There are gifts of speaking in different languages, but those gifts will stop. There is the gift of knowledge, but it will come to an end. [9]The reason is that our knowledge and our ability to prophesy are not perfect. [10]But when perfection comes, the things that are not perfect will end. [11]When I was a child, I talked like a child, I thought like a child, I reasoned like a child. When I became a man, I stopped those childish ways. [12]It is the same with us. Now we see a dim reflection, as if we were looking into a mirror, but then we shall see clearly. Now I know only a part, but then I will know fully, as God has known me. [13]So these three things continue forever: faith, hope, and love. And the greatest of these is love.

DESIRE SPIRITUAL GIFTS

14 You should seek after love, and you should truly want to have the spiritual gifts, especially the gift of prophecy. [2]I will explain why. Those who have the gift of speaking in different languages[n] are not speaking to people; they are speaking to God. No one understands them; they are speaking secret things through the Spirit. [3]But those who prophesy are speaking to people to give them strength, encouragement, and comfort. [4]The ones who speak in different languages are helping only

EXPERTS ANSWER YOUR QUESTIONS

Q. *I was witnessing to one of my best friends, and I blew it. I pushed too hard, and she's cut me off as a friend.*

A. God gives believers the task of telling others about Jesus, not changing them. You're figuring that out. Tell your friend you care a ton about her and apologize for being too pushy. Maybe you'll get her back as a friend. It's her choice.

Q. *This guy from school wants to take a road trip and go see places where he says aliens have landed. Do aliens exist? What does God say? What should I say?*

A. The Bible doesn't say anything about little green guys or any other kind of aliens. Some think that means there aren't any. If God can make people on this planet, he certainly could make them on other planets and in other galaxies. But don't start arguments about little things that make no difference in your relationship with others.

Q. *Do people become ghosts or angels when they die?*

A. Neither. Angels are not dead people. God created them separately from humans. And the dead don't come back to earth as ghosts to talk to their friends and guide them like lots of movies say they do. When a believer dies, his spirit returns to God who made it.

12:28; 13:1; 14:2 languages This can also be translated "tongues." 13:3 Verse 3 Other Greek copies read: "hand over my body in order that I may brag."

themselves, but those who prophesy are helping the whole church. [5]I wish all of you had the gift of speaking in different kinds of languages, but more, I wish you would prophesy. Those who prophesy are greater than those who can only speak in different languages—unless someone is there who can explain what is said so that the whole church can be helped.

[6]Brothers and sisters, will it help you if I come to you speaking in different languages? No! It will help you only if I bring you a new truth or some new knowledge, or prophecy, or teaching. [7]It is the same as with lifeless things that make sounds—like a flute or a harp. If they do not make clear musical notes, you will not know what is being played. [8]And in a war, if the trumpet does not give a clear sound, who will prepare for battle? [9]It is the same with you. Unless you speak clearly with your tongue, no one can understand what you are saying. You will be talking into the air! [10]It may be true that there are all kinds of sounds in the world, and none is without meaning. [11]But unless I understand the meaning of what someone says to me, I will be a foreigner to him, and he will be a for-

eigner to me. [12]It is the same with you. Since you want spiritual gifts very much, seek most of all to have the gifts that help the church grow stronger.

[13]The one who has the gift of speaking in a different language should pray for the gift to interpret what is spoken. [14]If I pray in a different language, my spirit is praying, but my mind does nothing. [15]So what should I do? I will pray with my spirit, but I will also pray with my mind. I will sing with my spirit, but I will also sing with my mind. [16]If you praise God with your spirit, those persons there without understanding cannot say amen[n] to your prayer of thanks, because they do not know what you are saying. [17]You may be thanking God in a good way, but the other person is not helped.

[18]I thank God that I speak in different kinds of languages more than all of you. [19]But in the church meetings I would rather speak five words I understand in order to teach others than thousands of words in a different language.

[20]Brothers and sisters, do not think like children. In evil things be like babies, but in your thinking you should be like adults. [21]It is written in the Scriptures:

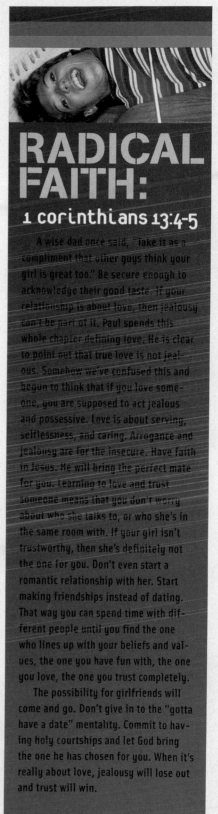

RADICAL FAITH:
1 corinthians 13:4-5

A wise dad once said, "Take it as a compliment that other guys think your girl is great too." Be secure enough to acknowledge their good taste. If your relationship is about love, then jealousy can't be part of it. Paul spends this whole chapter defining love. He is clear to point out that true love is not jealous. Somehow we've confused this and begun to think that if you love someone, you are supposed to act jealous and possessive. Love is about serving, selflessness, and caring. Arrogance and jealousy are for the insecure. Have faith in Jesus. He will bring the perfect mate for you. Learning to love and trust someone means that you don't worry about who she talks to, or who she's in the same room with. If your girl isn't trustworthy, then she's definitely not the one for you. Don't even start a romantic relationship with her. Start making friendships instead of dating. That way you can spend time with different people until you find the one who lines up with your beliefs and values, the one you have fun with, the one you love, the one you trust completely.

The possibility for girlfriends will come and go. Don't give in to the "gotta have a date" mentality. Commit to having holy courtships and let God bring the one he has chosen for you. When it's really about love, jealousy will lose out and trust will win.

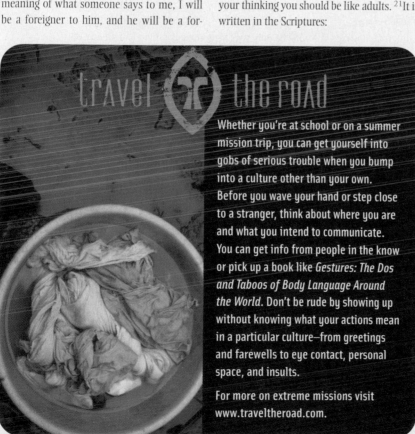

travel the road

Whether you're at school or on a summer mission trip, you can get yourself into gobs of serious trouble when you bump into a culture other than your own. Before you wave your hand or step close to a stranger, think about where you are and what you intend to communicate. You can get info from people in the know or pick up a book like *Gestures: The Dos and Taboos of Body Language Around the World*. Don't be rude by showing up without knowing what your actions mean in a particular culture—from greetings and farewells to eye contact, personal space, and insults.

For more on extreme missions visit www.traveltheroad.com.

14:16 amen To say amen means to agree with the things that were said.

DO'S & DON'TS

- **Do get answers to your toughest spiritual questions.**

- **Do rid your life of pornography.**

- **Do date girls who don't flash skin.**

- **Do take the lead in keeping your relationships pure.**

- **Don't make your parents pick up the phone when it's always for you.**

- **Don't go over on your cell phone minutes.**

- **Don't say anything about someone that you wouldn't say to their face.**

- **Don't forget how to write cursive.**

"With people who use strange words and
foreign languages
I will speak to these people.
But even then they will not listen to me,"
Isaiah 28:11-12

says the Lord.

22So the gift of speaking in different kinds of languages is a proof for those who do not believe, not for those who do believe. And prophecy is for people who believe, not for those who do not believe. 23Suppose the whole church meets together and everyone speaks in different languages. If some people come in who do not understand or do not believe, they will say you are crazy. 24But suppose everyone is prophesying and some people come in who do not believe or do not understand. If everyone is prophesying, their sin will be shown to them, and they will be judged by all that they hear. 25The secret things in their hearts will be made known. So they will bow down and worship God saying, "Truly, God is with you."

MEETINGS SHOULD HELP THE CHURCH

26So, brothers and sisters, what should you do? When you meet together, one person has a song, and another has a teaching. Another has a new truth from God. Another speaks in a different language,[n] and another person interprets that language. The purpose of all these things should be to help the church grow strong. 27When you meet together, if anyone speaks in a different language, it should be only two, or not more than three, who speak. They should speak one after the other, and someone else should interpret. 28But if there is no interpreter, then those who speak in a different language should be quiet in the church meeting. They should speak only to themselves and to God.

29Only two or three prophets should speak, and the others should judge what they say. 30If a message from God comes to another person who is sitting, the first speaker should stop. 31You can all prophesy one after the other. In this way all the people can be taught and encouraged. 32The spirits of prophets are under the control of the prophets themselves. 33God is not a God of confusion but a God of peace.

As is true in all the churches of God's people, 34women should keep quiet in the church meetings. They are not allowed to speak, but they must yield to this rule as the law says. 35If they want to learn something, they should ask their own husbands at home. It is shameful for a woman to speak in the church meeting. 36Did God's teaching come from you? Or are you the only ones to whom it has come?

37Those who think they are prophets or spiritual persons should understand that what I am writing to you is the Lord's command. 38Those who ignore this will be ignored by God.

39So my brothers and sisters, you should truly want to prophesy. But do not stop people from using the gift of speaking in different kinds of languages. 40But let everything be done in a right and orderly way.

THE GOOD NEWS ABOUT CHRIST

15 Now, brothers and sisters, I want you to remember the Good News I brought to you. You received this Good News and continue strong in it. 2And you are being saved by it if you con-

MEN OF THE SWORD

THOMAS

"Doubting Thomas" has a bad rep, but he was a guy with some honest questions. He was the only disciple who hadn't seen Jesus alive from the dead. Frankly, he doubted the whole story. He vowed he would only believe when he was able to put his fingers on the nail wounds in Jesus' hand—and jab the side where Jesus had been cut open by a soldier's sword. When Jesus appeared in a locked room to all the disciples including Thomas, Jesus told him, "Put your finger here, and look at my hands. Put your hand here in my side. Stop being an unbeliever and believe." Thomas replied, "My Lord and my God!" He had seen enough to know Jesus was really alive.

—John 20:24-29

 14:26 language This can also be translated "tongue."

tinue believing what I told you. If you do not, then you believed for nothing.

[3] I passed on to you what I received, of which this was most important: that Christ died for our sins, as the Scriptures say; [4] that he was buried and was raised to life on the third day as the Scriptures say; [5] and that he was seen by Peter and then by the twelve apostles. [6] After that, Jesus was seen by more than five hundred of the believers at the same time. Most of them are still living today, but some have died. [7] Then he was seen by James and later by all the apostles. [8] Last of all he was seen by me—as by a person not born at the normal time. [9] All the other apostles are greater than I am. I am not even good enough to be called an apostle, because I persecuted the church of God. [10] But God's grace has made me what I am, and his grace to me was not wasted. I worked harder than all the other apostles. (But it was not I really; it was God's grace that was with me.) [11] So if I preached to you or the other apostles preached to you, we all preach the same thing, and this is what you believed.

WE WILL BE RAISED FROM THE DEAD

[12] Now since we preached that Christ was raised from the dead, why do some of you say that people will not be raised from the dead? [13] If no one is ever raised from the dead, then Christ has not been raised. [14] And if Christ has not been raised, then our preaching is worth nothing, and your faith is worth nothing. [15] And also, we are guilty of lying about God, because we testified of him that he raised Christ from the dead. But if people are not raised from the dead, then God never raised Christ. [16] If the dead are not raised, Christ has not been raised either. [17] And if Christ has not been raised, then your faith has nothing to it; you are still guilty of your sins. [18] And those in Christ who have already died are lost. [19] If our hope in Christ is for this life only, we should be pitied more than anyone else in the world.

[20] But Christ has truly been raised from the dead—the first one and proof that those who sleep in death will also be raised. [21] Death has come because of what one man did, but the rising from death also comes because of one man. [22] In Adam all of us die. In the same way, in Christ all of us will be made alive again. [23] But everyone will be raised to life in the right order. Christ was first to be raised. When Christ comes again, those who belong to him will be raised to life, [24] and then the end will come. At that time Christ will destroy all rulers, authorities, and powers, and he will hand over the kingdom to God the Father. [25] Christ must rule until he puts all enemies under his control. [26] The last enemy to be destroyed will be death. [27] The Scripture says

HOW TO TELEPORT LIKE A TREKKIE

In a move that resembles Scotty beaming up Captain Kirk, researchers in quantum optics at the Australian National University made a beam of light disappear in one place and reappear a few feet away. It's some funky Star Trek physics, though scientists point out that they moved photons—particles of electromagnetic energy—rather than atoms. While you might wish you could instantly teleport yourself to a sunny South American beach, that would take computers capable of tracking and reassembling the trillions and trillions of atoms that make up your body. That won't happen anytime soon. But it goes to show: The only way to chase a fantastic dream is to start trying.

that God put all things under his control.[n] When it says "all things" are under him, it is clear this does not include God himself. God is the One who put everything under his control. [28]After everything has been put under the Son, then he will put himself under God, who had put all things under him. Then God will be the complete ruler over everything.

[29]If the dead are never raised, what will people do who are being baptized for the dead? If the dead are not raised at all, why are people being baptized for them?

[30]And what about us? Why do we put ourselves in danger every hour? [31]I die every day. That is true, brothers and sisters, just as it is true that I brag about you in Christ Jesus our Lord. [32]If I fought wild animals in Ephesus only with human hopes, I have gained nothing. If the dead are not raised, "Let us eat and drink, because tomorrow we will die."[n]

[33]Do not be fooled: "Bad friends will ruin good habits." [34]Come back to your right way of thinking and stop sinning. Some of you do not know God—I say this to shame you.

WHAT KIND OF BODY WILL WE HAVE?

[35]But someone may ask, "How are the dead raised? What kind of body will they have?" [36]Foolish person! When you sow a seed, it must die in the ground before it can live and grow. [37]And when you sow it, it does not have the same "body" it will have later. What you sow is only a bare seed, maybe wheat or something else. [38]But God gives it a body that he has planned for it, and God gives each kind of seed its own body. [39]All things made of flesh are not the same: People have one kind of flesh, animals have another, birds have another, and fish have another. [40]Also there are heavenly bodies and earthly bodies. But the beauty of the heavenly bodies is one kind, and the beauty of the earthly bodies is another. [41]The sun has one kind of beauty, the moon has another beauty, and the stars have another. And each star is different in its beauty.

[42]It is the same with the dead who are raised to life. The body that is "planted" will ruin and decay, but it is raised to a life that cannot be destroyed. [43]When the body is "planted," it is without honor, but it is raised in glory. When the body is "planted," it is weak, but when it is raised, it is powerful. [44]The body that is "planted" is a physical body. When it is raised, it is a spiritual body.

There is a physical body, and there is also a spiritual body. [45]It is written in the Scriptures: "The first man, Adam, became a living person."[n] But the last Adam became a spirit that gives life. [46]The spiritual did not come first, but the physical and then the spiritual. [47]The first man came from the dust of the earth. The second man came from heaven. [48]People who belong to the earth are like the first man of earth. But those people who belong to heaven are like the man of heaven. [49]Just as we were made like the man of earth, so we will also be made like the man of heaven.

[50]I tell you this, brothers and sisters: Flesh and blood cannot have a part in the kingdom of God. Something that will ruin cannot have a part in something that never ruins. [51]But look! I tell you this secret: We will not all sleep in death, but we will all be changed. [52]It will take only a second—as quickly as an eye blinks—when the last trumpet sounds. The trumpet will sound, and those who have died will be raised to live forever, and we will all be changed. [53]This body that can be destroyed must clothe itself with something that can

1 JOHN 4:18 "WHERE GOD'S LOVE IS, THERE IS NO FEAR, BECAUSE GOD'S PERFECT LOVE DRIVES OUT FEAR."

never be destroyed. And this body that dies must clothe itself with something that can never die. [54]So this body that can be destroyed will clothe itself with that which can never be destroyed, and this body that dies will clothe itself with that which can never die. When this happens, this Scripture will be made true:

"Death is destroyed forever in victory."
                                    Isaiah 25:8

[55]"Death, where is your victory?

Death, where is your pain?"   *Hosea 13:14*

[56]Death's power to hurt is sin, and the power of sin is the law. [57]But we thank God! He gives us the victory through our Lord Jesus Christ.

[58]So my dear brothers and sisters, stand strong. Do not let anything change you. Always give yourselves fully to the work of the Lord, because you know that your work in the Lord is never wasted.

THE GIFT FOR OTHER BELIEVERS

16 Now I will write about the collection of money for God's people. Do

 15:27 God put . . . control. From Psalm 8:6.   **15:32** "Let us . . . die." Quotation from Isaiah 22:13; 56:12.   **15:45** "The first . . . person." Quotation from Genesis 2:7.

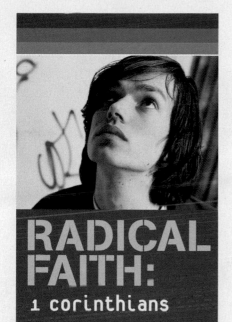

RADICAL FAITH:
1 corinthians
15:47-48

Call it amazing. God takes a handful of dirt and makes a man. Very humble beginnings for people who think so highly of themselves. Have you felt jealous of anyone lately? Do you think you deserve more than you have? Are you mad at God because your family doesn't have some of the comforts other families do? Maybe it's time to remember where you came from—dust. Yep, you (and all the people you're jealous of) are just a bunch of dust.

Your life is a gift. It's a blessing to be on earth and to be able to enjoy life. You've got the freedom to choose what you're going to do with your life. The point is to make something out of the gifts God has given you. Your body, mind, emotions, and personality are specially crafted by God for his purpose. God wants you to use the time you've got on earth and the gifts you've been given to glorify him. Your glory comes later. Paul says that everyone in heaven will have a body like the glorified Christ. There's a lot to do between now and the time you get to heaven, so get that old, dusty body in gear. God has great things for you!

the same thing I told the Galatian churches to do: [2]On the first day of every week, each one of you should put aside money as you have been blessed. Save it up so you will not have to collect money after I come. [3]When I arrive, I will send whomever you approve to take your gift to Jerusalem. I will send them with letters of introduction, [4]and if it seems good for me to go also, they will go along with me.

PAUL'S PLANS

[5]I plan to go through Macedonia, so I will come to you after I go through there. [6]Perhaps I will stay with you for a time or even all winter. Then you can help me on my trip, wherever I go. [7]I do not want to see you now just in passing. I hope to stay a longer time with you if the Lord allows it. [8]But I will stay at Ephesus until Pentecost, [9]because a good opportunity for a great and growing work has been given to me now. And there are many people working against me.

[10]If Timothy comes to you, see to it that he has nothing to fear with you, because he is working for the Lord just as I am. [11]So none of you should treat Timothy as unimportant, but help him on his trip in peace so that he can come back to me. I am expecting him to come with the brothers.

[12]Now about our brother Apollos: I strongly encouraged him to visit you with the other brothers. He did not at all want to come now; he will come when he has the opportunity.

PAUL ENDS HIS LETTER

[13]Be alert. Continue strong in the faith. Have courage, and be strong. [14]Do everything in love.

[15]You know that the family of Stephanas were the first believers in Southern Greece and that they have given themselves to the service of God's people. I ask you, brothers and sisters, [16]to follow the leading of people like these and anyone else who works and serves with them.

[17]I am happy that Stephanas, Fortunatus, and Achaicus have come. You are not here, but they have filled your place. [18]They have refreshed my spirit and yours. You should

10 RANDOM WAYS TO FRESHEN YOUR PRAYERS

1. WRITE OUT YOUR WORDS.

2. KEEP TRACK OF PRAYERS YOU PRAY AND LOOK FOR ANSWERS.

3. SWAP PRAYER REQUESTS WITH A BUDDY EACH MORNING.

4. PRAY OUT LOUD.

5. PICK THE WORDS OF A PSALM AND SAY THEM TO GOD.

6. PRAY WITH A GROUP.

7. ASK YOUR PARENTS HOW YOU CAN PRAY FOR THEM.

8. POUR OUT YOUR DEEPEST HURTS.

9. SPEAK THE WORDS OF YOUR FAVORITE WORSHIP SONG.

10. TELL GOD WHAT YOU REALLY THINK.

recognize the value of people like these.

[19]The churches in the country of Asia send greetings to you. Aquila and Priscilla greet you in the Lord, as does the church that meets in their house. [20]All the brothers and sisters here send greetings. Give each other a holy kiss when you meet.

[21]I, Paul, am writing this greeting with my own hand.

[22]If anyone does not love the Lord, let him be separated from God—lost forever!

Come, O Lord!

[23]The grace of the Lord Jesus be with you.

[24]My love be with all of you in Christ Jesus.

2 CORINTHIANS

When we first meet the church at Corinth, it is in crisis mode. Paul started and trained the church, but he has been absent for several years. Chaos now reigns in the church. Arguments have broken out about who is coming to church, how Christians should behave, and how they should worship. Paul performs some emergency church triage by sending a letter and making a personal visit to address the problems.

A year later the church at Corinth is still struggling. Some men who claim to be apostles arrive in Corinth and begin luring the church leaders away from Paul's leadership. The letter never says exactly what these false apostles are teaching, but Paul accuses the imposters of repackaging the Good News with a different Jesus, spirit, and gospel (11:4).

When Paul catches wind of what's going on in Corinth, he goes on a rampage. He battles for the hearts and minds of the Corinthians, knowing full well this is a fight he may lose. Someone concerned about his or her reputation or personal pride might walk away from this one. But not Paul. He refuses to back off. He genuinely cares about the Corinthian people. And he'll do whatever it takes—regardless of the heartache or humiliation—to win them back to the true Jesus, the true Spirit, and the genuine message.

SEPTEMBER

Labor Day is always on the first Monday of September. Squeeze in one last summer party.

1
September is Self-Improvement Month. Got something to work on?

2
Pray for a Person of Influence: It's Keanu Reeves' birthday.

3

4
Get together with some friends and pray for your school year.

5

6
The *Mayflower* sailed for the New World in 1620—thank the Lord for your country today.

7

8

9
Pray for a Person of Influence: Adam Sandler.

10

11
Pray for all the families of the victims of the 9/11 terror attacks—pray that they will encounter peace today.

12
Little Rock High School was ordered to admit black students in 1958—love others without prejudice today and always.

13
Sing today in church—even if you grunt.

14
Surprise your mom with a hug.

15

16
Sit with someone you don't know very well at lunch.

17

18
Celebrate National Play-Doh® Day.

19
Get into National Talk Like a Pirate Day.

20

21
Go to a football game tonight and ponder whether God chooses sides.

22

23
Cook dinner tonight and give your parents a rest—and tell them thanks for everything they do.

24
Pray for a Person of Influence: Today is Will Smith's Birthday.

24
Sneak some zucchini onto your neighbor's step. Gently place it—don't throw it.

26
Pray for a Person of Influence: Today is Serena Williams' birthday.

27
Do your part to celebrate Ask a Stupid Question Day.

28
Pray for a Person of Influence: Wish Gwyneth Paltrow a happy birthday.

29

30
The Frisbee® was invented today in 1958—play a little Ultimate with friends.

1 From Paul, an apostle of Christ Jesus. I am an apostle because that is what God wanted. Also from Timothy our brother in Christ.

To the church of God in Corinth, and to all of God's people everywhere in Southern Greece:

[2]Grace and peace to you from God our Father and the Lord Jesus Christ.

PAUL GIVES THANKS TO GOD

[3]Praise be to the God and Father of our Lord Jesus Christ. God is the Father who is full of mercy and all comfort. [4]He comforts us every time we have trouble, so when others have trouble, we can comfort them with the same comfort God gives us. [5]We share in the many sufferings of Christ. In the same way, much comfort comes to us through Christ. [6]If we have troubles, it is for your comfort and salvation, and if we have comfort, you also have comfort. This helps you to accept patiently the same sufferings we have. [7]Our hope for you is strong, knowing that you share in our sufferings and also in the comfort we receive.

[8]Brothers and sisters,[n] we want you to know about the trouble we suffered in Asia. We had great burdens there that were beyond our own strength. We even gave up hope of living. [9]Truly, in our own hearts we believed we would die. But this happened so we would not trust in ourselves but in God, who raises people from the dead. [10]God saved us from these great dangers of death, and he will continue to save us. We have put our hope in him, and he will save us again. [11]And you can help us with your prayers. Then many people will give thanks for us—that God blessed us because of their many prayers.

THE CHANGE IN PAUL'S PLANS

[12]This is what we are proud of, and I can say it with a clear conscience: In everything we have done in the world, and especially with you, we have had an honest and sincere heart from God. We did this by God's grace, not by the kind of wisdom the world has. [13-14]We write to you only what you can read and understand. And I hope that as you have understood some things about us, you may come to know everything about us. Then you can be proud of us, as we will be proud of you on the day our Lord Jesus Christ comes again.

[15]I was so sure of all this that I made plans to visit you first so you could be blessed twice. [16]I planned to visit you on my way to Macedonia and again on my way back. I wanted to get help from you for my trip to Judea. [17]Do you think that I made these plans without really meaning it? Or maybe you think I make

✓ COUNT ON IT

2 CORINTHIANS 1:3-4

Trouble can come in all sizes. There's the kind you get yourself into, like staying out too late or tossing water balloons at passing cars. There's the kind that other people cause for you, like when somebody tells somebody else something you said when you said something totally different. And there's also the kind that just sort of hits you out of the blue, like when your best friend gets hurt in a car wreck or your grandmother dies on an operating table.

But God's comfort comes in colors to match every problem. It fits every hole left behind by someone you love. It soothes every wound that's opened by the daggers of jealousy and anger. It covers every sin with the hope that Christ's blood can forgive completely—and his discipline can keep you from ever visiting this awful place again.

God's comfort—so real, so refreshing—can appear in a Bible verse, a dad's reassuring hand on your shoulder, a series of events. But it's always there. And it's always yours. And it's always God.

travel the road

God doesn't intend for any Christian to stand on the sideline when it comes to missions. He wants each of us actively in the game. That doesn't necessarily mean he plans for you to head to the far end of the planet as a *goer*. For every person who goes to the mission field, God needs dozens of *senders*, people committed to supporting the *goers* with prayer and money. And while you figure out your long-term role, your mission field is right under your feet. God has made you to speak for him right here, right now (2 Corinthians 5:20).

For more on extreme missions visit www.traveltheroad.com.

1:8 **Brothers and sisters** Although the Greek text says "Brothers" here and throughout this book, Paul's words were meant for the entire church, including men and women.

plans as the world does, so that I say yes, yes and at the same time no, no.

¹⁸But if you can believe God, you can believe that what we tell you is never both yes and no. ¹⁹The Son of God, Jesus Christ, that Silas and Timothy and I preached to you, was not yes and no. In Christ it has always been yes. ²⁰The yes to all of God's promises is in Christ, and through Christ we say yes to the glory of God. ²¹Remember, God is the One who makes you and us strong in Christ. God made us his chosen people. ²²He put his mark on us to show that we are his, and he put his Spirit in our hearts to be a guarantee for all he has promised.

²³I tell you this, and I ask God to be my witness that this is true: The reason I did not come back to Corinth was to keep you from being punished or hurt. ²⁴We are not trying to control your faith. You are strong in faith. But we are workers with you for your own joy.

2 So I decided that my next visit to you would not be another one to make you sad. ²If I make you sad, who will make me glad? Only you can make me glad—particularly the person whom I made sad. ³I wrote you a letter for this reason: that when I came to you I would not be made sad by the people who should make me happy. I felt sure of all of you, that you would share my joy. ⁴When I wrote to you before, I was very troubled and unhappy in my heart, and I wrote with many tears. I did not write to make you sad, but to let you know how much I love you.

FORGIVE THE SINNER

⁵Someone there among you has caused sadness, not to me, but to all of you. I mean he caused sadness to all in some way. (I do not want to make it sound worse than it really is.) ⁶The punishment that most of you gave him is enough for him. ⁷But now you should forgive him and comfort him to keep him from having too much sadness and giving up completely. ⁸So I beg you to show that you love him. ⁹I wrote you to test you and to see if you obey in everything. ¹⁰If you forgive someone,

STARLIGHT CHILDREN'S FOUNDATION believes that reducing pain during therapy starts with the funny bone. The whole family struggles when a child is sick—and the day-to-day joys of childhood often take a back seat to the rigors of treatment and hospitalization. Starlight's core programs restore some of the laughter and happiness that a serious illness takes away from kids and those who love them.

Starlight's in-hospital services provide distractive entertainment, often reducing the need for pain medication and easing the stress, loneliness, isolation, and boredom that often accompany a child's hospital stay. Starlight Sites provide inviting environments within the hospital where children and their families can relax, play, and interact with each other. Starlight Fun Centers and PC Pals provide bedside entertainment, interaction, and education.

Out of the hospital, Starlight kids and their families can relax and regroup through family outings. Starlight's programs show that sometimes laughter is the best medicine.

To help make a sick child happy, go to www.starlight.org.

RADICAL FAITH:

2 corinthians 2:15-16

When you do what God wants instead of acting like all the people around you, Paul says that you are, figuratively speaking, a perfume. For some people that perfume smells wonderful. These people are inspired by your relationship with Jesus. If they haven't met him, they see the peace you have, the way it really makes you happy to follow him, and they want what you have. If they do know Jesus, your example encourages them to keep getting closer to him.

Unfortunately, there are others who think your life really stinks. The fact that you do things they wouldn't do—take up for someone who everyone else is picking on, stay straight-faced when you hear a dirty joke, refuse to drink at a party—that bugs them a lot. They can make things pretty unpleasant for you, but they're hurting themselves more than they hurt you and they don't even realize it. By giving you a hard time, they're pushing away Jesus—and knowing him is the whole reason they were born!

I also forgive him. And what I have forgiven—if I had anything to forgive—I forgave it for you, as if Christ were with me. [11]I did this so that Satan would not win anything from us, because we know very well what Satan's plans are.

PAUL'S CONCERN IN TROAS

[12]When I came to Troas to preach the Good News of Christ, the Lord gave me a good opportunity there. [13]But I had no peace, because I did not find my brother Titus. So I said good-bye to them at Troas and went to Macedonia.

VICTORY THROUGH CHRIST

[14]But thanks be to God, who always leads us in victory through Christ. God uses us to spread his knowledge everywhere like a sweet-smelling perfume. [15]Our offering to God is this: We are the sweet smell of Christ among those who are being saved and among those who are being lost. [16]To those who are lost, we are the smell of death that brings death, but to those who are being saved, we are the smell of life that brings life. So who is able to do this work? [17]We do not sell the word of God for a profit as many other people do. But in Christ we speak the truth before God, as messengers of God.

SERVANTS OF THE NEW AGREEMENT

3 Are we starting to brag about ourselves again? Do we need letters of introduction to you or from you, like some other people? [2]You yourselves are our letter, written on our hearts, known and read by everyone. [3]You show that you are a letter from Christ sent through us. This letter is not written with ink but with the Spirit of the living God. It is not written on stone tablets[n] but on human hearts.

[4]We can say this, because through Christ we feel certain before God. [5]We are not saying that we can do this work ourselves. It is God who makes us able to do all that we do. [6]He made us able to be servants of a new agreement from himself to his people. This new agreement is not a written law, but it is of the Spirit. The written law brings death, but the Spirit gives life.

[7]The law that brought death was written in words on stone. It came with God's glory, which made Moses' face so bright that the Israelites could not continue to look at it. But that glory later disappeared. [8]So surely the new way that brings the Spirit has even more glory. [9]If the law that judged people guilty of sin had glory, surely the new way that makes

MUSIC REVIEWS

SHAUN GROVES: TWILIGHT

Twilight is a contemporary pop effort for Shaun Groves, who opened for Michael W. Smith's recent tour. Even though the album features Groves' strong vocals and catchy arrangements, it's as unmistakably lyric-driven as his first release, *Invitation to Eavesdrop*—a disc nominated for six Doves. "Here I Am" is about authentic, God-focused worship. Talking about the pressure believers feel to constantly get new feelings out of praising the Lord, Groves told worshipleader.com, "Worship is [either] true or false—there are no levels of worship." He wrote "I Love You" for a friend who had been hiding sin out of terror that he would be slammed and rejected by the church if he was honest.

WHY IT ROCKS: GROVES SHOWS HOW HUMAN FRAILTY NEEDS GOD'S PERFECTION.

 3:3 stone tablets Meaning the Law of Moses that was written on stone tablets (Exodus 24:12; 25:16).

HOW TO BUY A BEAUTIFUL BOUQUET

So you want to buy a girl some flowers. Beware: Your guy friends might spot your car if you park outside a flower shop. But the next time you shop for snacks in a big supermarket, stop by the flower cart. While it's tough to go wrong as long as you don't pick something wilted or dead, put some thought into your purchase: Is your girl dressy or casual? Is she a wild mix or a quieter all-one-kind type of girl? Is she flashy or more subdued? Aim for a flower set that matches her personality, then drop your purchase into a protective bag, grab a free little packet of the powder that keeps flowers fresh, and march to the checkout stand like you buy flowers all the time. Buying flowers is like a million other things in a relationship: You might not understand why something's so special. But she will.

WAYS TO WALK THE WALK

2 corinthians 5:7

WORD: We walk by faith, not by sight.

WALK IT: Don't demand proof from God before you trust him. Take a leap of faith today—like signing up for a mission trip, loving someone you hate, obeying him when you don't feel like it.

2 corinthians 5:14-15

WORD: Christ died for you, so live for him.

WALK IT: Figure out the biggest thing that keeps you from following God. Then weigh that against God's total love for you in Jesus. Which wins? When you don't feel like living as a Christian, look deeply at what Jesus did for you.

people right with God has much greater glory. [10]That old law had glory, but it really loses its glory when it is compared to the much greater glory of this new way. [11]If that law which disappeared came with glory, then this new way which continues forever has much greater glory.

[12]We have this hope, so we are very bold. [13]We are not like Moses, who put a covering over his face so the Israelites would not see it. The glory was disappearing, and Moses did not want them to see it end. [14]But their minds were closed, and even today that same covering hides the meaning when they read the old agreement. That covering is taken away only through Christ. [15]Even today, when they read the law of Moses, there is a covering over their minds. [16]But when a person changes and follows the Lord, that covering is taken away. [17]The Lord is the Spirit, and where the Spirit of the Lord is, there is freedom. [18]Our faces, then, are not covered. We all show the Lord's glory, and we are being changed to be like him. This change in us brings ever greater glory, which comes from the Lord, who is the Spirit.

PREACHING THE GOOD NEWS

4 God, with his mercy, gave us this work to do, so we don't give up. [2]But we have turned away from secret and shameful ways. We use no trickery, and we do not change the teaching of God. We teach the truth plainly, showing everyone who we are. Then they can know in their hearts what kind of people we are in God's sight. [3]If the Good News that we preach is hidden, it is hidden only to those who are lost. [4]The devil who rules this world has blinded the minds of those who do not believe. They cannot see the light of the Good News—the Good News about the glory of Christ, who is exactly like God. [5]We do not preach about ourselves, but we preach that Jesus Christ is Lord and that we are your servants for Jesus. [6]God once said, "Let the light shine out of the darkness!" This is the same God who made his light shine in our hearts by letting us know the glory of God that is in the face of Christ.

SPIRITUAL TREASURE IN CLAY JARS

[7]We have this treasure from God, but we are like clay jars that hold the treasure. This shows that the great power is from God, not from us. [8]We have troubles all around us, but we are not defeated. We do not know what to do, but we do not give up the hope of living. [9]We are persecuted, but God does not leave us. We are hurt sometimes, but we are not destroyed. [10]We carry the death of Jesus in our own bodies so that the life of Jesus can also be

seen in our bodies. [11]We are alive, but for Jesus we are always in danger of death so that the life of Jesus can be seen in our bodies that die. [12]So death is working in us, but life is working in you.

[13]It is written in the Scriptures, "I believed, so I spoke."[n] Our faith is like this, too. We believe, and so we speak. [14]God raised the Lord Jesus from the dead, and we know that God will also raise us with Jesus. God will bring us together with you, and we will stand before him. [15]All these things are for you. And so the grace of God that is being given to more and more people will bring increasing thanks to God for his glory.

LIVING BY FAITH

[16]So we do not give up. Our physical body is becoming older and weaker, but our spirit inside us is made new every day. [17]We have small troubles for a while now, but they are helping us gain an eternal glory that is much greater than the troubles. [18]We set our eyes not on what we see but on what we cannot see. What we see will last only a short time, but what we cannot see will last forever.

5 We know that our body—the tent we live in here on earth—will be destroyed. But when that happens, God will have a house for us. It will not be a house made by human hands; instead, it will be a home in heaven that will last forever. [2]But now we groan in this tent. We want God to give us our heavenly home, [3]because it will clothe us so we will not be naked. [4]While we live in this body, we have burdens, and we groan. We do not want to be naked, but we want to be clothed with our heavenly home. Then this body that dies will be fully covered with life. [5]This is what God made us for, and he has given us the Spirit to be a guarantee for this new life.

[6]So we always have courage. We know that while we live in this body, we are away from the Lord. [7]We live by what we believe, not by what we can see. [8]So I say that we have courage. We really want to be away from this body and be at home with the Lord. [9]Our only goal is to please God whether we live here or there, [10]because we must all stand before Christ to be judged. Each of us will receive what we should get—good or bad—for the things we did in the earthly body.

RADICAL FAITH:

2 corinthians 5:1-2

Your body is just a temporary home. That's right, it's just like a tent—a place for the real you, your spirit, to live. It's important to exercise, eat right, and take care of your body, but someday your tent is going to check out of here. That's just the natural cycle of life. Your body cannot live forever, but, thank God, death is not the end. You're on your way to a much greater place—a place where there's no more sadness, a place we've all heard about, a place called heaven!

Your body may be like a tent down here on earth, but someday you're going to live in a home that God himself has prepared just for you. Just think—he made the whole world in seven days, but he's still working on your eternal home. Your mind can't even imagine how awesome that place will be! So don't be discouraged with your home here on earth. It won't be long, and you'll be walking those streets of gold!

RELATIONSHIPS

"God gives the lonely a home" (Psalm 68:6). When your folks rule the roost and your siblings act like chickens with their heads whacked off, it's normal to squawk. Yet when it comes right down to it, your family is your flock. They're the people you'll be related to for the rest of your life. So take time today to stop and appreciate your family. It'll keep the coop from feeling cramped.

4:13 "I . . . spoke." Quotation from Psalm 116:10.

2 corinthians 10:5

WORD: We make sure that every thought lines up with what Christ thinks.

WALK IT: The best way to push negative, lustful, or selfish thoughts out of your head is to crowd them out with good thoughts. Do something new today to fill your mind with good stuff—like reading your Bible, listening to Christian music, or talking with a Christian friend.

✓ COUNT ON IT

**2 CORINTHIANS
7:6**

Paul is so honest. He wasn't always standing on a spiritual mountaintop, and he doesn't mind admitting it. He spends a lot of time in this book talking about his suffering, worry, tears, and broken heart. He doesn't try to pretend that just because he loves Jesus, nothing hard ever happens. He admits to his struggles and hardships. He talks about the troubles he's faced. He is real and vulnerable.

Somehow over time, Christians have lost sight of Paul's example. Somehow we've replaced honesty with pretending. Too many Christians pretend that their lives are happy and suffer in total silence. They won't admit to their own needs and weaknesses, yet wonder why God doesn't do something. God will bring cheer and comfort to those who are in need. Do you need God to comfort you? Do you need some cheering up? Then talk to the Lord. Be honest with some people who are close to you. Be brave enough to say, "I love God, but life is tough right now." God may use the Holy Spirit, or the body of believers, or the truth of his Word—but he will bring cheer to people in need.

BECOMING FRIENDS WITH GOD

[11]Since we know what it means to fear the Lord, we try to help people accept the truth about us. God knows what we really are, and I hope that in your hearts you know, too. [12]We are not trying to prove ourselves to you again, but we are telling you about ourselves so you will be proud of us. Then you will have an answer for those who are proud about things that can be seen rather than what is in the heart. [13]If we are out of our minds, it is for God. If we have our right minds, it is for you. [14]The love of Christ controls us, because we know that One died for all, so all have died. [15]Christ died for all so that those who live would not continue to live for themselves. He died for them and was raised from the dead so that they would live for him.

[16]From this time on we do not think of anyone as the world does. In the past we thought of Christ as the world thinks, but we no longer think of him in that way. [17]If anyone belongs to Christ, there is a new creation. The old things have gone; everything is made new! [18]All this is from God. Through Christ, God made peace between us and himself, and God gave us the work of telling everyone about the peace we can have with him. [19]God was in Christ, making peace between the world and himself. In Christ, God did not hold the world guilty of its sins. And he gave us this message of peace. [20]So we have been sent to speak for Christ. It is as if God is calling to you through us. We speak for Christ when we beg you to be at peace with God. [21]Christ had no sin, but God made him become sin so that in Christ we could become right with God.

6 We are workers together with God, so we beg you: Do not let the grace that you received from God be for nothing. [2]God says,

"At the right time I heard your prayers.
On the day of salvation I helped you."

Isaiah 49:8

I tell you that the "right time" is now, and the "day of salvation" is now.

[3]We do not want anyone to find fault with our work, so nothing we do will be a problem for anyone. [4]But in every way we show we are servants of God: in accepting many hard things, in troubles, in difficulties, and in great problems. [5]We are beaten and thrown into prison. We meet those who become upset with us and start riots. We work hard, and sometimes we get no sleep or food. [6]We show we are servants of God by our pure lives, our understanding, patience, and kindness, by the Holy Spirit, by true love, [7]by speaking the truth, and by God's power. We use our right living to defend ourselves against everything. [8]Some people honor us, but others blame us. Some people say evil things about us, but others say good things. Some people say we are liars, but we speak the truth. [9]We are not known, but we are well known. We seem to be dying, but we continue to live. We are punished, but we are not killed. [10]We have much sadness, but we are always rejoicing. We are poor, but we are making many people rich in faith. We have nothing, but really we have everything.

[11]We have spoken freely to you in Corinth and have opened our hearts to you. [12]Our feelings of love for you have not stopped, but you have stopped your feelings of love for us.

[13]I speak to you as if you were my children. Do to us as we have done—open your hearts to us.

WARNING ABOUT NON-CHRISTIANS

[14]You are not the same as those who do not believe. So do not join yourselves to them. Good and bad do not belong together. Light and darkness cannot share together. [15]How can Christ and Belial, the devil, have any agreement? What can a believer have together with a nonbeliever? [16]The temple of God cannot have any agreement with idols, and we are the temple of the living God. As God said: "I will live with them and walk with them. And I will be their God, and they will be my people."[n]

[17]"Leave those people,
and be separate, says the Lord.
Touch nothing that is unclean,
and I will accept you."

Isaiah 52:11; Ezekiel 20:34, 41

[18]"I will be your father,
and you will be my sons and daughters,
says the Lord Almighty."

2 Samuel 7:14

7 Dear friends, we have these promises from God, so we should make ourselves pure—free from anything that makes body or soul unclean. We should try to become holy in the way we live, because we respect God.

PAUL'S JOY

[2]Open your hearts to us. We have not done wrong to anyone, we have not ruined the faith of anyone, and we have not cheated anyone. [3]I do not say this to blame you. I told you before that we love you so much we would live or die with you. [4]I feel very sure of you and am very proud of you. You give me much comfort, and in all of our troubles I have great joy.

[5]When we came into Macedonia, we had no rest. We found trouble all around us. We had fighting on the outside and fear on the inside. [6]But God, who comforts those who are troubled, comforted us when Titus came. [7]We were comforted, not only by his coming but also by the comfort you gave him. Titus told us about your wish to see me and that you are very sorry for what you did. He also told me about your great care for me, and when I heard this, I was much happier.

[8]Even if my letter made you sad, I am not sorry I wrote it. At first I was sorry, because it made you sad, but you were sad only for a short time. [9]Now I am happy, not because you were made sad, but because your sorrow made you change your lives. You became sad in the way God wanted you to, so you were not hurt by us in any way. [10]The kind of sorrow God wants makes people change their

GET OUT THERE

YOUTH SERVICE AMERICA (YSA) aims to make service and service-learning the common expectation and common experience of all young people in America. YSA is a resource center which partners with thousands of organizations committed to increasing the quality and quantity of volunteer opportunities for young people in America, ages 5–25, to serve locally, nationally, and globally. Servenet.org is YSA's award-winning website and the most comprehensive site on the Internet dedicated to service and volunteering. Home to a broad national database of local volunteer opportunities, events, jobs, news, effective practices, and quotes, SERVEnet also matches the skills, experiences, and enthusiasm of volunteers who wish to help with organizations that need them.

For more information go to www.ysa.org or www.servenet.org.

 6:16 "I . . . people." Quotation from Leviticus 26:11–12; Jeremiah 32:38; Ezekiel 37:27.

RADICAL FAITH:

2 corinthians 8:9

Jesus had it all. In heaven, he had angels singing his praises all day long. He'd been sitting at God's right hand ever since the beginning of time. He ruled the whole universe and walked on streets of gold comfortable, adored, worshiped. Then, one day, it was decision time. Someone had to go to earth. God loved his people so much that he couldn't stand to watch them suffer and wander. The humans needed someone like them to explain God's plan and purpose. So God sent Jesus to be like the people and to live among them on earth. He poured his glorious body into one like ours, gave up all the magnificence of heaven just to help us learn how to live and be right with God. He became poor so that we could know the riches of heaven—joy in a busted world, love when hearts are broken, peace when chaos is reigning, and other blessings. Jesus said that his riches have become ours by our faith in him. That's great news—you're rich!

hearts and lives. This leads to salvation, and you cannot be sorry for that. But the kind of sorrow the world has brings death. [11]See what this sorrow—the sorrow God wanted you to have—has done to you: It has made you very serious. It made you want to prove you were not wrong. It made you angry and afraid. It made you want to see me. It made you care. It made you want the right thing to be done. You proved you were innocent in the problem. [12]I wrote that letter, not because of the one who did the wrong or because of the person who was hurt. I wrote the letter so you could see, before God, the great care you have for us. [13]That is why we were comforted.

Not only were we very comforted, we were even happier to see that Titus was so happy. All of you made him feel much better. [14]I bragged to Titus about you, and you showed that I was right. Everything we said to you was true, and you have proved that what we bragged about to Titus is true. [15]And his love for you is stronger when he remembers that you were all ready to obey. You welcomed him with respect and fear. [16]I am very happy that I can trust you fully.

CHRISTIAN GIVING

8 And now, brothers and sisters, we want you to know about the grace God gave the churches in Macedonia. [2]They have been tested by great troubles, and they are very poor. But they gave much because of their great joy. [3]I can tell you that they gave as much as they were able and even more than they could afford. No one told them to do it. [4]But they begged and pleaded with us to let them share in this service for God's people. [5]And they gave in a way we did not expect: They first gave themselves to the Lord and to us. This is what God wants. [6]So we asked Titus to help you finish this special work of grace since he is the one who started it. [7]You are rich in everything—in faith, in speaking, in knowledge, in truly wanting to help, and in the love you learned from us. In the same way, be strong also in the grace of giving.

[8]I am not commanding you to give. But I want to see if your love is true by comparing you with others that really want to help. [9]You know the grace of our Lord Jesus Christ. You know that Christ was rich, but for you he

EXPERTS ANSWER YOUR QUESTIONS

Q. *Do you think cloning is OK?*

A. Just because people figure out how to do something, that doesn't mean they use that knowledge wisely. Some potential uses for cloning are trying to play God. Some want to clone people or use genetic engineering to create people more to their own liking. It's not a lot different from Hitler's attempt to create an ultimate race, and we know how that turned out.

Q. *How do I deal with my parents' divorce? It's hard for me to really trust God, and I even give up on God half the time. How can I trust in God when I think that he did all of this?*

A. If you believe that the Bible is true, then you can believe that God didn't do all this. He is incapable of doing evil. It really stinks that your parents couldn't work it out, but now you need to figure out what God is going to teach you through this. Remember that the testing of your faith develops perseverance. And perseverance leads to perfection.

Q. *My parents are getting divorced, and I have to choose which one to move in with. What do I do?*

A. Go to the house where you'll spend the most time with your parent, where you'll be most spiritually nourished, and you'll get to be in Christian fellowship. If this is both, then pray real hard. God will let you know.

RANDOM THINGS TO PRAY FOR

1. YOUR FAMILY
2. YOUR FRIENDS
3. WORLD LEADERS
4. UNDERPRIVILEGED PEOPLE AROUND THE WORLD
5. WISDOM
6. INTEGRITY
7. CELEBRITIES
8. YOUR PRINCIPAL AND TEACHERS
9. YOUR FUTURE WIFE
10. YOUR FUTURE CHILDREN

WAYS TO WALK THE WALK

2 corinthians 10:17

WORD: If you're going to brag, then brag about God.

WALK IT: What accomplishments do you sport on your sleeve, as obvious as patches on a letter jacket? Tell someone today that God is the reason for your success.

became poor so that by his becoming poor you might become rich.

[10]This is what I think you should do: Last year you were the first to want to give, and you were the first who gave. [11]So now finish the work you started. Then your "doing" will be equal to your "wanting to do." Give from what you have. [12]If you want to give, your gift will be accepted. It will be judged by what you have, not by what you do not have. [13]We do not want you to have troubles while other people are at ease, but we want everything to be equal. [14]At this time you have plenty. What you have can help others who are in need. Then later, when they have plenty, they can help you when you are in need, and all will be equal. [15]As it is written in the Scriptures, "The person who gathered more did not have too much, nor did the person who gathered less have too little."[n]

TITUS AND HIS COMPANIONS HELP

[16]I thank God because he gave Titus the same love for you that I have. [17]Titus accepted what we asked him to do. He wanted very much to go to you, and this was his own idea. [18]We are sending with him the brother who is praised by all the churches because of his service in preaching the Good News. [19]Also, this brother was chosen by the churches to go with us when we deliver this gift of money. We are doing this service to bring glory to the Lord and to show that we really want to help.

[20]We are being careful so that no one will criticize us for the way we are handling this large gift. [21]We are trying hard to do what the Lord accepts as right and also what people think is right.

[22]Also, we are sending with them our brother, who is always ready to help. He has proved this to us in many ways, and he wants to help even more now, because he has much faith in you.

[23]Now about Titus—he is my partner who is working with me to help you. And about the other brothers—they are sent from the churches, and they bring glory to Christ. [24]So show these men the proof of your love and the reason we are proud of you. Then all the churches can see it.

HELP FOR FELLOW CHRISTIANS

9 I really do not need to write you about this help for God's people. [2]I know you want to help. I have been bragging about this to the people in Macedonia, telling them that you in Southern Greece have been ready to give since last year. And your desire to give has made most of them ready to give also. [3]But I am sending the brothers to you so that our bragging about you in this will not be empty words. I want you to be ready, as I said you would be. [4]If any of the people from Macedonia come with me and find that you are not ready, we will be ashamed that we were so sure of you. (And you will be ashamed, too!) [5]So I thought I should ask these brothers to go to you before we do. They will finish getting in order the generous gift you promised so it will be ready when we come. And it will be a generous gift—not one that you did not want to give.

[6]Remember this: The person who plants a little will have a small harvest, but the person who plants a lot will have a big harvest. [7]Each one should give as you have decided in your heart to give. You should not be sad when you give, and you should not give because you feel forced to give. God loves the person who gives happily. [8]And God can give you more blessings than you need. Then you will always have plenty of everything—enough to give to every good work. [9]It is written in the Scriptures:

"He gives freely to the poor.
The things he does are right and will
continue forever." *Psalm 112:9*

[10]God is the One who gives seed to the farmer and bread for food. He will give you all the seed you need and make it grow so there will be a great harvest from your goodness. [11]He will make you rich in every way so that you can always give freely. And your giving through us will cause many to give thanks to God. [12]This service you do not only helps the needs of God's people, it also brings many more thanks to God. [13]It is a proof of your faith. Many people will praise God because you obey the Good News of Christ—the gospel you say you believe—and because you freely share with them and with all others. [14]And when they pray, they will wish they could be with you because of the great grace that God has given you. [15]Thanks be to God for his gift that is too wonderful for words.

8:15 "The person . . . little." Quotation from Exodus 16:18.

PAUL DEFENDS HIS MINISTRY

10 I, Paul, am begging you with the gentleness and the kindness of Christ. Some people say that I am easy on you when I am with you and bold when I am away. [2]They think we live in a worldly way, and I plan to be very bold with them when I come. I beg you that when I come I will not need to use that same boldness with you. [3]We do live in the world, but we do not fight in the same way the world fights. [4]We fight with weapons that are different from those the world uses. Our weapons have power from God that can destroy the enemy's strong places. We destroy people's arguments [5]and every proud thing that raises itself against the knowledge of God. We capture every thought and make it give up and obey Christ. [6]We are ready to punish anyone there who does not obey, but first we want you to obey fully.

[7]You must look at the facts before you. If you feel sure that you belong to Christ, you must remember that we belong to Christ just as you do. [8]It is true that we brag freely about the authority the Lord gave us. But this authority is to build you up, not to tear you down. So I will not be ashamed. [9]I do not want you to think I am trying to scare you with my letters. [10]Some people say, "Paul's letters are powerful and sound important, but when he is with us, he is weak. And his speaking is nothing." [11]They should know this: We are not there with you now, so we say these things in letters. But when we are there with you, we will show the same authority that we show in our letters.

[12]We do not dare to compare ourselves with those who think they are very important. They use themselves to measure themselves, and they judge themselves by what they themselves are. This shows that they know nothing. [13]But we will not brag about things outside the work that was given us to do. We will limit our bragging to the work that God gave us, and this includes our work with you. [14]We are not bragging too much, as we would be if we had not already come to you. But we have come to you with the Good News of Christ. [15]We limit our bragging to the work that is ours, not what others have done. We hope that as your faith continues to grow, you will help our work to grow much larger. [16]We want to tell the Good News in the areas beyond your city. We do not want to brag about work that has already been done in another person's area. [17]But, "If someone wants to brag, he should brag only about the Lord."[n] [18]It is not those who say they are good who are accepted but those who the Lord thinks are good.

PAUL AND THE FALSE APOSTLES

11 I wish you would be patient with me even when I am a little foolish, but you are already doing that. [2]I am jealous over you with a jealousy that comes from God. I promised to give you to Christ, as your

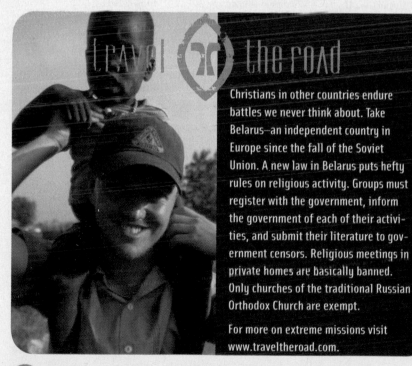

Christians in other countries endure battles we never think about. Take Belarus—an independent country in Europe since the fall of the Soviet Union. A new law in Belarus puts hefty rules on religious activity. Groups must register with the government, inform the government of each of their activities, and submit their literature to government censors. Religious meetings in private homes are basically banned. Only churches of the traditional Russian Orthodox Church are exempt.

For more on extreme missions visit www.traveltheroad.com.

BIBLE BASICS

Baptism is a public acknowledgment of Jesus Christ. A person is covered with water—some use sprinkling, some pouring, some dunking—as a symbol of their commitment to God. It's a practice that comes from the New Testament. Even before Christ began his ministry, John the Baptist baptized people in the wilderness, and Jesus himself was actually baptized by John. It's a public way to show your belief in God, and it symbolizes death to your old self by leaving it behind as you come up with a new life.

10:17 "If . . . Lord." Quotation from Jeremiah 9:24.

only husband. ³But I am afraid that your minds will be led away from your true and pure following of Christ just as Eve was tricked by the snake with his evil ways. ⁴You are very patient with anyone who comes to you and preaches a different Jesus from the one we preached. You are very willing to accept a spirit or gospel that is different from the Spirit and Good News you received from us.

⁵I do not think that those "great apostles" are any better than I am. ⁶I may not be a trained speaker, but I do have knowledge. We have shown this to you clearly in every way.

⁷I preached God's Good News to you without pay. I made myself unimportant to make you important. Do you think that was wrong? ⁸I accepted pay from other churches, taking their money so I could serve you. ⁹If I needed something when I was with you, I did not trouble any of you. The brothers who came from Macedonia gave me all that I needed. I did not allow myself to depend on you in any way, and I will never depend on you. ¹⁰No one in Southern Greece will stop me from bragging about that. I say this with the truth of Christ in me. ¹¹And why do I not depend on you? Do you think it is because I do not love you? God knows that I love you.

¹²And I will continue doing what I am doing now, because I want to stop those people from having a reason to brag. They would like to say that the work they brag about is the same as ours. ¹³Such men are not

true apostles but are workers who lie. They change themselves to look like apostles of Christ. ¹⁴This does not surprise us. Even Satan changes himself to look like an angel of light.ⁿ ¹⁵So it does not surprise us if Satan's servants also make themselves look like servants who work for what is right. But in the end they will be punished for what they do.

PAUL TELLS ABOUT HIS SUFFERINGS

¹⁶I tell you again: No one should think I am a fool. But if you think so, accept me as you would accept a fool. Then I can brag a little, too. ¹⁷When I brag because I feel sure of myself, I am not talking as the Lord would talk but as a fool. ¹⁸Many people are bragging about their lives in the world. So I will brag too. ¹⁹You are wise, so you will gladly be patient with fools! ²⁰You are even patient with those who order you around, or use you, or trick you, or think they are better than you, or hit you in the face. ²¹It is shameful to me to say this, but we were too "weak" to do those things to you!

But if anyone else is brave enough to brag, then I also will be brave and brag. (I am talking as a fool.) ²²Are they Hebrews?ⁿ So am I. Are they Israelites? So am I. Are they from Abraham's family? So am I. ²³Are they serving Christ? I am serving him more. (I am crazy to talk like this.) I have worked much harder than they. I have been in prison more often. I have been hurt more in beatings. I have been near death many times. ²⁴Five

times the Jews have given me their punishment of thirty-nine lashes with a whip. ²⁵Three different times I was beaten with rods. One time I was almost stoned to death. Three times I was in ships that wrecked, and one of those times I spent a night and a day in the sea. ²⁶I have gone on many travels and have been in danger from rivers, thieves, my own people, the Jews, and those who are not Jews. I have been in danger in cities, in places where no one lives, and on the sea. And I have been in danger with false Christians. ²⁷I have done hard and tiring work, and many times I did not sleep. I have been hungry and thirsty, and many times I have been without food. I have been cold and without clothes. ²⁸Besides all this, there is on me every day the load of my concern for all the churches. ²⁹I feel weak every time someone is weak, and I feel upset every time someone is led into sin.

³⁰If I must brag, I will brag about the things that show I am weak. ³¹God knows I am not lying. He is the God and Father of the Lord Jesus Christ, and he is to be praised forever. ³²When I was in Damascus, the governor under King Aretas wanted to arrest me, so he put guards around the city. ³³But my friends lowered me in a basket through a hole in the city wall. So I escaped from the governor.

A SPECIAL BLESSING IN PAUL'S LIFE

12 I must continue to brag. It will do no good, but I will

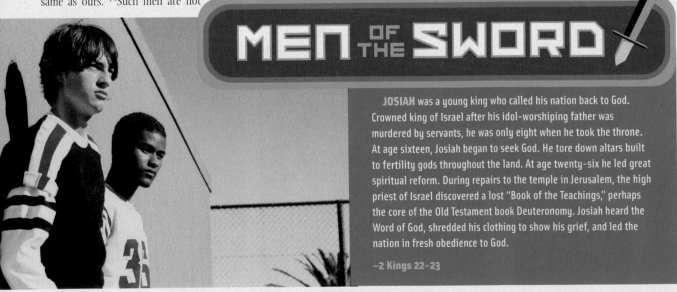

MEN OF THE SWORD

JOSIAH was a young king who called his nation back to God. Crowned king of Israel after his idol-worshiping father was murdered by servants, he was only eight when he took the throne. At age sixteen, Josiah began to seek God. He tore down altars built to fertility gods throughout the land. At age twenty-six he led great spiritual reform. During repairs to the temple in Jerusalem, the high priest of Israel discovered a lost "Book of the Teachings," perhaps the core of the Old Testament book Deuteronomy. Josiah heard the Word of God, shredded his clothing to show his grief, and led the nation in fresh obedience to God.

—2 Kings 22–23

11:14 angel of light Messenger from God. The devil fools people so that they think he is from God.   11:22 Hebrews A name for the Jews that some Jews were very proud of.

talk now about visions and revelations[n] from the Lord. [2]I know a man in Christ who was taken up to the third heaven fourteen years ago. I do not know whether the man was in his body or out of his body, but God knows. [3-4]And I know that this man was taken up to paradise.[n] I don't know if he was in his body or away from his body, but God knows. He heard things he is not able to explain, things that no human is allowed to tell. [5]I will brag about a man like that, but I will not brag about myself, except about my weaknesses. [6]But if I wanted to brag about myself, I would not be a fool, because I would be telling the truth. But I will not brag about myself. I do not want people to think more of me than what they see me do or hear me say.

[7]So that I would not become too proud of the wonderful things that were shown to me, a painful physical problem[n] was given to me. This problem was a messenger from Satan, sent to beat me and keep me from being too proud. [8]I begged the Lord three times to take this problem away from me. [9]But he said to me, "My grace is enough for you. When you are weak, my power is made perfect in you." So I am very happy to brag about my weaknesses. Then Christ's power can live in me. [10]For this reason I am happy when I have weaknesses, insults, hard times, sufferings, and all kinds of troubles for Christ. Because when I am weak, then I am truly strong.

PAUL'S LOVE FOR THE CHRISTIANS

[11]I have been talking like a fool, but you made me do it. You are the ones who should say good things about me. I am worth nothing, but those "great apostles" are not worth any more than I am! [12]When I was with you, I patiently did the things that prove I am an apostle—signs, wonders, and miracles. [13]So you received everything that the other churches have received. Only one thing was different: I was not a burden to you. Forgive me for this!

[14]I am now ready to visit you the third time, and I will not be a burden to you. I want nothing from you, except you. Children should not have to save up to give to their parents. Parents should save to give to their children. [15]So I am happy to give everything I have for you, even myself. If I love you more, will you love me less?

[16]It is clear I was not a burden to you, but you think I was tricky and lied to catch you. [17]Did I cheat you by using any of the messengers I sent to you? No, you know I did not. [18]I asked Titus to go to you, and I sent our brother with him. Titus did not cheat you, did he? No, you know that Titus and I did the same thing and with the same spirit.

[19]Do you think we have been defending ourselves to you all this time? We have been speaking in Christ and before God. You are our dear friends, and everything we do is to make you stronger. [20]I am afraid that when I come, you will not be what I want you to be, and I will not be what you want me to be. I am afraid that among you there may be arguing, jealousy, anger, selfish fighting, evil talk, gossip, pride, and confusion. [21]I am afraid that when I come to you again, my God will make me ashamed before you. I may be saddened by many of those who have sinned because they have not changed their hearts or turned from their sexual sins and the shameful things they have done.

FINAL WARNINGS AND GREETINGS

13 I will come to you for the third time. "Every case must be proved by two or three witnesses."[n] [2]When I was with you the second time, I gave a warning to those who had sinned. Now I am away from you, and I give a warning to all the others. When I come to you again, I will not be easy with them. [3]You want proof that Christ is speaking through me. My proof is that he is not weak among you, but he is powerful. [4]It is true that he was weak when he was killed on the cross, but he lives now by God's power. It is true that we are weak in Christ, but for you we will be alive in Christ by God's power.

[5]Look closely at yourselves. Test yourselves to see if you are living in the faith. You know that Jesus Christ is in you—unless you fail the test. [6]But I hope you will see that we ourselves have not failed the test. [7]We pray to God that you will not do anything wrong. It is not important to see that we have passed the test, but it is important that you do what is right, even if it seems we have failed. [8]We cannot do anything against the truth, but only for the truth. [9]We are happy to be weak, if you are strong, and we pray that you will become complete. [10]I am writing this while I am away from you so that when I come I will not have to be harsh in my use of authority. The Lord gave me this authority to build you up, not to tear you down.

[11]Now, brothers and sisters, I say good-bye. Try to be complete. Do what I have asked you to do. Agree with each other, and live in peace. Then the God of love and peace will be with you.

[12]Greet each other with a holy kiss. [13]All of God's holy people send greetings to you.

[14]The grace of the Lord Jesus Christ, the love of God, and the fellowship of the Holy Spirit be with you all.

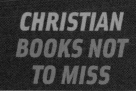

CHRISTIAN BOOKS NOT TO MISS

1. *MERE CHRISTIANITY*
   BY C.S. LEWIS

2. *PILGRIM'S PROGRESS*
   BY JOHN BUNYAN

3. *WILD AT HEART*
   BY JOHN ELDREDGE

4. *MY UTMOST FOR HIS HIGHEST*
   BY OSWALD CHAMBERS

5. *WAIT FOR ME*
   BY REBECCA ST. JAMES

6. *IN HIS STEPS*
   BY CHARLES M. SHELDON

7. *WITNESSING 101*
   BY TIM BAKER

8. *THE RULES: TEN TO LIVE BY*
   BY M. NICHOLAS

9. *WITH CHRIST IN THE SCHOOL OF PRAYER*
   BY ANDREW MURRAY

10. *THE BIG BUCKS*
    BY ELIZABETH PATTON

 12:1 revelations Revelation is making known a truth that was hidden.   12:3-4 paradise Another word for heaven.   12:7 painful physical problem Literally, "thorn in the flesh."   13:1 "Every . . . witnesses." Quotation from Deuteronomy 19:15.

GALATIANS

A spiritual coach gets worked up about the gospel

Sometimes it feels like Bible is devoid of emotion. The cold, hard facts of history don't exactly leap off the page. Well, if you've ever felt that way... try Galatians. It's the most emotionally charged book of the Bible. You can almost see veins pop out on Paul's neck as he confronts some badly misguided Christians.

What's the big deal? For starters, Paul has made clear that God saves us by our trusting in Christ alone, not by our doing religious things. The believers in Galatia obviously don't buy it. Instead, they've bought the message of some missionaries who teach that Christians have to obey Jewish laws to get right with God. Paul is adamant that because Christ has come, keeping the Law has nothing to do with salvation. So, with an emotionally charged response, Paul reminds the Galatians of the miracles and the gift of the Holy Spirit they experienced when he was still in the area. He fires away, asking them how they actually received God's Spirit. Did they have to work to get it? Nope. How in the world can they be so stupid? (Hey...those are Paul's words!)

It's hard to understand the rage and intensity that drive Paul as he speaks some of the harshest words in Scripture. Yet when he detonates his anger all over the Galatians and the people leading them in the wrong direction, he sounds oddly familiar—like a furious but loving parent reading the riot act to a child who just did something incredibly stupid and nearly got killed. Been there? Then you will recognize that love is behind this scream, calling God's people back from the brink of disaster.

1 From Paul, an apostle. I was not chosen to be an apostle by human beings, nor was I sent from human beings. I was made an apostle through Jesus Christ and God the Father who raised Jesus from the dead. [2]This letter is also from all those of God's family[n] who are with me.

To the churches in Galatia:[n]

[3]Grace and peace to you from God our Father and the Lord Jesus Christ. [4]Jesus gave himself for our sins to free us from this evil world we live in, as God the Father planned. [5]The glory belongs to God forever and ever. Amen.

THE ONLY GOOD NEWS

[6]God, by his grace through Christ, called you to become his people. So I am amazed that you are turning away so quickly and believing something different than the Good News. [7]Really, there is no other Good News. But some people are confusing you; they want to change the Good News of Christ. [8]We preached to you the Good News. So if we ourselves, or even an angel from heaven, should preach to you something different, we should be judged guilty! [9]I said this before, and now I say it again: You have already accepted the Good News. If anyone is preaching something different to you, he should be judged guilty!

[10]Do you think I am trying to make people accept me? No, God is the One I am trying to please. Am I trying to please people? If I still wanted to please people, I would not be a servant of Christ.

PAUL'S AUTHORITY IS FROM GOD

[11]Brothers and sisters,[n] I want you to know that the Good News I preached to you was not made up by human beings. [12]I did not get it from humans, nor did anyone teach it to me, but Jesus Christ showed it to me.

[13]You have heard about my past life in the Jewish religion. I attacked the church of God and tried to destroy it. [14]I was becoming a leader in the Jewish religion, doing better than most other Jews of my age. I tried harder than anyone else to follow the teachings handed down by our ancestors.

[15]But God had special plans for me and set me apart for his work even before I was born. He called me through his grace [16]and showed his son to me so that I might tell the Good News about him to those who are not Jewish. When God called me, I did not get advice or help from any person. [17]I did not go to Jerusalem to see those who were apostles before I was. But, without waiting, I went away to Arabia and later went back to Damascus.

[18]After three years I went to Jerusalem to meet Peter and stayed with him for fifteen days. [19]I met no other apostles, except James, the brother of the Lord. [20]God knows that these things I write are not lies. [21]Later, I went to the areas of Syria and Cilicia.

[22]In Judea the churches in Christ had never met me. [23]They had only heard it said, "This man who was attacking us is now preaching the same faith that he once tried to destroy." [24]And these believers praised God because of me.

OTHER APOSTLES ACCEPTED PAUL

2 After fourteen years I went to Jerusalem again, this time with Barnabas. I also took Titus with me. [2]I went because God showed me I should go. I met with the believers there, and

PROJECT PLAN-IT! helps you turn ideas into action, whatever you aim to do. It's an easy, interactive series of online questions and templates that allow you and your friends to plan your service project or program. It's a part of Youth Service America. At the end of Project Plan-It! you will be able to print out your own project plan, funding proposal, press release, service-learning reflection plan, and other helpful resources. You will also be able to post your project on SERVEnet and convert your project/program into your own website.

To use Project Plan-It, visit www.ysa.org/planit.

1:2 those . . . family The Greek text says "brothers." **1:2 Galatia** Probably the same country where Paul preached and began churches on his first missionary trip. Read the Book of Acts, chapters 13 and 14. **1:11 Brothers and sisters** Although the Greek text says "Brothers" here and throughout this book, Paul's words were meant for the entire church, including men and women.

issues

SOCIAL ACTIVISM

HOW MUCH DOES IT MATTER that you're socially involved? How big should it be in your life? Well, there are over 2,300 verses in Scripture that command us to take care of the poor, feed the hungry, and clothe the naked. So look for a way to live that out day to day. Get on www.volunteermatch.org today, and see what opportunities are available in your neighborhood. Or check out the newspaper, magazine, website, or other media outlet you use most, and find out what's going on with an issue you care about. Stuff envelopes, raise cash, volunteer your time, do whatever it takes to make a difference in the lives of those less fortunate than you.

in private I told their leaders the Good News that I preach to the non-Jewish people. I did not want my past work and the work I am now doing to be wasted. ³Titus was with me, but he was not forced to be circumcised, even though he was a Greek. ⁴We talked about this problem because some false believers had come into our group secretly. They came in like spies to overturn the freedom we have in Christ Jesus. They wanted to make us slaves. ⁵But we did not give in to those false believers for a minute. We wanted the truth of the Good News to continue for you.

⁶Those leaders who seemed to be important did not change the Good News that I preach. (It doesn't matter to me if they were "important" or not. To God everyone is the same.) ⁷But these leaders saw that I had been given the work of telling the Good News to those who are not Jewish, just as Peter had the work of telling the Jews. ⁸God gave Peter the power to work as an apostle for the Jewish people. But he also gave me the power to work as an apostle for those who are not Jews. ⁹James, Peter, and John, who seemed to be the leaders, understood that God had given me this special grace, so they accepted Barnabas and me. They agreed that they would go to the Jewish people and that we should go to those who are not Jewish. ¹⁰The only thing they asked us was to remember to help the poor—something I really wanted to do.

PAUL SHOWS THAT PETER WAS WRONG

¹¹When Peter came to Antioch, I challenged him to his face, because he was wrong. ¹²Peter ate with the non-Jewish people until some Jewish people sent from James came to Antioch. When they arrived, Peter stopped eating with those who weren't Jewish, and he separated himself from them. He was afraid of the Jews. ¹³So Peter was a hypocrite, as were the other Jewish believers who joined with him. Even Barnabas was influenced by what these Jewish believers did. ¹⁴When I saw they were not following the truth of the Good News, I spoke to Peter in front of them all. I said, "Peter, you are a Jew, but you are not living like a Jew. You are living like those who are not Jewish. So why do you now try to force those who are not Jewish to live like Jews?"

¹⁵We were not born as non-Jewish "sinners," but as Jews. ¹⁶Yet we know that a person is made right with God not by following the law, but by trusting in Jesus Christ. So we, too, have put our faith in Christ Jesus, that we might be made right with God because we trusted in Christ. It is not because we followed the law, because no one can be made right with God by following the law.

¹⁷We Jews came to Christ, trying to be made right with God, and it became clear that we are sinners, too. Does this mean that Christ encourages sin? No! ¹⁸But I would really be wrong to begin teaching again those things that I gave

GALATIANS 3:26

You are God's child, and he is your Father. But how? Because you put your faith in Jesus. What is faith? Belief without proof. Hebrews 11:1 says, "Faith means being sure of the things we hope for and knowing that something is real even if we do not see it." Even though you've never seen God, you know he exists. Because you know he exists, you put your faith in him.

God cares for you the same way an earthly father takes care of his children, only better. God is concerned with every detail of your life. He wants to give you good things. He wants to see you grow up and be everything he's designed you to be. He really wants you to know him—deeply and powerfully. How can you get to know your Father better? By spending time with him in prayer and by studying his Word.

You're God's child. You're a prince in his kingdom because the King is your Dad! He loves you so much that he's adopted you as his very own. By faith, take your place as a child of God.

the road

You might assume that missions only happens when a North American family packs up and moves overseas. While western countries are still heavy senders of missionaries, the majority of Protestant missionaries now come from the non-Western world. In fact, the countries that send the most missionaries aren't places like the United States, Britain, or Germany, but India, South Korea, Brazil, and Nigeria.

For more on extreme missions visit www.traveltheroad.com.

EXPERTS ANSWER YOUR QUESTIONS

Q. *I have a friend who talks about suicide sometimes. I don't think he would do it, but he wonders what it would be like. How can I help him?*

A. By yourself, you can't help him. If you have a friend who even mentions suicide, tell a qualified adult like a counselor, pastor, or a suicide hotline. This isn't dissing your age or abilities. It's just that none of us has the smarts to handle that heavy info alone. If you think it's crazy to involve an adult, consider how you will feel if your friend hurts himself and you maybe could have stopped it.

Q. *Last night after Bible study a girl I know well told me she was raped the day before. What should I do?*

A. The best thing you can do is believe her—and help her get help. It's fantastic that you're concerned, but it's not your job to counsel her in-depth. A recent rape victim should immediately visit an emergency room, where she will be guided to appropriate care. Someone raped back in the past should get help by seeing a pastor or other counselor.

up. [19]It was the law that put me to death, and I died to the law so that I can now live for God. [20]I was put to death on the cross with Christ, and I do not live anymore—it is Christ who lives in me. I still live in my body, but I live by faith in the Son of God who loved me and gave himself to save me. [21]By saying these things I am not going against God's grace. Just the opposite, if the law could make us right with God, then Christ's death would be useless.

BLESSING COMES THROUGH FAITH

3 You people in Galatia were told very clearly about the death of Jesus Christ on the cross. But you were foolish; you let someone trick you. [2]Tell me this one thing: How did you receive the Holy Spirit? Did you receive the Spirit by following the law? No, you received the Spirit because you heard the Good News and believed it. [3]You began your life in Christ by the Spirit. Now are you trying to make it complete by your own power? That is foolish. [4]Were all your experiences wasted? I hope not! [5]Does God give you the Spirit and work miracles among you because you follow the law? No, he does these things because you heard the Good News and believed it.

[6]The Scriptures say the same thing about Abraham: "Abraham believed God, and God accepted Abraham's faith, and that faith made him right with God."[n] [7]So you should know that the true children of Abraham are those who have faith. [8]The Scriptures, telling what would happen in the future, said that God would make the non-Jewish people right through their faith. This Good News was told to Abraham beforehand, as the Scripture says: "All nations will be blessed through you."[n] [9]So all who believe as Abraham believed are blessed just as Abraham was. [10]But those who depend on following the law to make them right are under a curse, because the Scriptures say, "Anyone will be cursed who does not always obey what is written in the Book of the Law."[n] [11]Now it is clear that no one can be made right with God by the law, because the Scriptures say, "Those who are right with God will live by trusting in him."[n] [12]The law is not based on faith. It says, "A person who obeys these

RANDOM THINGS TO LOOK FOR IN A GODLY GIRL

1. JOY
2. HONESTY
3. WARMTH
4. RESPECT
5. PATIENCE
6. HUMOR
7. FRIENDLINESS
8. SELF-ESTEEM
9. STAMINA
10. KINDNESS

things will live because of them."[n] [13]Christ took away the curse the law put on us. He changed places with us and put himself under that curse. It is written in the Scriptures, "Anyone whose body is displayed on a tree[n] is cursed." [14]Christ did this so that God's blessing promised to Abraham might come through Jesus Christ to those who are not Jews. Jesus died so that by our believing we could receive the Spirit that God promised.

THE LAW AND THE PROMISE

[15]Brothers and sisters, let us think in human terms: Even an agreement made between two persons is firm. After that agreement is accepted by both people, no one can stop it or add anything to it. [16]God made promises both to Abraham and to his descendant. God did not say, "and to your descendants." That would mean many people. But God said, "and to your descendant." That means only one person; that person is Christ. [17]This is what I mean: God had an agreement with Abraham and promised to keep it. The law, which came four hundred thirty years later, cannot change that agreement and so destroy God's promise to Abraham. [18]If the law could give us

Abraham's blessing, then the promise would not be necessary. But that is not possible, because God freely gave his blessings to Abraham through the promise he had made.

[19] So what was the law for? It was given to show that the wrong things people do are against God's will. And it continued until the special descendant, who had been promised, came. The law was given through angels who used Moses for a mediator[n] to give the law to people. [20] But a mediator is not needed when there is only one side, and God is only one.

THE PURPOSE OF THE LAW OF MOSES

[21] Does this mean that the law is against God's promises? Never! That would be true only if the law could make us right. But God did not give a law that can bring life. [22] Instead, the Scriptures showed that the whole world is bound by sin. This was so the promise would be given through faith to people who believe in Jesus Christ.

[23] Before this faith came, we were all held prisoners by the law. We had no freedom until God showed us the way of faith that was coming. [24] In other words, the law was our guardian leading us to Christ so that we could be made right with God through faith. [25] Now the way of faith has come, and we no longer live under a guardian.

[26-27] You were all baptized into Christ, and so you were all clothed with Christ. This means that you are all children of God through faith in Christ Jesus. [28] In Christ, there is no difference between Jew and Greek, slave and free person, male and female. You are all the same

in Christ Jesus. [29] You belong to Christ, so you are Abraham's descendants. You will inherit all of God's blessings because of the promise God made to Abraham.

4 I want to tell you this: While those who will inherit their fathers' property are still children, they are no different from slaves. It does not matter that the children own everything. [2] While they are children, they must obey those who are chosen to care for them. But when the children reach the age set by their fathers, they are free. [3] It is the same for us. We were once like children, slaves to the useless rules of this world. [4] But when the right time came, God sent his Son who was born of a woman and lived under the law. [5] God did this so he could buy freedom for those who were under the law and so we could become his children.

[6] Since you are God's children, God sent the Spirit of his Son into your hearts, and the Spirit cries out, "Father."[n] [7] So now you are not a slave; you are God's child, and God will give you the blessing he promised, because you are his child.

PAUL'S LOVE FOR THE CHRISTIANS

[8] In the past you did not know God. You were slaves to gods that were not real. [9] But now you know the true God. Really, it is God who knows you. So why do you turn back to those weak and useless rules you followed before? Do you want to be slaves to those things again? [10] You still follow teachings about special days, months, seasons, and years. [11] I am afraid for you, that my work for you has been wasted.

[12] Brothers and sisters, I became like you, so I beg you to become like me. You were very good to me before. [13] You remember that it was because of an illness that I came to you the first time, preaching the Good News. [14] Though my sickness was a trouble for you, you did not hate me or make me leave. But you welcomed me as an angel from God, as if I were Jesus Christ himself! [15] You were very happy then, but where is that joy now? I am ready to testify that you would have taken out your eyes and given them to me if that were possible. [16] Now am I your enemy because I tell you the truth?

[17] Those people[n] are working hard to persuade you, but this is not good for you. They want to persuade you to turn against us and follow only them. [18] It is good for people to

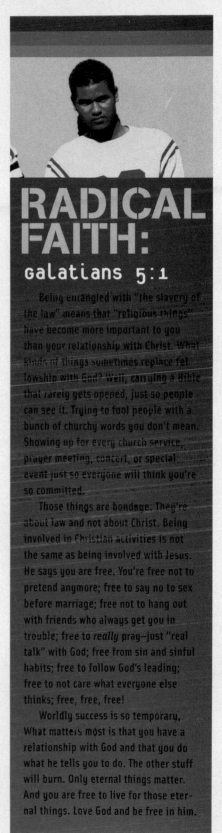

3:19 mediator A person who helps one person talk to or give something to another person. **4:6 "Father"** Literally, "Abba, Father." Jewish children called their fathers "Abba." **4:17 Those people** They are the false teachers who were bothering the believers in Galatia (Galatians 1:7).

RADICAL FAITH:

galatians 5:17

God's Word tells us to love the Lord with all of our heart, with all of our soul, and with all of our strength (see Deuteronomy 6:4-5). When you first got saved, you gave your heart to Jesus first. You didn't give him your soul or your strength first. You gave him your heart.

Satan will always counterfeit what God does, and do the exact opposite. He'll always go after your mind first, because he knows that if he can get something into your mind and get you to think continually about it, then he can get you to do it. That's why it's so important to realize that you can control your thoughts and desires.

Sin always starts in the mind. It's not sin to have an evil thought—that's temptation; but it is wrong to dwell on and entertain those thoughts. To make it simpler: A bird can lay an egg on your head, but only you can let him build a nest in your hair!

James 1:13-15 reminds us that if we think about sin long enough, we'll desire to sin. If we want to sin, we will eventually sin. After sin is done, it will leave us dead. That's why it's so important to walk in the Spirit and feed your mind with the Word of God.

show interest in you, but only if their purpose is good. This is always true, not just when I am with you. [19]My little children, again I feel the pain of childbirth for you until you truly become like Christ. [20]I wish I could be with you now and could change the way I am talking to you, because I do not know what to think about you.

THE EXAMPLE OF HAGAR AND SARAH

[21]Some of you still want to be under the law. Tell me, do you know what the law says? [22]The Scriptures say that Abraham had two sons. The mother of one son was a slave woman, and the mother of the other son was a free woman. [23]Abraham's son from the slave woman was born in the normal human way. But the son from the free woman was born because of the promise God made to Abraham.

[24]This story teaches something else: The two women are like the two agreements between God and his people. One agreement is the law that God made on Mount Sinai,[n] and the people who are under this agreement are like slaves. The mother named Hagar is like that agreement. [25]She is like Mount Sinai in Arabia and is a picture of the earthly Jewish city of Jerusalem. This city and its people, the Jews, are slaves to the law. [26]But the heavenly Jerusalem, which is above, is like the free woman. She is our mother. [27]It is written in the Scriptures:

"Be happy, Jerusalem.
    You are like a woman who never gave
        birth to children.
Start singing and shout for joy.
    You never felt the pain of giving birth,
but you will have more children
    than the woman who has a husband."

Isaiah 54:1

[28]My brothers and sisters, you are God's children because of his promise, as Isaac was then. [29]The son who was born in the normal way treated the other son badly. It is the same today. [30]But what does the Scripture say? "Throw out the slave woman and her son. The son of the slave woman should not inherit anything. The son of the free woman should receive it all."[n] [31]So, my brothers and sisters, we are not children of the slave woman, but of the free woman.

KEEP YOUR FREEDOM

5 We have freedom now, because Christ made us free. So stand strong. Do not change and go back into the slavery of the law. [2]Listen, I Paul tell you that if you go back to the law by being circumcised, Christ does you no good. [3]Again, I warn every man: If you allow yourselves to be circumcised, you must follow all the law. [4]If you try to be made right with God through the law, your life with Christ is over—you have left God's grace. [5]But we have the true hope that comes from being made right with God, and by the Spirit we wait eagerly for this hope. [6]When we are in Christ Jesus, it is not important if we are circumcised or not. The important thing is faith—the kind of faith that works through love.

[7]You were running a good race. Who stopped you from following the true way? [8]This change did not come from the One who chose you. [9]Be careful! "Just a little yeast makes the whole batch of dough rise." [10]But I trust in the Lord that you will not believe those different ideas. Whoever is confusing you with such ideas will be punished.

[11]My brothers and sisters, I do not teach that a man must be circumcised. If I teach circumcision, why am I still being attacked? If I still taught circumcision, my preaching about the cross would not be a problem. [12]I wish the people who are bothering you would castrate[n] themselves!

[13]My brothers and sisters, God called you to be free, but do not use your freedom as an excuse to do what pleases your sinful self. Serve each other with love. [14]The whole law is made complete in this one command: "Love your neighbor as you love yourself."[n] [15]If you go on hurting each other and tearing each other apart, be careful, or you will completely destroy each other.

THE SPIRIT AND HUMAN NATURE

[16]So I tell you: Live by following the Spirit. Then you will not do what your sinful selves want. [17]Our sinful selves want what is against the Spirit, and the Spirit wants what is against our sinful selves. The two are against each other, so you cannot do just what you please. [18]But if the Spirit is leading you, you are not under the law.

[19]The wrong things the sinful self does are clear: being sexually unfaithful, not being pure, taking part in sexual sins, [20]worshiping gods, doing witchcraft, hating, making trouble, being

4:24 **Mount Sinai** Mountain in Arabia where God gave his Law to Moses (Exodus 19 and 20).   4:30 "**Throw . . . all.**" Quotation from Genesis 21:10.   5:12 **castrate** To cut off part of the male sex organ. Paul uses this word because it is similar to "circumcision." Paul wanted to show that he is very upset with the false teachers.   5:14 "**Love . . . yourself.**" Quotation from Leviticus 19:18.

DO'S & DON'TS

- **Do let your parents know what you're watching.**

- **Do let your parents hear what you're listening to.**

- **Do let someone strong hold you accountable for where you go online.**

- **Do wear a helmet.**

- **Don't always want what others have.**

- **Don't push your way to the front of the line.**

- **Don't focus on the bad things that happen to you.**

- **Don't get played.**

jealous, being angry, being selfish, making people angry with each other, causing divisions among people, [21]feeling envy, being drunk, having wild and wasteful parties, and doing other things like these. I warn you now as I warned you before: Those who do these things will not inherit God's kingdom. [22]But the Spirit produces the fruit of love, joy, peace, patience, kindness, goodness, faithfulness, [23]gentleness, self-control. There is no law that says these things are wrong. [24]Those who belong to Christ Jesus have crucified their own sinful selves. They have given up their old selfish feelings and the evil things they wanted to do. [25]We get our new life from the Spirit, so we should follow the Spirit. [26]We must not be proud or make trouble with each other or be jealous of each other.

HELP EACH OTHER

6 Brothers and sisters, if someone in your group does something wrong, you who are spiritual should go to that person and gently help make him right again. But be careful, because you might be tempted to sin, too. [2]By helping each other with your troubles, you truly obey the law of Christ. [3]If anyone thinks he is important when he really is not, he is only fooling himself. [4]Each person should judge his own actions and not compare himself with others. Then he can be proud for what he himself has done. [5]Each person must be responsible for himself.

[6]Anyone who is learning the teaching of God should share all the good things he has with his teacher.

LIFE IS LIKE PLANTING A FIELD

[7]Do not be fooled: You cannot cheat God. People harvest only what they plant. [8]If they plant to satisfy their sinful selves, their sinful selves will bring them ruin. But if they plant to please the Spirit, they will receive eternal life from the Spirit. [9]We must not become tired of doing good. We will receive our harvest of eternal life at the right time if we do not give up. [10]When we have the opportunity to help anyone, we should do it. But we should give special attention to those who are in the family of believers.

PAUL ENDS HIS LETTER

[11]See what large letters I use to write this myself. [12]Some people are trying to force you to be circumcised so the Jews will accept them. They are afraid they will be attacked if they follow only the cross of Christ." [13]Those who are circumcised do not obey the law themselves, but they want you to be circumcised so they can brag about what they forced you to do. [14]I hope I will never brag about things like that. The cross of our Lord Jesus Christ is my only reason for bragging. Through the cross of Jesus my world was crucified, and I died to the world. [15]It is not important if a man is circumcised or uncircumcised. The important thing is being the new people God has made. [16]Peace and mercy to those who follow this rule—and to all of God's people.

[17]So do not give me any more trouble. I have scars on my body that show" I belong to Christ Jesus.

[18]My brothers and sisters, the grace of our Lord Jesus Christ be with your spirit. Amen.

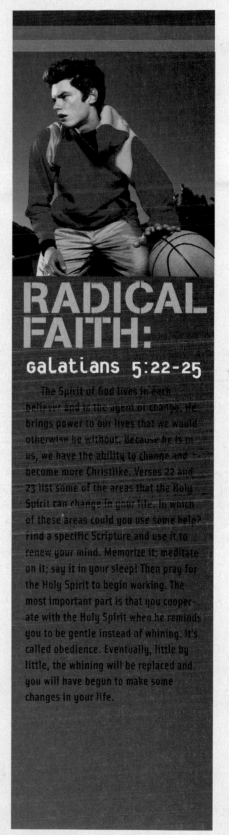

RADICAL FAITH:
galatians 5:22-25

The Spirit of God lives in each believer and is the agent of change. He brings power to our lives that we would otherwise be without. Because he is in us, we have the ability to change and become more Christlike. Verses 22 and 23 list some of the areas that the Holy Spirit can change in your life. In which of these areas could you use some help? Find a specific Scripture and use it to renew your mind. Memorize it; meditate on it; say it in your sleep! Then pray for the Holy Spirit to begin working. The most important part is that you cooperate with the Holy Spirit when he reminds you to be gentle instead of whining. It's called obedience. Eventually, little by little, the whining will be replaced and you will have begun to make some changes in your life.

 6:12 cross of Christ Paul uses the cross as a picture of the Good News, the story of Christ's death and rising from the dead to pay for our sins. The cross, or Christ's death, was God's way to save us. **6:17 that show** Many times Paul was beaten and whipped by people who were against him because he was teaching about Christ. The scars were from these beatings.

EPHESIANS

A word to the ultimate New Testament church

Paul had a vision for the church. He intended for it to have a lot of meetings. He dreamed of churches getting bogged down with boring committees. He hoped that someday we'd spend 100 percent of our time counting the number of warm bodies in the church.

Not really. Actually Paul *does* lay out the job of the church in this book, and it has nothing to do with agendas or number-crunching. The church's job is to be the people of faith—God's people. Paul can't help but remind us what we were like before we

knew Jesus. But he contrasts that ugly truth with the reality of the new persons we are becoming. So, how do we measure our success? The measuring is God's job. But the goals before us, says Paul, are unity among believers, following the Spirit within us, maturing our faith, defeating spiritual forces allied against us, and (maybe the hardest job of all) getting along with the people we live with every day. Can the church ever hope to accomplish all of this? Yep. But only with God's help.

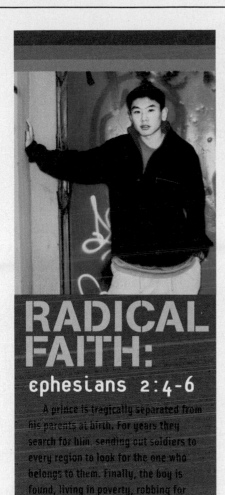

RADICAL FAITH:

ephesians 2:4-6

A prince is tragically separated from his parents at birth. For years they search for him, sending out soldiers to every region to look for the one who belongs to them. Finally, the boy is found, living in poverty, robbing for food, and acting like a savage. A soldier tells the boy about his father. His father is king of the entire country. In an instant, the beggar child has a new position. He is the son of a king. The one who thought he had no family has become royalty. He has a new life, new power, and a new home. He even has a place to sit beside his father's throne. You too are the child of a King. God has been merciful. He knew that you were dead in your sins, ruled by selfish desires, and destined for eternal punishment. He loved you and graciously gave you new life. With your new life has come new power and a new home with Christ in heaven.

WAYS TO WALK THE WALK

ephesians 2:10

WORD: God has outfitted you to do good works.

WALK IT: Flip through the "Get Out There" features in *REFUEL*—or talk to a teacher or youth leader about ways to serve. Make a decision today to do something cool in God's name.

ephesians 4:29

WORD: Mouth check: Ask yourself, "Is this helpful to say?"

WALK IT: Ask a friend to tell you when you spout off for the next week. Let him or her point out when you say things that hurt rather than help people.

ephesians 4:32

WORD: Forgive as God has forgiven you.

WALK IT: Think of a friend who has bruised you or busted up your friendship. Forgive that person in your heart, and muster the courage to tell him or her you forgive them.

1 From Paul, an apostle of Christ Jesus. I am an apostle because that is what God wanted.

To God's holy people living in Ephesus, believers in Christ Jesus:

²Grace and peace to you from God our Father and the Lord Jesus Christ.

SPIRITUAL BLESSINGS IN CHRIST

³Praise be to the God and Father of our Lord Jesus Christ. In Christ, God has given us every spiritual blessing in the heavenly world. ⁴That is, in Christ, he chose us before the world was made so that we would be his holy people—people without blame before him. ⁵Because of his love, God had already decided to make us his own children through Jesus Christ. That was what he wanted and what pleased him, ⁶and it brings praise to God because of his wonderful grace. God gave that grace to us freely, in Christ, the One he loves. ⁷In Christ we are set free by the blood of his death, and so we have forgiveness of sins. How rich is God's grace, ⁸which he has given to us so fully and freely. God, with

full wisdom and understanding, ⁹let us know his secret purpose. This was what God wanted, and he planned to do it through Christ. ¹⁰His goal was to carry out his plan, when the right time came, that all things in heaven and on earth would be joined together in Christ as the head.

¹¹In Christ we were chosen to be God's people, because from the very beginning God had decided this in keeping with his plan. And he is the One who makes everything agree with what he decides and wants. ¹²We are the first people who hoped in Christ, and we were chosen so that we would bring praise to God's glory. ¹³So it is with you. When you heard the true teaching—the Good News about your salvation—you believed in Christ. And in Christ, God put his special mark of ownership on you by giving you the Holy Spirit that he had promised. ¹⁴That Holy Spirit is the guarantee that we will receive what God promised for his people until God gives full freedom to those who are his—to bring praise to God's glory.

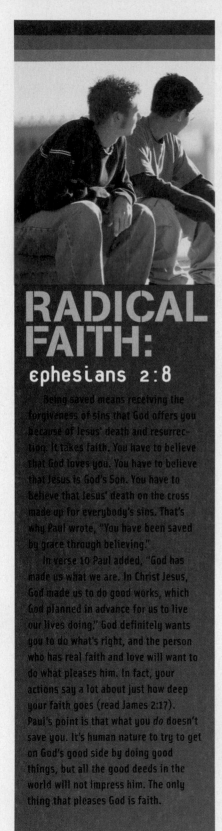

RADICAL FAITH:

ephesians 2:8

Being saved means receiving the forgiveness of sins that God offers you because of Jesus' death and resurrection. It takes faith. You have to believe that God loves you. You have to believe that Jesus is God's Son. You have to believe that Jesus' death on the cross made up for everybody's sins. That's why Paul wrote, "You have been saved by grace through believing."

In verse 10 Paul added, "God has made us what we are. In Christ Jesus, God made us to do good works, which God planned in advance for us to live our lives doing." God definitely wants you to do what's right, and the person who has real faith and love will want to do what pleases him. In fact, your actions say a lot about just how deep your faith goes (read James 2:17). Paul's point is that what you *do* doesn't save you. It's human nature to try to get on God's good side by doing good things, but all the good deeds in the world will not impress him. The only thing that pleases God is faith.

PAUL'S PRAYER

[15]That is why since I heard about your faith in the Lord Jesus and your love for all God's people, [16]I have not stopped giving thanks to God for you. I always remember you in my prayers, [17]asking the God of our Lord Jesus Christ, the glorious Father, to give you a spirit of wisdom and revelation so that you will know him better. [18]I pray also that you will have greater understanding in your heart so you will know the hope to which he has called us and that you will know how rich and glorious are the blessings God has promised his holy people. [19]And you will know that God's power is very great for us who believe. That power is the same as the great strength [20]God used to raise Christ from the dead and put him at his right side in the heavenly world. [21]God has put Christ over all rulers, authorities, powers, and kings, not only in this world but also in the next. [22]God put everything under his power and made him the head over everything for the church, [23]which is Christ's body. The church is filled with Christ, and Christ fills everything in every way.

WE NOW HAVE LIFE

2 In the past you were spiritually dead because of your sins and the things you did against God. [2]Yes, in the past you lived the way the world lives, following the ruler of the evil powers that are above the earth. That same spirit is now working in those who refuse to obey God. [3]In the past all of us lived like them, trying to please our sinful selves and doing all the things our bodies and minds wanted. We should have suffered God's anger because of the way we were. We were the same as all other people.

[4]But God's mercy is great, and he loved us very much. [5]Though we were spiritually dead because of the things we did against God, he gave us new life with Christ. You have been saved by God's grace. [6]And he raised us up with Christ and gave us a seat with him in the heavens. He did this for those in Christ Jesus [7]so that for all future time he could show the very great riches of his grace by being kind to us in Christ Jesus. [8]I mean that you have been saved by grace through believing. You did not

RANDOM THINGS TO KNOW ABOUT BEING A GODLY GUY

1. THEY DON'T HIT GIRLS.
2. THEY DON'T CHEW WITH THEIR MOUTH OPEN.
3. THEY DON'T BELCH.
4. THEY AREN'T ARROGANT.
5. THEY DON'T BACKSTAB.
6. THEY KNOW THEIR BODIES ARE TEMPLES OF GOD.
7. THEY RESPECT OTHERS.
8. THEY DON'T DITCH THEIR FAMILIES.
9. THEY DON'T TALK SMUT ABOUT THEIR DATES.
10. THEY ARE LOYAL FRIENDS.

save yourselves; it was a gift from God. [9]It was not the result of your own efforts, so you cannot brag about it. [10]God has made us what we are. In Christ Jesus, God made us to do good works, which God planned in advance for us to live our lives doing.

ONE IN CHRIST

[11]You were not born Jewish. You are the people the Jews call "uncircumcised."[n] Those who call you "uncircumcised" call themselves "circumcised." (Their circumcision is only something they themselves do on their bodies.) [12]Remember that in the past you were without Christ. You were not citizens of Israel, and you had no part in the agreements[n] with the promise that God made to his people. You had no hope, and you did not know God. [13]But now in Christ Jesus, you who were far away

---

 2:11 uncircumcised People not having the mark of circumcision as the Jews had.   **2:12 agreements** The agreements that God gave to his people in the Old Testament.

WAYS TO WALK THE WALK

ephesians 5:18

WORD: Don't get drunk or abuse drugs.

WALK IT: The Word says it straight. Is there anything you're doing that breaks this command? Get help to break a bad habit.

ephesians 6:10

WORD: Be strong in God, not yourself.

WALK IT: Today when you want to rub your brains, brawn, or beauty in someone's face, step back. Stop whatever it was you were about to do or say, and instead tell God thanks for his gifts to you.

✓ COUNT ON IT

EPHESIANS 2:10

Most days just seem to go by like every other day. Same old stuff. Same old everything. Blah blah blah. One day runs into another one. You close your eyes and wake up to do it all over again. Doesn't seem like much of a plan, does it?

Maybe not. But God has an exciting plan for your life—a plan that will give you purpose and fulfillment beyond your wildest dreams. Following God's plan takes commitment from you. You don't just accidentally fulfill what he's planned for you to do. You've got to seek God and ask him to reveal his plan to you and to give you understanding about how you can fulfill it. Then, you've got to determine to make every day count for him and for his plan.

Pay attention to every decision you face—even the ones that seem so insignificant. Take seriously every person you meet—even the ones you don't like. Embrace every situation you find yourself in—even the ones that seem to make no sense at all. They're shaping you, molding you, preparing you for the next decision, the next person, the next situation.

Lose yourself in doing what God wants with every aspect of your life. Live your life in light of his plan!

from God are brought near through the blood of Christ's death. [14]Christ himself is our peace. He made both Jewish people and those who are not Jews one people. They were separated as if there were a wall between them, but Christ broke down that wall of hate by giving his own body. [15]The Jewish law had many commands and rules, but Christ ended that law. His purpose was to make the two groups of people become one new people in him and in this way make peace. [16]It was also Christ's purpose to end the hatred between the two groups, to make them into one body, and to bring them back to God. Christ did all this with his death on the cross. [17]Christ came and preached peace to you who were far away from God, and to those who were near to God. [18]Yes, it is through Christ we all have the right to come to the Father in one Spirit.

[19]Now you who are not Jewish are not foreigners or strangers any longer, but are citizens together with God's holy people. You belong to God's family. [20]You are like a building that was built on the foundation of the apostles and prophets. Christ Jesus himself is the most important stone[n] in that building, [21]and that whole building is joined together in Christ. He makes it grow and become a holy temple in the Lord. [22]And in Christ you, too, are being built together with the Jews into a place where God lives through the Spirit.

PAUL'S WORK IN TELLING THE GOOD NEWS

3 So I, Paul, am a prisoner of Christ Jesus for you who are not Jews. [2]Surely you have heard that God gave me this work through his grace to help you. [3]He let me know his secret by showing it to me. I have already written a little about this. [4]If you read what I wrote then, you can see that I truly understand the secret about the Christ. [5]People who lived in other times were not told that secret. But now, through the Spirit, God has shown that secret to his holy apostles and prophets. [6]This is that secret: that through the Good News those who are not Jews will share with the Jews in God's blessing. They belong to the same body, and they share together in the promise that God made in Christ Jesus.

[7]By God's special gift of grace given to me through his power, I became a servant to tell that Good News. [8]I am the least important of all God's people, but God gave me this gift—to tell those who are not Jews the Good News about the riches of Christ, which are too great to understand fully. [9]And God gave me the work of telling all people about the plan for his secret, which has been hidden in him since the beginning of time. He is the One who created everything. [10]His purpose was that through the church all the rulers and powers in the heavenly world will now know God's wisdom,

2:20 **most important stone** Literally, "cornerstone." The first and most important stone in a building.

which has so many forms. [11]This agrees with the purpose God had since the beginning of time, and he carried out his plan through Christ Jesus our Lord. [12]In Christ we can come before God with freedom and without fear. We can do this through faith in Christ. [13]So I ask you not to become discouraged because of the sufferings I am having for you. My sufferings are for your glory.

THE LOVE OF CHRIST

[14]So I bow in prayer before the Father [15]from whom every family in heaven and on earth gets its true name. [16]I ask the Father in his great glory to give you the power to be strong inwardly through his Spirit. [17]I pray that Christ will live in your hearts by faith and that your life will be strong in love and be built on love. [18]And I pray that you and all God's holy people will have the power to understand the greatness of Christ's love—how wide and how long and how high and how deep that love is. [19]Christ's love is greater than anyone can ever know, but I pray that you will be able to know that love. Then you can be filled with the fullness of God.

[20]With God's power working in us, God can do much, much more than anything we can ask or imagine. [21]To him be glory in the church and in Christ Jesus for all time, forever and ever. Amen.

THE UNITY OF THE BODY

4 I am in prison because I belong to the Lord. God chose you to be his people, so I urge you now to live the life to which God called you. [2]Always be humble, gentle, and patient, accepting each other in love. [3]You are joined together with peace through the Spirit, so make every effort to continue together in this way. [4]There is one body and one Spirit, and God called you to have one hope. [5]There is one Lord, one faith, and one baptism. [6]There is one God and Father of everything. He rules everything and is everywhere and is in everything.

[7]Christ gave each one of us the special gift of grace, showing how generous he is. [8]That is why it says in the Scriptures,

"When he went up to the heights,
    he led a parade of captives,
    and he gave gifts to people."   *Psalm 68:18*

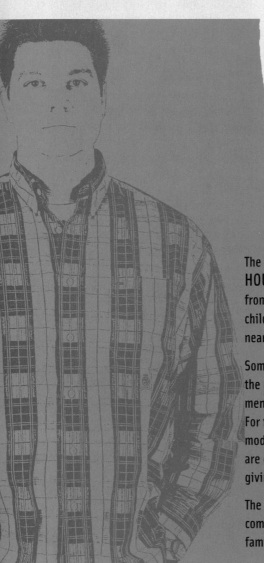

GET OUT THERE

The idea behind **RONALD MCDONALD HOUSE** is simple: provide a "home-away-from-home" for families of seriously ill children who are receiving treatment at nearby hospitals.

Some children travel great distances to get the medical attention. In-hospital treatment may last a day, a year, or even longer. For the families of these children, accommodations can be hard to come by. Options are often limited to costly hotels or unforgiving hospital chairs and benches.

The Ronald McDonald House provides a comfortable temporary residence where family members can sleep, eat, relax, and find support from other families in similar situations. In return, families are asked to make a donation ranging from $5 to $20 per day; if that isn't possible, their stay is free.

At Ronald McDonald House Charities, the supporters with the biggest hearts are often children and teens who are eager to help kids just like them. You can contact your local House to arrange donations, ask about specific toys or other items they need, or get suggestions for a grocery list to stock the kitchens to make it easy for families to fix quick meals and snacks when they have the chance.

Join in at www.rmhc.com.

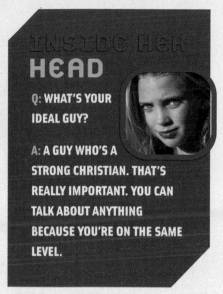
[9]When it says, "He went up," what does it mean? It means that he first came down to the earth. [10]So Jesus came down, and he is the same One who went up above all the heaven. Christ did that to fill everything with his presence. [11]And Christ gave gifts to people—he made some to be apostles, some to be prophets, some to go and tell the Good News, and some to have the work of caring for and teaching God's people. [12]Christ gave those gifts to prepare God's holy people for the work of serving, to make the body of Christ stronger. [13]This work must continue until we are all joined together in the same faith and in the same knowledge of the Son of God. We must become like a mature person, growing until we become like Christ and have his perfection.

[14]Then we will no longer be babies. We will not be tossed about like a ship that the waves carry one way and then another. We will not be influenced by every new teaching we hear from people who are trying to fool us. They make plans and try any kind of trick to fool people into following the wrong path. [15]No! Speaking the truth with love, we will grow up in every way into Christ, who is the head.

[16]The whole body depends on Christ, and all the parts of the body are joined and held together. Each part does its own work to make the whole body grow and be strong with love.

THE WAY YOU SHOULD LIVE

[17]In the Lord's name, I tell you this. Do not continue living like those who do not believe. Their thoughts are worth nothing. [18]They do not understand, and they know nothing, because they refuse to listen. So they cannot have the life that God gives. [19]They have lost all feeling of shame, and they use their lives for doing evil. They continually want to do all kinds of evil. [20]But what you learned in Christ was not like this. [21]I know that you heard about him, and you are in him, so you were taught the truth that is in Jesus. [22]You were taught to leave your old self—to stop living the evil way you lived before. That old self becomes worse, because people are fooled by the evil things they want to do. [23]But you were taught to be made new in your hearts, [24]to become a new person. That new person is made to be like God—made to be truly good and holy.

[25]So you must stop telling lies. Tell each other the truth, because we all belong to each other in the same body.[n] [26]When you are angry, do not sin, and be sure to stop being angry before the end of the day. [27]Do not give the devil a way to defeat you. [28]Those who are stealing must stop stealing and start working. They should earn an honest living for themselves. Then they will have something to share with those who are poor.

[29]When you talk, do not say harmful things, but say what people need—words that will help others become stronger. Then what you say will do good to those who listen to you. [30]And do not make the Holy Spirit sad. The Spirit is God's proof that you belong to him. God gave you the Spirit to show that God will make you free when the final day comes. [31]Do not be bitter or angry or mad. Never

 4:25 Tell . . . body. Quotation from Zechariah 8:16.

BIBLE BASICS

Prayer is just talking with God. You can tell him about whatever is going on in your world. You can tell him how great he is, or chat with him about what a drag a teacher is being or the loneliness you feel when things go rough with your friends. You can tell him anything. You can pray with your eyes wide open anytime you want, or set aside a specific time to talk to him. God loves for us to talk with him and listen to him, so do it as much as you can.

shout angrily or say things to hurt others. Never do anything evil. ³²Be kind and loving to each other, and forgive each other just as God forgave you in Christ.

LIVING IN THE LIGHT

5 You are God's children whom he loves, so try to be like him. ²Live a life of love just as Christ loved us and gave himself for us as a sweet-smelling offering and sacrifice to God.

³But there must be no sexual sin among you, or any kind of evil or greed. Those things are not right for God's holy people. ⁴Also, there must be no evil talk among you, and you must not speak foolishly or tell evil jokes. These things are not right for you. Instead, you should be giving thanks to God. ⁵You can be sure of this: No one will have a place in the kingdom of Christ and of God who sins sexually, or does evil things, or is greedy. Anyone who is greedy is serving a false god.

⁶Do not let anyone fool you by telling you things that are not true, because these things will bring God's anger on those who do not obey him. ⁷So have nothing to do with them. ⁸In the past you were full of darkness, but now you are full of light in the Lord. So live like children who belong to the light. ⁹Light brings every kind of goodness, right living, and truth. ¹⁰Try to learn what pleases the Lord. ¹¹Have nothing to do with the things done in darkness, which are not worth anything. But show that they are wrong. ¹²It is shameful even to talk about what those people do in secret. ¹³But the light makes all things easy to see, ¹⁴and everything that is made easy to see can become light. This is why it is said:

"Wake up, sleeper!
  Rise from death,
and Christ will shine on you."

¹⁵So be very careful how you live. Do not live like those who are not wise, but live wisely. ¹⁶Use every chance you have for doing good, because these are evil times. ¹⁷So do not be foolish but learn what the Lord wants you to do. ¹⁸Do not be drunk with wine, which will ruin you, but be filled with the Spirit. ¹⁹Speak to each other with psalms, hymns, and spiritual songs, singing and making music in your hearts to the Lord. ²⁰Always give thanks to God the Father for everything, in the name of our Lord Jesus Christ.

WIVES AND HUSBANDS

²¹Yield to obey each other because you respect Christ.

²²Wives, yield to your husbands, as you do to the Lord, ²³because the husband is the head of the wife, as Christ is the head of the church. And he is the Savior of the body, which is the church.

EXPERTS ANSWER YOUR QUESTIONS

Q. *I'm almost sixteen and I've never kissed a girl—not a real kiss, I mean. What am I doing wrong?*

A. Here's a question to answer your question. What will kissing a girl prove to you? You don't need it to demonstrate to the guys that you're a man. Or that you aren't a loser. Or even that girls think you're okay. After all, girls aren't trophies to win. Talk to God and wait for him to bring the right girl into your life. Then a kiss will mean way more.

Q. *My girlfriend isn't a Christian, but she's nicer than any of the Christian girls I know—probably better morals too. What's so wrong about dating her?*

A. If you're a Christian, the problem with dating a non-Christian is that dating ultimately leads to marriage—and that God definitely rules out marrying non-Christians. Honestly, you really never know when you'll decide that the girl you're going with is the one you want to stick tight to for life. Why drive down a dead-end road?

[24]As the church yields to Christ, so you wives should yield to your husbands in everything.

[25]Husbands, love your wives as Christ loved the church and gave himself for it [26]to make it belong to God. Christ used the word to make the church clean by washing it with water. [27]He died so that he could give the church to himself like a bride in all her beauty. He died so that the church could be pure and without fault, with no evil or sin or any other wrong thing in it. [28]In the same way, husbands should love their wives as they love their own bodies. The man who loves his wife loves himself. [29]No one ever hates his own body, but feeds and takes care of it. And that is what Christ does for the church, [30]because we are parts of his body. [31]The Scripture says, "So a man will leave his father and mother and be united with his wife, and the two will become one body."[n] [32]That secret is very important—I am talking about Christ and the church. [33]But each one of you must love his wife as he loves himself, and a wife must respect her husband.

CHILDREN AND PARENTS

6 Children, obey your parents as the Lord wants, because this is the right thing to do. [2]The command says, "Honor your father and mother."[n] This is the first command that has a promise with it— [3]"Then everything will be well with you, and you will have a long life on the earth."[n]

[4]Fathers, do not make your children angry, but raise them with the training and teaching of the Lord.

SLAVES AND MASTERS

[5]Slaves, obey your masters here on earth with fear and respect and from a sincere heart, just as you obey Christ. [6]You must do this not only while they are watching you, to please them. With all your heart you must do what God wants as people who are obeying Christ. [7]Do your work with enthusiasm. Work as if you were serving the Lord, not as if you were serving only men and women. [8]Remember that the Lord will give a reward to everyone, slave or free, for doing good.

[9]Masters, in the same way, be good to your

LUKE 18:38 "THE BLIND MAN CRIED OUT, 'JESUS, SON OF DAVID, HAVE MERCY ON ME!'"

slaves. Do not threaten them. Remember that the One who is your Master and their Master is in heaven, and he treats everyone alike.

WEAR THE FULL ARMOR OF GOD

[10]Finally, be strong in the Lord and in his great power. [11]Put on the full armor of God so that you can fight against the devil's evil tricks. [12]Our fight is not against people on earth but against the rulers and authorities and the powers of this world's darkness, against the spiritual powers of evil in the heavenly world. [13]That is why you need to put on God's full armor. Then on the day of evil you will be able to stand strong. And when you have finished the whole fight, you will still be standing. [14]So stand strong, with the belt of truth tied around your waist and the protection of right living on your chest. [15]On your feet wear the Good News of peace to help you stand strong. [16]And also use the shield of faith with which you can stop all the burning arrows of the Evil One. [17]Accept God's salvation as your helmet, and take the sword of the Spirit, which is the word of God. [18]Pray in the Spirit at all times with all kinds of prayers, asking for everything you need. To do this you must always be ready and never give up. Always pray for all God's people.

[19]Also pray for me that when I speak, God will give me words so that I can tell the secret of the Good News without fear. [20]I have been sent to preach this Good News, and I am doing that now, here in prison. Pray that when I preach the Good News I will speak without fear, as I should.

FINAL GREETINGS

[21]I am sending to you Tychicus, our brother whom we love and a faithful servant of the Lord's work. He will tell you everything that is happening with me. Then you will know how I am and what I am doing. [22]I am sending him to you for this reason—so that you will know how we are, and he can encourage you.

[23]Peace and love with faith to you from God the Father and the Lord Jesus Christ. [24]Grace to all of you who love our Lord Jesus Christ with love that never ends.

5:31 "So . . . body." Quotation from Genesis 2:24.   6:2 "Honor . . . mother." Quotation from Exodus 20:12; Deuteronomy 5:16.   6:3 "Then . . . earth." Quotation from Exodus 20:12; Deuteronomy 5:16.

PHILIPPIANS

A LETTER OF JOY BETWEEN TRUE FRIENDS

Imagine this: You're locked up in prison. The conditions are gross. The food rots. It's dark and damp. Rats scramble over you at night, keeping you awake. In the midst of this misery, you get a chance to write your friends a letter. What will you say?

Paul was there. So what does he write about? The fact that he's crazy happy!

He hasn't gone insane. Paul says he's happy that he has friends who haven't forgotten him. He's even happy that he's suffering for Christ, because his imprisonment is inspiring other Christians to preach more boldly. He says if death is part of God's plan for him, he will be happy to be with Christ, which is a wildly better place than where he is now. Yet he longs to hang out in this life so he can continue to help his friends in Philippi.

Paul wants the Philippians to experience this same peaceful joy when they reflect on their lives. So, he advises them to discover one of the things it means to be saved. So, what does it mean, according to Paul? It means to be more than happy. It means to experience joy that cuts deep into your soul. Joy that fills you no matter what happens. No matter where you are. Locked up in prison? Living a dead-end life? Get joy. Never mind the rats.

1 From Paul and Timothy, servants of Christ Jesus.

To all of God's holy people in Christ Jesus who live in Philippi, including your elders and deacons:

[2] Grace and peace to you from God our Father and the Lord Jesus Christ.

PAUL'S PRAYER

[3] I thank my God every time I remember you, [4] always praying with joy for all of you. [5] I thank God for the help you gave me while I preached the Good News—help you gave from the first day you believed until now. [6] God began doing a good work in you, and I am sure he will continue it until it is finished when Jesus Christ comes again.

[7] And I know that I am right to think like this about all of you, because I have you in my heart. All of you share in God's grace with me while I am in prison and while I am defending and proving the truth of the Good News. [8] God knows that I want to see you very much, because I love all of you with the love of Christ Jesus.

[9] This is my prayer for you: that your love will grow more and more; that you will have knowledge and understanding with your love; [10] that you will see the difference between good and bad and will choose the good; that you will be pure and without wrong for the coming of Christ; [11] that you will do many good things with the help of Christ to bring glory and praise to God.

PAUL'S TROUBLES HELP THE WORK

[12] I want you brothers and sisters[n] to know that what has happened to me has helped to spread the Good News. [13] All the palace guards

philippians 2:4

WORD: Pay attention to others, not just yourself.

WALK IT: Ask what's up with a friend, and bite your lip when you want to tell what's going on with you. There's nothing wrong with sharing your stuff. But see if you can listen to a friend's needs and concerns for fifteen minutes without interrupting

philippians 2:14

WORD: Do everything without grumbling or arguing.

WALK IT: Check how you talk for the next week. Clamp your mouth shut if you're about to spew or complain. If you really need to speak up, do it without an attitude.

philippians 2:15

WORD: Make an effort to stand out from the cruel and nasty people around you.

WALK IT: As you live life today, ask yourself if people would know you follow Jesus just by looking at you. How are you different from everyone else? Make a break with a harmful thing you do just to fit in.

RELATIONSHIPS

"Whoever does not care for his own relatives, especially his own family members, has turned against the faith and is worse than someone who does not believe in God" (1 Timothy 5:8). Some days you might wish you were the only son of Bill Gates, set to inherit the keys to the front door. But God has bigger and better plans for you in your real-life family. He's put you together to care for each other. To live, laugh, and chow down together. Is your family a top priority with you?

1:12 **brothers and sisters** Although the Greek text says "brothers" here and throughout this book, Paul's words were meant for the entire church, including men and women.

and everyone else knows that I am in prison because I am a believer in Christ. [14]Because I am in prison, most of the believers have become more bold in Christ and are not afraid to speak the word of God.

[15]It is true that some preach about Christ because they are jealous and ambitious, but others preach about Christ because they want to help. [16]They preach because they have love, and they know that God gave me the work of defending the Good News. [17]But the others preach about Christ for selfish and wrong reasons, wanting to make trouble for me in prison.

[18]But it doesn't matter. The important thing is that in every way, whether for right or wrong reasons, they are preaching about Christ. So I am happy, and I will continue to be happy. [19]Because you are praying for me and the Spirit of Jesus Christ is helping me, I know this trouble will bring my freedom. [20]I expect and hope that I will not fail Christ in anything but that I will have the courage now, as always, to show the greatness of Christ in my life here on earth, whether I live or die. [21]To me the only important thing about living is Christ, and dying would be profit for me. [22]If I continue living in my body, I will be able to work for the Lord. I do not know what to choose—living or dying. [23]It is hard to choose between the two. I want to leave this life and be with Christ, which is much better, [24]but you need me here in my body. [25]Since I am sure of this, I know I will stay with you to help you grow and have joy in your faith. [26]You will be very happy in Christ Jesus when I am with you again.

[27]Only one thing concerns me: Be sure that you live in a way that brings honor to the Good News of Christ. Then whether I come and visit you or am away from you, I will hear that you are standing strong with one purpose, that you work together as one for the faith of the Good News, [28]and that you are not afraid of those who are against you. All of this is proof that your enemies will be destroyed but that you will be saved by God. [29]God gave you the honor not only of believing in Christ but also of suffering for him, both of which bring glory to Christ. [30]When I was with you, you saw the struggles I had, and you hear about the struggles I am having now. You yourselves are having the same kind of struggles.

2 Does your life in Christ give you strength? Does his love comfort you? Do we share together in the spirit? Do you have mercy and kindness? [2]If so, make me very happy by having the same thoughts, sharing the same love, and having one mind and purpose. [3]When you do things, do not let selfishness or pride be your guide. Instead, be humble and give more honor to others than to yourselves. [4]Do not be interested only in your own life, but be interested in the lives of others.

BE UNSELFISH LIKE CHRIST

[5]In your lives you must think and act like Christ Jesus.

[6]Christ himself was like God in everything.
But he did not think that being equal
with God was something to be used
for his own benefit.
[7]But he gave up his place with God and
made himself nothing.
He was born to be a man
and became like a servant.
[8]And when he was living as a man,
he humbled himself and was fully
obedient to God,
even when that caused his death—
death on a cross.
[9]So God raised him to the highest place.
God made his name greater than every
other name
[10]so that every knee will bow to the name
of Jesus—
everyone in heaven, on earth,
and under the earth.
[11]And everyone will confess that Jesus Christ
is Lord
and bring glory to God the Father.

BE THE PEOPLE GOD WANTS YOU TO BE

[12]My dear friends, you have always obeyed God when I was with you. It is even more important that you obey now while I am away from you. Keep on working to complete your salvation with fear and trembling, [13]because God is working in you to help you want to do and be able to do what pleases him.

[14]Do everything without complaining or arguing. [15]Then you will be innocent and without any wrong. You will be God's children without fault. But you are living with crooked

RANDOM WAYS TO MAKE A DIFFERENCE IN YOUR SCHOOL

1. START A PRAYER GROUP.
2. MAKE SOME NEW FRIENDS.
3. PRAY FOR YOUR TEACHER.
4. HELP THE CLEANING STAFF AFTER SCHOOL HOURS.
5. ORGANIZE A GROUP TO RAISE MONEY FOR CHARITY.
6. PRAY AT THE POLE.
7. DON'T RIP ON UNDERCLASSMEN.
8. TAKE ON A CAMPUS BEAUTIFICATION PROJECT.
9. LEAD A BIBLE STUDY.
10. PRAY FOR YOUR SCHOOL.

and mean people all around you, among whom you shine like stars in the dark world. [16]You offer the teaching that gives life. So when Christ comes again, I can be happy because my work was not wasted. I ran the race and won.

[17]Your faith makes you offer your lives as a sacrifice in serving God. If I have to offer my own blood with your sacrifice, I will be happy and full of joy with all of you. [18]You also should be happy and full of joy with me.

TIMOTHY AND EPAPHRODITUS

[19]I hope in the Lord Jesus to send Timothy to you soon. I will be happy to learn how you are. [20]I have no one else like Timothy, who truly cares for you. [21]Other people are interested only in their own lives, not in the work of Jesus Christ. [22]You know the kind of person Timothy is. You know he has served with me in telling the Good News, as a son serves his father. [23]I plan to

send him to you quickly when I know what will happen to me. [24]I am sure that the Lord will help me to come to you soon.

[25]Epaphroditus, my brother in Christ, works and serves with me in the army of Christ. When I needed help, you sent him to me. I think now that I must send him back to you, [26]because he wants very much to see all of you. He is worried because you heard that he was sick. [27]Yes, he was sick, and nearly died, but God had mercy on him and me too so that I would not have more sadness. [28]I want very much to send him to you so that when you see him you can be happy, and I can stop worrying about you. [29]Welcome him in the Lord with much joy. Give honor to people like him, [30]because he almost died for the work of Christ. He risked his life to give me the help you could not give in your service to me.

THE IMPORTANCE OF CHRIST

3 My brothers and sisters, be full of joy in the Lord. It is no trouble for me to write the same things to you again, and it will help you to be more ready. [2]Watch out for those who do evil, who are like dogs, who demand to cut[n] the body. [3]We are the ones who are truly circumcised. We worship God through his Spirit, and our pride is in Christ Jesus. We do not put trust in ourselves or anything we can do,

[4]although I might be able to put trust in myself. If anyone thinks he has a reason to trust in himself, he should know that I have greater reason for trusting in myself. [5]I was circumcised eight days after my birth. I am from the people of Israel and the tribe of Benjamin. I am a Hebrew, and my parents were Hebrews. I had a strict view of the law, which is why I became a Pharisee. [6]I was so enthusiastic I tried to hurt the church. No one could find fault with the way I obeyed the law of Moses. [7]Those things were important to me, but now I think they are worth nothing because of Christ. [8]Not only those things, but I think that all things are worth nothing compared with the greatness of knowing Christ Jesus my Lord. Because of him, I have lost all those things, and now I know they are worthless trash. This allows me to have Christ [9]and to belong to him. Now I am right with God, not because I followed the law, but because I believed in Christ. God uses my faith to make me right with him. [10]I want to know Christ and the power that raised him from the dead. I want to share in his sufferings and become like him in his death. [11]Then I have hope that I myself will be raised from the dead.

CONTINUING TOWARD OUR GOAL

[12]I do not mean that I am already as God wants me to be. I have not yet reached that

RADICAL FAITH:
philippians 4:8

Mom is probably more concerned with the lyrics of the songs than the style of music. So put your CD collection through the Philippians 4:8 test. Do any of the lyrics oppose the teaching of Paul in verse 8? If what you are listening to makes you think about things that are impure, wrong, or immoral, it fails the test. What you put into your mind simmers there and eventually comes back out. So throw out the stuff that's trash and let Mom know that you've cleaned out the music she's been worried about. Wailing guitar riffs may still make Mom's head throb, but a good pair of headphones should bring her some relief. Next time you buy a CD, give it the "4:8" test and ask yourself if God would be pleased.

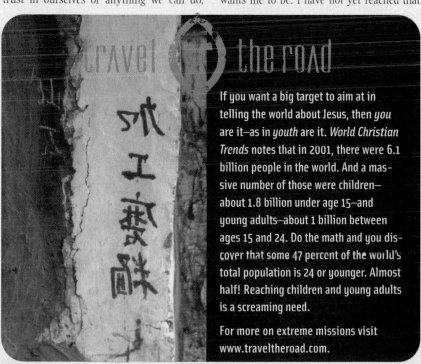

travel the road

If you want a big target to aim at in telling the world about Jesus, then *you* are it—as in *youth* are it. *World Christian Trends* notes that in 2001, there were 6.1 billion people in the world. And a massive number of those were children—about 1.8 billion under age 15—and young adults—about 1 billion between ages 15 and 24. Do the math and you discover that some 47 percent of the world's total population is 24 or younger. Almost half! Reaching children and young adults is a screaming need.

For more on extreme missions visit www.traveltheroad.com.

 3:2 cut The word in Greek is like the word "circumcise," but it means "to cut completely off."

goal, but I continue trying to reach it and to make it mine. Christ wants me to do that, which is the reason he made me his. [13]Brothers and sisters, I know that I have not yet reached that goal, but there is one thing I always do. Forgetting the past and straining toward what is ahead, [14]I keep trying to reach the goal and get the prize for which God called me through Christ to the life above.

[15]All of us who are spiritually mature should think this way, too. And if there are things you do not agree with, God will make them clear to you. [16]But we should continue following the truth we already have.

[17]Brothers and sisters, all of you should try to follow my example and to copy those who live the way we showed you. [18]Many people live like enemies of the cross of Christ. I have often told you about them, and it makes me cry to tell you about them now. [19]In the end, they will be destroyed. They do whatever their bodies want, they are proud of their shameful acts, and they think only about earthly things. [20]But our homeland is in heaven, and we are waiting for our Savior, the Lord Jesus Christ, to come from heaven. [21]By his power to rule all things, he will change our simple bodies and make them like his own glorious body.

WHAT THE CHRISTIANS ARE TO DO

4 My dear brothers and sisters, I love you and want to see you. You bring me joy and make me proud of you, so stand strong in the Lord as I have told you.

[2]I ask Euodia and Syntyche to agree in the Lord. [3]And I ask you, my faithful friend, to help these women. They served with me in telling the Good News, together with Clement and others who worked with me, whose names are written in the book of life.[n]

[4]Be full of joy in the Lord always. I will say again, be full of joy.

[5]Let everyone see that you are gentle and kind. The Lord is coming soon. [6]Do not worry about anything, but pray and ask God for everything you need, always giving thanks. [7]And God's peace, which is so great we cannot understand it, will keep your hearts and minds in Christ Jesus.

[8]Brothers and sisters, think about the things that are good and worthy of praise. Think about the things that are true and honorable and right and pure and beautiful and respected. [9]Do what you learned and received from me, what I told you, and what you saw me do. And the God who gives peace will be with you.

PAUL THANKS THE CHRISTIANS

[10]I am very happy in the Lord that you have shown your care for me again. You continued to care about me, but there was no way for you to show it. [11]I am not telling you this because I need anything. I have learned to be satisfied with the things I have and with everything that happens. [12]I know how to live when I am poor, and I know how to live when I have plenty. I have learned the secret of being happy at any time in everything that happens, when I have enough to eat and when I go hungry, when I have more than I need and when I do not have enough. [13]I can do all things through Christ, because he gives me strength.

[14]But it was good that you helped me when I needed it. [15]You Philippians remember when I first preached the Good News there. When I left Macedonia, you were the only church that gave me help. [16]Several times you sent me things I needed when I was in Thessalonica. [17]Really, it is not that I want to receive gifts from you, but I want you to have the good that comes from giving. [18]And now I have everything, and more. I have all I need, because Epaphroditus brought your gift to me. It is like a sweet-smelling sacrifice offered to God, who accepts that sacrifice and is pleased with it. [19]My God will use his wonderful riches in Christ Jesus to give you everything you need. [20]Glory to our God and Father forever and ever! Amen.

[21]Greet each of God's people in Christ. Those who are with me send greetings to you. [22]All of God's people greet you, particularly those from the palace of Caesar.

[23]The grace of the Lord Jesus Christ be with you all.

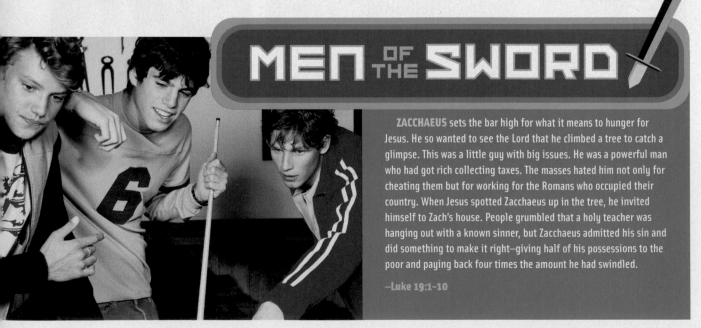

MEN OF THE SWORD

ZACCHAEUS sets the bar high for what it means to hunger for Jesus. He so wanted to see the Lord that he climbed a tree to catch a glimpse. This was a little guy with big issues. He was a powerful man who had got rich collecting taxes. The masses hated him not only for cheating them but for working for the Romans who occupied their country. When Jesus spotted Zacchaeus up in the tree, he invited himself to Zach's house. People grumbled that a holy teacher was hanging out with a known sinner, but Zacchaeus admitted his sin and did something to make it right—giving half of his possessions to the poor and paying back four times the amount he had swindled.

—Luke 19:1–10

 4:3 book of life God's book that has the names of all God's chosen people (Revelation 3:5; 21:27).

COLOSSIANS

JESUS IS THE PREEMINENT LORD OF THE UNIVERSE

Paul's facing a real challenge. He's discovered a new religion is popping up that approaches its beliefs like many of us hit the buffet. Sure, it starts with a big spoonful of Christianity. But it also loads up the plate with heaping servings from other religions. This pile of assorted spirituality looks mouthwatering to people in the area. It teaches that angels exist. It honors religious holidays. And it urges people to seek God. All of this looks so familiar, in fact, that it makes the Christians of Colossae wonder if this new teaching is simply a more insightful way of interpreting old truths.

Paul insists that this isn't a good religion. It's actually just another set of human teachings. For the people who are getting confused, Paul has this advice: Follow Jesus. Simple truth...but often so very difficult to do.

This letter was written to warn followers of Christ to stay clear of this deceptive religion.

1 From Paul, an apostle of Christ Jesus. I am an apostle because that is what God wanted. Also from Timothy, our brother.

[2] To the holy and faithful brothers and sisters[n] in Christ that live in Colossae:

Grace and peace to you from God our Father.

[3] In our prayers for you we always thank God, the Father of our Lord Jesus Christ, [4] because we have heard about the faith you have in Christ Jesus and the love you have for all of God's people. [5] You have this faith and love because of your hope, and what you hope for is kept safe for you in heaven. You learned about this hope when you heard the message about the truth, the Good News [6] that was told to you. Everywhere in the world that Good News is bringing blessings and is growing. This has happened with you, too, since you heard the Good News and understood the truth about the grace of God. [7] You learned about God's grace from Epaphras, whom we love. He works together with us and is a faithful servant of Christ for us. [8] He also told us about the love you have from the Holy Spirit.

[9] Because of this, since the day we heard about you, we have continued praying for you, asking God that you will know fully what he wants. We pray that you will also have great wisdom and understanding in spiritual things [10] so that you will live the kind of life that honors and pleases the Lord in every way. You will produce fruit in every good work and grow in the knowledge of God. [11] God will strengthen you with his own great power so that you will not give up when troubles come, but you will be patient. [12] And you will joyfully give thanks to the Father who has made you able to have a share in all that he has prepared for his people in the kingdom of light. [13] God has freed us from the power of darkness, and he brought us into the kingdom of his dear Son. [14] The Son paid for our sins, and in him we have forgiveness.

THE IMPORTANCE OF CHRIST

[15] No one can see God, but Jesus Christ is exactly like him. He ranks higher than everything that has been made. [16] Through his power all things were made—things in heaven and on earth, things seen and unseen, all powers, authorities, lords, and rulers. All things were made through Christ and for Christ. [17] He was there before anything was made, and all things continue because of him. [18] He is the head of the body, which is the church. Everything comes from him. He is the first one who was raised from the dead. So in all things Jesus has first place. [19] God was pleased for all of himself to live in Christ. [20] And through Christ, God has brought all things back to himself again—things on earth and things in heaven. God made peace through the blood of Christ's death on the cross.

[21] At one time you were separated from God. You were his enemies in your minds, and the evil things you did were against God. [22] But now God has made you his friends again. He did this through Christ's death in the body so

COLOSSIANS 2:13-14

We think we're pretty slick with our big-screen TVs and surround-sound systems. But wonder what God's got in store for the day of judgment, when every person who's ever lived has to stand before him and give account of their lives?

This is just a wild guess—highly unproven—but can't you just imagine some gigantic movie screen, out in the middle of this huge mass of people, playing surveillance camera footage of their secret sins, their bad thoughts, their evil intentions—right there in front of their mamas and everybody?

If that scenario is even remotely true, what do you think would be on your tape? The time you let your sister's pet mouse loose? The day you got mad and told your dad you hated him—and thought something worse?

If you've asked Christ into your heart, your own personal private showing will have been somehow, mysteriously erased . . . deleted from memory by a nail-scarred hand.

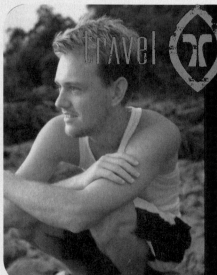

The Good News about Jesus isn't just spread by grown-ups. Every Saturday, teens from a three-thousand-member church hit a marketplace in Campinas, a city of a million people in southern Brazil—not to shop, but to do an evangelistic outreach using puppets. They're well on their way to their goal of helping a thousand people trust in Christ in a year.

For more on extreme missions visit www.traveltheroad.com.

 1:2 brothers and sisters Although the Greek text says "brothers" here and throughout this book, Paul's words were meant for the entire church, including men and women.

that he might bring you into God's presence as people who are holy, with no wrong, and with nothing of which God can judge you guilty. [23]This will happen if you continue strong and sure in your faith. You must not be moved away from the hope brought to you by the Good News that you heard. That same Good News has been told to everyone in the world, and I, Paul, help in preaching that Good News.

PAUL'S WORK FOR THE CHURCH

[24]I am happy in my sufferings for you. There are things that Christ must still suffer through his body, the church. I am accepting, in my body, my part of these things that must be suffered. [25]I became a servant of the church because God gave me a special work to do that helps you, and that work is to tell fully the message of God. [26]This message is the secret that was hidden from everyone since the beginning of time, but now it is made known to God's holy people. [27]God decided to let his people know this rich and glorious secret which he has for all people. This secret is Christ himself, who is in you. He is our only hope for glory. [28]So we continue to preach Christ to each person, using all wisdom to warn and to teach everyone, in order to bring each one into God's presence as a mature person in Christ. [29]To do this, I work and struggle, using Christ's great strength that works so powerfully in me.

2 I want you to know how hard I work for you, those in Laodicea, and others who have never seen me. [2]I want them to be strengthened and joined together with love so that they may be rich in their understanding. This leads to their knowing fully God's secret, that is, Christ himself. [3]In him all the treasures of wisdom and knowledge are safely kept.

[4]I say this so that no one can fool you by arguments that seem good, but are false. [5]Though I am absent from you in my body, my heart is with you, and I am happy to see your good lives and your strong faith in Christ.

CONTINUE TO LIVE IN CHRIST

[6]As you received Christ Jesus the Lord, so continue to live in him. [7]Keep your roots deep in him and have your lives built on him. Be strong in the faith, just as you were taught, and always be thankful.

[8]Be sure that no one leads you away with false and empty teaching that is only human, which comes from the ruling spirits of this world, and not from Christ. [9]All of God lives in Christ fully (even when Christ was on earth), [10]and you have a full and true life in Christ, who is ruler over all rulers and powers.

[11]Also in Christ you had a different kind of circumcision, a circumcision not done by hands. It was through Christ's circumcision, that is, his death, that you were made free from the power of your sinful self. [12]When you were baptized, you were buried with Christ, and you were raised up with him through your faith in God's power that was shown when he raised Christ from the dead. [13]When you were spiritually

GET OUT THERE ➤

Every day, the plague of AIDS takes 8,000 lives in Africa. That means there are now 13 million AIDS orphans in Africa, and more every day. DATA aims to raise awareness about this crisis by focusing on *d-a-t-a*: the unpayable *debts*, uncontrolled spread of *AIDS,* and burdensome *trade* rules, which keep *Africans* poor. They are asking people in the world's wealthy nations—the United States, the nations of Europe, Canada, and Japan—to respond quickly and generously to this emergency.

In industrialized nations, we have the power to make a difference and save millions of lives. Visit www.data.org to learn how you can keep the world's promise to Africa.

OCTOBER

Switch to Standard Time on the last Sunday of October—turn your clocks back one hour.

1 Get lost with some friends in a corn maze.

2

3

4

5 Read 1 Timothy today.

6

7 Pray for a Person of Influence: Priest Holmes gets older today.

8 Pray for a Person of Influence: Matt Damon has a birthday.

9

10 Pray for a Person of Influence: Brett Favre turns a year older

11

12 Columbus Day. Read up on what it was like for those guys to cross the Atlantic.

13 Go for a walk with your family and look at the changing leaves.

14 Drive the speed limit today and every day.

15

16 Boss's Day. Do something nice for the man or woman who signs your check.

17 Pray for a Person of Influence: Eminem celebrates his birthday today.

18

19

20

21 Save some money you would normally spend on yourself—and put it aside for Christmas gifts.

22

23 Tell your parents something good that happened at school today.

24

25

26 Get back on track if school isn't going well.

27

28 Pray for a Person of Influence: Bill Gates is one year older.

29 Be a man and fire up a leafblower today.

30 Change the time on the VCR.

31 Make a deal with a friend: Surprise your families by raking both yards.

Halloween: Find a fun way to honor God today.

RADICAL FAITH:

colossians 3:20

In his wisdom, the Lord has put people in places of authority over you. When you are a student, the Lord calls you to obey your parents, your teachers, coaches, and leaders at your church. Even as an adult you will still be under the rule of government and called to submit to the leadership of church elders. God works out his will in your life through the authority that he has allowed. By obeying your parents or other leaders, you are obeying God. God says that it pleases him when you obey your parents. So even when you disagree with them, or feel frustrated, remember that obedience to them is a gift that you are giving to God.

dead because of your sins and because you were not free from the power of your sinful self, God made you alive with Christ, and he forgave all our sins. [14]He canceled the debt, which listed all the rules we failed to follow. He took away that record with its rules and nailed it to the cross. [15]God stripped the spiritual rulers and powers of their authority. With the cross, he won the victory and showed the world that they were powerless.

DON'T FOLLOW PEOPLE'S RULES

[16]So do not let anyone make rules for you about eating and drinking or about a religious feast, a New Moon Festival, or a Sabbath day. [17]These things were like a shadow of what was to come. But what is true and real has come and is found in Christ. [18]Do not let anyone disqualify you by making you humiliate yourself and worship angels. Such people enter into visions, which fill them with foolish pride because of their human way of thinking. [19]They do not hold tightly to Christ, the head. It is from him that all the parts of the body are cared for and held together. So it grows in the way God wants it to grow.

[20]Since you died with Christ and were made free from the ruling spirits of the world, why do you act as if you still belong to this world by following rules like these: [21]"Don't eat this," "Don't taste that," "Don't even touch that thing"? [22]These rules refer to earthly things that are gone as soon as they are used. They are only man-made commands and teachings. [23]They seem to be wise, but they are only part of a man-made religion. They make people pretend not to be proud and make them punish their bodies, but they do not really control the evil desires of the sinful self.

YOUR NEW LIFE IN CHRIST

3 Since you were raised from the dead with Christ, aim at what is in heaven, where Christ is sitting at the right hand of God. [2]Think only about the things in heaven, not the things on earth. [3]Your old sinful self has died, and your new life is kept with Christ in God. [4]Christ is our life, and when he comes again, you will share in his glory.

[5]So put all evil things out of your life: sexual sinning, doing evil, letting evil thoughts

RANDOM WAYS TO BE A COOL BROTHER

1. DON'T RIP ON YOUR SIBS WHEN THEY GET ON YOUR NERVES.
2. TAKE YOUR SIBS OUT FOR ICE CREAM OR COFFEE.
3. LET YOUR SISTER WEAR YOUR OLD SWEATSHIRTS.
4. BE KIND TO THEIR FRIENDS.
5. LET THEM TAKE YOU TO ONE OF THEIR FAVORITE PLACES.
6. PLAN A FUN OUTING FOR YOUR PARENTS TOGETHER.
7. DON'T TEASE YOUR SIBS WHEN THEIR FRIENDS ARE AROUND.
8. LISTEN TO THEIR PROBLEMS.
9. GIVE YOUR BROTHER SOME CLOTHES YOU HAVEN'T WORN IN A WHILE.
10. PATIENTLY TEACH THEM TO DO STUFF YOU ALREADY DO WELL.

control you, wanting things that are evil, and greed. This is really serving a false god. [6]These things make God angry.[n] [7]In your past, evil life you also did these things.

[8]But now also put these things out of your life: anger, bad temper, doing or saying things to hurt others, and using evil words when you talk. [9]Do not lie to each other. You have left your old sinful life and the things you did before. [10]You have begun to live the new life, in which you are being made new and are becoming like the One who made you. This new life brings you the true knowledge of God. [11]In the new life there is no difference

 3:6 These . . . angry Some Greek copies add: "against the people who do not obey God."

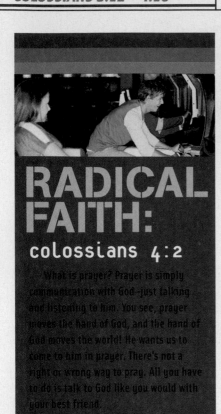

RADICAL FAITH:
colossians 4:2

What is prayer? Prayer is simply communication with God—just talking and listening to him. You see, prayer moves the hand of God, and the hand of God moves the world! He wants us to come to him in prayer. There's not a right or wrong way to pray. All you have to do is talk to God like you would with your best friend.

A lot of people have the idea that prayer is only talking to God. That's only half of it. You really can't communicate with someone without another important activity—listening. Prayer is a two-way street. Not only does God want you to talk to him; he also wants to talk to you. How can God talk to you? Through his Word.

Try it right now. Whatever need you have, go to God in prayer, and then pick this Bible back up and let God speak to you from his Word. But don't just get in a habit of praying when you're in a bind. God wants you to be in continual prayer, talking to him throughout the day. Start every day with a quiet time—moments that are reserved for you and God. Prayer can only happen when the two of you are spending time together. If you were to only talk to a close friend once in a while, what would happen? Your friendship wouldn't be that close. If we expect our relationship with Christ to be strong, we must never stop praying. Kick it up a notch today!

between Greeks and Jews, those who are circumcised and those who are not circumcised, or people who are foreigners, or Scythians.[n] There is no difference between slaves and free people. But Christ is in all believers, and Christ is all that is important.

[12]God has chosen you and made you his holy people. He loves you. So always do these things: Show mercy to others, be kind, humble, gentle, and patient. [13]Get along with each other, and forgive each other. If someone does wrong to you, forgive that person because the Lord forgave you. [14]Do all these things; but most important, love each other. Love is what holds you all together in perfect unity. [15]Let the peace that Christ gives control your thinking, because you were all called together in one body[n] to have peace. Always be thankful. [16]Let the teaching of Christ live in you richly. Use all wisdom to teach and instruct each other by singing psalms, hymns, and spiritual songs with thankfulness in your hearts to God. [17]Everything you do or say should be done to obey Jesus your Lord. And in all you do, give thanks to God the Father through Jesus.

YOUR NEW LIFE WITH OTHER PEOPLE

[18]Wives, yield to the authority of your husbands, because this is the right thing to do in the Lord.

[19]Husbands, love your wives and be gentle with them.

[20]Children, obey your parents in all things, because this pleases the Lord.

[21]Fathers, do not nag your children. If you are too hard to please, they may want to stop trying.

[22]Slaves, obey your masters in all things. Do not obey just when they are watching you, to gain their favor, but serve them honestly, because you respect the Lord. [23]In all the work you are doing, work the best you can. Work as if you were doing it for the Lord, not for people. [24]Remember that you will receive your reward from the Lord, which he promised to his people. You are serving the Lord Christ. [25]But remember that anyone who does wrong will be punished for that wrong, and the Lord treats everyone the same.

4 Masters, give what is good and fair to your slaves. Remember that you have a Master in heaven.

WHAT THE CHRISTIANS ARE TO DO

[2]Continue praying, keeping alert, and always thanking God. [3]Also pray for us that God will give us an opportunity to tell people his message. Pray that we can preach the secret that God has made known about Christ. This is why I am in prison. [4]Pray that I can speak in a way that will make it clear, as I should.

[5]Be wise in the way you act with people who are not believers, making the most of every opportunity. [6]When you talk, you should always be kind and pleasant so you will be able to answer everyone in the way you should.

NEWS ABOUT THE PEOPLE WITH PAUL

[7]Tychicus is my dear brother in Christ and a faithful minister and servant with me in the Lord. He will tell you all the things that are happening to me. [8]This is why I am sending him: so you may know how we are and he may encourage you. [9]I send him with Onesimus, a faithful and dear brother in Christ, and one of your group. They will tell you all that has happened here.

[10]Aristarchus, a prisoner with me, and Mark, the cousin of Barnabas, greet you. (I have already told you what to do about Mark. If he comes, welcome him.) [11]Jesus, who is called Justus, also greets you. These are the only Jewish believers who work with me for the kingdom of God, and they have been a comfort to me.

[12]Epaphras, a servant of Jesus Christ, from your group, also greets you. He always prays for you that you will grow to be spiritually mature and have everything God wants for you. [13]I know he has worked hard for you and the people in Laodicea and in Hierapolis. [14]Demas and our dear friend Luke, the doctor, greet you.

[15]Greet the brothers in Laodicea. And greet Nympha and the church that meets in her house. [16]After this letter is read to you, be sure it is also read to the church in Laodicea. And you read the letter that I wrote to Laodicea. [17]Tell Archippus, "Be sure to finish the work the Lord gave you."

[18]I, Paul, greet you and write this with my own hand. Remember me in prison. Grace be with you.

 3:11 Scythians The Scythians were known as very wild and cruel people. **3:15 body** The spiritual body of Christ, meaning the church or his people.

1 THESSALONIANS

ANSWERS TO QUESTIONS ABOUT CHRIST'S RETURN

Everyone was stoked when Jesus walked the earth. His miracles, his teachings, and his service were bigger than their wildest hopes. Now that their Master is gone, they long to experience all that again. They are gripped by his promise to come back to earth. And they can't wait for him to return so they can have a king to look up to. It's all they think about.

Can you blame them? Without their Messiah around, physically, they feel like outcasts...like religious criminals. This unorganized core of converts had only their experience of salvation to bind them together, and now they're struggling to survive like street kids in a dangerous city. And even though they have their faith to unite them, they feel they suffer alone. Living for Jesus seems impossible in their sprawling port city that teems with immorality, greed, and deception. Besides that, their worship of Jesus as God's Son and as ruler of the heavenly kingdom pits them against the Jews who insist that God had no son—not to mention the Romans, who worship the emperor.

For the Thessalonians, and all Christians who feel out of sync in their world, Paul encourages them to put their energy on working hard, living honorable lives, and earning the respect of others. It's okay to look forward to Jesus' return. It's understandable to be concerned about persecution. But Paul's message nudges them to shift their attention away from their suffering and focus on what they do right now in life.

1 From Paul, Silas, and Timothy.
To the church in Thessalonica, the church in God the Father and the Lord Jesus Christ:

Grace and peace to you.

THE FAITH OF THE THESSALONIANS

[2]We always thank God for all of you and mention you when we pray. [3]We continually recall before God our Father the things you have done because of your faith and the work you have done because of your love. And we thank him that you continue to be strong because of your hope in our Lord Jesus Christ.

[4]Brothers and sisters,[n] God loves you, and we know he has chosen you, [5]because the Good News we brought to you came not only with words, but with power, with the Holy Spirit, and with sure knowledge that it is true. Also you know how we lived when we were with you in order to help you. [6]And you became like us and like the Lord. You suffered much, but still you accepted the teaching with the joy that comes from the Holy Spirit. [7]So you became an example to all the believers in Macedonia and Southern Greece. [8]And the Lord's teaching spread from you not only into Macedonia and Southern Greece, but now your faith in God has become known every-where. So we do not need to say anything about it. [9]People everywhere are telling about the way you accepted us when we were there with you. They tell how you stopped worshiping idols and began serving the living and true God. [10]And you wait for God's Son, whom God raised from the dead, to come from heaven. He is Jesus, who saves us from God's angry judgment that is sure to come.

PAUL'S WORK IN THESSALONICA

2 Brothers and sisters, you know our visit to you was not a failure. [2]Before we came to you, we suffered in Philippi. People there insulted us, as you know, and many people were against us. But our God helped us to be brave and to tell you his Good News. [3]Our appeal does not come from lies or wrong reasons, nor were we trying to trick you. [4]But we speak the Good News because God tested us and trusted us to do it. When we speak, we are not trying to please people, but God, who tests our hearts. [5]You know that we never tried to influence you by saying nice things about you. We were not trying to get your money; we had no selfishness to hide from you. God knows that this is true. [6]We were not looking for human praise, from you or anyone else, [7]even

WAYS TO WALK THE WALK

1 Thessalonians 2:4

WORD: Pleasing God and pleasing people don't always mix.

WALK IT: Set your watch to beep every hour today. When it beeps, ask yourself whether at that moment you are more concerned with pleasing God or pleasing people. Talk to God about the times you put people first.

1 Thessalonians 4:3-4

WORD: Stay clear of sexual sin. It can't get any clearer.

WALK IT: Sexual impurity is a big issue in the Bible because it wreaks havoc in people's lives. If you're falling short of God's standard, talk to him. Get help from a mature Christian male to break loose from sin.

✓ COUNT ON IT

1 THESSALONIANS 1:9-10

The return of Jesus is an incredible source of hope for all believers! We have hope for many reasons, but the one Paul mentions here is that Jesus will save us from God's wrath. God is love and he loves all people and wants them to be saved (see 1 John 4:8-10). But the day will come when God will pour out his anger on those who have not believed. The great white throne judgment will be a specific time of anger (Revelation 20:11-15), and the great tribulation (Revelation 6–19) will be another. The anger of God is also poured out on earth, where unbelievers live without the Holy Spirit and without the power and presence of God. Their lives have fallen under the power of Satan.

As a Christian, you can rest in the promise that Jesus saves you from God's anger over sinful human rebellion. You will be kept from it because you are covered with the blood of Jesus. That is, because Jesus is the Lord of your life and you have accepted his work on the cross, God's anger is satisfied. Thank Jesus today for sparing you from God's anger on the day of judgment.

 1:4 Brothers and sisters Although the Greek text says "Brothers" here and throughout this book, Paul's words were meant for the entire church, including men and women.

though as apostles of Christ we could have used our authority over you.

But we were very gentle with you, like a mother caring for her little children. [8]Because we loved you, we were happy to share not only God's Good News with you, but even our own lives. You had become so dear to us! [9]Brothers and sisters, I know you remember our hard work and difficulties. We worked night and day so we would not burden any of you while we preached God's Good News to you.

[10]When we were with you, we lived in a holy and honest way, without fault. You know this is true, and so does God. [11]You know that we treated each of you as a father treats his own children. [12]We encouraged you, we urged you, and we insisted that you live good lives for God, who calls you to his glorious kingdom.

[13]Also, we always thank God because when you heard his message from us, you accepted it as the word of God, not the words of humans. And it really is God's message which works in you who believe. [14]Brothers and sisters, your experiences have been like those of God's churches in Christ that are in Judea.[n] You suffered from the people of your own country, as they suffered from the Jews, [15]who killed both the Lord Jesus and the prophets and forced us to leave that country. They do not please God and are against all people. [16]They try to stop us from teaching those who are not Jews so they may be saved. By doing this, they are increasing their sins to the limit. The anger of God has come to them at last.

PAUL WANTS TO VISIT THEM AGAIN

[17]Brothers and sisters, though we were separated from you for a short time, our thoughts were still with you. We wanted very much to see you and tried hard to do so. [18]We wanted to come to you. I, Paul, tried to come more than once, but Satan stopped us. [19]You are our hope, our joy, and the crown we will take pride in when our Lord Jesus Christ comes. [20]Truly you are our glory and our joy.

3 When we could not wait any longer, we decided it was best to stay in Athens alone [2]and send Timothy to you. Timothy, our brother, works with us for God and helps us tell people the Good News about Christ. We sent him to strengthen and encourage you in your faith [3]so none of you would be upset by these

troubles. You yourselves know that we must face these troubles. [4]Even when we were with you, we told you we all would have to suffer, and you know it has happened. [5]Because of this, when I could wait no longer, I sent Timothy to you so I could learn about your faith. I was afraid the devil had tempted you, and then our hard work would have been wasted.

[6]But Timothy now has come back to us from you and has brought us good news about your faith and love. He told us that you always remember us in a good way and that you want to see us just as much as we want to see you. [7]So, brothers and sisters, while we have much trouble and suffering, we are encouraged about you because of your faith. [8]Our life is really full if you stand strong in the Lord. [9]We have so much joy before our God because of you. We cannot thank him enough for all the joy we feel. [10]Night and day we continue praying with all our heart that we can see you again and give you all the things you need to make your faith strong.

[11]Now may our God and Father himself and our Lord Jesus prepare the way for us to come to you. [12]May the Lord make your love grow more and multiply for each other and for all people so that you will love others as we love you. [13]May your hearts be made strong so that you will be holy and without fault before our God and Father when our Lord Jesus comes with all his holy ones.

A LIFE THAT PLEASES GOD

4 Brothers and sisters, we taught you how to live in a way that will please God, and you are living that way. Now we ask and encourage you in the Lord Jesus to live that way even more. [2]You know what we told you to do by the authority of the Lord Jesus. [3]God wants you to be holy and to stay away from sexual sins. [4]He wants each of you to learn to control your own body[n] in a way that is holy and honorable. [5]Don't use your body for sexual sin like the people who do not know God. [6]Also, do not wrong or cheat another Christian in this way. The Lord will punish people who do those things as we have already told you and warned you. [7]God called us to be holy and does not want us to live in sin. [8]So the person who refuses to obey this teaching is disobeying God, not simply a human teaching. And God is the One who gives us his Holy Spirit.

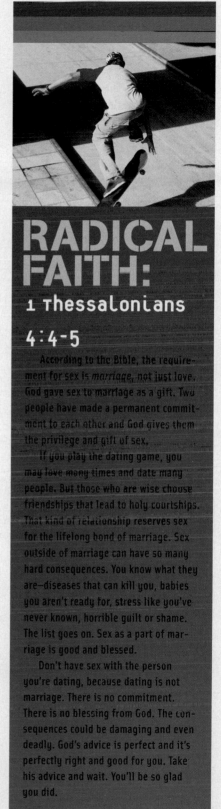

RADICAL FAITH:

1 Thessalonians 4:4-5

According to the Bible, the requirement for sex is *marriage*, not just love. God gave sex to marriage as a gift. Two people have made a permanent commitment to each other and God gives them the privilege and gift of sex.

If you play the dating game, you may love many times and date many people. But those who are wise choose friendships that lead to holy courtships. That kind of relationship reserves sex for the lifelong bond of marriage. Sex outside of marriage can have so many hard consequences. You know what they are—diseases that can kill you, babies you aren't ready for, stress like you've never known, horrible guilt or shame. The list goes on. Sex as a part of marriage is good and blessed.

Don't have sex with the person you're dating, because dating is not marriage. There is no commitment. There is no blessing from God. The consequences could be damaging and even deadly. God's advice is perfect and it's perfectly right and good for you. Take his advice and wait. You'll be so glad you did.

2:14 **Judea** The Jewish land where Jesus lived and taught and where the church first began.   4:4 **learn . . . body** This might also mean "learn to live with your own wife."

[9]We do not need to write you about having love for your Christian family, because God has already taught you to love each other. [10]And truly you do love the Christians in all of Macedonia. Brothers and sisters, now we encourage you to love them even more.

[11]Do all you can to live a peaceful life. Take care of your own business, and do your own work as we have already told you. [12]If you do, then people who are not believers will respect you, and you will not have to depend on others for what you need.

THE LORD'S COMING

[13]Brothers and sisters, we want you to know about those Christians who have died so you will not be sad, as others who have no hope. [14]We believe that Jesus died and that he rose again. So, because of him, God will raise with Jesus those who have died. [15]What we tell you now is the Lord's own message. We who are living when the Lord comes again will not go before those who have already died. [16]The Lord himself will come down from heaven with a loud command, with the voice of the archangel,[n] and with the trumpet call of God. And those who have died believing in Christ will rise first. [17]After that, we who are still alive will be gathered up with them in the clouds to meet the Lord in the air. And we will be with the Lord forever. [18]So encourage each other with these words.

BE READY FOR THE LORD'S COMING

5 Now, brothers and sisters, we do not need to write you about times and dates. [2]You know very well that the day the Lord comes again will be a surprise, like a thief that comes in the night. [3]While people are saying, "We have peace and we are safe," they will be destroyed quickly. It is like pains that come quickly to a woman having a baby. Those people will not escape. [4]But you, brothers and sisters, are not living in darkness, and so that day will not surprise you like a thief. [5]You are all people who belong to the light and to the day. We do not belong to the night or to darkness. [6]So we should not be like other people who are sleeping, but we should be alert and have self-control. [7]Those who sleep, sleep at night. Those who get drunk, get drunk at night. [8]But we belong to the day, so we should control ourselves. We should wear faith and love to protect us, and the hope of salvation should be our helmet. [9]God did not choose us to suffer his anger but to have salvation through our Lord Jesus Christ. [10]Jesus died for us so that we can live together with him, whether we are alive or dead when he comes. [11]So encourage each other and give each other strength, just as you are doing now.

FINAL INSTRUCTIONS AND GREETINGS

[12]Now, brothers and sisters, we ask you to appreciate those who work hard among you, who lead you in the Lord and teach you.

[13]Respect them with a very special love because of the work they do.

Live in peace with each other. [14]We ask you, brothers and sisters, to warn those who do not work. Encourage the people who are afraid. Help those who are weak. Be patient with everyone. [15]Be sure that no one pays back wrong for wrong, but always try to do what is good for each other and for all people.

[16]Always be joyful. [17]Pray continually, [18]and give thanks whatever happens. That is what God wants for you in Christ Jesus.

[19]Do not hold back the work of the Holy Spirit. [20]Do not treat prophecy as if it were unimportant. [21]But test everything. Keep what is good, [22]and stay away from everything that is evil.

[23]Now may God himself, the God of peace, make you pure, belonging only to him. May your whole self—spirit, soul, and body—be kept safe and without fault when our Lord Jesus Christ comes. [24]You can trust the One who calls you to do that for you.

[25]Brothers and sisters, pray for us.

[26]Give each other a holy kiss when you meet. [27]I tell you by the authority of the Lord to read this letter to all the believers.

[28]The grace of our Lord Jesus Christ be with you.

travel the road

Don't listen to people who say it's stupid to send missionaries to foreign countries. Yep, some Christians say we should stop sending missionaries altogether. It's true that a missionary family from North America or Europe might need $50,000 a year to get to a foreign land—and that those dollars could support dozens of local workers. But until the Good News about Jesus is told in every corner of earth, we need workers to go where no Christian has gone before. That's pricey—but priceless.

For more on extreme missions visit www.traveltheroad.com.

4:16 archangel The leader among God's angels or messengers.

2THESSALONIANS

GET ON WITH LIVING AND SERVING GOD

• **In 2 Thessalonians**, Paul threw cold water on a bunch of people who quit their jobs to hang out at church waiting for Jesus to show up once again on earth. Once Paul had their attention, he told them that while it's a good thing to look forward to Christ's return, they needed to get a life. Paul's poke at the Thessalonians reminds us that none of us know the date or hour of Christ's return, so we should stop waiting around and get on with our lives, our work, and our serving. Paul is no fan of laziness. He calls the Thessalonians to get out there and earn their keep. In this way, Christians can be respected as hard workers and lawful people. Good call, Paul.

COUNT ON IT

2 THESSALONIANS 1:6-8

Been laughed at lately? Taken any jabs for being a Christian? Been made fun of because you did the right thing? Take heart, because relief is on its way. When Jesus comes, he promises to give you rest from your troubles. You won't have to fight anymore. Jesus will take over with his powerful angels and a flaming fire. He will take care of your enemies and all who would persecute you. Sometimes the battle is bigger than you are. The trouble seems overwhelming. Be courageous enough to know which battles belong to the Lord, and leave them for him to fight.

1 From Paul, Silas, and Timothy. To the church in Thessalonica in God our Father and the Lord Jesus Christ:

[2] Grace and peace to you from God the Father and the Lord Jesus Christ.

PAUL TALKS ABOUT GOD'S JUDGMENT

[3] We must always thank God for you, brothers and sisters.[n] This is only right, because your faith is growing more and more, and the love that every one of you has for each other is increasing. [4] So we brag about you to the other churches of God. We tell them about the way you continue to be strong and have faith even though you are being treated badly and are suffering many troubles.

[5] This is proof that God is right in his judgment. He wants you to be counted worthy of his kingdom for which you are suffering. [6] God will do what is right. He will give trouble to those who trouble you. [7] And he will give rest to you who are troubled and to us also when the Lord Jesus appears with burning fire from heaven with his powerful angels. [8] Then he will punish those who do not know God and who do not obey the Good News about our Lord Jesus Christ. [9] Those people will be punished with a destruction that continues forever. They will be kept away from the Lord and from his great power. [10] This will happen on the day when the Lord Jesus comes to receive glory because of his holy people. And all the people who have believed will be amazed at Jesus. You will be in that group, because you believed what we told you.

[11] That is why we always pray for you, asking our God to help you live the kind of life he called you to live. We pray that with his power God will help you do the good things you want and perform the works that come from your faith. [12] We pray all this so that the name of our Lord Jesus Christ will have glory in you, and you will have glory in him. That glory comes from the grace of our God and the Lord Jesus Christ.

EVIL THINGS WILL HAPPEN

2 Brothers and sisters, we have something to say about the coming of our Lord Jesus Christ and the time when we will meet together with him. [2] Do not become easily upset in your thinking or afraid if you hear that the day of the Lord has already come. Someone may say this in a prophecy or in a message or in a letter as if it came from us. [3] Do not let anyone fool you in any way. That day of the Lord will not come until the turning away[n] from God happens and the Man of Evil, who is on his way to hell, appears. [4] He will be against and put himself above anything called God or anything that people worship. And that Man of Evil will even go into God's Temple and sit there and say that he is God.

[5] I told you when I was with you that all this would happen. Do you not remember? [6] And

RADICAL FAITH:

2 Thessalonians 2:13

When you gave your heart to Jesus, you became a new person—"a new creation" (see 2 Corinthians 5:17). The old you disappeared, and you were transformed from darkness to light—from death to life! Now God wants you to be changed into his likeness, and he has equipped you to do this by his Spirit. The Holy Spirit puts in you the desire not to sin—not just the desire, but also the ability. Sin doesn't have authority over you anymore. You are free! We all need to submit ourselves to God, by remaining set apart for him. As you begin to do this, it will become easier to walk in his will.

Walking in God's will is nothing more than walking in obedience to him and to his Word. That's when the true blessings of God will begin to flow in your life. When Paul writes you are chosen to be "saved by the Spirit that makes you holy," he is telling you that the Holy Spirit has given you the power to live a holy life—a life that pleases and serves God. He is the One who makes you holy!

RADICAL FAITH:

2 Thessalonians 3:13

"So why have I kept my heart pure? Why have I kept my hands from doing wrong?" (Psalm 73:13). Can you relate to this person's frustration? You tell the truth, even when it costs you, because you trust God to reward you for it. You help other people to try to make their lives better. Those are good reasons, but sometimes you just don't see those things happening. It's enough to make you want to give up.

Paul says you must not give up. How can you keep from getting tired of doing the right thing when it seems like it's getting you nowhere? Well, it takes some faith. You have to believe that God's going to do what he promised he would—even when his timetable is different from yours (and it usually is). You also have to continually fill up with God's Spirit. If you don't do that, you're like a car that's about to run out of gas. He keeps you going—you can't do it yourself.

Finally, you have to have your priorities straight. Ask yourself: Am I doing this to get results or am I doing it to please God? The answer makes all the difference.

now you know what is stopping that Man of Evil so he will appear at the right time. [7]The secret power of evil is already working in the world, but there is one who is stopping that power. And he will continue to stop it until he is taken out of the way. [8]Then that Man of Evil will appear, and the Lord Jesus will kill him with the breath that comes from his mouth and will destroy him with the glory of his coming. [9]The Man of Evil will come by the power of Satan. He will have great power, and he will do many different false miracles, signs, and wonders. [10]He will use every kind of evil to trick those who are lost. They will die, because they refused to love the truth. (If they loved the truth, they would be saved.) [11]For this reason God sends them something powerful that leads them away from the truth so they will believe a lie. [12]So all those will be judged guilty who did not believe the truth, but enjoyed doing evil.

YOU ARE CHOSEN FOR SALVATION

[13]Brothers and sisters, whom the Lord loves, God chose you from the beginning to be saved. So we must always thank God for you. You are saved by the Spirit that makes you holy and by your faith in the truth. [14]God used the Good News that we preached to call you to be saved so you can share in the glory of our Lord Jesus Christ. [15]So, brothers and sisters, stand strong and continue to believe the teachings we gave you in our speaking and in our letter.

[16-17]May our Lord Jesus Christ himself and God our Father encourage you and strengthen you in every good thing you do and say. God loved us, and through his grace he gave us a good hope and encouragement that continues forever.

PRAY FOR US

3 And now, brothers and sisters, pray for us that the Lord's teaching will continue to spread quickly and that people will give honor to that teaching, just as happened with you. [2]And pray that we will be protected from stubborn and evil people, because not all people believe.

[3]But the Lord is faithful and will give you strength and will protect you from the Evil One. [4]The Lord makes us feel sure that you are doing and will continue to do the things we told you. [5]May the Lord lead your hearts into God's love and Christ's patience.

RANDOM WAYS TO SHOW YOUR MOM YOU LOVE HER

1. OFFER TO HELP BEFORE SHE ASKS.

2. DON'T FUSS ABOUT POSING FOR CHRISTMAS PICTURES.

3. OBEY THE FIRST TIME.

4. DON'T MAKE HER REPEAT HERSELF.

5. DON'T PUT EMPTY MILK CARTONS BACK IN THE FRIDGE.

6. CHANGE THE EMPTY TOILET PAPER ROLL.

7. LEARN TO DO LAUNDRY.

8. TAXI YOUR SIBS WITHOUT COMPLAINING.

9. GIVE HER HUGS.

10. PICK UP YOUR DIRTY SOCKS AND BOXERS.

THE DUTY TO WORK

[6]Brothers and sisters, by the authority of our Lord Jesus Christ we command you to stay away from any believer who refuses to work and does not follow the teaching we gave you. [7]You yourselves know that you should live as we live. We were not lazy when we were with you. [8]And when we ate another person's food, we always paid for it. We worked very hard night and day so we would not be an expense to any of you. [9]We had the right to ask you to help us, but we worked to take care of ourselves so we would be an example for you to follow. [10]When we were with you, we gave you this rule: "Anyone who refuses to work should not eat."

BIBLE BASICS

The Garden of Eden is where the first people lived. In the Old Testament, the first chapter of Genesis tells how God created people and placed them in this flawless paradise. There was no sin, and Adam and Eve (the world's first couple) were in an unspoiled relationship with God. When Adam and Eve blew off God's rules, he banished them from the garden.

MUSIC REVIEWS

CHRIS RICE: RUN THE EARTH/WATCH THE SKY

Chris Rice has been a Gen-X *and* Gen-Y favorite since long before this release, his sixth. Hey, it's hard to resist a guy who hesitated to enter the music industry because he didn't want it to mess up his calling—as a camp counselor. And even after becoming widely known, he still preferred singing at smaller youth gatherings to staging big concerts. Rice sheds light on everyday life with crafted songs that are always humble and simple but never canned. The basic idea behind the album title is this: Life is a delight, so have a blast, but remember your destiny and focus on your future home.

WHY IT ROCKS: WHEN YOU LISTEN TO CHRIS RICE, YOU'LL WISH HE WAS ACTUALLY IN YOUR LIVING ROOM.

WAYS TO WALK THE WALK

2 Thessalonians 2:15

WORD: We should believe the truth of Scripture.

WALK IT: Read the Bible for thirty minutes every day this week. A guy needs to know what he's talking about when he goes out into the world.

2 Thessalonians 3:12

WORD: Don't be a loudmouth.

WALK IT: Focus on listening today. Don't be loud or overly obnoxious. Just watch people and hear what they have to say. What difference did it make in your day?

¹¹We hear that some people in your group refuse to work. They do nothing but busy themselves in other people's lives. ¹²We command those people and beg them in the Lord Jesus Christ to work quietly and earn their own food. ¹³But you, brothers and sisters, never become tired of doing good.

¹⁴If some people do not obey what we tell you in this letter, then take note of them. Have nothing to do with them so they will feel ashamed. ¹⁵But do not treat them as enemies. Warn them as fellow believers.

FINAL WORDS

¹⁶Now may the Lord of peace give you peace at all times and in every way. The Lord be with all of you.

¹⁷I, Paul, end this letter now in my own handwriting. All my letters have this to show they are from me. This is the way I write.

¹⁸The grace of our Lord Jesus Christ be with you all.

1 TIMOTHY

A LETTER FROM A FATHER TO HIS SPIRITUAL SON

Timothy was like a son to Paul. Paul loved him so much he took him on trips and talked to him about the deep stuff of life and faith. Like a band on tour, Paul and Timothy hit the road together and spread the Good News in Turkey, Greece, and Italy. When Paul spent two years getting the church going in Corinth, Timothy was right there as his assistant pastor. But Timothy had a lot to learn, and Paul had a lot to teach. God used their relationship to let us listen in on instructions for doing church right, being faithful to our calling, and following Christ. In his first letter to Timothy, Paul had two heavy items on his to-do list: offering guidance on leading the church and opposing false teachings by guys who seemed true. He accomplished both with instructions for regular worship as well as a mandatory resume for leadership.

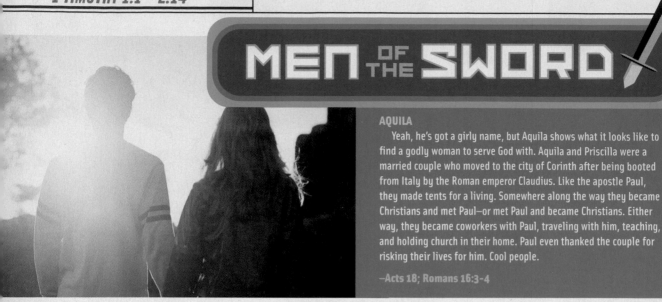

MEN OF THE SWORD

AQUILA

Yeah, he's got a girly name, but Aquila shows what it looks like to find a godly woman to serve God with. Aquila and Priscilla were a married couple who moved to the city of Corinth after being booted from Italy by the Roman emperor Claudius. Like the apostle Paul, they made tents for a living. Somewhere along the way they became Christians and met Paul—or met Paul and became Christians. Either way, they became coworkers with Paul, traveling with him, teaching, and holding church in their home. Paul even thanked the couple for risking their lives for him. Cool people.

—Acts 18; Romans 16:3-4

1 From Paul, an apostle of Christ Jesus, by the command of God our Savior and Christ Jesus our hope.

[2] To Timothy, a true child to me because you believe:

Grace, mercy, and peace from God the Father and Christ Jesus our Lord.

WARNING AGAINST FALSE TEACHING

[3] I asked you to stay longer in Ephesus when I went into Macedonia so you could command some people there to stop teaching false things. [4] Tell them not to spend their time on stories that are not true and on long lists of names in family histories. These things only bring arguments; they do not help God's work, which is done in faith. [5] The purpose of this command is for people to have love, a love that comes from a pure heart and a good conscience and a true faith. [6] Some people have missed these things and turned to useless talk. [7] They want to be teachers of the law, but they do not understand either what they are talking about or what they are sure about.

[8] But we know that the law is good if someone uses it lawfully. [9] We also know that the law is not made for good people but for those who are against the law and for those who refuse to follow it. It is for people who are against God and are sinful, who are not holy and have no religion, who kill their fathers and mothers, who murder, [10] who take part in sexual sins, who have sexual relations with people of the same sex, who sell slaves, who tell lies, who speak falsely, and who do anything

against the true teaching of God. [11] That teaching is part of the Good News of the blessed God that he gave me to tell.

THANKS FOR GOD'S MERCY

[12] I thank Christ Jesus our Lord, who gave me strength, because he trusted me and gave me this work of serving him. [13] In the past I spoke against Christ and persecuted him and did all kinds of things to hurt him. But God showed me mercy, because I did not know what I was doing. I did not believe. [14] But the grace of our Lord was fully given to me, and with that grace came the faith and love that are in Christ Jesus.

[15] What I say is true, and you should fully accept it: Christ Jesus came into the world to save sinners, of whom I am the worst. [16] But I was given mercy so that in me, the worst of all sinners, Christ Jesus could show that he has patience without limit. His patience with me made me an example for those who would believe in him and have life forever. [17] To the King that rules forever, who will never die, who cannot be seen, the only God, be honor and glory forever and ever. Amen.

[18] Timothy, my child, I am giving you a command that agrees with the prophecies that were given about you in the past. I tell you this so you can follow them and fight the good fight. [19] Continue to have faith and do what you know is right. Some people have rejected this, and their faith has been shipwrecked. [20] Hymenaeus and Alexander have done that, and I have given them to Satan so they will

learn not to speak against God.

SOME RULES FOR MEN AND WOMEN

2 First, I tell you to pray for all people, asking God for what they need and being thankful to him. [2] Pray for rulers and for all who have authority so that we can have quiet and peaceful lives full of worship and respect for God. [3] This is good, and it pleases God our Savior, [4] who wants all people to be saved and to know the truth. [5] There is one God and one way human beings can reach God. That way is through Christ Jesus, who is himself human. [6] He gave himself as a payment to free all people. He is proof that came at the right time. [7] That is why I was chosen to tell the Good News and to be an apostle. (I am telling the truth; I am not lying.) I was chosen to teach those who are not Jews to believe and to know the truth.

[8] So, I want the men everywhere to pray, lifting up their hands in a holy manner, without anger and arguments.

[9] Also, women should wear proper clothes that show respect and self-control, not using braided hair or gold or pearls or expensive clothes. [10] Instead, they should do good deeds, which is right for women who say they worship God.

[11] Let a woman learn by listening quietly and being ready to cooperate in everything. [12] But I do not allow a woman to teach or to have authority over a man, but to listen quietly, [13] because Adam was formed first and then Eve. [14] And Adam was not tricked, but the

woman was tricked and became a sinner. [15]But she will be saved through having children if they continue in faith, love, and holiness, with self-control.

ELDERS IN THE CHURCH

3 What I say is true: Anyone wanting to become an elder desires a good work. [2]An elder must not give people a reason to criticize him, and he must have only one wife. He must be self-controlled, wise, respected by others, ready to welcome guests, and able to teach. [3]He must not drink too much wine or like to fight, but rather be gentle and peaceable, not loving money. [4]He must be a good family leader, having children who cooperate with full respect. [5](If someone does not know how to lead the family, how can that person take care of God's church?) [6]But an elder must not be a new believer, or he might be too proud of himself and be judged guilty just as the devil was. [7]An elder must also have the respect of people who are not in the church so he will not be criticized by others and caught in the devil's trap.

DEACONS IN THE CHURCH

[8]In the same way, deacons must be respected by others, not saying things they do not mean. They must not drink too much wine or try to get rich by cheating others. [9]With a clear conscience they must follow the secret of the faith that God made known to us. [10]Test them first. Then let them serve as deacons if you find nothing wrong in them. [11]In the same way, women[n] must be respected by others. They must not speak evil of others. They must be self-controlled and trustworthy in everything. [12]Deacons must have only one wife and be good leaders of their children and their own families. [13]Those who serve well as deacons are making an honorable place for themselves, and they will be very bold in their faith in Christ Jesus.

THE SECRET OF OUR LIFE

[14]Although I hope I can come to you soon, I am writing these things to you now. [15]Then, even if I am delayed, you will know how to live in the family of God. That family is the church of the living God, the support and foundation of the truth. [16]Without doubt, the secret of our life of worship is great:

He was shown to us in a human body,
  proved right in spirit,
and seen by angels.

  He was preached to those who
    are not Jews,
believed in by the world,
  and taken up in glory.

A WARNING ABOUT FALSE TEACHERS

4 Now the Holy Spirit clearly says that in the later times some people will stop believing the faith. They will follow spirits that lie and teachings of demons. [2]Such teachings come from the false words of liars whose consciences are destroyed as if by a hot iron. [3]They forbid people to marry and tell them not to eat certain foods which God created to be eaten with thanks by people who believe and know the truth. [4]Everything God made is good, and nothing should be refused if it is accepted with thanks, [5]because it is made holy by what God has said and by prayer.

BE A GOOD SERVANT OF CHRIST

[6]By telling these things to the brothers and sisters,[n] you will be a good servant of Christ Jesus. You will be made strong by the words of the faith and the good teaching which you have been following. [7]But do not follow foolish stories that disagree with God's truth, but train yourself to serve God. [8]Training your body helps you in some ways, but serving God helps you in every way by bringing you blessings in this life and in the future life, too. [9]What I say is true, and you should fully accept it. [10]This is why we work and struggle: We hope in the living God who is the Savior of all people, especially of those who believe.

[11]Command and teach these things. [12]Do not let anyone treat you as if you are unimportant because you are young. Instead, be an example to the believers with your words, your actions, your love, your faith, and your pure life. [13]Until I come, continue to read the Scriptures to the people, strengthen them, and teach them. [14]Use the gift you have, which was given to you through prophecy when the group of elders laid their hands on[n] you. [15]Continue to do those things; give your life to doing them so your progress may be seen by everyone. [16]Be careful in your life and in your teaching. If you continue to live and teach rightly, you will save both yourself and those who listen to you.

RULES FOR LIVING WITH OTHERS

5 Do not speak angrily to an older man, but plead with him as if he

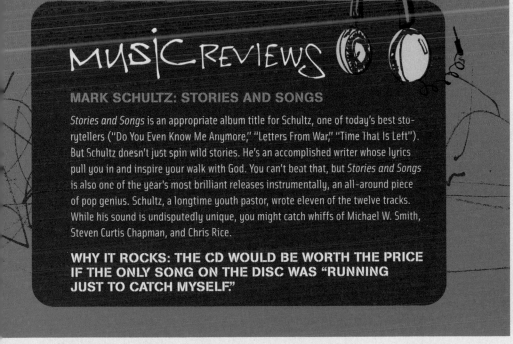

3:11 women This might mean the wives of the deacons, or it might mean women who serve in the same way as deacons.　4:6 brothers and sisters Although the Greek text says "brothers" here and throughout this book, Paul's words refer to the entire church, including men and women.　4:14 laid their hands on The laying on of hands had many purposes, including the giving of a blessing, power, or authority.

RELATIONSHIPS

"Religion that God accepts as pure and without fault is this: caring for orphans or widows who need help..." (James 1:27). The powerful people of this world take care of themselves. God takes care of the rest. Not that God doesn't love the world's bigshots. But he roots for people who feel shoved to the background. When you're figuring out who you want to spend time with, think past the usual crowd. Look out for the left out—older relatives, little sibs, loners at school. Hanging with them is at the core of what it means to be a believer.

were your father. Treat younger men like brothers, [2]older women like mothers, and younger women like sisters. Always treat them in a pure way.

[3]Take care of widows who are truly widows. [4]But if a widow has children or grandchildren, let them first learn to do their duty to their own family and to repay their parents or grandparents. That pleases God. [5]The true widow, who is all alone, puts her hope in God and continues to pray night and day for God's help. [6]But the widow who uses her life to please herself is really dead while she is alive. [7]Tell the believers to do these things so that no one can criticize them. [8]Whoever does not care for his own relatives, especially his own family members, has turned against the faith and is worse than someone who does not believe in God.

[9]To be on the list of widows, a woman must be at least sixty years old. She must have been faithful to her husband. [10]She must be known for her good works—works such as raising her children, welcoming strangers, washing the feet of God's people, helping those in trouble, and giving her life to do all kinds of good deeds.

[11]But do not put younger widows on that list. After they give themselves to Christ, they are pulled away from him by their physical needs, and then they want to marry again. [12]They will be judged for not doing what they first promised to do. [13]Besides that, they learn to waste their time, going from house to house. And they not only waste their time but also begin to gossip and busy themselves with other people's lives, saying things they should not say. [14]So I want the younger widows to marry, have children, and manage their homes. Then no enemy will have any reason to criticize them. [15]But some have already turned away to follow Satan.

[16]If any woman who is a believer has widows in her family, she should care for them herself. The church should not have to care for them. Then it will be able to take care of those who are truly widows.

[17]The elders who lead the church well should receive double honor, especially those who work hard by speaking and teaching, [18]because the Scripture says: "When an ox is working in the grain, do not cover its mouth to keep it from eating,"[n] and "A worker should be given his pay."[n]

[19]Do not listen to someone who accuses an elder, without two or three witnesses. [20]Tell those who continue sinning that they are wrong. Do this in front of the whole church so that the others will have a warning.

[21]Before God and Christ Jesus and the chosen angels, I command you to do these things without showing favor of any kind to anyone.

[22]Think carefully before you lay your hands on[n] anyone, and don't share in the sins of others. Keep yourself pure.

[23]Stop drinking only water, but drink a little wine to help your stomach and your frequent sicknesses.

[24]The sins of some people are easy to see even before they are judged, but the sins of others are seen only later. [25]So also good deeds are easy to see, but even those that are not easily seen cannot stay hidden.

6 All who are slaves under a yoke should show full respect to their masters so no one will speak against God's name and our teaching. [2]The slaves whose masters are believers should not show their masters any less respect because they are believers. They should serve their masters even better, because they are helping believers they love.

You must teach and preach these things.

FALSE TEACHING AND TRUE RICHES

[3]Anyone who has a different teaching does not agree with the true teaching of our Lord Jesus Christ and the teaching that shows the true way to serve God. [4]This person is full of pride and understands nothing, but is sick with a love for arguing and fighting about words. This brings jealousy, fighting, speaking against others, evil mistrust, [5]and constant quarrels from those who have evil minds and have lost the truth. They think that serving God is a way to get rich.

[6]Serving God does make us very rich, if we are satisfied with what we have. [7]We brought nothing into the world, so we can take nothing out. [8]But, if we have food and clothes, we will be satisfied with that. [9]Those who want to become rich bring temptation to themselves and are caught in a trap. They want many foolish and harmful things that ruin and destroy people. [10]The love of money causes all kinds

5:18 "When . . . eating," Quotation from Deuteronomy 25:4.   5:18 "A worker . . . pay." Quotation from Luke 10:7.   5:22 lay your hands on The laying on of hands had many purposes, including the giving of a blessing, power, or authority.

306

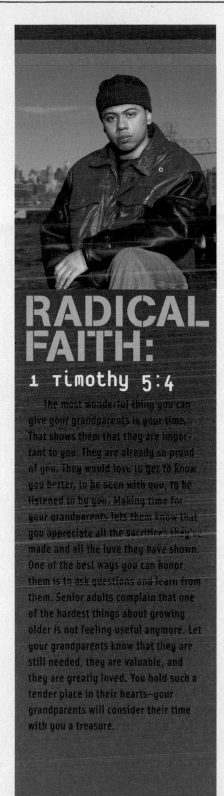

RADICAL FAITH:
1 Timothy 5:4

The most wonderful thing you can give your grandparents is your time. That shows them that they are important to you. They are already so proud of you. They would love to get to know you better, to be seen with you, to be listened to by you. Making time for your grandparents lets them know that you appreciate all the sacrifices they've made and all the love they have shown. One of the best ways you can honor them is to ask questions and learn from them. Senior adults complain that one of the hardest things about growing older is not feeling useful anymore. Let your grandparents know that they are still needed, they are valuable, and they are greatly loved. You hold such a tender place in their hearts—your grandparents will consider their time with you a treasure.

of evil. Some people have left the faith, because they wanted to get more money, but they have caused themselves much sorrow.

SOME THINGS TO REMEMBER

[11]But you, man of God, run away from all those things. Instead, live in the right way, serve God, have faith, love, patience, and gentleness. [12]Fight the good fight of faith, grabbing hold of the life that continues forever. You were called to have that life when you confessed the good confession before many witnesses. [13]In the sight of God, who gives life to everything, and of Christ Jesus, I give you a command. Christ Jesus made the good confession when he stood before Pontius Pilate. [14]Do what you were commanded to do without wrong or blame until our Lord Jesus Christ comes again. [15]God will make that happen at the right time. He is the blessed and only Ruler, the King of all kings and the Lord of all lords. [16]He is the only One who never dies. He lives in light so bright no one can go near it. No one has ever seen God, or can see him. May honor and power belong to God forever. Amen.

[17]Command those who are rich with things of this world not to be proud. Tell them to hope in God, not in their uncertain riches. God richly gives us everything to enjoy. [18]Tell the rich people to do good, to be rich in doing good deeds, to be generous and ready to share. [19]By doing that, they will be saving a treasure for themselves as a strong foundation for the future. Then they will be able to have the life that is true life.

[20]Timothy, guard what God has trusted to you. Stay away from foolish, useless talk and from the arguments of what is falsely called "knowledge." [21]By saying they have that "knowledge," some have missed the true faith.

Grace be with you.

EXPERTS ANSWER YOUR QUESTIONS

Q. *One of my best friends actually slapped me in the face yesterday. She told me I was a total hypocrite—one person at school and another person at church. She's right. What should I do?*

A. It's no fun to get slapped, but it sounds like she knocked some sense into you. Start by making a list of what you've been doing at school—and at church. Which way do you want to live? Talk to God about each point and ask your pastor for support. And ask your slappy friend to pray for you instead.

Q. *Is something wrong with me? All I think about is sex.*

A. No. Nothing's wrong with you. Your hormones are kicking in. That's a wild ride, and part of it is that sex is always on your mind. But don't make it worse by fantasizing and thinking of ways to act on it. When the thoughts come, know they are just human, think about something more appropriate, and go on with your life. You can control your thoughts by not spending hours dreaming about them. Stay in control and you will be fine.

2 TIMOTHY

ENCOURAGEMENT TO BE STRONG IN THE FAITH

This letter is a follow-up to Paul's first letter to Timothy—probably written from within the walls of a jail! Of all the Pastoral Epistles—the how-to-do-church letters of 1 and 2 Timothy as well as Titus—this one is the most personal. Paul wrote his spiritual son Timothy this second letter with advice to renew the importance of Scripture and to remind him that holy living is essential. Paul warns Timothy that times of trouble are on the way, attacks both from forces outside the church and false teachers inside the church. He encourages Timothy to endure throughout these times with faithfulness and to lead the church with fortitude in the face of Paul's own imminent martyrdom. As Timothy perseveres, Paul tells him above all to keep on preaching the Good News. Like a good coach, Paul takes Timothy under his wing and tells him how to win the second half of a crushing ball game.

1 From Paul, an apostle of Christ Jesus by the will of God. God sent me to tell about the promise of life that is in Christ Jesus.

[2]To Timothy, a dear child to me:

Grace, mercy, and peace to you from God the Father and Christ Jesus our Lord.

ENCOURAGEMENT FOR TIMOTHY

[3]I thank God as I always mention you in my prayers, day and night. I serve him, doing what I know is right as my ancestors did. [4]Remembering that you cried for me, I want very much to see you so I can be filled with

> **MATTHEW 20:28 "THE SON OF MAN DID NOT COME TO BE SERVED. HE CAME TO SERVE OTHERS AND TO GIVE HIS LIFE AS A RANSOM FOR MANY PEOPLE."**

joy. [5]I remember your true faith. That faith first lived in your grandmother Lois and in your mother Eunice, and I know you now have that same faith. [6]This is why I remind you to keep using the gift God gave you when I laid my hands on[n] you. Now let it grow, as a small flame grows into a fire. [7]God did not give us a spirit that makes us afraid but a spirit of power and love and self-control.

[8]So do not be ashamed to tell people about our Lord Jesus, and do not be ashamed of me, in prison for the Lord. But suffer with me for the Good News. God, who gives us the strength to do that, [9]saved us and made us his holy people. That was not because of anything we did ourselves but because of God's purpose and grace. That grace was given to us through Christ Jesus before time began, [10]but it is now shown to us by the coming of our Savior Christ Jesus. He destroyed death, and through the Good News he showed us the way to have life that cannot be destroyed. [11]I was chosen to tell that Good News and to be an apostle and a teacher. [12]I am suffering now because I tell the Good News, but I am not ashamed, because I know Jesus, the One in whom I have believed. And I am sure he is able to protect what he has trusted me with until that day.[n] [13]Follow the pattern of true teachings that you heard from me in faith and love, which are in Christ Jesus. [14]Protect the truth that you were given; protect it with the help of the Holy Spirit who lives in us.

[15]You know that everyone in the country of Asia has left me, even Phygelus and Hermogenes. [16]May the Lord show mercy to the family of Onesiphorus, who has often helped me and was not ashamed that I was in prison. [17]When he came to Rome, he looked eagerly for me until he found me. [18]May the Lord allow him to find mercy from the Lord on that day. You know how many ways he helped me in Ephesus.

A LOYAL SOLDIER OF CHRIST JESUS

2 You then, Timothy, my child, be strong in the grace we have in Christ Jesus. [2]You should teach people whom you can trust the things you and many others have heard me say. Then they will be able to teach others. [3]Share in the troubles we have like a good soldier of Christ Jesus. [4]A soldier wants to please the enlisting officer, so no one serving in the army wastes time with everyday matters. [5]Also an athlete who takes part in a contest must obey all the rules in order to win. [6]The farmer who works hard should be the first person to get some of the food that was grown. [7]Think about what I am saying, because the Lord will give you the ability to understand everything.

[8]Remember Jesus Christ, who was raised from the dead, who is from the family of David. This is the Good News I preach, [9]and I am suffering because of it to the point of being bound with chains like a criminal. But God's teaching is not in chains. [10]So I patiently accept all these troubles so that those whom God has chosen can have the salvation that is in Christ Jesus. With that salvation comes glory that never ends.

[11]This teaching is true:

If we died with him, we will also live with him.

[12]If we accept suffering, we will also rule with him.

If we refuse to accept him, he will refuse to accept us.

INSIDE HER HEAD

Q: WHAT DO YOU THINK OF A GUY WHO GETS ALONG WITH HIS PARENTS?

A: THAT'S REALLY GOOD. IT JUST SHOWS THAT HE CAN WORK WITH PEOPLE EVEN IF HE DOESN'T ALWAYS AGREE WITH THEM. I THINK IT MEANS HE'LL TREAT ME BETTER.

WAYS TO WALK THE WALK

2 Timothy 1:6

WORD: We should let our gifts grow.

WALK IT: Don't hide your talents because you might be shy about showing them. God gave them to you for a reason. Be a man. Do the good stuff God gave you to do.

2 Timothy 1:8

WORD: We should not be ashamed of the Good News.

WALK IT: Tell at least one person the story of the Good News this week.

 1:6 **laid my hands on** The laying on of hands had many purposes, including the giving of a blessing, power, or authority. 1:12 **day** The day Christ will come to judge all people and take his people to live with him.

13If we are not faithful, he will still be faithful,

because he cannot be false to himself.

A WORKER PLEASING TO GOD

14Continue teaching these things, warning people in God's presence not to argue about words. It does not help anyone, and it ruins those who listen. 15Make every effort to give yourself to God as the kind of person he will accept. Be a worker who is not ashamed and who uses the true teaching in the right way. 16Stay away from foolish, useless talk, because that will lead people further away from God. 17Their evil teaching will spread like a sickness inside the body. Hymenaeus and Philetus are like that. 18They have left the true teaching, saying that the rising from the dead has already taken place, and so they are destroying the faith of some people. 19But God's strong foundation continues to stand. These words

PSALM 86:11 "TEACH ME TO RESPECT YOU COMPLETELY."

are written on the seal: "The Lord knows those who belong to him,"[n] and "Everyone who wants to belong to the Lord must stop doing wrong."

20In a large house there are not only things made of gold and silver, but also things made of wood and clay. Some things are used for special purposes, and others are made for ordinary jobs. 21All who make themselves clean from evil will be used for special purposes. They will be made holy, useful to the Master, ready to do any good work.

22But run away from the evil young people like to do. Try hard to live right and to have faith, love, and peace, together with those who trust in the Lord from pure hearts. 23Stay away from foolish and stupid arguments, because you know they grow into quarrels. 24And a servant of the Lord must not quarrel but must be kind to everyone, a good teacher, and patient. 25The Lord's servant must gently teach those who disagree. Then maybe God will let

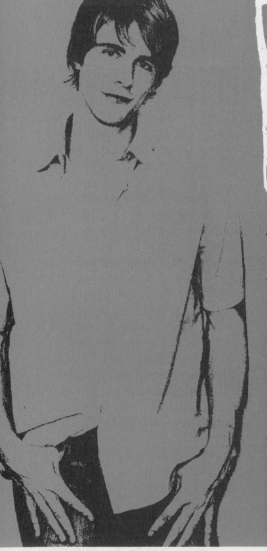

GET OUT THERE

The **CHERNOBYL CHILDREN'S PROJECT** is Ireland's leading charity specializing in alleviating the suffering of victims caused by the world's worst nuclear accident at Chernobyl. It was born as a result of receiving a heart-rending message from Belarusian and Ukrainian doctors, which said: "SOS appeal. . . . Help us to get the children out." The CCP exists to provide humanitarian support to the victims still living in the stricken regions of Belarus, Western Russia, and Northern Ukraine.

The Project saw that the human impact of the Chernobyl disaster had to be dealt with. The Project was anxious not only to apply a healing bandage and has, at a very practical level, devised and implemented fourteen aid programs, each of which is designed to tackle a different consequence of the disaster.

The child victims at Chernobyl offer living proof of the impact of such a technological disaster on human society. Their lives are a testimony to its ravages, but they offer hope and inspiration that such a tragedy will not happen anywhere else on this fragile planet.

Get involved by visiting www.adiccp.org.

 2:19 "The Lord . . . him" Quotation from Numbers 16:5.

HOW TO GET RID OF AN EARWORM

An earworm is a song that runs through your head over...and over...and over. It's a tune—even a tune you hate—that gets stuck in your head. Almost everyone gets earworms, but so far the only treatment is to spin up a CD that you like better. Sounds like the way to get rid of ungodly thoughts. Telling yourself "Don't covet that guy's Viper!" doesn't stop you from wanting to steal that sweet car. You can only shove out bad thoughts with something better, like telling God you're grateful for your '90 Corolla.

them change their minds so they can accept the truth. ²⁶And they may wake up and escape from the trap of the devil, who catches them to do what he wants.

THE LAST DAYS

3 Remember this! In the last days there will be many troubles, ²because people will love themselves, love money, brag, and be proud. They will say evil things against others and will not obey their parents or be thankful or be the kind of people God wants. ³They will not love others, will refuse to forgive, will gossip, and will not control themselves. They will

be cruel, will hate what is good, ⁴will turn against their friends, and will do foolish things without thinking. They will be conceited, will love pleasure instead of God, ⁵and will act as if they serve God but will not have his power. Stay away from those people. ⁶Some of them go into homes and get control of silly women who are full of sin and are led by many evil desires. ⁷These women are always learning new teachings, but they are never able to understand the truth fully. ⁸Just as Jannes and Jambres were against Moses, these people are against the truth. Their thinking has been ruined, and they have failed in trying to follow the faith. ⁹But they will not be successful in what they do, because as with Jannes and Jambres, everyone will see that they are foolish.

OBEY THE TEACHINGS

¹⁰But you have followed what I teach, the way I live, my goal, faith, patience, and love. You know I never give up. ¹¹You know how I have been hurt and have suffered, as in Antioch, Iconium, and Lystra. I have suffered, but the Lord saved me from all those troubles. ¹²Everyone who wants to live as God desires, in Christ Jesus, will be hurt. ¹³But people who are evil and cheat others will go from bad to worse. They will fool others, but they will also be fooling themselves.

¹⁴But you should continue following the teachings you learned. You know they are true, because you trust those who taught you. ¹⁵Since you were a child you have known the Holy Scriptures which are able to make you wise. And that wisdom leads to salvation through faith in Christ Jesus. ¹⁶All Scripture is given by God and is useful for teaching, for showing people what is wrong in their lives, for correcting faults, and for teaching how to live right. ¹⁷Using the Scriptures, the person who serves God will be capable, having all that is needed to do every good work.

4 I give you a command in the presence of God and Christ Jesus, the One who will judge the living and the dead, and by his coming and his kingdom: ²Preach the Good News. Be ready at all times, and tell people what they need to do. Tell them when they are wrong. Encourage them with great patience and careful teaching, ³because the time will come when people will not listen to the true teaching but

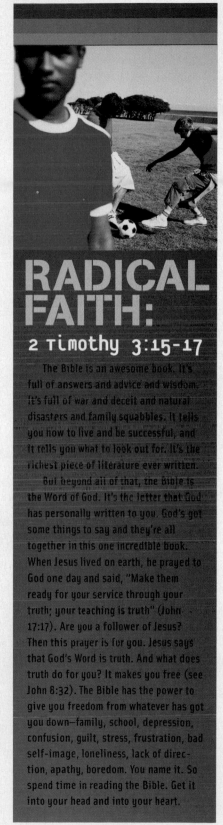

RADICAL FAITH:
2 Timothy 3:15-17

The Bible is an awesome book. It's full of answers and advice and wisdom. It's full of war and deceit and natural disasters and family squabbles. It tells you how to live and be successful, and it tells you what to look out for. It's the richest piece of literature ever written.

But beyond all of that, the Bible is the Word of God. It's the letter that God has personally written to you. God's got some things to say and they're all together in this one incredible book. When Jesus lived on earth, he prayed to God one day and said, "Make them ready for your service through your truth; your teaching is truth" (John 17:17). Are you a follower of Jesus? Then this prayer is for you. Jesus says that God's Word is truth. And what does truth do for you? It makes you free (see John 8:32). The Bible has the power to give you freedom from whatever has got you down—family, school, depression, confusion, guilt, stress, frustration, bad self-image, loneliness, lack of direction, apathy, boredom. You name it. So spend time in reading the Bible. Get it into your head and into your heart.

RANDOM VERSES TO PRAY FOR YOUR LIFE

1. MATTHEW 6:31-34
2. 2 CORINTHIANS 1:3-4
3. JOHN 3:16-18
4. EPHESIANS 6:11-17
5. JAMES 1:19-20
6. COLOSSIANS 3:12-14
7. 1 PETER 5:5
8. MATTHEW 6:14-15
9. ROMANS 15:30
10. ROMANS 12:3

WAYS TO WALK THE WALK

2 Timothy 2:22

WORD: Guys need Christian friends as they follow God.

WALK IT: Take a look at your friends. Who helps you get closer to God? Who drags you away? Get plenty of friends who follow God. Figure out how to influence the others for good.

2 Timothy 3:14

WORD: The Scriptures are true.

WALK IT: Follow the teachings of the Bible today with bold confidence. Don't be ashamed of them. Share them with others, because they are total truth.

will find many more teachers who please them by saying the things they want to hear. [4]They will stop listening to the truth and will begin to follow false stories. [5]But you should control yourself at all times, accept troubles, do the work of telling the Good News, and complete all the duties of a servant of God.

[6]My life is being given as an offering to God, and the time has come for me to leave this life. [7]I have fought the good fight, I have finished the race, I have kept the faith. [8]Now, a crown is being held for me—a crown for being right with God. The Lord, the judge who judges rightly, will give the crown to me on that day[n]—not only to me but to all those who have waited with love for him to come again.

PERSONAL WORDS

[9]Do your best to come to me as soon as you can, [10]because Demas, who loved this world, left me and went to Thessalonica. Crescens went to Galatia, and Titus went to Dalmatia. [11]Luke is the only one still with me. Get Mark and bring him with you when you come, because he can help me in my work here. [12]I sent Tychicus to Ephesus. [13]When I was in Troas, I left my coat there with Carpus. So when you come, bring it to me, along with my books, particularly the ones written on parchment.[n] [14]Alexander the metalworker did many harmful things against me. The Lord will punish him for what he did. [15]You also should be careful that he does not hurt you, because he fought strongly against our teaching.

[16]The first time I defended myself, no one helped me; everyone left me. May they be forgiven. [17]But the Lord stayed with me and gave me strength so I could fully tell the Good News to all those who are not Jews. So I was saved from the lion's mouth. [18]The Lord will save me when anyone tries to hurt me, and he will bring me safely to his heavenly kingdom. Glory forever and ever be the Lord's. Amen.

FINAL GREETINGS

[19]Greet Priscilla and Aquila and the family of Onesiphorus. [20]Erastus stayed in Corinth, and I left Trophimus sick in Miletus. [21]Try as hard as you can to come to me before winter.

Eubulus sends greetings to you. Also Pudens, Linus, Claudia, and all the brothers and sisters in Christ greet you.

[22]The Lord be with your spirit. Grace be with you.

DO'S & DON'TS

- **Do think about your future.**

- **Do get strong and in shape.**

- **Do ask your mom if she needs help.**

- **Do ask your dad how you can help.**

- **Don't settle for any god but God.**

- **Don't be scared about your future.**

- **Don't get stuck on yourself.**

- **Don't be cruel when others can't do what you can.**

4:8 day The day Christ will come to judge all people and take his people to live with him.   **4:13 parchment** A writing paper made from the skins of sheep.

TITUS

TRUTH CAN MAKE EVEN THUGS CHRISTLIKE

Like Timothy, Titus was a traveling companion of Paul. Titus, however, settled down in Crete, an isle of pirates and thugs. He took on a tough job. To help him out with a little advice, Paul wrote a letter of general teachings for the church. In this letter, he talks about the roles of leaders in the church, proper behavior for various groups of people, and finally an ethical program for believers to live in a hostile world in accordance with Jesus' teachings of meekness, obedience, and gentleness. Paul describes in detail how Titus' church should be run in Crete, truths that still tell us how to get along. Pastoring a renegade church was a real challenge, but Paul knew that Titus could handle these guys.

TITUS 2:14

Sometimes people think that God's grace is nothing more than the forgiveness of sins. It would be enough if that's all there was to it—just the forgiveness of every sin in your whole life—even the ones you won't commit for another twenty or thirty years.

But God knows you need more than just a clean slate to become all he wants you to be. You also need a heart that's tender toward him, a mind that can be made to think like his, and a soul that yields its will to the wishes of his Spirit. This verse tells you that he "gave himself for us so he might pay the price to free us . . . and to make us pure people who belong only to him. . . ." You're included.

But gentle and patient to the end, he's also allowed your heart to be tested. He's also given you the power to stand up to temptation. Anything that doesn't agree with God or his Word is temptation. Know his Word so well that you are quick to recognize temptation. When you see it, run.

Your pure heart can feel impure sometimes. If it does, get clean. Ask God's forgiveness and receive it. His forgiveness purifies you.

He's changed your heart forever. Go and live like you believe it.

1 From Paul, a servant of God and an apostle of Jesus Christ. I was sent to help the faith of God's chosen people and to help them know the truth that shows people how to serve God. [2]That faith and that knowledge come from the hope for life forever, which God promised to us before time began. And God cannot lie. [3]At the right time God let the world know about that life through preaching. He trusted me with that work, and I preached by the command of God our Savior.

[4]To Titus, my true child in the faith we share:

Grace and peace from God the Father and Christ Jesus our Savior.

TITUS' WORK IN CRETE

[5]I left you in Crete so you could finish doing the things that still needed to be done and so you could appoint elders in every town, as I directed you. [6]An elder must not be guilty of doing wrong, must have only one wife, and must have believing children. They must not be known as children who are wild and do not cooperate. [7]As God's manager, an elder must not be guilty of doing wrong, being selfish, or becoming angry quickly. He must not drink too much wine, like to fight, or try to get rich by cheating others. [8]An elder must be ready to welcome guests, love what is good, be wise, live right, and be holy and self-controlled. [9]By holding on to the trustworthy word just as we teach it, an elder can help people by using true teaching, and he can show those who are against the true teaching that they are wrong.

[10]There are many people who refuse to cooperate, who talk about worthless things and lead others into the wrong way—mainly those who say all who are not Jews must be circumcised. [11]These people must be stopped, because they are upsetting whole families by teaching things they should not teach, which they do to get rich by cheating people. [12]Even one of their own prophets said, "Cretans are always liars, evil animals, and lazy people who do nothing but eat." [13]The words that prophet said are true. So firmly tell those people they are wrong so they may become strong in the faith, [14]not accepting Jewish false stories and the commands of people who reject the truth. [15]To those who are pure, all things are pure, but to those who are full of sin and do not

believe, nothing is pure. Both their minds and their consciences have been ruined. [16]They say they know God, but their actions show they do not accept him. They are hateful people, they refuse to obey, and they are useless for doing anything good.

FOLLOWING THE TRUE TEACHING

2 But you must tell everyone what to do to follow the true teaching. [2]Teach older men to be self-controlled, serious, wise, strong in faith, in love, and in patience.

[3]In the same way, teach older women to be holy in their behavior, not speaking against others or enslaved to too much wine, but teaching what is good. [4]Then they can teach the young women to love their husbands, to love their children, [5]to be wise and pure, to be good workers at home, to be kind, and to yield to their husbands. Then no one will be able to criticize the teaching God gave us.

[6]In the same way, encourage young men to be wise. [7]In every way be an example of doing good deeds. When you teach, do it with honesty and seriousness. [8]Speak the truth so that you cannot be criticized. Then those who are against you will be ashamed because there is nothing bad to say about us.

[9]Slaves should yield to their own masters at all times, trying to please them and not arguing with them. [10]They should not steal from them but should show their masters they can be fully trusted so that in everything they do they will make the teaching of God our Savior attractive.

[11]That is the way we should live, because God's grace that can save everyone has come. [12]It teaches us not to live against God nor to do the evil things the world wants to do. Instead, that grace teaches us to live now in a wise and right way and in a way that shows we serve God. [13]We should live like that while we wait for our great hope and the coming of the glory of our great God and Savior Jesus Christ. [14]He gave himself for us so he might pay the price to free us from all evil and to make us pure people who belong only to him—people who are always wanting to do good deeds.

[15]Say these things and encourage the people and tell them what is wrong in their lives, with all authority. Do not let anyone treat you as if you were unimportant.

DO'S & DON'TS

- Do pay back people what you owe them.

- Do your own laundry.

- Do take one for the team.

- Do tell your parents what's going on in your head.

- Don't make excuses.

- Don't be afraid to raise your hand.

- Don't rip on people who can't afford cool clothes.

- Don't let anger run your life.

THE RIGHT WAY TO LIVE

3 Remind the believers to yield to the authority of rulers and government leaders, to obey them, to be ready to do good, [2]to speak no evil about anyone, to live in peace, and to be gentle and polite to all people.

[3]In the past we also were foolish. We did not obey, we were wrong, and we were slaves to many things our bodies wanted and enjoyed. We spent our lives doing evil and being jealous. People hated us, and we hated each other. [4]But when the kindness and love of God our Savior was shown, [5]he saved us because of his mercy. It was not because of good deeds we did to be right with him. He saved us through the washing that made us new people through the Holy Spirit. [6]God poured out richly upon us that Holy Spirit through Jesus Christ our Savior. [7]Being made right with God by his grace, we could have the hope of receiving the life that never ends.

[8]This teaching is true, and I want you to be sure the people understand these things. Then those who believe in God will be careful to use their lives for doing good. These things are good and will help everyone.

[9]But stay away from those who have foolish arguments and talk about useless family

RANDOM THINGS TO DO WITH YOUR DAD

1. ASK HIM TO TEACH YOU HOW TO CHANGE A TIRE.

2. GO FISHING.

3. TEACH HIM HOW TO SKATE-BOARD.

4. DO HIS HOBBY FOR AN AFTERNOON.

5. TAKE HIM TO A GUY MOVIE.

6. SIT NEXT TO HIM IN CHURCH.

7. LISTEN TO HIM TELL STORIES ABOUT WHEN HE WAS A KID.

8. WALK OR RUN TOGETHER.

9. BUILD SOMETHING BIG.

10. LEARN HOW TO TIE A TIE.

travel the road

Ephesians 6:12 says that "our fight is not against people on earth but against the rulers and authorities and the powers of this world's darkness, against the spiritual powers of evil in the heavenly world." So when Christians talk about "spiritual warfare," they don't mean bullying people into believing; they mean that we should pray for God's love to shine into a world where Satan has real power. The battle between good and evil is often hottest and most obvious at the forefront of missions—so if you know a missionary, pray for him or her right now.

For more on extreme missions visit www.traveltheroad.com.

histories and argue and quarrel about the law. Those things are worth nothing and will not help anyone. [10]After a first and second warning, avoid someone who causes arguments. [11]You can know that such people are evil and sinful; their own sins prove them wrong.

SOME THINGS TO REMEMBER

[12]When I send Artemas or Tychicus to you, make every effort to come to me at Nicopolis, because I have decided to stay there this winter. [13]Do all you can to help Zenas the lawyer and Apollos on their journey so that they have everything they need. [14]Our people must learn to use their lives for doing good deeds to provide what is necessary so that their lives will not be useless.

[15]All who are with me greet you. Greet those who love us in the faith.

Grace be with you all.

PHILEMON

HOW CHRIST MAKES A DIFFERENCE IN RELATIONSHIPS

The runaway slave Onesimus had become a Christian while staying with Paul, yet after a while Paul knew Onesimus needed to return to his master and make things right. So Paul wrote to Philemon, a sort of reference letter for Onesimus that asked for Philemon's forgiveness and acceptance back into his home and church. Paul never really talks about slavery being good or bad, just how all people should treat each other. (In Galatians 3:26-29 Paul taught that in Christ all people are equal, a principle that Christians later took up as inspiration to abolish slavery in England and the Americas.) Instead of trying to start a revolution to fight the system, Paul works for the moment on changing the people inside the system through brotherly love. Because Onesimus and Philemon were both part of the church, he wanted to demonstrate the love that should or could be shown among God's people.

[1]From Paul, a prisoner of Christ Jesus, and from Timothy, our brother.

To Philemon, our dear friend and worker with us; [2]to Apphia, our sister; to Archippus, a worker with us; and to the church that meets in your home:

[3]Grace and peace to you from God our Father and the Lord Jesus Christ.

PHILEMON'S LOVE AND FAITH

[4]I always thank my God when I mention you in my prayers, [5]because I hear about the love you have for all God's holy people and the faith you have in the Lord Jesus. [6]I pray that the faith you share may make you understand every blessing we have in Christ. [7]I have great joy and comfort, my brother, because the love you have shown to God's people has refreshed them.

PSALM 145:8 "THE LORD IS KIND AND SHOWS MERCY. HE DOES NOT BECOME ANGRY QUICKLY BUT IS FULL OF LOVE."

ACCEPT ONESIMUS AS A BROTHER

[8]So, in Christ, I could be bold and order you to do what is right. [9]But because I love you, I am pleading with you instead. I, Paul, an old man now and also a prisoner for Christ Jesus [10]am pleading with you for my child Onesimus, who became my child while I was in prison. [11]In the past he was useless to you, but now he has become useful for both you and me.

[12]I am sending him back to you, and with him I am sending my own heart. [13]I wanted to keep him with me so that in your place he might help me while I am in prison for the Good News. [14]But I did not want to do anything without asking you first so that any good you do for me will be because you want to do it, not because I forced you. [15]Maybe Onesimus was separated from you for a short time so you could have him back forever— [16]no longer as a slave, but better than a slave, as a loved brother. I love him very much, but you will love him even more, both as a person and as a believer in the Lord.

[17]So if you consider me your partner, welcome Onesimus as you would welcome me. [18]If he has done anything wrong to you or if he owes you anything, charge that to me. [19]I, Paul, am writing this with my own hand. I will pay it back, and I will say nothing about what you owe me for your own life. [20]So, my brother, I ask that you do this for me in the Lord: Refresh my heart in Christ. [21]I write this letter, knowing that you will do what I ask you and even more.

[22]One more thing—prepare a room for me in which to stay, because I hope God will answer your prayers and I will be able to come to you.

FINAL GREETINGS

[23]Epaphras, a prisoner with me for Christ Jesus, sends greetings to you. [24]And also Mark, Aristarchus, Demas, and Luke, workers together with me, send greetings.

[25]The grace of our Lord Jesus Christ be with your spirit.

EXPERTS ANSWER YOUR QUESTIONS

Q. *I know porn can be abusive and gross. But what's so bad about looking at tasteful photos of beautiful women?*

A. You might have good taste, but that isn't the point. You're burning into your brain images of women who aren't your wife-to-be. No real-world woman can compete with the airbrushed perfection of soft porn beauties. But God has something better waiting for you—a unique, genuine, 3-D woman. Wait for that gift.

Q. *What's the difference between pornography and art?*

A. If it's art, you can look at it with your mother.

Q. *I was looking for help with my porn problem. I told another Christian guy, and we wound up surfing together.*

A. AAAAARGH! You're not supposed to get slammed like that. You get thunderous applause for admitting a problem that affects countless guys. Difficult as it is, keep looking for a good accountability partner. You can surf to www.exxit.org or www.pureintimacy.org for starters.

WAYS TO WALK THE WALK

philemon 7

WORD: We should show compassion to others.

WALK IT: Find a concrete way to be kind today. Need ideas? Look around at school. Ask a friend how you can help. Check with your parents to see if you can do an extra chore today.

HEBREWS

jesus is the new and greatest prophet, priest, and king

Every group of people has tags and labels they use to identify themselves as part of their group. For the Jews, their biggest tags were the rituals and rules God had given them back in Old Testament times. The Law, as these rules were called, represented God's agreement with the Jews. The writer of Hebrews (some scholars think it was Paul, some Apollos, some Priscilla—or none of the above) walked back through the whole history of the Jews starting with their earliest and most famous ancestors, Abraham and Moses. Doing this demonstrated a huge point: Jesus was greater than any of their ancestors! He was the new prophet, priest, and king. The writer was trying to convince his Jewish readers that Jesus was indeed the Messiah that all their ancestors had pointed them toward. Maybe the most famous chapter of Hebrews is chapter 11. The writer spells out that "you've got to have faith," telling what it is and how to live it.

GOD SPOKE THROUGH HIS SON

1 In the past God spoke to our ancestors through the prophets many times and in many different ways. [2]But now in these last days God has spoken to us through his Son. God has chosen his Son to own all things, and through him he made the world. [3]The Son reflects the glory of God and shows exactly what God is like. He holds everything together with his powerful word. When the Son made people clean from their sins, he sat down at the right side of God, the Great One in heaven. [4]The Son became much greater than the angels, and God gave him a name that is much greater than theirs.

[5]This is because God never said to any of the angels,

"You are my Son.
    Today I have become your Father."

Psalm 2:1

Nor did God say of any angel,

"I will be his Father,
    and he will be my Son."   *2 Samuel 7:14*

[6]And when God brings his firstborn Son into the world, he says,

"Let all God's angels worship him."[n]

Psalm 97:7

[7]This is what God said about the angels:

"God makes his angels become like winds.
    He makes his servants become like
        flames of fire."   *Psalm 104:4*

[8]But God said this about his Son:

"God, your throne will last forever
    and ever.

You will rule your kingdom with
    fairness.
[9]You love right and hate evil,
    so God has chosen you from among
        your friends;
    he has set you apart with much joy."

Psalm 45:6-7

[10]God also says,

"Lord, in the beginning you made the earth,
    and your hands made the skies.
[11]They will be destroyed, but you will
        remain.
    They will all wear out like clothes.
[12]You will fold them like a coat.
    And, like clothes, you will change them.
But you never change,
    and your life will never end."

Psalm 102:25-27

[13]And God never said this to an angel:

"Sit by me at my right side
    until I put your enemies under your
        control."[n]   *Psalm 110:1*

[14]All the angels are spirits who serve God and are sent to help those who will receive salvation.

OUR SALVATION IS GREAT

2 So we must be more careful to follow what we were taught. Then we will not stray away from the truth. [2]The teaching God spoke through angels was shown to be true, and anyone who did not follow it or obey it received the punishment that was earned. [3]So surely we also will be punished if we ignore this great salvation. The Lord himself first told about this salvation, and it was proven true to us by those who heard him. [4]God also proved it by using wonders, great signs, many kinds of miracles, and by giving people gifts through the Holy Spirit, just as he wanted.

CHRIST BECAME LIKE HUMANS

[5]God did not choose angels to be the rulers of the new world that was coming, which is what we have been talking about. [6]It is written in the Scriptures,

"Why are people important to you?
    Why do you take care of human
        beings?

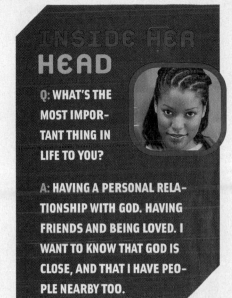

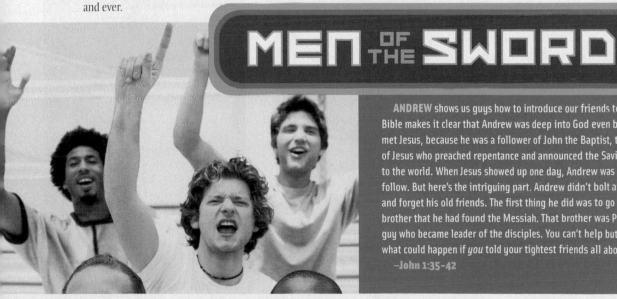

MEN OF THE SWORD

ANDREW shows us guys how to introduce our friends to Jesus. The Bible makes it clear that Andrew was deep into God even before he met Jesus, because he was a follower of John the Baptist, the cousin of Jesus who preached repentance and announced the Savior's arrival to the world. When Jesus showed up one day, Andrew was primed to follow. But here's the intriguing part. Andrew didn't bolt after Jesus and forget his old friends. The first thing he did was to go tell his brother that he had found the Messiah. That brother was Peter, the guy who became leader of the disciples. You can't help but wonder what could happen if *you* told your tightest friends all about Jesus.

—John 1:35-42

 1:6 "Let . . . him." These words are found in Deuteronomy 32:43 in the Septuagint, the Greek version of the Old Testament, and in a Hebrew copy among the Dead Sea Scrolls. 1:13 until . . . control Literally, "until I make your enemies a footstool for your feet."

LOOK COOL
TIPS ON YOURSELF

No guy wants to be told what to wear, or be controlled by what others think. Yet your clothes say loads about you, not just to your peers but to the adults in your life. Your teachers and coaches all watch what you wear and stow an opinion somewhere in the back of their brains. Others from parents to police quickly draw conclusions about who you are by how you skin yourself. It might not be right, but it's a fact. What do your clothes say about who you are as God's guy?

[7]You made them a little lower than the
   angels
   and crowned them with glory and honor.
[8]You put all things under their control."

Psalm 8:4-6

When God put everything under their control, there was nothing left that they did not rule. Still, we do not yet see them ruling over everything. [9]But we see Jesus, who for a short time was made lower than the angels. And now he is wearing a crown of glory and honor because he suffered and died. And by God's grace, he died for everyone.

[10]God is the One who made all things, and all things are for his glory. He wanted to have many children share his glory, so he made the One who leads people to salvation perfect through suffering.

[11]Jesus, who makes people holy, and those who are made holy are from the same family.

So he is not ashamed to call them his brothers and sisters.[n] [12]He says,

"Then, I will tell my fellow Israelites about
   you;
   I will praise you in the public meeting."

Psalm 22:22

[13]He also says,

"I will trust in God." *Isaiah 8:17*

And he also says,

"I am here, and with me are the children
   God has given me." *Isaiah 8:18*

[14]Since these children are people with physical bodies, Jesus himself became like them. He did this so that, by dying, he could destroy the one who has the power of death—the devil—[15]and free those who were like slaves all their lives because of their fear of death. [16]Clearly, it is not angels that Jesus helps, but the people who are from Abraham.[n] [17]For this reason Jesus had to be made like his brothers in every way so he could be their merciful and faithful high priest in service to God. Then Jesus could bring forgiveness for their sins. [18]And now he can help those who are tempted, because he himself suffered and was tempted.

JESUS IS GREATER THAN MOSES

3 So all of you holy brothers and sisters, who were called by God, think about Jesus, who was sent to us and is the high priest of our faith. [2]Jesus was faithful to God as Moses was in God's family. [3]Jesus has more honor than Moses, just as the builder of a house has more honor than the house itself. [4]Every house is built by someone, but the builder of everything is God himself. [5]Moses was faithful in God's family as a servant, and he told what God would say in the future. [6]But Christ is faithful as a Son over God's house. And we are God's house if we keep on being very sure about our great hope.

WE MUST CONTINUE TO FOLLOW GOD

[7]So it is as the Holy Spirit says:

"Today listen to what he says.
[8]Do not be stubborn as in the past
   when you turned against God,
   when you tested God in the desert.
[9]There your ancestors tried me and
   tested me
   and saw the things I did for forty years.
[10]I was angry with them.
   I said, 'They are not loyal to me
   and have not understood my ways.'

✓ COUNT ON IT

HEBREWS 2:18

It's not unusual to hear somebody excuse personal faults by saying, "Well, that's just the way I am"—as if it would be unfair to expect anything better out of him or her. It's true that everybody has flaws and everyone is susceptible to some temptations. Some people have a hard time being nice when things aren't going well for them; some people are tempted to cheat because they're so driven to make a good grade; some people are sucked in by the buzz they get from drinking or drugs. That's the way they are.

But Jesus never said that it was okay to do wrong because you have a weakness. He told people to do the right thing anyway. He wasn't being heartless. He wasn't looking down from some ivory tower, shouting, "You must resist temptation!" He was flesh and blood, just like you. He knew what it was like to be tempted. He isn't leaving you to overcome your weaknesses all by yourself. He's right there with you, giving you the strength to make the right choice. He's saying, "You can do it!" He's God. He's given you the strength to overcome and he knows you can!

2:11 brothers and sisters Although the Greek text says "brothers" here and throughout this book, the writer's words were meant for the entire church, including men and women. **2:16 Abraham** Most respected ancestor of the Jews. Every Jew hoped to see Abraham.

320

[11]I was angry and made a promise,
'They will never enter my rest.' "[n]

Psalm 95:7-11

[12]So brothers and sisters, be careful that none of you has an evil, unbelieving heart that will turn you away from the living God. [13]But encourage each other every day while it is "today."[n] Help each other so none of you will become hardened because sin has tricked you. [14]We all share in Christ if we keep till the end the sure faith we had in the beginning. [15]This is what the Scripture says:

"Today listen to what he says.

Do not be stubborn as in the past
when you turned against God."

Psalm 95:7-8

[16]Who heard God's voice and was against him? It was all those people Moses led out of Egypt. [17]And with whom was God angry for forty years? He was angry with those who sinned, who died in the desert. [18]And to whom was God talking when he promised that they would never enter his rest? He was talking to those who did not obey him. [19]So we see they were not allowed to enter and have God's rest, because they did not believe.

4 Now, since God has left us the promise that we may enter his rest, let us be very careful so none of you will fail to enter.

[2]The Good News was preached to us just as it was to them. But the teaching they heard did not help them, because they heard it but did not accept it with faith. [3]We who have believed are able to enter and have God's rest. As God has said,

"I was angry and made a promise,

'They will never enter my rest.' " *Psalm 95:11*

But God's work was finished from the time he made the world. [4]In the Scriptures he talked about the seventh day of the week: "And on the seventh day God rested from all his works."[n] [5]And again in the Scripture God said, "They will never enter my rest."

[6]It is still true that some people will enter God's rest, but those who first heard the way to be saved did not enter, because they did not obey. [7]So God planned another day, called "today." He spoke about that day through David a long time later in the same Scripture used before:

"Today listen to what he says.

Do not be stubborn." *Psalm 95:7-8*

[8]We know that Joshua[n] did not lead the people into that rest, because God spoke later about another day. [9]This shows that the rest[n] for God's people is still coming. [10]Anyone who enters God's rest will rest from his work as God did. [11]Let us try as hard as we can to enter

RELATIONSHIPS

"All of you must yield to the government rulers. No one rules unless God has given him the power to rule, and no one rules now without that power from God" (Romans 13:1). You've been busted—by a parent, a teacher, a police officer. For stuff like lying, cheating, or stealing. So what do you do with that? When you get caught, God wants you to learn from the experience. He doesn't put authority figures in your life just to catch you being bad. He uses them to steer you toward doing good. But you have to want to go there. Do you?

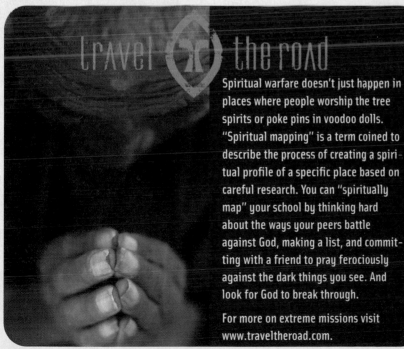

travel the road

Spiritual warfare doesn't just happen in places where people worship the tree spirits or poke pins in voodoo dolls. "Spiritual mapping" is a term coined to describe the process of creating a spiritual profile of a specific place based on careful research. You can "spiritually map" your school by thinking hard about the ways your peers battle against God, making a list, and committing with a friend to pray ferociously against the dark things you see. And look for God to break through.

For more on extreme missions visit www.traveltheroad.com.

 3:11 rest A place of rest God promised to give his people. **3:13 "today"** This word is taken from verse 7. It means that it is important to do these things now. **4:4 "And . . . works."** Quotation from Genesis 2:2. **4:8 Joshua** After Moses died, Joshua became leader of the Jewish people and led them into the land that God promised to give them. **4:9 rest** Literally, "sabbath rest," meaning a sharing in the rest that God began after he created the world.

God's rest so that no one will fail by following the example of those who refused to obey.

[12]God's word is alive and working and is sharper than a double-edged sword. It cuts all the way into us, where the soul and the spirit are joined, to the center of our joints and bones. And it judges the thoughts and feelings in our hearts. [13]Nothing in all the world can be hidden from God. Everything is clear and lies open before him, and to him we must explain the way we have lived.

JESUS IS OUR HIGH PRIEST

[14]Since we have a great high priest, Jesus the Son of God, who has gone into heaven, let us hold on to the faith we have. [15]For our high priest is able to understand our weaknesses. When he lived on earth, he was tempted in every way that we are, but he did not sin. [16]Let us, then, feel very sure that we can come before God's throne where there is grace.

There we can receive mercy and grace to help us when we need it.

5 Every high priest is chosen from among other people. He is given the work of going before God for them to offer gifts and sacrifices for sins. [2]Since he himself is weak, he is able to be gentle with those who do not understand and who are doing wrong things. [3]Because he is weak, the high priest must offer sacrifices for his own sins and also for the sins of the people.

[4]To be a high priest is an honor, but no one chooses himself for this work. He must be called by God as Aaron[n] was. [5]So also Christ did not choose himself to have the honor of being a high priest, but God chose him. God said to him,

"You are my Son.
    Today I have become your Father."

Psalm 2:7

[6]And in another Scripture God says,
"You are a priest forever,
    a priest like Melchizedek."[n]   *Psalm 110:4*

[7]While Jesus lived on earth, he prayed to God and asked God for help. He prayed with loud cries and tears to the One who could save him from death, and his prayer was heard because he trusted God. [8]Even though Jesus was the Son of God, he learned obedience by what he suffered. [9]And because his obedience was perfect, he was able to give eternal salvation to all who obey him. [10]In this way God made Jesus a high priest, a priest like Melchizedek.

WARNING AGAINST FALLING AWAY

[11]We have much to say about this, but it is hard to explain because you are so slow to understand. [12]By now you should be teachers, but you need someone to teach you again the first lessons of God's message. You still need

BIG BROTHERS/BIG SISTERS has been the nation's preeminent youth-service organization for nearly a century. They have a proven success in creating and nurturing relationships between adults and children.

The service is based on volunteers. Big Brothers and Big Sisters are, foremost, friends to children: They share everyday activities, expand horizons, and experience the joy in even the simplest events. Within those little moments lies the big magic that a Big Brother or Big Sister brings to the life of a young person. Today, Big Brothers/Big Sisters serves hundreds of thousands of children in 5,000 communities across the country.

Nobody else is doing the work that Big Brothers/Big Sisters does in exactly the way they do it. That's why America counts on Big Brothers/Big Sisters.

To get involved, visit www.bbbsa.org.

5:4 Aaron Aaron was Moses' brother and the first Jewish high priest.   **5:6 Melchizedek** A priest and king who lived in the time of Abraham. (Read Genesis 14:17–24.)

RADICAL FAITH:
Hebrews 3:13

Most of us feel insecure when we are in a new place, doing new things, or meeting new people. Somehow we forget everything that is good and strong about ourselves. We can only see our weaknesses and think about our failures. You may have a friend who needs some encouragement in this area.

Verse 13 says he may need it every day. That's what being in the body of Christ is all about. Christians are supposed to encourage one another and remind each other that they are children of a loving God—empowered by his strength and covered by his grace. It's your official job as a Christian to encourage your friend. Be there when he needs you and cheer him on. There will come a day when you'll be the one who needs it. Your friend will be happy to return the favor.

the teaching that is like milk. You are not ready for solid food. [13]Anyone who lives on milk is still a baby and knows nothing about right teaching. [14]But solid food is for those who are grown up. They have practiced in order to know the difference between good and evil.

6 So let us go on to grown-up teaching. Let us not go back over the beginning lessons we learned about Christ. We should not again start teaching about faith in God and about turning away from those acts that lead to death. [2]We should not return to the teaching about baptisms,[n] about laying on of hands,[n] about the raising of the dead and eternal judgment. [3]And we will go on to grown-up teaching if God allows.

[4]Some people cannot be brought back again to a changed life. They were once in God's light, and enjoyed heaven's gift, and shared in the Holy Spirit. [5]They found out how good God's word is, and they received the powers of his new world. [6]But they fell away from Christ. It is impossible to bring them back to a changed life again, because they are nailing the Son of God to a cross again and are shaming him in front of others.

[7]Some people are like land that gets plenty of rain. The land produces a good crop for those who work it, and it receives God's blessings. [8]Other people are like land that grows thorns and weeds and is worthless. It is in danger of being cursed by God and will be destroyed by fire.

DO'S & DON'TS

- *Do wear a watch and show up on time.*
- *Do what you promised.*
- *Do empty the dishwasher.*
- *Do pitch in to pick up, dust, and vacuum.*
- *Don't take matters into your own hands.*
- *Don't wish evil on your enemies.*
- *Don't tease girls about their weight.*
- *Don't point and laugh.*

[9]Dear friends, we are saying this to you, but we really expect better things from you that will lead to your salvation. [10]God is fair; he will not forget the work you did and the love you showed for him by helping his people. And he will remember that you are still helping them

WAYS TO WALK THE WALK

Hebrews 2:15

WORD: Jesus has freed us from our fear of death.

WALK IT: Don't be stupid with your life. But when you get scared about where you're headed when you die, remind yourself ten times that you belong to God.

Hebrews 6:10

WORD: God is fair.

WALK IT: Are you bugged by something not going your way? Does it seem the whole world is slamming you? God is fair. He makes things right. Don't complain.

 6:2 **baptisms** The word here may refer to Christian baptism, or it may refer to the Jewish ceremonial washings.   6:2 **laying on of hands** The laying on of hands had many purposes, including the giving of a blessing, power, or authority.

EXPERTS ANSWER YOUR QUESTIONS

Q. *Is it a sin to masturbate?*

A. The Bible doesn't specifically address masturbation. But can it be separated from lust? The Bible forbids that, doesn't it? And besides, getting that kind of solo physical release is unhelpful because it trains you to be selfish about your sexuality.

Q. *Most Christians are way too rigid about sex. It's just fun. I want to do it whenever, wherever, and with who-ever I can.*

A. You're not impressed by what the Bible teaches about purity, but ask yourself this: Do you honestly want your future bride to be someone who thinks that sex is "just fun," and has been with a bunch of guys who think that way too?

Q. *My girlfriend just broke up with me. I really want her back. What should I do?*

A. Give her space. You can't force a girl to like you. Be strong, confident, an even better guy than when she dated you. Get on with life and see if she comes back.

11 We want each of you to go on with the same hard work all your lives so you will surely get what you hope for. 12 We do not want you to become lazy. Be like those who through faith and patience will receive what God has promised.

13 God made a promise to Abraham. And as there is no one greater than God, he used himself when he swore to Abraham, 14 saying, "I will surely bless you and give you many descendants."[n] 15 Abraham waited patiently for this to happen, and he received what God promised.

16 People always use the name of someone greater than themselves when they swear. The oath proves that what they say is true, and this ends all arguing. 17 God wanted to prove that his promise was true to those who would get what he promised. And he wanted them to understand clearly that his purposes never change, so he made an oath. 18 These two things cannot change: God cannot lie when he makes a promise, and he cannot lie when he makes an oath. These things encourage us who came to God for safety. They give us strength to hold on to the hope we have been given. 19 We have this hope as an anchor for the soul, sure and strong. It enters behind the curtain in the Most Holy Place in heaven, 20 where Jesus has gone ahead of us and for us. He has become the high priest forever, a priest like Melchizedek.[n]

THE PRIEST MELCHIZEDEK

7 Melchizedek[n] was the king of Salem and a priest for God Most High. He met Abraham when Abraham was coming back after defeating the kings. When they met, Melchizedek blessed Abraham, 2 and Abraham gave him a tenth of everything he had brought back from the battle. First, Melchizedek's name means "king of goodness," and he is king of Salem, which means "king of peace." 3 No one knows who Melchizedek's father or mother was,[n] where he came from, when he was born, or when he died. Melchizedek is like the Son of God; he continues being a priest forever.

4 You can see how great Melchizedek was. Abraham, the great father, gave him a tenth of everything that he won in battle. 5 Now the law says that those in the tribe of Levi who become priests must collect a tenth from the people—their own people—even though the priests and the people are from the family of Abraham. 6 Melchizedek was not from the tribe of Levi, but he collected a tenth from Abraham. And he blessed Abraham, the man who had God's promises. 7 Now everyone knows that the more important person blesses the less important person. 8 Priests receive a tenth, even though they are only men who live and then die. But Melchizedek, who received a tenth from Abraham, continues living, as the Scripture says. 9 We might even say that Levi, who receives a tenth, also paid it when Abraham paid Melchizedek a tenth. 10 Levi was not yet born, but he was in the body of his ancestor when Melchizedek met Abraham.

11 The people were given the law[n] based on a system of priests from the tribe of Levi, but they could not be made perfect through that system. So there was a need for another priest

TOP TEN WAYS TO HONOR YOUR DAD

1. **LOOK HIM IN THE EYE WHEN HE TALKS.**
2. **OBEY THE FIRST TIME.**
3. **ASK FOR HIS ADVICE.**
4. **DON'T WASTE MONEY.**
5. **LET HIM PICK THE RESTAURANT.**
6. **HUMOR HIM IN THE LITTLE THINGS.**
7. **LAUGH AT HIS JOKES.**
8. **IMAGINE LIFE IN HIS SHOES.**
9. **HELP YOUR MOM WITHOUT BEING TOLD.**
10. **DON'T THREATEN TO PUT HIM IN A REST HOME.**

6:14 "I . . . descendants." Quotation from Genesis 22:17.   6:20; 7:1 Melchizedek A priest and king who lived in the time of Abraham. (Read Genesis 14:17–24.)   7:3 No . . . was Literally, "Melchizedek was without father, without mother, without genealogy."
7:11 The . . . law This refers to the people of Israel who were given the Law of Moses.

NOVEMBER

Elections are held on the Tuesday after the first Monday in November! Vote!

1 How's school? Write a thank-you note to a teacher today.

2

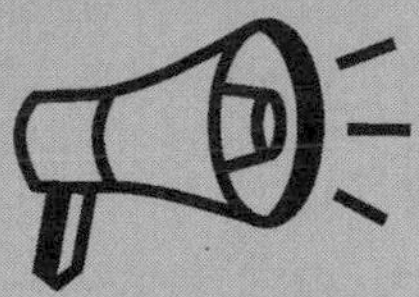

3 Think hard about why you're thankful for your parents—and tell them.

4

5

6 It's Dunce Day. Live it up.

7

8 Take your brother to the mall and buy him a gift, just to be cool.

9 Brush up on your CPR skills.

10

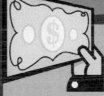

11 Veteran's Day: Honor those vets who protect our country. Go to a cemetery for a multi-gun salute.

12 Pray for a Person of Influence: It's Sammy Sosa's birthday.

13

14 Figure out what you want to get your family members for Christmas—and go shop.

15

16 Don't let it slide by unnoticed: It's National Pizza With The Works Except Anchovies Day.

17

18

19 Get the family car ready for holiday travels by topping off all the fluids.

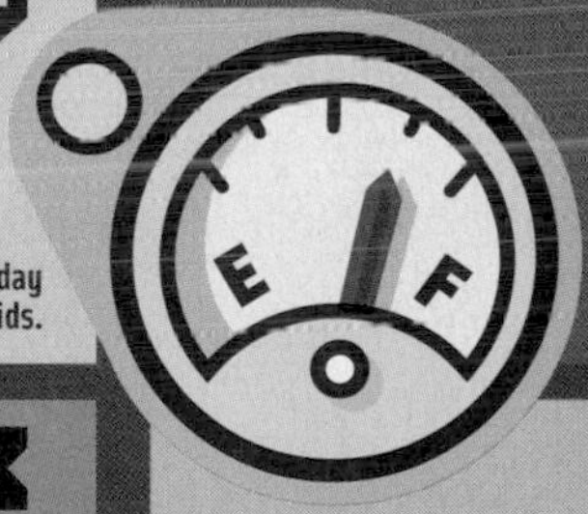

20

21 Read the Book of Acts chapter by chapter this month.

22

23 Visit your grandparents or some elderly folks in a nursing home this weekend.

24 Take your mom out for dinner tonight.

25 Put on a Christian CD today and get psyched up.

26

27 Round up some friends for a party.

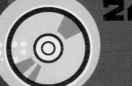

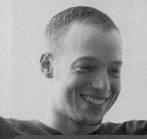

28

29 It's Square Dance Day. If you're square, dance.

30 Pray for a Person of Influence: Ben Stiller turns another year older today.

Thanksgiving is the fourth Thursday in November. Celebrate with the family, and consider going out in the community today to help others who have less than you.

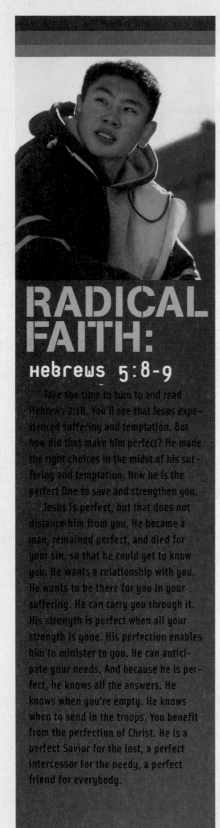

RADICAL FAITH:

Hebrews 5:8-9

Take the time to turn to and read Hebrews 2:18. You'll see that Jesus experienced suffering and temptation. But how did that make him perfect? He made the right choices in the midst of his suffering and temptation. Now he is the perfect One to save and strengthen you.

Jesus is perfect, but that does not distance him from you. He became a man, remained perfect, and died for your sin, so that he could get to know you. He wants a relationship with you. He wants to be there for you in your suffering. He can carry you through it. His strength is perfect when all your strength is gone. His perfection enables him to minister to you. He can anticipate your needs. And because he is perfect, he knows all the answers. He knows when you're empty. He knows when to send in the troops. You benefit from the perfection of Christ. He is a perfect Savior for the lost, a perfect intercessor for the needy, a perfect friend for everybody.

to come, a priest like Melchizedek, not Aaron. [12]And when a different kind of priest comes, the law must be changed, too. [13]We are saying these things about Christ, who belonged to a different tribe. No one from that tribe ever served as a priest at the altar. [14]It is clear that our Lord came from the tribe of Judah, and Moses said nothing about priests belonging to that tribe.

JESUS IS LIKE MELCHIZEDEK

[15]And this becomes even more clear when we see that another priest comes who is like Melchizedek.[n] [16]He was not made a priest by human rules and laws but through the power of his life, which continues forever. [17]It is said about him,

> "You are a priest forever,
> a priest like Melchizedek."
>
> *Psalm 110:4*

[18]The old rule is now set aside, because it was weak and useless. [19]The law of Moses could not make anything perfect. But now a better hope has been given to us, and with this hope we can come near to God. [20]It is important that God did this with an oath. Others became priests without an oath, [21]but Christ became a priest with God's oath. God said:

> "The Lord has made a promise
> and will not change his mind.
> 'You are a priest forever.' "
>
> *Psalm 110:4*

[22]This means that Jesus is the guarantee of a better agreement[n] from God to his people.

[23]When one of the other priests died, he could not continue being a priest. So there were many priests. [24]But because Jesus lives forever, he will never stop serving as priest. [25]So he is able always to save those who come to God through him because he always lives, asking God to help them.

[26]Jesus is the kind of high priest we need. He is holy, sinless, pure, not influenced by sinners, and he is raised above the heavens. [27]He is not like the other priests who had to offer sacrifices every day, first for their own sins, and then for the sins of the people. Christ offered his sacrifice only once and for all time when he offered himself. [28]The law chooses high priests who are people with weaknesses, but the word of God's oath came later than the law. It made God's Son to be the high priest, and that Son has been made perfect forever.

✓COUNT ON IT

HEBREWS 6:17-18

Do you ever doubt God? Maybe you doubt the whole thing—God, the Bible, and all the Jesus stuff. Do you think that everyone who believes must be out to lunch? Maybe you do believe in God, but aren't sure that he's really going to come through for you. Hebrews says that the hope of Christ is right in front of you— "the hope we have been given." You are holding a record of the promises God has made to you. He has told the truth. He has kept his promises. His vows have never changed. Be encouraged to run to him because he never lies. You've got to make up your mind to believe that and you've got to decide that you are going to believe his Word. Until you've made that commitment, you'll constantly struggle with doubt.

The truth of his Word will replace your doubt. John 8:32 says "the truth will make you free." So immerse yourself in these pages. Commit to do more than just slide your eyes over the words. Really concentrate and study the Bible prayerfully. Read about how God has kept his promises. Read about the incredibly deep and powerful love he has for you. Read about his longing to know you and to be with you forever. Get these words into your heart and into your mind. Pretty soon, all your doubts will be replaced with the absolute certainty of God and of his truth.

7:15 **Melchizedek** A priest and king who lived in the time of Abraham. (Read Genesis 14:17–24.)
7:22 **agreement** God gives a contract or agreement to his people. For the Jews, this agreement was the Law of Moses. But now God has given a better agreement to his people through Christ.

INSIDE HER
HEAD

Q: DO YOU DO
BLIND DATES?

A: IT DEPENDS
WHO THINKS WE SHOULD MEET.

JESUS IS OUR HIGH PRIEST

8 Here is the point of what we are saying: We have a high priest who sits on the right side of God's throne in heaven. [2]Our high priest serves in the Most Holy Place, the true place of worship that was made by God, not by humans.

[3]Every high priest has the work of offering gifts and sacrifices to God. So our high priest must also offer something to God. [4]If our high priest were now living on earth, he would not be a priest, because there are already priests here who follow the law by offering gifts to God. [5]The work they do as priests is only a copy and a shadow of what is in heaven. This is why God warned Moses when he was ready to build the Holy Tent: "Be very careful to make everything by the plan I showed you on the mountain."[n] [6]But the priestly work that has been given to Jesus is much greater than the work that was given to the other priests. In the same way, the new agreement that Jesus brought from God to his people is much greater than the old one. And the new agreement is based on promises of better things.

[7]If there had been nothing wrong with the first agreement,[n] there would have been no need for a second agreement. [8]But God found something wrong with his people. He says:

"Look, the time is coming, says the Lord,
    when I will make a new agreement
  with the people of Israel
    and the people of Judah.
[9]It will not be like the agreement
    I made with their ancestors
  when I took them by the hand
    to bring them out of Egypt.

But they broke that agreement,
    and I turned away from
      them, says the Lord.
[10]This is the agreement I will
      make
  with the people of Israel at
      that time, says the Lord.
I will put my teachings in their minds
    and write them on their hearts.
I will be their God,
    and they will be my people.
[11]People will no longer have to teach their
      neighbors and relatives
    to know the Lord,
  because all people will know me,
    from the least to the most important.
[12]I will forgive them for the wicked things
      they did,
    and I will not remember their sins
      anymore."   *Jeremiah 31.31-34*

[13]God called this a new agreement, so he has made the first agreement old. And anything that is old and worn out is ready to disappear.

THE OLD AGREEMENT

9 The first agreement[n] had rules for worship and a man-made place for worship. [2]The Holy Tent was set up for this. The first area in the Tent was called the Holy Place. In it were the lamp and the table with the bread that was made holy for God. [3]Behind the second curtain was a room called the Most Holy Place. [4]In it was a golden altar for burning incense and the Ark covered with gold that held the old agreement. Inside this Ark was a golden jar of manna, Aaron's rod that once grew leaves, and the stone tablets of the old agreement. [5]Above the Ark were the creatures that showed God's glory, whose wings reached over the lid. But we cannot tell everything about these things now.

[6]When everything in the Tent was made ready in this way, the priests went into the first room every day to worship. [7]But only the high priest could go into the second room, and he did that only once a year. He could never enter the inner room without taking blood with him, which he offered to God for himself and for sins the people did without knowing they did them. [8]The Holy Spirit uses this to show that the way into the Most Holy Place was not open while the system of the old Holy Tent was still being used. [9]This is an example for the present time. It shows that the gifts and sacrifices offered cannot make the conscience of the worshiper perfect. [10]These gifts and sacrifices were only about food and drink and special washings. They were rules for the body, to be followed until the time of God's new way.

THE NEW AGREEMENT

[11]But when Christ came as the high priest of the good things we now have, he entered the greater and more perfect tent. It is not made by humans and does not belong to this world. [12]Christ entered the Most Holy Place only

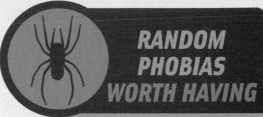

RANDOM PHOBIAS WORTH HAVING

1. **AICHMOPHOBIA—FEAR OF NEEDLES**

2. **ARACHNIPHOBIA—FEAR OF SPIDERS**

3. **MYXOPHOBIA—FEAR OF SLIME**

4. **HELMINTHOPHOBIA—FEAR OF BEING INFESTED WITH WORMS**

5. **NUCLEOMITUPHOBIA—FEAR OF NUCLEAR WEAPONS**

6. **COULROPHOBIA—FEAR OF CLOWNS**

7. **PLACOPHOBIA—FEAR OF TOMBSTONES**

8. **HIPPOPOTOMONSTROSES-QUIPPEDALIOPHOBIA—FEAR OF LONG WORDS**

9. **SESQUIPEDALOPHOBIA—MORE FEAR OF LONG WORDS**

10. **STYGIOPHOBIA—FEAR OF HELL**

8:5 "Be . . . mountain." Quotation from Exodus 25:40.   8:7 **first agreement** The contract God gave the Jewish people when he gave them the Law of Moses.   9:1 **first agreement** The contract God gave the Jewish people when he gave them the Law of Moses.

once—and for all time. He did not take with him the blood of goats and calves. His sacrifice was his own blood, and by it he set us free from sin forever. [13]The blood of goats and bulls and the ashes of a cow are sprinkled on the people who are unclean, and this makes their bodies clean again. [14]How much more is done by the blood of Christ. He offered himself through the eternal Spirit[n] as a perfect sacrifice to God. His blood will make our consciences pure from useless acts so we may serve the living God.

[15]For this reason Christ brings a new agreement from God to his people. Those who are called by God can now receive the blessings he has promised, blessings that will last forever. They can have those things because Christ died so that the people who lived under the first agreement could be set free from sin.

[16]When there is a will,[n] it must be proven that the one who wrote that will is dead. [17]A will means nothing while the person is alive; it can be used only after the person dies. [18]This is why even the first agreement could not begin without blood to show death. [19]First, Moses told all the people every command in the law. Next he took the blood of calves and mixed it with water. Then he used red wool and a branch of the hyssop plant to sprinkle it on the book of the law and on all the people. [20]He said, "This is the blood that begins the Agreement that God commanded you to obey."[n] [21]In the same way, Moses sprinkled the blood on the Holy Tent and over all the things used in worship. [22]The law says that almost everything must be made clean by blood, and sins cannot be forgiven without blood to show death.

CHRIST'S DEATH TAKES AWAY SINS

[23]So the copies of the real things in heaven had to be made clean by animal sacrifices. But the real things in heaven need much better sacrifices. [24]Christ did not go into the Most Holy Place made by humans, which is only a copy of the real one. He went into heaven itself and is there now before God to help us. [25]The high priest enters the Most Holy Place once every year with blood that is not his own. But Christ did not offer himself many times. [26]Then he would have had to suffer many times since the world was made. But Christ came only once and for all time at just the right time to take away all sin by sacrificing himself. [27]Just as everyone must die once and be judged, [28]so Christ was offered as a sacrifice one time to take away the sins of many people. And he will

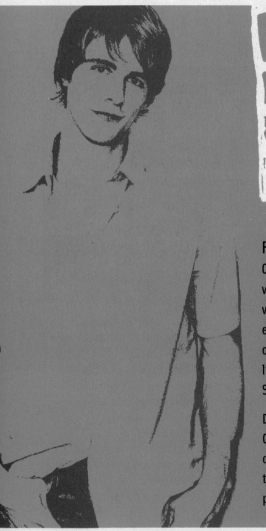

FEED THE CHILDREN is a nonprofit, Christian, charitable organization providing physical, spiritual, educational, vocational/technical, psychological, economic, and medical assistance and other necessary aid to children, families, and persons in need in the United States and internationally.

During their 24-year history, Feed The Children has created and developed one of the world's largest private organizations dedicated to feeding hungry people. Last year, Feed The Children shipped 63 million pounds of food and 24 million pounds of other essentials to children and families in all 50 states and in 51 foreign countries. Feed The Children supplements 484,453 meals a day, worldwide. Their system is fast and efficient. They deliver the food to partner organizations that speed it to over 60,000 other groups who work with the hungry. The food is provided at no cost to the recipients.

For more information, go to www.feedthechildren.org.

 9:14 Spirit This refers to the Holy Spirit, to Christ's own spirit, or to the spiritual and eternal nature of his sacrifice. **9:16 will** A legal document that shows how a person's money and property are to be distributed at the time of death. This is the same word in Greek as "agreement" in verse 15. **9:20 "This . . . obey."** Quotation from Exodus 24:8.

come a second time, not to offer himself for sin, but to bring salvation to those who are waiting for him.

10 The law is only an unclear picture of the good things coming in the future; it is not the real thing. The people under the law offer the same sacrifices every year, but these sacrifices can never make perfect those who come near to worship God. ²If the law could make them perfect, the sacrifices would have already stopped. The worshipers would be made clean, and they would no longer have a sense of sin. ³But these sacrifices remind them of their sins every year, ⁴because it is impossible for the blood of bulls and goats to take away sins.

⁵So when Christ came into the world, he said:

"You do not want sacrifices and offerings,
but you have prepared a body for me.
⁶You do not ask for burnt offerings
and offerings to take away sins.
⁷Then I said, 'Look, I have come.
It is written about me in the book.
God, I have come to do what you want.' "

Psalm 40:6-8

⁸In this Scripture he first said, "You do not want sacrifices and offerings. You do not ask for burnt offerings and offerings to take away sins." (These are all sacrifices that the law commands.) ⁹Then he said, "Look, I have come to do what you want." God ends the first system of sacrifices so he can set up the new system.

¹⁰And because of this, we are made holy through the sacrifice Christ made in his body once and for all time.

¹¹Every day the priests stand and do their religious service, often offering the same sacrifices. Those sacrifices can never take away sins. ¹²But after Christ offered one sacrifice for sins, forever, he sat down at the right side of God. ¹³And now Christ waits there for his enemies to be put under his power. ¹⁴With one sacrifice he made perfect forever those who are being made holy.

¹⁵The Holy Spirit also tells us about this. First he says:

¹⁶"This is the agreement*ⁿ* I will make
with them at that time, says the Lord.
I will put my teachings in their hearts
and write them on their minds."

Jeremiah 31:33

¹⁷Then he says:

"Their sins and the evil things they do —
I will not remember anymore."

Jeremiah 31:34

¹⁸Now when these have been forgiven, there is no more need for a sacrifice for sins.

CONTINUE TO TRUST GOD

¹⁹So, brothers and sisters, we are completely free to enter the Most Holy Place without fear because of the blood of Jesus' death. ²⁰We can enter through a new and living way that Jesus opened for us. It leads through the curtain—Christ's body. ²¹And since we have a

---

WAYS TO WALK THE WALK

Hebrews 6:18

WORD: God cannot lie.

WALK IT: Really believe that what God says is true. Dare to live a radical life because you take God at his word.

Hebrews 10:25

WORD: A guy needs to be part of a church.

WALK IT: If you're not plugged in, start the search this week. If you're already part of a growing group of Christians, take the next step by getting there more often or going deeper by joining a small group.

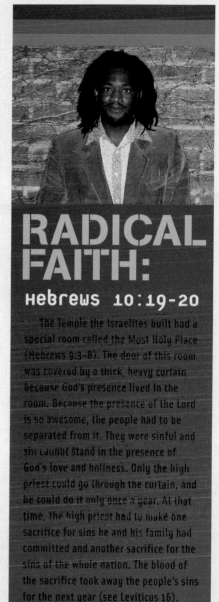

RADICAL FAITH:
Hebrews 10:19-20

The Temple the Israelites built had a special room called the Most Holy Place (Hebrews 9:3-8). The door of this room was covered by a thick, heavy curtain because God's presence lived in the room. Because the presence of the Lord is so awesome, the people had to be separated from it. They were sinful and sin cannot stand in the presence of God's love and holiness. Only the high priest could go through the curtain, and he could do it only once a year. At that time, the high priest had to make one sacrifice for sins he and his family had committed and another sacrifice for the sins of the whole nation. The blood of the sacrifice took away the people's sins for the next year (see Leviticus 16).

At the moment Jesus died on the cross, the curtain in front of the Most Holy Place was torn from top to bottom (see Matthew 27:51). God's presence was made available to everyone! It's like God had been sitting behind a locked door for years and years; and only the high priest had the key. Then Jesus came along and unlocked that door for everyone. His blood takes away the sins of everyone who trusts in him. Now he's the High Priest. Enter God's presence freely and as often as you want!

10:16 **agreement** God gives a contract or agreement to his people. For the Jews, this agreement was the Law of Moses. But now God has given a better agreement to his people through Christ.

great priest over God's house, [22]let us come near to God with a sincere heart and a sure faith, because we have been made free from a guilty conscience, and our bodies have been washed with pure water. [23]Let us hold firmly to the hope that we have confessed, because we can trust God to do what he promised.

[24]Let us think about each other and help each other to show love and do good deeds. [25]You should not stay away from the church meetings, as some are doing, but you should meet together and encourage each other. Do this even more as you see the day[n] coming.

[26]If we decide to go on sinning after we have learned the truth, there is no longer any sacrifice for sins. [27]There is nothing but fear in waiting for the judgment and the terrible fire that will destroy all those who live against God. [28]Anyone who refused to obey the law of Moses was found guilty from the proof given by two or three witnesses. He was put to death without mercy. [29]So what do you think should be done to those who do not respect the Son of God, who look at the blood of the agreement that made them holy as no different from others' blood, who insult the Spirit of God's grace? Surely they should have a much worse punishment. [30]We know that God said, "I will punish those who do wrong; I will repay

travel the road

The Good News about Jesus goes forward when Christians march on their knees. If you're aiming to pray for world missions, grab a copy of *Operation World*. It's a huge collection of information, providing facts and figures about every country in the world. Sure, it's an encyclopedic homework helper. But its real focus is detailing country-by-country prayer concerns, with data set up to help you pray around the world each year. You can catch the online version at www.gmi.org/ow/.

For more on extreme missions visit www.traveltheroad.com.

them."[n] And he also said, "The Lord will judge his people."[n] [31]It is a terrible thing to fall into the hands of the living God.

[32]Remember those days in the past when you first learned the truth. You had a hard struggle with many sufferings, but you continued strong. [33]Sometimes you were hurt and attacked before crowds of people, and sometimes you shared with those who were being treated that way. [34]You helped the prisoners. You even had joy when all that you owned was taken from you, because you knew you had something better and more lasting.

[35]So do not lose the courage you had in the past, which has a great reward. [36]You must hold on, so you can do what God wants and receive what he has promised. [37]For in a very short time,

"The One who is coming will come
    and will not be delayed.
[38]The person who is right with me
    will live by trusting in me.
But if he turns back with fear,
    I will not be pleased with him."

Habakkuk 2:3-4

[39]But we are not those who turn back and are lost. We are people who have faith and are saved.

WHAT IS FAITH?

11 Faith means being sure of the things we hope for and knowing that something is real even if we do not see it. [2]Faith is the reason we remember great people who lived in the past.

 10:25 day The day Christ will come to judge all people and take his people to live with him.   **10:30** "I . . . them." Quotation from Deuteronomy 32:35.   **10:30** "The Lord . . . people." Quotation from Deuteronomy 32:36; Psalm 135:14.

330

[3]It is by faith we understand that the whole world was made by God's command so what we see was made by something that cannot be seen.

[4]It was by faith that Abel offered God a better sacrifice than Cain did. God said he was pleased with the gifts Abel offered and called Abel a good man because of his faith. Abel died, but through his faith he is still speaking.

[5]It was by faith that Enoch was taken to heaven so he would not die. He could not be found, because God had taken him away. Before he was taken, the Scripture says that he was a man who truly pleased God. [6]Without faith no one can please God. Anyone who comes to God must believe that he is real and that he rewards those who truly want to find him.

[7]It was by faith that Noah heard God's warnings about things he could not yet see. He obeyed God and built a large boat to save his family. By his faith, Noah showed that the world was wrong, and he became one of those who are made right with God through faith.

[8]It was by faith Abraham obeyed God's call to go to another place God promised to give him. He left his own country, not knowing where he was to go. [9]It was by faith that he lived like a foreigner in the country God promised to give him. He lived in tents with Isaac and Jacob, who had received that same promise from God. [10]Abraham was waiting for the city[n] that has real foundations—the city planned and built by God.

[11]He was too old to have children, and Sarah could not have children. It was by faith that Abraham was made able to become a father, because he trusted God to do what he had promised. [12]This man was so old he was almost dead, but from him came as many descendants as there are stars in the sky. Like the sand on the seashore, they could not be counted.

[13]All these great people died in faith. They did not get the things that God promised his people, but they saw them coming far in the future and were glad. They said they were like visitors and strangers on earth. [14]When people say such things, they show they are looking for a country that will be their own. [15]If they had been thinking about the country they had left, they could have gone back. [16]But they were waiting for a better country—a heavenly country. So God is

not ashamed to be called their God, because he has prepared a city for them.

[17]It was by faith that Abraham, when God tested him, offered his son Isaac as a sacrifice. God made the promises to Abraham, but Abraham was ready to offer his own son as a sacrifice. [18]God had said, "The descendants I promised you will be from Isaac."[n] [19]Abraham believed that God could raise the dead, and really, it was as if Abraham got Isaac back from death.

[20]It was by faith that Isaac blessed the future of Jacob and Esau. [21]It was by faith that Jacob, as he was dying, blessed each one of Joseph's sons. Then he worshiped as he leaned on the top of his walking stick.

[22]It was by faith that Joseph, while he was dying, spoke about the Israelites leaving Egypt and gave instructions about what to do with his body.

[23]It was by faith that Moses' parents hid him for three months after he was born. They saw that Moses was a beautiful baby, and they were not afraid to disobey the king's order.

[24]It was by faith that Moses, when he grew up, refused to be called the son of the king of Egypt's daughter. [25]He chose to suffer with God's people instead of enjoying sin for a short time. [26]He thought it was better to suffer for the Christ than to have all the treasures of Egypt, because he was looking for God's reward. [27]It was by faith that Moses left Egypt and was not afraid of the king's anger. Moses continued strong as if he could see the God that no one can see. [28]It was by faith that Moses prepared the Passover and spread the blood on the doors so the one who brings death would not kill the firstborn sons of Israel.

[29]It was by faith that the people crossed the Red Sea as if it were dry land. But when the Egyptians tried it, they were drowned.

[30]It was by faith that the walls of Jericho fell after the people had marched around them for seven days.

[31]It was by faith that Rahab, the prostitute, welcomed the spies and was not killed with those who refused to obey God.

[32]Do I need to give more examples? I do not have time to tell you about Gideon, Barak, Samson, Jephthah, David, Samuel, and the prophets. [33]Through their faith they defeated

BIBLE BASICS

Holiness is absolute perfection. Only God is holy. He has never sinned, never made a mistake, never done anything wrong. God demands that people be holy also. That's a problem, because it's impossible. The only option is for us to ask Jesus to be our Savior and claim his reputation as our own. That way, God looks at Jesus' perfect record and sees us as his flawless people instead of the sinful messes we are. Holiness is also a lifestyle that says, "Anything that I do or say will honor Christ."

kingdoms. They did what was right, received God's promises, and shut the mouths of lions. [34]They stopped great fires and were saved from being killed with swords. They were weak, and yet were made strong. They were powerful in battle and defeated other armies. [35]Women received their dead relatives raised back to life. Others

11:10 **city** The spiritual "city" where God's people live with him. Also called "the heavenly Jerusalem." (See Hebrews 12:22.) 11:18 "**The descendants . . . Isaac.**" Quotation from Genesis 21:12.

HOW TO DATE A SUPERMODEL

Miss Teen America might not sit next to you in school, but you've still got a shot at the world's most beautiful women. And it isn't about how they look on the outside. Yeah, you've heard that beauty is more than skin-deep. Sure, you know that beauty is in the eye of the beholder. But there's more to it than that. You've got to know how to spot the real lookers. Proverbs 31:30 says it straight: "Charm can fool you, and beauty can trick you, but a woman who respects the Lord should be praised." When you set your heart on a girl who knows God well, you get beauty that blazes from the inside... beauty that comes from a girl respecting herself as God's temple.

were tortured and refused to accept their freedom so they could be raised from the dead to a better life. [36]Some were laughed at and beaten. Others were put in chains and thrown into prison. [37]They were stoned to death, they were cut in half, and they were killed with swords. Some wore the skins of sheep and goats. They were poor, abused, and treated badly. [38]The world was not good enough for them! They wandered in deserts and mountains, living in caves and holes in the earth.

[39]All these people are known for their faith, but none of them received what God had promised. [40]God planned to give us something better so that they would be made perfect, but only together with us.

FOLLOW JESUS' EXAMPLE

12 We have around us many people whose lives tell us what faith means. So let us run the race that is before us and never give up. We should remove from our lives anything that would get in the way and the sin that so easily holds us back. [2]Let us look only to Jesus, the One who began our faith and who makes it perfect. He suffered death on the cross. But he accepted the shame as if it were nothing because of the joy that God put before him. And now he is sitting at the right side of God's throne. [3]Think about Jesus' example. He held on while wicked people were doing evil things to him. So do not get tired and stop trying.

GOD IS LIKE A FATHER

[4]You are struggling against sin, but your struggles have not yet caused you to be killed. [5]You have forgotten the encouraging words that call you his children:

"My child, don't think the Lord's discipline
is worth nothing,
and don't stop trying when he corrects
you.
[6]The Lord disciplines those he loves,
and he punishes everyone he accepts as
his child."   *Proverbs 3:11-12*

[7]So hold on through your sufferings, because they are like a father's discipline. God is treating you as children. All children are disciplined by their fathers. [8]If you are never disciplined (and every child must be disciplined), you are not true children. [9]We have all had fathers here on earth who disciplined us, and we respected them. So it is even more important that we accept discipline from the Father of our spirits so we will have life. [10]Our fathers on earth disciplined us for a short time in the way they thought was best. But God disciplines us to help us, so we can become holy as he is. [11]We do not enjoy being disciplined. It is painful, but later, after we have learned from it, we have peace, because we start living in the right way.

BE CAREFUL HOW YOU LIVE

[12]You have become weak, so make yourselves strong again. [13]Live in the right way so that you will be saved and your weakness will not cause you to be lost.

[14]Try to live in peace with all people, and try to live free from sin. Anyone whose life is

> ## LUKE 19:40 "BUT JESUS ANSWERED, 'I TELL YOU, IF MY FOLLOWERS DIDN'T SAY THESE THINGS, THEN THE STONES WOULD CRY OUT.'"

not holy will never see the Lord. [15]Be careful that no one fails to receive God's grace and begins to cause trouble among you. A person like that can ruin many of you. [16]Be careful that no one takes part in sexual sin or is like Esau and never thinks about God. As the oldest son, Esau would have received everything from his father, but he sold all that for a single meal. [17]You remember that after Esau did this, he wanted to get his father's blessing, but his father refused. Esau could find no way to change what he had done, even though he wanted the blessing so much that he cried.

[18]You have not come to a mountain that can be touched and that is burning with fire. You have not come to darkness, sadness, and storms. [19]You have not come to the noise of a trumpet or to the sound of a voice like the one the people of Israel heard and begged not to hear another word. [20]They did not want to hear the command: "If anything, even an animal, touches the mountain, it must be put to death with stones."[n] [21]What they saw was so terrible that Moses said, "I am shaking with fear."[n]

[22]But you have come to Mount Zion,[n] to the city of the living God, the heavenly Jerusalem. You have come to thousands of angels gathered together with joy. [23]You have come to the meeting of God's firstborn[n] children whose names are written in heaven. You have come to God, the judge of all people, and to the spirits of good people who have been made perfect. [24]You have

 12:20 "If . . . stones." Quotation from Exodus 19:12–13.   **12:21** "I . . . fear." Quotation from Deuteronomy 9:19.   **12:22 Mount Zion** Another name for Jerusalem, here meaning the spiritual city of God's people.
12:23 firstborn The first son born in a Jewish family was given the most important place in the family and received special blessings. All of God's children are like that.

come to Jesus, the One who brought the new agreement from God to his people, and you have come to the sprinkled blood[n] that has a better message than the blood of Abel.[n]

25So be careful and do not refuse to listen when God speaks. Others refused to listen to him when he warned them on earth, and they did not escape. So it will be worse for us if we refuse to listen to God who warns us from heaven. 26When he spoke before, his voice shook the earth, but now he has promised, "Once again I will shake not only the earth but also the heavens."[n] 27The words "once again" clearly show us that everything that was made—things that can be shaken—will be destroyed. Only the things that cannot be shaken will remain.

28So let us be thankful, because we have a kingdom that cannot be shaken. We should worship God in a way that pleases him with respect and fear, 29because our God is like a fire that burns things up.

13 Keep on loving each other as brothers and sisters. 2Remember to welcome strangers, because some who have done this have welcomed angels without knowing it. 3Remember those who are in prison as if you were in prison with them. Remember those who are suffering as if you were suffering with them.

4Marriage should be honored by everyone, and husband and wife should keep their marriage pure. God will judge as guilty those who take part in sexual sins. 5Keep your lives free from the love of money, and be satisfied with what you have. God has said,

"I will never leave you;
    I will never forget you."   *Deuteronomy 31:6*
6So we can be sure when we say,

"I will not be afraid, because the Lord is
    my helper.
People can't do anything to me."
                                    Psalm 118:6

7Remember your leaders who taught God's message to you. Remember how they lived and died, and copy their faith. 8Jesus Christ is the same yesterday, today, and forever.

9Do not let all kinds of strange teachings lead you into the wrong way. Your hearts should be strengthened by God's grace, not by obeying rules about foods, which do not help those who obey them.

10We have a sacrifice, but the priests who serve in the Holy Tent cannot eat from it. 11The high priest carries the blood of animals into the Most Holy Place where he offers this blood for sins. But the bodies of the animals are burned outside the camp. 12So Jesus also suffered outside the city to make his people holy with his own blood. 13So let us go to Jesus outside the camp, holding on as he did when we are abused.

14Here on earth we do not have a city that lasts forever, but we are looking for the city that we will have in the future. 15So through Jesus let us always offer to God our sacrifice of praise, coming from lips that speak his name. 16Do not forget to do good to others, and share with them, because such sacrifices please God.

17Obey your leaders and act under their authority. They are watching over you, because they are responsible for your souls. Obey them so that they will do this work with joy, not sadness. It will not help you to make their work hard.

18Pray for us. We are sure that we have a clear conscience, because we always want to do the right thing. 19I especially beg you to pray so that God will send me back to you soon.

20-21I pray that the God of peace will give you every good thing you need so you can do what he wants. God raised from the dead our Lord Jesus, the Great Shepherd of the sheep, because of the blood of his death. His blood began the eternal agreement that God made with his people. I pray that God will do in us what pleases him, through Jesus Christ, and to him be glory forever and ever. Amen.

22My brothers and sisters, I beg you to listen patiently to this message I have written to encourage you, because it is not very long. 23I want you to know that our brother Timothy has been let out of prison. If he arrives soon, we will both come to see you.

24Greet all your leaders and all of God's people. Those from Italy send greetings to you.

25Grace be with you all.

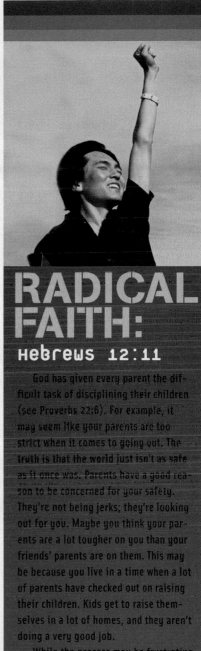

RADICAL FAITH:
Hebrews 12:11

God has given every parent the difficult task of disciplining their children (see Proverbs 22:6). For example, it may seem like your parents are too strict when it comes to going out. The truth is that the world just isn't as safe as it once was. Parents have a good reason to be concerned for your safety. They're not being jerks; they're looking out for you. Maybe you think your parents are a lot tougher on you than your friends' parents are on them. This may be because you live in a time when a lot of parents have checked out on raising their children. Kids get to raise themselves in a lot of homes, and they aren't doing a very good job.

While the process may be frustrating and hard at times, be thankful that you have parents who love you and want to do what God has called them to do. Believe it or not, when you look back on these years, you will thank your parents for caring so much about you. Try to learn from their correction. More freedom is always given to those who become responsible. Begin to apply these lessons and see what happens!

12:24 **sprinkled blood** The blood of Jesus' death.   12:24 **Abel** The son of Adam and Eve, who was killed by his brother Cain (Genesis 4:8).   12:26 **"Once . . . heavens."** Quotation from Haggai 2:6, 21.

JAMES

HOW TO LIVE OUT THE CHRISTIAN FAITH EVERY DAY

All through his writings Paul hammers home the fact that we get right with God through faith in Jesus—not by what we do. James, however, teaches us to look at faith from a different angle. He's all for having the right beliefs. But he's all about *doing* something to prove that faith! The beliefs we confess with our words should match the way we act. James goes so far as to say that if our actions don't match our faith, then our faith is worthless. James reminds us that we are playing with holy fire when we say we believe. We can't be superficial about our beliefs, and when we say we believe we make a promise that changes everything we do. What is religion? Religion is taking care of orphans and widows and keeping ourselves pure from the world's influences. What is faith without action? Nothing! So put your money where your mouth is. Just do it.

1 From James, a servant of God and of the Lord Jesus Christ.

To all of God's people who are scattered everywhere in the world:

Greetings.

FAITH AND WISDOM

²My brothers and sisters," when you have many kinds of troubles, you should be full of joy, ³because you know that these troubles test your faith, and this will give you patience. ⁴Let your patience show itself perfectly in what you do. Then you will be perfect and complete and will have everything you need. ⁵But if any of you needs wisdom, you should ask God for it. He is generous and enjoys giving to all people, so he will give you wisdom. ⁶But when you ask God, you must believe and not doubt. Anyone who doubts is like a wave in the sea, blown up and down by the wind. ⁷⁻⁸Such doubters are thinking two different things at the same time, and they cannot decide about anything they do. They should not think they will receive anything from the Lord.

TRUE RICHES

⁹Believers who are poor should be proud, because God has made them spiritually rich. ¹⁰Those who are rich should be proud, because God has shown them that they are spiritually poor. The rich will die like a wild flower in the grass. ¹¹The sun rises with burning heat and dries up the plants. The flower falls off, and its beauty is gone. In the same way the rich will die while they are still taking care of business.

TEMPTATION IS NOT FROM GOD

¹²When people are tempted and still continue strong, they should be happy. After they have proved their faith, God will reward them with life forever. God promised this to all those who love him. ¹³When people are tempted, they should not say, "God is tempting me." Evil cannot tempt God, and God himself does not tempt anyone. ¹⁴But people are tempted when their own evil desire leads them away and traps them. ¹⁵This desire leads to sin, and then the sin grows and brings death.

¹⁶My dear brothers and sisters, do not be fooled about this. ¹⁷Every good action and every perfect gift is from God. These good gifts come down from the Creator of the sun, moon, and stars, who does not change like their shifting shadows. ¹⁸God decided to give us life through the word of truth so we might be the most important of all the things he made.

LISTENING AND OBEYING

¹⁹My dear brothers and sisters, always be willing to listen and slow to speak. Do not become angry easily, ²⁰because anger will not help you live the right kind of life God wants. ²¹So put out of your life every evil thing and every kind of wrong. Then in gentleness accept God's teaching that is planted in your hearts, which can save you.

²²Do what God's teaching says; when you only listen and do nothing, you are fooling yourselves. ²³Those who hear God's teaching and do nothing are like people who look at themselves in a mirror. ²⁴They see their faces and then go away and quickly forget what they looked like. ²⁵But the truly happy people are those who carefully study God's perfect law that makes people free,

MEN OF THE SWORD

TIMOTHY was a one-of-a-kind friend and advocate for the Good News. Timothy's mother and grandmother taught him the Scriptures when he was little, but the apostle Paul likely played a large role in his belief in Jesus, calling Timothy his son in the faith. Timothy often traveled with Paul, but when Paul was unable to travel he sent Timothy—and that lets us glimpse Timothy's true greatness. Paul promised the Philippians he would send Timothy, saying, "I have no one else like Timothy, who truly cares for you. Other people are interested only in their own lives, not in the work of Jesus Christ." Paul and Timothy were so close that six New Testament letters list both men as authors (2 Corinthians, Philippians, Colossians, 1 and 2 Thessalonians, and Philemon), and two of the most practical books in the New Testament are letters from Paul guiding Timothy in his job as a young pastor.

—1 and 2 Timothy, Philippians 2:20–21

 1:2 brothers and sisters Although the Greek text says "brothers" here and throughout this book, James's words were meant for the entire church, including men and women.

JAMES 2:5

Maybe you'll find a lot of money, or stumble onto a fortune, or marry into royalty. Most people spend all of their lives trying to build a kingdom or to win one. They haven't heard the news that we're already heirs to a kingdom—the eternal kingdom of God—the one that doesn't rot, or fade away, or go broke.

Where are you spending your time? Building a kingdom on earth, or building the kingdom of heaven. Think for a moment. Do you know your grandfather's name? Easy? How about your great-grandfather's name? Harder, but okay. Now, what's your great-great-grandfather's name? Stumped? It's the sad truth. In about three or four generations, no one will remember your name either. Oh, it'll be written down somewhere, but you'll be long gone. Your earthly kingdom won't matter anymore. If you're a Christian, you'll be with Jesus, sharing in the kingdom he has for you. There, you'll matter forever.

and they continue to study it. They do not forget what they heard, but they obey what God's teaching says. Those who do this will be made happy.

THE TRUE WAY TO WORSHIP GOD

26People who think they are religious but say things they should not say are just fooling themselves. Their "religion" is worth nothing. 27Religion that God accepts as pure and without fault is this: caring for orphans or widows who need help, and keeping yourself free from the world's evil influence.

LOVE ALL PEOPLE

2 My dear brothers and sisters, as believers in our glorious Lord Jesus Christ, never think some people are more important than others. 2Suppose someone comes into your church meeting wearing nice clothes and a gold ring. At the same time a poor person comes in wearing old, dirty clothes. 3You show special attention to the one wearing nice clothes and say, "Please, sit here in this good seat." But you say to the poor person, "Stand over there," or, "Sit on the floor by my feet." 4What are you doing? You are making some people more important than others, and with evil thoughts you are deciding that one person is better.

5Listen, my dear brothers and sisters! God chose the poor in the world to be rich with faith and to receive the kingdom God promised to those who love him. 6But you show no respect to the poor. The rich are always trying to control your lives. They are the ones who take you to court. 7And they are the ones who speak against Jesus, who owns you.

8This royal law is found in the Scriptures: "Love your neighbor as you love yourself."[n] If you obey this law, you are doing right. 9But if you treat one person as being more important than another, you are sinning. You are guilty of breaking God's law. 10A person who follows all of God's law but fails to obey even one command is guilty of breaking all the commands in that law. 11The same God who said, "You must not be guilty of adultery,"[n] also said, "You must not murder anyone."[n] So if you do not take part in adultery but you murder someone, you are guilty of breaking all of God's law. 12In everything you say and do, remember that you will

RANDOM THINGS TO DO OUTSIDE

1. SLEEP.
2. READ.
3. WATCH TV.
4. CLIP YOUR TOENAILS.
5. BUILD A SAND CASTLE.
6. STUDY.
7. PLAY WITH YOUR OLD ACTION FIGURES.
8. COOK.
9. THROW DARTS.
10. PLAY MONOPOLY.

be judged by the law that makes people free. 13So you must show mercy to others, or God will not show mercy to you when he judges you. But the person who shows mercy can stand without fear at the judgment.

FAITH AND GOOD WORKS

14My brothers and sisters, if people say they have faith, but do nothing, their faith is worth nothing. Can faith like that save them? 15A brother or sister in Christ might need clothes or food. 16If you say to that person, "God be with you! I hope you stay warm and get plenty to eat," but you do not give what that person needs, your words are worth nothing. 17In the same way, faith that is alone—that does nothing—is dead.

18Someone might say, "You have faith, but I have deeds." Show me your faith without doing anything, and I will show you my faith by what I do. 19You believe there is one God. Good! But the demons believe that, too, and they tremble with fear.

20You foolish person! Must you be shown that faith that does nothing is worth nothing?

2:8 "Love . . . yourself." Quotation from Leviticus 19:18.   2:11 "You . . . adultery." Quotation from Exodus 20:14 and Deuteronomy 5:18.   2:11 "You . . . anyone." Quotation from Exodus 20:13 and Deuteronomy 5:17.

WAYS TO WALK THE WALK

James 1:2-3

WORD: If you face trials with joy, you'll discover patience.

WALK IT: What is stressing you out right now? Find three things about that ugly situation that you can be thankful for. Tell them to someone who knows you're suffering, and help them see how God is helping you through.

James 1:15

WORD: Sin grows and brings death.

WALK IT: You're probably not a mass murderer. But what about "little" sins in your life? Make a list. Be bold and work one by one to quit those sins before they grow huge.

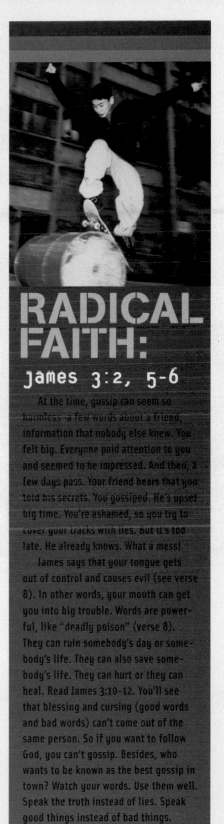

RADICAL FAITH:

James 3:2, 5-6

At the time, gossip can seem so harmless—a few words about a friend, information that nobody else knew. You felt big. Everyone paid attention to you and seemed to be impressed. And then, a few days pass. Your friend hears that you told his secrets. You gossiped. He's upset big time. You're ashamed, so you try to cover your tracks with lies. But it's too late. He already knows. What a mess!

James says that your tongue gets out of control and causes evil (see verse 8). In other words, your mouth can get you into big trouble. Words are powerful, like "deadly poison" (verse 8). They can ruin somebody's day or somebody's life. They can also save somebody's life. They can hurt or they can heal. Read James 3:10-12. You'll see that blessing and cursing (good words and bad words) can't come out of the same person. So if you want to follow God, you can't gossip. Besides, who wants to be known as the best gossip in town? Watch your words. Use them well. Speak the truth instead of lies. Speak good things instead of bad things.

[21] Abraham, our ancestor, was made right with God by what he did when he offered his son Isaac on the altar. [22] So you see that Abraham's faith and the things he did worked together. His faith was made perfect by what he did. [23] This shows the full meaning of the Scripture that says: "Abraham believed God, and God accepted Abraham's faith, and that faith made him right with God."[n] And Abraham was called God's friend.[n] [24] So you see that people are made right with God by what they do, not by faith only.

[25] Another example is Rahab, a prostitute, who was made right with God by something she did. She welcomed the spies into her home and helped them escape by a different road.

[26] Just as a person's body that does not have a spirit is dead, so faith that does nothing is dead!

CONTROLLING THE THINGS WE SAY

3 My brothers and sisters, not many of you should become teachers, because you know that we who teach will be judged more strictly. [2] We all make many mistakes. If people never said anything wrong, they would be perfect and able to control their entire selves, too. [3] When we put bits into the mouths of horses to make them obey us, we can control their whole bodies. [4] Also a ship is very big, and it is pushed by strong winds. But a very small rudder controls that big ship, making it go wherever the pilot wants. [5] It is the same with the tongue. It is a small part of the body, but it brags about great things.

A big forest fire can be started with only a little flame. [6] And the tongue is like a fire. It is a whole world of evil among the parts of our bodies. The tongue spreads its evil through the whole body. The tongue is set on fire by hell, and it starts a fire that influences all of life. [7] People can tame every kind of wild animal, bird, reptile, and fish, and they have tamed them, [8] but no one can tame the tongue. It is wild and evil and full of deadly poison. [9] We use our tongues to praise our Lord and Father, but then we curse people, whom God made like himself. [10] Praises and curses come from the same mouth! My brothers and sisters, this should not happen. [11] Do good and bad water flow from the same spring? [12] My brothers and sisters, can a fig tree make olives, or can a grapevine make figs? No! And a well full of salty water cannot give good water.

TRUE WISDOM

[13] Are there those among you who are truly wise and understanding? Then they should show it by living right and doing good things with a gentleness that comes from wisdom. [14] But if you are selfish and have bitter jealousy in your hearts, do not brag. Your bragging is a lie that hides the truth. [15] That kind of

2:23 "Abraham . . . God." Quotation from Genesis 15:6.   **2:23 God's friend** These words about Abraham are found in 2 Chronicles 20:7 and Isaiah 41:8.

337

GET OUT THERE

GRAFFITI HURTS is a grassroots community education program developed by Keep America Beautiful, Inc. The Graffiti Hurts Program is dedicated to raising awareness about the harmful effects of graffiti vandalism on communities and how it can be stopped without confrontation. At the heart of the Graffiti Hurts Program are four goals: educate citizens about the importance of graffiti prevention and abatement; provide local municipalities with a platform for delivering graffiti prevention messages; utilize local organizations and Keep America Beautiful affiliates to provide opportunities to give back through community service; and create healthier, safer, and more livable community environments. The Graffiti Hurts Program also helps communities initiate local graffiti prevention activities and educate youth and adults about the impact of graffiti vandalism.

To get a kit telling how you can help, visit www.graffitihurts.org.

"wisdom" does not come from God but from the world. It is not spiritual; it is from the devil. [16]Where jealousy and selfishness are, there will be confusion and every kind of evil. [17]But the wisdom that comes from God is first of all pure, then peaceful, gentle, and easy to please. This wisdom is always ready to help those who are troubled and to do good for others. It is always fair and honest. [18]People who work for peace in a peaceful way plant a good crop of right-living.

GIVE YOURSELVES TO GOD

4 Do you know where your fights and arguments come from? They come from the selfish desires that war within you. [2]You want things, but you do not have them. So you are ready to kill and are jealous of other people, but you still cannot get what you want. So you argue and fight. You do not get what you want, because you do not ask God. [3]Or when you ask, you do not receive because the reason you ask is wrong. You want things so you can use them for your own pleasures.

[4]So, you are not loyal to God! You should know that loving the world is the same as hating God. Anyone who wants to be a friend of the world becomes God's enemy. [5]Do you think the Scripture means nothing that says, "The Spirit that God made to live in us wants us for himself alone"?[n] [6]But God gives us even more grace, as the Scripture says,

"God is against the proud,
   but he gives grace to the humble."

Proverbs 3:34

[7]So give yourselves completely to God. Stand against the devil, and the devil will run from you. [8]Come near to God, and God will come near to you. You sinners, clean sin out of your lives. You who are trying to follow God and the world at the same time, make your thinking pure. [9]Be sad, cry, and weep! Change your laughter into crying and your joy into sadness. [10]Don't be too proud in the Lord's presence, and he will make you great.

YOU ARE NOT THE JUDGE

[11]Brothers and sisters, do not tell evil lies about each other. If you speak against your fellow believers or judge them, you are judging and speaking against the law they follow. And when you are judging the law, you are no longer a follower of the law. You have become a

4:5 **"The Spirit . . . alone"** These words may be from Exodus 20:5.

LOOK COOL

TIPS ON YOURSELF

One of a guy's best friends is an iron. No, not a nine iron. The hot kind that stomps wrinkles out of your clothes. Knowing how to iron will both shock your mother and save your coolness when your clothes exit the dryer looking worse than when they went in. Ironing most guy stuff is simple. Five tips: 1) Read the clothing label and set the iron for the right temperature—cotton gets hot, silk and wool get medium, and fabrics not found in nature get a cool iron. 2) Try a little steam on stubborn wrinkles, but too much leaves your clothes feeling soggy. 3) Move the iron around to spare your clothes a meltdown. 4) Unplug the iron when you're done. 5) Like in life, practice first on something you don't mind wrecking.

judge. ¹²God is the only Lawmaker and Judge. He is the only One who can save and destroy. So it is not right for you to judge your neighbor.

LET GOD PLAN YOUR LIFE

¹³Some of you say, "Today or tomorrow we will go to some city. We will stay there a year, do business, and make money." ¹⁴But you do not know what will happen tomorrow! Your life is like a mist. You can see it for a short time, but then it goes away. ¹⁵So you should say, "If the Lord wants, we will live and do this or that." ¹⁶But now you are proud and you brag. All of this bragging is wrong. ¹⁷Anyone who knows the right thing to do, but does not do it, is sinning.

A WARNING TO THE RICH

5 You rich people, listen! Cry and be very sad because of the troubles that are coming to you. ²Your riches have rotted, and your clothes have been eaten by moths. ³Your gold and silver have rusted, and that rust will be a proof that you were wrong. It will eat your bodies like fire. You saved your treasure for the last days. ⁴The pay you did not give the workers who mowed your fields cries out against you, and the cries of the workers have been heard by the Lord All-Powerful. ⁵Your life on earth was full of rich living and pleasing yourselves with everything you wanted. You made yourselves fat, like an animal ready to be killed. ⁶You have judged guilty and then murdered innocent people, who were not against you.

BE PATIENT

⁷Brothers and sisters, be patient until the Lord comes again. A farmer patiently waits for his valuable crop to grow from the earth and for it to receive the autumn and spring rains. ⁸You, too, must be patient. Do not give up hope, because the Lord is coming soon. ⁹Brothers and sisters, do not complain against each other or you will be judged guilty. And the Judge is ready to come! ¹⁰Brothers and sisters, follow the example of the prophets who spoke for the Lord. They suffered many hard things, but they were patient. ¹¹We say they are happy because they did not give up. You have heard about Job's patience, and you know the Lord's purpose for him in the end. You know the Lord is full of mercy and is kind.

BE CAREFUL WHAT YOU SAY

¹²My brothers and sisters, above all, do not use an oath when you make a promise. Don't use the name of heaven, earth, or anything else to prove what you say. When you mean yes, say only yes, and when you mean no, say only no so you will not be judged guilty.

THE POWER OF PRAYER

¹³Anyone who is having troubles should pray. Anyone who is happy should sing praises. ¹⁴Anyone who is sick should call the church's elders. They should pray for and pour oil on the person*[n]* in the name of the Lord. ¹⁵And the prayer that is said with faith will make the sick person well; the Lord will heal that person. And if the person has sinned, the sins will be forgiven. ¹⁶Confess your sins to each other

✓COUNT ON IT

JAMES 4:6, 10

The way up with God, the way toward honor, is to be humble. God is looking for young men and women who will be genuinely humble. He doesn't want a fake humility that says, "I'm really a nothing," but is conceited and arrogant on the inside. Some people think that humility means really believing that you are a nothing. No way. *True humility is knowing and recognizing who God is and who you are.* God says that, through Christ, you can do all things (see Philippians 4:13). He rejoices and sings because of you (see Zephaniah 3:17). You are not a nothing!

Being humble does not mean acting like a doormat. It means that you know for certain that you are strong through Jesus Christ. It means that you are secure enough to serve others and not care what people think. You're strong enough to be seen with people who aren't popular. You're secure enough to really care about someone who often gets left out and you show it.

Pride and arrogance have no place with God. Jesus measures strength not by how cool you act, but by your humility. Look at John 13:3-17. You'll see a great picture of Jesus' humility. Working on humility in your life will help you be more like him. And that's what it's all about.

5:14 pour oil on the person Oil was used in the name of the Lord as a sign that the person was now set apart for God's special attention and care.

MUSIC REVIEWS

JARS OF CLAY: WHO WE ARE INSTEAD

The first all-new release from Jars of Clay in nearly two years, *Who We Are Instead* features the band's signature acoustic pop sound with distinct flavors of folk, blues, country, and gospel sprinkled throughout the album. The scheme works. The tracks flow together to create an interconnected vibe that's smooth, mellow, and relaxing. Though the style of *Who We Are Instead* doesn't clone any previous Jars CD, Dan Haseltine's vocals remain unmistakable—and hardcore followers will note that the songwriting and presentation dig as deep as ever. This bold and creative CD might be Jar's most impressive effort to date.

WHY IT ROCKS: CHOICE TUNES THAT SHOW HOW FAITH CAN BE BOTH SIMPLE AND PROFOUND.

and pray for each other so God can heal you. When a believing person prays, great things happen. [17]Elijah was a human being just like us. He prayed that it would not rain, and it did not rain on the land for three and a half years! [18]Then Elijah prayed again, and the rain came down from the sky, and the land produced crops again.

SAVING A SOUL

[19]My brothers and sisters, if one of you wanders away from the truth, and someone helps that person come back, [20]remember this: Anyone who brings a sinner back from the wrong way will save that sinner's soul from death and will cause many sins to be forgiven.

WAYS TO WALK THE WALK

James 3:17

WORD: Real wisdom is pure and peaceful.

WALK IT: Do the five-second rule when you speak. Before you split your lips, count to five. Ask yourself: Do you have something better to say? Is there a kinder way to say it? What's your motivation? Should you not say anything at all?

James 5:12

WORD: We should not swear with oaths.

WALK IT: Go one full week without saying "I swear!" Then see if you can go longer.

1 PETER

ORDER AND SUPPORT FOR CHRISTIANS FACING HOSTILITY

Peter's name literally means "the Rock." And over time Peter became super-solid in his trust in God. When he was arrested and threatened with the death sentence, Peter still told the courts, "We must obey God, not human authority" (Acts 5:29). When it came to doing what the people in charge said to do, Peter knew it was his duty as a Christian to obey. But when those people forced him to choose between following a command of Jesus or doing what he was told, he stuck with Jesus and didn't back down from anybody. In this letter, Peter wrote to Christians being persecuted by powers outside the church. Being faced with torture and death for what they believed, they needed hope to keep the faith strong. Peter came through with encouragement and perspective, reminding them that even when they faced physical danger, their souls would be safe. Peter also taught women how to be women and men how to be men, telling each to honor the other. Just when Christians felt their world was in disarray, Peter provided order and support in their time of need.

RELATIONSHIPS

"Forgive that person because the Lord forgave you" (Colossians 3:13). Someone hurts you, and your first reaction is to take a swing. Even if you need to take steps to address the problem, God's requirement doesn't change: Forgive! When you forgive, you refuse to hold a wrong against a person. God commands us to forgive. Over and over. Even the same people who do the same sin over and over. It sounds weird until you realize it's exactly what God has done for us.

1 From Peter, an apostle of Jesus Christ. To God's chosen people who are away from their homes and are scattered all around the countries of Pontus, Galatia, Cappadocia, Asia, and Bithynia. [2]God planned long ago to choose you by making you his holy people, which is the Spirit's work. God wanted you to obey him and to be made clean by the blood of the death of Jesus Christ.

Grace and peace be yours more and more.

WE HAVE A LIVING HOPE

[3]Praise be to the God and Father of our Lord Jesus Christ. In God's great mercy he has caused us to be born again into a living hope, because Jesus Christ rose from the dead. [4]Now we hope for the blessings God has for his children. These blessings, which cannot be destroyed or be spoiled or lose their beauty, are kept in heaven for you. [5]God's power protects you through your faith until salvation is shown to you at the end of time. [6]This makes you very happy, even though now for a short time different kinds of troubles may make you sad. [7]These troubles come to prove that your faith is pure. This purity of faith is worth more than gold, which can be proved to be pure by fire but will ruin. But the purity of your faith will bring you praise and glory and honor when Jesus Christ is shown to you. [8]You have not seen Christ, but still you love him. You cannot see him now, but you believe in him. So you are filled with a joy that cannot be explained, a joy full of glory. [9]And you are receiving the goal of your faith—the salvation of your souls.

[10]The prophets searched carefully and tried to learn about this salvation. They prophesied about the grace that was coming to you. [11]The Spirit of Christ was in the prophets, telling in advance about the sufferings of Christ and about the glory that would follow those sufferings. The prophets tried to learn about what the Spirit was showing them, when those things would happen, and what the world would be like at that time. [12]It was shown them that their service was not for themselves but for you, when they told about the truths you have now heard. Those who preached the Good News to you told you those things with the help of the Holy Spirit who was sent from heaven—things into which angels desire to look.

A CALL TO HOLY LIVING

[13]So prepare your minds for service and have self-control. All your hope should be for the gift of grace that will be yours when Jesus Christ is shown to you. [14]Now that you are obedient children of God do not live as you did in the past. You did not understand, so you did the evil things you wanted. [15]But be holy in all you do, just as God, the One who called you, is holy. [16]It is written in the Scriptures: "You must be holy, because I am holy."[n]

[17]You pray to God and call him Father, and he judges each person's work equally. So while you are here on earth, you should live with respect for God. [18]You know that in the past you were living in a worthless way, a way passed down from the people who lived before you. But you were saved from that useless life. You were bought, not with something that ruins like gold or silver, [19]but with the precious blood of Christ, who was like a pure and perfect lamb. [20]Christ was chosen before the world was made, but he was shown to the world in these last times for your sake. [21]Through Christ you believe in God, who raised Christ from the dead and gave him glory. So your faith and your hope are in God.

[22]Now that you have made your souls pure by obeying the truth, you can have true love for your Christian brothers and sisters.[n] So love each other deeply with all your heart. [23]You have been born again, and this new life did not come from something that dies, but

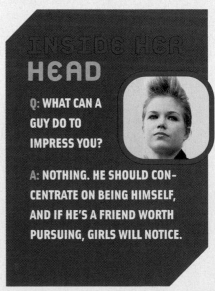

INSIDE HER HEAD

Q: WHAT CAN A GUY DO TO IMPRESS YOU?

A: NOTHING. HE SHOULD CONCENTRATE ON BEING HIMSELF, AND IF HE'S A FRIEND WORTH PURSUING, GIRLS WILL NOTICE.

1:16 "You must be . . . holy." Quotation from Leviticus 11:45; 19:2; 20:7.   1:22 brothers and sisters Although the Greek text says "brothers" here and throughout this book, Peter's words were meant for the entire church, including men and women.

from something that cannot die. You were born again through God's living message that continues forever. ²⁴The Scripture says,

"All people are like the grass,
and all their glory is like the flowers of the field.
The grass dies and the flowers fall,
²⁵   but the word of the Lord will live forever."

Isaiah 40:6-8

And this is the word that was preached to you.

JESUS IS THE LIVING STONE

2 So then, rid yourselves of all evil, all lying, hypocrisy, jealousy, and evil speech. ²As newborn babies want milk, you should want the pure and simple teaching. By it you can grow up and be saved, ³because you have already examined and seen how good the Lord is.

⁴Come to the Lord Jesus, the "stone"ⁿ that lives. The people of the world did not want this stone, but he was the stone God chose, and he was precious. ⁵You also are like living stones, so let yourselves be used to build a spiritual temple—to be holy priests who offer spiritual sacrifices to God. He will accept those sacrifices through Jesus Christ. ⁶The Scripture says:

"I will put a stone in the ground in Jerusalem.
Everything will be built on this important and precious rock.
Anyone who trusts in him
will never be disappointed." *Isaiah 28:16*

⁷This stone is worth much to you who believe. But to the people who do not believe,

"the stone that the builders rejected
has become the cornerstone."

Psalm 118:22

⁸Also, he is

"a stone that causes people to stumble,
a rock that makes them fall." *Isaiah 8:14*

They stumble because they do not obey what God says, which is what God planned to happen to them.

⁹But you are a chosen people, royal priests, a holy nation, a people for God's own possession. You were chosen to tell about the wonderful acts of God, who called you out of darkness into his wonderful light. ¹⁰At one time you were not a people, but now you are God's people. In the past you had never received mercy, but now you have received God's mercy.

RADICAL FAITH:
1 peter 3:3-4

Think this is just for girls? Peter says that beauty has more to do with the inside than the outside. But even for guys, God cares about your heart and your attitude more than looks or physique. If you ask him, God will reveal to you the "looks" he created inside you. He created you for a purpose. Your life gives him real pleasure. He thinks you're impressive. You're valuable to him. Can you see what he sees?

If you feel like God created you for something more than Mr. Universe contests, then begin to search and pray for his purpose. Ask him to show you your strengths and help you use them. The most attractive people in the world are the ones who are confident about their purpose. They know what their life is supposed to be about, and they are hard at work to fulfill God's plan for them.

If you can't stand the way you look, then ask God to show you what he has in mind for you. Ask him to make you into a guy who looks into the mirror and likes the reflection no matter what it looks like. Focus on the awesome things he has built into you. Ask him to replace your insecurity with his purpose.

WAYS TO WALK THE WALK

1 peter 1:15

WORD: God wants you to obey him.

WALK IT: Find one passage of Scripture today that's hard to follow through on and do it. Obey God.

1 peter 1:18

WORD: You have been saved from a pointless life.

WALK IT: Spend fifteen minutes a day praying about God's purpose for your life until you feel sure you have found it.

1 peter 3:15

WORD: Respect for God should occupy every corner of your mind.

WALK IT: God knows what you think—not just what you say and do. How do you think about him? Focus today on being thankful that he rules your life.

2:4 "stone" The most important stone in God's spiritual temple or house (his people).

COUNT ON IT

1 PETER 3:12

You've tried praying. But you've wondered if it does any good. You feel like you're just launching words into dead air and thinking they'll magically make a difference. Why talk when no one's listening?

The guy who wrote this particular book knew the feeling. Rough-and-tumble Peter, sidekick to a mysterious traveling man from Nazareth named Jesus, saw everything he dreamed about blow up in his face as his Lord was led away to die. This is what he gave up a good-paying job for? Ridicule? Embarrassment? Maybe even the end of his life? "Why me, God?" he must have cried into the heavens.

But God *was* doing something more loving than an easy answer would have done. He was letting Peter do some searching, to prove to himself that his faith was in God and not in his blessings.

Your ceiling may seem dark and silent. But God *is* watching. And listening. And waiting. And working. And one day, you'll wonder why you thought he wasn't.

LIVE FOR GOD

[11] Dear friends, you are like foreigners and strangers in this world. I beg you to avoid the evil things your bodies want to do that fight against your soul. [12] People who do not believe are living all around you and might say that you are doing wrong. Live such good lives that they will see the good things you do and will give glory to God on the day when Christ comes again.

YIELD TO EVERY HUMAN AUTHORITY

[13] For the Lord's sake, yield to the people who have authority in this world: the king, who is the highest authority, [14] and the leaders who are sent by him to punish those who do wrong and to praise those who do right. [15] It is God's desire that by doing good you should stop foolish people from saying stupid things about you. [16] Live as free people, but do not use your freedom as an excuse to do evil. Live as servants of God. [17] Show respect for all people: Love the brothers and sisters of God's family, respect God, honor the king.

JOHN 20:31 "THESE ARE WRITTEN SO THAT YOU MAY BELIEVE THAT JESUS IS THE CHRIST, THE SON OF GOD."

FOLLOW CHRIST'S EXAMPLE

[18] Slaves, yield to the authority of your masters with all respect, not only those who are good and kind, but also those who are dishonest. [19] A person might have to suffer even when it is unfair, but if he thinks of God and stands the pain, God is pleased. [20] If you are beaten for doing wrong, there is no reason to praise you for being patient in your punishment. But if you suffer for doing good, and you are patient, then God is pleased. [21] This is what you were called to do, because Christ suffered for you and gave you an example to follow. So you should do as he did.
[22] "He had never sinned,
    and he had never lied."   *Isaiah 53:9*
[23] People insulted Christ, but he did not insult them in return. Christ suffered, but he did not threaten. He let God, the One who judges rightly, take care of him. [24] Christ carried our sins in his body on the cross so we would stop

HOW TO STRIKE IT RICH

When you were a little guy maybe you tried to make a pile of money selling gift wrap, but even your mom wasn't buying. Right now maybe you can't wait to be old enough to buy a winning Powerball ticket or to sign a multimillion dollar bonus to play major league ball. And when you're an adult you might try to make your millions on insider trading or by sinking your every penny into a frozen yogurt stand. Here's a slow yet sure formula to amass cash: Save 10 percent of every dollar you ever make. Bank at least 25 percent of every raise you earn. Slam into your savings account 50 percent of whatever unexpected cash comes your way. God doesn't want you infatuated with money. But he wants you to be a wise money manager.

living for sin and start living for what is right. And you are healed because of his wounds. [25] You were like sheep that wandered away, but

1 peter 5:6

WORD: If you want to get to the top, you need to lower yourself.

WALK IT: God blesses you when you submit to him. Check your life to discover one way you're not letting God rule your life. Tell him that he truly is the boss of you, and live that way.

1 peter 5:7

WORD: You don't have to be a tough guy—especially not in front of God.

WALK IT: God cares about everything that causes you pain. Talk to him about the things that rip you apart. Tell him about the good things too.

BIBLE BASICS

The **Second Coming** is what Christians call the end-of-the-world event when Jesus will return to earth and call his followers up into heaven. Some believe he will reign on earth for a thousand years, then create a new heaven and new earth. People disagree over whether Jesus will come and take his followers before the horrible events of the end times or after them. All we know for sure is that God is faithful to those he loves. Either way, he will take care of us.

now you have come back to the Shepherd and Protector of your souls.

WIVES AND HUSBANDS

3 In the same way, you wives should yield to your husbands. Then, if some husbands do not obey God's teaching, they will be persuaded to believe without anyone's saying a word to them. They will be persuaded by the way their wives live. ²Your husbands will see the pure lives you live with your respect for God. ³It is not fancy hair, gold jewelry, or fine clothes that should make you beautiful. ⁴No, your beauty should come from within you—the beauty of a gentle and quiet spirit that will never be destroyed and is very precious to God. ⁵In this same way the holy women who lived long ago and followed God made themselves beautiful, yielding to their own husbands. ⁶Sarah obeyed Abraham, her husband, and called him her master. And you women are true children of Sarah if you always do what is right and are not afraid.

⁷In the same way, you husbands should live with your wives in an understanding way, since they are weaker than you. But show them respect, because God gives them the same blessing he gives you—the grace that gives true life. Do this so that nothing will stop your prayers.

SUFFERING FOR DOING RIGHT

⁸Finally, all of you should be in agreement, understanding each other, loving each other as family, being kind and humble. ⁹Do not do wrong to repay a wrong, and do not insult to repay an insult. But repay with a blessing, because you yourselves were called to do this so that you might receive a blessing. ¹⁰The Scripture says,

"A person must do these things
  to enjoy life and have many happy days.
He must not say evil things,
  and he must not tell lies.
¹¹He must stop doing evil and do good.
  He must look for peace and work for it.
¹²The Lord sees the good people
  and listens to their prayers.
But the Lord is against
  those who do evil." *Psalm 34:12-16*

¹³If you are trying hard to do good, no one can really hurt you. ¹⁴But even if you suffer for doing right, you are blessed.

"Don't be afraid of what they fear;
  do not dread those things." *Isaiah 8:12-13*

¹⁵But respect Christ as the holy Lord in your hearts. Always be ready to answer everyone who asks you to explain about the hope you have, ¹⁶but answer in a gentle way and with respect. Keep a clear conscience so that those who speak evil of your good life in Christ will be

made ashamed. ¹⁷It is better to suffer for doing good than for doing wrong if that is what God wants. ¹⁸Christ himself suffered for sins once. He was not guilty, but he suffered for those who are guilty to bring you to God. His body was killed, but he was made alive in the spirit.

[19]And in the spirit he went and preached to the spirits in prison [20]who refused to obey God long ago in the time of Noah. God was waiting patiently for them while Noah was building the boat. Only a few people—eight in all—were saved by water. [21]And that water is like baptism that now saves you—not the washing of dirt from the body, but the promise made to God from a good conscience. And this is because Jesus Christ was raised from the dead. [22]Now Jesus has gone into heaven and is at God's right side ruling over angels, authorities, and powers.

CHANGE YOUR LIVES

4 Since Christ suffered while he was in his body, strengthen yourselves with the same way of thinking Christ had. The person who has suffered in the body is finished with

received a gift to use to serve others. Be good servants of God's various gifts of grace. [11]Anyone who speaks should speak words from God. Anyone who serves should serve with the strength God gives so that in everything God will be praised through Jesus Christ. Power and glory belong to him forever and ever. Amen.

SUFFERING AS A CHRISTIAN

[12]My friends, do not be surprised at the terrible trouble which now comes to test you. Do not think that something strange is happening to you. [13]But be happy that you are sharing in Christ's sufferings so that you will be happy and full of joy when Christ comes again in glory. [14]When people insult you because you follow Christ, you are blessed, because the glorious Spirit, the Spirit of God, is with you. [15]Do not

forced. That is how God wants it. Do it because you are happy to serve, not because you want money. [3]Do not be like a ruler over people you are responsible for, but be good examples to them. [4]Then when Christ, the Chief Shepherd, comes, you will get a glorious crown that will never lose its beauty.

[5]In the same way, younger people should be willing to be under older people. And all of you should be very humble with each other.

"God is against the proud,
　but he gives grace to the humble."

Proverbs 3:34

[6]Be humble under God's powerful hand so he will lift you up when the right time comes. [7]Give all your worries to him, because he cares about you.

MORE THAN 150 THOUSAND FIRST-YEAR COLLEGE STUDENTS DROP OUT OF SCHOOL WITH ALCOHOL- OR DRUG-RELATED PROBLEMS.

–LOS ANGELES TIMES

sin. [2]Strengthen yourselves so that you will live here on earth doing what God wants, not the evil things people want. [3]In the past you wasted too much time doing what nonbelievers enjoy. You were guilty of sexual sins, evil desires, drunkenness, wild and drunken parties, and hateful idol worship. [4]Nonbelievers think it is strange that you do not do the many wild and wasteful things they do, so they insult you. [5]But they will have to explain this to God, who is ready to judge the living and the dead. [6]For this reason the Good News was preached to those who are now dead. Even though they were judged like all people, the Good News was preached to them so they could live in the spirit as God lives.

USE GOD'S GIFTS WISELY

[7]The time is near when all things will end. So think clearly and control yourselves so you will be able to pray. [8]Most importantly, love each other deeply, because love will cause many sins to be forgiven. [9]Open your homes to each other, without complaining. [10]Each of you has

suffer for murder, theft, or any other crime, nor because you trouble other people. [16]But if you suffer because you are a Christian, do not be ashamed. Praise God because you wear that name. [17]It is time for judgment to begin with God's family. And if that judging begins with us, what will happen to those people who do not obey the Good News of God?

[18]"If it is very hard for a good person
　　to be saved,
　the wicked person and the sinner
　　will surely be lost!"[n]

[19]So those who suffer as God wants should trust their souls to the faithful Creator as they continue to do what is right.

THE FLOCK OF GOD

5 Now I have something to say to the elders in your group. I also am an elder. I have seen Christ's sufferings, and I will share in the glory that will be shown to us. I beg you to [2]shepherd God's flock, for whom you are responsible. Watch over them because you want to, not because you are

[8]Control yourselves and be careful! The devil, your enemy, goes around like a roaring lion looking for someone to eat. [9]Refuse to give in to him, by standing strong in your faith. You know that your Christian family all over the world is having the same kinds of suffering.

[10]And after you suffer for a short time, God, who gives all grace, will make everything right. He will make you strong and support you and keep you from falling. He called you to share in his glory in Christ, a glory that will continue forever. [11]All power is his forever and ever. Amen.

FINAL GREETINGS

[12]I wrote this short letter with the help of Silas, who I know is a faithful brother in Christ. I wrote to encourage you and to tell you that this is the true grace of God. Stand strong in that grace.

[13]The church in Babylon, who was chosen like you, sends you greetings. Mark, my son in Christ, also greets you. [14]Give each other a kiss of Christian love when you meet.

Peace to all of you who are in Christ.

4:18 **"If . . . lost!"** Quotation from Proverbs 11:31 in the Septuagint, the Greek version of the Old Testament.

issues

MEDIA

JUST LIKE YOU CHOOSE to do your body good or harm every time you eat, you choose to help or hurt your faith every time you spin a CD, tune the radio, or flip on the TV. The wrong choices in media can be just as detrimental to your spiritual health as artery-clogging foods can be to your physical health. So how often do you think about making media choices that help you pull close to God? A lot of stuff gives you the spiritual equivalent of a beer belly.

Other ungood stuff makes you a heart attack waiting to happen. But the best stuff helps you build spiritual muscle. Head to www.pluggedinonline.com for reviews of all kinds of media, and www.screenit.com for detailed movie reviews.

2 PETER

DEFENSE AGAINST FALSE TEACHERS

In his second letter, Peter warned Christians to watch out for traitors inside the church. These persecutors took the form of false teachers who taught doctrines that would thrash faith rather than build it up. This letter reads a lot like an episode of *America's Most Wanted*, one of those shows that hunts down criminals at large. Peter writes that these false teachers profess to know Christ, but they live immoral lives and take advantage of others (2:13-14). For these Christians, even though their bodies weren't in physical danger, their souls were in a risky position. In this short little letter, Peter offers something of a "last testament" of his teachings and beliefs against the confusion of false teaching.

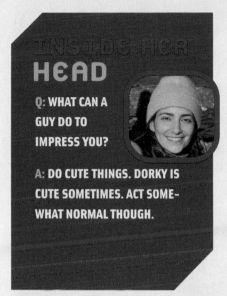
1 From Simon Peter, a servant and apostle of Jesus Christ.

To you who have received a faith as valuable as ours, because our God and Savior Jesus Christ does what is right. ²Grace and peace be given to you more and more, because you truly know God and Jesus our Lord.

GOD HAS GIVEN US BLESSINGS

³Jesus has the power of God, by which he has given us everything we need to live and to serve God. We have these things because we know him. Jesus called us by his glory and goodness. ⁴Through these he gave us the very great and precious promises. With these gifts you can share in being like God, and the world will not ruin you with its evil desires.

⁵Because you have these blessings, do your best to add these things to your lives: to your faith, add goodness; and to your goodness, add knowledge; ⁶and to your knowledge, add self-control; and to your self-control, add patience; and to your patience, add service for God; ⁷and to your service for God, add kindness for your brothers and sisters in Christ; and to this kindness, add love. ⁸If all these things are in you

PSALM 91:11 "HE HAS PUT HIS ANGELS IN CHARGE OF YOU TO WATCH OVER YOU WHEREVER YOU GO."

and are growing, they will help you to be useful and productive in your knowledge of our Lord Jesus Christ. ⁹But anyone who does not have these things cannot see clearly. He is blind and has forgotten that he was made clean from his past sins.

¹⁰My brothers and sisters,ⁿ try hard to be certain that you really are called and chosen by God. If you do all these things, you will never fall. ¹¹And you will be given a very great welcome into the eternal kingdom of our Lord and Savior Jesus Christ.

¹²You know these things, and you are very strong in the truth, but I will always help you remember them. ¹³I think it is right for me to help you remember as long as I am in this body. ¹⁴I know I must soon leave this body, as our Lord Jesus Christ has shown me. ¹⁵I will try my best so that you may be able to remember these things even after I am gone.

WE SAW CHRIST'S GLORY

¹⁶When we told you about the powerful coming of our Lord Jesus Christ, we were not telling just smart stories that someone invented. But we saw the greatness of Jesus with our own eyes. ¹⁷Jesus heard the voice of God, the Greatest Glory, when he received honor and glory from God the Father. The voice said, "This is my Son, whom I love, and I am very pleased with him." ¹⁸We heard that voice from heaven while we were with Jesus on the holy mountain.

¹⁹This makes us more sure about the message the prophets gave. It is good for you to follow closely what they said as you would follow a light shining in a dark place, until the day begins and the morning star rises in your hearts. ²⁰Most of all, you must understand this: No prophecy in the Scriptures ever comes from the prophet's own interpretation. ²¹No prophecy ever came from what a person wanted to say, but people led by the Holy Spirit spoke words from God.

FALSE TEACHERS

2 There used to be false prophets among God's people, just as you will have some false teachers in your group. They will secretly teach things that are wrong—teachings that will cause people to be lost. They will even refuse to accept the Master, Jesus, who bought their freedom. So they will bring quick ruin on

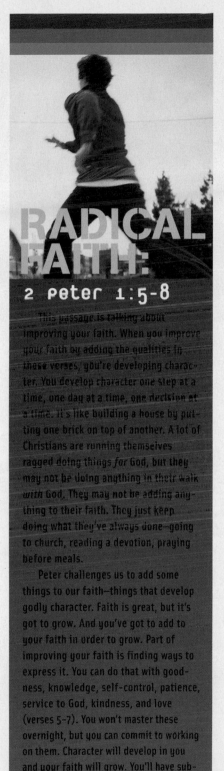

RADICAL FAITH:
2 Peter 1:5-8

This passage is talking about improving your faith. When you improve your faith by adding the qualities in these verses, you're developing character. You develop character one step at a time, one day at a time, one decision at a time. It's like building a house by putting one brick on top of another. A lot of Christians are running themselves ragged doing things *for* God, but they may not be doing anything in their walk *with* God. They may not be adding anything to their faith. They just keep doing what they've always done—going to church, reading a devotion, praying before meals.

Peter challenges us to add some things to our faith—things that develop godly character. Faith is great, but it's got to grow. And you've got to add to your faith in order to grow. Part of improving your faith is finding ways to express it. You can do that with goodness, knowledge, self-control, patience, service to God, kindness, and love (verses 5-7). You won't master these overnight, but you can commit to working on them. Character will develop in you and your faith will grow. You'll have substance and credibility in your life. You'll begin to look more and more like Jesus.

 1:10 brothers and sisters Although the Greek text reads "brothers" here and throughout this book, Peter's words were meant for the entire church, including men and women.

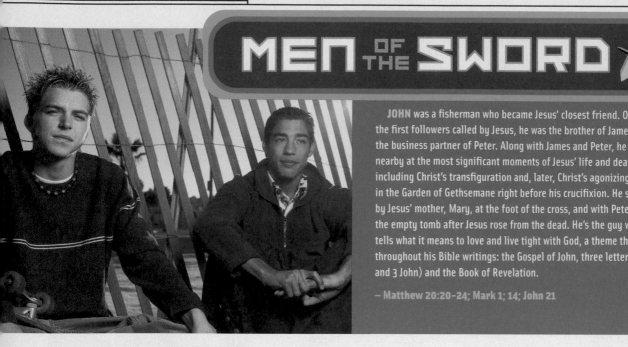

MEN OF THE SWORD

JOHN was a fisherman who became Jesus' closest friend. One of the first followers called by Jesus, he was the brother of James and the business partner of Peter. Along with James and Peter, he was nearby at the most significant moments of Jesus' life and death, including Christ's transfiguration and, later, Christ's agonizing prayer in the Garden of Gethsemane right before his crucifixion. He stood by Jesus' mother, Mary, at the foot of the cross, and with Peter ran to the empty tomb after Jesus rose from the dead. He's the guy who tells what it means to love and live tight with God, a theme that runs throughout his Bible writings: the Gospel of John, three letters (1, 2, and 3 John) and the Book of Revelation.

– Matthew 20:20–24; Mark 1; 14; John 21

themselves. [2]Many will follow their evil ways and say evil things about the way of truth. [3]Those false teachers only want your money, so they will use you by telling you lies. Their judgment spoken against them long ago is still coming, and their ruin is certain.

[4]When angels sinned, God did not let them go free without punishment. He sent them to hell and put them in caves of darkness where they are being held for judgment. [5]And God punished the world long ago when he brought a flood to the world that was full of people who were against him. But God saved Noah, who preached about being right with God, and seven other people with him. [6]And God also destroyed the evil cities of Sodom and

his good heart was hurt by the evil things he saw and heard.) [9]So the Lord knows how to save those who serve him when troubles come. He will hold evil people and punish them, while waiting for the Judgment Day. [10]That punishment is especially for those who live by doing the evil things their sinful selves want and who hate authority.

These false teachers are bold and do anything they want. They are not afraid to speak against the angels. [11]But even the angels, who are much stronger and more powerful than false teachers, do not accuse them with insults before the Lord. [12]But these people speak against things they do not understand. They are like animals that act without think-

delight in trickery while eating meals with you. [14]Every time they look at a woman they want her, and their desire for sin is never satisfied. They lead weak people into the trap of sin, and they have taught their hearts to be greedy. God will punish them! [15]These false teachers left the right road and lost their way, following the way Balaam went. Balaam was the son of Beor, who loved being paid for doing wrong. [16]But a donkey, which cannot talk, told Balaam he was sinning. It spoke with a man's voice and stopped the prophet's crazy thinking.

[17]Those false teachers are like springs without water and clouds blown by a storm. A place in the blackest darkness has been kept

MORE THAN 40 PERCENT OF TEENS TALK TO FAMILY OR FRIENDS ABOUT RELIGIOUS MATTERS IN A TYPICAL DAY. ABOUT 40 PERCENT TALK POLITICS. –BARNA RESEARCH GROUP

Gomorrah[n] by burning them until they were ashes. He made those cities an example of what will happen to those who are against God. [7]But he saved Lot from those cities. Lot, a good man, was troubled because of the filthy lives of evil people. [8](Lot was a good man, but because he lived with evil people every day,

ing, animals born to be caught and killed. And, like animals, these false teachers will be destroyed. [13]They have caused many people to suffer, so they themselves will suffer. That is their pay for what they have done. They take pleasure in openly doing evil, so they are like dirty spots and stains among you. They

for them. [18]They brag with words that mean nothing. By their evil desires they lead people into the trap of sin—people who are just beginning to escape from others who live in error. [19]They promise them freedom, but they themselves are not free. They are slaves of things that will be destroyed. For people are slaves of

 2:6 Sodom and Gomorrah Two cities God destroyed because the people were so evil.

anything that controls them. [20]They were made free from the evil in the world by knowing our Lord and Savior Jesus Christ. But if they return to evil things and those things control them, then it is worse for them than it was before. [21]Yes, it would be better for them to have never known the right way than to know it and to turn away from the holy teaching that was given to them. [22]What they did is like this true saying: "A dog goes back to what it has thrown up,"[n] and, "After a pig is washed, it goes back and rolls in the mud."

of all who are against God.

[8]But do not forget this one thing, dear friends: To the Lord one day is as a thousand years, and a thousand years is as one day. [9]The Lord is not slow in doing what he promised—the way some people understand slowness. But God is being patient with you. He does not want anyone to be lost, but he wants all people to change their hearts and lives.

[10]But the day of the Lord will come like a

WAYS TO WALK THE WALK

2 peter 3:3

WORD: People will laugh at you for your faith.

WALK IT: Don't care. Can you do that? Put your rep on the line for Christ.

JESUS WILL COME AGAIN

3 My friends, this is the second letter I have written you to help your honest minds remember. [2]I want you to think about the words the holy prophets spoke in the past, and remember the command our Lord and Savior gave us through your apostles. [3]It is most important for you to understand what will happen in the last days. People will laugh at you. They will live doing the evil things they want to do. [4]They will say, "Jesus promised to come again. Where is he? Our fathers have died, but the world continues the way it has been since it was made." [5]But they do not want to remember what happened long ago. By the word of God heaven was made, and the earth was made from water and with water. [6]Then the world was flooded and destroyed with water. [7]And that same word of God is keeping heaven and earth that we now have in order to be destroyed by fire. They are being kept for the Judgment Day and the destruction

thief. The skies will disappear with a loud noise. Everything in them will be destroyed by fire, and the earth and everything in it will be burned up.[n] [11]In that way everything will be destroyed. So what kind of people should you be? You should live holy lives and serve God, [12]as you wait for and look forward to the coming of the day of God. When that day comes, the skies will be destroyed with fire, and everything in them will melt with heat. [13]But God made a promise to us, and we are waiting for a new heaven and a new earth where goodness lives.

[14]Dear friends, since you are waiting for this to happen, do your best to be without sin and without fault. Try to be at peace with God. [15]Remember that we are saved because our Lord is patient. Our dear brother Paul told you the same thing when he wrote to you with the wisdom that God gave him. [16]He writes about this in all his letters. Some things in Paul's letters are hard to understand, and people who

are ignorant and weak in faith explain these things falsely. They also falsely explain the other Scriptures, but they are destroying themselves by doing this.

[17]Dear friends, since you already know about this, be careful. Do not let those evil people lead you away by the wrong they do. Be careful so you will not fall from your strong faith. [18]But grow in the grace and knowledge of our Lord and Savior Jesus Christ. Glory be to him now and forever! Amen.

1 JOHN

BACK TO THE BASICS OF CHRISTIANITY

You know how you struggle to learn a new skateboarding trick or a great play on the ball field? Then, boom! Something suddenly clicks and you get it? It's the same with following Jesus. Grabbing hold of a single big concept can be all it takes to launch us to a whole new level of understanding. For the follower John, that concept was love. He wanted to show God's love to people so they could show God's love to one another. And John felt urgent about it. In his first letter, John explores the doctrine of love, expanding on the famous words of Christ he recorded in John 3:16. He talks about Christ being our example, the new commandment, and how Jesus overcomes the world with the love of God. He tells us how to get right with God when we have blown it. In all, John passes along the secret of how to love our neighbor, how to love God, and how to love ourselves. And if we listen up, we get it.

1 We write you now about what has always existed, which we have heard, we have seen with our own eyes, we have looked at, and we have touched with our hands. We write to you about the Word[n] that gives life. [2]He who gives life was shown to us. We saw him and can give proof about it. And now we announce to you that he has life that continues forever. He was with God the Father and was shown to us. [3]We announce to you what we have seen and heard, because we want you also to have fellowship with us. Our fellowship is with God the Father and with his Son, Jesus Christ. [4]We write this to you so you can be full of joy with us.

GOD FORGIVES OUR SINS

[5]Here is the message we have heard from Christ and now announce to you: God is light,[n] and in him there is no darkness at all. [6]So if we say we have fellowship with God, but we continue living in darkness, we are liars and do not follow the truth. [7]But if we live in the light, as God is in the light, we can share fellowship with each other. Then the blood of Jesus, God's Son, cleanses us from every sin.

[8]If we say we have no sin, we are fooling ourselves, and the truth is not in us. [9]But if we confess our sins, he will forgive our sins, because we can trust God to do what is right. He will cleanse us from all the wrongs we have done. [10]If we say we have not sinned, we make God a liar, and we do not accept God's teaching.

JESUS IS OUR HELPER

2 My dear children, I write this letter to you so you will not sin. But if anyone does sin, we have a helper in the presence of the Father—Jesus Christ, the One who does what is right. [2]He is the way our sins are taken away, and not only our sins but the sins of all people.

[3]We can be sure that we know God if we obey his commands. [4]Anyone who says, "I know God," but does not obey God's commands is a liar, and the truth is not in that person. [5]But if someone obeys God's teaching, then in that person God's love has truly reached its goal. This is how we can be sure we are living in God: [6]Whoever says that he lives in God must live as Jesus lived.

THE COMMAND TO LOVE OTHERS

[7]My dear friends, I am not writing a new command to you but an old command you have had from the beginning. It is the teaching you have already heard. [8]But also I am writing a new command to you, and you can see its truth in Jesus and in you, because the darkness is passing away, and the true light is already shining.

[9]Anyone who says, "I am in the light,"[n] but hates a brother or sister,[n] is still in the darkness. [10]Whoever loves a brother or sister lives in the light and will not cause anyone to stumble in his faith. [11]But whoever hates a brother or sister is in darkness, lives in darkness, and does not know where to go, because the darkness has made that person blind.

[12]I write to you, dear children,
because your sins are forgiven
through Christ.
[13]I write to you, parents,
because you know the One who existed
from the beginning.
I write to you, young people,
because you have defeated the
Evil One.
[14]I write to you, children,
because you know the Father.
I write to you, parents,
because you know the One who existed
from the beginning.
I write to you, young people,
because you are strong;
the teaching of God lives in you,
and you have defeated the Evil One.

[15]Do not love the world or the things in the world. If you love the world, the love of the Father is not in you. [16]These are the ways of the world: wanting to please our sinful selves, wanting the sinful things we see, and being too proud of what we have. None of these come from the Father, but all of them come from the world. [17]The world and everything that people want in it are passing away, but the person who does what God wants lives forever.

REJECT THE ENEMIES OF CHRIST

[18]My dear children, these are the last days. You have heard that the enemy of Christ is coming, and now many enemies of Christ are already here. This is how we know that these are the last days. [19]These enemies of Christ were in our fellowship, but they left us. They never really belonged to us; if they had been a

1 JOHN 2:1

There's a certain sick feeling that comes after you've done something you shouldn't have done. Maybe it's dread or anger or guilt or shame or all of the above—and more—rolled into one big downer of depressing disgust.

But all you want to do is hide from God, to wait until the feeling passes, to go listen to some music or watch some TV and let your mind just go to mush. That's too bad, because Jesus is just waiting for you to call for help. He's waiting to pick you up with one nail-scarred hand, and hold the other one out before his Father—to show that the price has been paid, the debt has been canceled, the way of forgiveness has been paved with cleansing blood.

That's what an Advocate does. He's our counsel for the defense. Call him up. He's ready and waiting right now.

1:1 Word The Greek word is "logos," meaning any kind of communication. Here, it means Christ, who was the way God told people about himself. **1:5; 2:9 light** Here, it is used as a symbol of God's goodness or truth. **2:9 brother or sister** Although the Greek text says "brother" here and throughout this book, the writer's words were meant for the entire church, including men and women.

1 JOHN 2:25

Here is the most awesome promise in all of Scripture. Jesus Christ has promised us eternal life. Could anyone else keep that promise besides the Lord God himself? Would you believe anyone else if they promised you the same thing? The magnificent truth is that no one else, living or dead, can offer you eternal life. Some other religions claim multiple lives or reincarnation for their followers, but where are their resurrected sons? There are none. The Resurrection of Christ is proof that he holds the power over death. The Resurrection is the basis of our faith and the proof that this promise is real. Only Jesus Christ gives eternal life. Your faith in him will be rewarded. The reward is all the fellowship, love, and joy of heaven. Commit your heart and life to Christ. Decide that you're going to stick with him—no matter what. Don't miss out on the best that God has for you. He'll change your life, your stuff, your circumstances; but best of all, he'll change you forever.

part of us, they would have stayed with us. But they left, and this shows that none of them really belonged to us.

[20]You have the gift[n] that the Holy One gave you, so you all know the truth. [21]I do not write to you because you do not know the truth but because you do know the truth. And you know that no lie comes from the truth.

[22]Who is the liar? It is the person who does not accept Jesus as the Christ. This is the enemy of Christ: the person who does not accept the Father and his Son. [23]Whoever does not accept the Son does not have the Father. But whoever confesses the Son has the Father, too.

[24]Be sure you continue to follow the teaching you heard from the beginning. If you continue to follow what you heard from the beginning, you will stay in the Son and in the Father. [25]And this is what the Son promised to us—life forever.

[26]I am writing this letter about those people who are trying to lead you the wrong way. [27]Christ gave you a special gift that is still in you, so you do not need any other teacher. His gift teaches you about everything, and it is true, not false. So continue to live in Christ, as his gift taught you.

[28]Yes, my dear children, live in him so that when Christ comes back, we can be without fear and not be ashamed in his presence. [29]If you know that Christ is all that is right, you know that all who do right are God's children.

WE ARE GOD'S CHILDREN

3 The Father has loved us so much that we are called children of God. And we really are his children. The reason the people in the world do not know us is that they have not known him. [2]Dear friends, now we are children of God, and we have not yet been shown what we will be in the future. But we know that when Christ comes again, we will be like him, because we will see him as he really is. [3]Christ is pure, and all who have this hope in Christ keep themselves pure like Christ.

[4]The person who sins breaks God's law. Yes, sin is living against God's law. [5]You know that Christ came to take away sins and that there is no sin in Christ. [6]So anyone who lives in Christ does not go on sinning. Anyone who goes on sinning has never really understood Christ and has never known him.

You probably mess with your hair more than any other part of how you look. It's all about you. Yet as long as your parents pay the barber, they deserve some say over how you wear your hair. Dads don't want their sons to look like juvenile delinquents. Most moms can be cool with hair cut short or left long, but they all hate the smell and feel of greasy unwashed hair. You can ditch hair hassles at home by learning to compromise with your parents. Unknotting hairballs is good practice for dealing with way bigger stuff.

[7]Dear children, do not let anyone lead you the wrong way. Christ is all that is right. So to be like Christ a person must do what is right. [8]The devil has been sinning since the beginning, so anyone who continues to sin belongs to the devil. The Son of God came for this purpose: to destroy the devil's work.

[9]Those who are God's children do not continue sinning, because the new life from God remains in them. They are not able to go on sinning, because they have become children of God. [10]So we can see who God's children are and who the devil's children are: Those who do not do what is right are not God's children, and those who do not love their brothers and sisters are not God's children.

WE MUST LOVE EACH OTHER

[11]This is the teaching you have heard from the beginning: We must love each other. [12]Do

2:20 gift This might mean the Holy Spirit, or it might mean teaching or truth as in verse 24.

not be like Cain who belonged to the Evil One and killed his brother. And why did he kill him? Because the things Cain did were evil, and the things his brother did were good.

¹³Brothers and sisters, do not be surprised when the people of the world hate you. ¹⁴We know we have left death and have come into life because we love each other. Whoever does not love is still dead. ¹⁵Everyone who hates a brother or sister is a murderer," and you know that no murderers have eternal life in them. ¹⁶This is how we know what real love is; Jesus gave his life for us. So we should give our lives for our brothers and sisters. ¹⁷Suppose someone has enough to live and sees a brother or sister in need, but does not help. Then God's love is not living in that person. ¹⁸My children, we should love people not only with words and talk, but by our actions and true caring.

¹⁹⁻²⁰This is the way we know that we belong to the way of truth. When our hearts make us feel guilty, we can still have peace before God. God is greater than our hearts, and he knows everything. ²¹My dear friends, if our hearts do not make us feel guilty, we can come without fear into God's presence. ²²And God gives us what we ask for because we obey God's commands and do what pleases him. ²³This is what God commands: that we believe in his Son, Jesus Christ, and that we love each other, just as he commanded. ²⁴The people who

obey God's commands live in God, and God lives in them. We know that God lives in us because of the Spirit God gave us.

WARNING AGAINST FALSE TEACHERS

4 My dear friends, many false prophets have gone out into the world. So do not believe every spirit, but test the spirits to see if they are from God. ²This is how you can know God's Spirit: Every spirit who confesses that Jesus Christ came to earth as a human is from God. ³And every spirit who refuses to say this about Jesus is not from God. It is the spirit of the enemy of Christ, which you have heard is coming, and now he is already in the world.

⁴My dear children, you belong to God and have defeated them; because God's Spirit, who is in you, is greater than the devil, who is in the world. ⁵And they belong to the world, so what they say is from the world, and the world listens to them. ⁶But we belong to God, and those who know God listen to us. But those who are not from God do not listen to us. That is how we know the Spirit that is true and the spirit that is false.

LOVE COMES FROM GOD

⁷Dear friends, we should love each other, because love comes from God. Everyone who loves has become God's child and knows God. ⁸Whoever does not love does not know God, because God is love. ⁹This is how God showed his love to us: He sent his one and only Son into the world so that we could have life through him. ¹⁰This is what real love is: It is not our love for God; it is God's love for us in sending his Son to be the way to take away our sins.

¹¹Dear friends, if God loved us that much we also should love each other. ¹²No one has ever seen God, but if we love each other, God

3:15 Everyone . . . murderer If one person hates a brother or sister, then in the heart that person has killed that brother or sister. Jesus taught about this sin to his followers (Matthew 5:21–26).

DECEMBER

1
World AIDS Day. Research the crisis around the world at www.datadata.org.

2

3
Pray for a Person of Influence: Ozzy Osbourne piles on yet another year today.

4

5
Read Luke 2 today to get in the Christmas mood.

6

7
Pick up a CD today to learn basic phrases in a new language.

8
Pray for a Person of Influence: It's Brad Pitt's birthday.

9
Eat Christmas cookies today.

10
Invite someone to church with you today.

11

12
Plan a worship service with some buds.

13

14
Buy presents for family members yourself—as in don't expect your mother to do it for you.

15

16
Start reading the prophecies in the Bible leading up to Christ's birth. Start with Isaiah 53.

17

18
Pray for a Person of Influence: Celebrate Steven Spielberg's birthday.

19
Christmas is just around the corner. Do you have all your gifts yet?

20

21
Pray for a Person of Influence: It's Kiefer Sutherland's birthday.

22
Ask your mom what you can do to relieve the holiday stress for her.

23

24
Christmas Eve. Gather the family around and read the story of Jesus' birth.

25

Christmas Day. Be extra kind today to all your relatives.

26
Go to a homeless shelter and share Christ's love this winter.

27

28
Pray for a Person of Influence: Denzel Washington is a year older.

29

30
Pray for two People of Influence: LeBron James and Tiger Woods share a birthday!

31
New Year's Eve. Throw a bash, and pray for the new year that lies ahead.

lives in us, and his love is made perfect in us.

13We know that we live in God and he lives in us, because he gave us his Spirit. 14We have seen and can testify that the Father sent his Son to be the Savior of the world. 15Whoever confesses that Jesus is the Son of God has God living inside, and that person lives in God. 16And so we know the love that God has for us, and we trust that love.

God is love. Those who live in love live in God, and God lives in them. 17This is how love is made perfect in us: that we can be without fear on the day God judges us, because in this world we are like him. 18Where God's love is, there is no fear, because God's perfect love drives out fear. It is punishment that makes a person fear, so love is not made perfect in the person who fears.

19We love because God first loved us. 20If people say, "I love God," but hate their brothers or sisters, they are liars. Those who do not love their brothers and sisters, whom they have seen, cannot love God, whom they have never seen. 21And God gave us this command: Those who love God must also love their brothers and sisters.

FAITH IN THE SON OF GOD

5 Everyone who believes that Jesus is the Christ is God's child, and whoever loves the Father also loves the Father's children. 2This is how we know we love God's children: when we love God and obey his commands. 3Loving God means obeying his commands. And God's commands are not too hard for us, 4because everyone who is a child of God conquers the world. And this is the victory that conquers the world—our faith. 5So the one who wins against the world is the person who believes that Jesus is the Son of God.

6Jesus Christ is the One who came by water*n* and blood.*n* He did not come by water only, but by water and blood. And the Spirit says that this is true, because the Spirit is the truth. 7So there are three witnesses that tell us about Jesus: 8the Spirit, the water, and the blood; and these three witnesses agree. 9We believe people when they say something is true. But what God says is more important, and he has told us the truth about his own Son. 10Anyone who believes in the Son of God has the truth that God told us. Anyone who does not believe makes God a liar, because that person does not believe what God told us about his Son. 11This is what God told us: God has given us eternal life, and this life is in his Son. 12Whoever has the Son has life, but whoever does not have the Son of God does not have life.

WE HAVE ETERNAL LIFE NOW

13I write this letter to you who believe in the Son of God so you will know you have eternal life. 14And this is the boldness we have in God's presence: that if we ask God for anything that agrees with what he wants, he hears us. 15If we know he hears us every time we ask him, we know we have what we ask from him.

16If anyone sees a brother or sister sinning (sin that does not lead to eternal death), that person should pray, and God will give the sinner life. I am talking about people whose sin does not lead to eternal death. There is sin that leads to death. I do not mean that a person should pray about that sin. 17Doing wrong is always sin, but there is sin that does not lead to eternal death.

18We know that those who are God's children do not continue to sin. The Son of God keeps them safe, and the Evil One cannot touch them. 19We know that we belong to God, but the Evil One controls the whole world. 20We also know that the Son of God has come and has given us understanding so that we can know the True One. And our lives are in the True One and in his Son, Jesus Christ. He is the true God and the eternal life.

21So, dear children, keep yourselves away from gods.

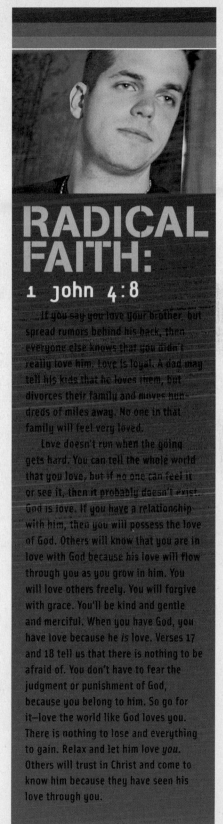

RADICAL FAITH:
1 john 4:8

If you say you love your brother, but spread rumors behind his back, then everyone else knows that you didn't really love him. Love is loyal. A dad may tell his kids that he loves them, but divorces their family and moves hundreds of miles away. No one in that family will feel very loved.

Love doesn't run when the going gets hard. You can tell the whole world that you love, but if no one can feel it or see it, then it probably doesn't exist. God is love. If you have a relationship with him, then you will possess the love of God. Others will know that you are in love with God because his love will flow through you as you grow in him. You will love others freely. You will forgive with grace. You'll be kind and gentle and merciful. When you have God, you have love because he *is* love. Verses 17 and 18 tell us that there is nothing to be afraid of. You don't have to fear the judgment or punishment of God, because you belong to him. So go for it—love the world like God loves you. There is nothing to lose and everything to gain. Relax and let him love *you*. Others will trust in Christ and come to know him because they have seen his love through you.

5:6 water This probably means the water of Jesus' baptism. **5:6 blood** This probably means the blood of Jesus' death.

2 JOHN

LOVE ONE ANOTHER, BUT BEWARE OF FALSE TEACHERS

In John's second letter, he tells the church how to hold tight to the truth. Actually, this brief note seems to address a particular church in Asia Minor. While John reviews the teachings of his first letter about love, he adds a second command not to show hospitality to false teachers. If anyone does, they are guilty of participation in their evil teachings. It's almost as if 2 John is an important P.S. to 1 John. As in, "Note to Heretics: Get outta there!" In thirteen verses, John warns true Christians against the fake evangelists traveling the land and preaching that spiritual things are good and physical things are evil. While this sounds pretty good, they actually went so far as to say that Jesus was only a spirit who looked human. Now that's heresy, but the believers are making the problem worse. These liars weren't just in the church. The believers had welcomed them into their homes! John warns Christians not to support these fakes. If people don't preach the genuine story of Jesus, don't let them in. Period.

RELATIONSHIPS

"If your fellow believer sins against you, go and tell him in private what he did wrong" (Matthew 18:15). You want to put a friendship back together. But where to start? Skip the usual backstabbing and go-betweens. In Matthew 18, Jesus outlines a pattern wise to follow no matter what the problem. Four steps: (1) Talk one-on-one with the person who hurt you. (2) If that first step flops, bring someone to back up your concerns. (3) If move two gets you nowhere, tell an authority. (4) If you still haven't solved the problem after step three, take a time-out from the relationship. Can you picture the pattern? Put it to use.

From the Elder.[n]

To the chosen lady[n] and her children:

I love all of you in the truth,[n] and all those who know the truth love you. [2]We love you because of the truth that lives in us and will be with us forever.

[3]Grace, mercy, and peace from God the Father and his Son, Jesus Christ, will be with us in truth and love.

[4]I was very happy to learn that some of your children are following the way of truth, as the Father commanded us. [5]And now, dear lady, this is not a new command but is the same command we have had from the beginning. I ask you that we all love each other. [6]And love means living the way God commanded us to live. As you have heard from the beginning, his command is this: Live a life of love.

[7]Many false teachers are in the world now who do not confess that Jesus Christ came to earth as a human. Anyone who does not confess this is a false teacher and an enemy of Christ. [8]Be careful yourselves that you do not lose everything you have worked for, but that you receive your full reward.

[9]Anyone who goes beyond Christ's teaching and does not continue to follow only his teaching does not have God. But whoever continues to follow the teaching of Christ has both the Father and the Son. [10]If someone comes to you and does not bring this teaching, do not welcome or accept that person into your house. [11]If you welcome such a person, you share in the evil work.

[12]I have many things to write to you, but I do not want to use paper and ink. Instead, I hope to come to you and talk face to face so we can be full of joy. [13]The children of your chosen sister[n] greet you.

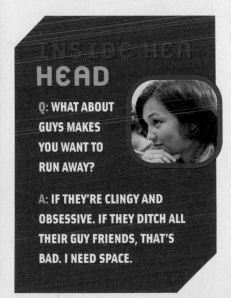

INSIDE HER HEAD

Q: WHAT ABOUT GUYS MAKES YOU WANT TO RUN AWAY?

A: IF THEY'RE CLINGY AND OBSESSIVE. IF THEY DITCH ALL THEIR GUY FRIENDS, THAT'S BAD. I NEED SPACE.

10 CHARACTER TRAITS GOD WANTS TO BUILD IN YOU

1. INTEGRITY
2. LOYALTY
3. PATIENCE
4. PURITY
5. GENEROSITY
6. FAITHFULNESS
7. GENTLENESS
8. SUBMISSIVENESS
9. COMPASSION
10. SELF-CONTROL

1 Elder "Elder" means an older person. It can also mean a special leader in the church (as in Titus 1:5). **1 lady** This might mean a woman, or in this letter it might mean a church. If it is a church, then "her children" would be the people of the church. **1 truth** The truth or "Good News" about Jesus Christ that joins all believers together. **13 sister** Sister of the "lady" in verse 1. This might be another woman or another church.

3 JOHN

GUIDELINES ABOUT CHRISTIAN HOSPITALITY

In this last of John's letters, he writes to encourage a friend, Gaius. You'd think that in the beginning years of Christianity believers were all happy and good to each other. But guess what? It didn't happen that way. Evil people with false teachings and void of godly love had infiltrated the church. These evil people worshiped two things only: power and prestige. So what does John do? He writes a letter filled with quick advice for beginners struggling with the issue. John's advice to believers is to keep doing what they know God wants them to do: Obey the truth, love others, and support those spreading the Good News, regardless of the risk. In this personal letter, he congratulates Gaius for obeying the true teachings about Jesus, and especially for showing hospitality to true Christian missionaries.

From the Elder.[n]

To my dear friend Gaius, whom I love in the truth:[n]

MARK 11:22 "JESUS ANSWERED, 'HAVE FAITH IN GOD.'"

[2]My dear friend, I know your soul is doing fine, and I pray that you are doing well in every way and that your health is good. [3]I was very happy when some brothers and sisters[n] came and told me about the truth in your life and how you are following the way of truth. [4]Nothing gives me greater joy than to hear that my children are following the way of truth.

[5]My dear friend, it is good that you help the brothers and sisters, even those you do not know. [6]They told the church about your love. Please help them to continue their trip in a way worthy of God. [7]They started out in service to Christ, and they have been accepting nothing from non-believers. [8]So we should help such people; when we do, we share in their work for the truth.

[9]I wrote something to the church, but Diotrephes, who loves to be their leader, will not listen to us. [10]So if I come, I will talk about what Diotrephes is doing, about how he lies and says evil things about us. But more than that, he refuses to accept the other brothers and sisters; he even stops those who do want to accept them and puts them out of the church.

[11]My dear friend, do not follow what is bad; follow what is good. The one who does good belongs to God. But the one who does evil has never known God.

[12]Everyone says good things about Demetrius, and the truth agrees with what they say. We also speak well of him, and you know what we say is true.

[13]I have many things I want to write you, but I do not want to use pen and ink. [14]I hope to see you soon and talk face to face. [15]Peace to you. The friends here greet you. Please greet each friend there by name.

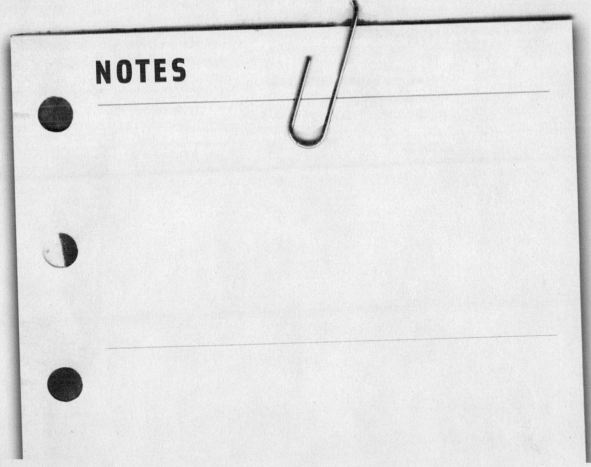

NOTES

1 Elder "Elder" means an older person. It can also mean a special leader in the church (as in Titus 1:5).　**1 truth** The truth or "Good News" about Jesus Christ that joins all believers together.　**3 brothers and sisters** Although the Greek text says "brothers" here and throughout this book, the writer's words were meant for the entire church, including men and women.

JUDE

Jude was a man with a mission. Even though Christianity hadn't been around for long, there were already lots of people twisting and turning the truth of the Good News to mean something totally different. Christians were bumping into people with great-sounding shortcuts to the total devotion Christ commanded. These people claimed to have found an easier, shorter, better way to live as a Christian. What was it? Well, since Jesus had forgiven people of their sins, they said that sin didn't matter anymore. In fact, they taught, Christians could sin all they wanted! Jude had no patience for this kind of trickery and lying. He wrote his letter to the church to straighten out these deceptions and to remind them that how we act does matter to God. He encourages believers to make God their Master and defend their beliefs by the way they live.

[1]From Jude, a servant of Jesus Christ and a brother of James.

To all who have been called by God. God the Father loves you, and you have been kept safe in Jesus Christ:

[2]Mercy, peace, and love be yours richly.

GOD WILL PUNISH SINNERS

[3]Dear friends, I wanted very much to write you about the salvation we all share. But I felt the need to write you about something else: I want to encourage you to fight hard for the faith that was given the holy people of God once and for all time. [4]Some people have secretly entered your group. Long ago the prophets wrote about these people who will be judged guilty. They are against God and have changed the grace of our God into a reason for sexual sin. They also refuse to accept Jesus Christ, our only Master and Lord.

[5]I want to remind you of some things you already know: Remember that the Lord saved his people by bringing them out of the land of Egypt. But later he destroyed all those who did not believe. [6]And remember the angels who did not keep their place of power but left their proper home. The Lord has kept these angels in darkness, bound with everlasting chains, to be judged on the great day. [7]Also remember the cities of Sodom and Gomorrah[n] and the other towns around them. In the same way they were full of sexual sin and people who desired sexual relations that God does not allow. They suffer the punishment of eternal fire, as an example for all to see.

[8]It is the same with these people who have entered your group. They are guided by dreams and make themselves filthy with sin. They reject God's authority and speak against the angels. [9]Not even the archangel[n] Michael, when he argued with the devil about who would have the body of Moses, dared to judge the devil guilty. Instead, he said, "The Lord punish you." [10]But these people speak against things they do not understand. And what they do know, by feeling, as dumb animals know things, are the very things that destroy them. [11]It will be terrible for them. They have followed the way of Cain, and for money they have given themselves to doing the wrong that Balaam did.

They have fought against God as Korah did, and like Korah, they surely will be destroyed. [12]They are like dirty spots in your special Christian meals you share. They eat with you and have no fear, caring only for themselves. They are clouds without rain, which the wind blows around. They are autumn trees without fruit that are pulled out of the ground. So they are twice dead. [13]They are like wild waves of the sea, tossing up their own shameful actions like foam. They are like stars that wander in the sky. A place in the blackest darkness has been kept for them forever.

[14]Enoch, the seventh descendant from Adam, said about these people: "Look, the Lord is coming with many thousands of his holy angels to [15]judge every person. He is coming to punish all who are against God for all the evil they have done against him. And he will punish the sinners who are against God for all the evil they have said against him."

[16]These people complain and blame others, doing the evil things they want to do. They brag about themselves, and they flatter others to get what they want.

A WARNING AND THINGS TO DO

[17]Dear friends, remember what the apostles of our Lord Jesus Christ said before. [18]They said to you, "In the last times there will be people who laugh about God, following their own evil desires which are against God." [19]These are the people who divide you, people whose thoughts are only of this world, who do not have the Spirit.

[20]But dear friends, use your most holy faith to build yourselves up, praying in the Holy Spirit. [21]Keep yourselves in God's love as you wait for the Lord Jesus Christ with his mercy to give you life forever.

[22]Show mercy to some people who have doubts. [23]Take others out of the fire, and save them. Show mercy mixed with fear to others, hating even their clothes which are dirty from sin.

PRAISE GOD

[24]God is strong and can help you not to fall. He can bring you before his glory without any wrong in you and can give you great joy. [25]He is the only God, the One who saves us. To him be glory, greatness, power, and authority through Jesus Christ our Lord for all time past, now, and forever. Amen.

BIBLE BASICS

Spiritual gifts are special abilities God gives believers to help people get close to him. The Bible mentions gifts like sharing the Good News, teaching, serving, and caring for others. It also lists gifts like speaking in tongues, prophecy, healing, and other supernatural gifts that many believe Christians can still experience today. The Bible makes it clear that God has given each person his or her own gifts and that all of us work together to make a *whole* body of believers.

REVELATION

THE FINAL SHOWDOWN BETWEEN GOD AND SATAN

The last book in the Bible was written by John after he had a bizarre vision while imprisoned for his faith on the isle of Patmos. If you could watch a movie of this revelation, it would be like Stephen King meets Stephen Spielberg: the best horror movie with special effects galore. John sees out-of-control creatures, the throne room of God, and the end times! Of course, scholars debate over what John really saw or whether these creatures and stories were symbols. And the meaning of some of the images John talks about are still a mystery today. The book teaches that God gives Satan and human evil some leeway in this world, but there will come a day when God will say, "Enough," and we will all be judged according to our faith and our works. In the end, those who have their faith in Christ's righteousness will be invited into God's presence forever, and Satan will be banished from the kingdom. It's a real and true happily-ever-after kind of story.

JOHN TELLS ABOUT THIS BOOK

1 This is the revelation[n] of Jesus Christ, which God gave to him, to show his servants what must soon happen. And Jesus sent his angel to show it to his servant John, [2]who has told everything he has seen. It is the word of God; it is the message from Jesus Christ. [3]Happy is the one who reads the words of God's message, and happy are the people who hear this message and do what is written in it. The time is near when all of this will happen.

JESUS' MESSAGE TO THE CHURCHES

[4]From John.

To the seven churches in the country of Asia:

Grace and peace to you from the One who is and was and is coming, and from the seven spirits before his throne, [5]and from Jesus Christ. Jesus is the faithful witness, the first among those raised from the dead. He is the ruler of the kings of the earth.

He is the One who loves us, who made us free from our sins with the blood of his death. [6]He made us to be a kingdom of priests who serve God his Father. To Jesus Christ be glory and power forever and ever! Amen.

[7]Look, Jesus is coming with the clouds, and everyone will see him, even those who stabbed him. And all peoples of the earth will cry loudly because of him. Yes, this will happen! Amen.

[8]The Lord God says, "I am the Alpha and the Omega.[n] I am the One who is and was and is coming. I am the Almighty."

[9]I, John, am your brother. All of us share with Christ in suffering, in the kingdom, and in patience to continue. I was on the island of Patmos,[n] because I had preached the word of God and the message about Jesus. [10]On the Lord's day I was in the Spirit, and I heard a loud voice behind me that sounded like a trumpet. [11]The voice said, "Write what you see in a book and send it to the seven churches: to Ephesus, Smyrna, Pergamum, Thyatira, Sardis, Philadelphia, and Laodicea."

[12]I turned to see who was talking to me. When I turned, I saw seven golden lampstands [13]and someone among the lampstands who was "like a Son of Man."[n] He was dressed in a long robe and had a gold band around his chest. [14]His head and hair were white like wool, as white as snow, and his eyes were like flames of fire. [15]His feet were like bronze that glows hot in a furnace, and his voice was like the noise of flooding water. [16]He held seven stars in his right hand, and a sharp double-edged

---

WAYS TO WALK THE WALK

Revelation 7:9

WORD: People from every tribe will worship God in heaven.

WALK IT: Find your part in spreading God's Good News all over the planet. You can pray for people who don't know God. You can help send missionaries. And you can ask God if and how you might go.

Revelation 16:7

WORD: God does get angry about sin.

WALK IT: Sin has consequences you can't escape. Strive to do what's right, and watch where you hang out. Don't be in the wrong place at the wrong time.

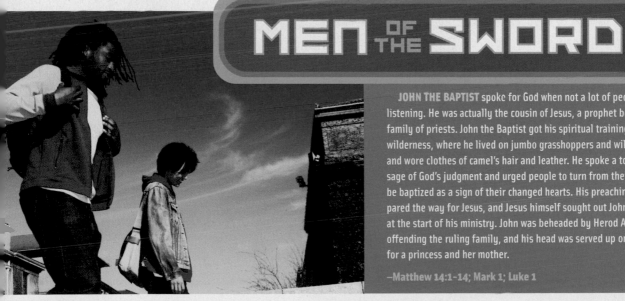

MEN OF THE SWORD

JOHN THE BAPTIST spoke for God when not a lot of people were listening. He was actually the cousin of Jesus, a prophet born into a family of priests. John the Baptist got his spiritual training in the wilderness, where he lived on jumbo grasshoppers and wild honey and wore clothes of camel's hair and leather. He spoke a tough message of God's judgment and urged people to turn from their sin and be baptized as a sign of their changed hearts. His preaching prepared the way for Jesus, and Jesus himself sought out John's baptism at the start of his ministry. John was beheaded by Herod Antipas for offending the ruling family, and his head was served up on a platter for a princess and her mother.

—Matthew 14:1–14; Mark 1; Luke 1

 1:1 revelation Making known truth that has been hidden. **1:8 Alpha and the Omega** The first and last letters of the Greek alphabet. This means "the beginning and the end." **1:9 Patmos** A small island in the Aegean Sea, near the coast of Asia Minor (modern Turkey). **1:13 "like . . . Man"** "Son of Man" is a name Jesus called himself.

sword came out of his mouth. He looked like the sun shining at its brightest time.

[17]When I saw him, I fell down at his feet like a dead man. He put his right hand on me and said, "Do not be afraid. I am the First and the Last. [18]I am the One who lives; I was dead, but look, I am alive forever and ever! And I hold the keys to death and to the place of the dead. [19]So write the things you see, what is now and what will happen later. [20]Here is the secret of the seven stars that you saw in my right hand and the seven golden lampstands: The seven lampstands are the seven churches, and the seven stars are the angels of the seven churches.

TO THE CHURCH IN EPHESUS

2 "Write this to the angel of the church in Ephesus:

"The One who holds the seven stars in his right hand and walks among the seven golden lampstands says this: [2]I know what you do, how you work hard and never give up. I know you do not put up with the false teachings of evil people. You have tested those who say they are apostles but really are not, and you found they are liars. [3]You have patience and have suffered troubles for my name and have not given up.

[4]"But I have this against you: You have left the love you had in the beginning. [5]So remember where you were before you fell. Change your hearts and do what you did at first. If you do not change, I will come to you and will take away your lampstand from its place. [6]But there is something you do that is right: You hate what the Nicolaitans[n] do, as much as I.

[7]"Every person who has ears should listen to what the Spirit says to the churches. To those who win the victory I will give the right to eat the fruit from the tree of life, which is in the garden of God.

TO THE CHURCH IN SMYRNA

[8]"Write this to the angel of the church in Smyrna:

"The One who is the First and the Last, who died and came to life again, says this: [9]I know your troubles and that you are poor, but really you are rich! I know the bad things some people say about you. They say they are Jews, but they are not true Jews. They are a synagogue that belongs to Satan. [10]Do not be afraid of what you are about to suffer. I tell you, the devil will put some of you in prison to test you, and you will suffer for ten days. But be faithful, even if you have to die, and I will give you the crown of life.

[11]"Everyone who has ears should listen to what the Spirit says to the churches. Those who win the victory will not be hurt by the second death.

TO THE CHURCH IN PERGAMUM

[12]"Write this to the angel of the church in Pergamum:

"The One who has the sharp, double-edged sword says this: [13]I know where you live. It is where Satan has his throne. But you are true to me. You did not refuse to tell about your faith in me even during the time of Antipas, my faithful witness who was killed in your city, where Satan lives.

[14]"But I have a few things against you: You have some there who follow the teaching of Balaam. He taught Balak how to cause the people of Israel to sin by eating food offered to idols and by taking part in sexual sins. [15]You also have some who follow the teaching of the Nicolaitans.[n] [16]So change your hearts and lives. If you do not, I will come to you quickly and fight against them with the sword that comes out of my mouth.

[17]"Everyone who has ears should listen to what the Spirit says to the churches.

"I will give some of the hidden manna to everyone who wins the victory. I will also give to each one who wins the victory a white stone with a new name written on it. No one knows this new name except the one who receives it.

TO THE CHURCH IN THYATIRA

[18]"Write this to the angel of the church in Thyatira:

"The Son of God, who has eyes that blaze like fire and feet like shining bronze, says this: [19]I know what you do. I know about your love, your faith, your service, and your patience. I

2:6, 15 **Nicolaitans** This is the name of a religious group that followed false beliefs and ideas.

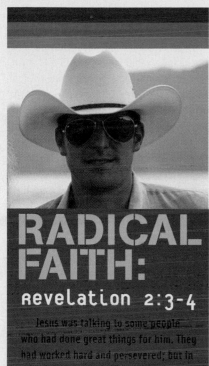

RADICAL FAITH:
revelation 2:3-4

Jesus was talking to some people who had done great things for him. They had worked hard and persevered; but in all of that, they somehow lost their first love for him. You probably know people like that. They go to church all the time, wear Christian t-shirts, and scream "Jesus" really loud at concerts. But they're missing a passion for him.

The Lord wants you to be known as a person who loves him. He'd rather have you be known as a gentle, humble lover of God than as the most eloquent preacher who just sounds good. All kinds of things will tempt you to love them more than you love Jesus, but don't give in. Hold on tight to your love for him. When other people walk away from an encounter with you, they should know one thing—that you have a passionate, fervent, fiery love for God that will not quit.

If you've gotten caught up in doing a bunch of stuff in the name of the Lord, slam on the brakes. Run into his presence. Pray and worship him. Start listening to him and hearing his voice. Let him melt your heart again. Ask him to rekindle your fire for him. Your service is made great because your love for him is great. Keep your passion burning for him!

know that you are doing more now than you did at first.

20"But I have this against you: You let that woman Jezebel spread false teachings. She says she is a prophetess, but by her teaching she leads my people to take part in sexual sins and to eat food that is offered to idols. 21I have given her time to change her heart and turn away from her sin, but she does not want to change. 22So I will throw her on a bed of suffering. And all those who take part in adultery with her will suffer greatly if they do not turn away from the wrongs she does. 23I will also kill her followers. Then all the churches will know I am the One who searches hearts and minds, and I will repay each of you for what you have done.

24"But others of you in Thyatira have not followed her teaching and have not learned what some call Satan's deep secrets. I say to you that I will not put any other load on you. 25Only continue in your loyalty until I come.

26"I will give power over the nations to everyone who wins the victory and continues to be obedient to me until the end.

27'You will rule over them with an iron rod, as when pottery is broken into pieces.'

Psalm 2:9

28This is the same power I received from my Father. I will also give him the morning star. 29Everyone who has ears should listen to what the Spirit says to the churches.

TO THE CHURCH IN SARDIS

3 "Write this to the angel of the church in Sardis:

"The One who has the seven spirits and the seven stars says this: I know what you do. People say that you are alive, but really you are dead. 2Wake up! Make yourselves stronger before what you have left dies completely. I have found that what you are doing is less than what my God wants. 3So do not forget what you have received and heard. Obey it, and change your hearts and lives. So you must wake up, or I will come like a thief, and you will not know when I will come to you. 4But you have a few there in Sardis who have kept their clothes unstained, so they will walk with me and will wear white clothes, because

RANDOM WAYS TO DEVELOP COMPASSION

1. **LISTEN TO THE STORIES OF INNER CITY FAMILIES.**

2. **VOLUNTEER IN THE CHURCH NURSERY.**

3. **SERVE AS A SUMMER MISSIONARY IN A THIRD-WORLD COUNTRY.**

4. **SPONSOR A NEEDY CHILD.**

5. **SLEEP OUTSIDE IN A CARDBOARD BOX.**

6. **MENTOR THE SON OF AN INMATE.**

7. **DO THE 30-HOUR FAMINE.**

8. **LEARN ABOUT SUFFERING CHRISTIANS AROUND THE WORLD.**

9. **HELP LEAD WORSHIP IN A JUVENILE LOCK-UP.**

10. **REHAB A HOUSE.**

they are worthy. 5Those who win the victory will be dressed in white clothes like them. And I will not erase their names from the book of life, but I will say they belong to me before my Father and before his angels. 6Everyone who has ears should listen to what the Spirit says to the churches.

TO THE CHURCH IN PHILADELPHIA

7"Write this to the angel of the church in Philadelphia:

"This is what the One who is holy and true, who holds the key of David, says. When he opens a door, no one can close it. And when he closes it, no one can open it. 8I know what you do. I have put an open door before you, which no one can close. I know you have a little strength, but you have obeyed my teaching and were not afraid to speak my name. [9]Those in the synagogue that belongs to Satan say they are Jews, but they are not true Jews; they are liars. I will make them come before you and bow at your feet, and they will know that I have loved you. [10]You have obeyed my teaching about not giving up your faith. So I will keep you from the time of trouble that will come to the whole world to test those who live on earth.

PSALM 139:13 "YOU MADE MY WHOLE BEING; YOU FORMED ME IN MY MOTHER'S BODY."

[11]"I am coming soon. Continue strong in your faith so no one will take away your crown. [12]I will make those who win the victory pillars in the temple of my God, and they will never have to leave it. I will write on them the name of my God and the name of the city of my God, the new Jerusalem,[n] that comes down out of heaven from my God. I will also write on them my new name. [13]Everyone who has ears should listen to what the Spirit says to the churches.

TO THE CHURCH IN LAODICEA

[14]"Write this to the angel of the church in Laodicea:

"The Amen,[n] the faithful and true witness, the beginning of all God has made, says this: [15]I know what you do, that you are not hot or cold. I wish that you were hot or cold! [16]But because you are lukewarm—neither hot, nor cold—I am ready to spit you out of my mouth. [17]You say, 'I am rich, and I have become wealthy and do not need anything.' But you do not know that you are really miserable, pitiful, poor, blind, and naked. [18]I advise you to buy from me gold made pure in fire so you can be truly rich. Buy from me white clothes so you can be clothed and so you can cover your shameful nakedness. Buy from me medicine to put on your eyes so you can truly see.

[19]"I correct and punish those whom I love. So be eager to do right, and change your hearts and lives. [20]Here I am! I stand at the door and knock. If you hear my voice and open the door, I will come in and eat with you, and you will eat with me.

[21]"Those who win the victory will sit with me on my throne in the same way that I won the victory and sat down with my Father on his throne. [22]Everyone who has ears should listen to what the Spirit says to the churches."

JOHN SEES HEAVEN

4 After the vision of these things I looked, and there before me was an open door in heaven. And the same voice that spoke to me before, that sounded like a trumpet, said, "Come up here, and I will show you what must happen after this." [2]Immediately I was in the Spirit, and before me was a throne in heaven, and someone was sitting on it. [3]The One who sat on the throne looked like precious stones, like jasper and carnelian. All around the throne was a rainbow the color of an emerald. [4]Around the throne there were twenty-four other thrones with twenty-four elders sitting on them. They were dressed in white and had golden crowns on their heads. [5]Lightning flashes and noises and thundering came from the throne. Before the throne seven lamps were burning, which are the seven spirits of God. [6]Also before the throne there was something that looked like a sea of glass, clear like crystal.

In the center and around the throne were four living creatures with eyes all over them, in front and in back. [7]The first living creature was like a lion. The second was like a calf. The third had a face like a man. The fourth was like a flying eagle. [8]Each of these four living creatures had six wings and was covered all over with eyes, inside and out. Day and night they never stop saying:

"Holy, holy, holy is the Lord God Almighty.
He was, he is, and he is coming."

[9]These living creatures give glory, honor, and thanks to the One who sits on the throne, who lives forever and ever. [10]Then the twenty-four elders bow down before the One who sits on the throne, and they worship him who lives forever and ever. They put their crowns down before the throne and say:

[11]"You are worthy, our Lord and God,
to receive glory and honor and power,
because you made all things.
Everything existed and was made,
because you wanted it."

5 Then I saw a scroll in the right hand of the One sitting on the throne. The scroll had writing on both sides and was kept closed with seven seals. [2]And I saw a powerful angel calling in a loud voice, "Who is worthy to break the seals and open the scroll?" [3]But

travel the road

The church in Africa glows red hot. It was the first continent to become majority Christian—over 50 percent—within the span of a century. More than 25 thousand people continue to come to faith each day, with 56 thousand Muslims becoming Christians during one summer in a major Kenyan city. And in one service in the ocean on the coast of Angola, ten thousand new believers were baptized in one day.

For more on extreme missions visit www.traveltheroad.com.

3:12 **Jerusalem** This name is used to mean the spiritual city God built for his people. See Revelation 21–22. 3:14 **Amen** Used here as a name for Jesus; it means to agree fully that something is true.

there was no one in heaven or on earth or under the earth who could open the scroll or look inside it. [4]I cried hard because there was no one who was worthy to open the scroll or look inside. [5]But one of the elders said to me, "Do not cry! The Lion[n] from the tribe of Judah, David's descendant, has won the victory so that he is able to open the scroll and its seven seals."

[6]Then I saw a Lamb standing in the center of the throne and in the middle of the four living creatures and the elders. The Lamb looked as if he had been killed. He had seven horns and seven eyes, which are the seven spirits of God that were sent into all the world. [7]The Lamb came and took the scroll from the right hand of the One sitting on the throne. [8]When he took the scroll, the four living creatures and the twenty-four elders bowed down before the Lamb. Each one of them had a harp and golden bowls full of incense, which are the prayers of God's holy people. [9]And they all sang a new song to the Lamb:

"You are worthy to take the scroll
    and to open its seals,
because you were killed,
    and with the blood of your death you
        bought people for God

MARK 12:17 "GIVE TO CAESAR THE THINGS THAT ARE CAESAR'S, AND GIVE TO GOD THE THINGS THAT ARE GOD'S."

from every tribe, language, people, and
    nation.
[10]You made them to be a kingdom of priests
        for our God,
    and they will rule on the earth."
[11]Then I looked, and I heard the voices of many angels around the throne, and the four living creatures, and the elders. There were thousands and thousands of angels, [12]saying in a loud voice:

"The Lamb who was killed is worthy
    to receive power, wealth, wisdom, and
        strength,
    honor, glory, and praise!"
[13]Then I heard all creatures in heaven and on earth and under the earth and in the sea saying:

"To the One who sits on the throne
        and to the Lamb
    be praise and honor and glory and power
        forever and ever."
[14]The four living creatures said, "Amen," and the elders bowed down and worshiped.

6 Then I watched while the Lamb opened the first of the seven seals. I heard one of the four living creatures say with a voice like thunder, "Come!" [2]I looked, and

GET OUT THERE →

SHARE OUR STRENGTH, one of the nation's leading anti-hunger, anti-poverty organizations, began in 1984 in the basement of a row house on Capitol Hill in Washington, DC. In the beginning, they organized a handful of chefs to cook for fundraisers. Today they mobilize thousands of individuals in the culinary industry to organize events, host dinners, teach cooking and nutrition classes to low-income families, and serve as anti-hunger advocates.

To bring even more resources to the fight against hunger and poverty, they build creative partnerships with a range of industries, including retail, financial services, and music—and create community wealth, resources generated through profitable enterprise to promise social change.

To learn more, go to www.strength.org.

 5:5 Lion Here refers to Christ.

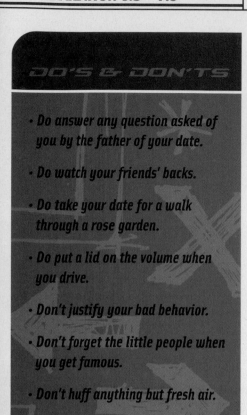

there before me was a white horse. The rider on the horse held a bow, and he was given a crown, and he rode out, determined to win the victory.

[3]When the Lamb opened the second seal, I heard the second living creature say, "Come!" [4]Then another horse came out, a red one. Its rider was given power to take away peace from the earth and to make people kill each other, and he was given a big sword.

[5]When the Lamb opened the third seal, I heard the third living creature say, "Come!" I looked, and there before me was a black horse, and its rider held a pair of scales in his hand. [6]Then I heard something that sounded like a voice coming from the middle of the four living creatures. The voice said, "A quart of wheat for a day's pay, and three quarts of barley for a day's pay, and do not damage the olive oil and wine!"

[7]When the Lamb opened the fourth seal, I heard the voice of the fourth living creature say, "Come!" [8]I looked, and there before me was a pale horse. Its rider was named death, and Hades[n] was following close behind him. They were given power over a fourth of the earth to kill people by war, by starvation, by disease, and by the wild animals of the earth.

[9]When the Lamb opened the fifth seal, I saw under the altar the souls of those who had been killed because they were faithful to the word of God and to the message they had received. [10]These souls shouted in a loud voice, "Holy and true Lord, how long until you judge the people of the earth and punish them for killing us?" [11]Then each one of them was given a white robe and was told to wait a short time longer. There were still some of their fellow servants and brothers and sisters[n] in the service of Christ who must be killed as they were. They had to wait until all of this was finished.

[12]Then I watched while the Lamb opened the sixth seal, and there was a great earthquake. The sun became black like rough black cloth, and the whole moon became red like blood. [13]And the stars in the sky fell to the earth like figs falling from a fig tree when the wind blows. [14]The sky disappeared as a scroll when it is rolled up, and every mountain and island was moved from its place.

[15]Then the kings of the earth, the rulers, the generals, the rich people, the powerful people, the slaves, and the free people hid themselves in caves and in the rocks on the mountains. [16]They called to the mountains and the rocks, "Fall on us. Hide us from the face of the One who sits on the throne and from the anger of the Lamb! [17]The great day for their anger has come, and who can stand against it?"

THE 144,000 PEOPLE OF ISRAEL

7 After the vision of these things I saw four angels standing at the four corners of the earth. The angels were holding the four winds of the earth to keep them from blowing on the land or on the sea or on any tree. [2]Then I saw another angel coming up from the east who had the seal of the living God. And he called out in a loud voice to the four angels to whom God had given power to harm the earth and the sea. [3]He said to them, "Do not harm the land or the sea or the trees until we mark with a sign the foreheads of the people who serve our God." [4]Then I heard how many people were marked with the sign. There were one hundred forty-four thousand from every tribe of the people of Israel.

[5]From the tribe of Judah twelve thousand
     were marked with the sign,

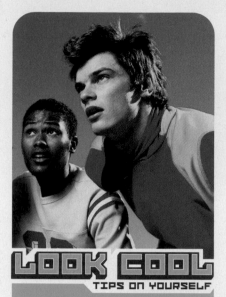

from the tribe of Reuben twelve thousand,
     from the tribe of Gad twelve thousand,
[6]from the tribe of Asher twelve thousand,
     from the tribe of Naphtali twelve
          thousand,
     from the tribe of Manasseh twelve
          thousand,
[7]from the tribe of Simeon twelve thousand,
     from the tribe of Levi twelve thousand,
     from the tribe of Issachar twelve thousand,
[8]from the tribe of Zebulun twelve thousand,
     from the tribe of Joseph twelve thousand,
     and from the tribe of Benjamin twelve
          thousand were marked with the sign.

THE GREAT CROWD WORSHIPS GOD

[9]After the vision of these things I looked, and there was a great number of people, so many that no one could count them. They were from every nation, tribe, people, and language of the earth. They were all standing before

6:8 Hades The unseen world of the dead.   6:11 brothers and sisters Although the Greek text says "brothers" here and throughout this book, both men and women would have been included.

the throne and before the Lamb, wearing white robes and holding palm branches in their hands. [10]They were shouting in a loud voice, "Salvation belongs to our God, who sits on the throne, and to the Lamb." [11]All the angels were standing around the throne and the elders and the four living creatures. They all bowed down on their faces before the throne and worshiped God, [12]saying, "Amen! Praise, glory, wisdom, thanks, honor, power, and strength belong to our God forever and ever. Amen!"

[13]Then one of the elders asked me, "Who are these people dressed in white robes? Where did they come from?"

[14]I answered, "You know, sir."

And the elder said to me, "These are the people who have come out of the great distress. They have washed their robes[n] and made them white in the blood of the Lamb. [15]Because of this, they are before the throne of God. They worship him day and night in his temple. And the One who sits on the throne will be present with them. [16]Those people will never be hungry again, and they will never be thirsty again. The sun will not hurt them, and no heat will burn them, [17]because the Lamb at the center of the throne will be their shepherd. He will lead them to springs of water that give life. And God will wipe away every tear from their eyes."

THE SEVENTH SEAL

8 When the Lamb opened the seventh seal, there was silence in heaven for about half an hour. [2]And I saw the seven angels who stand before God and to whom were given seven trumpets.

[3]Another angel came and stood at the altar, holding a golden pan for incense. He was given much incense to offer with the prayers of all God's holy people. The angel put this offering on the golden altar before the throne. [4]The smoke from the incense went up from the angel's hand to God with the prayers of God's people. [5]Then the angel filled the incense pan with fire from the altar and threw it on the earth, and there were flashes of lightning, thunder and loud noises, and an earthquake.

THE SEVEN ANGELS AND TRUMPETS

[6]Then the seven angels who had the seven trumpets prepared to blow them.

[7]The first angel blew his trumpet, and hail and fire mixed with blood were poured down on the earth. And a third of the earth, and all the green grass, and a third of the trees were burned up.

[8]Then the second angel blew his trumpet, and something that looked like a big mountain, burning with fire, was thrown into the sea. And a third of the sea became blood, [9]a third of the living things in the sea died, and a third of the ships were destroyed.

MUSIC REVIEWS

DEREK WEBB: SHE MUST AND SHALL GO FREE

She Must and Shall Go Free is the solo debut from Derek Webb, formerly a singer/songwriter with Caedmon's Call, a sound-and-style connection that listeners will immediately spot. The stunning title track helps to develop the main message: It's a call to Christ's bride, the church, to reject unfaithful compromise and live totally holy. Webb writes with a startling combination of blunt truth and tender love, pointing out that "truth is freedom—even truth that is hard to hear." The album's acoustic folk/pop style is so engaging that you might have a hard time taking it out of your player. Even if you do, you won't forget the words.

WHY IT ROCKS: WEBB'S LYRICS ARE ALL TRACEABLE TO SCRIPTURE.

 7:14 washed their robes This means they believed in Jesus so that their sins could be forgiven by Christ's blood.

RELATIONSHIPS

"Love each other deeply, because love will cause many sins to be forgiven" (1 Peter 4:8). Name your biggest beef about being corrected—at home, school, work. Somewhere near the top of everyone's list is the feeling you're being nagged for every little slip, sin, or mistake. It's very human, though, to turn around and do the same to others. People cause lots of big hurts worth confronting, evils you can't let slide. But all the little stuff of life? Let it go. Love will help you forget about it. Cut people the slack you want them to cut you.

[10]Then the third angel blew his trumpet, and a large star, burning like a torch, fell from the sky. It fell on a third of the rivers and on the springs of water. [11]The name of the star is Wormwood.[n] And a third of all the water became bitter, and many people died from drinking the water that was bitter.

[12]Then the fourth angel blew his trumpet, and a third of the sun, and a third of the moon, and a third of the stars were struck. So a third of them became dark, and a third of the day was without light, and also the night.

[13]While I watched, I heard an eagle that was flying high in the air cry out in a loud voice, "Trouble! Trouble! Trouble for those who live on the earth because of the remaining sounds of the trumpets that the other three angels are about to blow!"

9 Then the fifth angel blew his trumpet, and I saw a star fall from the sky to the earth. The star was given the key to the deep hole that leads to the bottomless pit. [2]Then it opened up the hole that leads to the bottomless pit, and smoke came up from the hole like smoke from a big furnace. Then the sun and sky became dark because of the smoke from the hole. [3]Then locusts came down to the earth out of the smoke, and they were given the power to sting like scorpions.[n] [4]They were told not to harm the grass on the earth or any plant or tree. They could harm only the people who did not have the sign of God on their foreheads. [5]These locusts were not given the power to kill anyone, but to cause pain to the people for five months. And the pain they felt was like the pain a scorpion gives when it stings someone. [6]During those days people will look for a way to die, but they will not find it. They will want to die, but death will run away from them.

[7]The locusts looked like horses prepared for battle. On their heads they wore what looked like crowns of gold, and their faces looked like human faces. [8]Their hair was like women's hair, and their teeth were like lions' teeth. [9]Their chests looked like iron breastplates, and the sound of their wings was like the noise of many horses and chariots hurrying into battle. [10]The locusts had tails with stingers like scorpions, and in their tails was their power to hurt people for five months. [11]The locusts had a king who was the angel of the bottomless pit. His name in the Hebrew language is Abaddon and in the Greek language is Apollyon.[n]

[12]The first trouble is past; there are still two other troubles that will come.

[13]Then the sixth angel blew his trumpet, and I heard a voice coming from the horns on the golden altar that is before God. [14]The voice said to the sixth angel who had the trumpet, "Free the four angels who are tied at

PSALM 139:16 "ALL THE DAYS PLANNED FOR ME WERE WRITTEN IN YOUR BOOK BEFORE I WAS ONE DAY OLD."

the great river Euphrates." [15]And they let loose the four angels who had been kept ready for this hour and day and month and year so they could kill a third of all people on the earth. [16]I heard how many troops on horses were in their army—two hundred million.

[17]The horses and their riders I saw in the vision looked like this: They had breastplates that were fiery red, dark blue, and yellow like sulfur. The heads of the horses looked like heads of lions, with fire, smoke, and sulfur coming out of their mouths. [18]A third of all the people on earth were killed by these three

WAYS TO WALK THE WALK

revelation 19:16

WORD: Jesus is King of Kings and Lord of Lords.

WALK IT: Don't wait for heaven. Let God reign in your life today, giving Jesus your absolute allegiance. Make it your life goal to obey your Master in everything.

 8:11 Wormwood Name of a very bitter plant; used here to give the idea of bitter sorrow. **9:3 scorpions** A scorpion is an insect that stings with a bad poison. **9:11 Abaddon, Apollyon** Both names mean "Destroyer."

terrible disasters coming out of the horses' mouths: the fire, the smoke, and the sulfur. [19]The horses' power was in their mouths and in their tails; their tails were like snakes with heads, and with them they hurt people.

[20]The other people who were not killed by these terrible disasters still did not change their hearts and turn away from what they had made with their own hands. They did not stop worshiping demons and idols made of gold, silver, bronze, stone, and wood—things that cannot see or hear or walk. [21]These people did not change their hearts and turn away from murder or evil magic, from their sexual sins or stealing.

THE ANGEL AND THE SMALL SCROLL

10 Then I saw another powerful angel coming down from heaven dressed in a cloud with a rainbow over his head. His face was like the sun, and his legs were like pillars of fire. [2]The angel was holding a small scroll open in his hand. He put his right foot on the sea and his left foot on the land. [3]Then he shouted loudly like the roaring of a lion. And when he shouted, the voices of seven thunders spoke. [4]When the seven thunders spoke, I started to write. But I heard a voice from heaven say, "Keep hidden what the seven thunders said, and do not write them down."

[5]Then the angel I saw standing on the sea and on the land raised his right hand to heaven, [6]and he made a promise by the power of the One who lives forever and ever. He is the One who made the skies and all that is in them, the earth and all that is in it, and the sea and all that is in it. The angel promised, "There will be no more waiting! [7]In the days when the seventh angel is ready to blow his trumpet, God's secret will be finished. This secret is the Good News God told to his servants, the prophets."

[8]Then I heard the same voice from heaven again, saying to me: "Go and take the open scroll that is in the hand of the angel that is standing on the sea and on the land."

[9]So I went to the angel and told him to give

GET OUT THERE

The **YOUTH CONSERVATION CORPS** is a summer employment program for young men and women ages 15 through 18, from all segments of society, who work, learn, and earn together by doing projects on public land. Since 1970, the Youth Conservation Corps program has operated as a work-earn-learn program for youth. The program is administered by the U.S. Department of Agriculture's Forest Service and the U.S. Department of the Interior's Fish and Wildlife Service and National Park Service.

The purpose of the Youth Conservation Corps program is to further the development and maintenance of the natural resources of the United States by America's youth, and in so doing to prepare them for the ultimate responsibility of maintaining and managing these resources for the American people.

Youth are provided an opportunity to increase their self-esteem and learn self-discipline. They learn work ethics, relate with peers and supervisors, and build lasting cultural bridges between youth from various social, economic, ethnic, and racial backgrounds. Work projects last approximately eight weeks.

For more information, go to www.fs.fed.us/people/programs/ycc.htm.

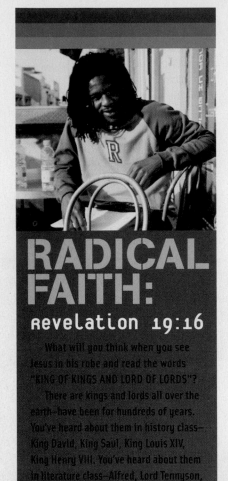

RADICAL FAITH:

Revelation 19:16

What will you think when you see Jesus in his robe and read the words "KING OF KINGS AND LORD OF LORDS"?

There are kings and lords all over the earth—have been for hundreds of years. You've heard about them in history class—King David, King Saul, King Louis XIV, King Henry VIII. You've heard about them in literature class—Alfred, Lord Tennyson, and George Gordon, Lord Byron.

Kings and lords are known primarily for their power, their wealth, their military might, and their positions as rulers over groups of people. Jesus Christ puts it all to shame. You talk about power. His power can raise the dead. You talk about wealth. His Father owns the cattle on a thousand hills (see Psalm 50:10). You talk about military might. He's raising up an army that will someday defeat the raging forces of Satan. You talk about a ruler. He rules the whole world. Philippians 2:10 says that "every knee will bow to the name of Jesus—everyone in heaven, on earth, and under the earth."

He is the King of all the kings who have ever ruled and the Lord of every lord. Go ahead. Enthrone him in your heart. You'll never find a more loving, merciful, gracious King.

me the small scroll. And he said to me, "Take the scroll and eat it. It will be sour in your stomach, but in your mouth it will be sweet as honey." [10]So I took the small scroll from the angel's hand and ate it. In my mouth it tasted sweet as honey, but after I ate it, it was sour in my stomach. [11]Then I was told, "You must prophesy again about many peoples, nations, languages, and kings."

THE TWO WITNESSES

11 I was given a measuring stick like a rod, and I was told, "Go and measure the temple of God and the altar, and count the people worshiping there. [2]But do not measure the yard outside the temple. Leave it alone, because it has been given to those who are not God's people. And they will trample on the holy city for forty-two months. [3]And I will give power to my two witnesses to prophesy for one thousand two hundred sixty days, and they will be dressed in rough cloth to show their sadness."

[4]These two witnesses are the two olive trees and the two lampstands that stand before the Lord of the earth. [5]And if anyone tries to hurt them, fire comes from their mouths and kills their enemies. And if anyone tries to hurt them in whatever way, in that same way that person will die. [6]These witnesses have the power to stop the sky from raining during the time they are prophesying. And they have power to make the waters become blood, and they have power to send every kind of trouble to the earth as many times as they want.

[7]When the two witnesses have finished telling their message, the beast that comes up from the bottomless pit will fight a war against them. He will defeat them and kill them. [8]The bodies of the two witnesses will lie in the street of the great city where the Lord was killed. This city is named Sodom[n] and Egypt, which has a spiritual meaning. [9]Those from every race of people, tribe, language, and nation will look at the bodies of the two witnesses for three and one-half days, and they will refuse to bury them. [10]People who live on the earth will rejoice and be happy because these two are dead. They will send each other gifts, because these two prophets brought much suffering to those who live on the earth.

Travel the road

Churches dot much of China, with millions attending each week. While the Chinese government recognizes official Catholic and Protestant organizations, members of these groups can't bring their children to church—and the government regulates what their churches can teach. Millions of additional Christians meet in illegal "house churches," meeting in homes, fields, or workplaces to study the Bible and pray. These Christians are often fined, beaten, and imprisoned for their beliefs. Get up-to-date news at the Center for Religious Freedom at www.freedomhouse.org.

For more on extreme missions visit www.traveltheroad.com.

11:8 Sodom City that God destroyed because the people were so evil.

HOW TO WRESTLE A STEER

This rodeo event is all about a crazy leap and catch. As you and your horse chase down a young ox five times your weight, you lean off your ride. Dangling by one stirruped foot, you lunge for the animal's horns. Got a good grasp? Then leap. You use your feet and body to skid the steer to a stop and knock it off balance. The clock stops when the animal is tackled to the ground with all four feet pointed in the same direction. The best guys can take down a steer in under four seconds in a rodeo competition. Sometimes a man has to do what a man has to do. Like grab a problem by the horns and toss it.

¹¹But after three and one-half days, God put the breath of life into the two prophets again. They stood on their feet, and everyone who saw them became very afraid. ¹²Then the two prophets heard a loud voice from heaven saying, "Come up here!" And they went up into heaven in a cloud as their enemies watched.

¹³In the same hour there was a great earthquake, and a tenth of the city was destroyed.

Seven thousand people were killed in the earthquake, and those who did not die were very afraid and gave glory to the God of heaven.

¹⁴The second trouble is finished. Pay attention: The third trouble is coming soon.

THE SEVENTH TRUMPET

¹⁵Then the seventh angel blew his trumpet. And there were loud voices in heaven, saying:

"The power to rule the world
now belongs to our Lord and his Christ,
and he will rule forever and ever."

¹⁶Then the twenty-four elders, who sit on their thrones before God, bowed down on their faces and worshiped God. ¹⁷They said:

"We give thanks to you, Lord God Almighty,
who is and who was,
because you have used your great power
and have begun to rule!

¹⁸The people of the world were angry,
but your anger has come.
The time has come to judge the dead,
and to reward your servants the prophets
and your holy people,
all who respect you, great and small.
The time has come to destroy those who
destroy the earth!"

¹⁹Then God's temple in heaven was opened. The Ark that holds the agreement God gave to his people could be seen in his temple. Then there were flashes of lightning, noises, thunder, an earthquake, and a great hailstorm.

THE WOMAN AND THE DRAGON

12 And then a great wonder appeared in heaven: A woman was clothed with the sun, and the moon was under her feet, and a crown of twelve stars was on her head. ²She was pregnant and cried out with pain, because she was about to give birth. ³Then another wonder appeared in heaven: There was a giant red dragon with seven heads and seven crowns on each head. He also had ten horns. ⁴His tail swept a third of the stars out of the sky and threw them down to the earth. He stood in front of the woman who was ready to give birth so he could eat her baby as soon as it was born. ⁵Then the woman gave birth to a son who will rule all the nations with an iron rod. And her child was taken up to God

BIBLE BASICS

Crucifixion was a hideous way that Romans executed people back during Bible times. Criminals were nailed to large planks of wood that were stood upright, and victims were left hanging there to suffocate. This was a cruel, public death; and the criminals were often beaten, ridiculed, and spat upon. Jesus was crucified because he claimed to be God's Son.

and to his throne. ⁶The woman ran away into the desert to a place God prepared for her where she would be taken care of for one thousand two hundred sixty days.

⁷Then there was a war in heaven. Michael[n] and his angels fought against the dragon, and the dragon and his angels fought back. ⁸But the dragon was not strong enough, and he and his angels lost their place in heaven. ⁹The giant dragon was thrown down out of heaven. (He is

that old snake called the devil or Satan, who tricks the whole world.) The dragon with his angels was thrown down to the earth.

[10]Then I heard a loud voice in heaven saying:

"The salvation and the power and the
  kingdom of our God
 and the authority of his Christ have now
  come.
The accuser of our brothers and sisters,
 who accused them day and night before
  our God,
 has been thrown down.
[11]And our brothers and sisters defeated him
 by the blood of the Lamb's death
 and by the message they preached.
They did not love their lives so much
 that they were afraid of death.
[12]So rejoice, you heavens
 and all who live there!
But it will be terrible for the earth and
  the sea,
 because the devil has come down
  to you!
He is filled with anger,
 because he knows he does not have
  much time."

[13]When the dragon saw he had been thrown down to the earth, he hunted for the woman who had given birth to the son. [14]But the woman was given the two wings of a great eagle so she could fly to the place prepared

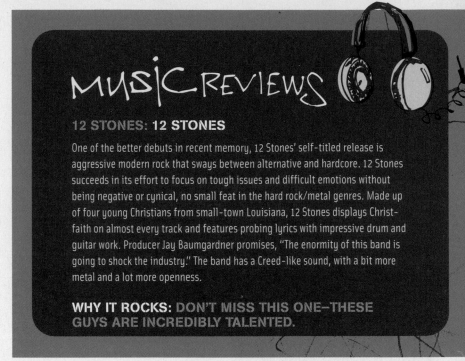

MUSIC REVIEWS

12 STONES: 12 STONES

One of the better debuts in recent memory, 12 Stones' self-titled release is aggressive modern rock that sways between alternative and hardcore. 12 Stones succeeds in its effort to focus on tough issues and difficult emotions without being negative or cynical, no small feat in the hard rock/metal genres. Made up of four young Christians from small-town Louisiana, 12 Stones displays Christ-faith on almost every track and features probing lyrics with impressive drum and guitar work. Producer Jay Baumgardner promises, "The enormity of this band is going to shock the industry." The band has a Creed-like sound, with a bit more metal and a lot more openness.

WHY IT ROCKS: DON'T MISS THIS ONE—THESE GUYS ARE INCREDIBLY TALENTED.

for her in the desert. There she would be taken care of for three and one-half years, away from the snake. [15]Then the snake poured water out of its mouth like a river toward the woman so the flood would carry her away. [16]But the earth helped the woman by opening its mouth and swallowing the river that came from the mouth of the dragon. [17]Then the dragon was very angry at the woman, and he went off to make war against all her other children—those who obey God's commands and who have the message Jesus taught.

[18]And the dragon stood on the seashore.

THE TWO BEASTS

13 Then I saw a beast coming up out of the sea. It had ten horns and seven heads, and there was a

MEN OF THE SWORD

JOSEPH was a young carpenter who obeyed God even when he was confused. He was the father of Jesus, but not biologically. Engaged to a young virgin named Mary, he was surprised to learn that his wife-to-be was pregnant. Engagement was such a serious matter in Bible times that ending an engagement required a formal divorce. Mary's pregnancy could have been punished by stoning, but Joseph decided to divorce her quietly. That's when an angel appeared to Joseph in a dream and explained that the baby growing inside Mary had been miraculously conceived by the Holy Spirit, and that the son Mary would bear would save the world from its sin. Joseph accepted God's word. He married Mary, staying apart from her sexually until after the birth of Jesus. And then he raised God's Son as his own.

—Matthew 1–2; Luke 1–2

crown on each horn. A name against God was written on each head. ²This beast looked like a leopard, with feet like a bear's feet and a mouth like a lion's mouth. And the dragon gave the beast all of his power and his throne and great authority. ³One of the heads of the beast looked as if it had been killed by a wound, but this death wound was healed. Then the whole world was amazed and followed the beast. ⁴People worshiped the dragon because he had given his power to the beast. And they also worshiped the beast, asking, "Who is like the beast? Who can make war against it?"

⁵The beast was allowed to say proud words and words against God, and it was allowed to use its power for forty-two months. ⁶It used its mouth to speak against God, against God's name, against the place where God lives, and against all those who live in heaven. ⁷It was given power to make war against God's holy people and to defeat them. It was given power over every tribe, people, language, and nation. ⁸And all who live on earth will worship the beast—all the people since the beginning of the world whose names are not written in the Lamb's book of life. The Lamb is the One who was killed.

⁹Anyone who has ears should listen:
¹⁰If you are to be a prisoner,
　then you will be a prisoner.
If you are to be killed with the sword,
　then you will be killed with the sword.
This means that God's holy people must have patience and faith.

¹¹Then I saw another beast coming up out of the earth. It had two horns like a lamb, but it spoke like a dragon. ¹²This beast stands before the first beast and uses the same power the first beast has. By this power it makes everyone living on earth worship the first beast, who had the death wound that was healed. ¹³And the second beast does great miracles so that it even makes fire come down from heaven to earth while people are watching. ¹⁴It fools those who live on earth by the

miracles it has been given the power to do. It does these miracles to serve the first beast. The second beast orders people to make an idol to honor the first beast, the one that was wounded by the deadly sword but sprang to life again. ¹⁵The second beast was given power to give life to the idol of the first one so that the idol could speak. And the second beast was given power to command all who will not worship the image of the beast to be killed. ¹⁶The second beast also forced all people, small and great, rich and poor, free and slave, to have a mark on their right hand or on their forehead. ¹⁷No one could buy or sell without this mark, which is the name of the beast or the number of its name. ¹⁸This takes wisdom. Let the one who has understanding find the meaning of the number, which is the number of a person. Its number is six hundred sixty-six.

THE SONG OF THE SAVED

14 Then I looked, and there before me was the Lamb standing on Mount Zion.ⁿ With him were one hundred forty-four thousand people who had his name and his Father's name written on their foreheads. ²And I heard a sound from heaven like the noise of flooding water and like the sound of loud thunder. The sound I heard was like people playing harps. ³And they sang a new song before the throne and before the four living creatures and the elders. No one could learn the new song except the one hundred forty-four thousand who had been bought from the earth. ⁴These are the ones who did not do sinful things with women, because they kept themselves pure. They follow the Lamb every place he goes. These one hundred forty-four thousand were bought from among the people of the earth as people to be offered to God and the Lamb. ⁵They were not guilty of telling lies; they are without fault.

THE THREE ANGELS

⁶Then I saw another angel flying high in the air. He had the eternal Good News to preach to

those who live on earth—to every nation, tribe, language, and people. ⁷He preached in a loud voice, "Fear God and give him praise, because the time has come for God to judge all people. So worship God who made the heavens, and the earth, and the sea, and the springs of water."

⁸Then the second angel followed the first angel and said, "Ruined, ruined is the great city of Babylon! She made all the nations drink the wine of the anger of her adultery."

⁹Then a third angel followed the first two angels, saying in a loud voice: "If anyone worships

RANDOM WORSHIP SONGS GUYS CAN GET INTO

1. "I COULD SING OF YOUR LOVE FOREVER" (DELIRIOUS)
2. "THE HEART OF WORSHIP" (MATT REDMAN)
3. "AGNUS DEI" (MICHAEL W. SMITH)
4. "I WANT TO KNOW YOU" (SONICFLOOD)
5. "YOU ARE MY STRONGHOLD" (WATERMARK)
6. "IT IS YOU" (NEWSBOYS)
7. "GOD OF WONDERS" (THIRD DAY)
8. "O PRAISE HIM (ALL THIS FOR A KING)" (DAVID CROWDER BAND)
9. "HERE I AM TO WORSHIP" (TIM HUGHES)
10. "FOREVER" (CHRIS TOMLIN)

ADVERTISING REVENUES AT MTV ARE ROUGHLY $1,000,000,000 A YEAR.
–BUSINESSWEEK

 14:1 Mount Zion Another name for Jerusalem; here meaning the spiritual city of God's people.

the beast and his idol and gets the beast's mark on the forehead or on the hand, [10]that one also will drink the wine of God's anger, which is prepared with all its strength in the cup of his anger. And that person will be put in pain with burning sulfur before the holy angels and the Lamb. [11]And the smoke from their burning pain will rise forever and ever. There will be no rest, day or night, for those who worship the beast and his idol or who get the mark of his name." [12]This means God's holy people must be patient. They must obey God's commands and keep their faith in Jesus.

[13]Then I heard a voice from heaven saying, "Write this: Happy are the dead who die from now on in the Lord."

The Spirit says, "Yes, they will rest from their hard work, and the reward of all they have done stays with them."

THE EARTH IS HARVESTED

[14]Then I looked, and there before me was a white cloud, and sitting on the white cloud was One who looked like a Son of Man.[n] He had a gold crown on his head and a sharp sickle[n] in his hand. [15]Then another angel came out of the temple and called out in a loud voice to the One who was sitting on the cloud, "Take your sickle and harvest from the earth, because the time to harvest has come, and the fruit of the earth is ripe." [16]So the One who was sitting on the cloud swung his sickle over the earth, and the earth was harvested.

[17]Then another angel came out of the temple in heaven, and he also had a sharp sickle. [18]And then another angel, who has power over the fire, came from the altar. This angel called to the angel with the sharp sickle, saying, "Take your sharp sickle and gather the bunches of grapes from the earth's vine, because its grapes are ripe." [19]Then the angel swung his sickle over the earth. He gathered the earth's grapes and threw them into the

HEIFER INTERNATIONAL

In the 1930s, a civil war raged in Spain. Dan West, a Midwestern farmer and Church of the Brethren youth worker, ladled out cups of milk to hungry children on both sides of the conflict. It struck him that what these families needed was "not a cup, but a cow." He asked his friends back home to donate heifers, a young cow that has not borne a calf, so hungry families could feed themselves. In return, they could help another family become self-reliant by passing on to them one of their gift animal's female calves. The idea of giving families a source of food rather than short-term relief caught on and has continued for more than 50 years. As a result, families in 115 countries have enjoyed better health, more income, and the joy of helping others. Your donation can provide for all or part of a heifer, water buffalo, or llama—or a gift of sheep, goats, pigs, rabbits, honey bees, or a whole flock of geese. Or your church can take the ultimate challenge and send an "ark" full of animal pairs all over the world!

Surf to www.heifer.org to find out more.

 14:14 Son of Man "Son of Man" is a name Jesus called himself.   **14:14 sickle** A farming tool with a curved blade. It was used to harvest grain.

great winepress of God's anger. ²⁰They were trampled in the winepress outside the city, and blood flowed out of the winepress as high as horses' bridles for a distance of about one hundred eighty miles.

THE LAST TROUBLES

15 Then I saw another wonder in heaven that was great and amazing. There were seven angels bringing seven disasters. These are the last disasters, because after them, God's anger is finished.

²I saw what looked like a sea of glass mixed with fire. All of those who had won the victory over the beast and his idol and over the number of his name were standing by the sea of glass. They had harps that God had given them. ³They sang the song of Moses, the servant of God, and the song of the Lamb:

"You do great and wonderful things,

Psalm 111:2

Lord God Almighty.   *Amos 3:13*

Everything the Lord does is right and true,

Psalm 145:17

King of the nations.

⁴Everyone will respect you, Lord, *Jeremiah 10:7*

and will honor you.

Only you are holy.

All the nations will come

and worship you,   *Psalm 86:9-10*

because the right things you have done

are now made known."   *Deuteronomy 32:4*

⁵After this I saw that the temple (the Tent of the Agreement) in heaven was opened. ⁶And the seven angels bringing the seven disasters came out of the temple. They were dressed in clean, shining linen and wore golden bands tied around their chests. ⁷Then one of the four living creatures gave to the seven angels seven golden bowls filled with the anger of God, who lives forever and ever. ⁸The temple was filled with smoke from the glory and the power of God, and no one could enter the temple until the seven disasters of the seven angels were finished.

THE BOWLS OF GOD'S ANGER

16 Then I heard a loud voice from the temple saying to the seven angels, "Go and pour out the seven bowls of God's anger on the earth."

²The first angel left and poured out his bowl on the land. Then ugly and painful sores came upon all those who had the mark of the beast and who worshiped his idol.

³The second angel poured out his bowl on the sea, and it became blood like that of a dead man, and every living thing in the sea died.

⁴The third angel poured out his bowl on the rivers and the springs of water, and they became blood. ⁵Then I heard the angel of the waters saying:

"Holy One, you are the One who is and
    who was.

You are right to decide to punish these
    evil people.

⁶They have poured out the blood of your
    holy people and your prophets.

So now you have given them blood to
    drink as they deserve."

⁷And I heard a voice coming from the altar saying:

"Yes, Lord God Almighty,

the way you punish evil people is right
    and fair."

MARK 12:17 "GIVE TO CAESAR THE THINGS THAT ARE CAESAR'S, AND GIVE TO GOD THE THINGS THAT ARE GOD'S."

⁸The fourth angel poured out his bowl on the sun, and he was given power to burn the people with fire. ⁹They were burned by the great heat, and they cursed the name of God, who had control over these disasters. But the people refused to change their hearts and lives and give glory to God.

¹⁰The fifth angel poured out his bowl on the throne of the beast, and darkness covered its kingdom. People gnawed their tongues because of the pain. ¹¹They also cursed the God of heaven because of their pain and the sores they had, but they refused to change their hearts and turn away from the evil things they did.

¹²The sixth angel poured out his bowl on the great river Euphrates so that the water in the river was dried up to prepare the way for the kings from the east to come. ¹³Then I saw three evil spirits that looked like frogs coming out of the mouth of the dragon, out of the

mouth of the beast, and out of the mouth of the false prophet. ¹⁴These evil spirits are the spirits of demons, which have power to do miracles. They go out to the kings of the whole world to gather them together for the battle on the great day of God Almighty.

¹⁵"Listen! I will come as a thief comes! Happy are those who stay awake and keep their clothes on so that they will not walk around naked and have people see their shame."

¹⁶Then the evil spirits gathered the kings together to the place that is called Armageddon in the Hebrew language.

¹⁷The seventh angel poured out his bowl into the air. Then a loud voice came out of the temple from the throne, saying, "It is finished!" ¹⁸Then there were flashes of lightning, noises, thunder, and a big earthquake—the worst earthquake that has ever happened since people have been on earth. ¹⁹The great city split into three parts, and the cities of the nations were destroyed. And God remembered the sins of Babylon the Great, so he gave that city the cup filled with the wine of his terrible anger. ²⁰Then every island ran away, and mountains disappeared. ²¹Giant hailstones, each weighing about a hundred pounds, fell from the sky upon people. People cursed God for the disaster of the hail, because this disaster was so terrible.

THE WOMAN ON THE ANIMAL

17 Then one of the seven angels who had the seven bowls came and

spoke to me. He said, "Come, and I will show you the punishment that will be given to the great prostitute, the one sitting over many waters. ²The kings of the earth sinned sexually with her, and the people of the earth became drunk from the wine of her sexual sin."

³Then the angel carried me away by the Spirit to the desert. There I saw a woman sitting on a red beast. It was covered with names against God written on it, and it had seven heads and ten horns. ⁴The woman was dressed in purple and red and was shining with the gold, precious jewels, and pearls she was wearing. She had a golden cup in her hand, a cup filled with evil things and the uncleanness of her sexual sin. ⁵On her forehead a title was written that was secret. This is what was written:

THE GREAT BABYLON
MOTHER OF PROSTITUTES
AND OF THE EVIL THINGS OF THE EARTH

⁶Then I saw that the woman was drunk with the blood of God's holy people and with the blood of those who were killed because of their faith in Jesus.

live on earth whose names have not been written in the book of life since the beginning of the world. They will be amazed when they see the beast, because he was once alive, is not alive now, but will come again.

⁹"You need a wise mind to understand this. The seven heads on the beast are seven mountains where the woman sits. ¹⁰And they are seven kings. Five of the kings have already been destroyed, one of the kings lives now, and another has not yet come. When he comes, he must stay a short time. ¹¹The beast that was once alive, but is not alive now, is also an eighth king. He belongs to the first seven kings, and he will go away to be destroyed.

¹²"The ten horns you saw are ten kings who have not yet begun to rule, but they will receive power to rule with the beast for one hour. ¹³All ten of these kings have the same purpose, and they will give their power and authority to the beast. ¹⁴They will make war against the Lamb, but the Lamb will defeat them, because he is Lord of lords and King of kings. He will defeat them with his called, chosen, and faithful followers."

¹⁵Then the angel said to me, "The waters that

about. ¹⁸The woman you saw is the great city that rules over the kings of the earth."

BABYLON IS DESTROYED

18 After the vision of these things, I saw another angel coming down from heaven. This angel had great power, and his glory made the earth bright. ²He shouted in a powerful voice:

"Ruined, ruined is the great city of
　Babylon!
She has become a home for demons
and a prison for every evil spirit,
　and a prison for every unclean bird and
　　unclean beast.
³She has been ruined, because all the
　peoples of the earth
　have drunk the wine of the desire of her
　　sexual sin.
She has been ruined also because the kings
　of the earth
　have sinned sexually with her,
and the merchants of the earth
　have grown rich from the great wealth of
　　her luxury."

⁴Then I heard another voice from heaven saying:

"Come out of that city, my people,
　so that you will not share in her sins,
　so that you will not receive the disasters
　　that will come to her.
⁵Her sins have piled up as high as the sky,
　and God has not forgotten the wrongs
　　she has done.
⁶Give that city the same as she gave to
　others.
　Pay her back twice as much as she did.
　Prepare wine for her that is twice as strong
　　as the wine she prepared for others.

When I saw the woman, I was very amazed. ⁷Then the angel said to me, "Why are you amazed? I will tell you the secret of this woman and the beast she rides—the one with seven heads and ten horns. ⁸The beast you saw was once alive but is not alive now. But soon it will come up out of the bottomless pit and go away to be destroyed. There are people who

you saw, where the prostitute sits, are peoples, races, nations, and languages. ¹⁶The ten horns and the beast you saw will hate the prostitute. They will take everything she has and leave her naked. They will eat her body and burn her with fire. ¹⁷God made the ten horns want to carry out his purpose by agreeing to give the beast their power to rule, until what God has said comes

⁷She gave herself much glory and rich
　living.
　Give her that much suffering and sadness.
　She says to herself, 'I am a queen sitting on
　　my throne.
　I am not a widow; I will never be sad.'
⁸So these disasters will come to her in one
　day:

death, and crying, and great hunger,
and she will be destroyed by fire,
because the Lord God who judges her is
powerful."

⁹The kings of the earth who sinned sexually with her and shared her wealth will see the smoke from her burning. Then they will cry and be sad because of her death. ¹⁰They will be afraid of her suffering and stand far away and say:

"Terrible! How terrible for you, great city,
powerful city of Babylon,
because your punishment has come in one
hour!"

¹¹And the merchants of the earth will cry and be sad about her, because now there is no one to buy their cargoes— ¹²cargoes of gold, silver, jewels, pearls, fine linen, purple cloth, silk, red cloth; all kinds of citron wood and all kinds of things made from ivory, expensive wood, bronze, iron, and marble; ¹³cinnamon, spice, incense, myrrh, frankincense, wine, olive oil, fine flour, wheat, cattle, sheep, horses, carriages, slaves, and human lives.

¹⁴The merchants will say,

"Babylon, the good things you wanted are
gone from you.
All your rich and fancy things have
disappeared.
You will never have them again."

¹⁵The merchants who became rich from selling to her will be afraid of her suffering and will stand far away. They will cry and be sad ¹⁶and say:

"Terrible! How terrible for the great city!
She was dressed in fine linen, purple
and red cloth,
and she was shining with gold, precious
jewels, and pearls!

¹⁷All these riches have been destroyed in one
hour!"

Every sea captain, every passenger, the sailors, and all those who earn their living from the sea stood far away from Babylon. ¹⁸As they saw the smoke from her burning, they cried out loudly, "There was never a city like this great city!" ¹⁹And they threw dust on their heads and cried out, weeping and being sad. They said:

"Terrible! How terrible for the great city!
All the people who had ships on the sea
became rich because of her
wealth!
But she has been destroyed in
one hour!"

²⁰Be happy because of this,
heaven!
Be happy, God's holy people and
apostles and prophets!
God has punished her because of what she
did to you."

²¹Then a powerful angel picked up a large stone, like one used for grinding grain, and threw it into the sea. He said:

"In the same way, the great city of Babylon
will be thrown down,
and it will never be found again.
²²The music of people playing harps and
other instruments, flutes, and trumpets,
will never be heard in you again.
No workman doing any job
will ever be found in you again.
The sound of grinding grain
will never be heard in you again.
²³The light of a lamp
will never shine in you again,
and the voices of a bridegroom and bride
will never be heard in you again.
Your merchants were the world's great
people,
and all the nations were tricked by your
magic.
²⁴You are guilty of the death of the prophets
and God's holy people
and all who have been killed on earth."

PEOPLE IN HEAVEN PRAISE GOD

19 After this vision and announcement I heard what sounded like a great many people in heaven saying:

"Hallelujah!ⁿ
Salvation, glory, and power belong to our
God,
²	because his judgments are true and right.
He has punished the prostitute
who made the earth evil with her sexual
sin.
He has paid her back for the death of his
servants."

³Again they said:

"Hallelujah!
She is burning, and her smoke will rise
forever and ever."

⁴Then the twenty-four elders and the four living creatures bowed down and worshiped God, who sits on the throne. They said:

"Amen, Hallelujah!"

⁵Then a voice came from the throne, saying:

"Praise our God, all you who serve him
and all you who honor him, both small
and great!"

⁶Then I heard what sounded like a great many people, like the noise of flooding water, and like the noise of loud thunder. The people were saying:

"Hallelujah!
Our Lord God, the Almighty, rules.
⁷Let us rejoice and be happy
and give God glory,
because the wedding of the Lamb has come,

19:1 **Hallelujah** This means "praise God!"

HOW TO LIFT A TON OF ANYTHING

Suppose a friend parks his Yugo on your foot. Back it up, right? But real men lift weights. Simple physics says your buddy can easily raise that bad boy enough to free your foot using a lever—a pole and a fulcrum, ala a teeter-totter. He doesn't have to lift the whole one-ton car to free your foot, so the formula looks something like this:

Force x Distance = Force x Distance
1,000 pounds x 1 inch = 100 pounds x 10 inches

To lift half a ton one inch, he needs to push the lever down with a force of a hundred pounds for a distance of ten inches. Push twice as hard or twice as far, and he could lift a whole ton. When it comes to life, God's Word is like that powerful lever. It makes you capable of doing great feats of strength. Check 2 Timothy 3:16-17 to see how.

and the Lamb's bride has made herself ready.

[8]Fine linen, bright and clean, was given to her to wear."

(The fine linen means the good things done by God's holy people.)

[9]And the angel said to me, "Write this: Happy are those who have been invited to the wedding meal of the Lamb!" And the angel said, "These are the true words of God."

[10]Then I bowed down at the angel's feet to worship him, but he said to me, "Do not worship me! I am a servant like you and your brothers and sisters who have the message of Jesus. Worship God, because the message about Jesus is the spirit that gives all prophecy."

revelation 22:18

WORD: If anyone adds to or takes away from the Scriptures, they will suffer disasters.

WALK IT: Study so you know what the Bible actually says. Don't mold the Bible's teachings to fit your wishes.

THE RIDER ON THE WHITE HORSE

[11]Then I saw heaven opened, and there before me was a white horse. The rider on the horse is called Faithful and True, and he is right when he judges and makes war. [12]His eyes are like burning fire, and on his head are many crowns. He has a name written on him, which no one but himself knows. [13]He is dressed in a robe dipped in blood, and his name is the Word of God. [14]The armies of heaven, dressed in fine linen, white and clean, were following him on white horses. [15]Out of the rider's mouth comes a sharp sword that he will use to defeat the nations, and he will rule them with a rod of iron. He will crush out the wine in the winepress of the terrible anger of God the Almighty. [16]On his robe and on his upper leg was written this name: KING OF KINGS AND LORD OF LORDS.

[17]Then I saw an angel standing in the sun, and he called with a loud voice to all the birds flying in the sky: "Come and gather together for the great feast of God [18]so that you can eat the bodies of kings, generals, mighty people, horses and their riders, and the bodies of all people—free, slave, small, and great."

[19]Then I saw the beast and the kings of the earth. Their armies were gathered together to make war against the rider on the horse and his army. [20]But the beast was captured and with him the false prophet who did the miracles for the beast. The false prophet had used these miracles to trick those who had the mark of the beast and worshiped his idol. The false prophet and the beast were thrown alive into the lake of fire that burns with sulfur. [21]And their armies were killed with the sword that came out of the mouth of the rider on the horse, and all the birds ate the bodies until they were full.

THE THOUSAND YEARS

20 I saw an angel coming down from heaven. He had the key to the bottomless pit and a large chain in his hand. [2]The angel grabbed the dragon, that old snake who is the devil and Satan, and tied him up for a thousand years. [3]Then he threw him into the bottomless pit, closed it, and locked it over him. The angel did this so he could not trick the people of the earth anymore until the thousand years were ended. After a thousand years he must be set free for a short time.

[4]Then I saw some thrones and people sitting

on them who had been given the power to judge. And I saw the souls of those who had been killed because they were faithful to the message of Jesus and the message from God. They had not worshiped the beast or his idol, and they had not received the mark of the beast on their foreheads or on their hands. They came back to life and ruled with Christ for a thousand years. [5](The others that were dead did not live again until the thousand years were ended.) This is the first raising of the dead. [6]Happy and holy are those who share in this first raising of the dead. The second death has no power over them. They will be priests for God and for Christ and will rule with him for a thousand years.

[7]When the thousand years are over, Satan will be set free from his prison. [8]Then he will go out to trick the nations in all the earth—Gog and Magog—to gather them for battle.

MARK 4:41 "WHO IS THIS? EVEN THE WIND AND THE WAVES OBEY HIM!"

There are so many people they will be like sand on the seashore. [9]And Satan's army marched across the earth and gathered around the camp of God's people and the city God loves. But fire came down from heaven and burned them up. [10]And Satan, who tricked them, was thrown into the lake of burning sulfur with the beast and the false prophet. There they will be punished day and night forever and ever.

PEOPLE OF THE WORLD ARE JUDGED

[11]Then I saw a great white throne and the One who was sitting on it. Earth and sky ran away from him and disappeared. [12]And I saw the dead, great and small, standing before the throne. Then books were opened, and the book of life was opened. The dead were judged by what they had done, which was written in the books. [13]The sea gave up the dead who were in it, and Death and Hades[n] gave up the dead who were in them. Each person was judged by what he had done. [14]And Death and Hades were thrown into the lake of fire. The lake of fire is the second death. [15]And anyone whose name

was not found written in the book of life was thrown into the lake of fire.

THE NEW JERUSALEM

21 Then I saw a new heaven and a new earth. The first heaven and the first earth had disappeared, and there was no sea anymore. [2]And I saw the holy city, the new Jerusalem,[n] coming down out of heaven from God. It was prepared like a bride dressed for her husband. [3]And I heard a loud voice from the throne, saying, "Now God's presence is with people, and he will live with them, and they will be his people. God himself will be with them and will be their God. [4]He will wipe away every tear from their eyes, and there will be no more death, sadness, crying, or pain, because all the old ways are gone."

[5]The One who was sitting on the throne said, "Look! I am making everything new!" Then he said, "Write this, because these words are true and can be trusted."

[6]The One on the throne said to me, "It is finished. I am the Alpha and the Omega,[n] the Beginning and the End. I will give free water from the spring of the water of life to anyone who is thirsty. [7]Those who win the victory will receive this, and I will be their God, and they will be my children. [8]But cowards, those who refuse to believe, who do evil things, who kill, who sin sexually, who do evil magic, who worship idols, and who tell lies—all these will have a place in the lake of burning sulfur. This is the second death."

[9]Then one of the seven angels who had the seven bowls full of the seven last troubles came to me, saying, "Come with me, and I will show you the bride, the wife of the Lamb." [10]And the angel carried me away by the Spirit to a very large and high mountain. He showed me the holy city, Jerusalem, coming down out of heaven from God. [11]It was shining with the glory of God and was bright like a very expensive jewel, like a jasper, clear as crystal. [12]The city had a great high wall with twelve gates with twelve angels at the gates, and on each gate was written the name of one of the twelve tribes of Israel. [13]There were three gates on the east, three on the north, three on the south, and three on the west. [14]The walls of the city were built on twelve foundation stones, and on the stones were written the names of the twelve apostles of the Lamb.

REVELATION 22:20

What if you were God? What if you'd spent years inspiring the Bible, making sure that the people who read it would have access to everything you wanted them to know? What would you tell them at the very end? Would you let your book just fizzle out with some kind of lame ending? Or would you let the whole work build up to one exciting, crucial climax?

God chose to end his Book with a thought that thrills some people and terrifies others. The end of the story is this: Jesus is coming back. And he's coming back soon. Christians should be the ones who are thrilled by this knowledge. It gives you so much hope! It gives you courage to live the challenging days you're living through right now. It gives you powerful motivation to get serious about answering God's call for your life. You want to be ready. You want to have your life right with God when the last trumpet sounds. You can't know the exact moment when he will arrive; you just know it's going to be soon.

Make your prayer the words of Revelation 22:20, "Amen. Come, Lord Jesus!" Do your part to be ready—be excited about his return. Get your heart tender and right before him. Share the news with those who don't know. It'll be the most awesome, most glorious moment the world has ever seen.

 20:13 Hades The place of the dead. **21:2 new Jerusalem** The spiritual city where God's people live with him. **21:6 Alpha and the Omega** The first and last letters of the Greek alphabet. This means "the beginning and the end."

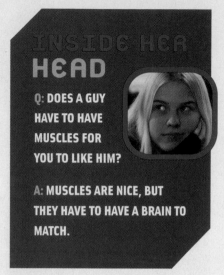

INSIDE HER HEAD

Q: DOES A GUY HAVE TO HAVE MUSCLES FOR YOU TO LIKE HIM?

A: MUSCLES ARE NICE, BUT THEY HAVE TO HAVE A BRAIN TO MATCH.

[15]The angel who talked with me had a measuring rod made of gold to measure the city, its gates, and its wall. [16]The city was built in a square, and its length was equal to its width. The angel measured the city with the rod. The city was twelve thousand stadia[n] long, twelve thousand stadia wide, and twelve thousand stadia high. [17]The angel also meas-ured the wall. It was one hundred forty-four cubits[n] high, by human measurements, which the angel was using. [18]The wall was made of jasper, and the city was made of pure gold, as pure as glass. [19]The foundation stones of the city walls were decorated with every kind of jewel. The first foundation was jasper, the sec-ond was sapphire, the third was chalcedony, the fourth was emerald, [20]the fifth was onyx, the sixth was carnelian, the seventh was chrysolite, the eighth was beryl, the ninth was topaz, the tenth was chrysoprase, the eleventh was jacinth, and the twelfth was amethyst. [21]The twelve gates were twelve pearls, each gate having been made from a single pearl. And the street of the city was made of pure gold as clear as glass.

[22]I did not see a temple in the city, because the Lord God Almighty and the Lamb are the city's temple. [23]The city does not need the sun or the moon to shine on it, because the glory of God is its light, and the Lamb is the city's lamp. [24]By its light the people of the world will walk, and the kings of the earth will bring their glory into it. [25]The city's gates will never be shut on any day, because there is no night there. [26]The glory and the honor of the nations will be brought into it. [27]Nothing unclean and no one who does shameful things or tells lies will ever go into it. Only those whose names are written in the Lamb's book of life will en-ter the city.

22 Then the angel showed me the river of the water of life. It was shining like crystal and was flowing from the throne of God and of the Lamb [2]down the mid-dle of the street of the city. The tree of life was on each side of the river. It produces fruit twelve times a year, once each month. The leaves of the tree are for the healing of all the nations. [3]Nothing that God judges guilty will be in that city. The throne of God and of the Lamb will be there, and God's servants will worship him. [4]They will see his face, and his name will be written on their foreheads. [5]There will never be night again. They will not need the light of a lamp or the light of the sun, because the Lord God will give them light. And they will rule as kings forever and ever.

[6]The angel said to me, "These words can be

PSALM 139:5 "YOU ARE ALL AROUND ME—IN FRONT AND IN BACK—AND HAVE PUT YOUR HAND ON ME."

trusted and are true." The Lord, the God of the spirits of the prophets, sent his angel to show his servants the things that must happen soon.

[7]"Listen! I am coming soon! Happy is the one who obeys the words of prophecy in this book."

[8]I, John, am the one who heard and saw these things. When I heard and saw them, I bowed down to worship at the feet of the an-gel who showed these things to me. [9]But the angel said to me, "Do not worship me! I am a servant like you, your brothers the prophets, and all those who obey the words in this book. Worship God!"

[10]Then the angel told me, "Do not keep se-cret the words of prophecy in this book, be-cause the time is near for all this to happen. [11]Let whoever is doing evil continue to do evil. Let whoever is unclean continue to be unclean. Let whoever is doing right continue to do right. Let whoever is holy continue to be holy."

[12]"Listen! I am coming soon! I will bring my reward with me, and I will repay each one of you for what you have done. [13]I am the Al-pha and the Omega,[n] the First and the Last, the Beginning and the End.

[14]"Happy are those who wash their robes[n] so that they will receive the right to eat the fruit from the tree of life and may go through the gates into the city. [15]Outside the city are the evil people, those who do evil magic, who sin sexually, who murder, who worship idols, and who love lies and tell lies.

[16]"I, Jesus, have sent my angel to tell you these things for the churches. I am the de-scendant from the family of David, and I am the bright morning star."

[17]The Spirit and the bride say, "Come!" Let the one who hears this say, "Come!" Let who-ever is thirsty come; whoever wishes may have the water of life as a free gift.

[18]I warn everyone who hears the words of the prophecy of this book: If anyone adds any-thing to these words, God will add to that per-son the disasters written about in this book. [19]And if anyone takes away from the words of this book of prophecy, God will take away that one's share of the tree of life and of the holy city, which are written about in this book.

[20]Jesus, the One who says these things are true, says, "Yes, I am coming soon."

Amen. Come, Lord Jesus!

[21]The grace of the Lord Jesus be with all. Amen.

 21:16 stadia One stadion was a distance of about two hundred yards; about one-eighth of a Roman mile. **21:17 cubits** A cubit is about half a yard, the length from the elbow to the tip of the little finger. **22:13 Alpha and the Omega** The first and last letters of the Greek alphabet. This means "the beginning and the end." **22:14 wash their robes** This means they believed and obeyed Jesus so that their sins could be forgiven by Christ's blood. The "washing" may refer to baptism (Acts 22:16).

BIBLE READING PLANS/
PRAYER CONCERNS

30 DAYS WITH JESUS

60 DAYS WITH PAUL

PRAYER CONCERNS

PRAYER CONCERNS

PRAYER CONCERNS

_____

_____

_____

_____

_____

_____

_____

_____

_____

_____

_____

_____

_____

_____

_____